THE WORLD'S MOST BEAUTIFUL CG CHARACTERS

EXOTIQUE 6™

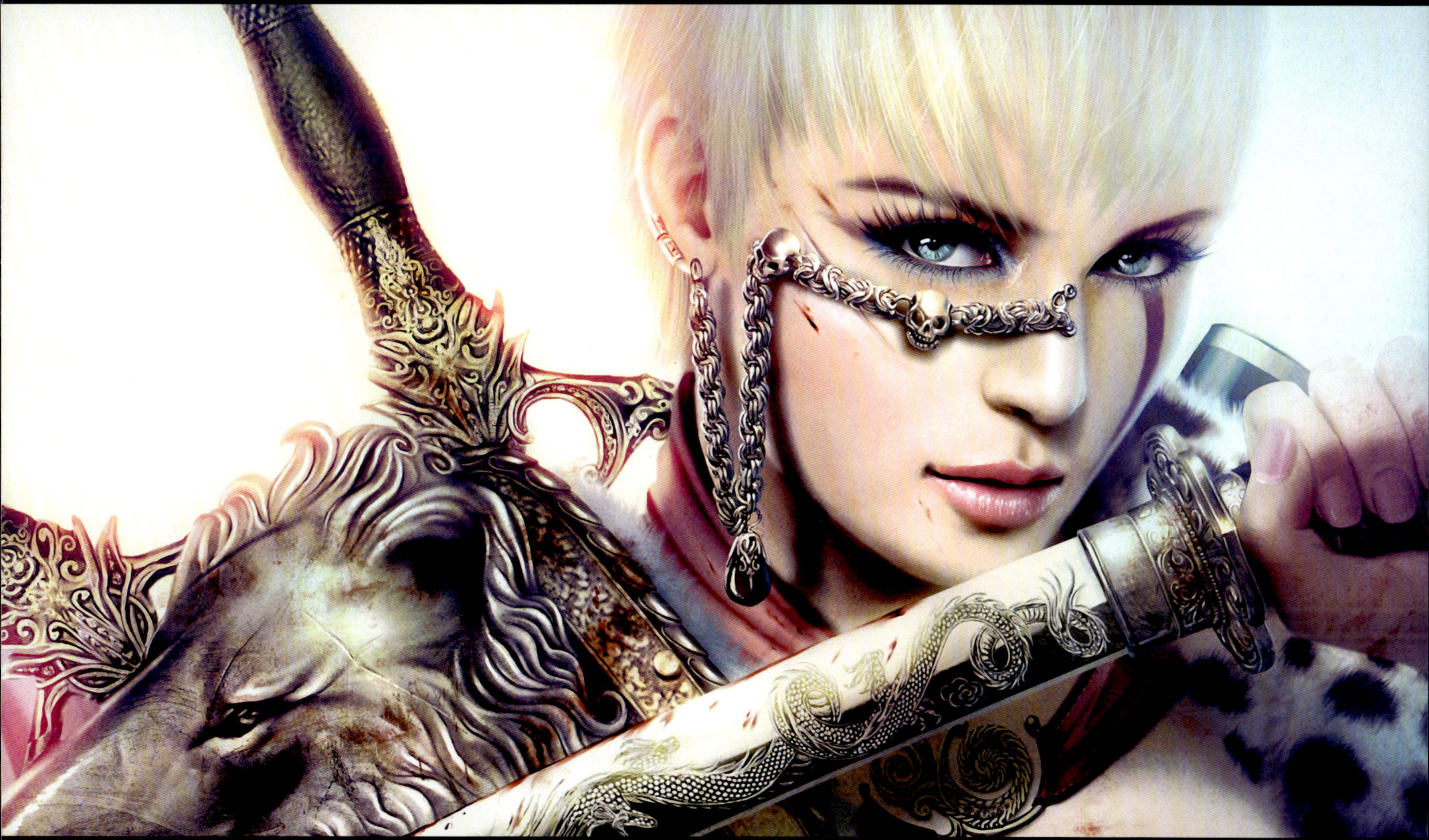

Edited by

EXOTIQUE 6™

Published
by
Ballistic Publishing
Finest digital art books in the known universe
134 Gilbert St
Adelaide, SA 5000
Australia

www.BallisticPublishing.com

Correspondence:
info@BallisticPublishing.com

First Edition published in Australia 2010
by Ballistic Publishing

Softcover Edition ISBN 978-1-921002-81-6
Special Edition ISBN 978-1-921002-80-9

Publisher/Managing Editor
Daniel Wade

Assistant Editor
Paul Hellard

Art Director
Lauren Stevens

Design & Image Processing
Lauren Stevens, Daniel Cox

Printing and binding
Everbest Printing (China):
www.everbest.com

Partners
The CGSociety (Computer Graphics Society):
www.CGSociety.org

Also available from Ballistic Publishing
EXPOSÉ 8 Softcover ISBN 978-1-921002-84-7
EXOTIQUE 5 Softcover ISBN 978-1-921002-69-4
The Art of UNCHARTED 2 ISBN 978-1-921002-71-7
The Art of God of War III ISBN 978-1-921002-72-4
d'artiste Character Modeling 3 ISBN 978-1-921002-67-0

Visit www.BallisticPublishing.com
for our complete range of titles.

Cover image credits

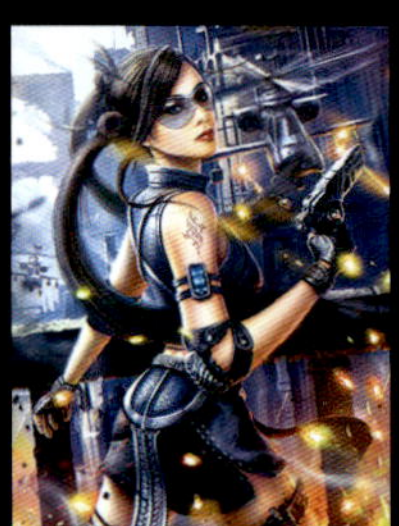

Catch
Photoshop
Bryan Sola,
THE PHILIPPINES
[Front cover: EXOTIQUE 6 Softcover edition], 164-165

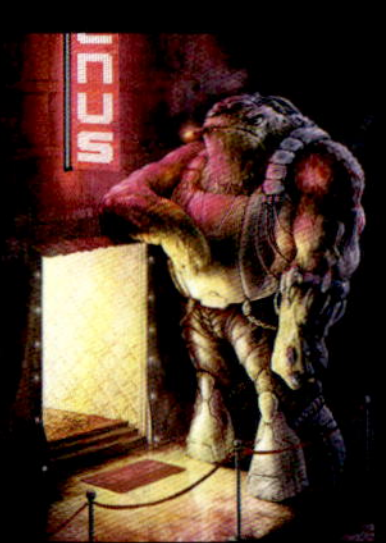

Golan Bouncer
Photoshop
Art Director: Arni Kristjan Gudmundsson
Client: Arni Kristjan Gudmundsson
Mark Molnar, NEW ZEALAND
[Back cover: EXOTIQUE 6 Softcover edition], 75

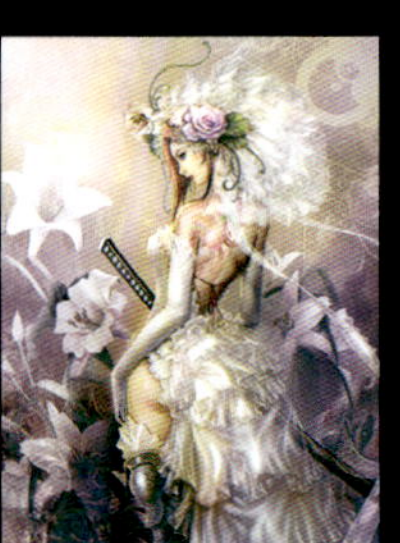

Revenge of the bride
Painter, Photoshop
Wan Hsienwei,
USERJOY Technology
Co. Ltd., TAIWAN
[Cover: EXOTIQUE 6 Special Edition], 44-45

/ BALLISTIC /

EDITORIAL

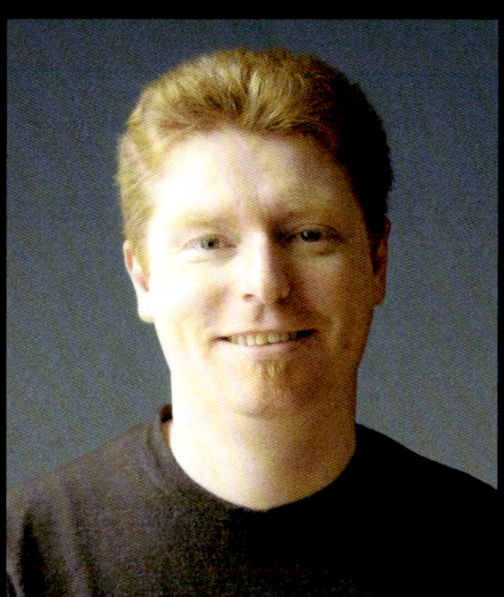

Daniel Wade | Publisher

Whenever someone asks me what Ballistic Publishing does, the easiest answer is to say we produce books on digital art. I then explain the different series we do, and how they're different in terms of whether they are a how-to book, or a gallery book, or a game art book. However, the question I enjoy answering most is why we do what we do—the reason that gets the team out of bed in the morning, and the reason we subject ourselves to deadlines. The answer can be one word, or thousands, but it boils down to this—inspiration. The most exciting, challenging and rewarding pursuit that drives us is being involved with talented artists and helping them to move others. The creative energy that surrounds artists, and their drive to continually push their own artistic boundaries is enormously inspiring, and as cheerleaders of the craft we love to see artists receive recognition for their efforts.

The physical part of our job which is to collect, and sort through thousands of pieces of art can be both exhilarating and disappointing. There's often more than ten times the amount of art entered than we can fit into one book, and we're always looking for ways to squeeze in more pieces—whether through clever design, more pages, or both. The disappointment comes with knowing that there are artists who deserve a place among their peers, but narrowly miss out because of the number of pages we can fit between the covers. Though the guilt can be overwhelming, it's offset by the many artists who continue to enter their work, and are eventually recognized.

Like the original digital art annual, EXPOSÉ, the EXOTIQUE series was created as a celebration of the huge amount of digital art being created both commercially and for artist's self-promotion in the character art genre. Each and every piece featured in EXOTIQUE 6 is worthy of praise, and we've taken every care to make sure we produced the best possible results by color-correcting each image by hand. It's this care that sets Ballistic Publishing books apart from any other.

The sixth title in the EXOTIQUE series brings together the world's most beautiful CG characters in science fiction, fantasy, anime, photorealism and stylized realism genres. With a record number of entries (approaching 3,000), we have included more character art than ever before to make it the biggest collection of new character art. Congratulations to all the artists who entered work for EXOTIQUE 6, and we hope you find the same level of inspiration in these pages as we have.

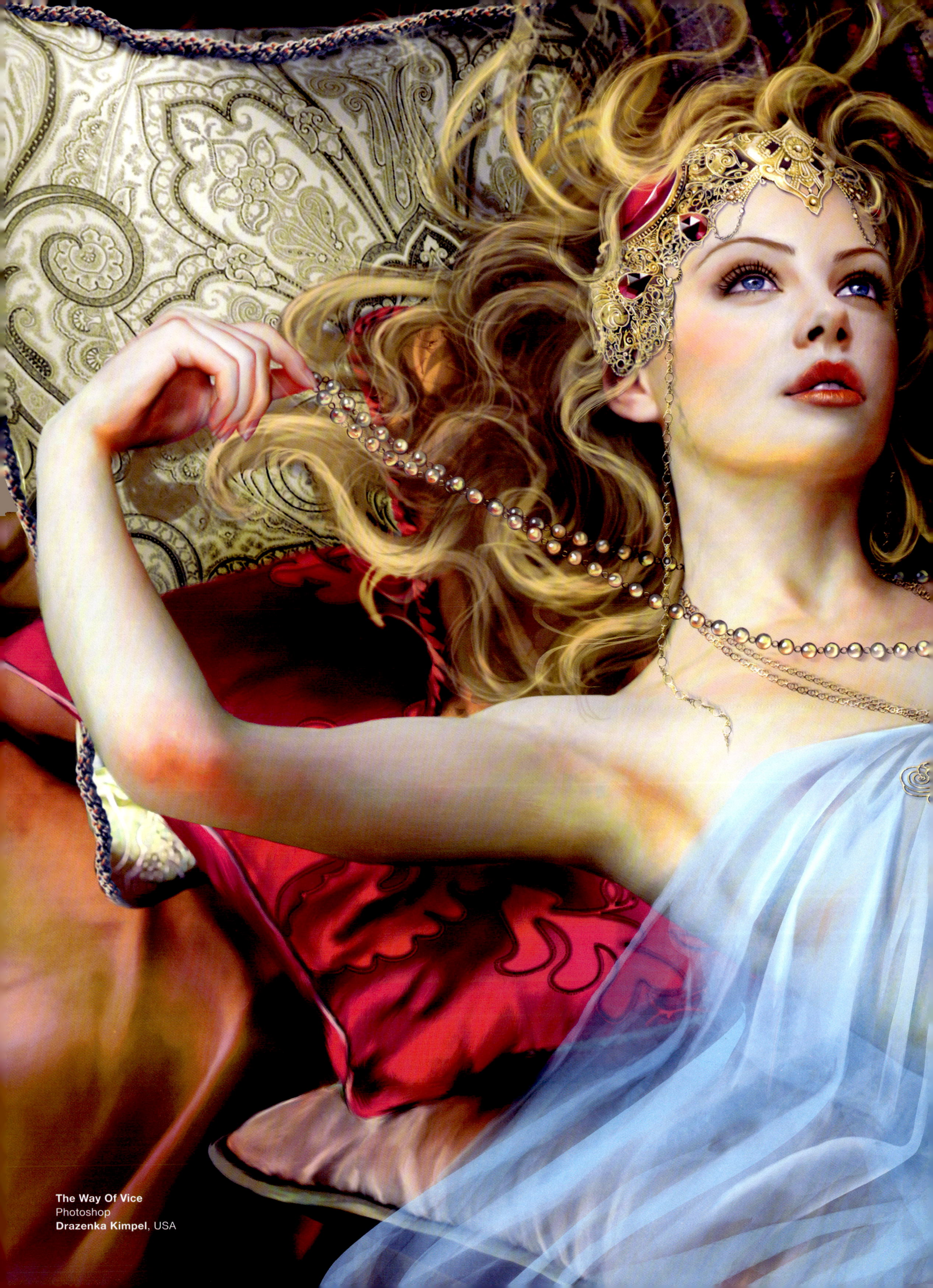

The Way Of Vice
Photoshop
Drazenka Kimpel, USA

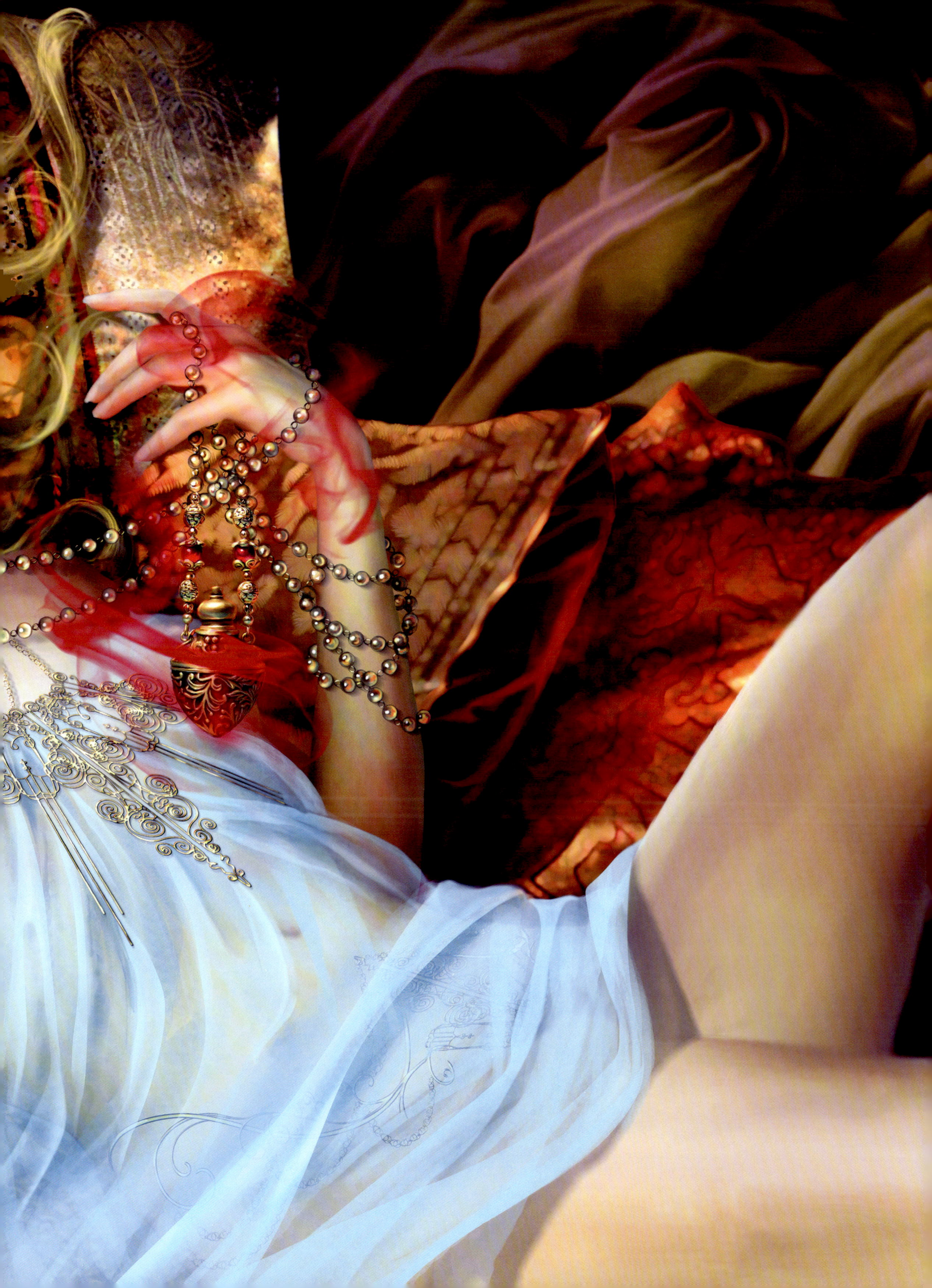

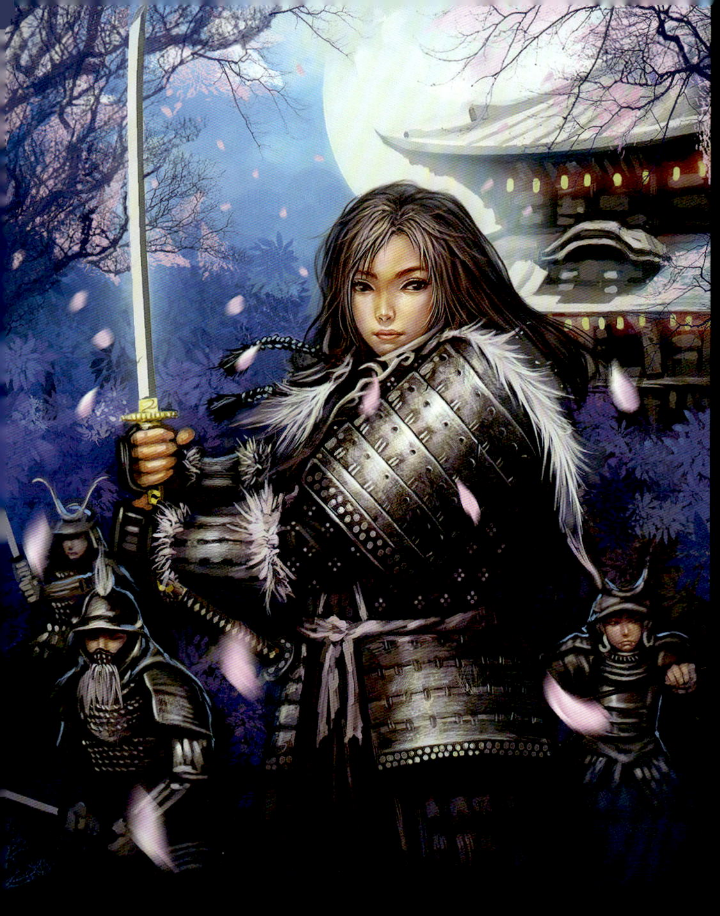

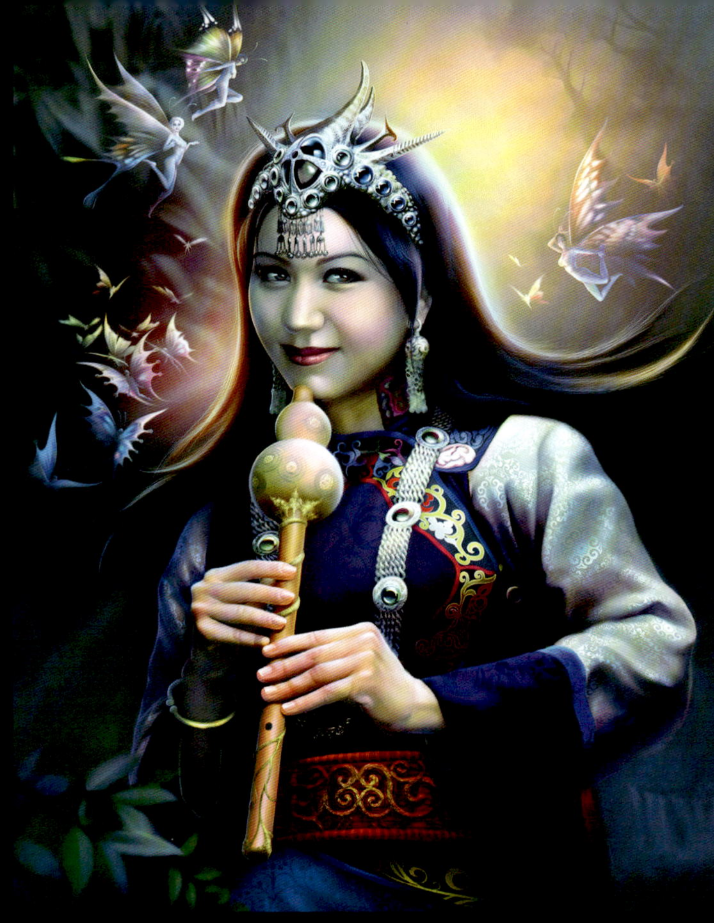

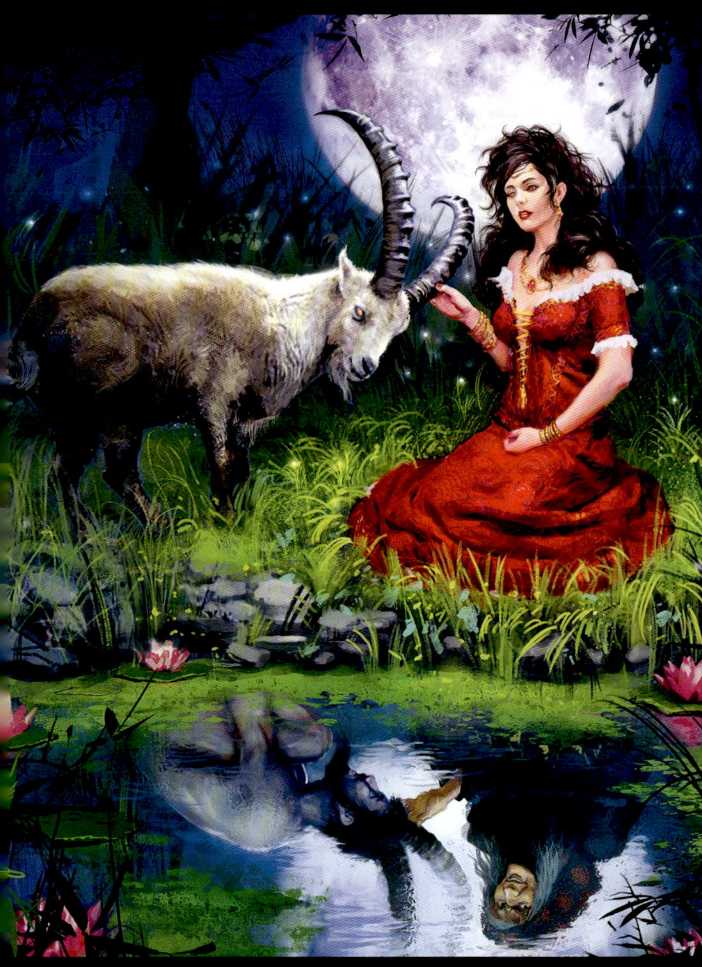

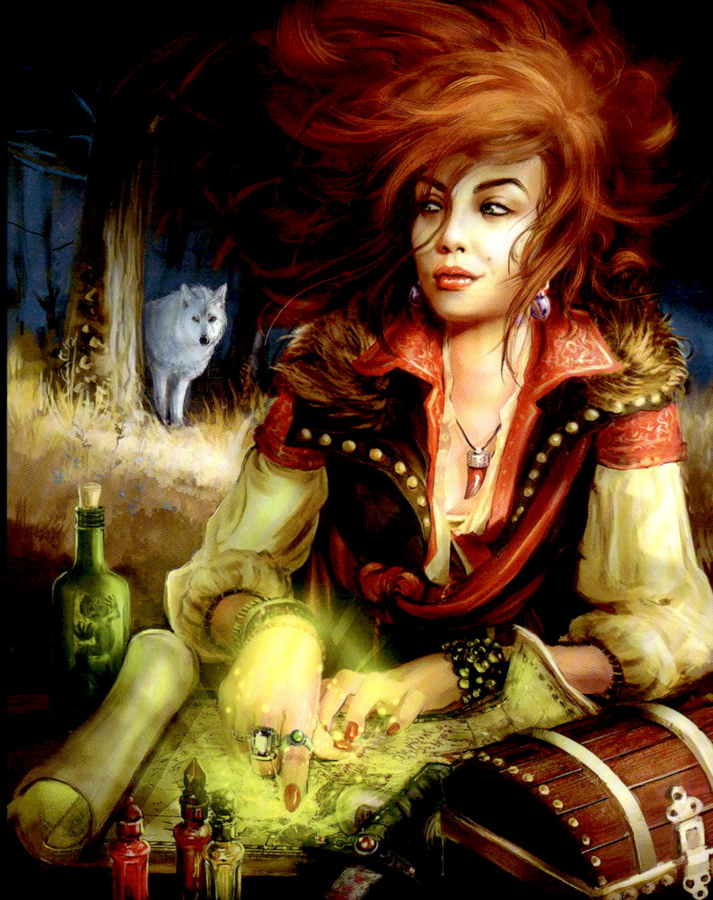

'Witch the Guardian' © Fabryka Słów

General
Photoshop
Sining Ma, CHINA
[top]

Witch From Wilzynska Valley
Photoshop
Client: Runa
Artur Sadlos, POLAND *[above]*

The Magic Flute
Painter, Photoshop
Bin Wee, CHINA
[top]

Witch the Guardian Vol.1: Cover
Photoshop
Client: Fabryka Słów
Milena Mlynarska, POLAND *[above]*

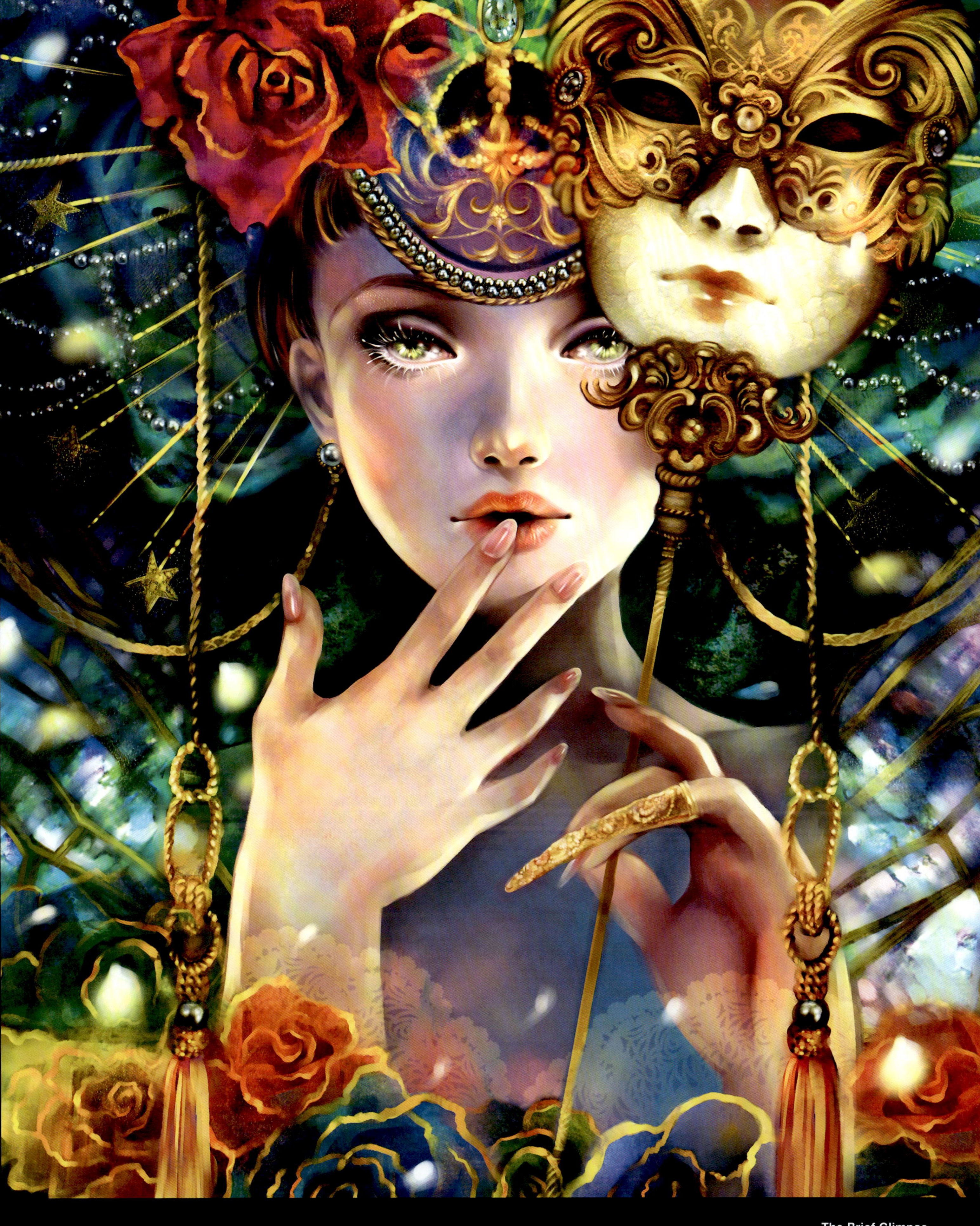

The Brief Glimpse
Photoshop, Painter
Schin Loong, USA

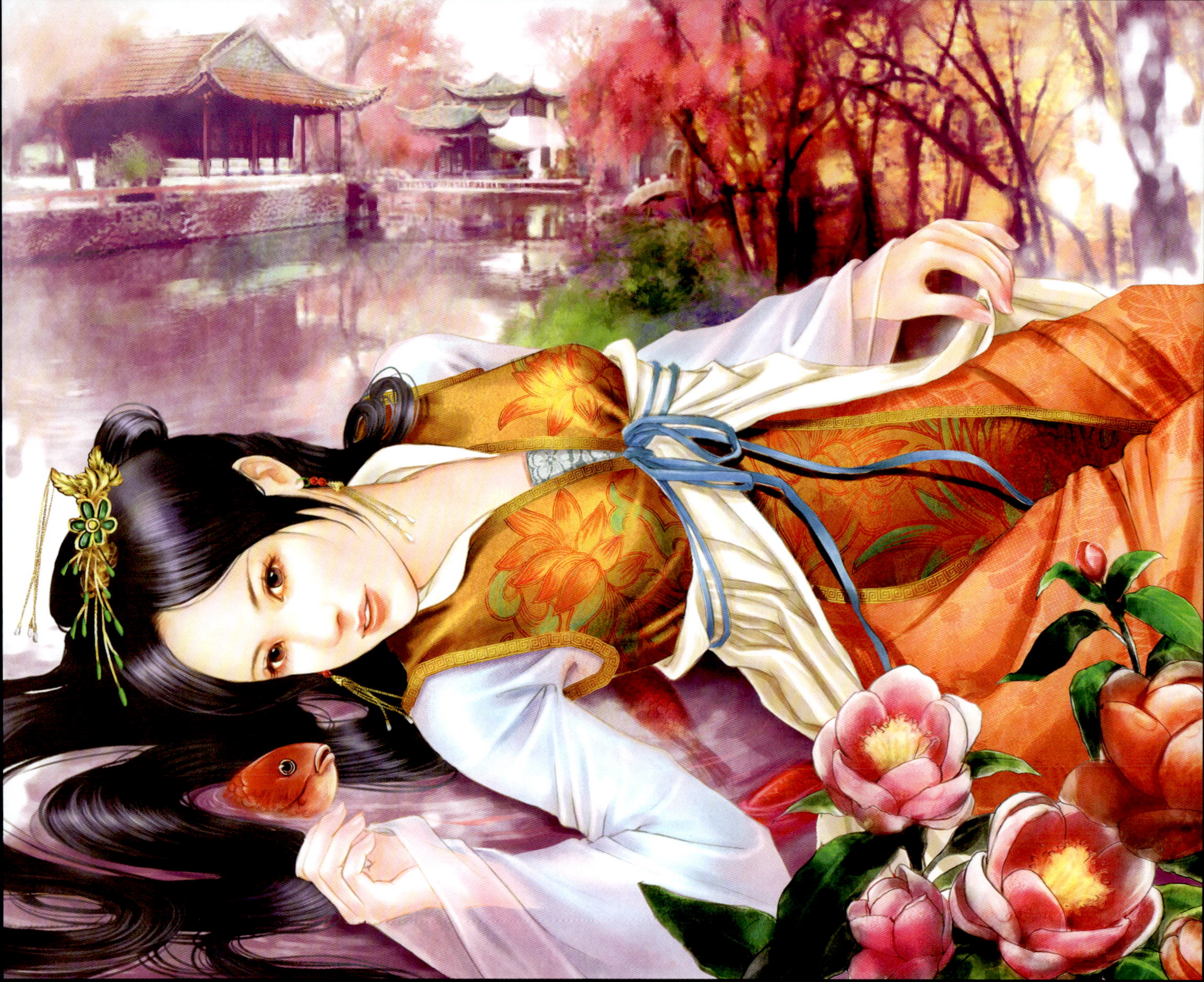

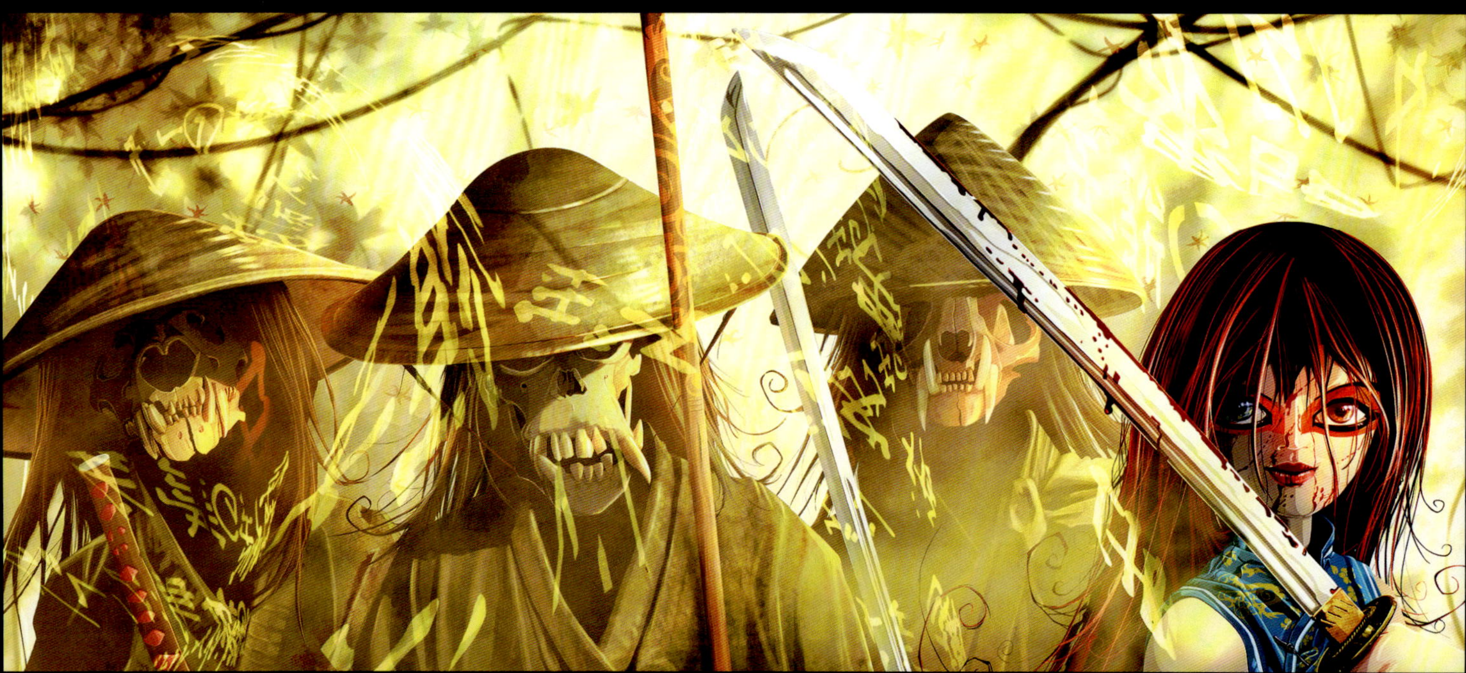

Fish Spirit
Painter
Wendy Wang, TAIWAN
[top]

Enter the Three
Photoshop, Illustrator, modo
Steve Sampson, GREAT BRITAIN
[above]

Kitsune
Photoshop
Helen Rusovich, UKRAINE
[right]

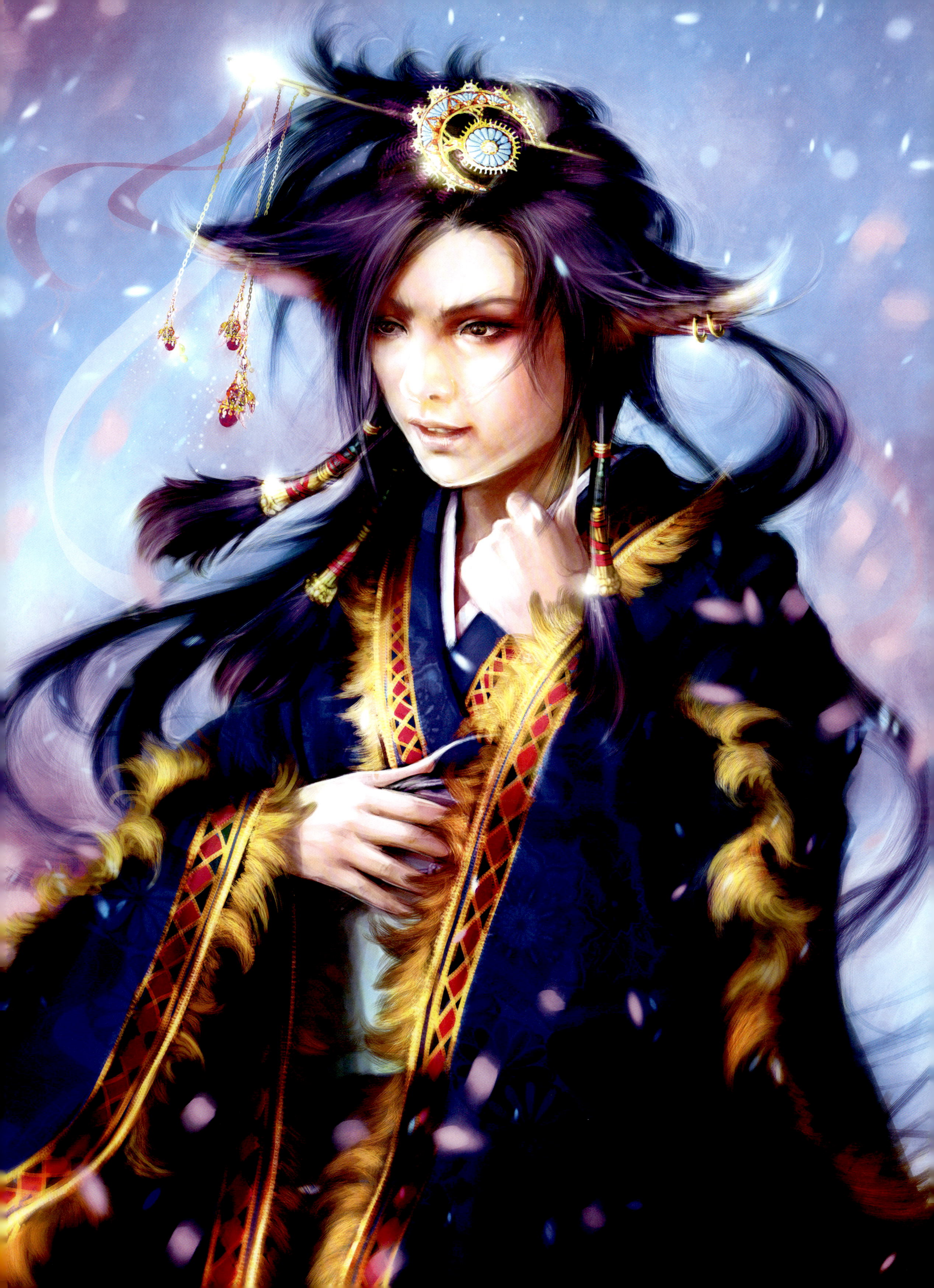

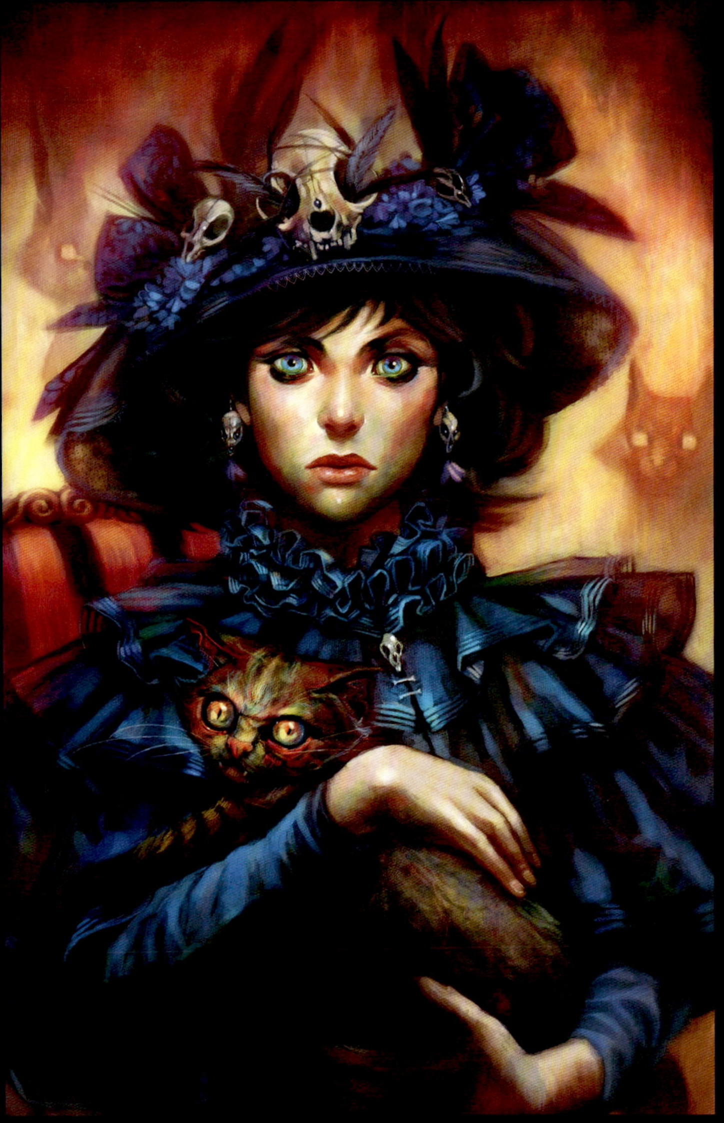

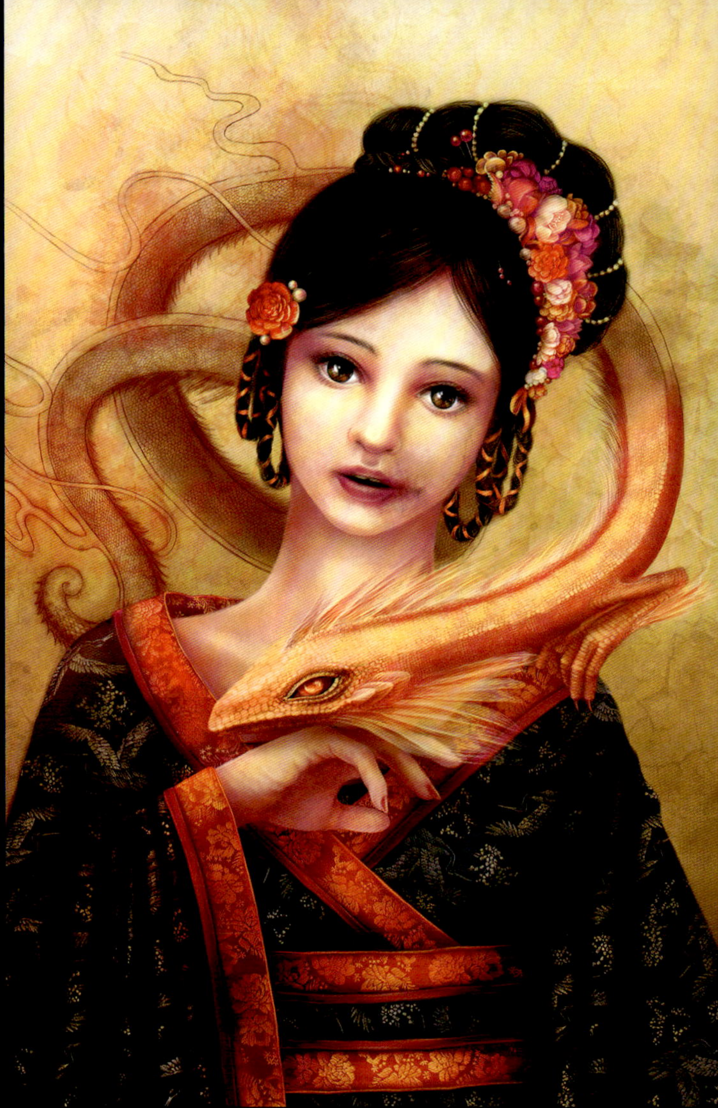

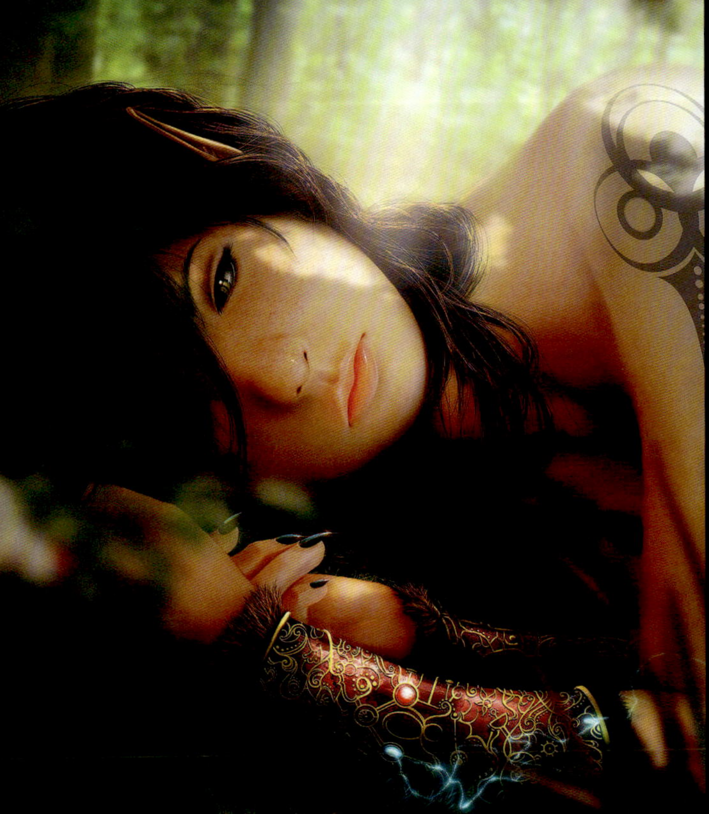

Out of the blue
Photoshop
Jeremie Fleury, FRANCE
[top left]

Imperfection
Photoshop
Magdalena Saramak,
POLAND
[above]

Daydreaming
Photoshop
Christopher Ang,
THE PHILIPPINES
[left]

Princess Peacock Eye
Photoshop
Elena 'Fish-KAart'
Klementyeva, RUSSIA
[right]

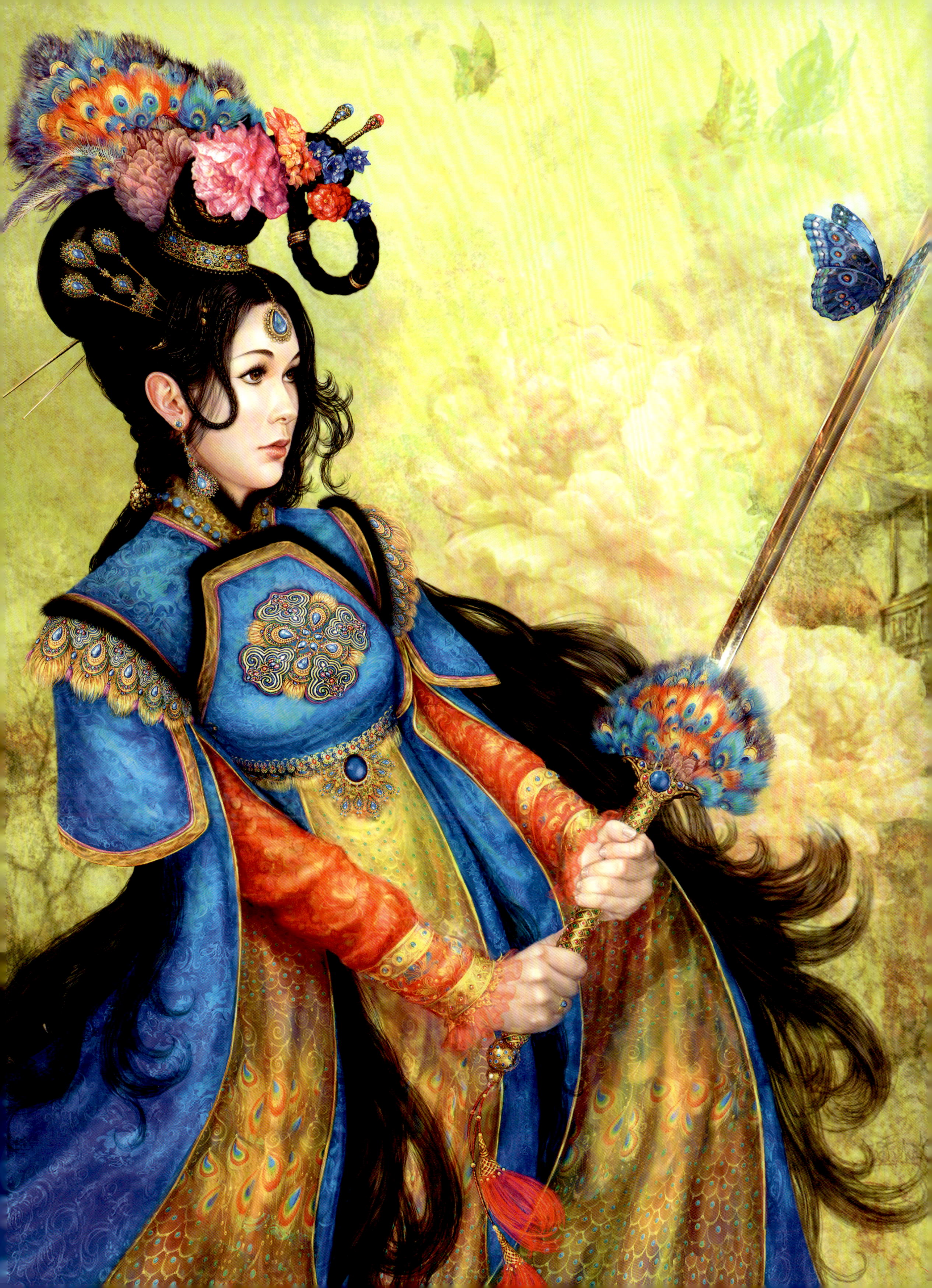

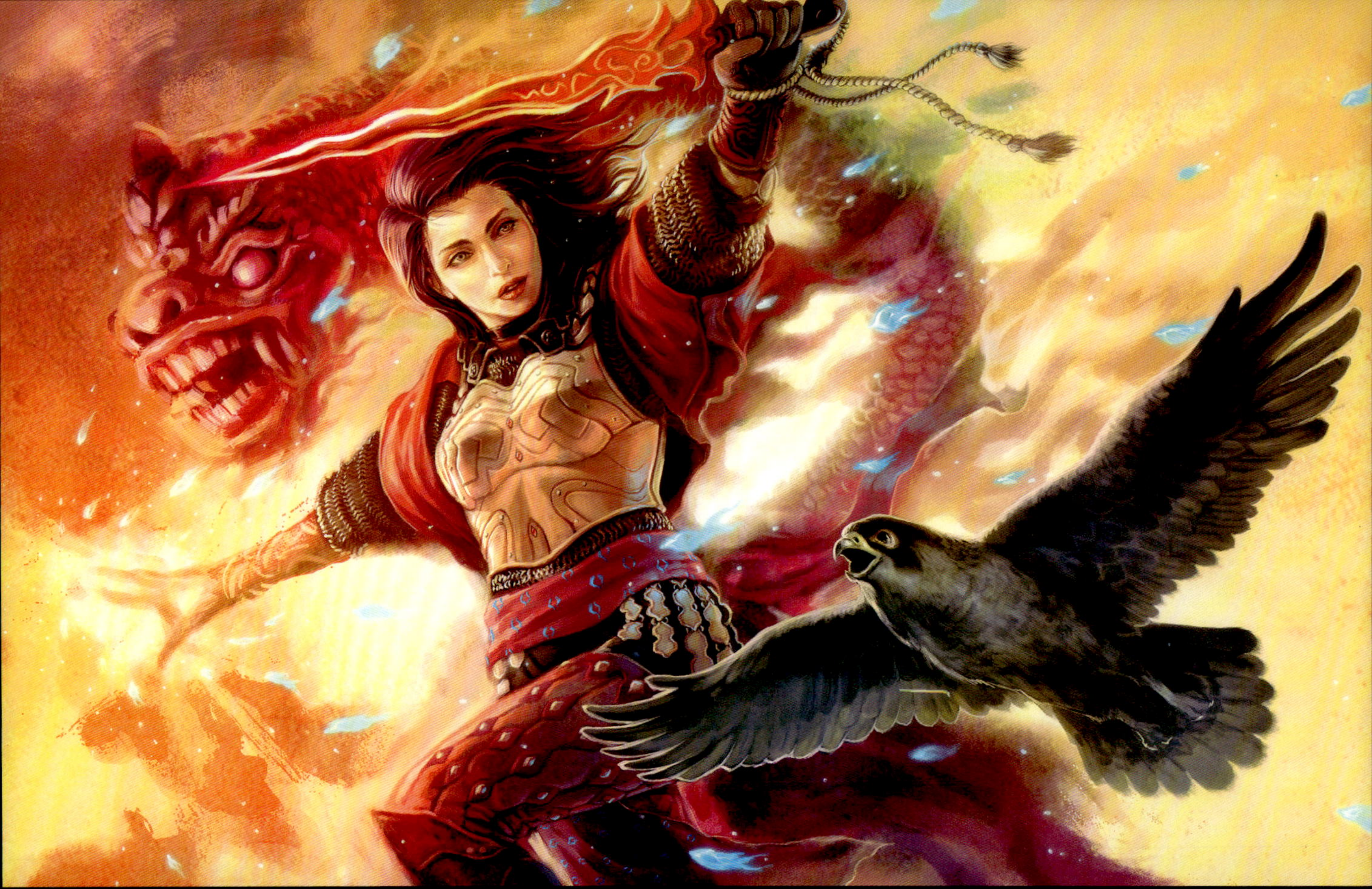

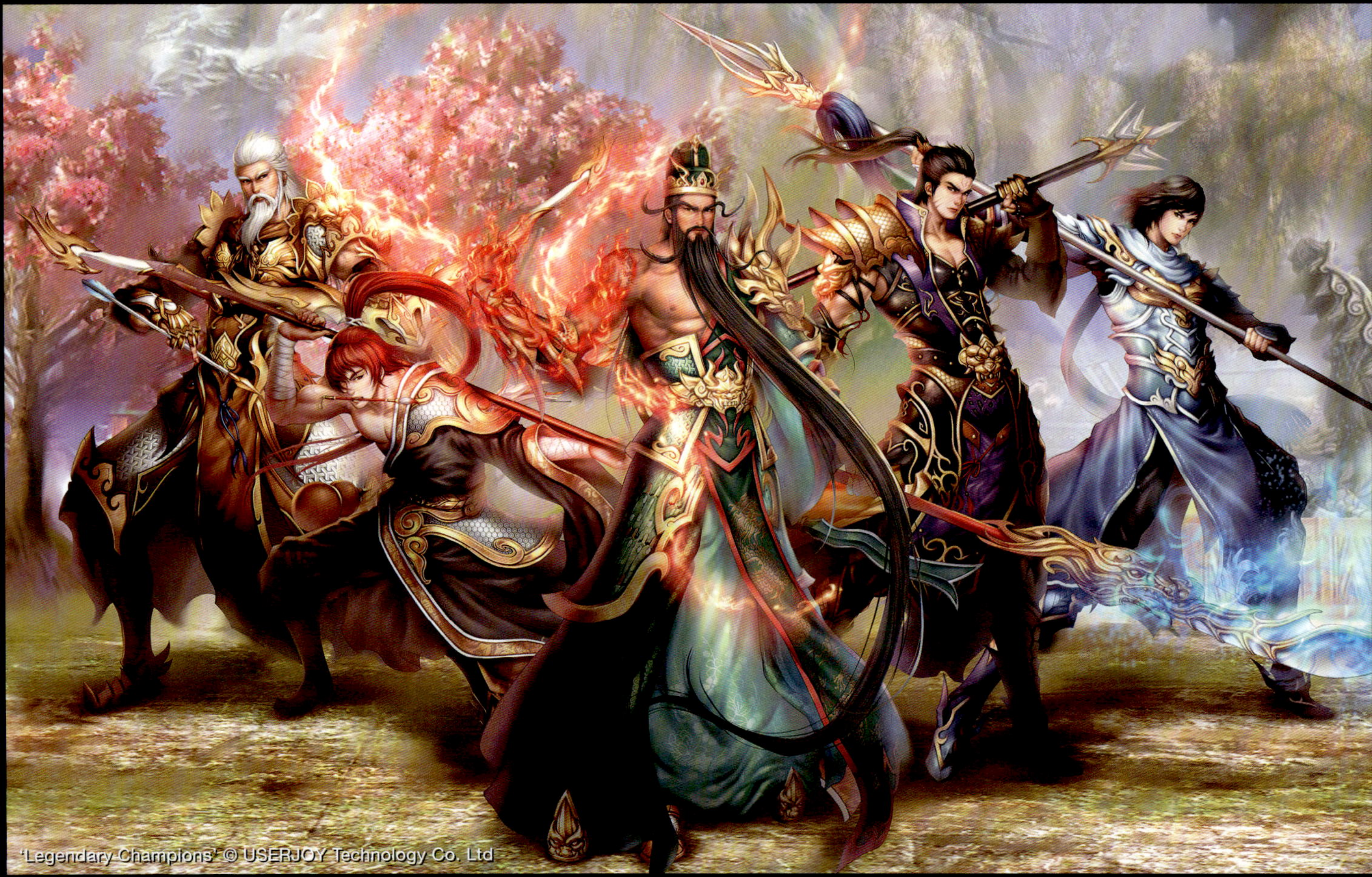

Nagasasra
Photoshop
Rafi Adrian Zulkarnain,
INDONESIA *[top]*

Legendary Champions: Five Tiger Warriors
Painter, Photoshop
Wan Hsienwei, USERJOY Technology Co. Ltd.,
TAIWAN *[above]*

Asian-inspired
Photoshop
Gracjana Zielinska,
POLAND *[right]*

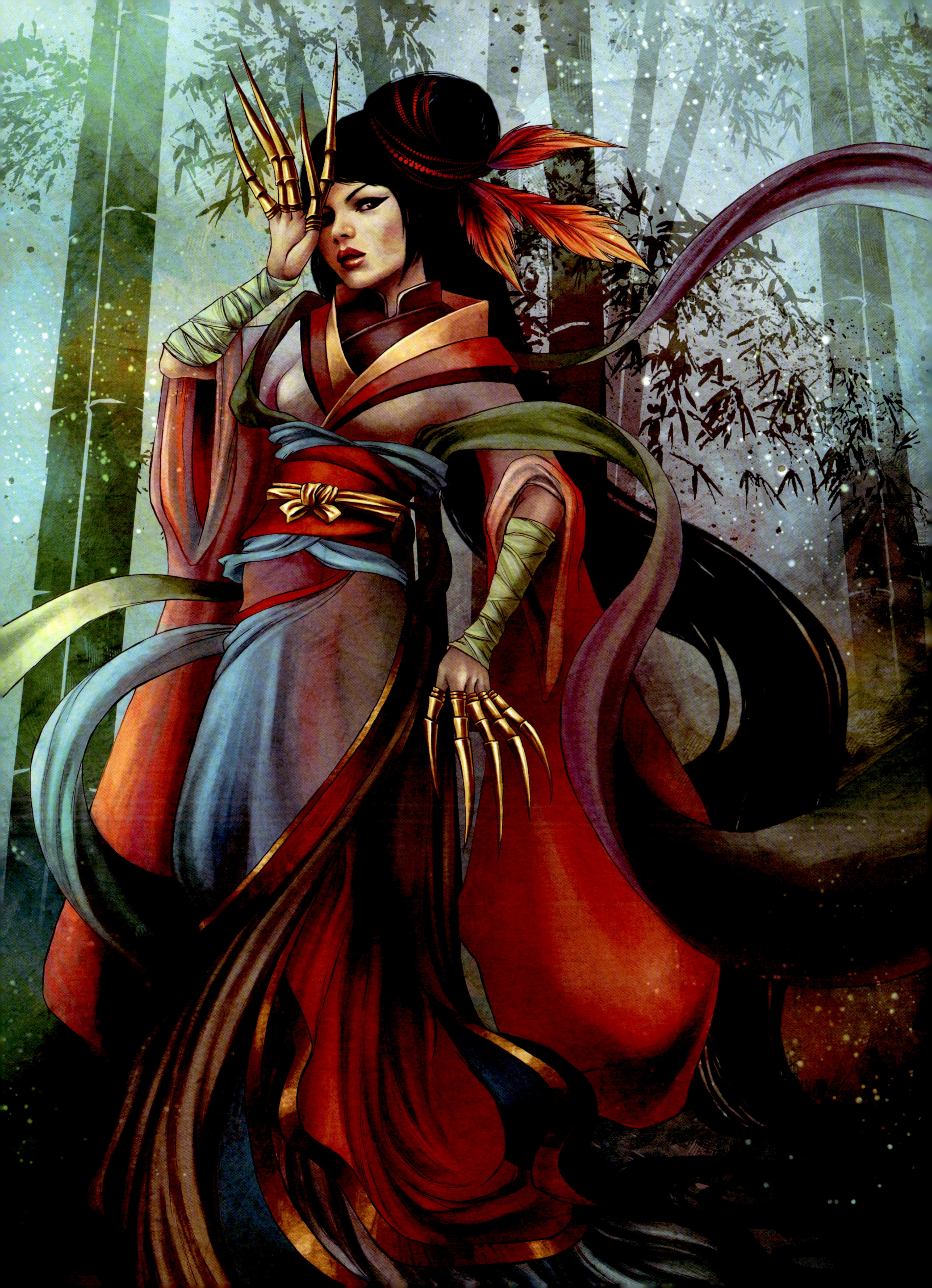

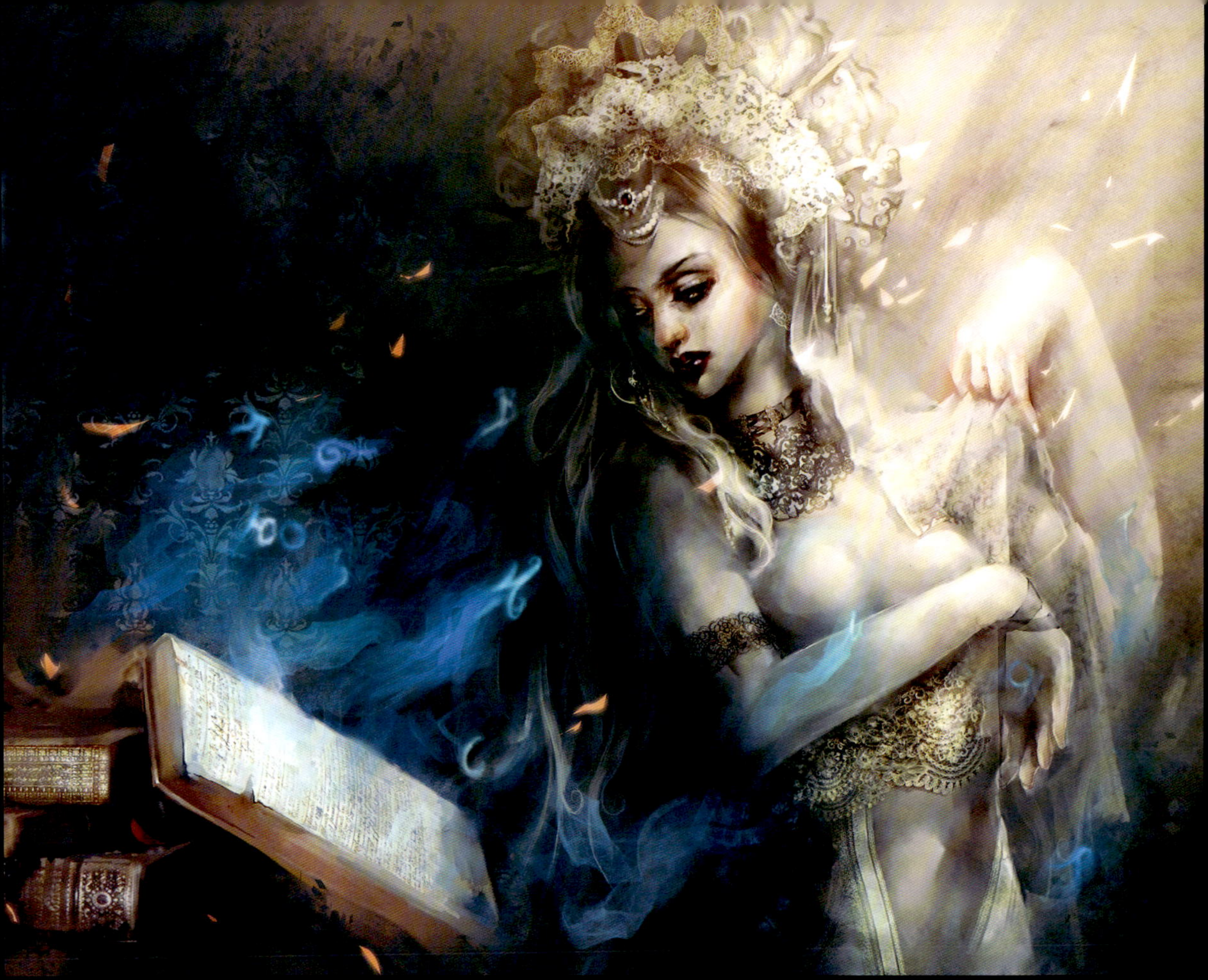

When words come to me
Photoshop
TE HU, USA
[left]

Magpies hope
Photoshop
Yundan Li, CHINA
[right]

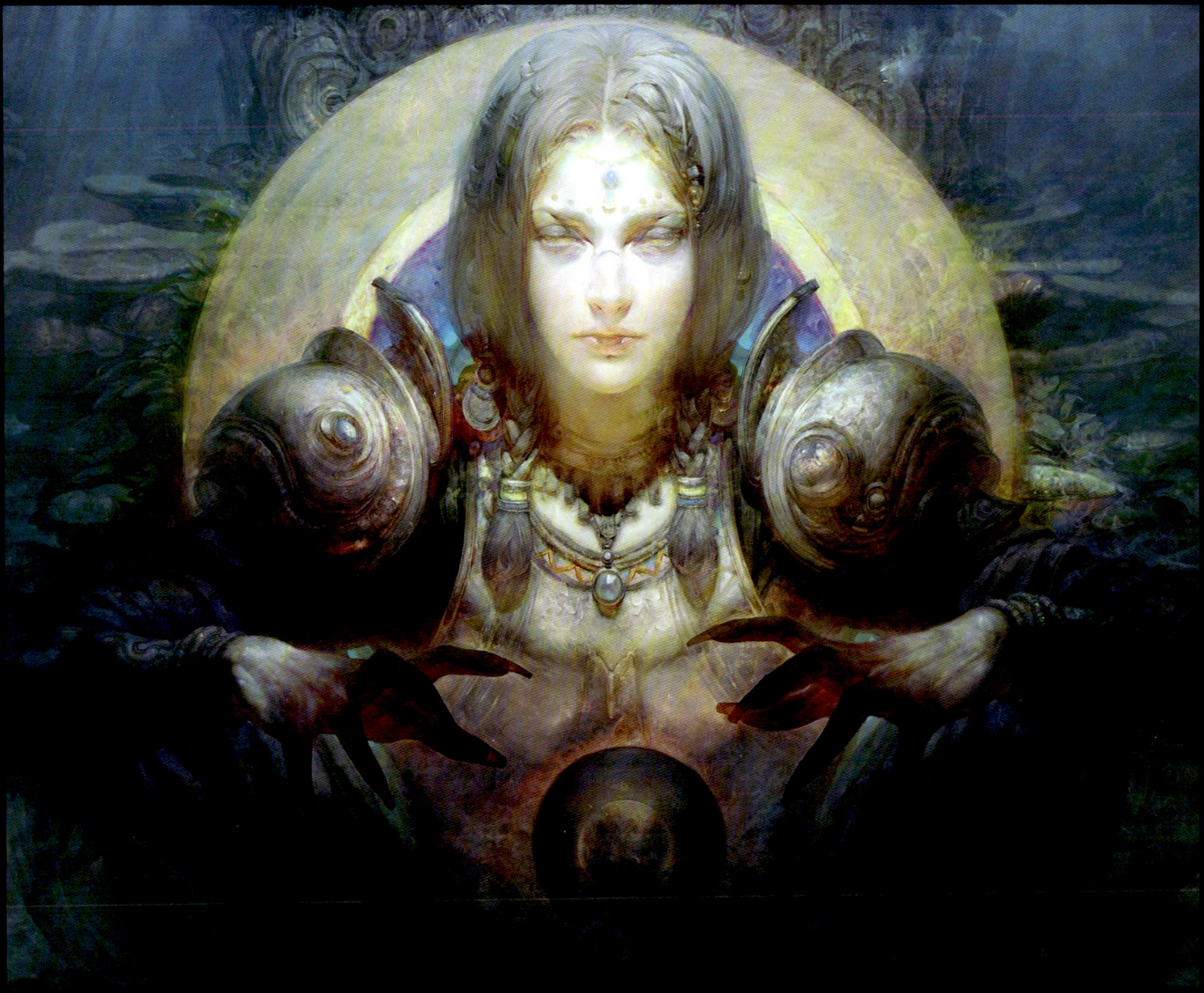

Blood glaze
Photoshop
Ruan Jia, CHINA
[left]

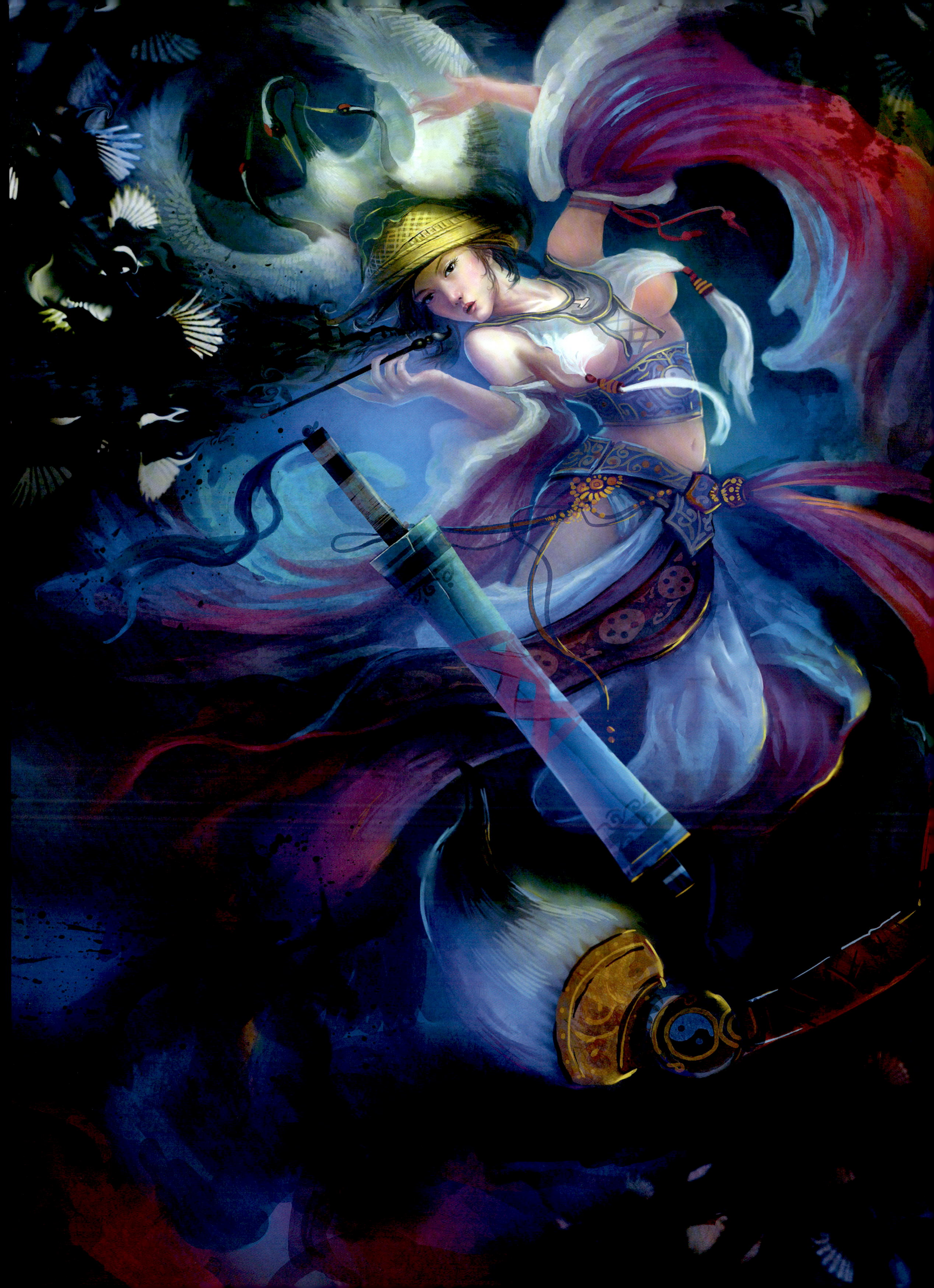

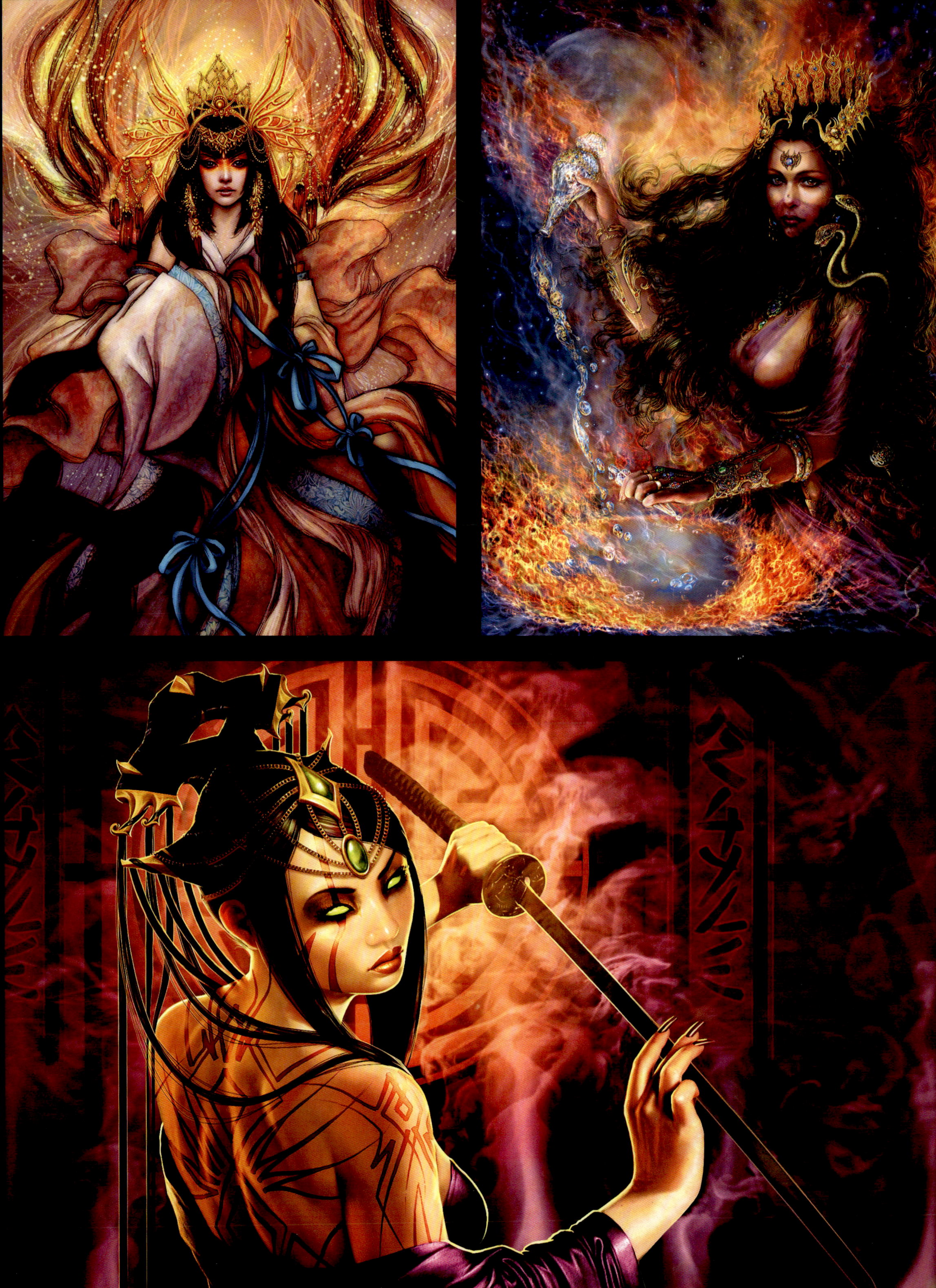

Asian-inspired
Photoshop
Gracjana Zielinska, POLAND
[far left]

E k a t h (Gekata)
Photoshop
Elena 'Fish-KAart' Klementyeva, RUSSIA
[left]

The Fairy of Oriental Star
Photoshop
Eldar Zakirov, UZBEKISTAN
[right]

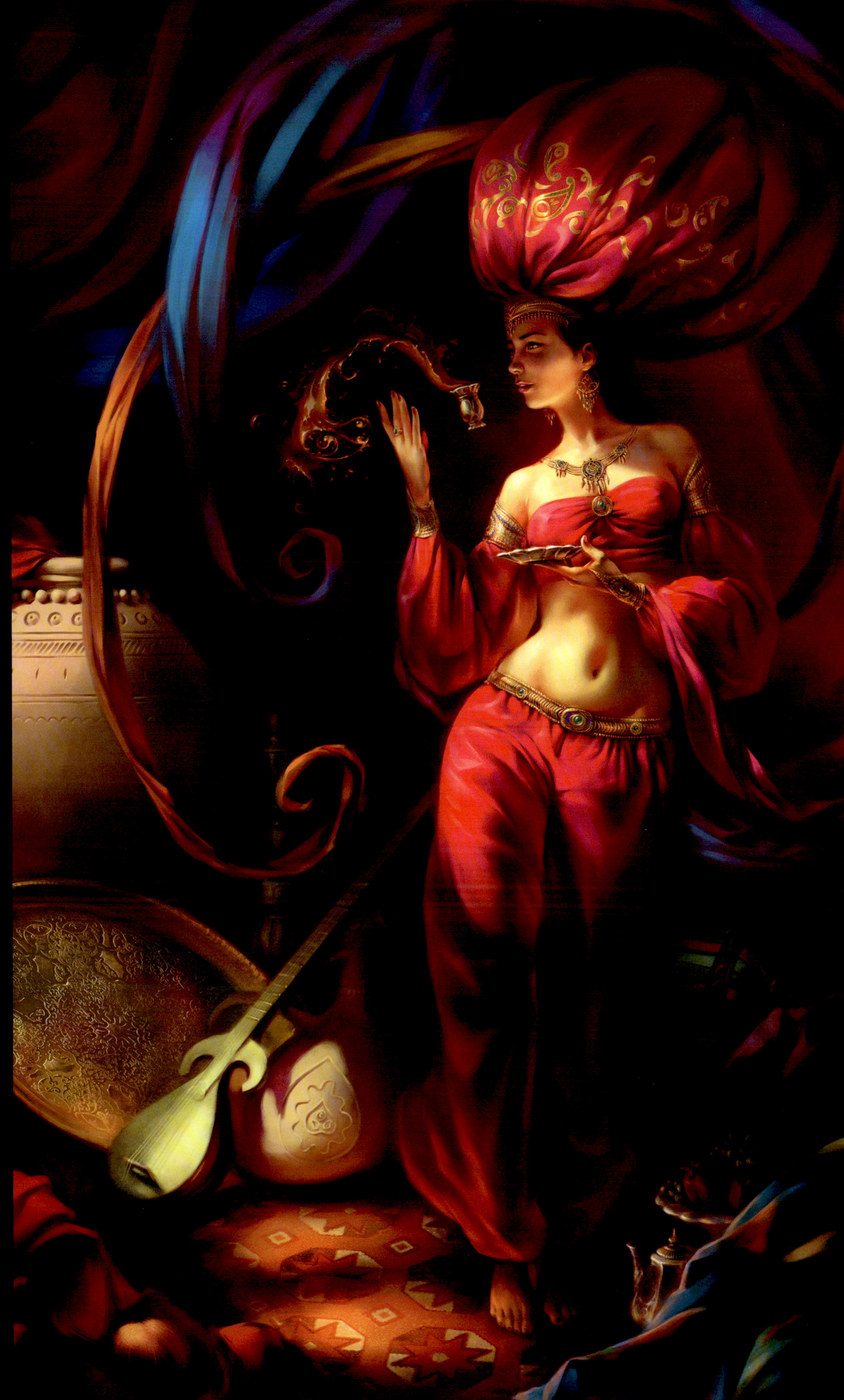

Legend of The Five Rings: Dark Beauty
Photoshop
Client: Alderac Entertainment Group
Steve Argyle, USA
[left]

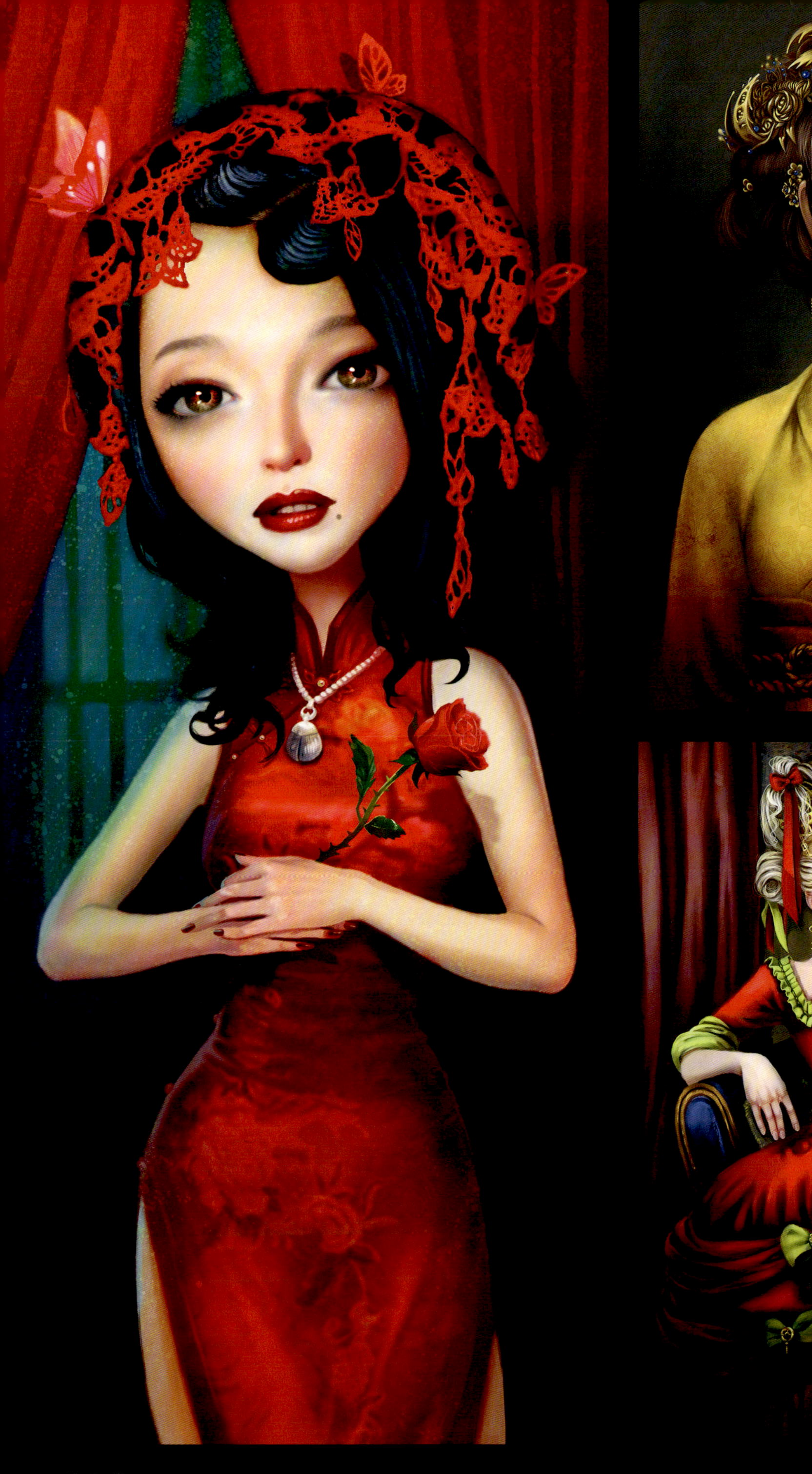

Butterfly
Photoshop
Jiansong Chain, Perfect World Co. Ltd,
CHINA *[above]*

The girl
Photoshop
Wing Liu, CHINA
[top]

Marie Antoinette
Photoshop
Nele Klumpe, GERMANY
[above]

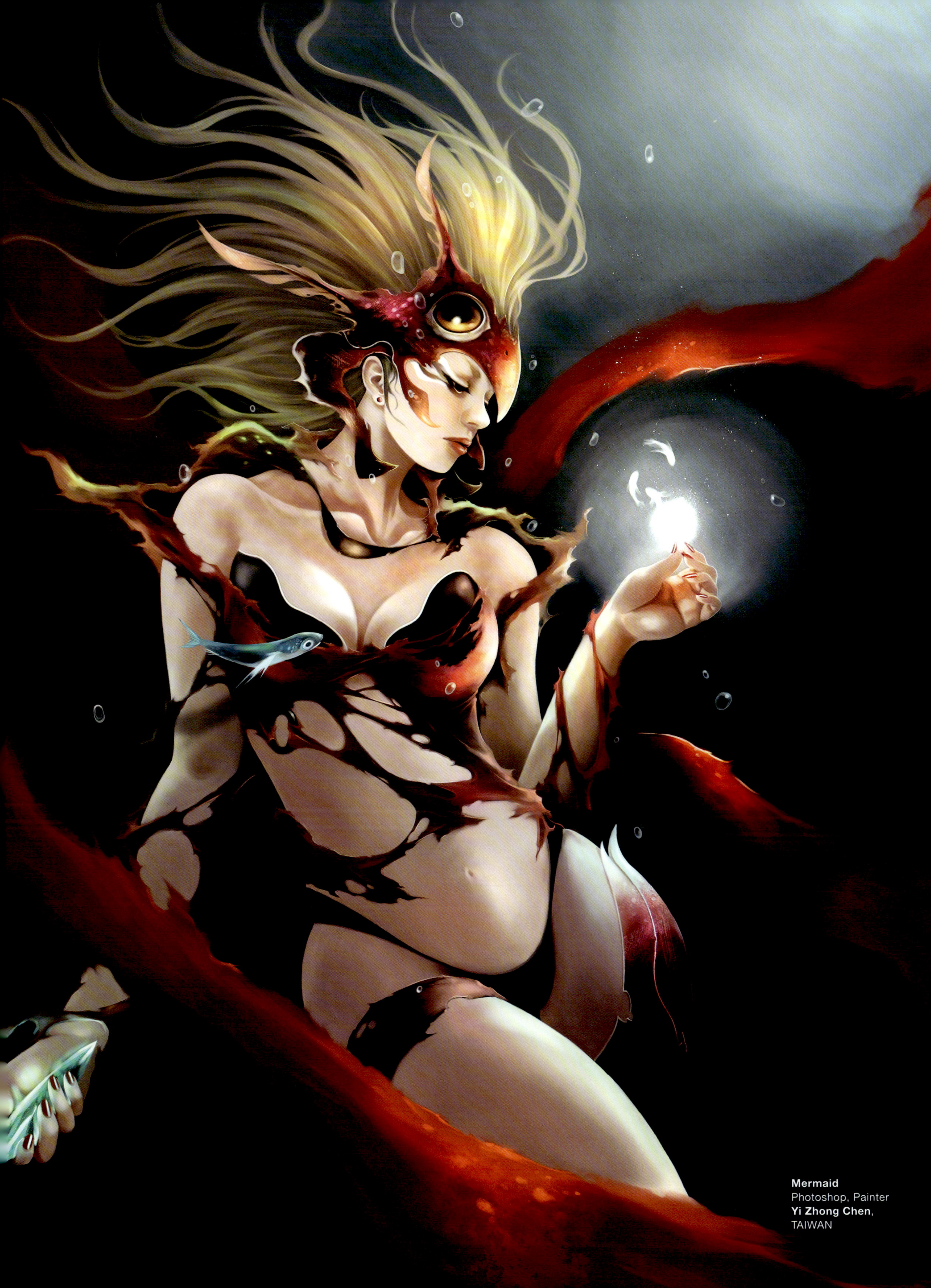

Mermaid
Photoshop, Painter
Yi Zhong Chen, TAIWAN

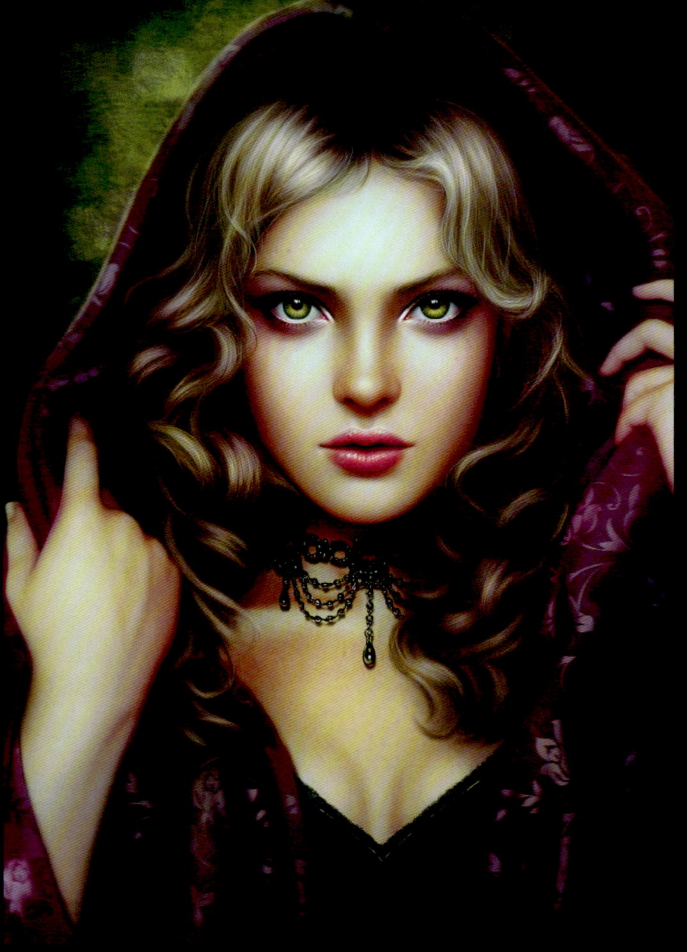

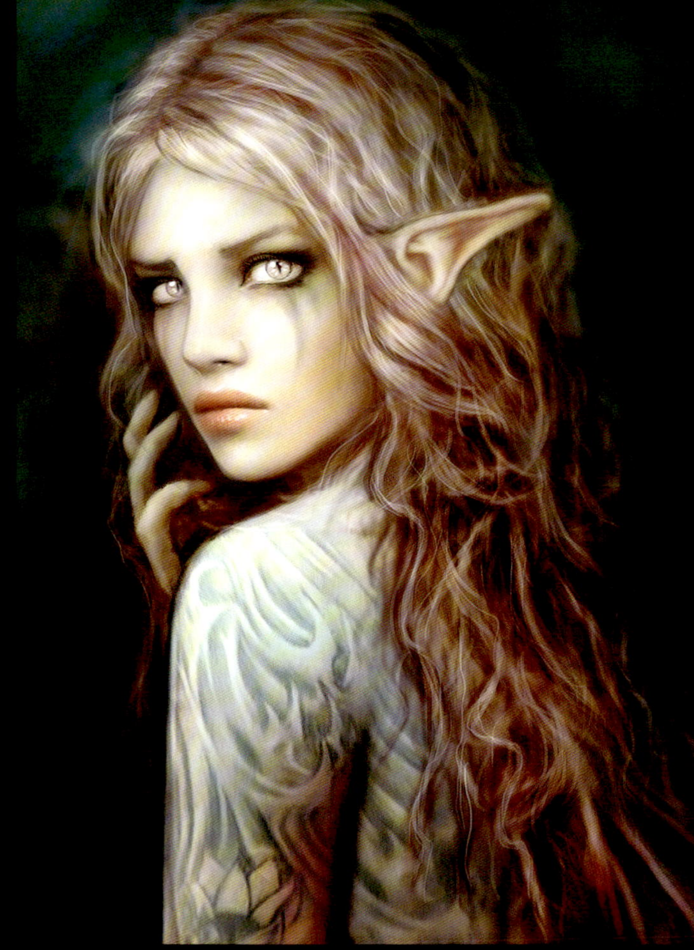

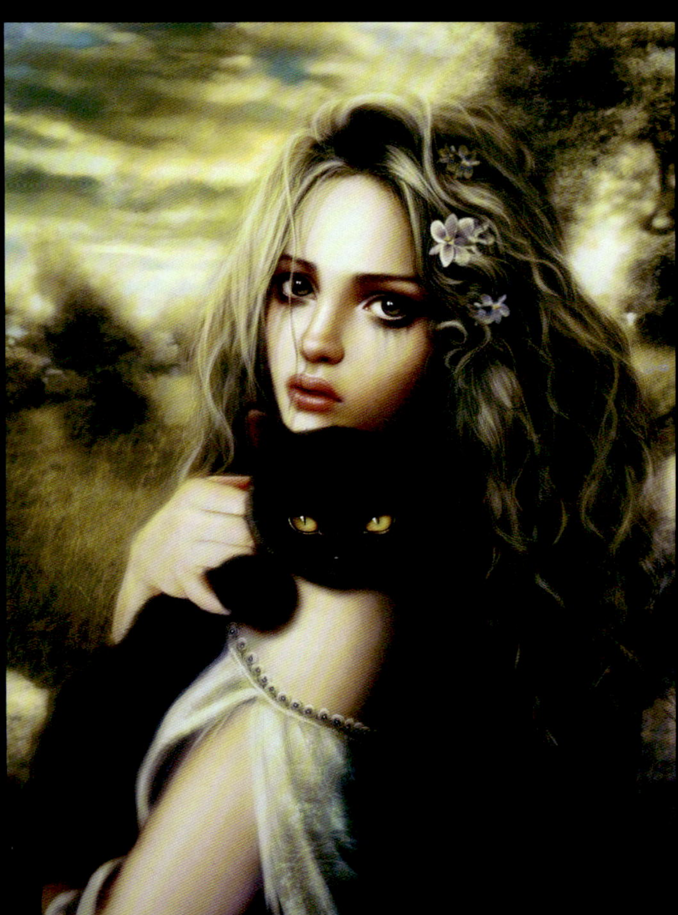

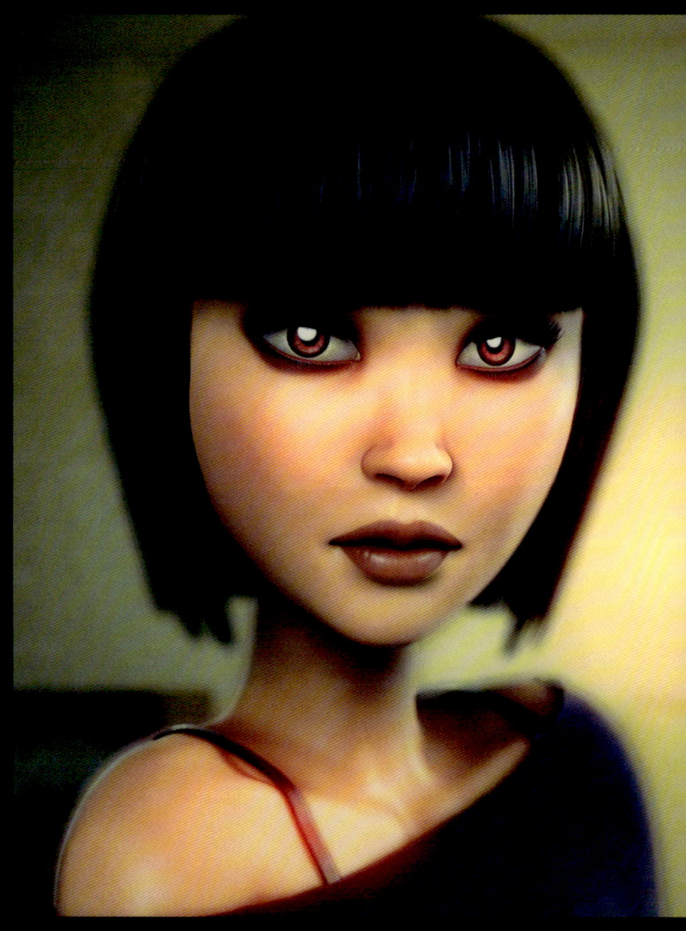

Look at me
Photoshop, Painter
Omar Diaz, SPAIN
[top]

Only You
Photoshop
Omar Diaz, SPAIN
[above]

Surrendered
Painter, Photoshop
Anne Pogoda, GERMANY
[top]

Patience
Maya, mental ray, Mudbox, Fusion
Lukasz Siudzinski, POLAND
[above]

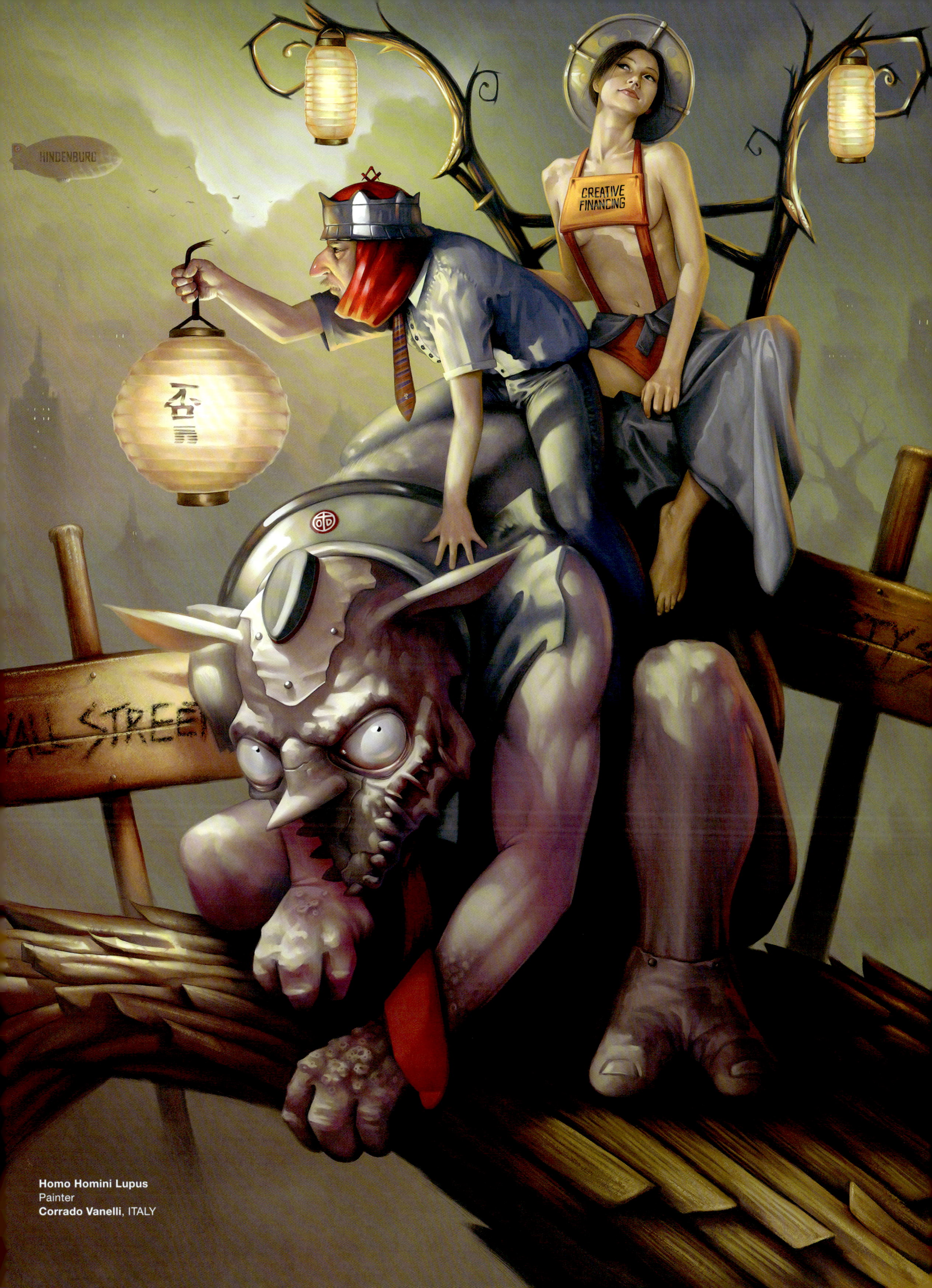

Homo Homini Lupus
Painter
Corrado Vanelli, ITALY

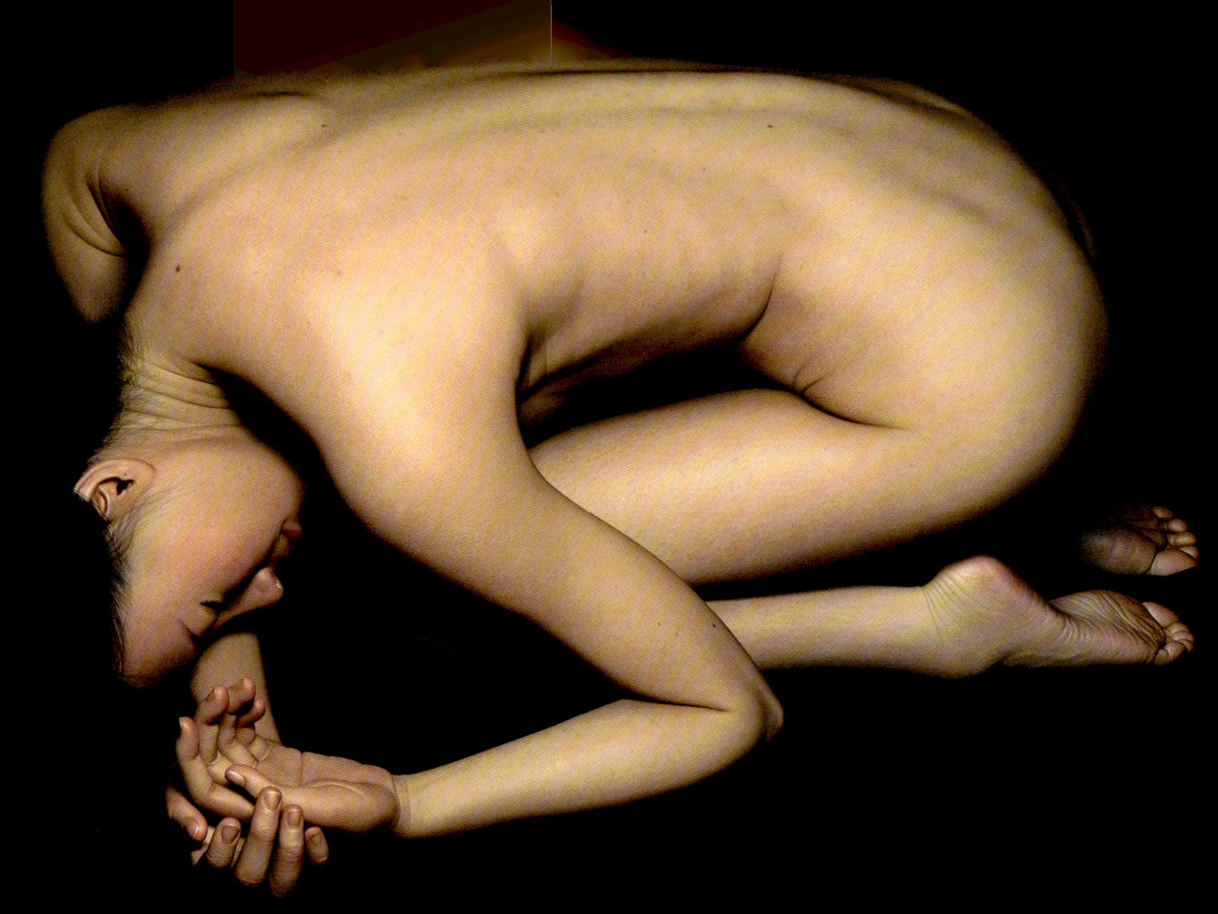

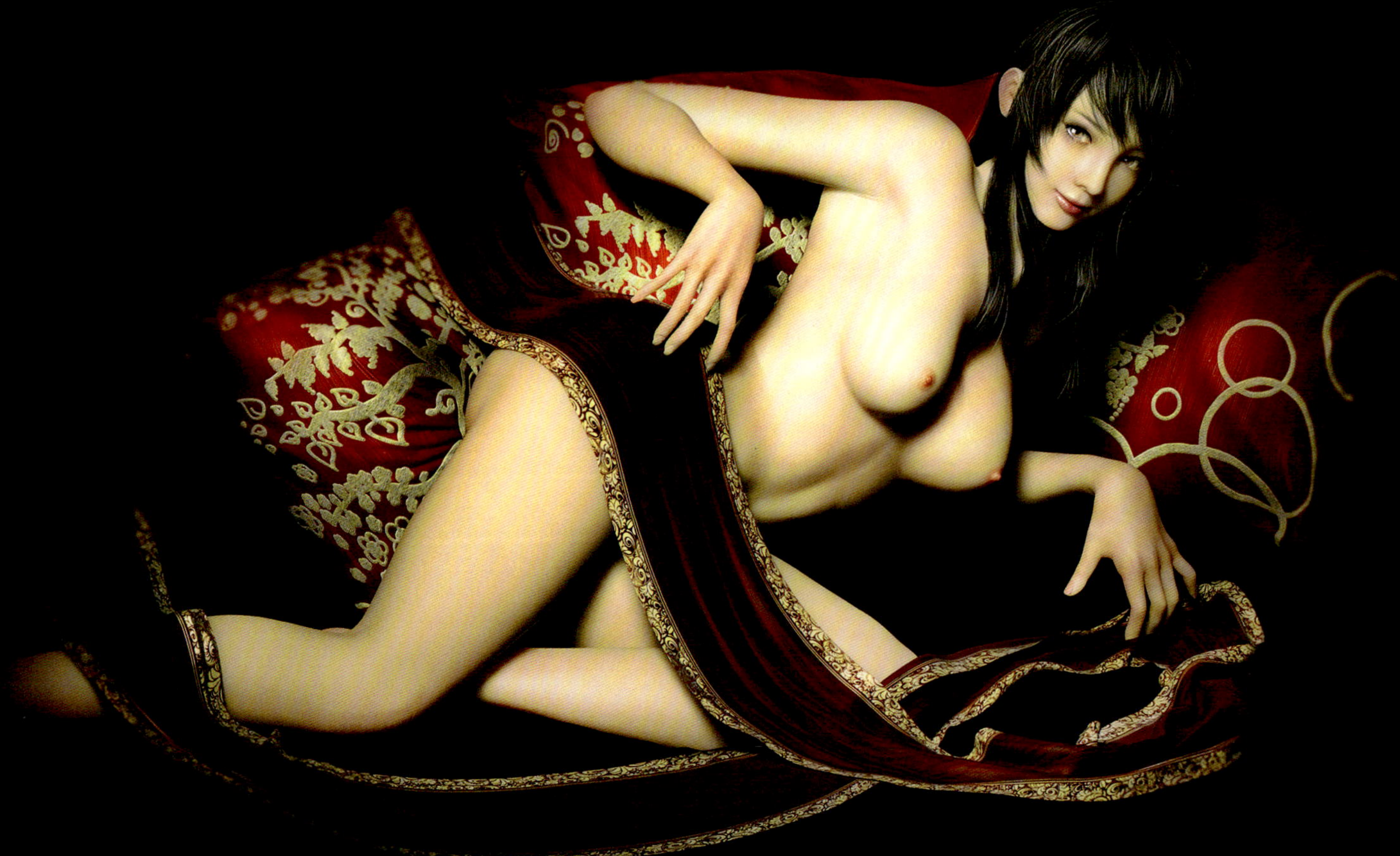

Nude woman
3ds Max, ZBrush, Photoshop, mental ray
Jian Xu, SINGAPORE
[top]

Vermillion and gold
BodyPaint 3D, Maya, mental ray, ZBrush
Dzung Phungdinh, VIETNAM
[above]

Akina in room
Photoshop
Michel Victor Oliveira, BRAZIL
[right]

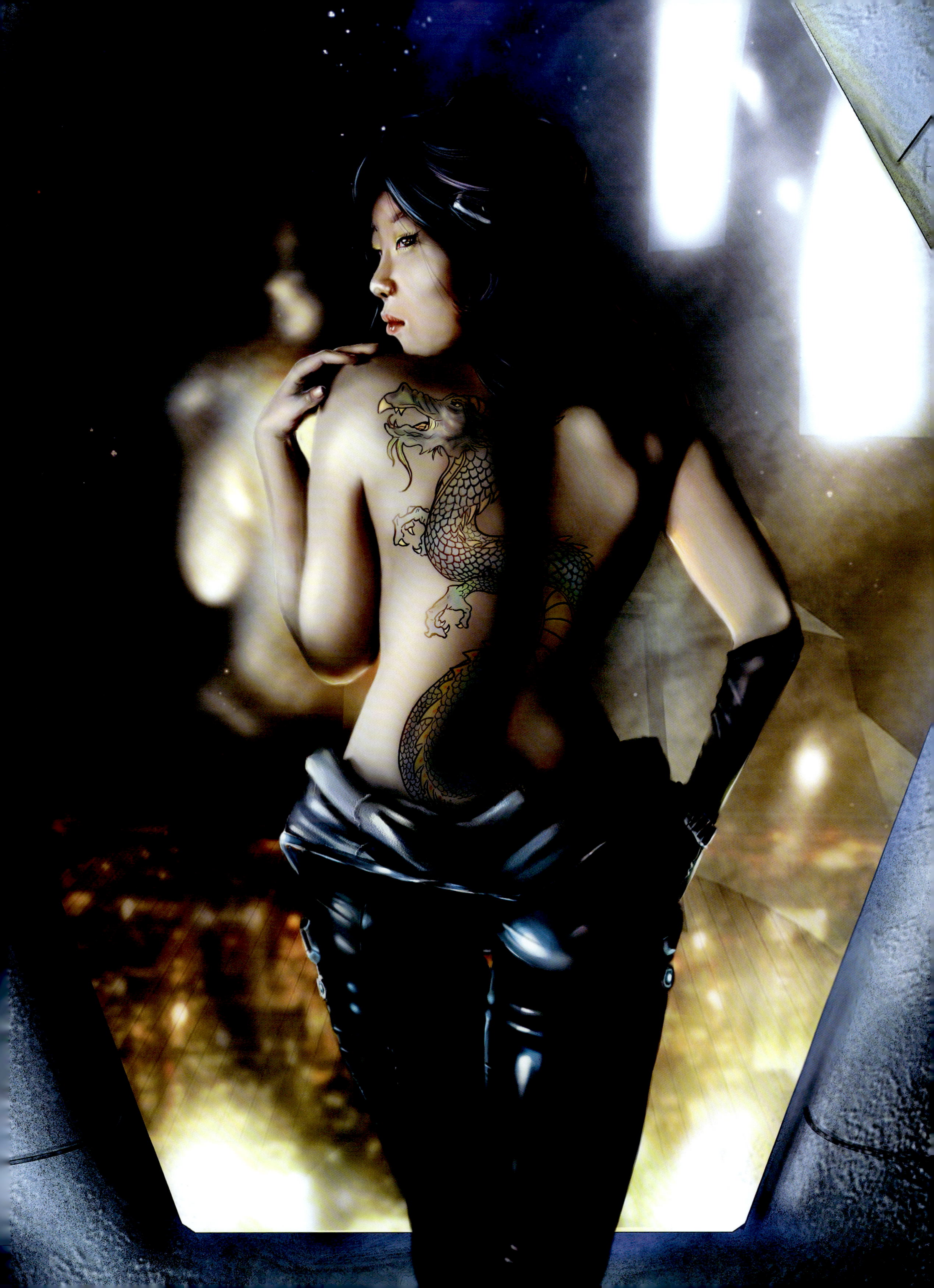

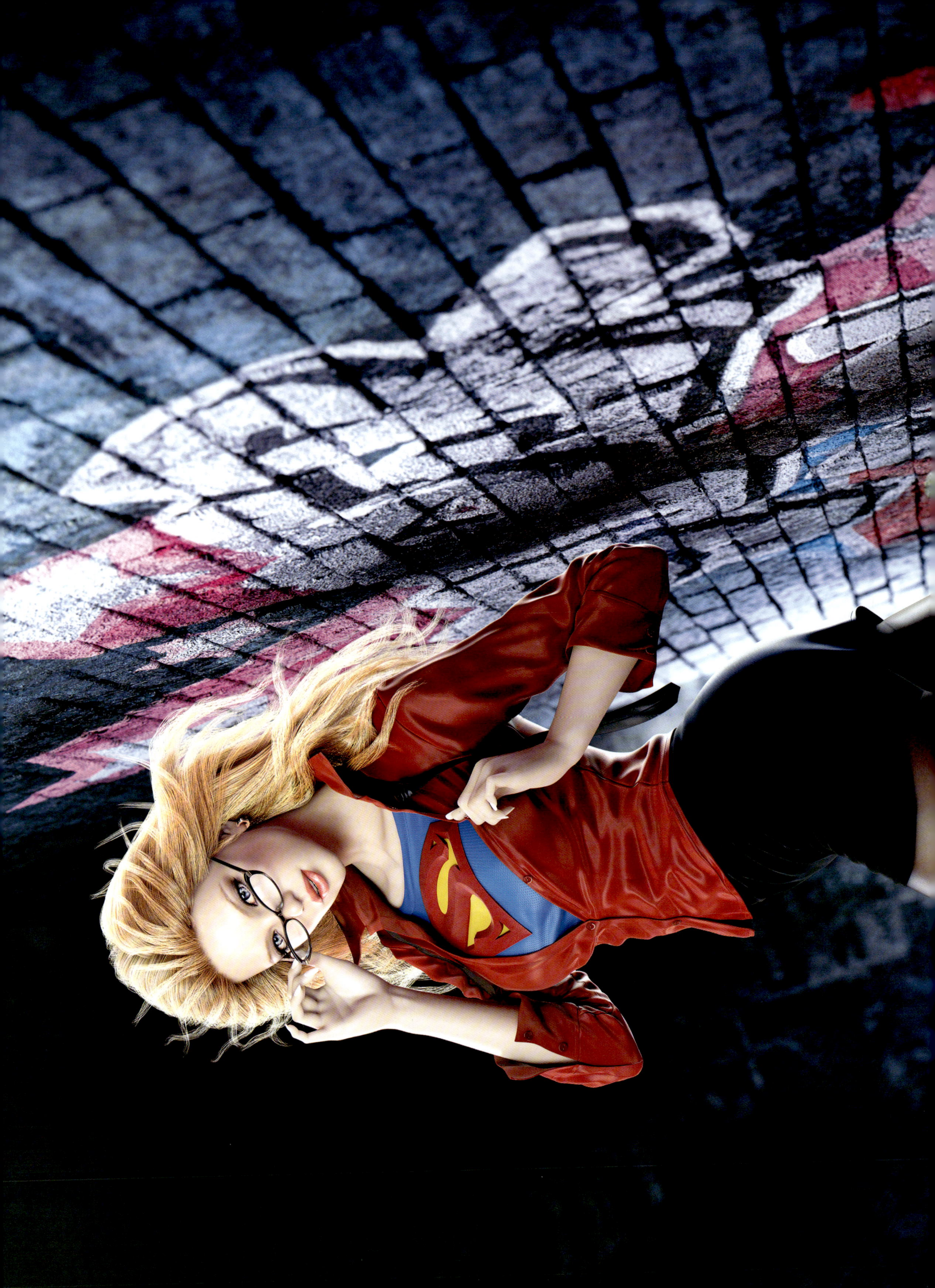

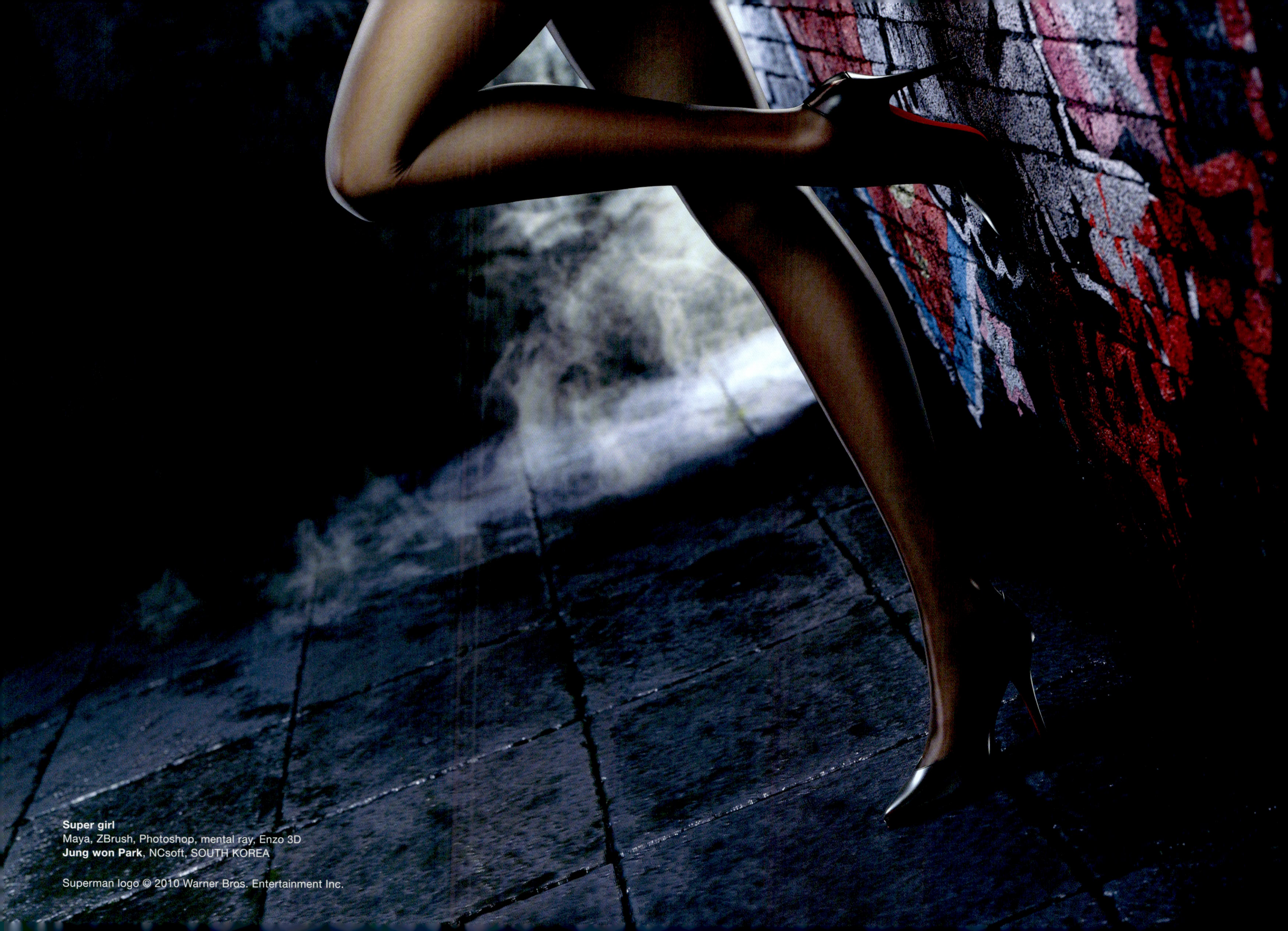

Super girl
Maya, ZBrush, Photoshop, mental ray, Enzo 3D
Jung won Park, NCsoft, SOUTH KOREA

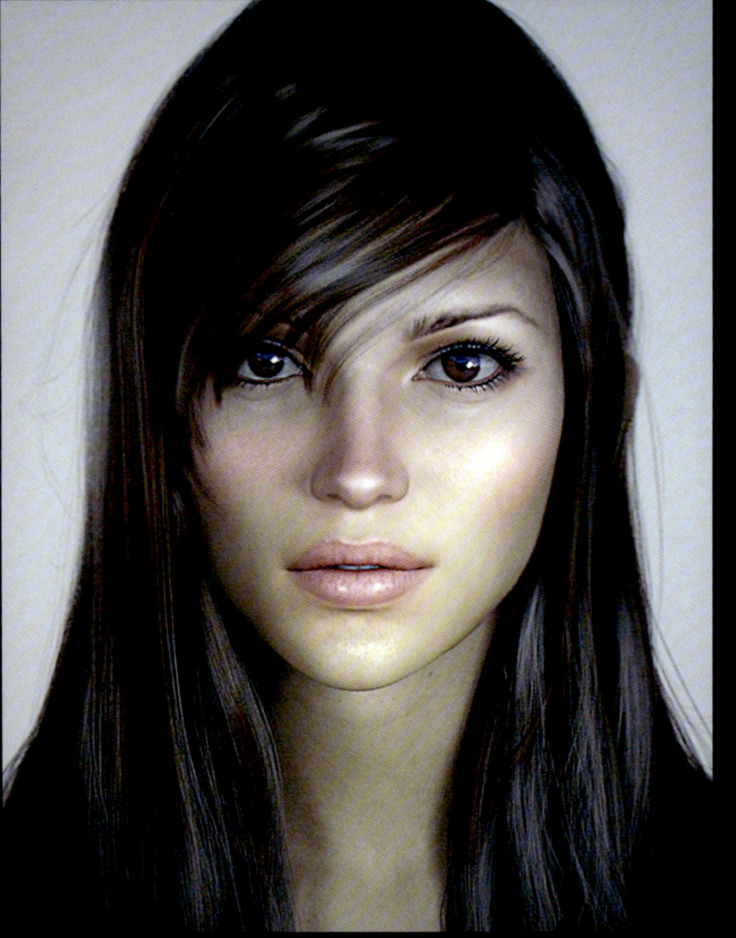

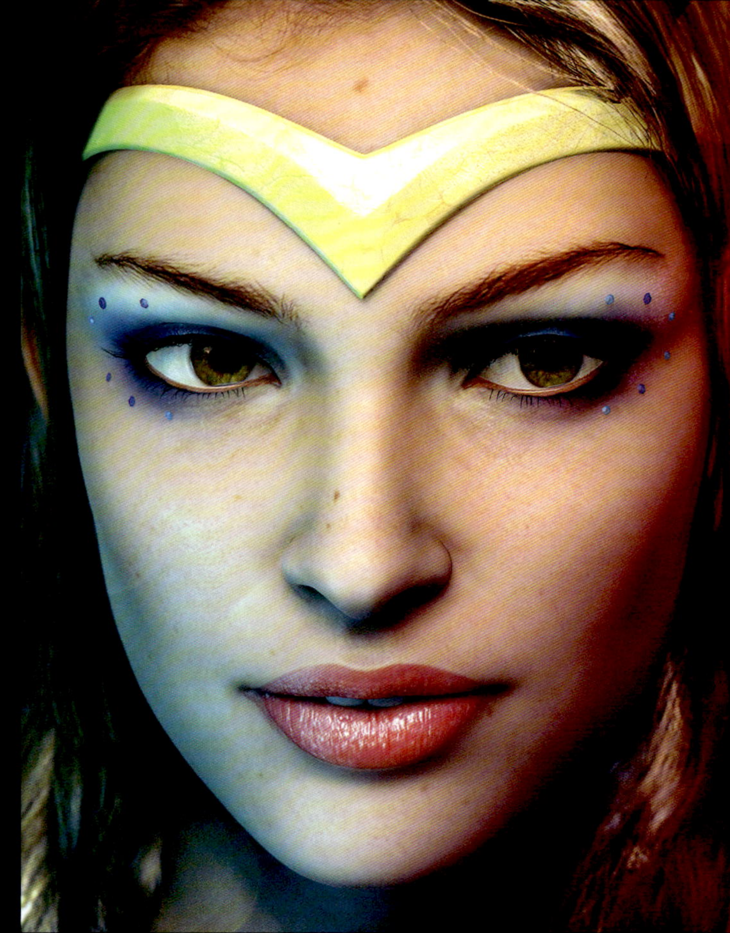

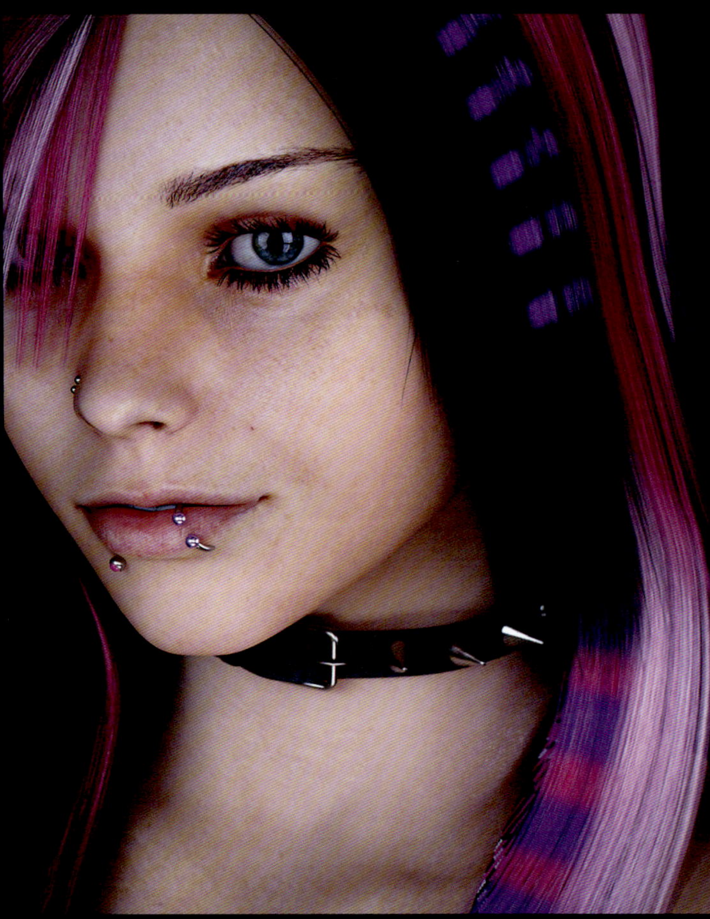

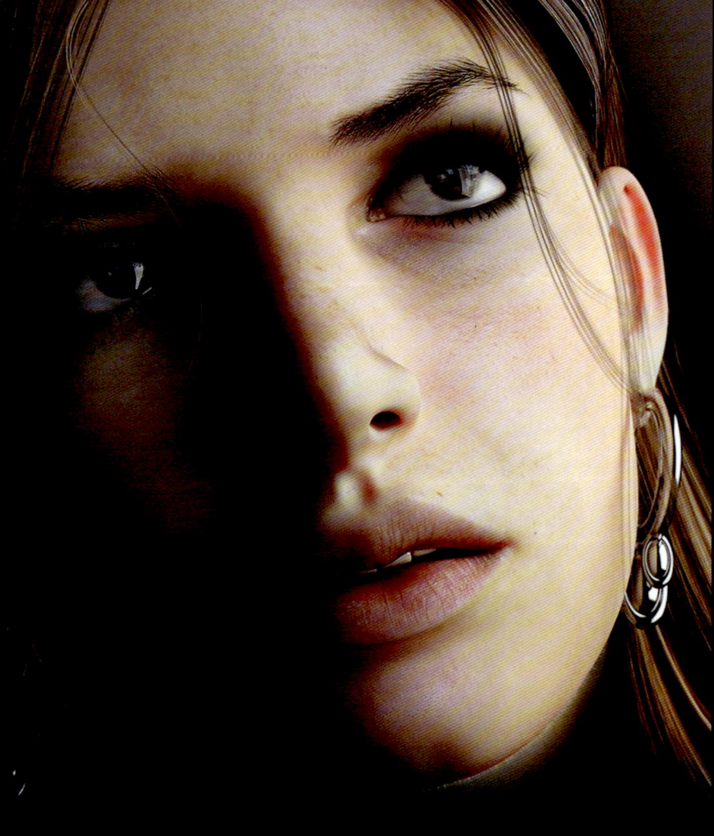

Violetta
Maya, Mudbox, mental ray, Photoshop
Roja Huchez,
CANADA
[top]

Shaina
3ds Max, V-Ray, Poser
Adam Potter,
AUSTRALIA
[above]

Superhero Girl: Close-up
Maya, Softimage, ZBrush, Photoshop
Thaddeus Maharaj,
TRINIDAD AND TOBAGO
[top]

Sad Woman
3ds Max, V-Ray, ZBrush, BodyPaint 3D
Kleber Silva,
BRAZIL
[above]

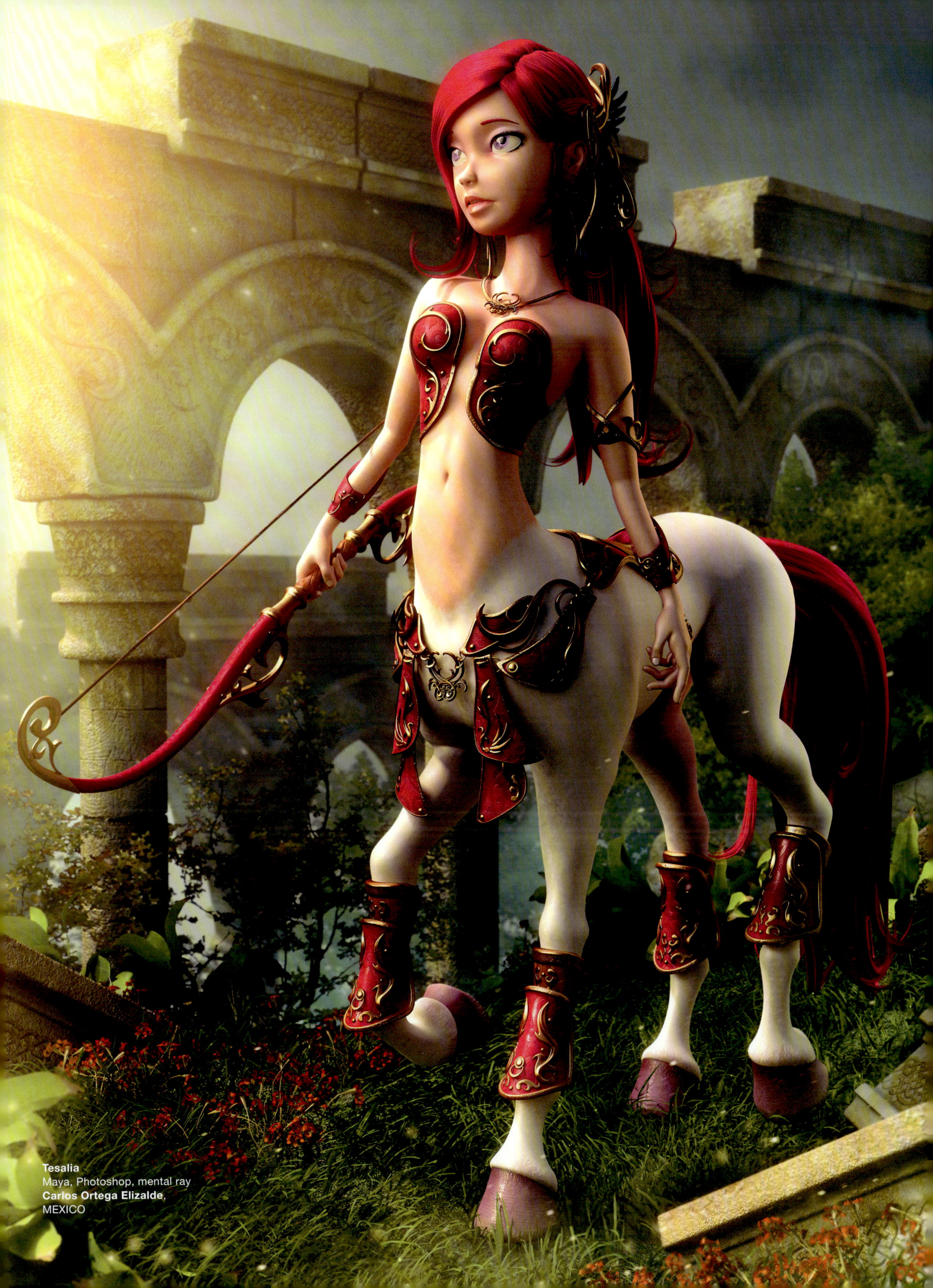

Tesalia
Maya, Photoshop, mental ray
Carlos Ortega Elizalde,
MEXICO

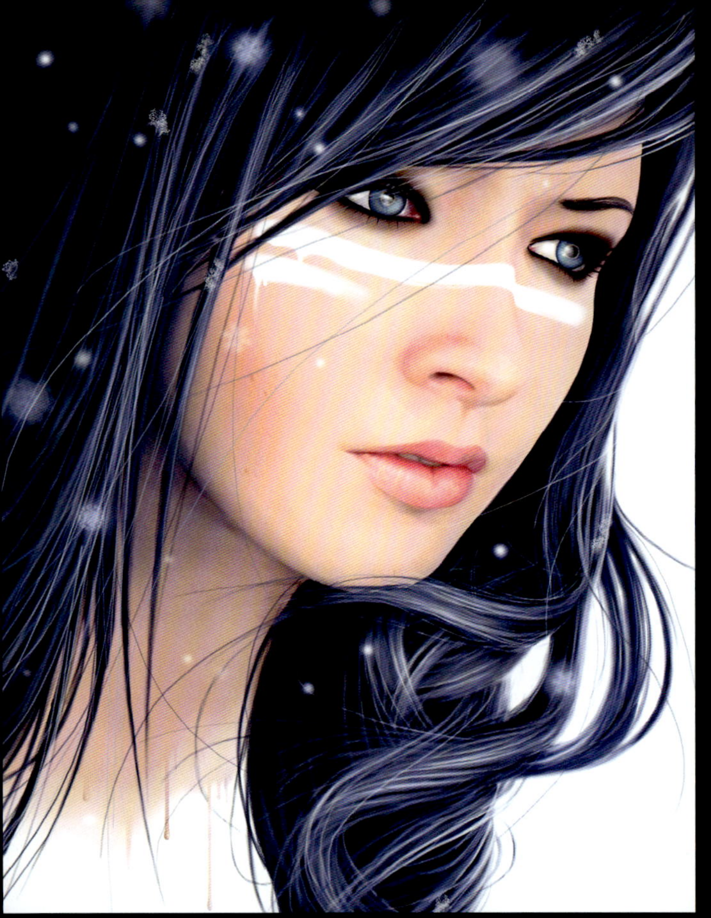

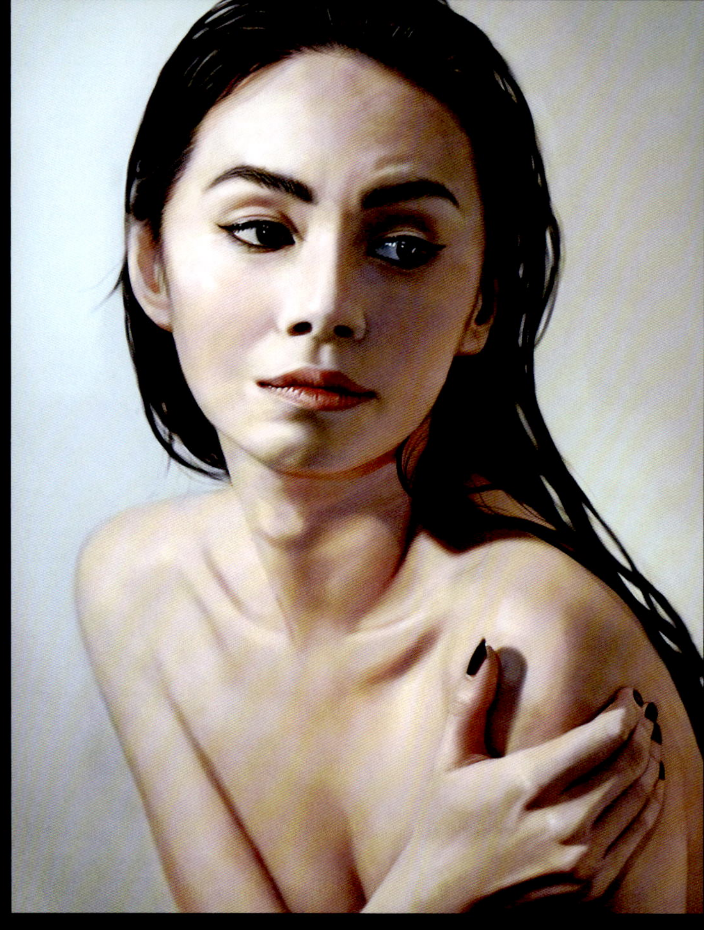

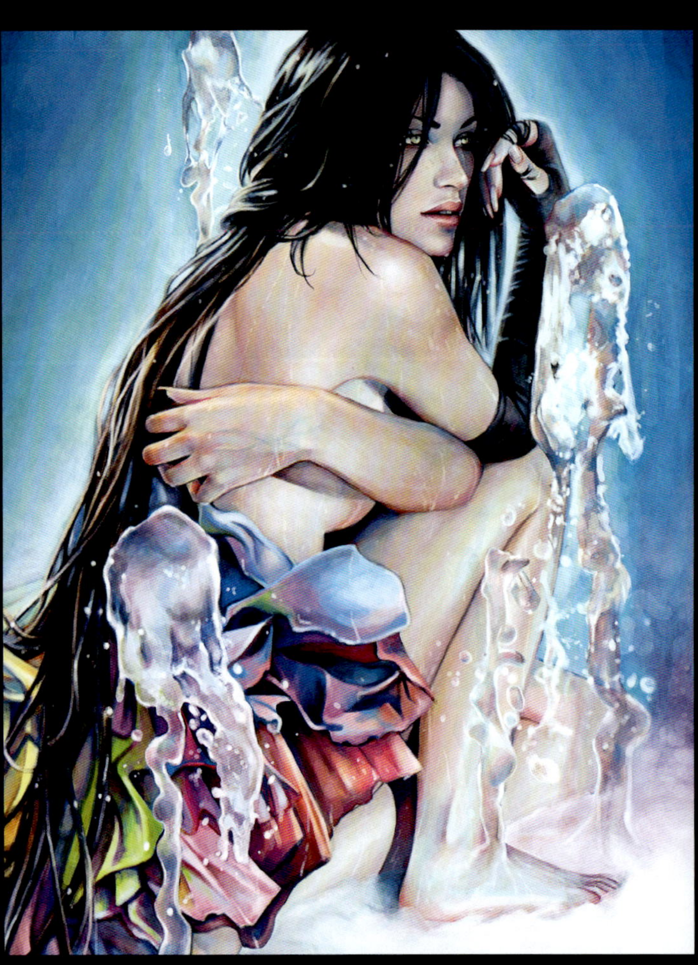

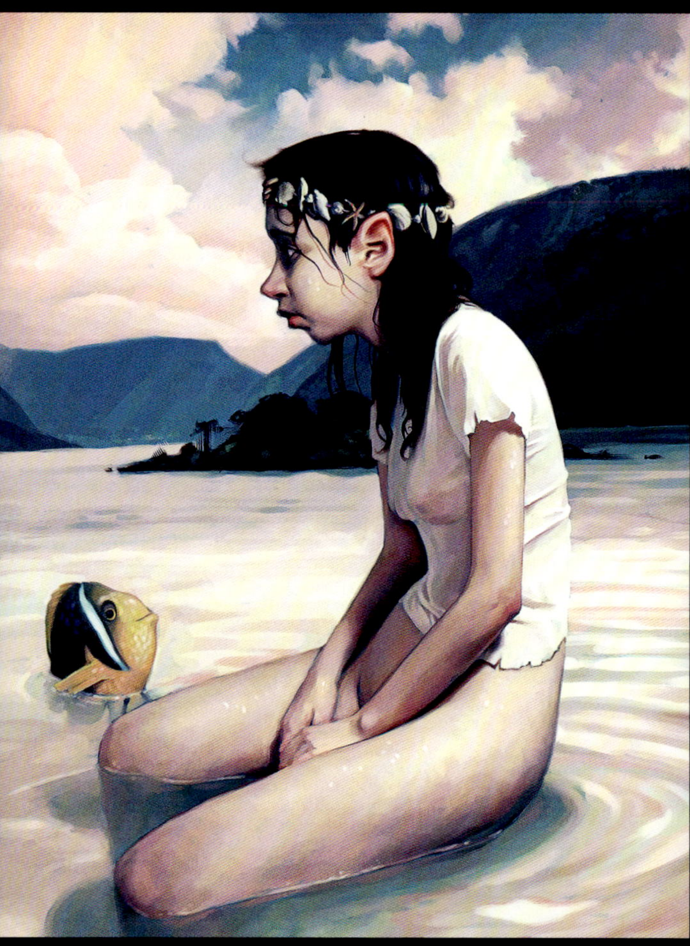

Frozen Beauty
Photoshop
Benjamin Friess, FRANCE
[top]

Summoning of the Muse
Photoshop, Painter
Marga Donaire, SPAIN
[above]

Burnette
Photoshop, Painter
Stephen Molyneaux, GREAT BRITAIN
[top]

Princess of the Seas
Photoshop
Ryan Mauskopf, USA
[above]

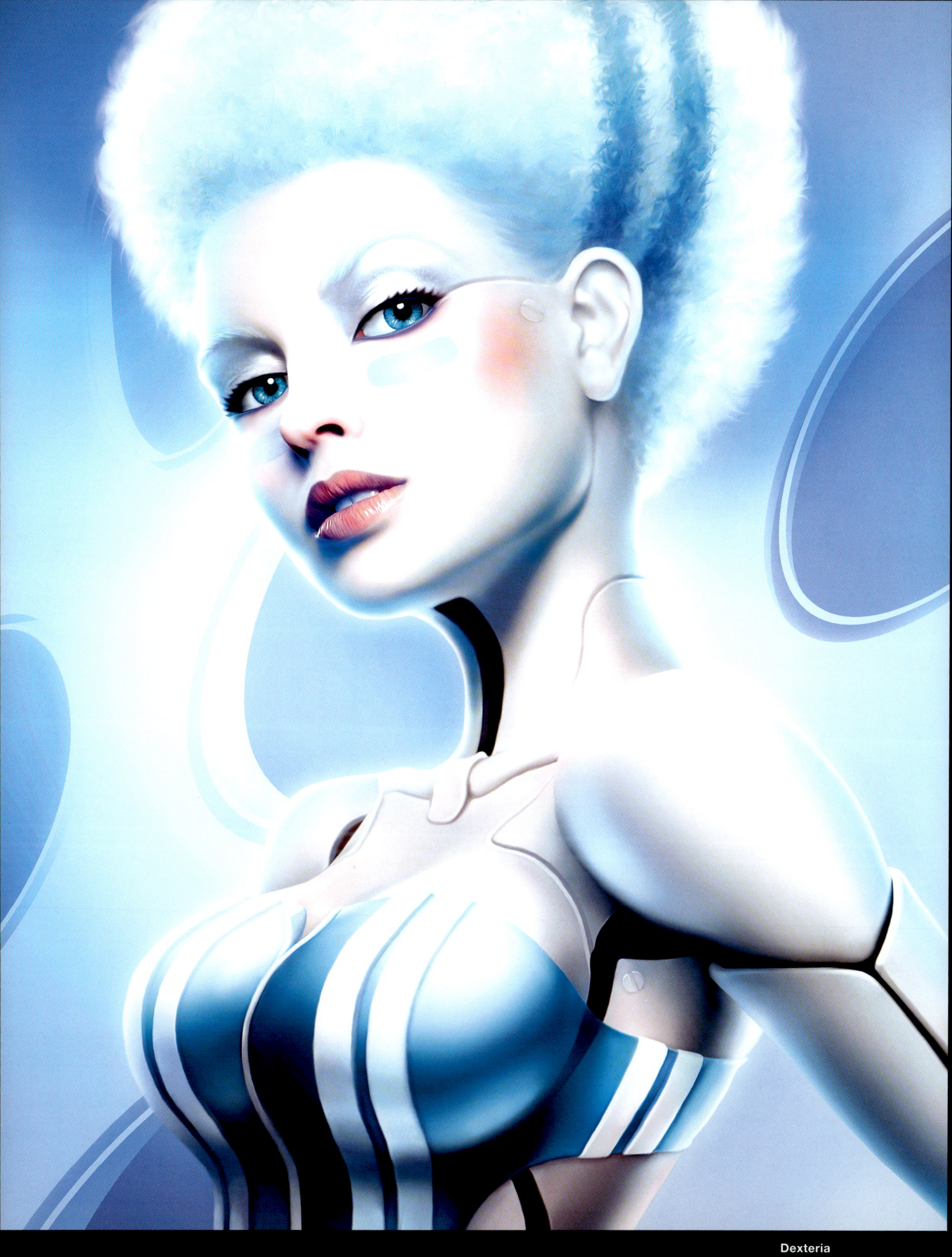

Dexteria
Photoshop
Photographer: Katja de Bruijn
Model: Vlada Varevko
Michael Oswald, USA

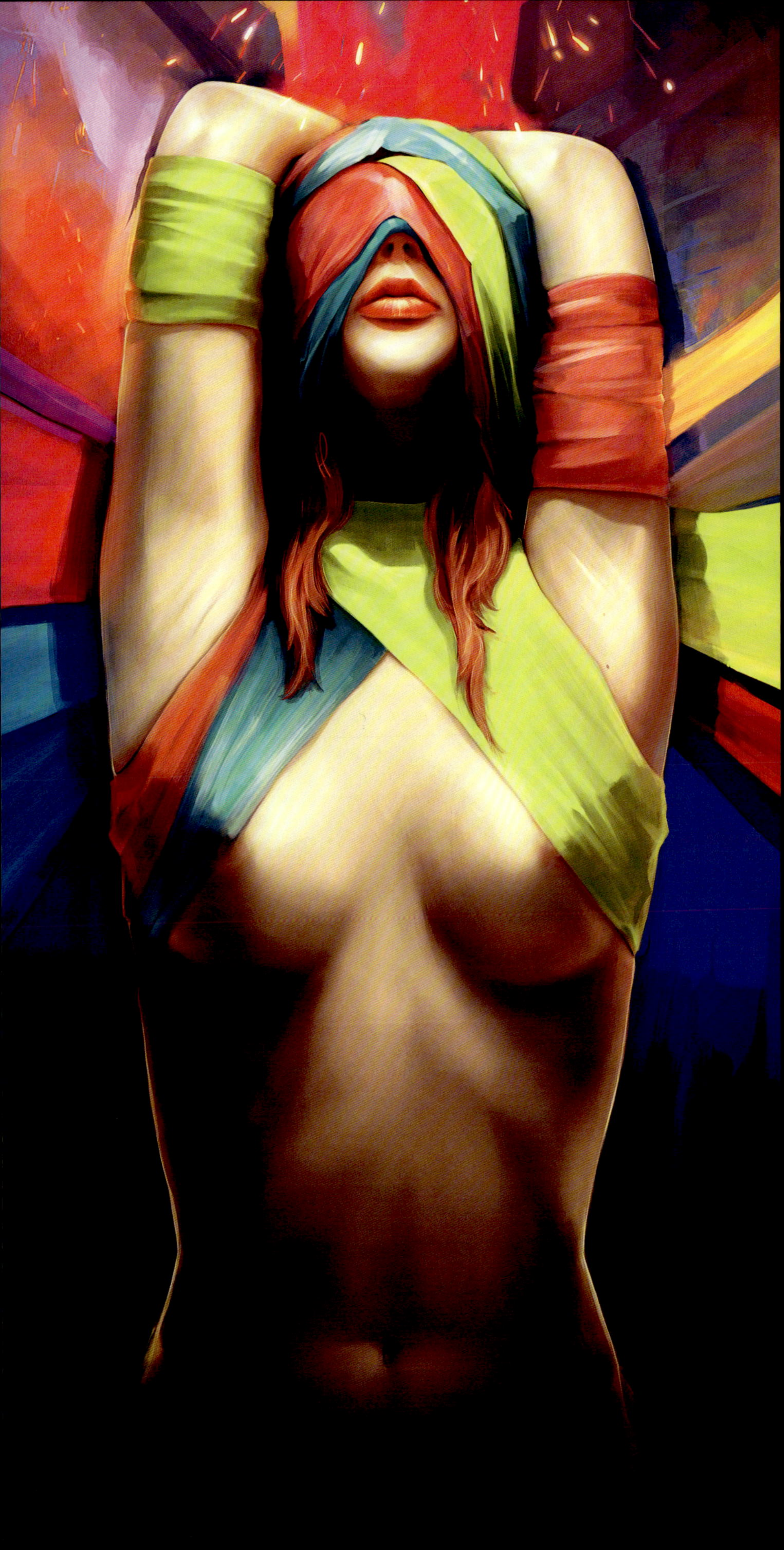

Blind Colors
Photoshop
Patryk Habryn, POLAND

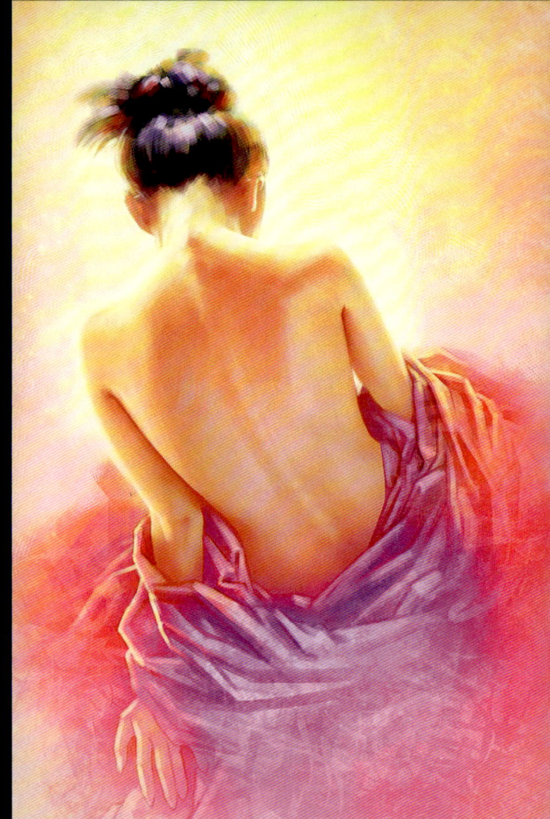

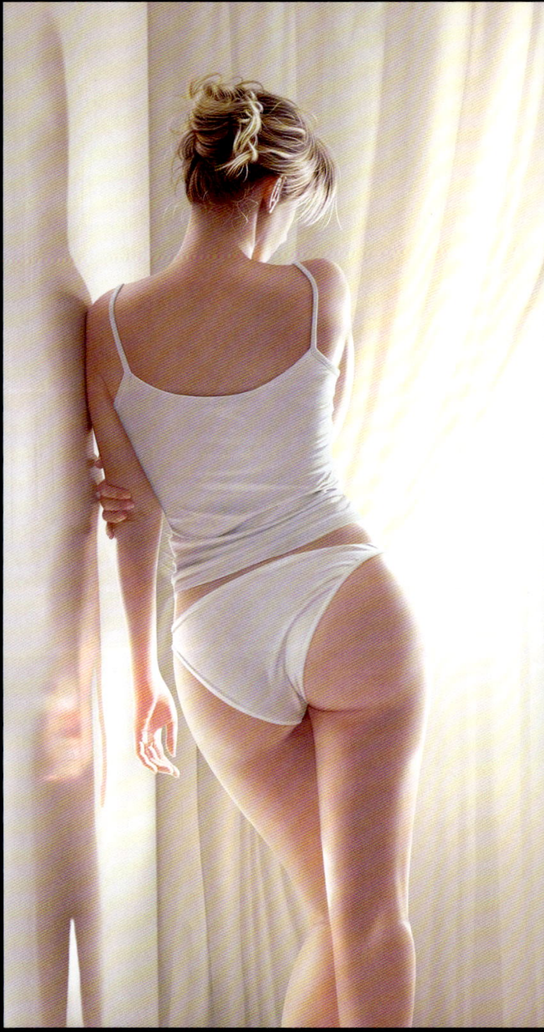

Soft Morning
Photoshop
Steve Argyle, USA

Here without you
Photoshop, Painter
Toni Rodriguez, SPAIN

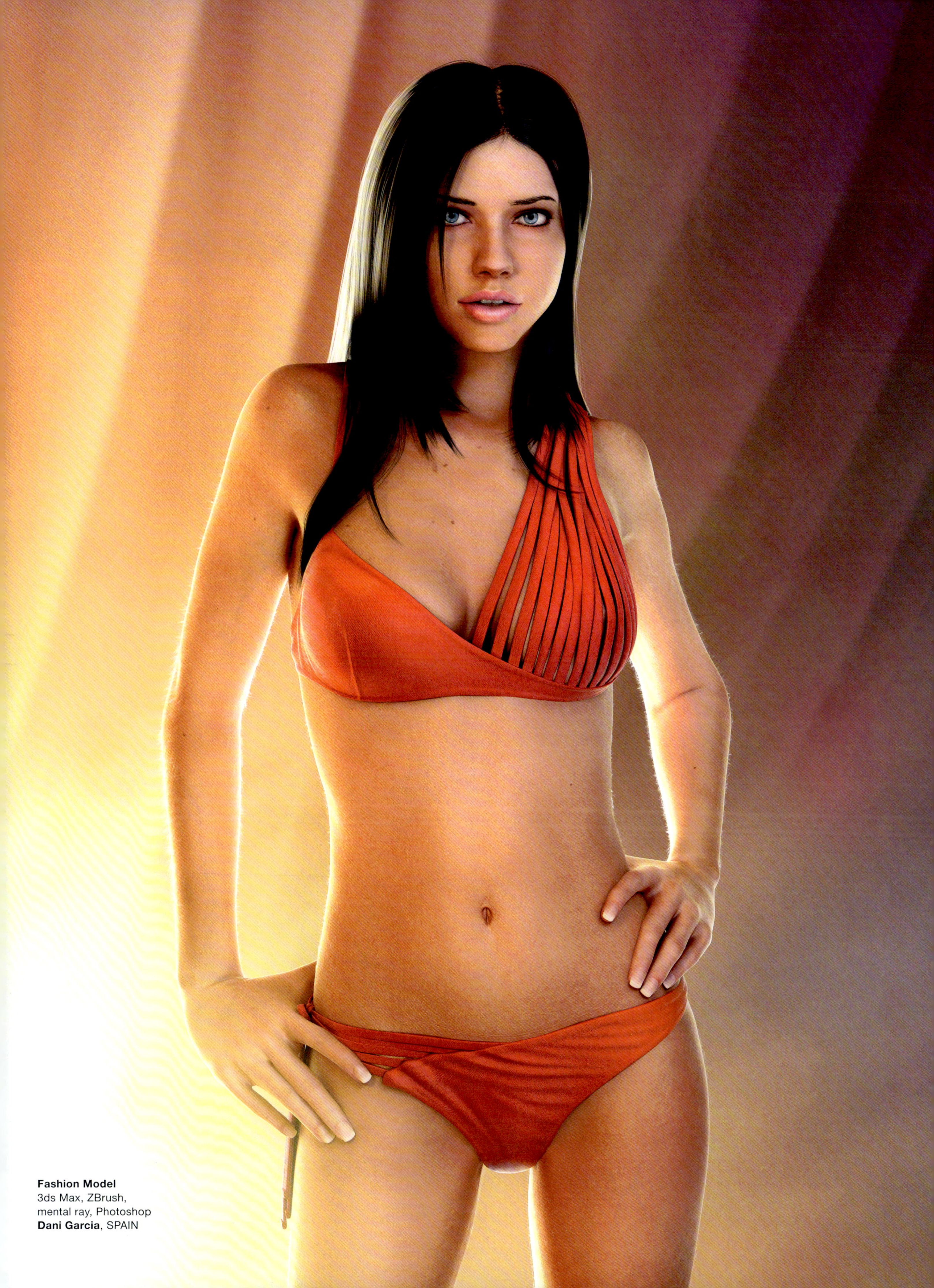

Fashion Model
3ds Max, ZBrush,
mental ray, Photoshop
Dani Garcia, SPAIN

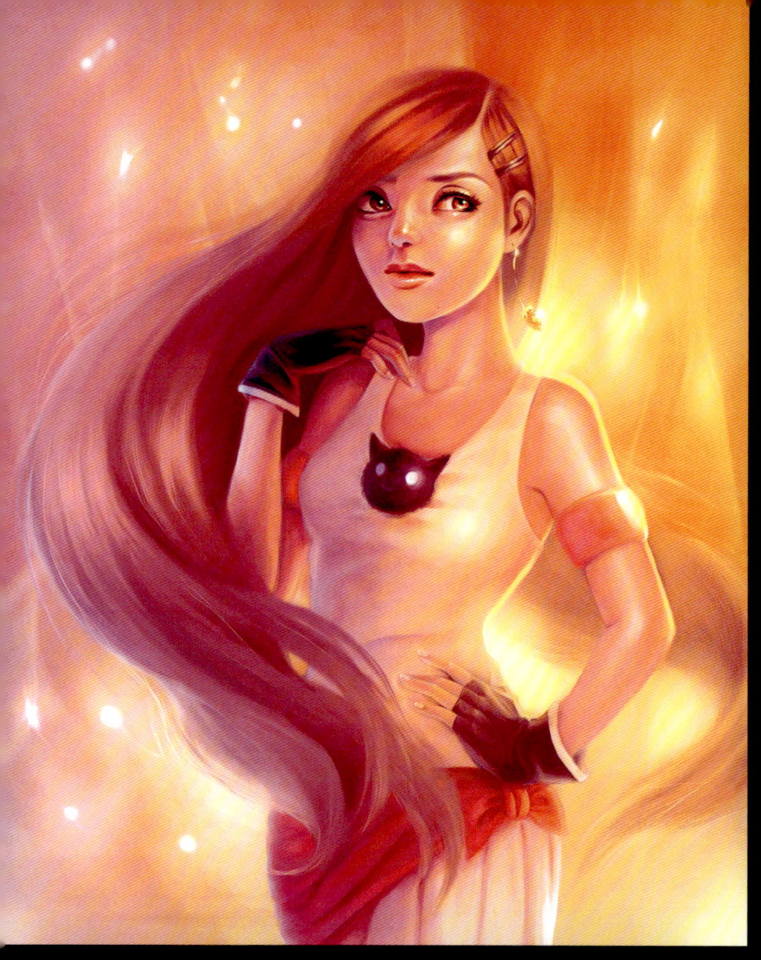

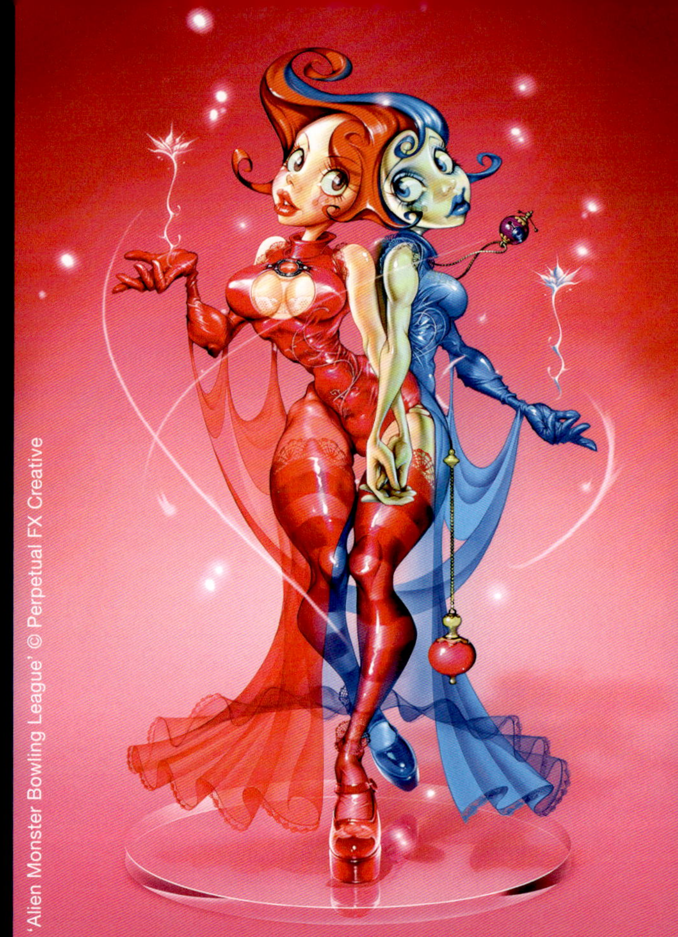

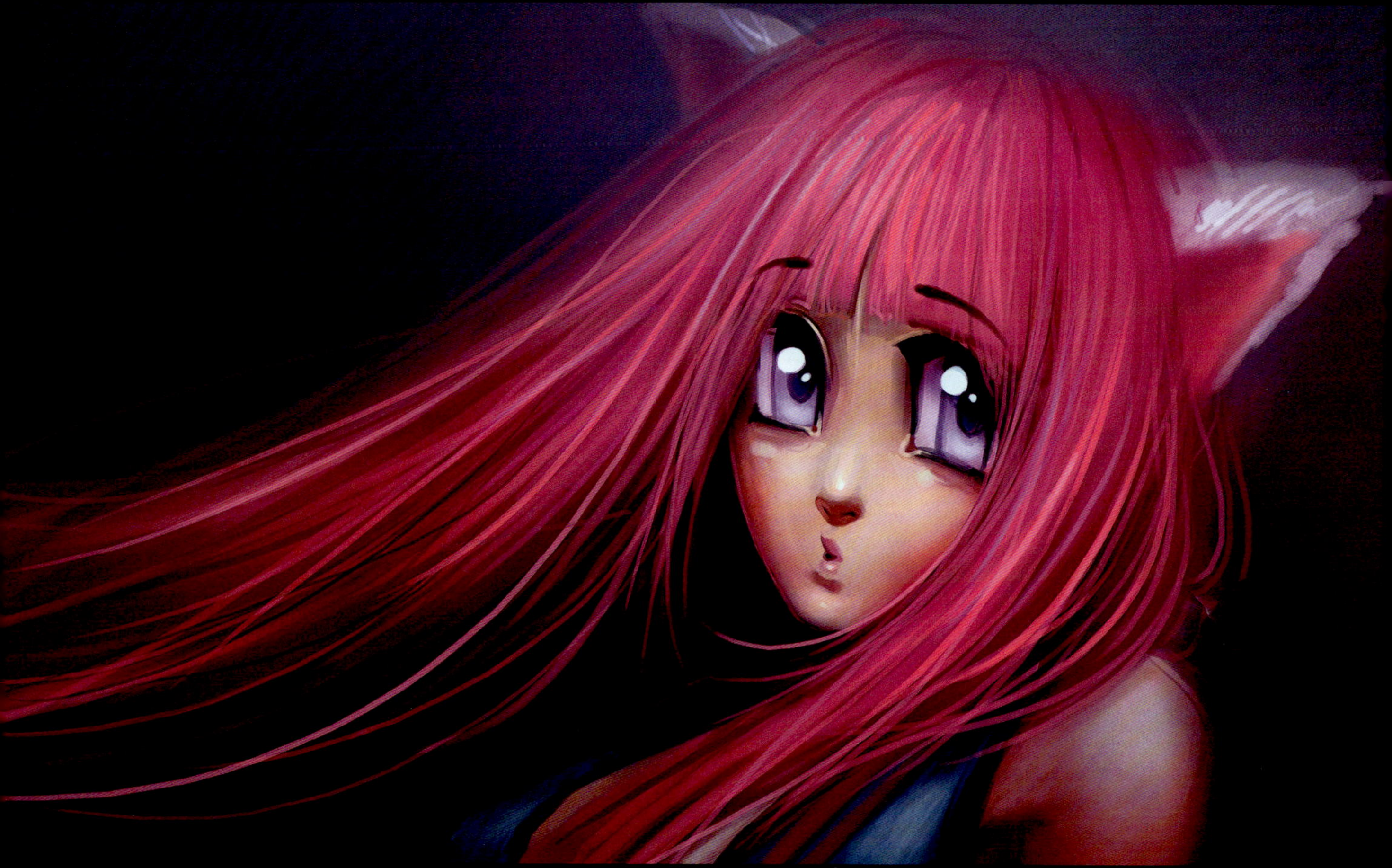

Fire
Photoshop
Doreen Haas, GERMANY
[top]

Kyu
Photoshop
Ejiwa Adaeze Ebenebe, NEW ZEALAND
[above]

Alien Monster Bowling League: Twins
Photoshop
Client: Perpetual FX Creative
Haitao Su, Suhaitao Studio, CHINA *[top]*

Jing Wu
Photoshop
Chen Kai, CHINA
[right]

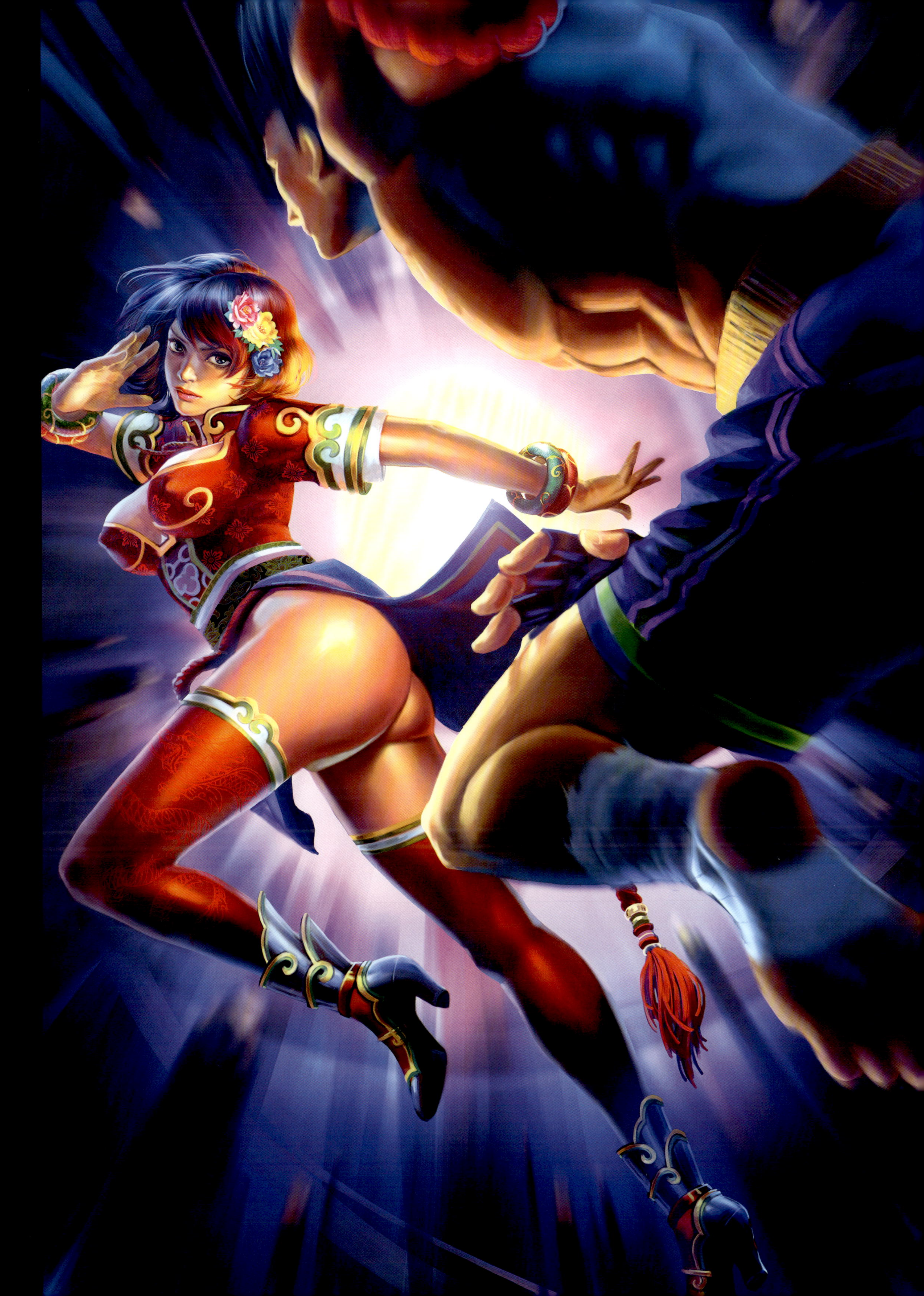

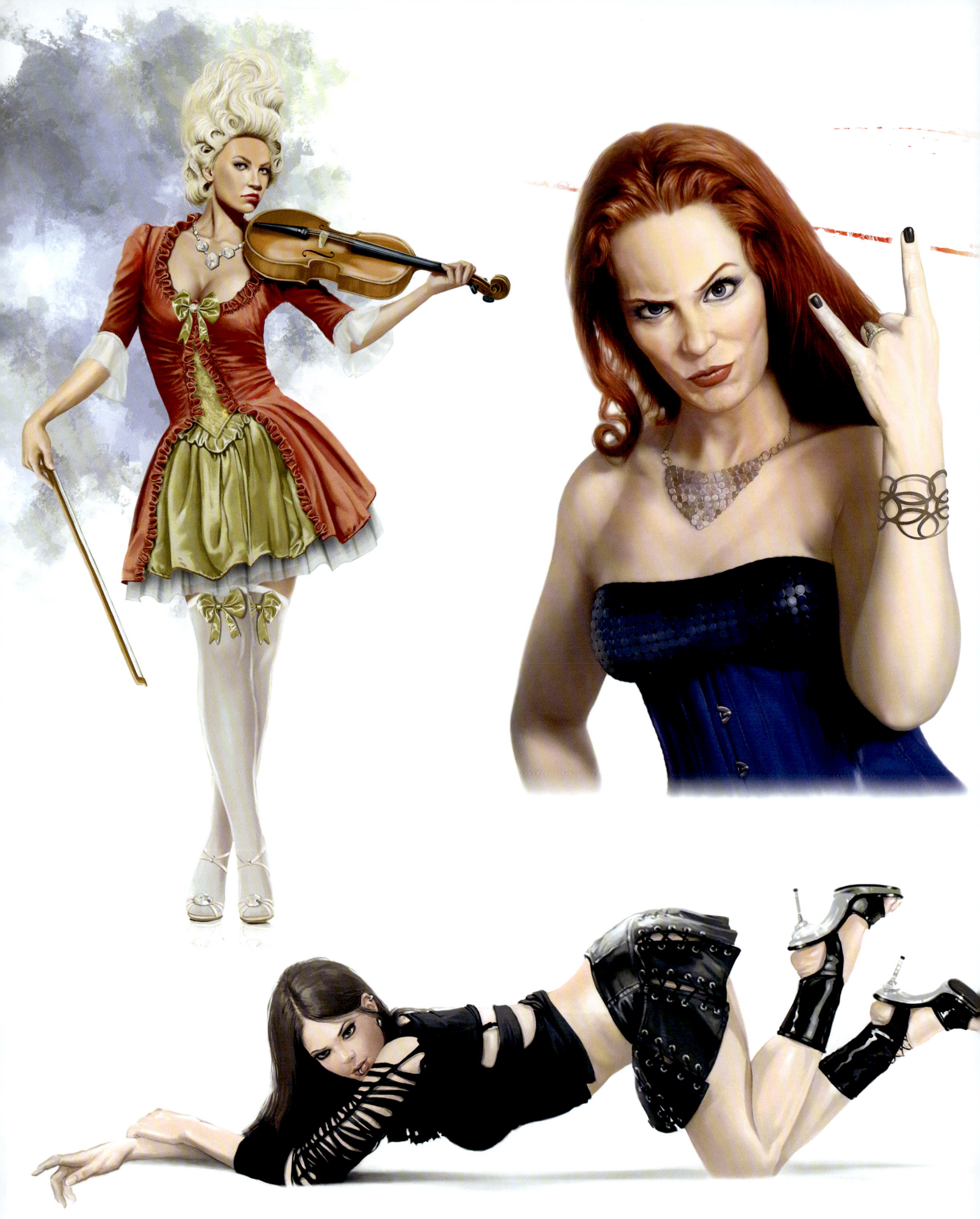

The Violin Singer
Photoshop
Cosmin Genete, ROMANIA
[top]

Black Widow
Photoshop
Ivan Kashubo, RUSSIA
[above]

Simone Rock
Photoshop
Ivan Kashubo, RUSSIA
[top]

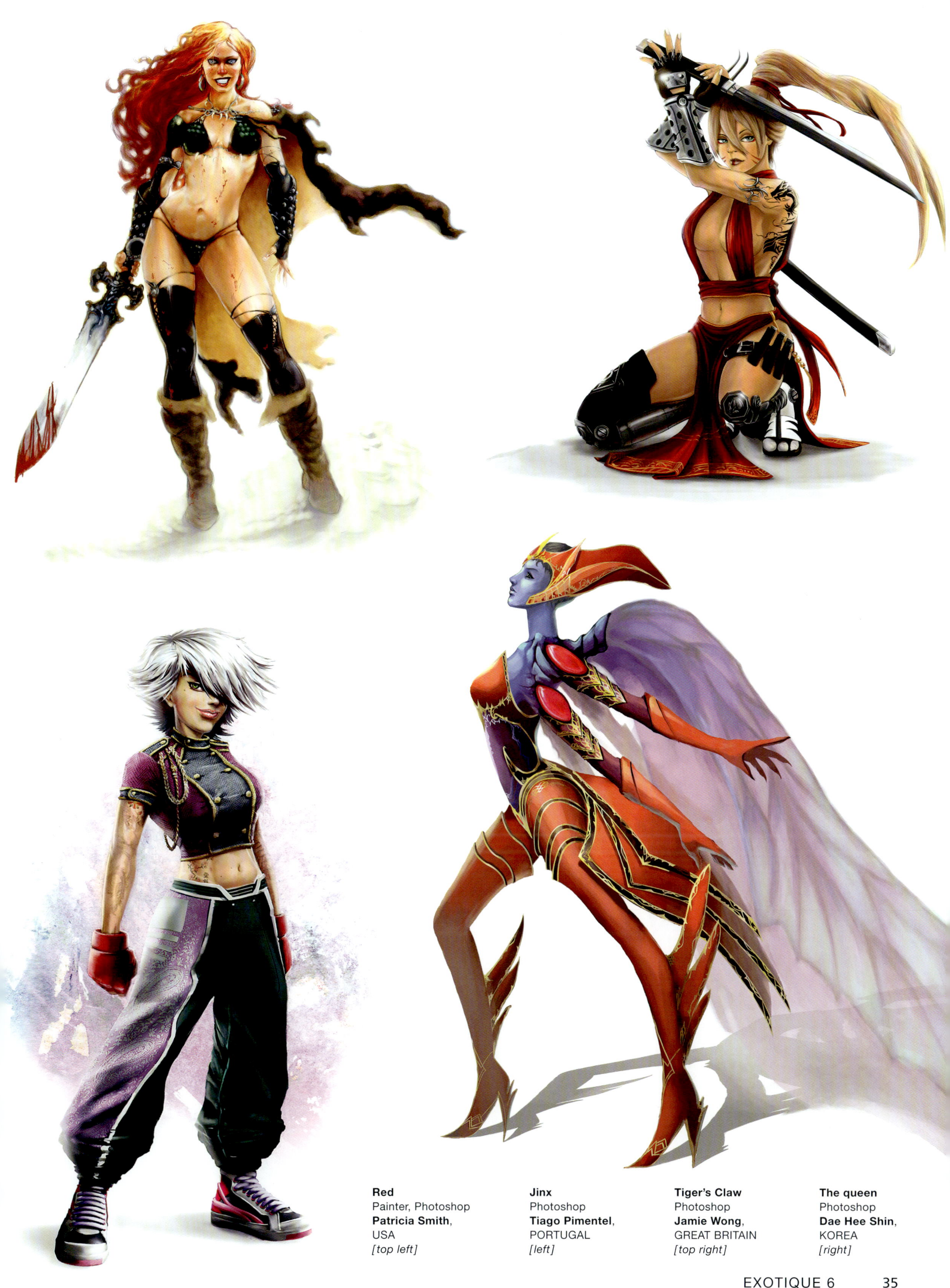

Red
Painter, Photoshop
Patricia Smith,
USA
[top left]

Jinx
Photoshop
Tiago Pimentel,
PORTUGAL
[left]

Tiger's Claw
Photoshop
Jamie Wong,
GREAT BRITAIN
[top right]

The queen
Photoshop
Dae Hee Shin,
KOREA
[right]

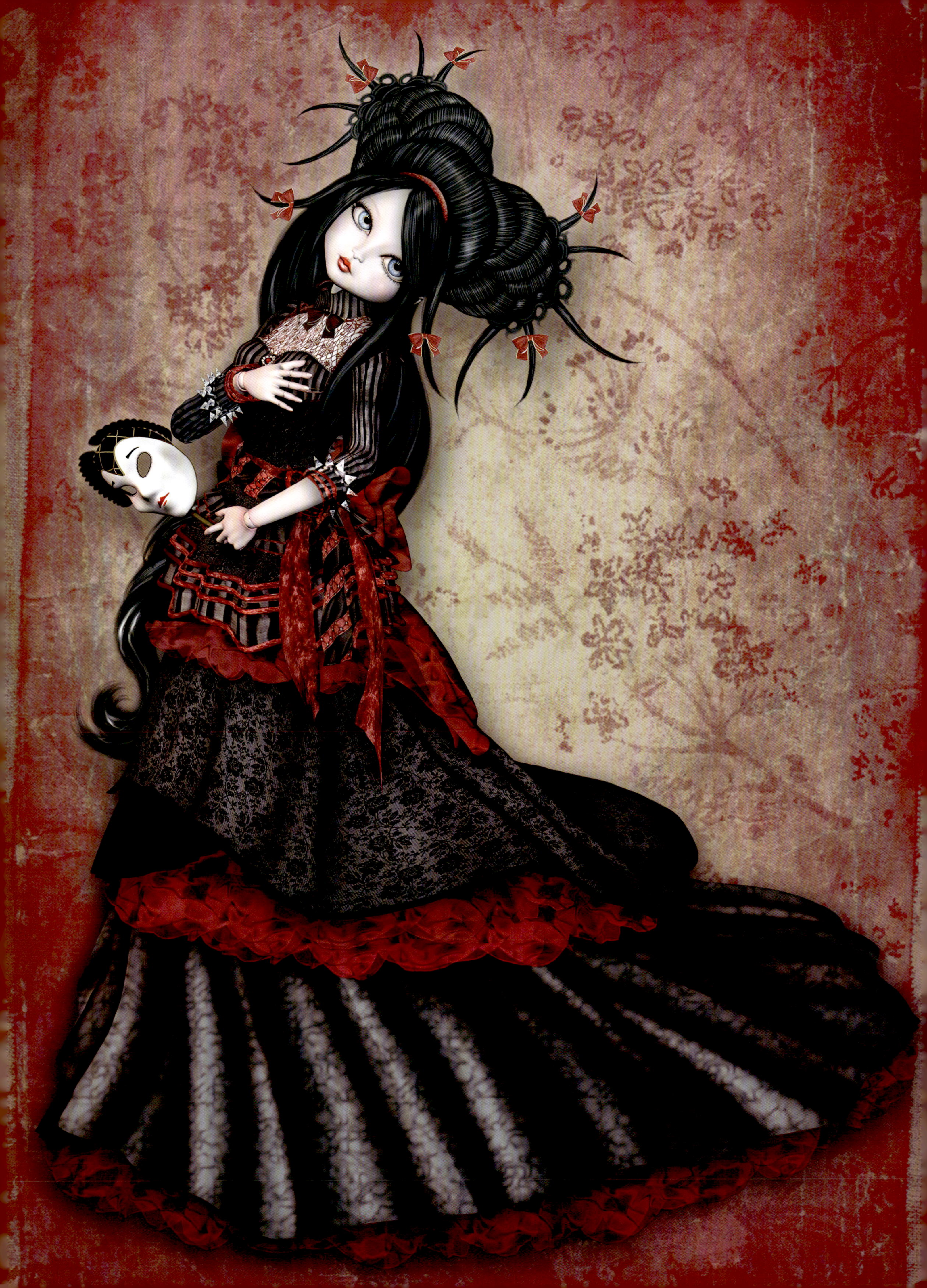

Bellina
DAZ Studio, Photoshop
Angela Newman, USA
[left]

Lady Ravendale
SketchBook Pro, Photoshop
Embiro and Jaysin,
DPI Studios.net, CANADA
[right]

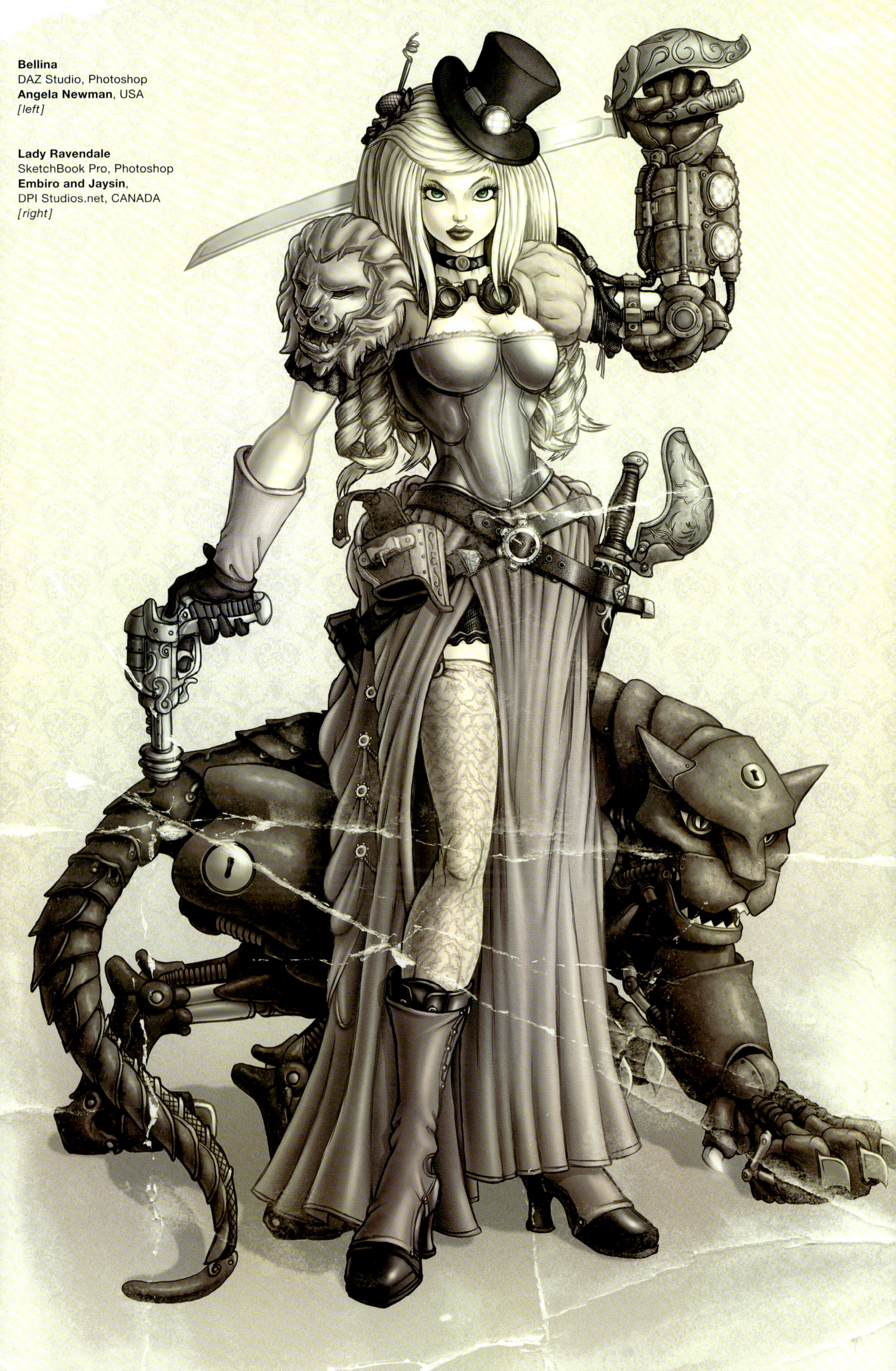

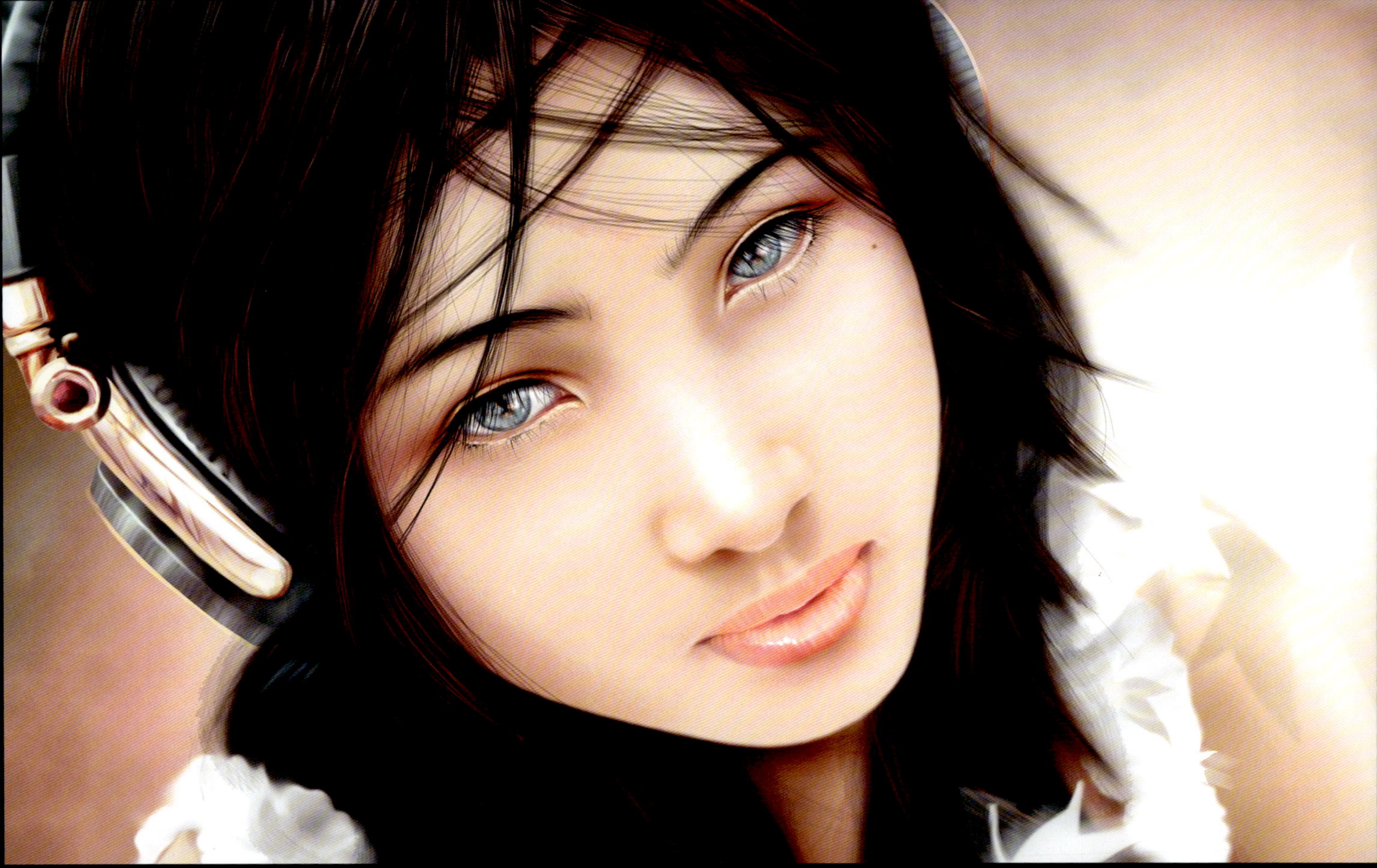

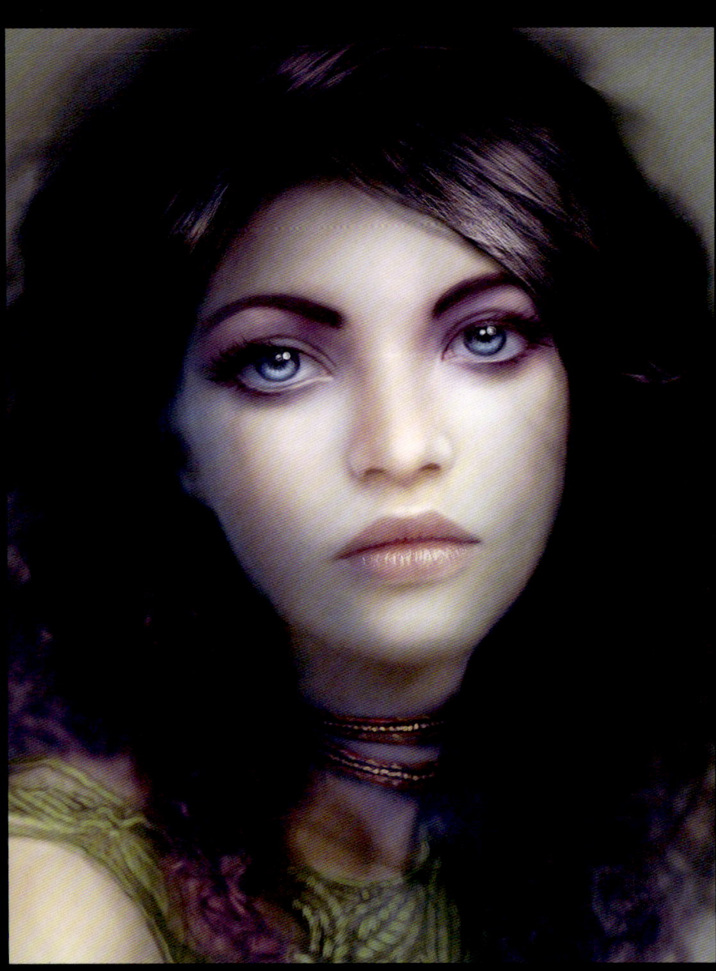

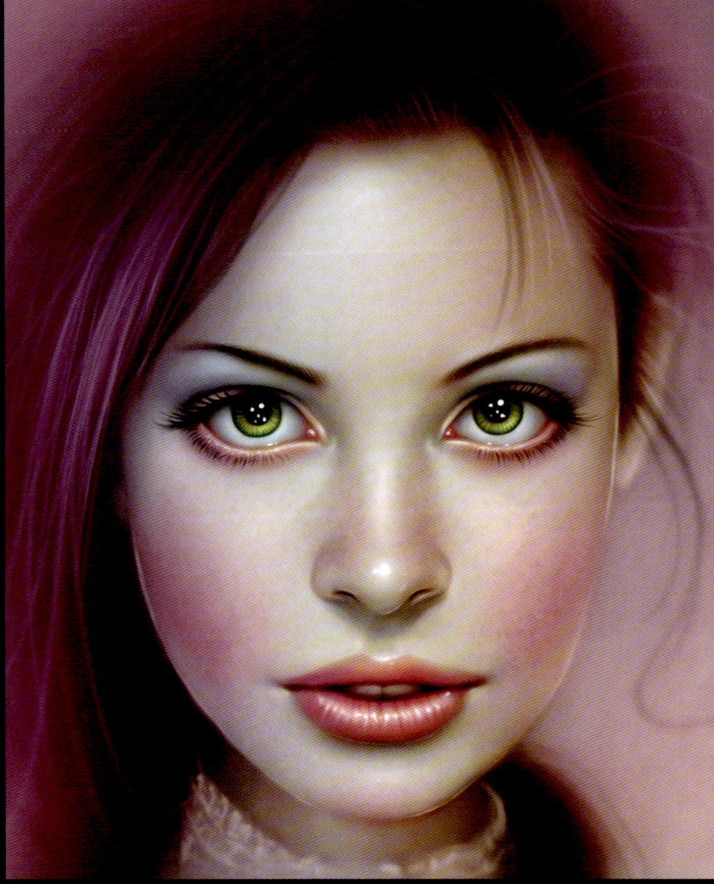

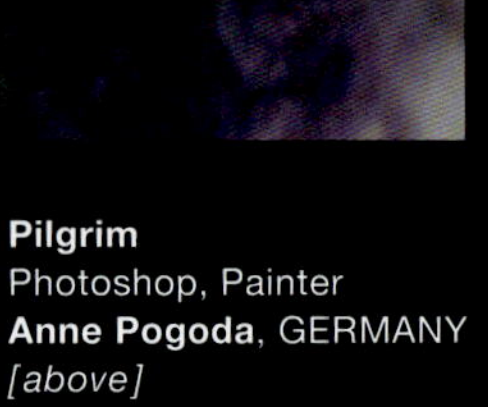

Katerina
Photoshop
Jared Castro, GUATEMALA
[top]

Pilgrim
Photoshop, Painter
Anne Pogoda, GERMANY
[above]

JEANNIE
Painter, Photoshop
Michael Hideux, FRANCE
[above]

Chang_e
Photoshop
Ruoxing Zhang, Shanghai HuaQi Network Technology Co., Ltd, CHINA *[right]*

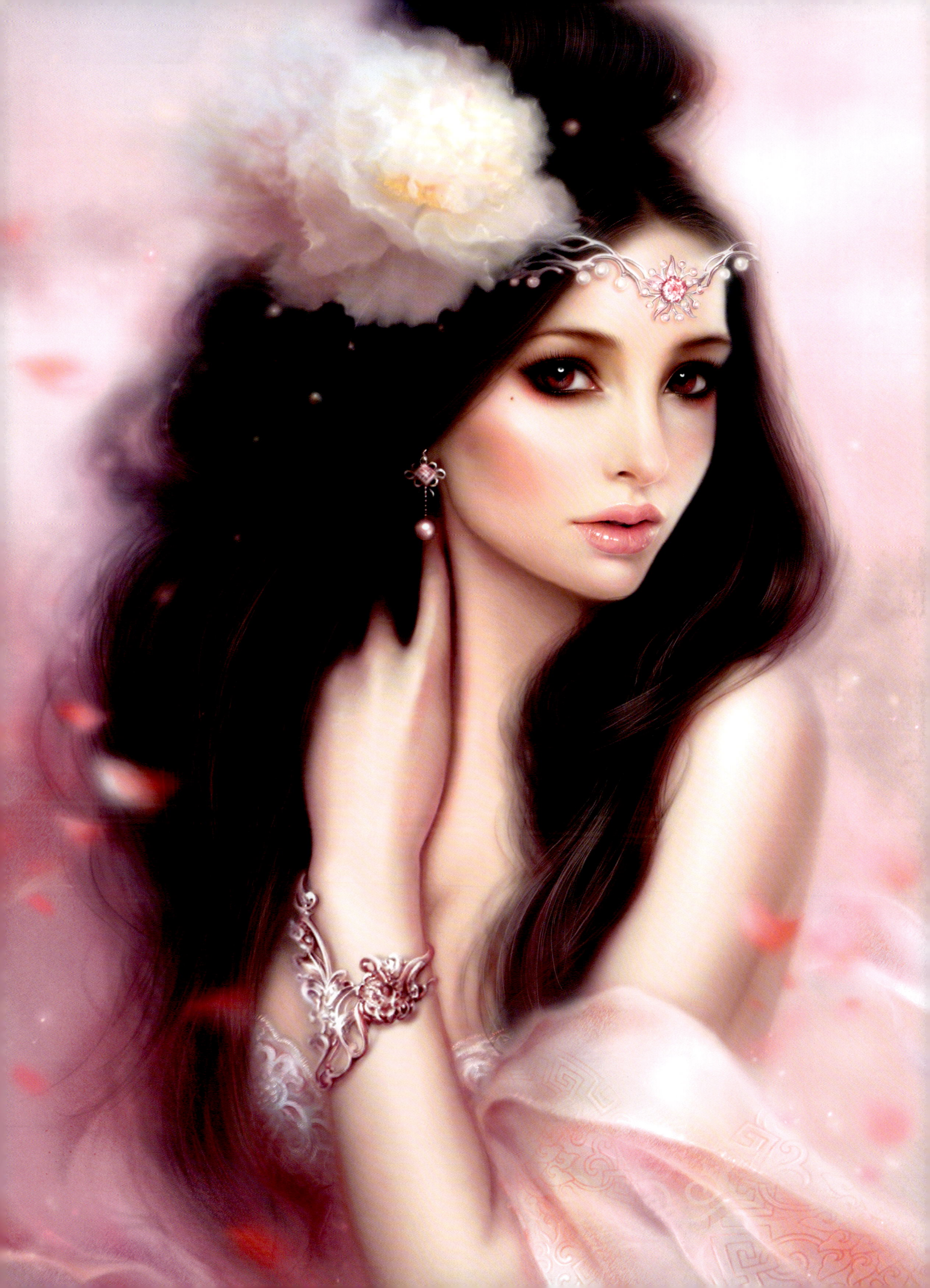

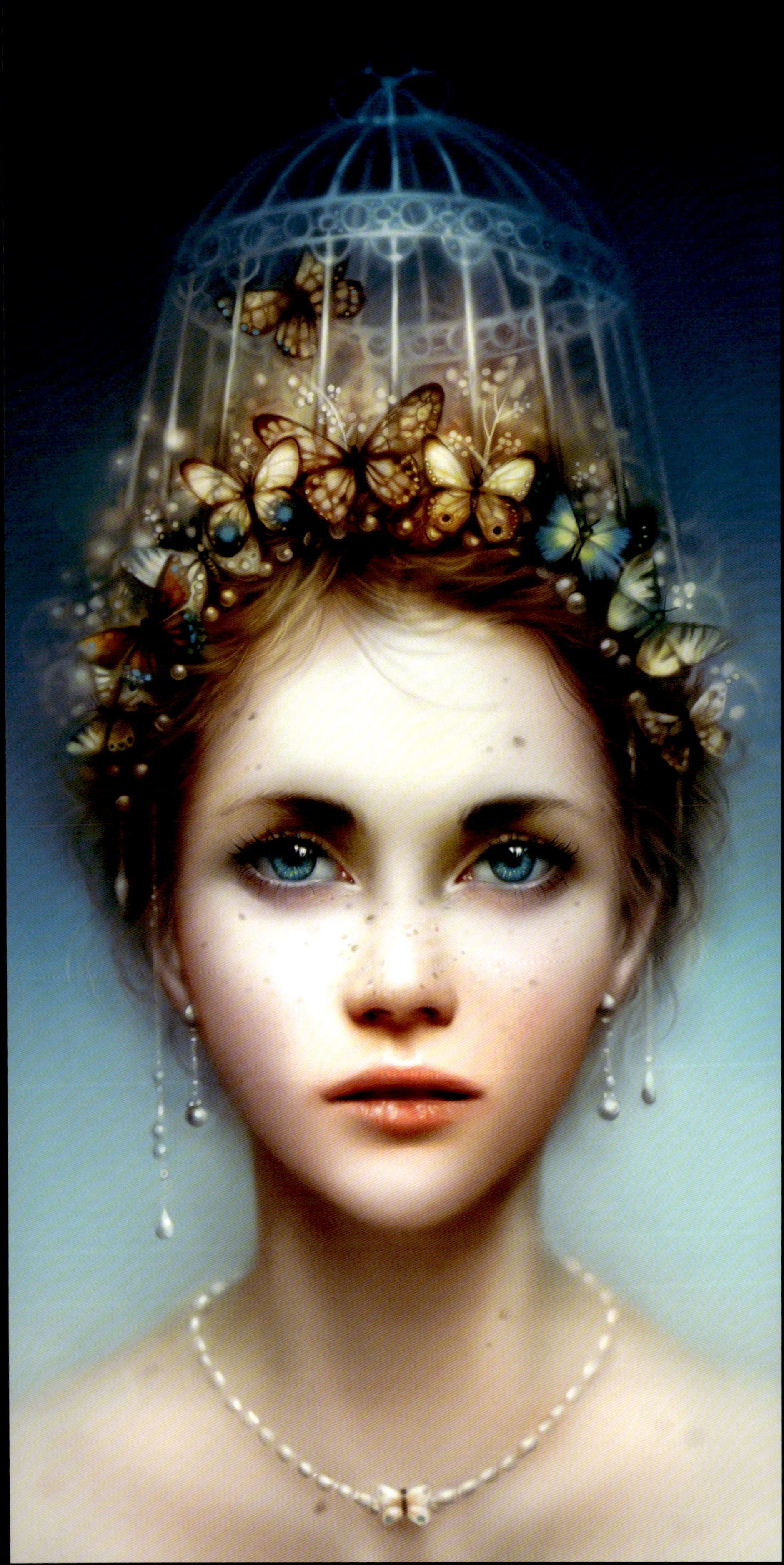

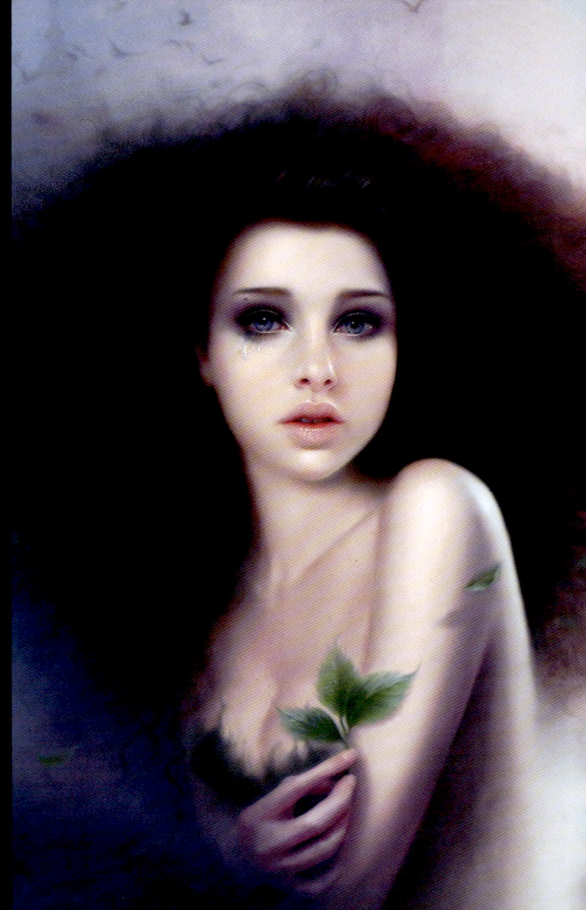

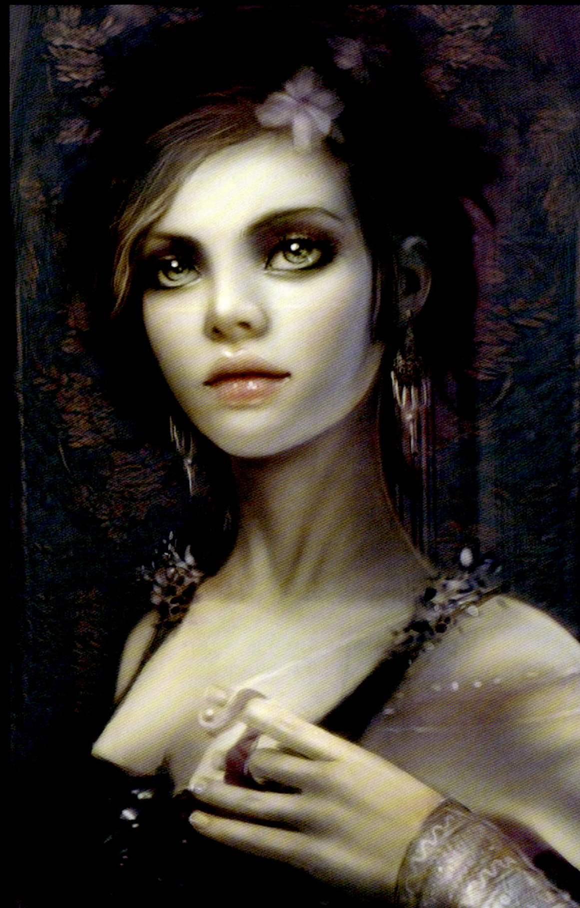

Caged
Photoshop
Anna Dittmann,
USA
[above]

Hope
Photoshop
Ruoxing Zhang, Shanghai HuaQi network technology Co. Ltd, CHINA
[top right]

Alice
Photoshop, Painter
Anne Pogoda,
GERMANY
[above]

Scimitar
Photoshop
Huang DaHong,
CHINA
[right]

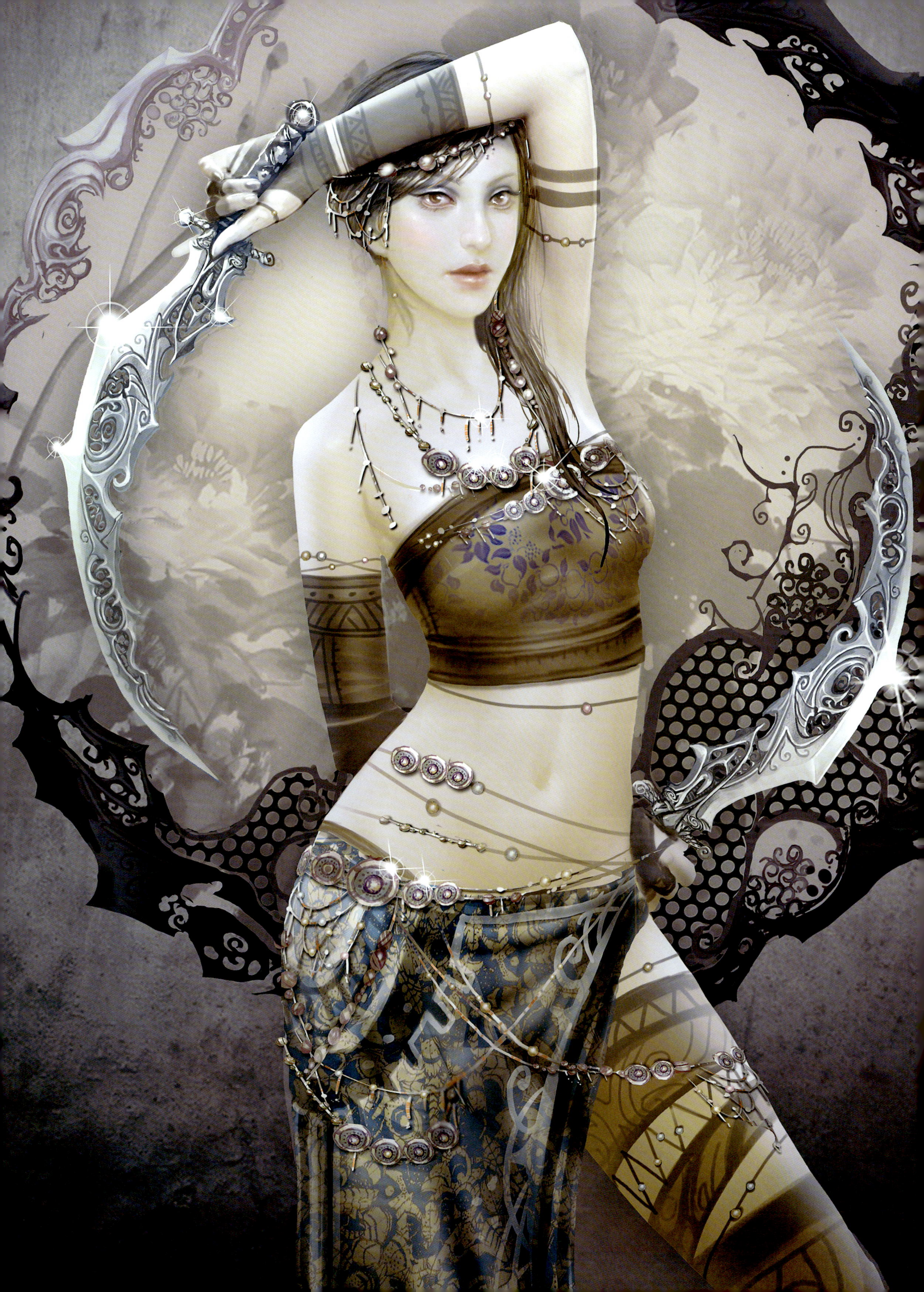

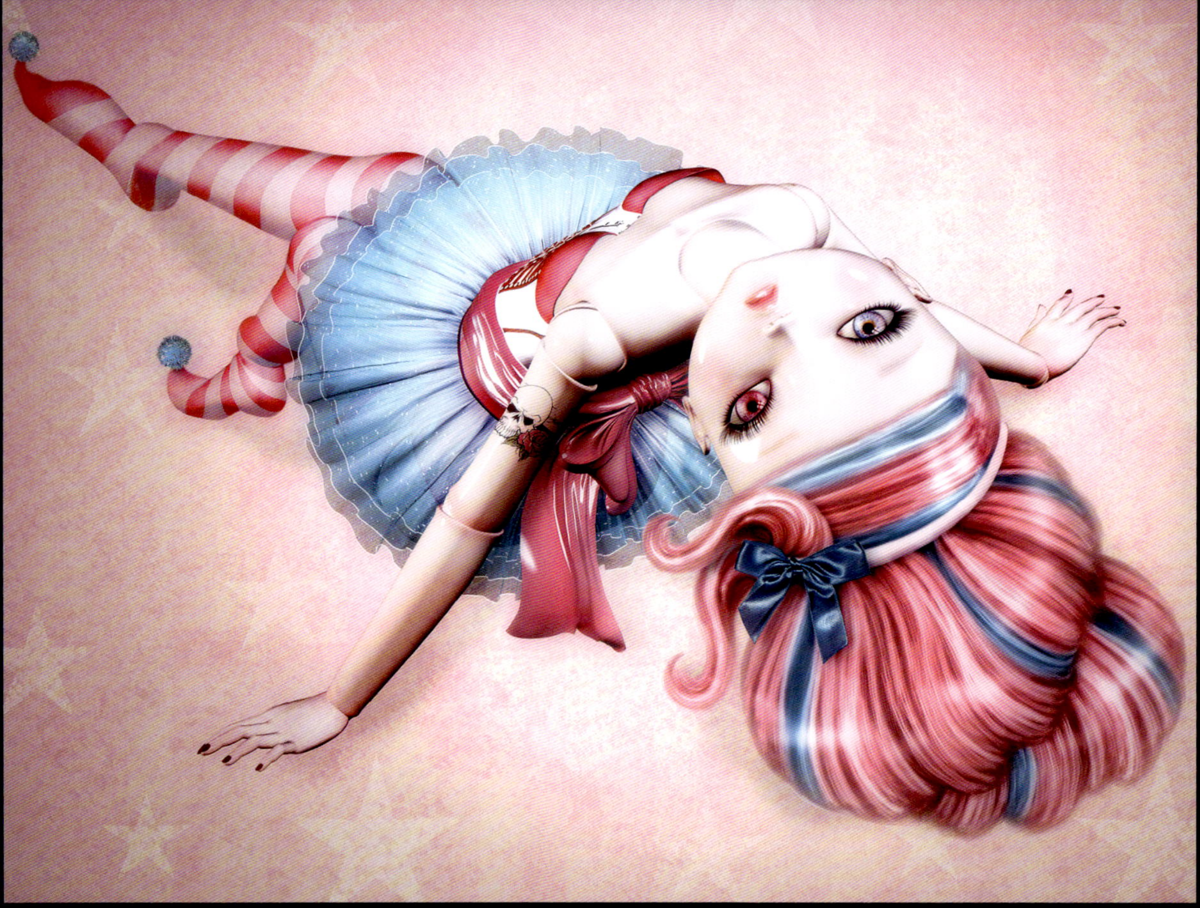

Alice
DAZ Studio, Photoshop
Angela Newman, USA
[left]

Under My Skin
Photoshop
Model: Daniella Bae
Michael Oswald, USA
[right]

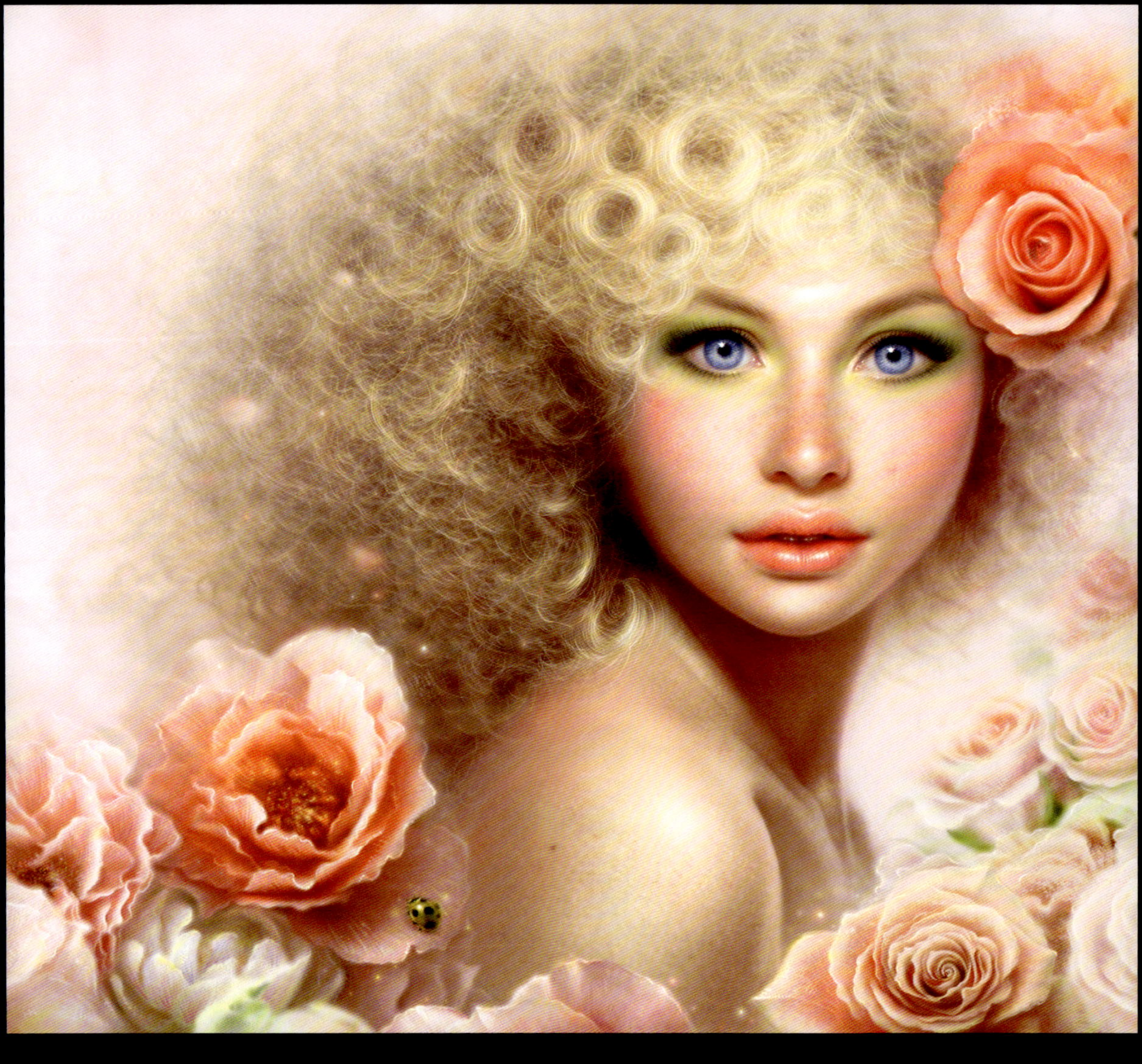

Angela
Photoshop
Ruoxing Zhang, Shanghai HuaQi network technology Co. Ltd, CHINA
[left]

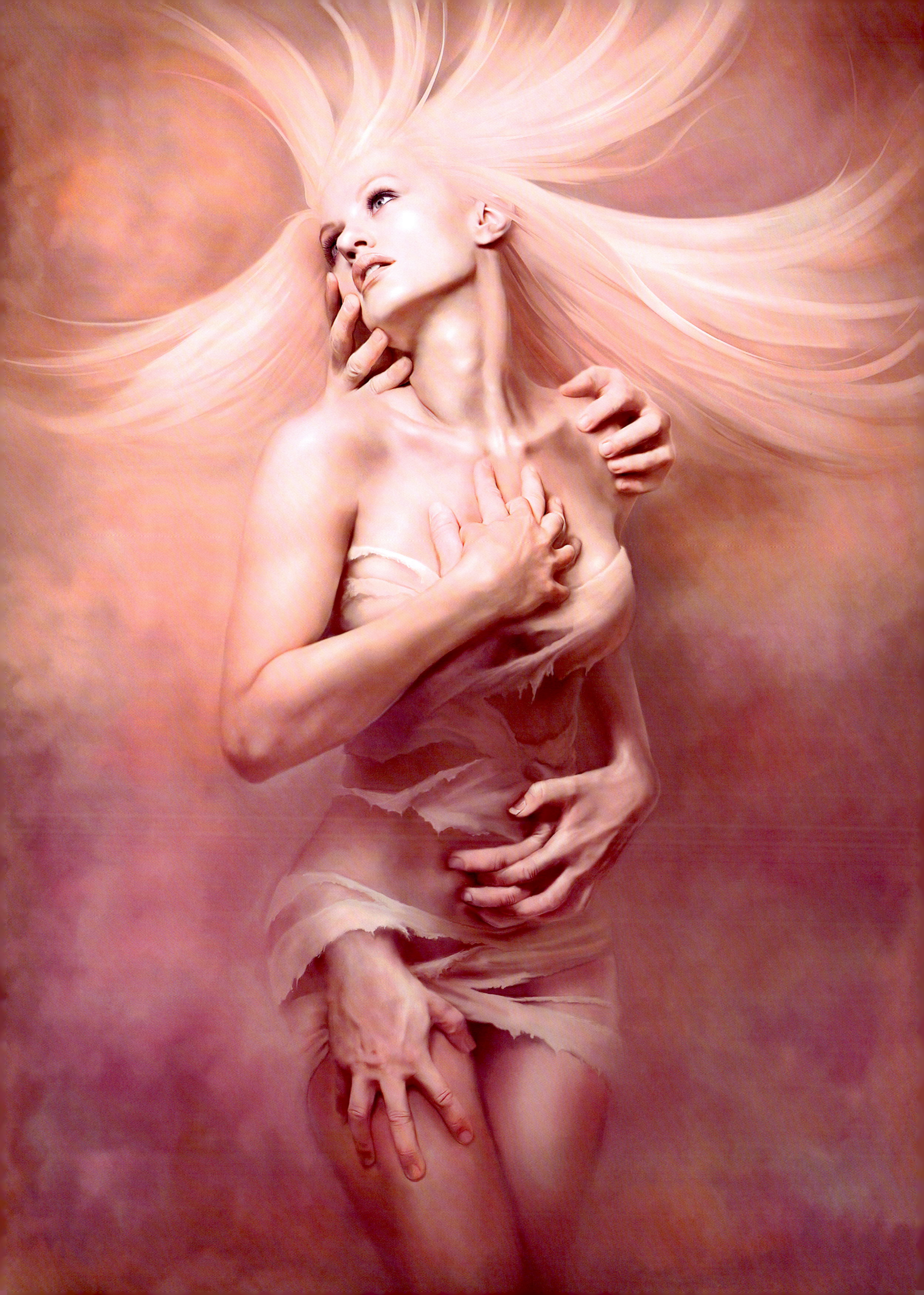

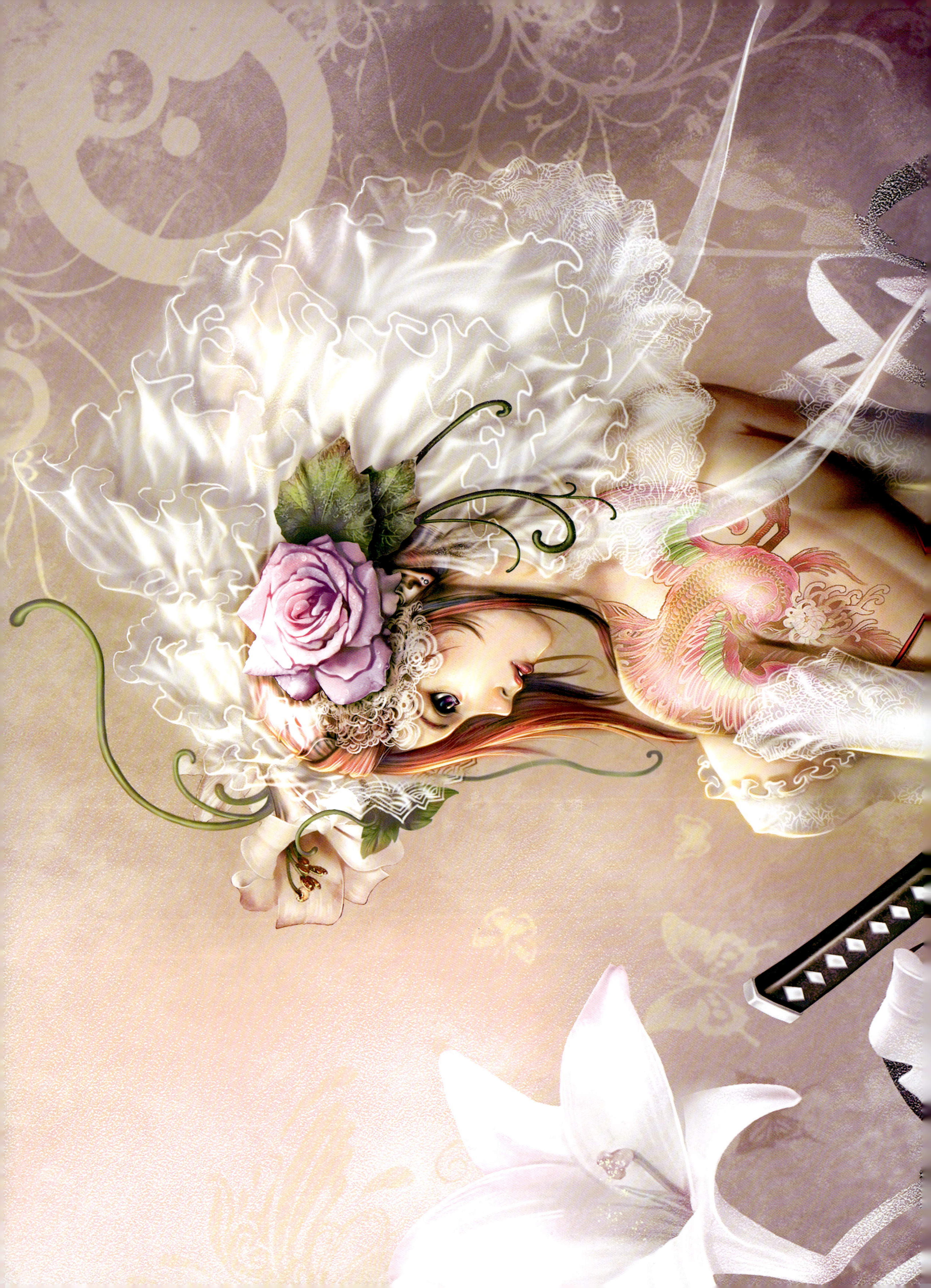

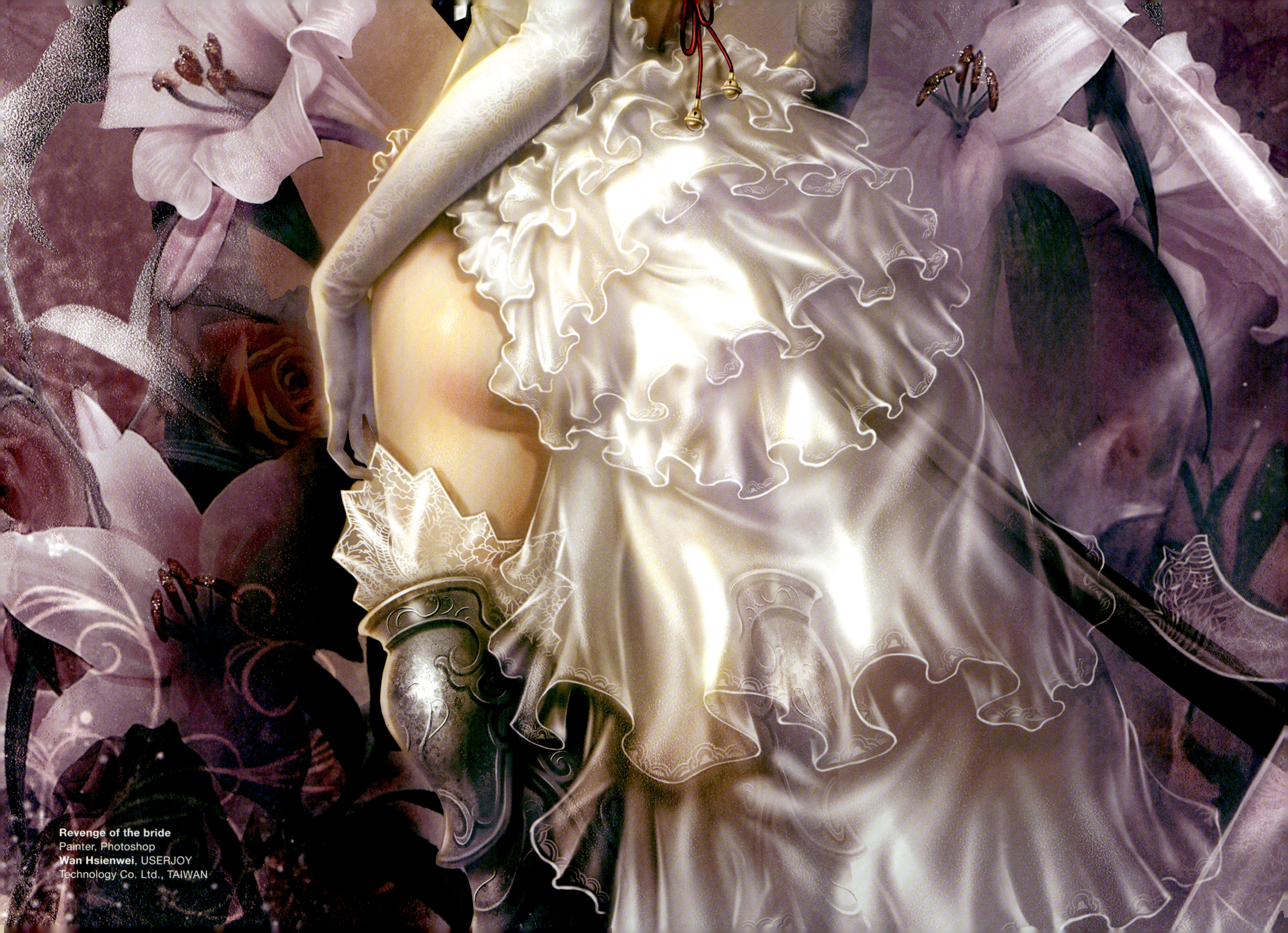

Revenge of the bride
Painter, Photoshop
Wan Hsienwei, USERJOY
Technology Co. Ltd., TAIWAN

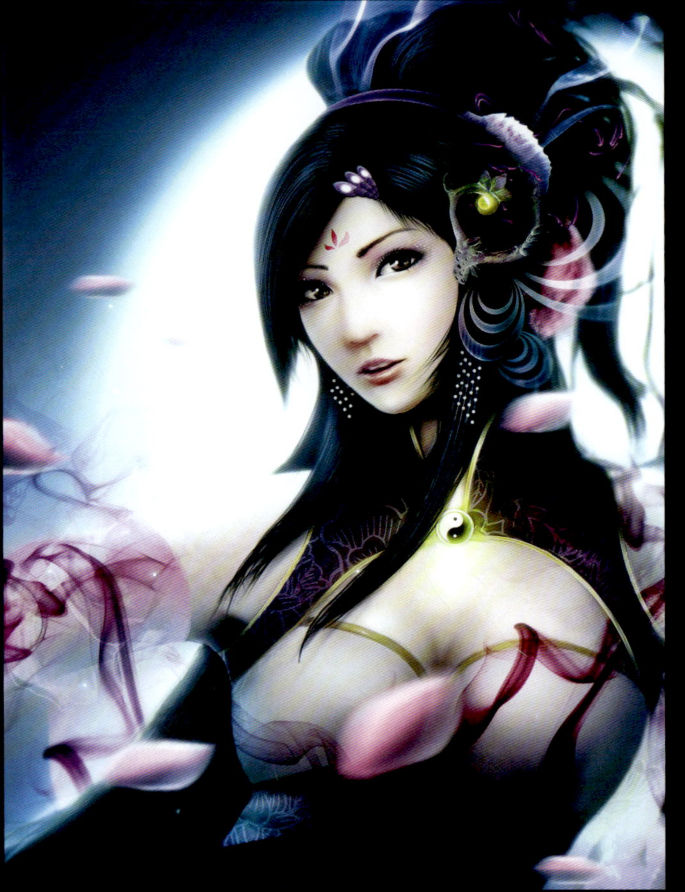

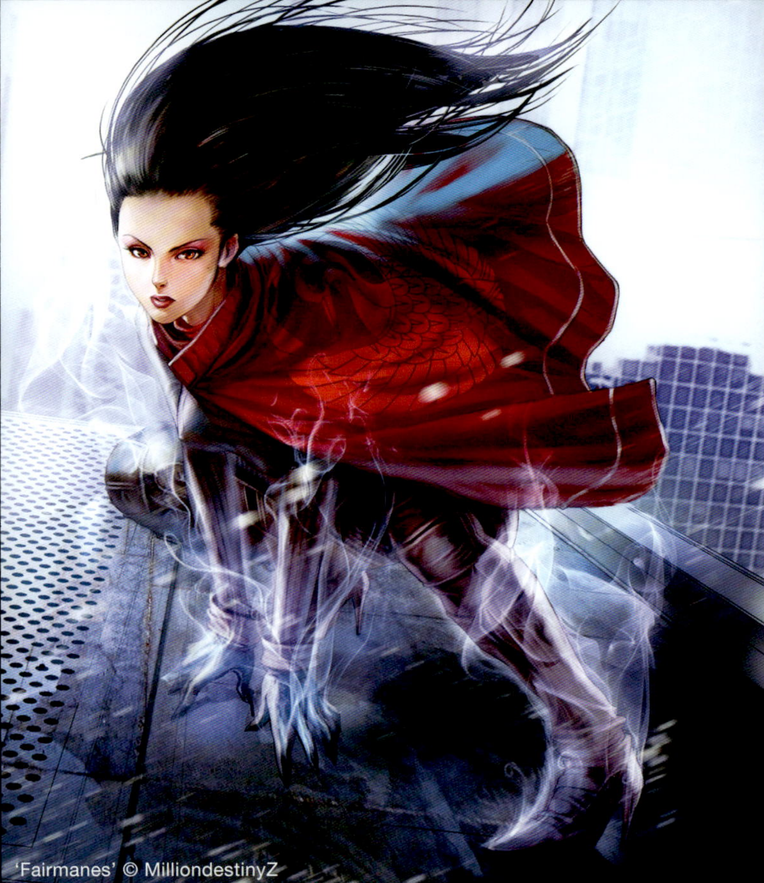

'Fairmanes' © MilliondestinyZ

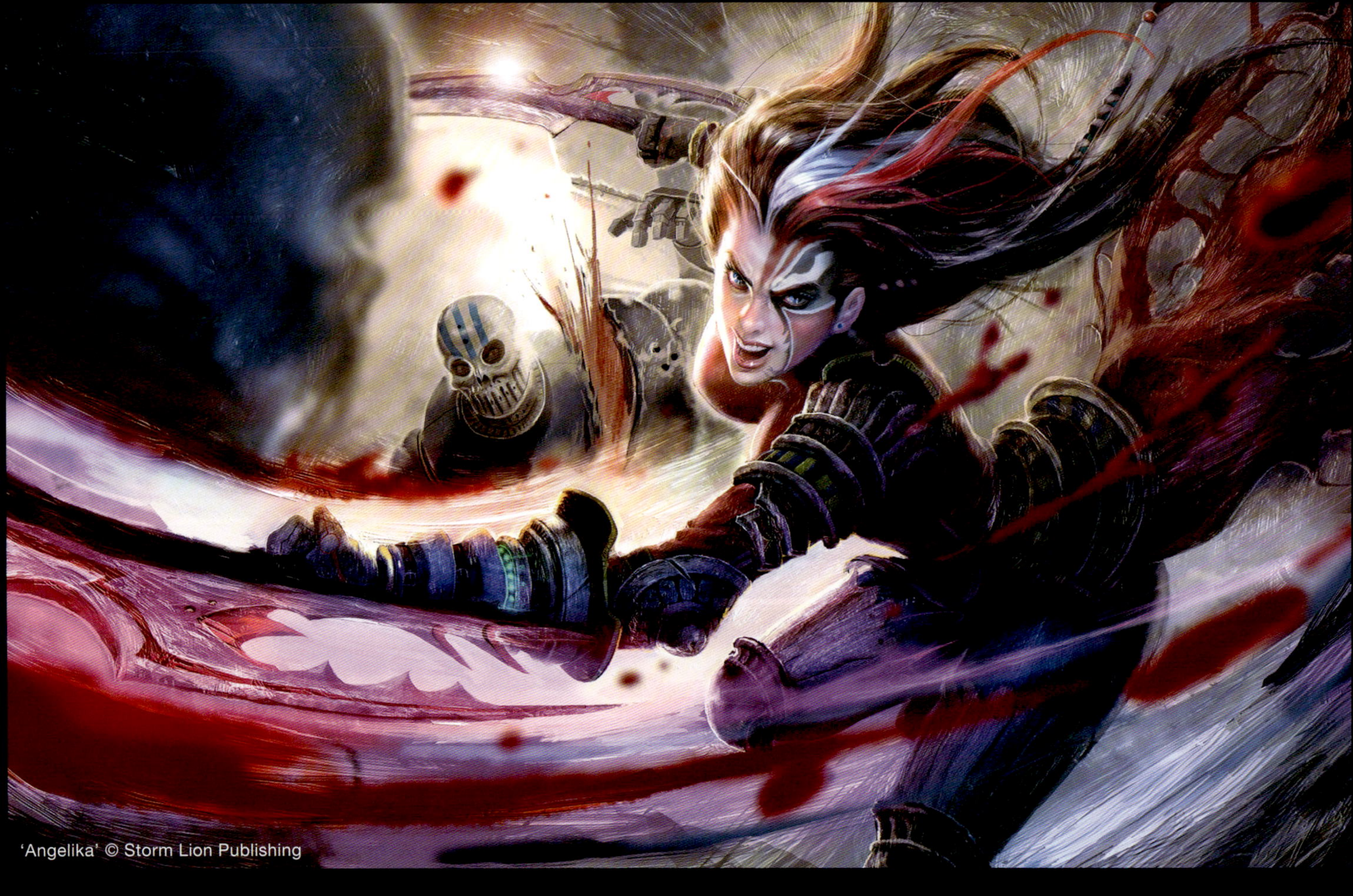

'Angelika' © Storm Lion Publishing

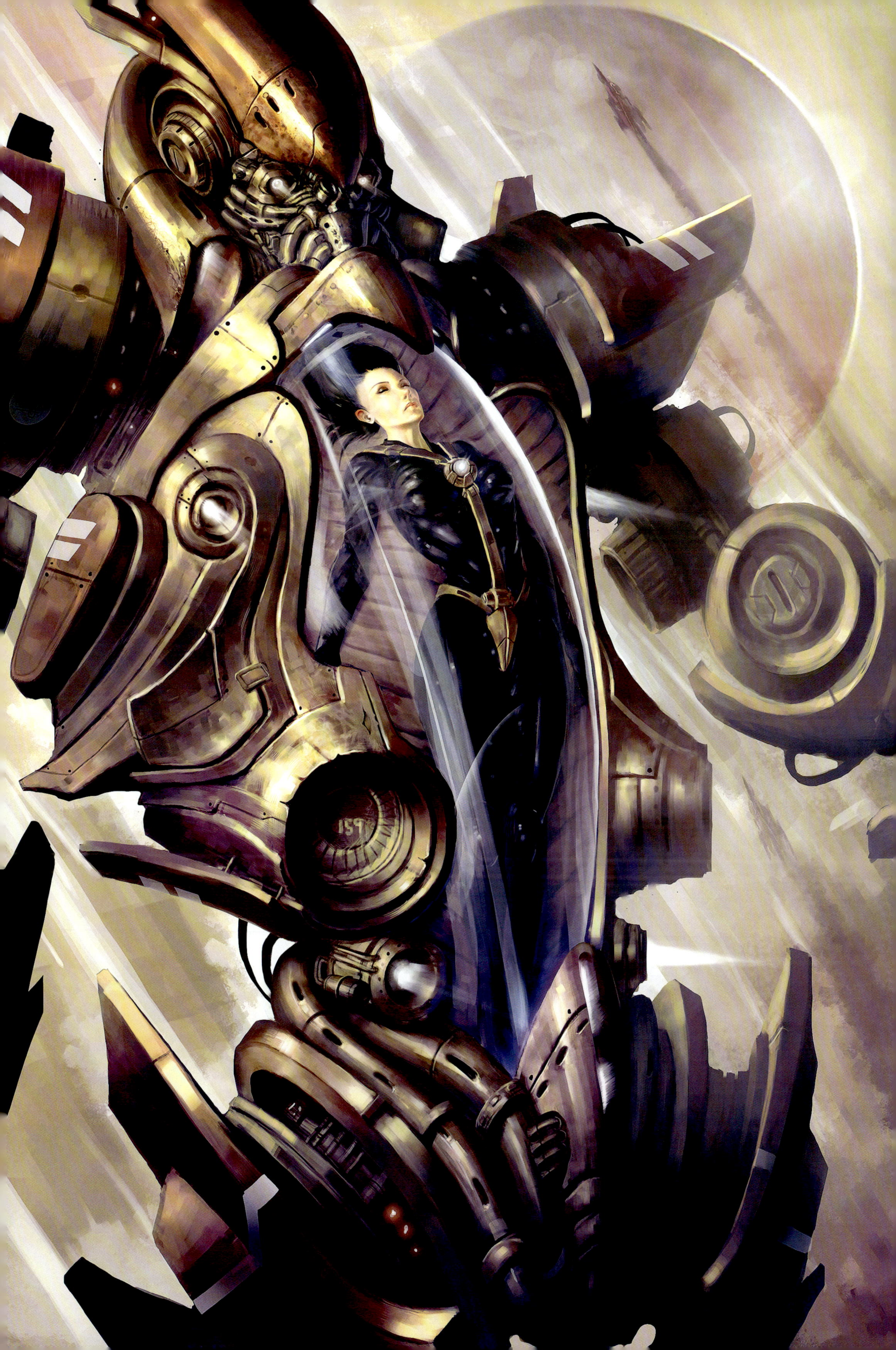

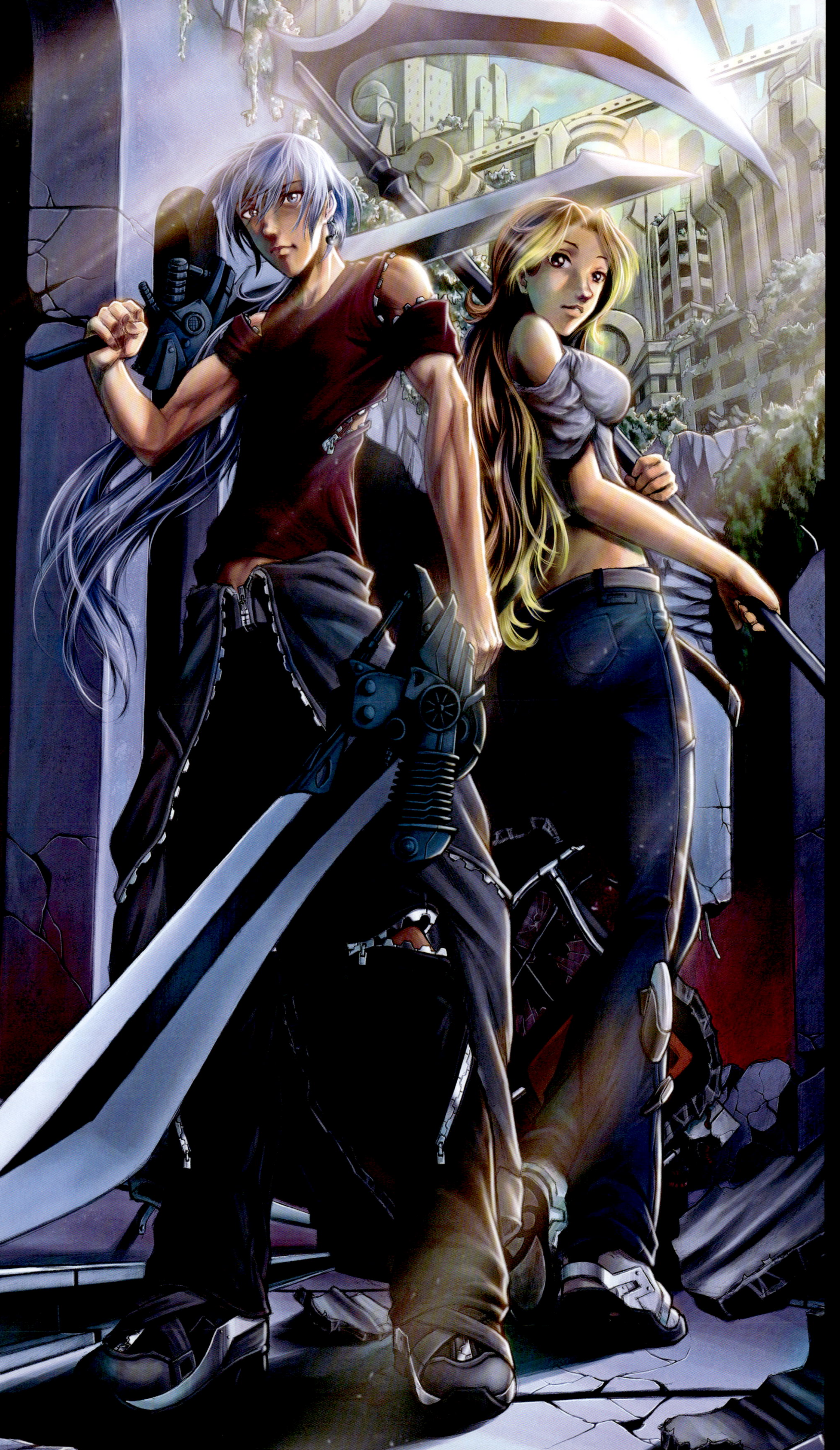

No World for Tomorrow
Photoshop
Gabriel Belluco, BRAZIL
[left]

Bambi the Zombie Slayer
Photoshop, Painter
Rudy-Jan Faber,
THE NETHERLANDS
[right]

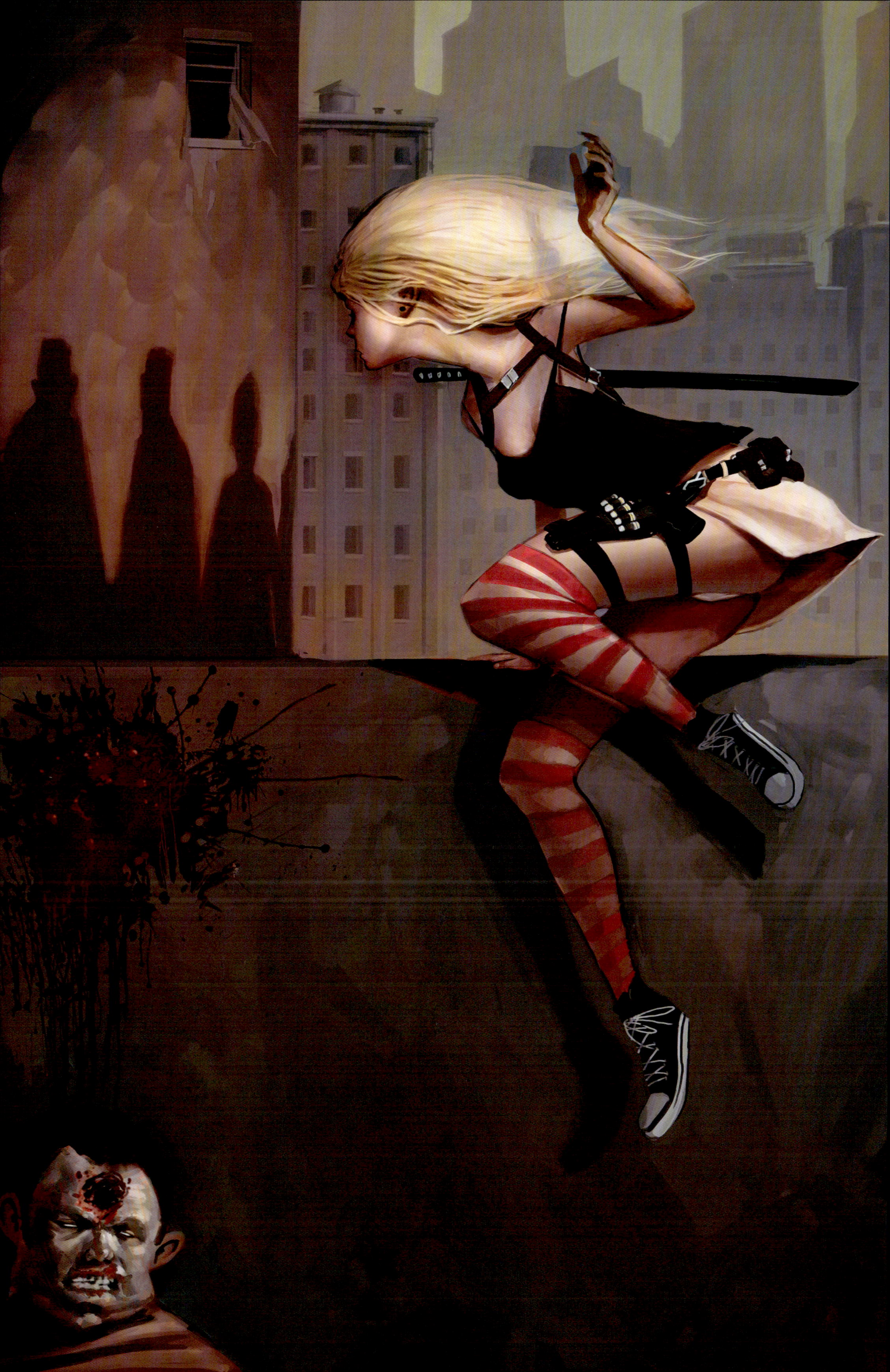

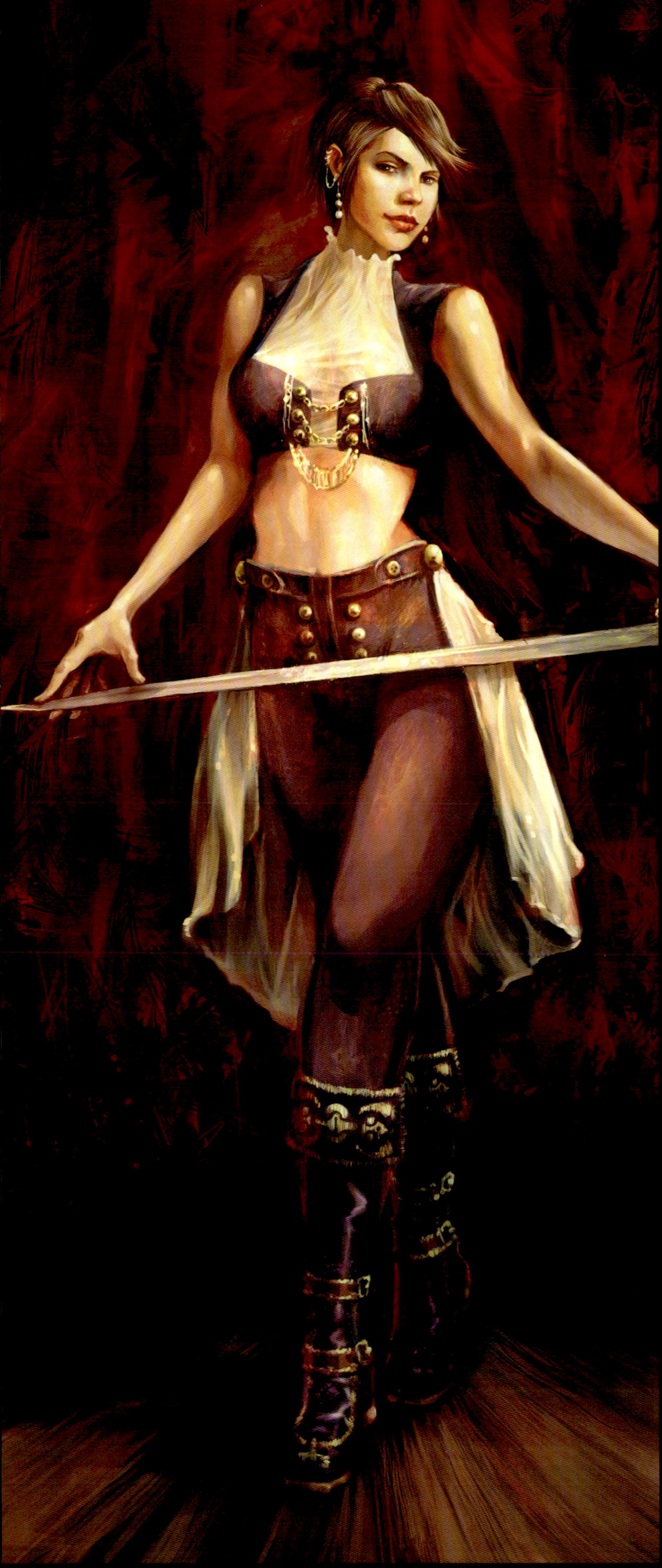

Captain
Photoshop
Claire Beard,

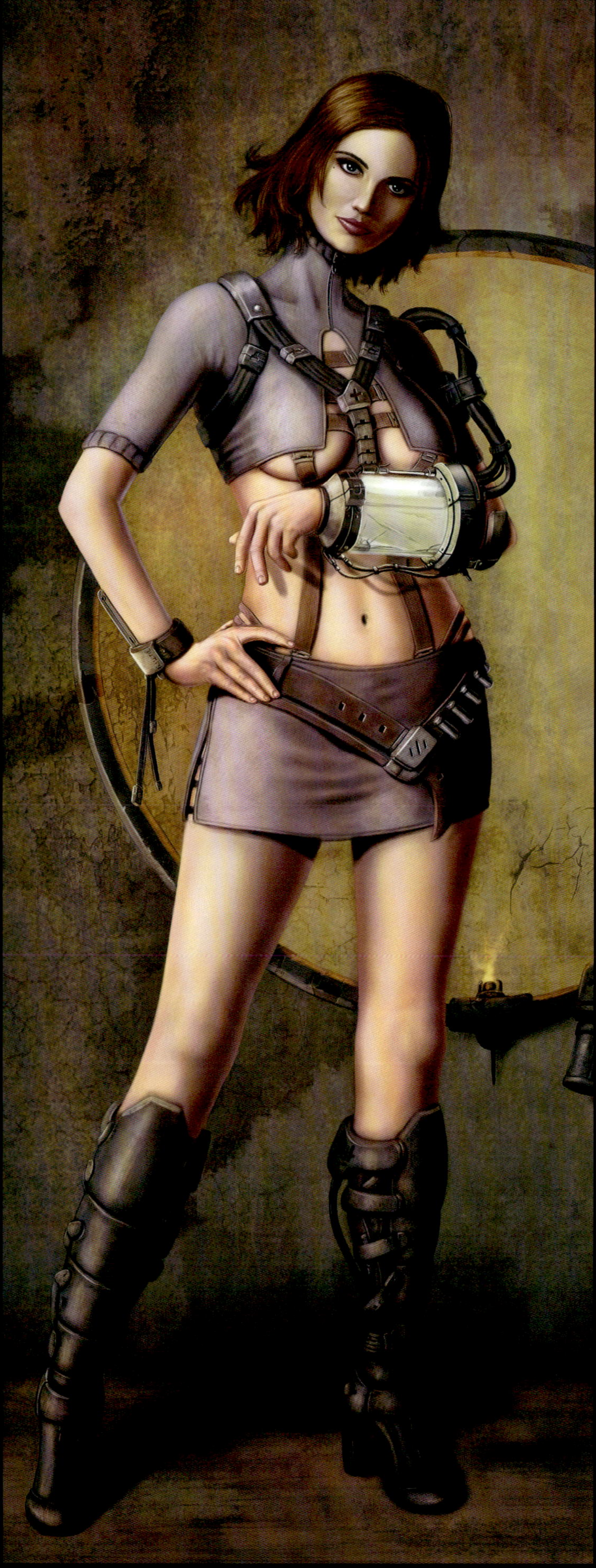

May
Photoshop
Arthur Gurin,

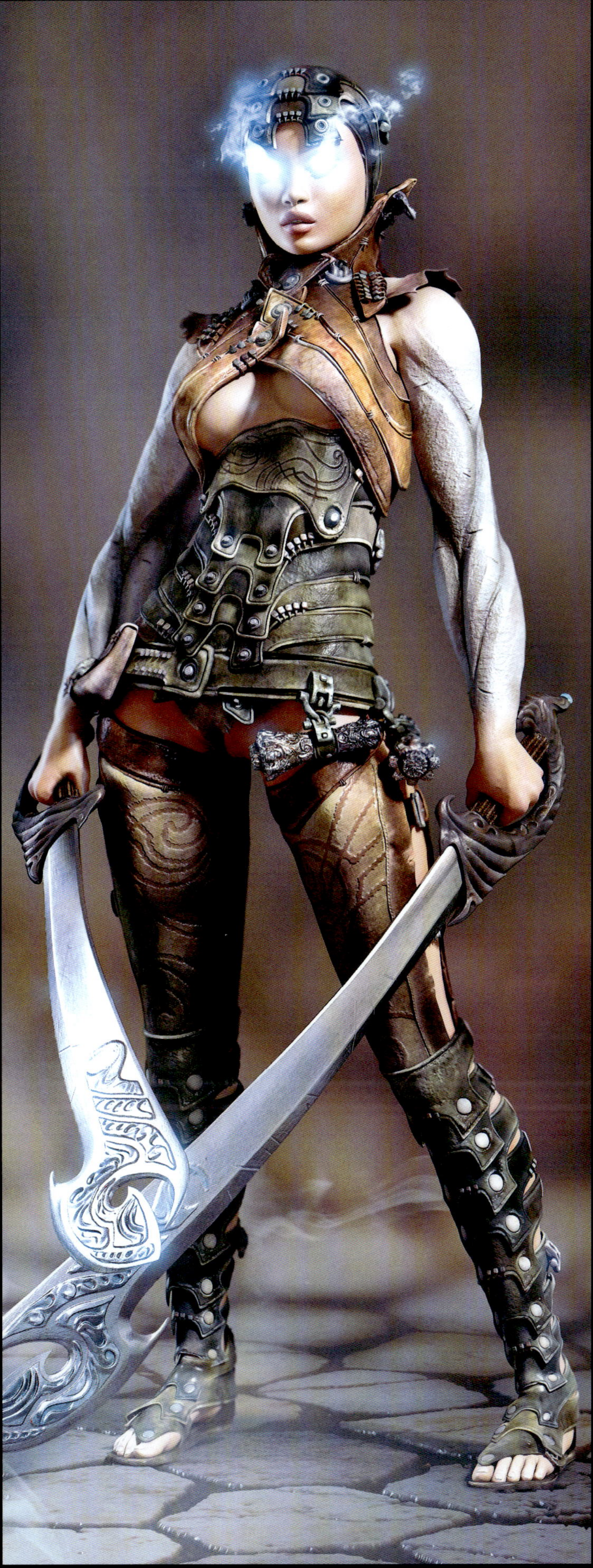

Hear No Evil
Maya, Photoshop, ZBrush, Poser
Siliphiel and As Shanim,

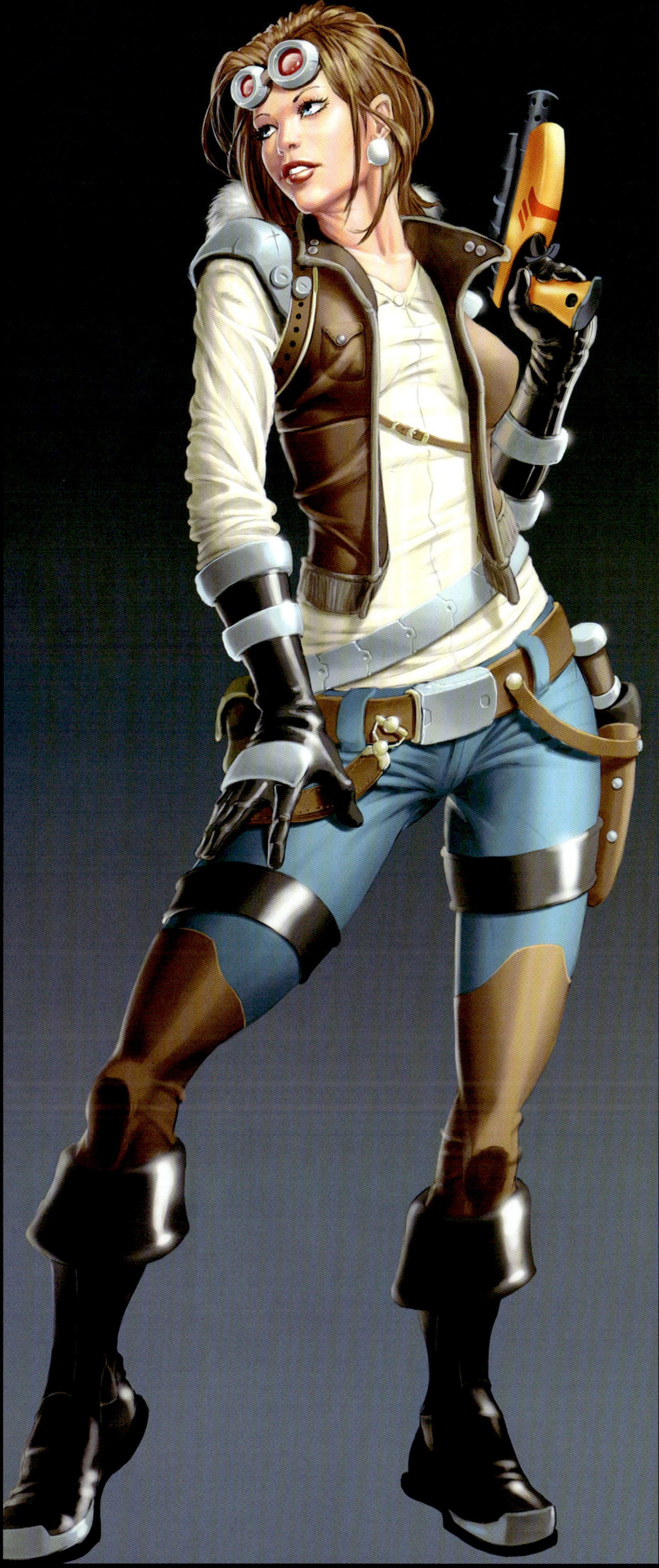

Smuggler
Photoshop
Ryan Hawkins,

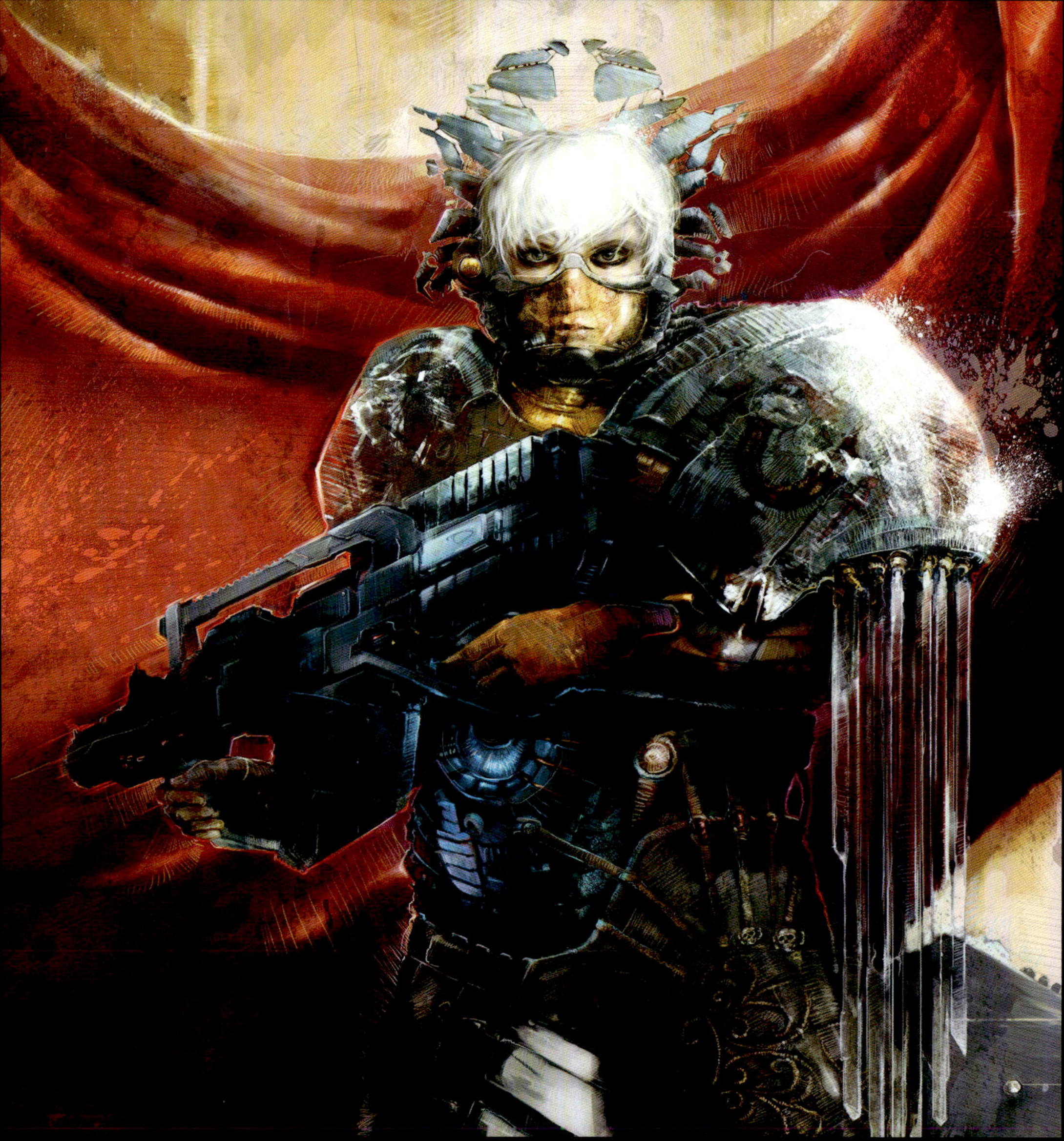

Aptitude
Photoshop
Paul Tysall, GREAT BRITAIN
[left]

Barbaric Lady
Photoshop
Lukasz Jaskolski, POLAND
[right]

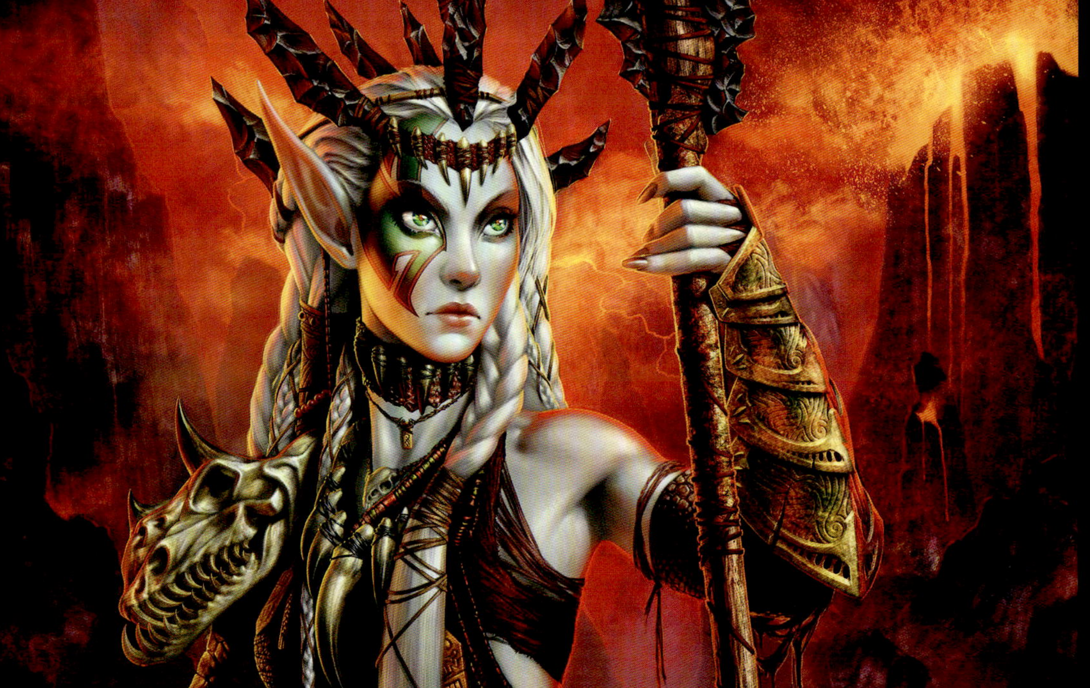

Magic: The Gathering (Bloodbraid Elf)
Photoshop
Client: Wizards of the Coast
Art Director: Jeremy Jarvis
Steve Argyle, USA
[left]

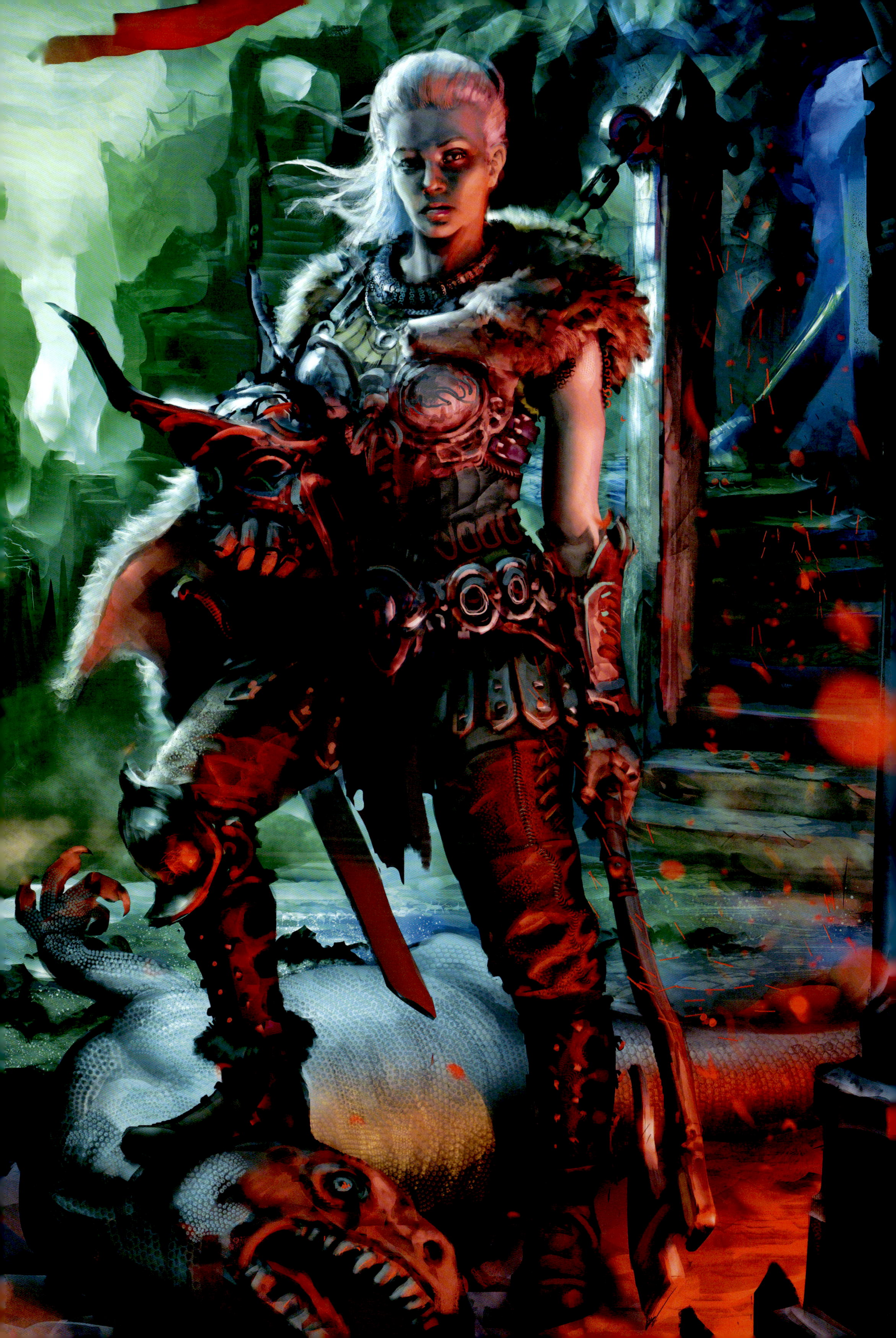

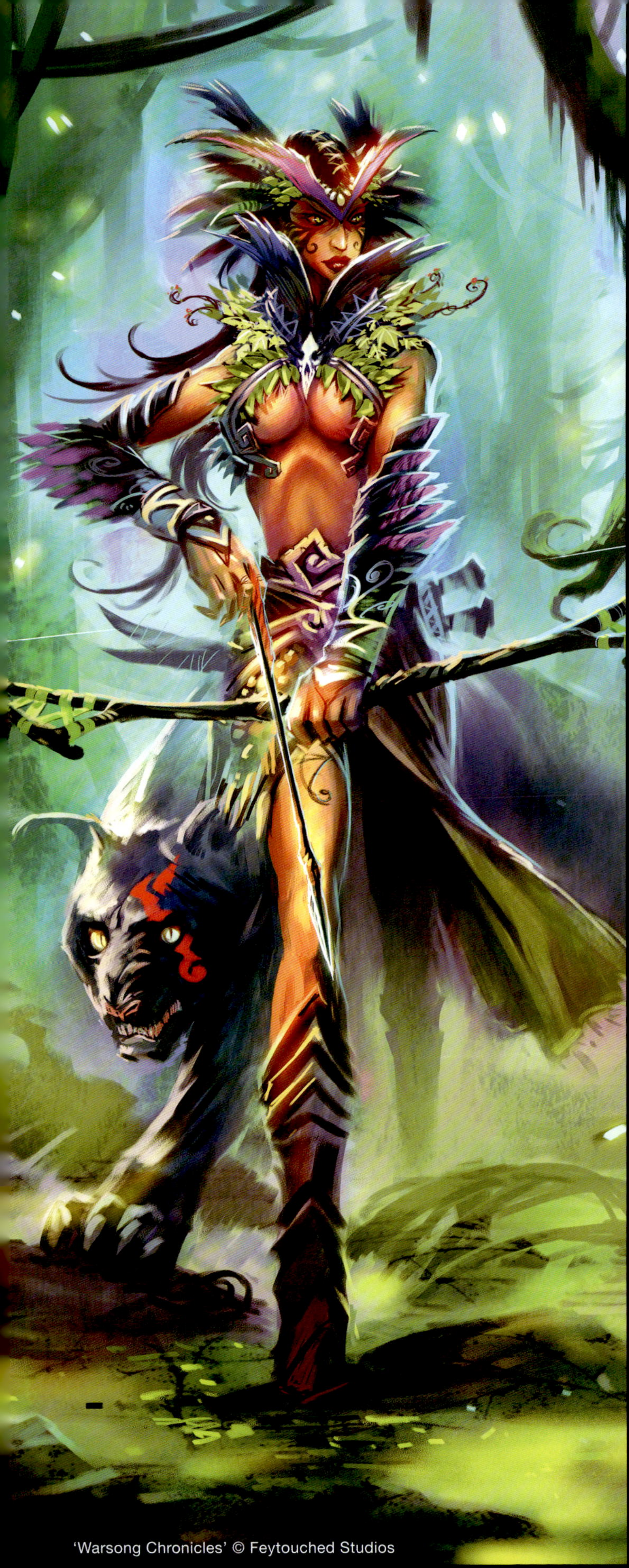

'Warsong Chronicles' © Feytouched Studios

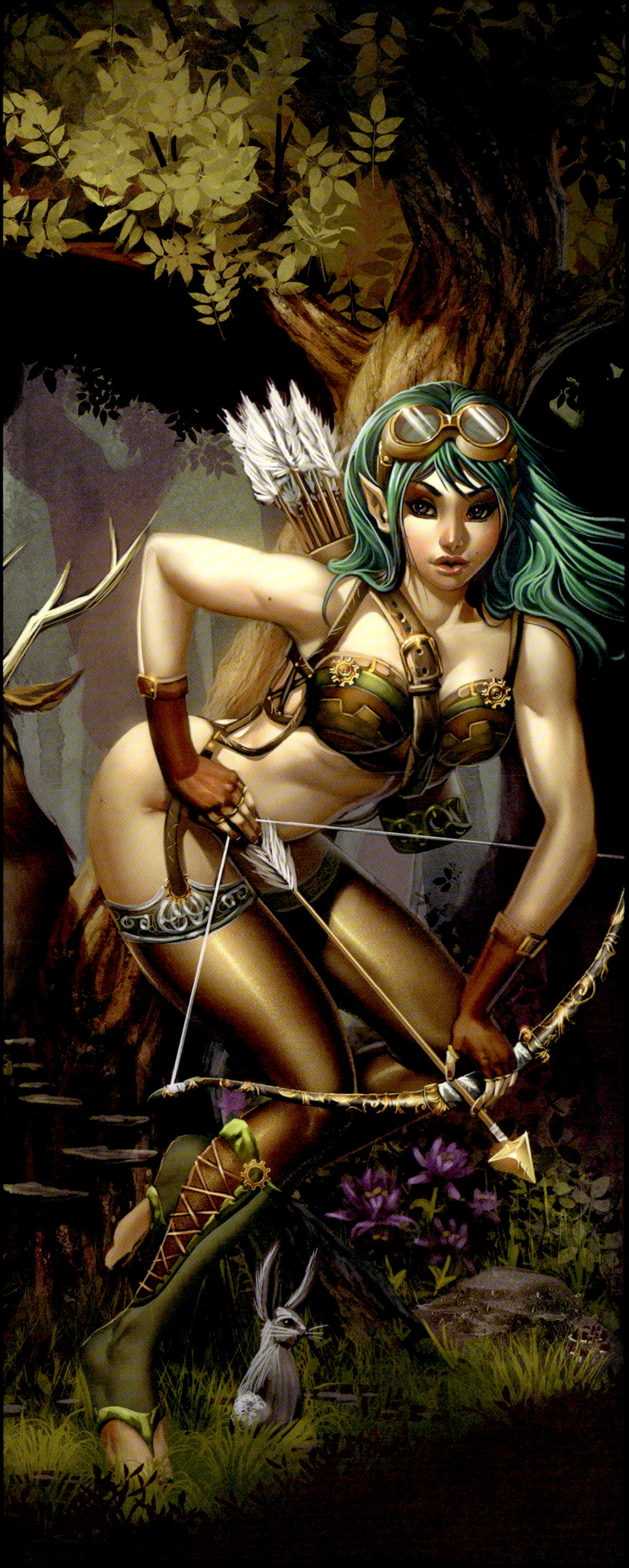

Warsong Chronicles: Pathfinder
Painter
Client: Feytouched Studios
Jian Guo, CHINA *[above]*

Hunteresque
Photoshop
Nei Ruffino, USA
[above]

Ghost ball
Photoshop
Huang DaHong, CHINA
[right]

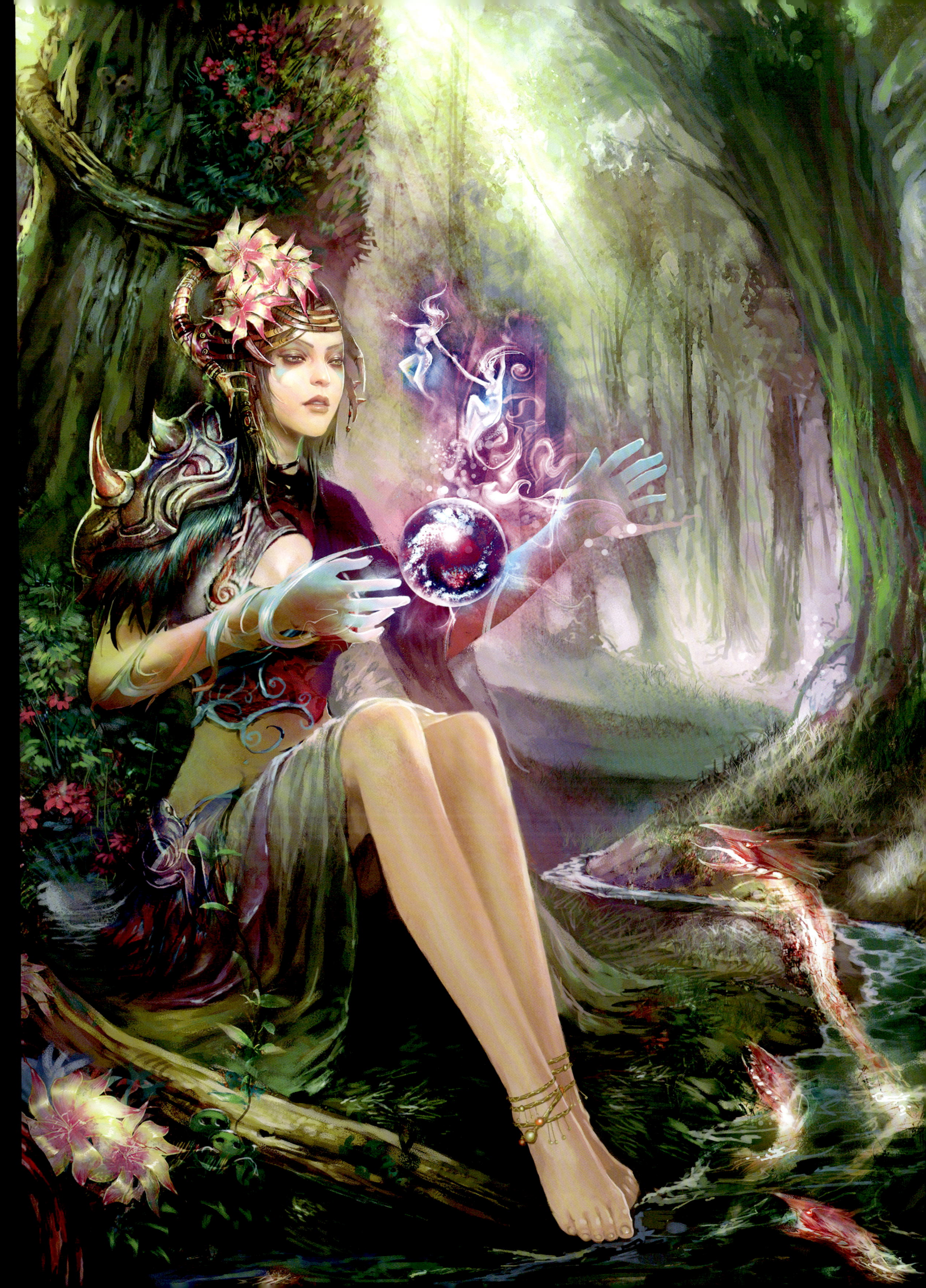

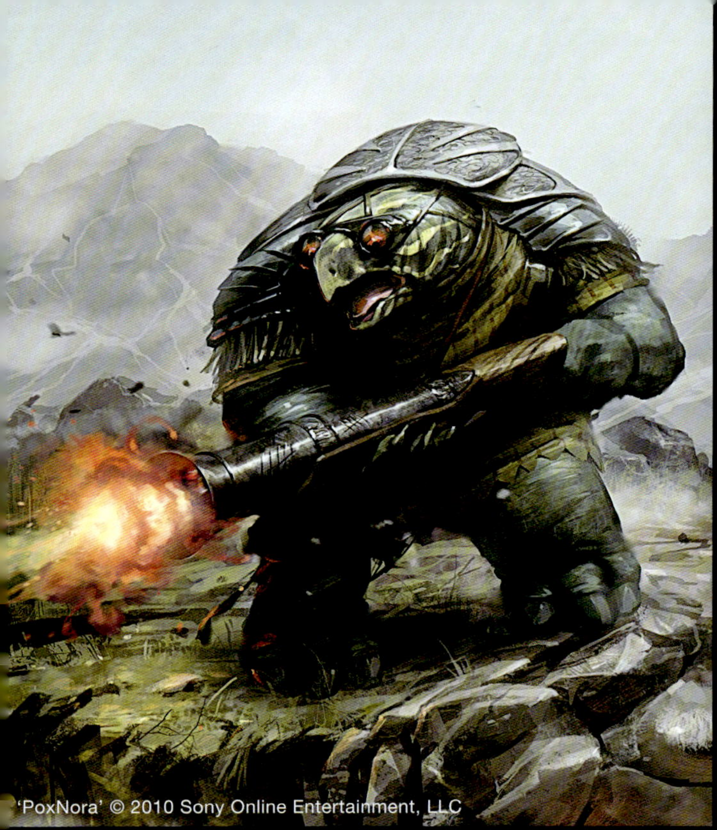

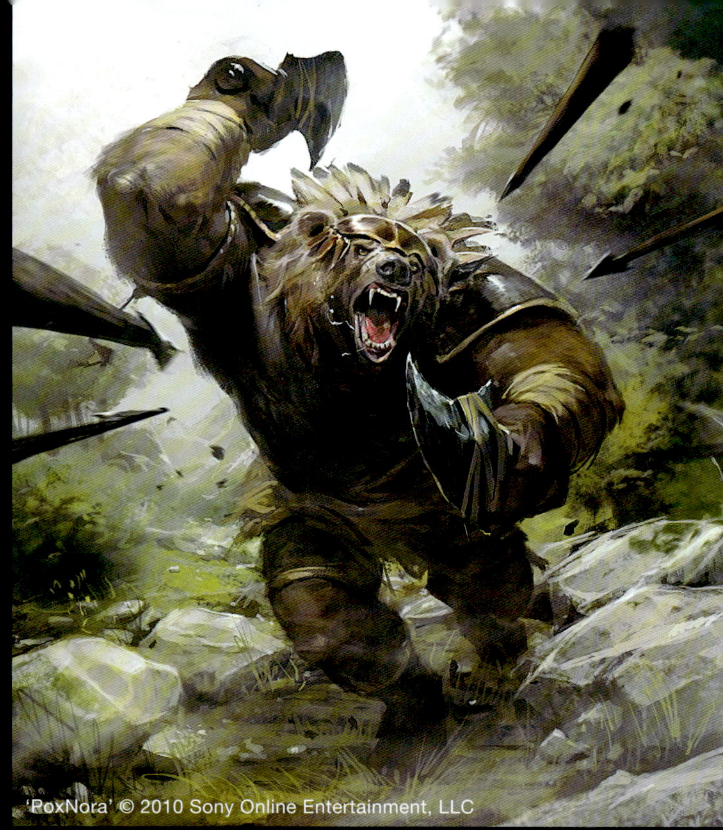

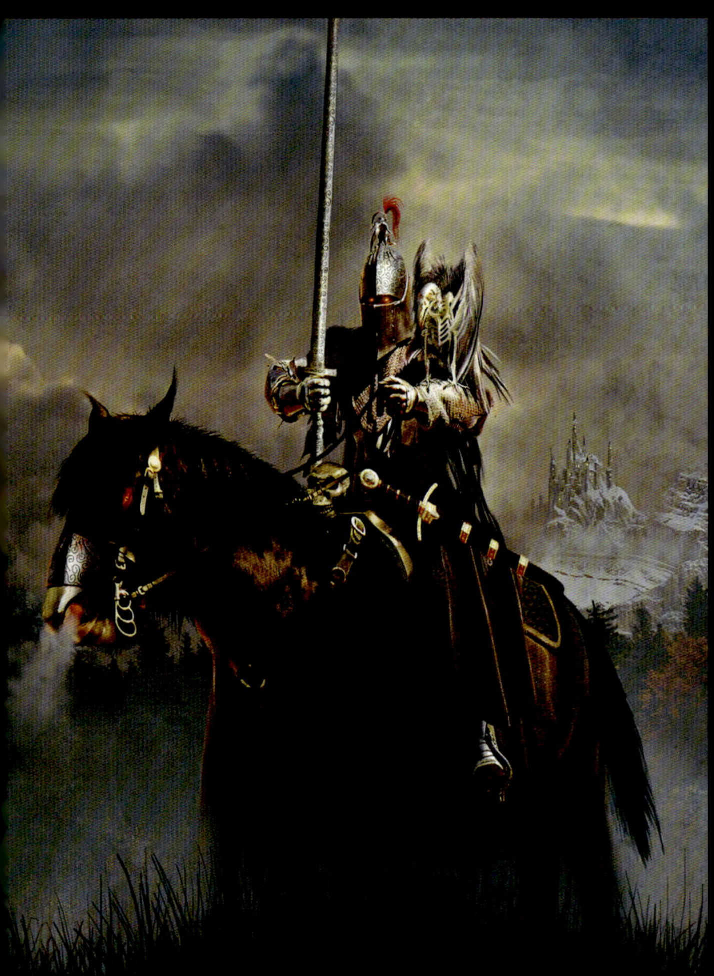

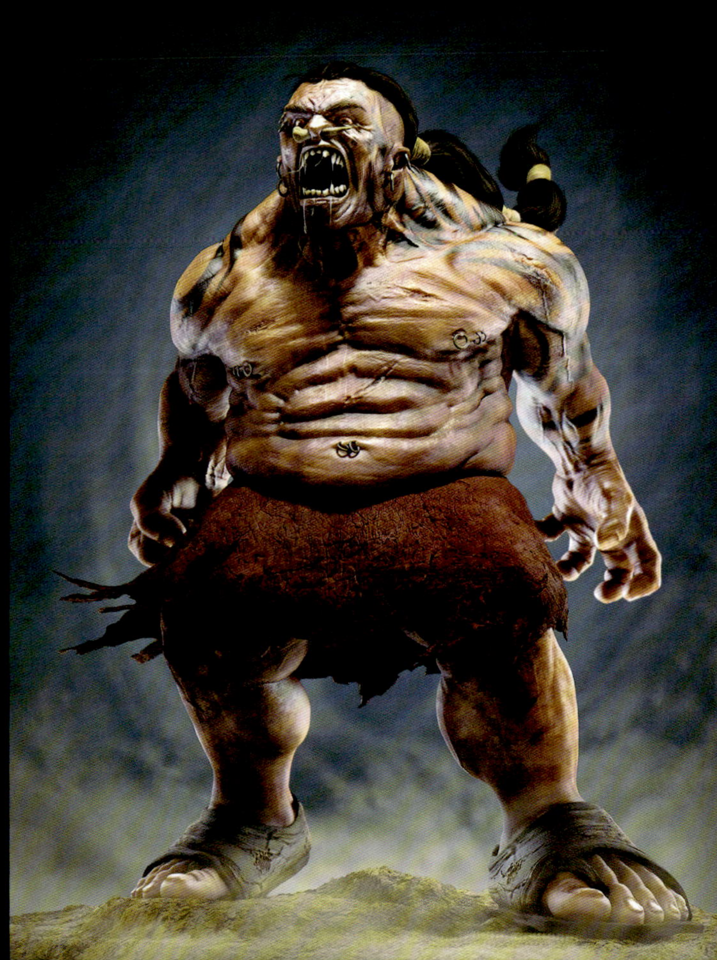

PoxNora: Tortun Heavy Repeater
Photoshop
Art Director: Bryan Rypkowski
Client: Sony Online Entertainment, LLC
Slawomir Maniak, POLAND *[top]*

Death Knight
Photoshop
Sarel Theron,
SOUTH AFRICA
[above]

PoxNora: Ailurite Brother
Photoshop
Art Director: Bryan Rypkowski
Client: Sony Online Entertainment, LLC
Slawomir Maniak, POLAND *[top]*

Screaming Giant
ZBrush, 3ds Max, V-Ray, Photoshop
Jesse Sandifer, Green Grass
Studios, LLC, USA
[above]

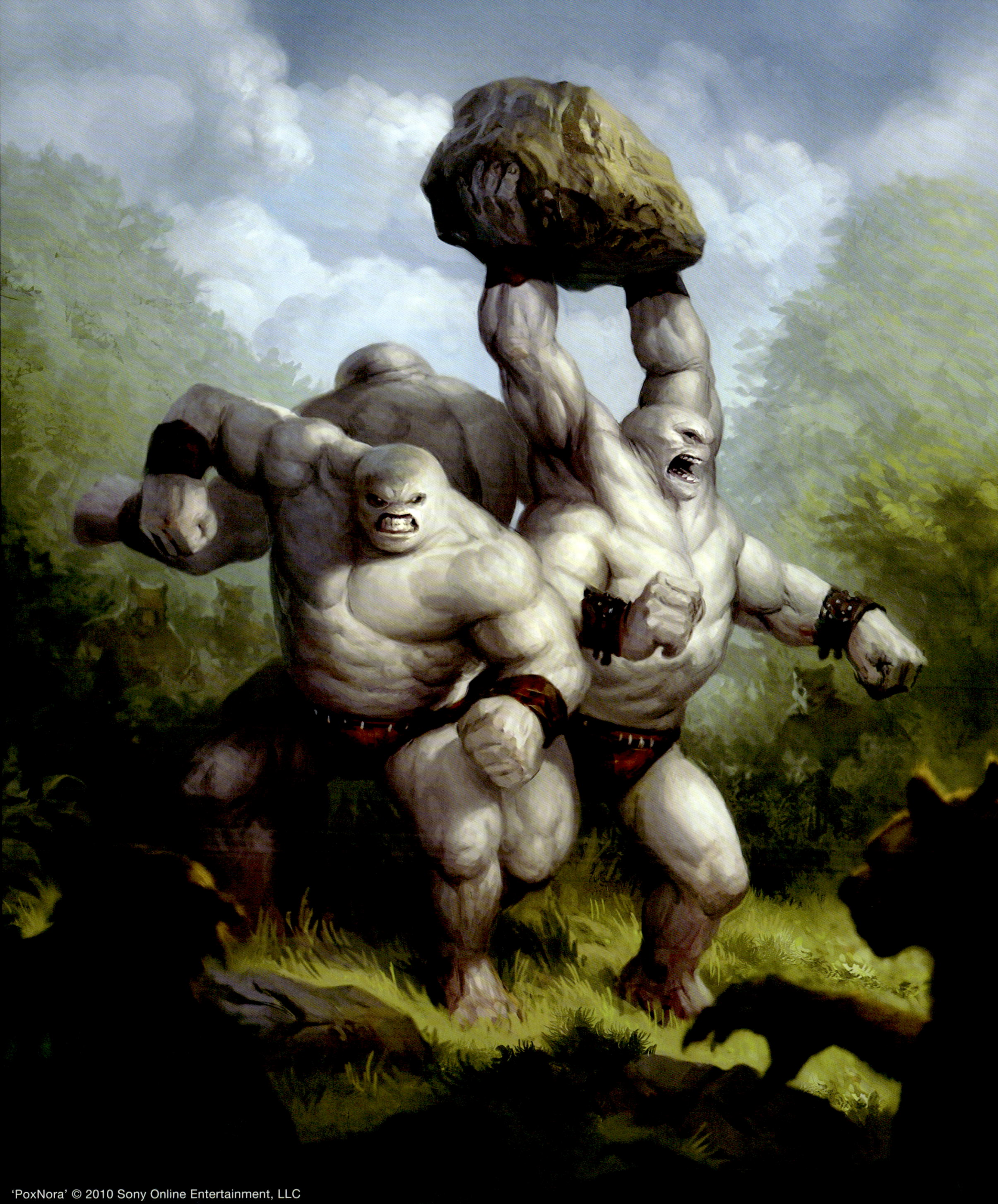

PoxNora: Groble Surplus
Photoshop
Art Director: Bryan Rypkowski
Client: Sony Online Entertainment, LLC

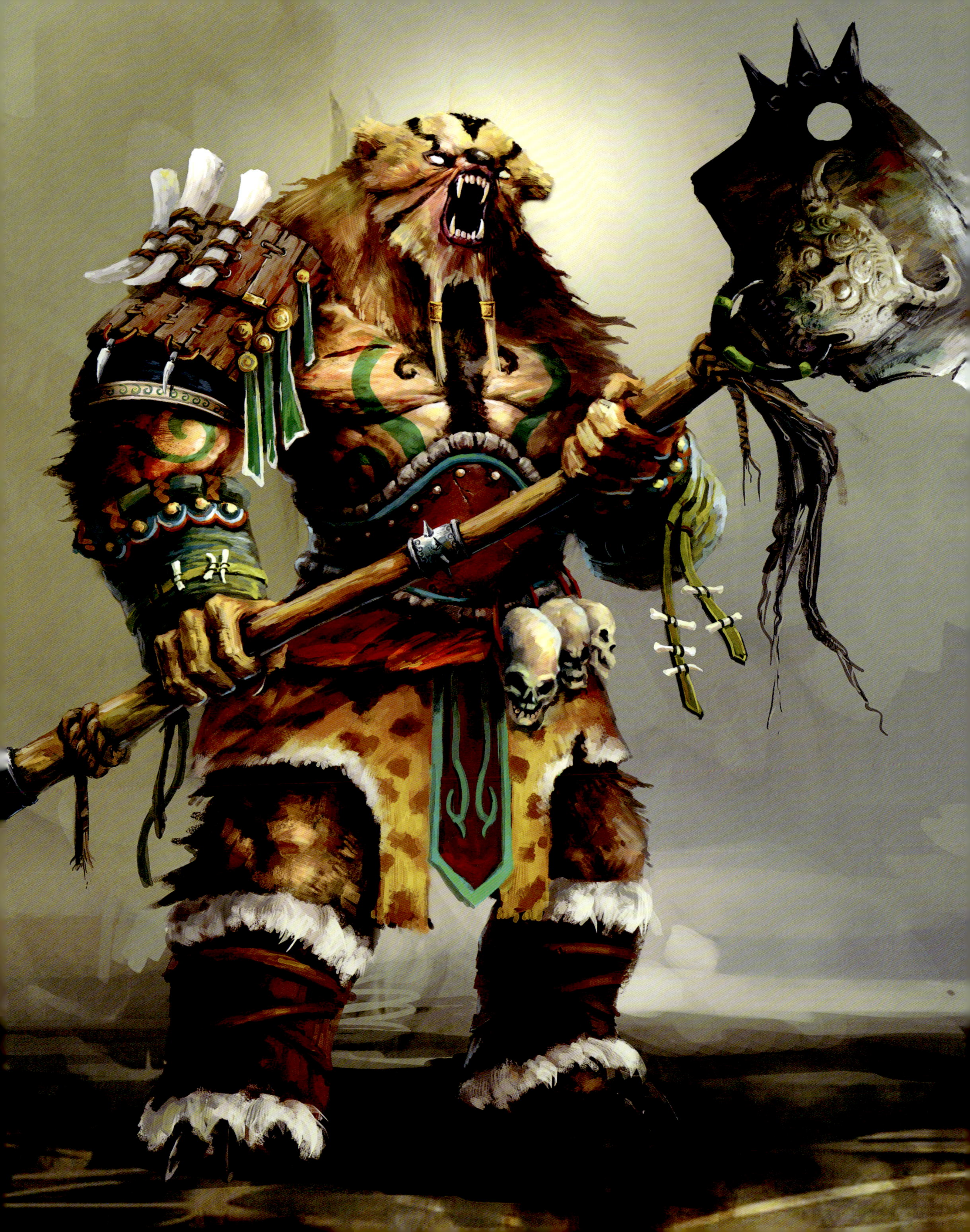

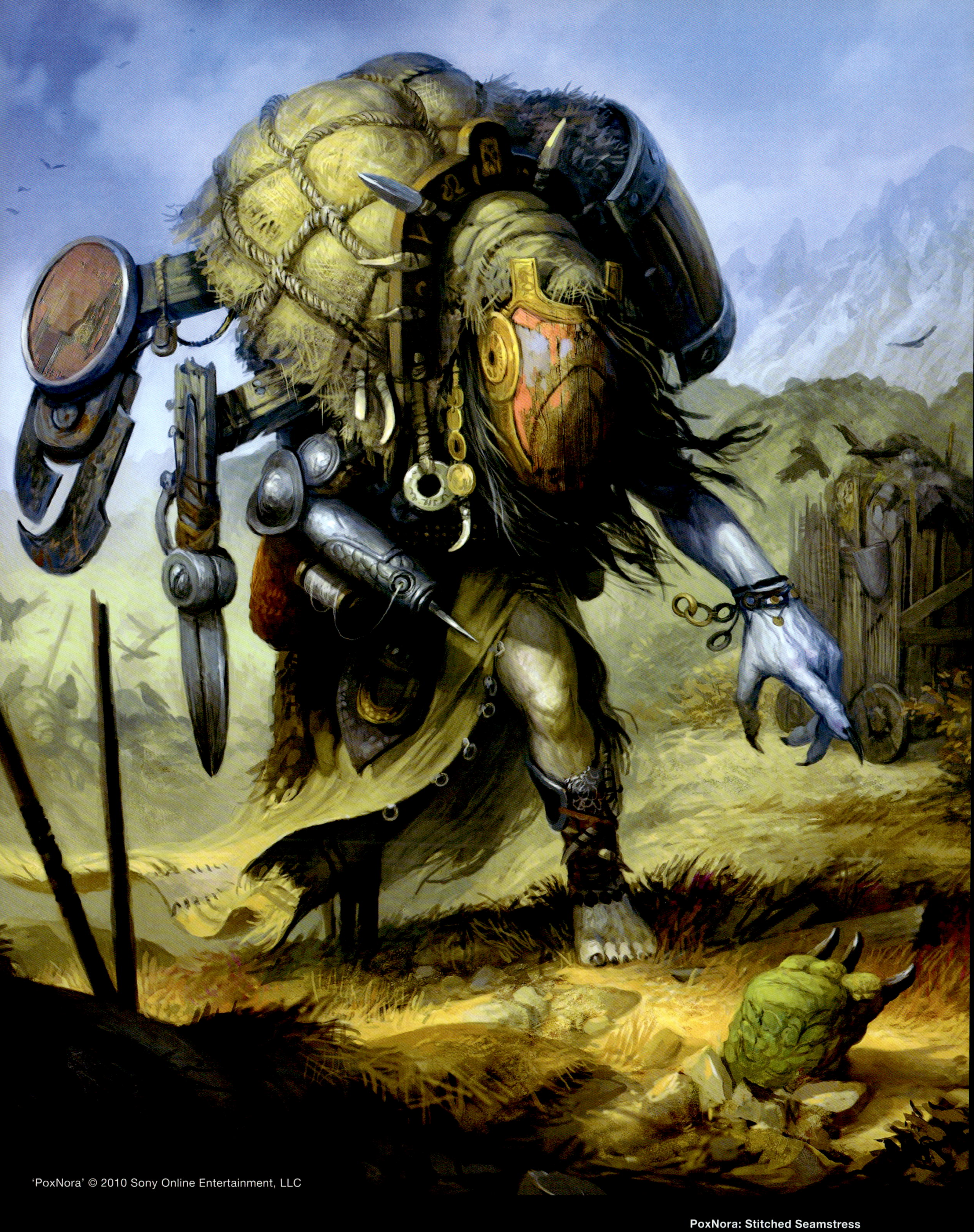

PoxNora: Stitched Seamstress
Photoshop
Art Director: Roger Chamberlain
Client: Sony Online Entertainment, LLC
Jakub Kasper, POLAND

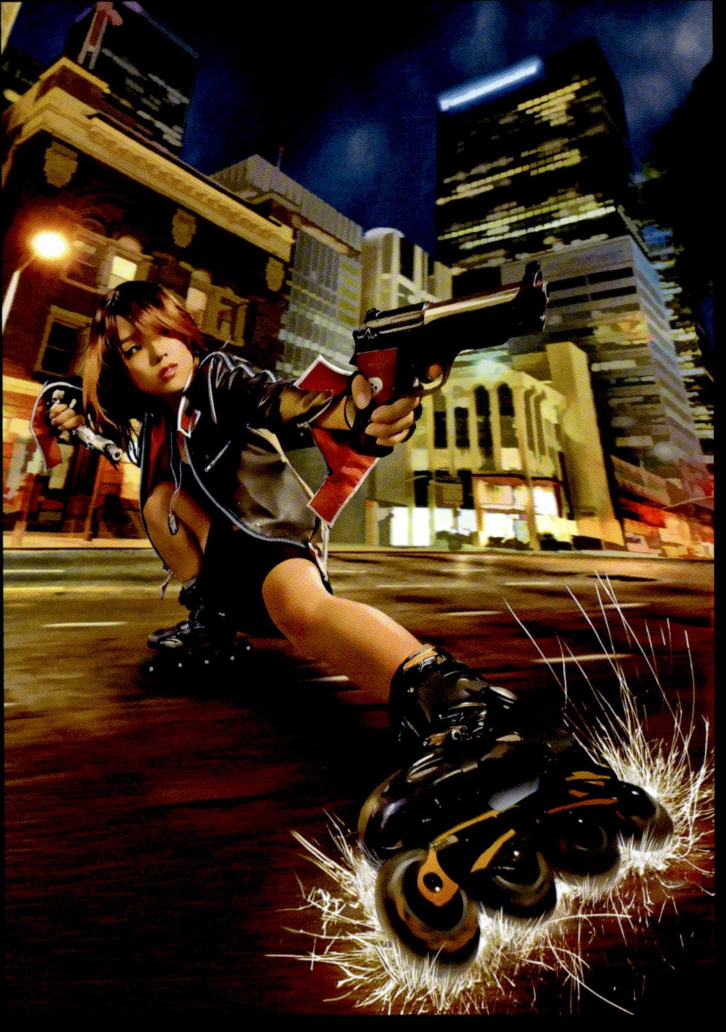

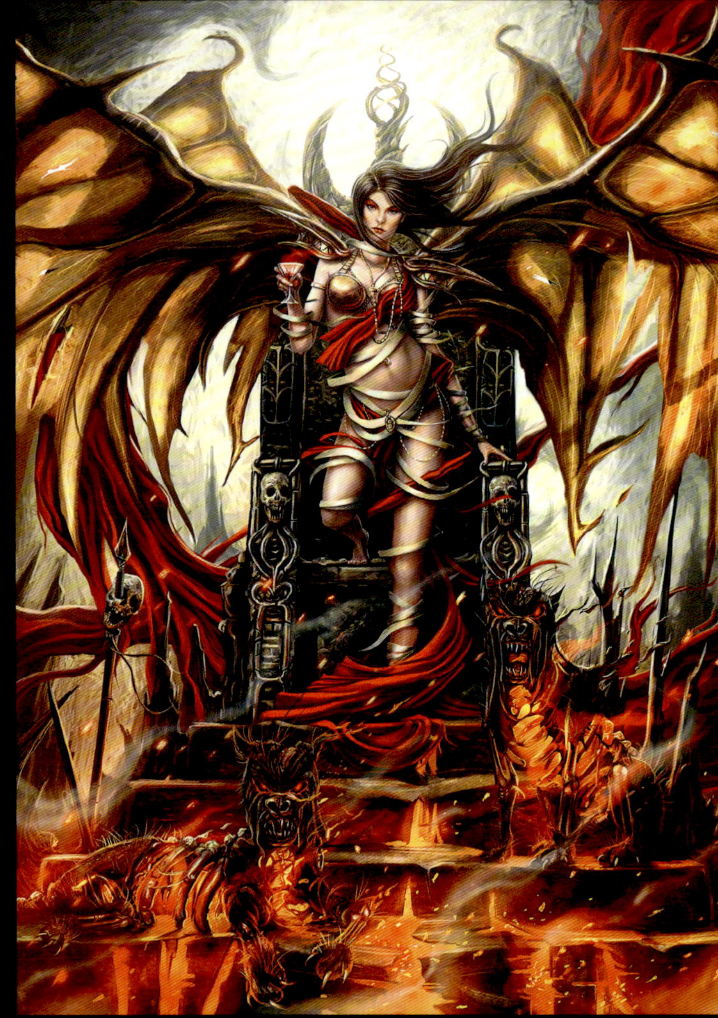

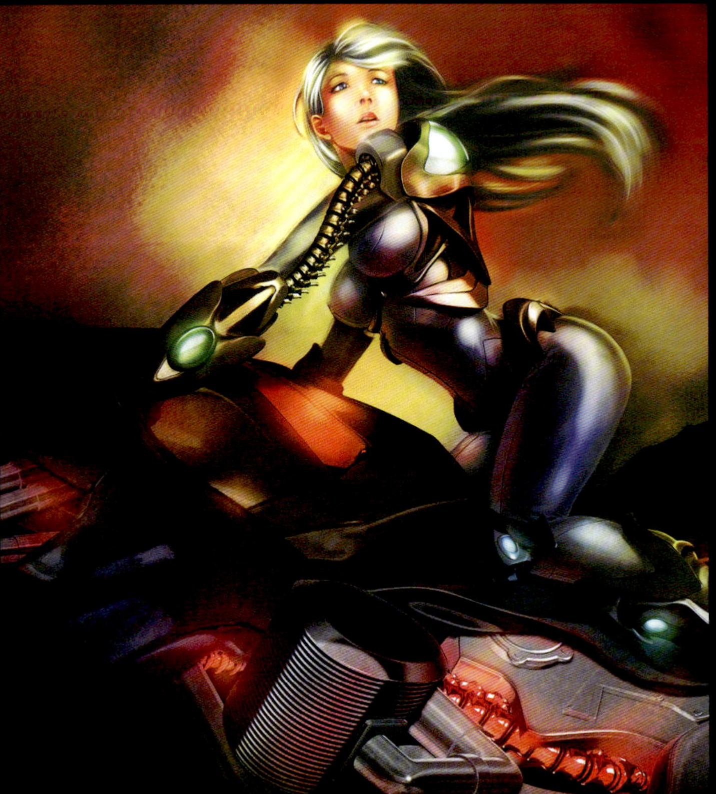

Girls of Action: Skate-by Shooting
Photoshop
Model: Akusesu
Client: Hollywood Ninja Pictures
Bruce Heinsius, USA
[top left]

The Life Giver
Photoshop
Bryan Sola, THE PHILIPPINES
[above]

Rider
Photoshop, ZBrush
Gabriel Belluco, BRAZIL
[left]

Lost Fleet 4
Photoshop
Client: Fabryka Słów
Artur Sadlos, POLAND
[right]

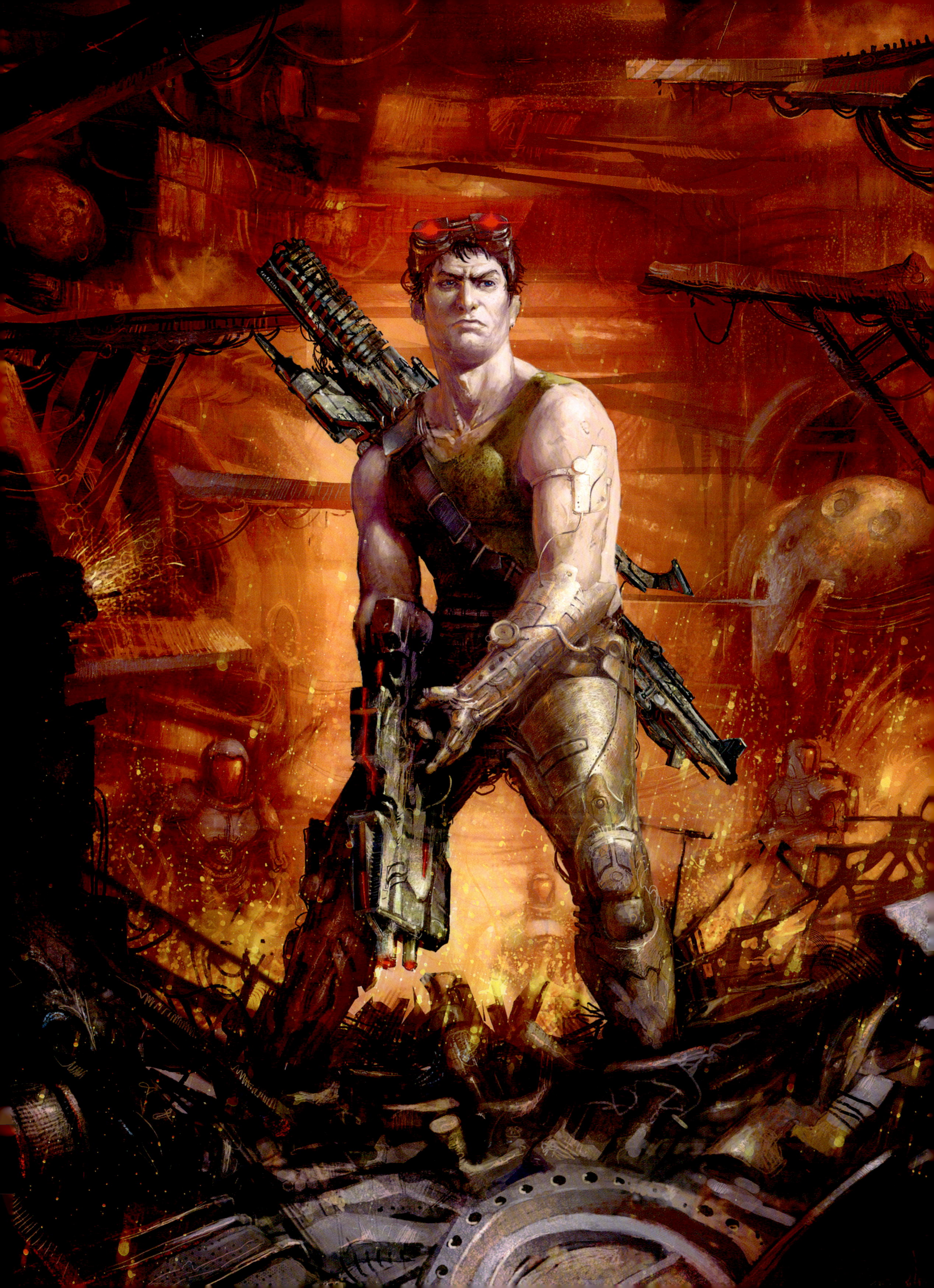

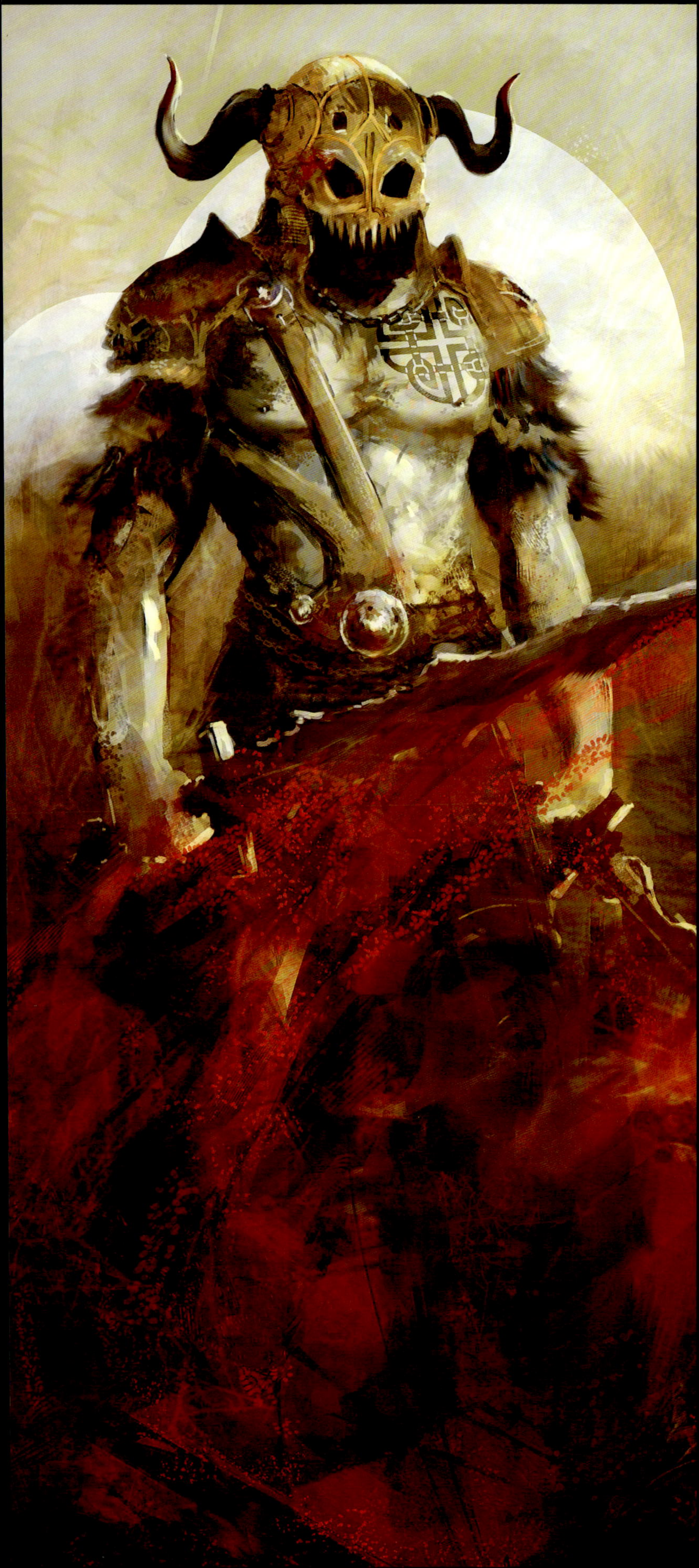

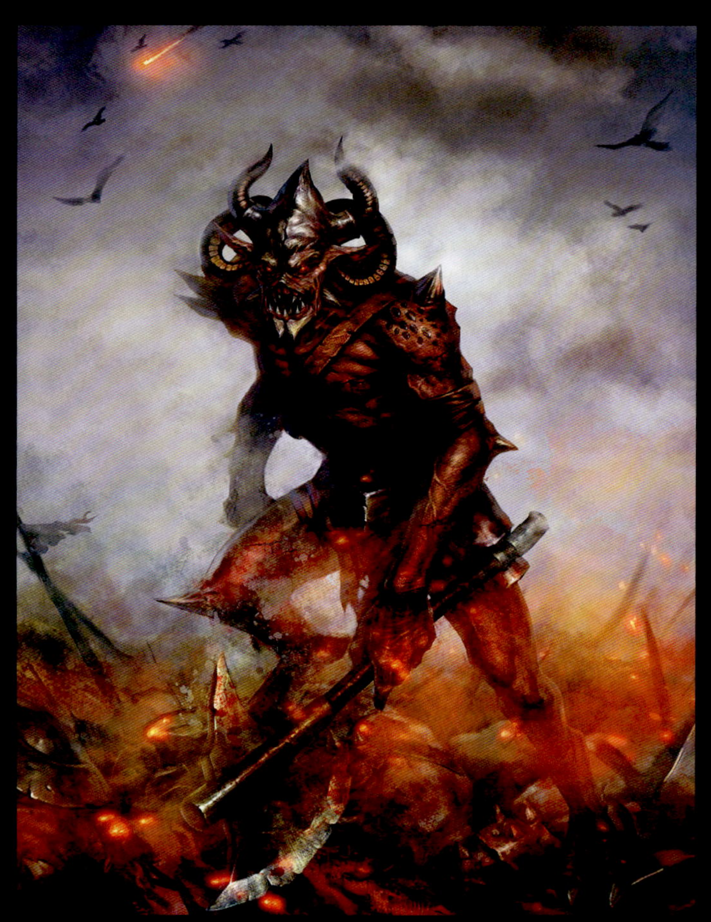

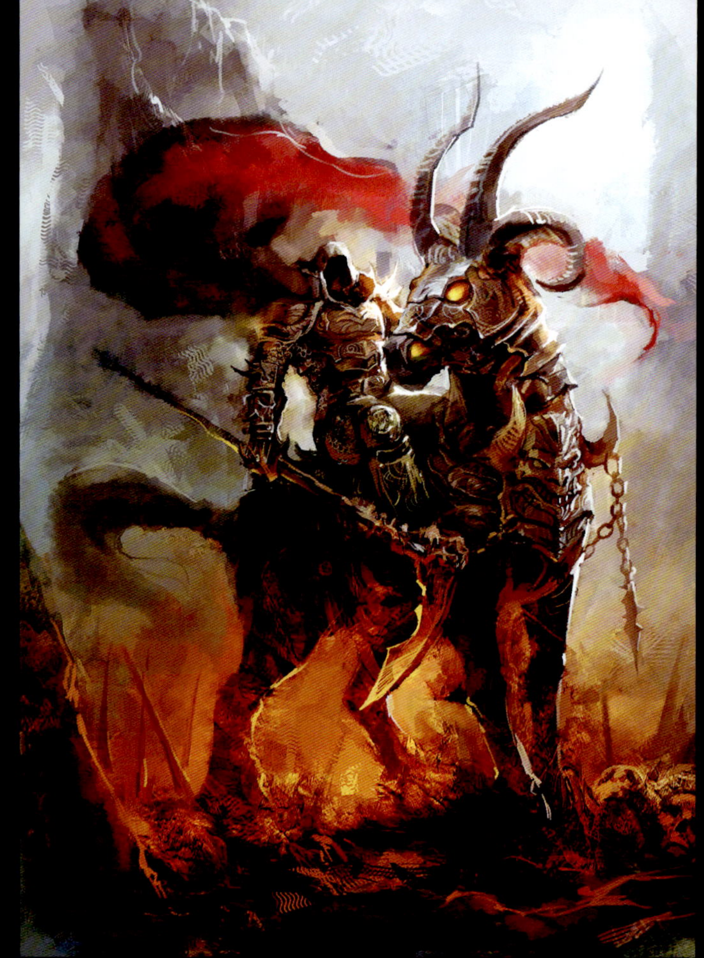

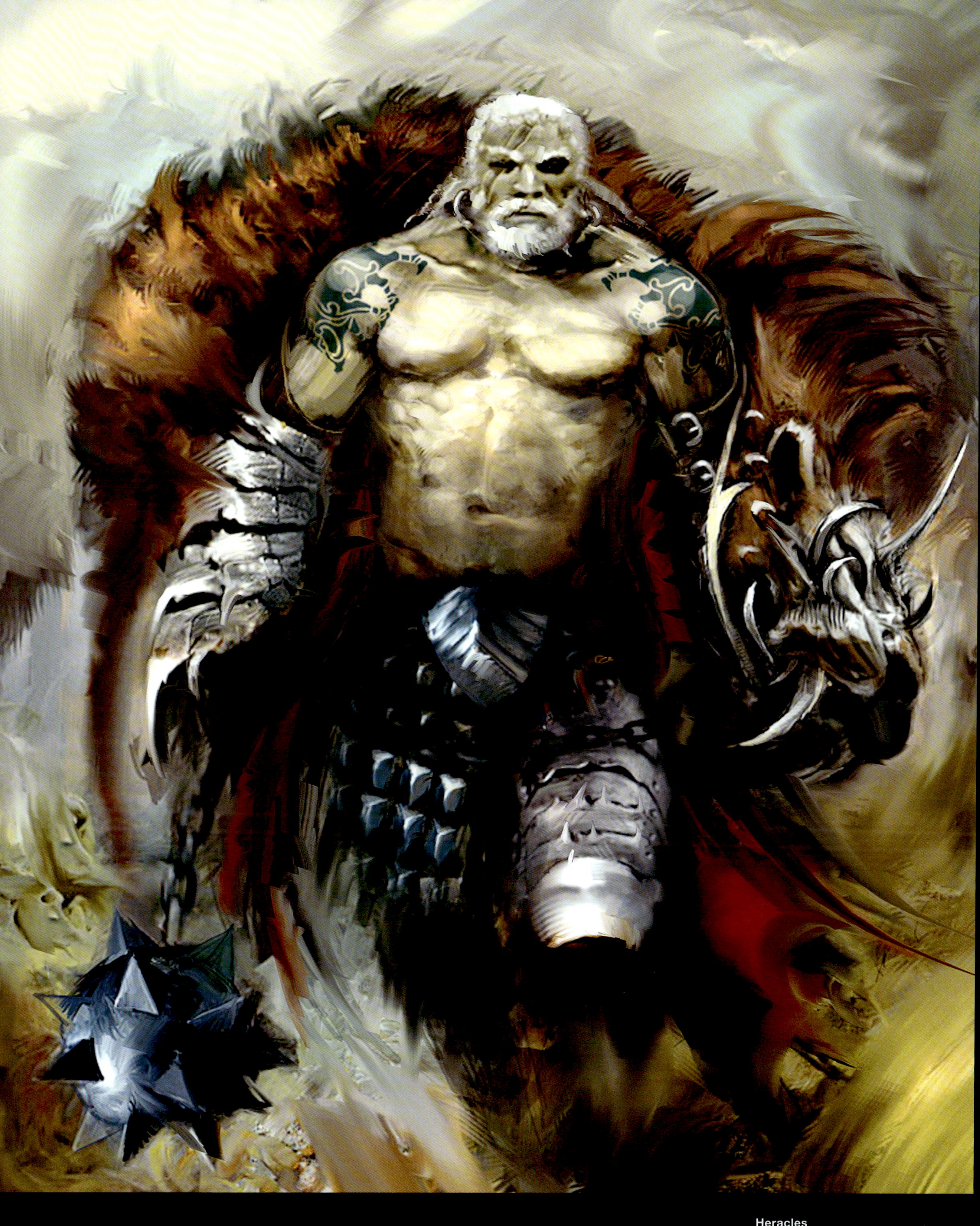

Heracles
Photoshop
Svet Mateev, NEW ZEALAND

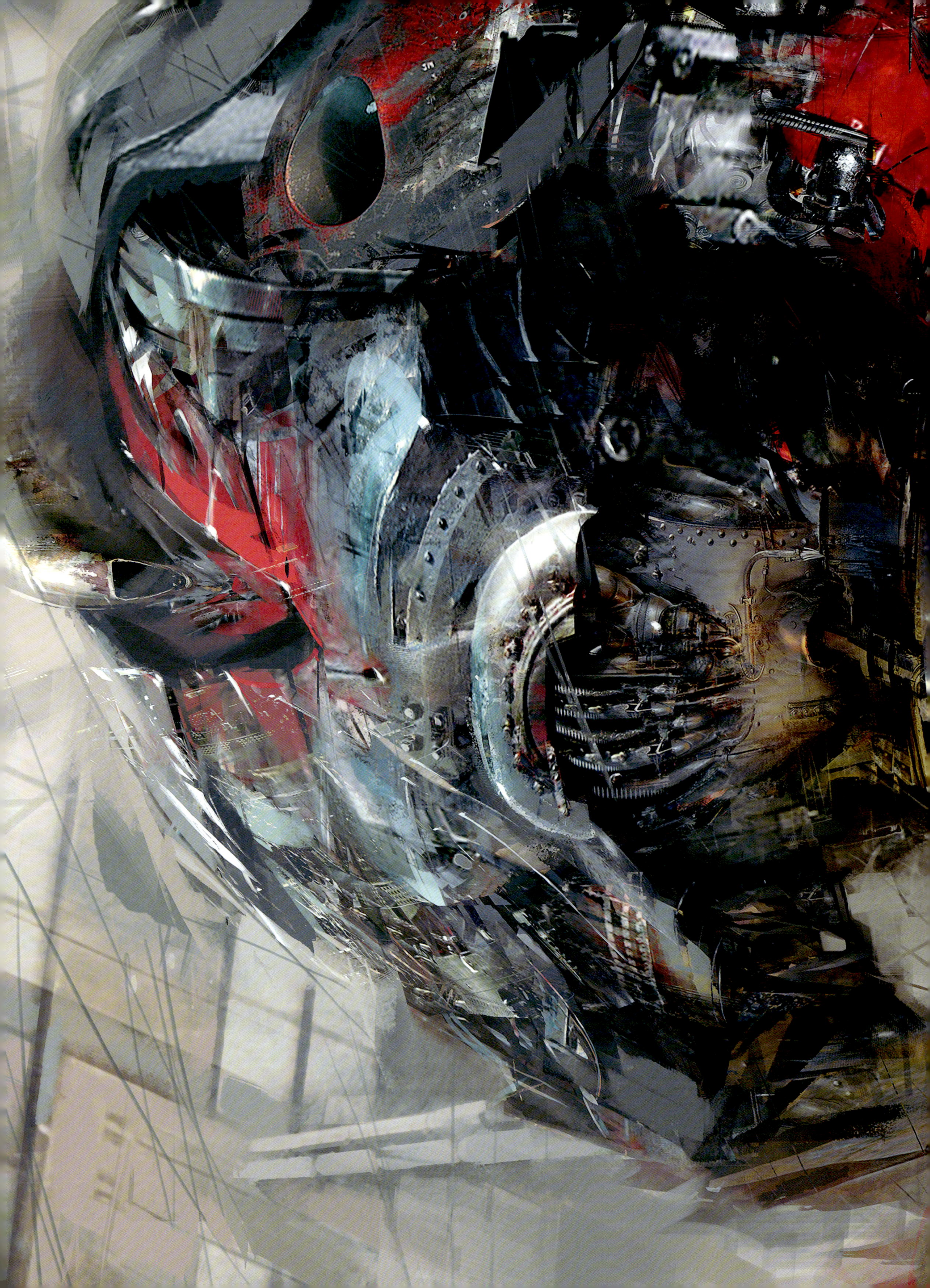

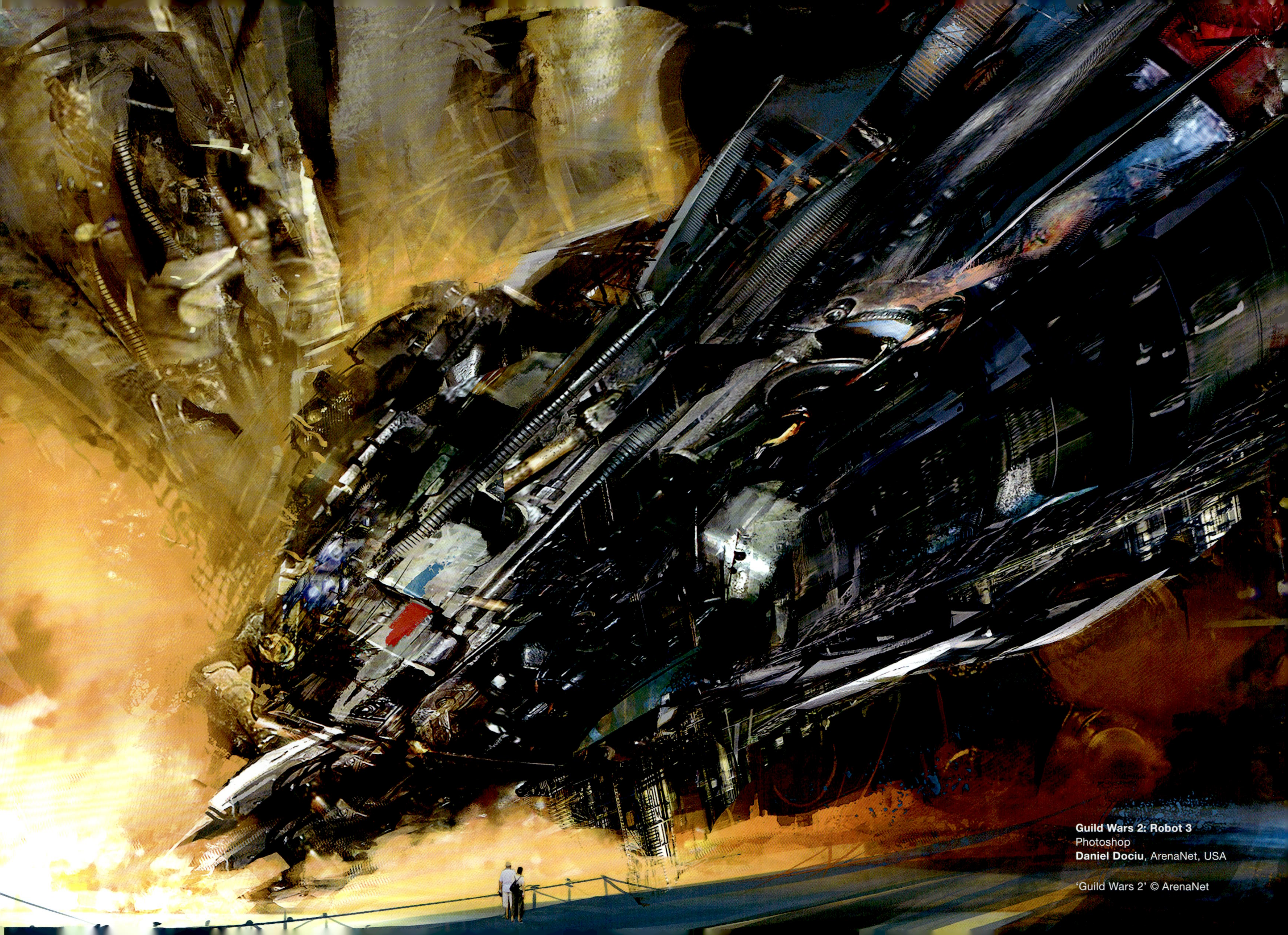

Guild Wars 2: Robot 3
Photoshop
Daniel Dociu, ArenaNet, USA

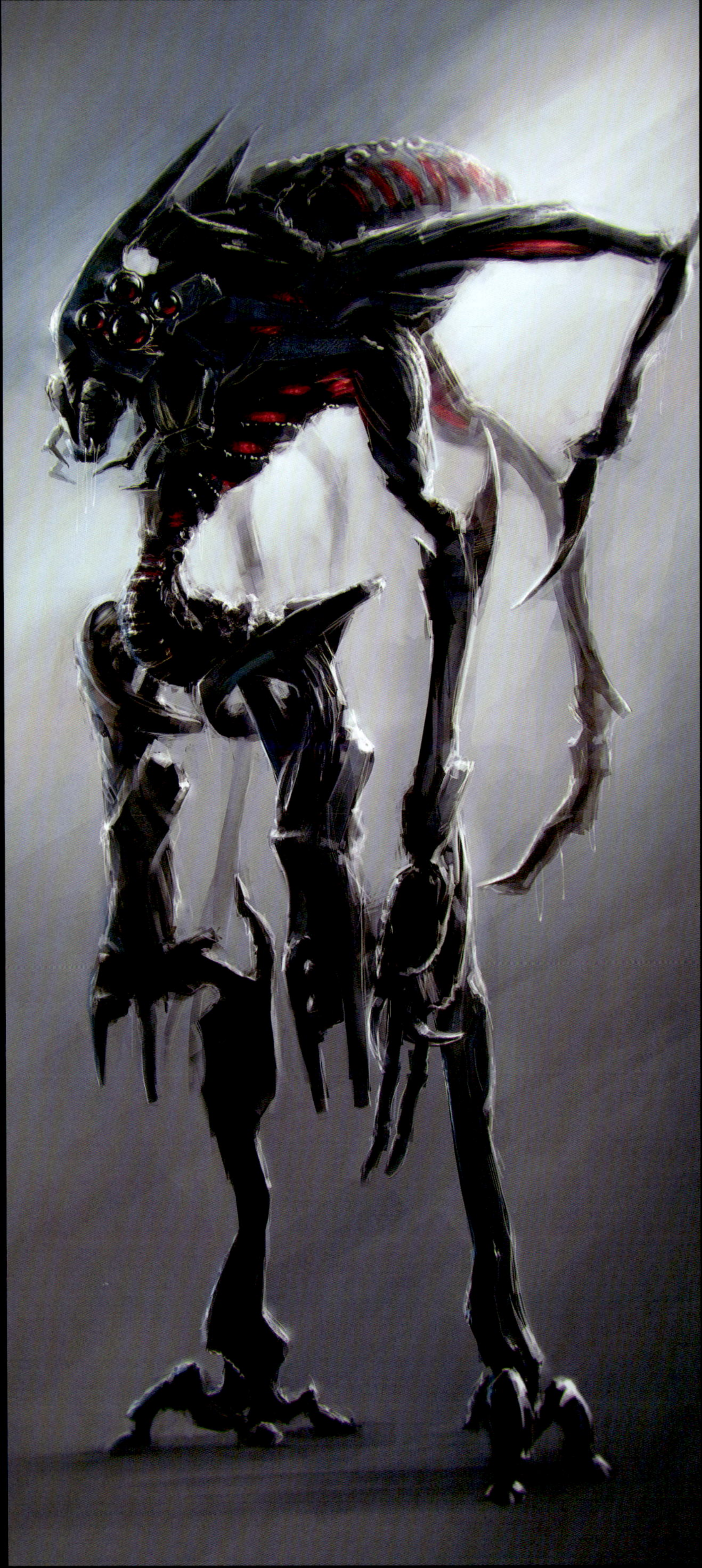

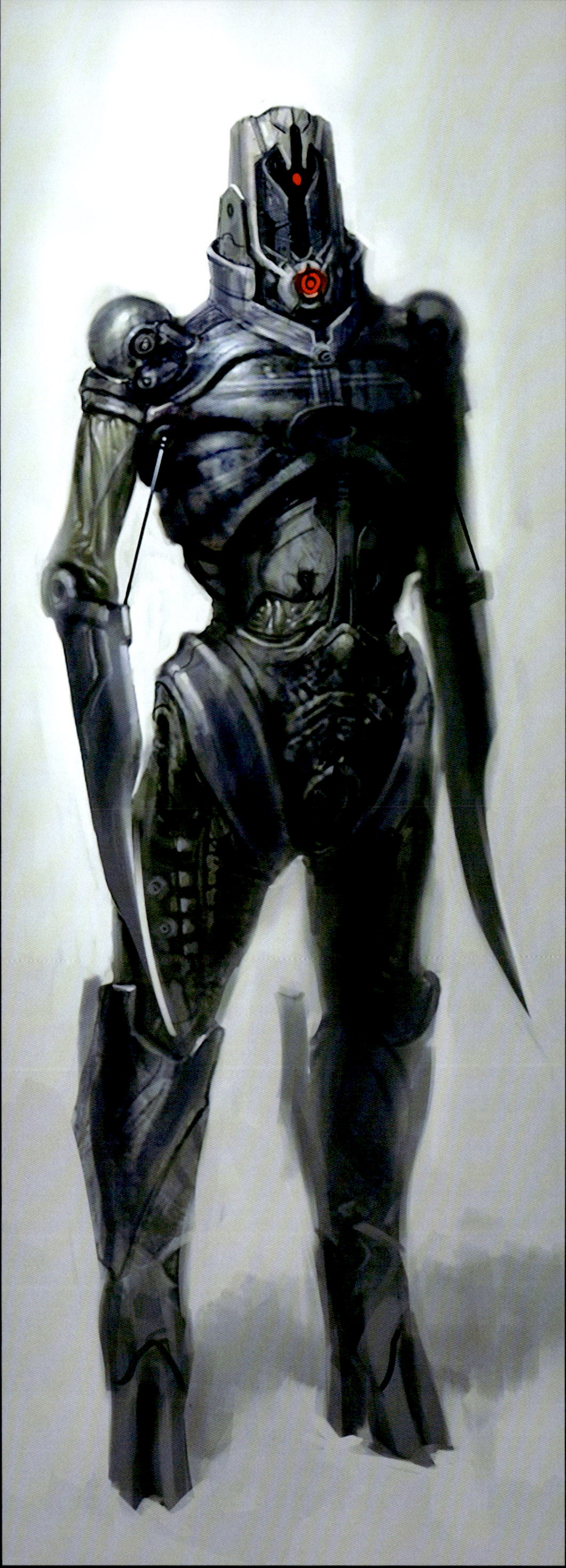

Insectorat warrior
Photoshop
Artem Borisov, RUSSIA
[above]

Robots
Photoshop
Waldek Kaminski, POLAND
[above]

The end of a century
Photoshop
Jong-Won Park, SOUTH KOREA
[right]

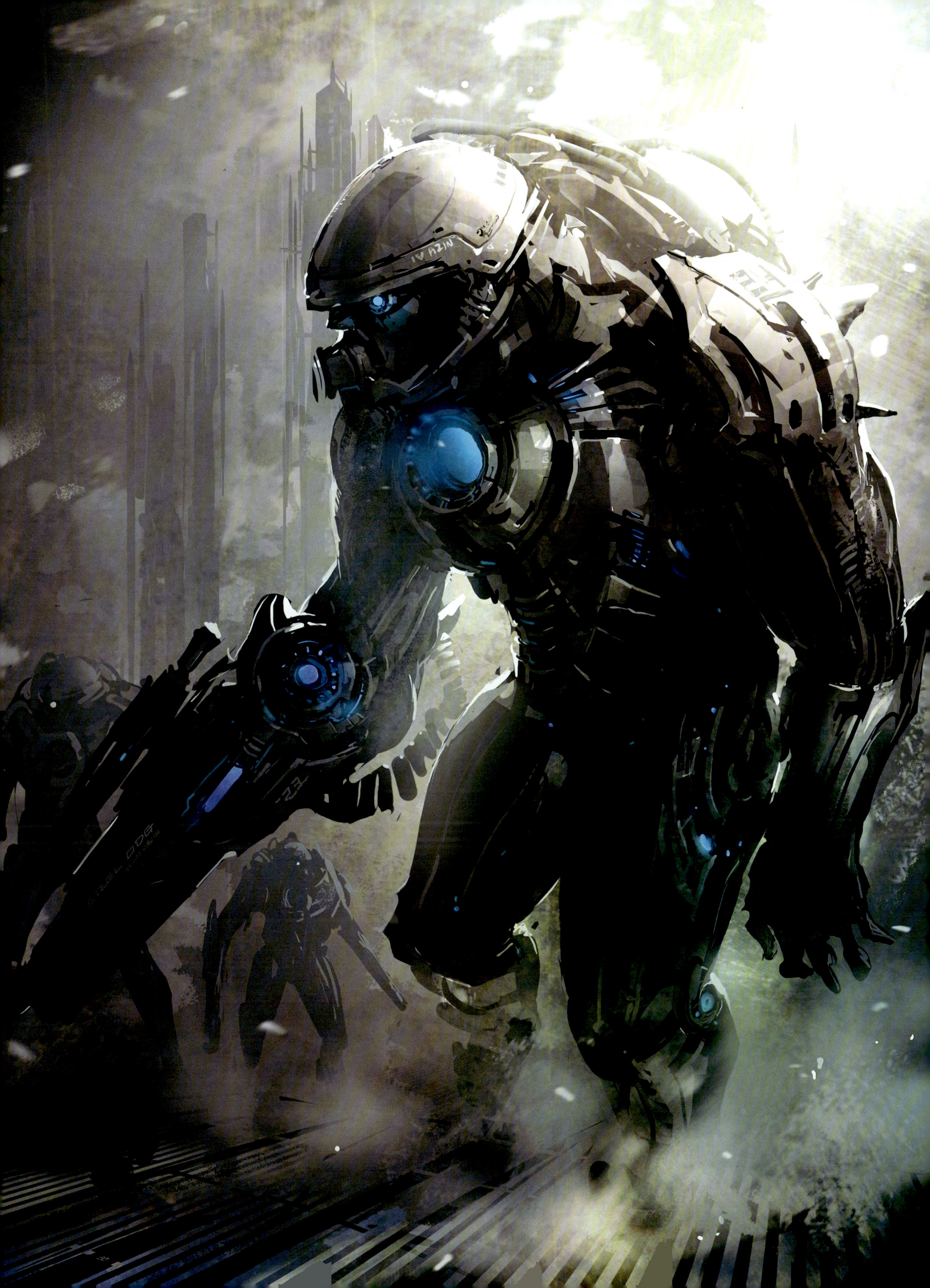

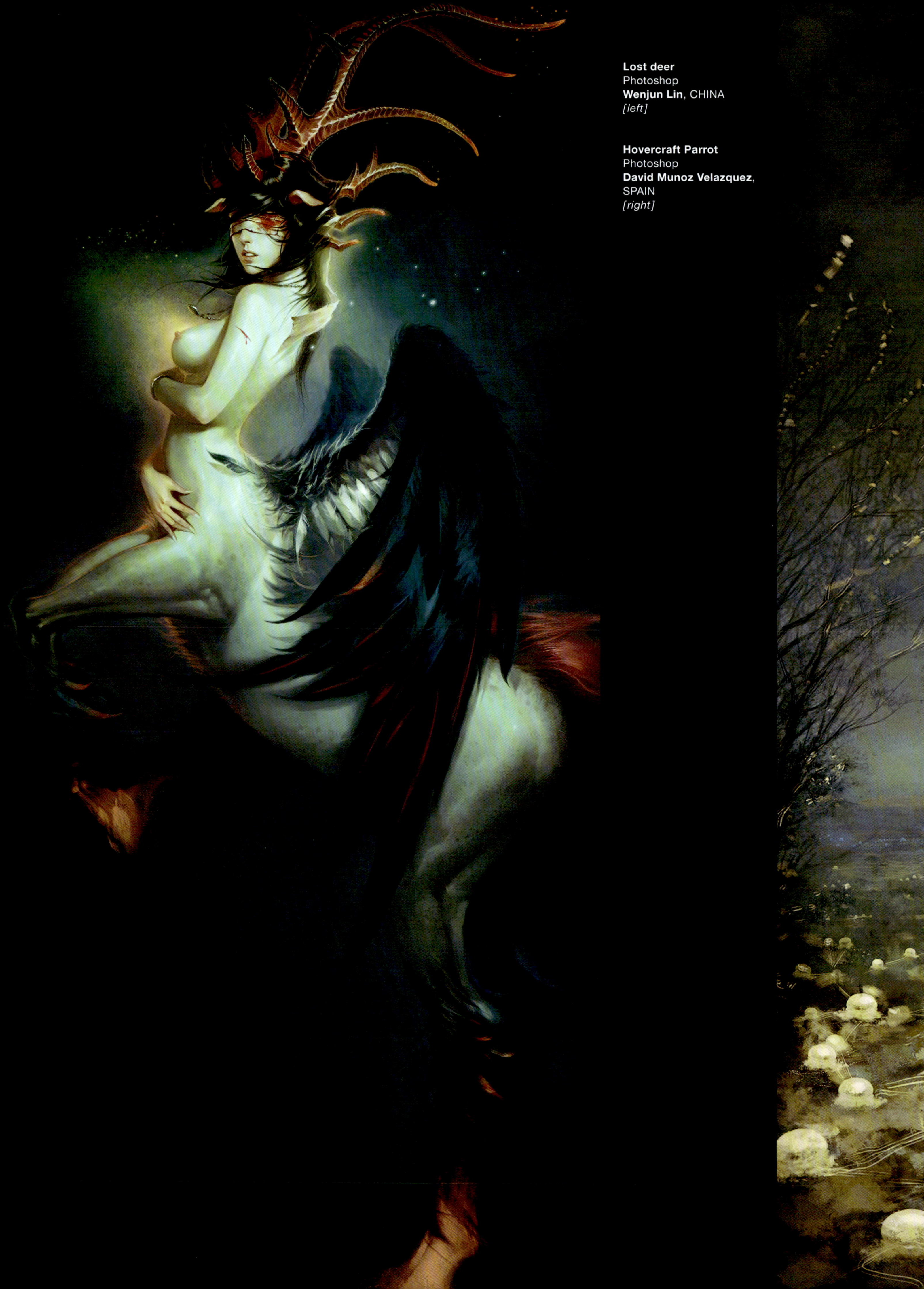

Lost deer
Photoshop
Wenjun Lin, CHINA
[left]

Hovercraft Parrot
Photoshop
David Munoz Velazquez,
SPAIN
[right]

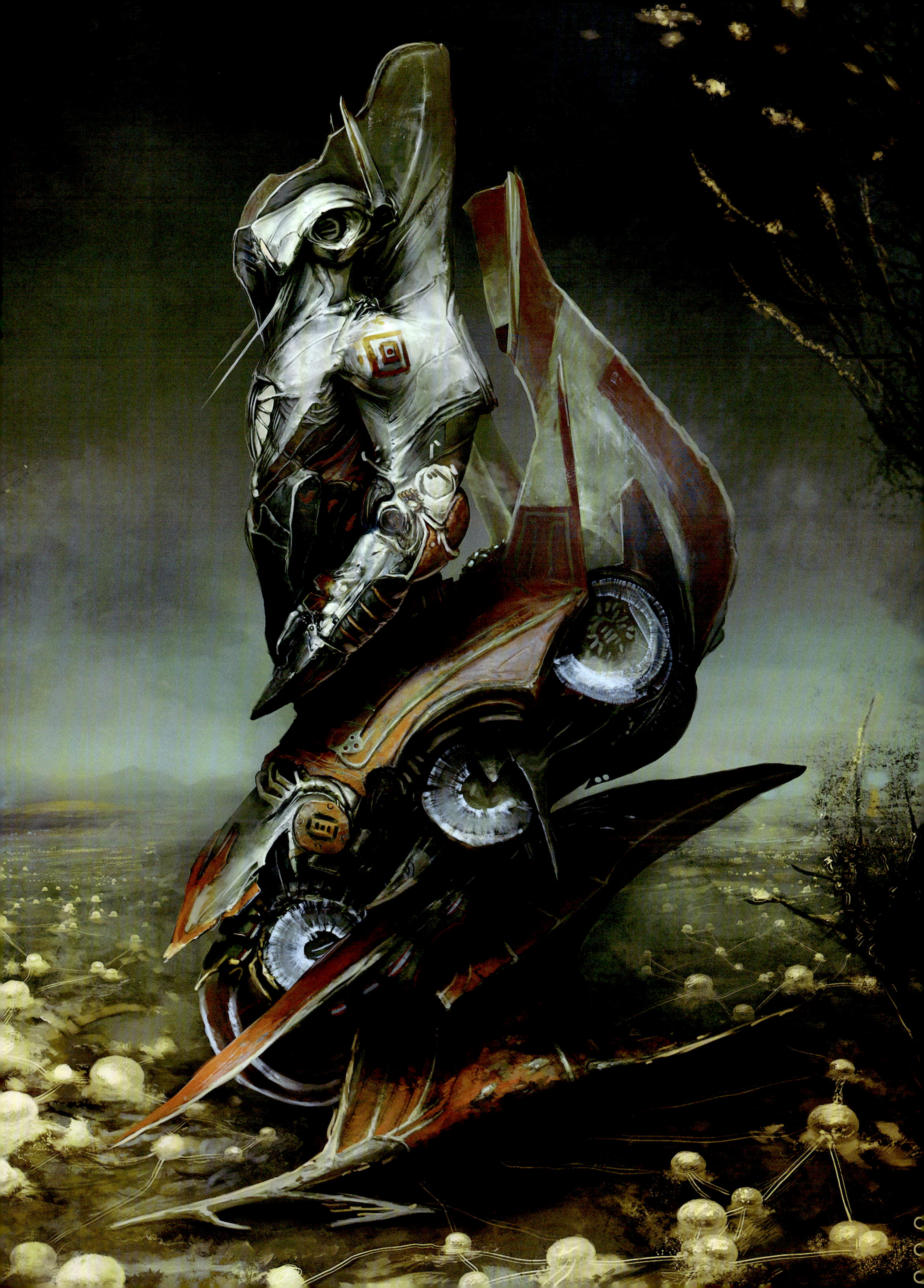

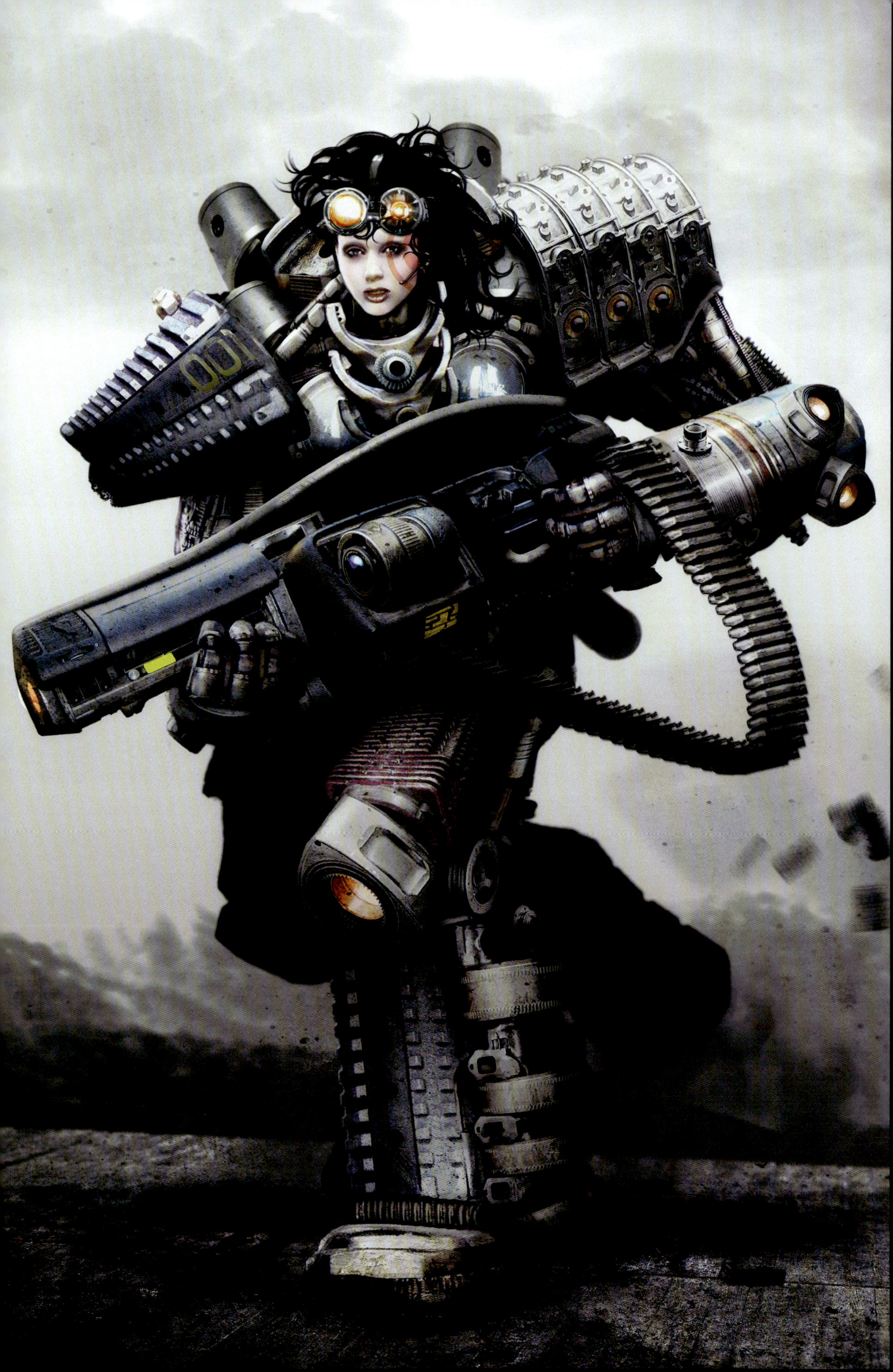

Laura Armour
Photoshop
Eddie Sharam, GREAT BRITAIN

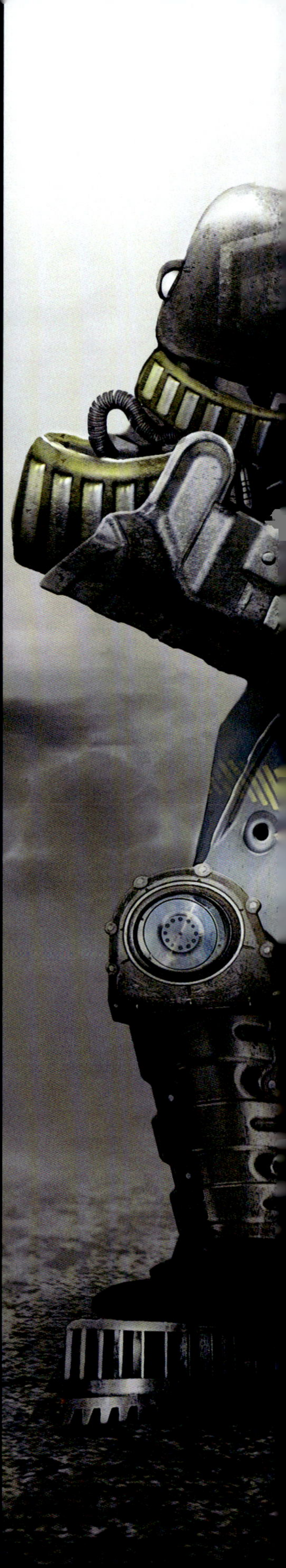

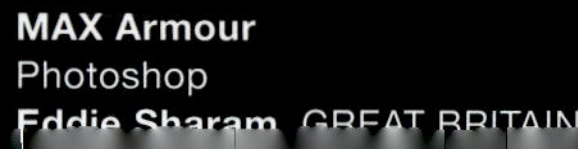

MAX Armour
Photoshop
Eddie Sharam, GREAT BRITAIN

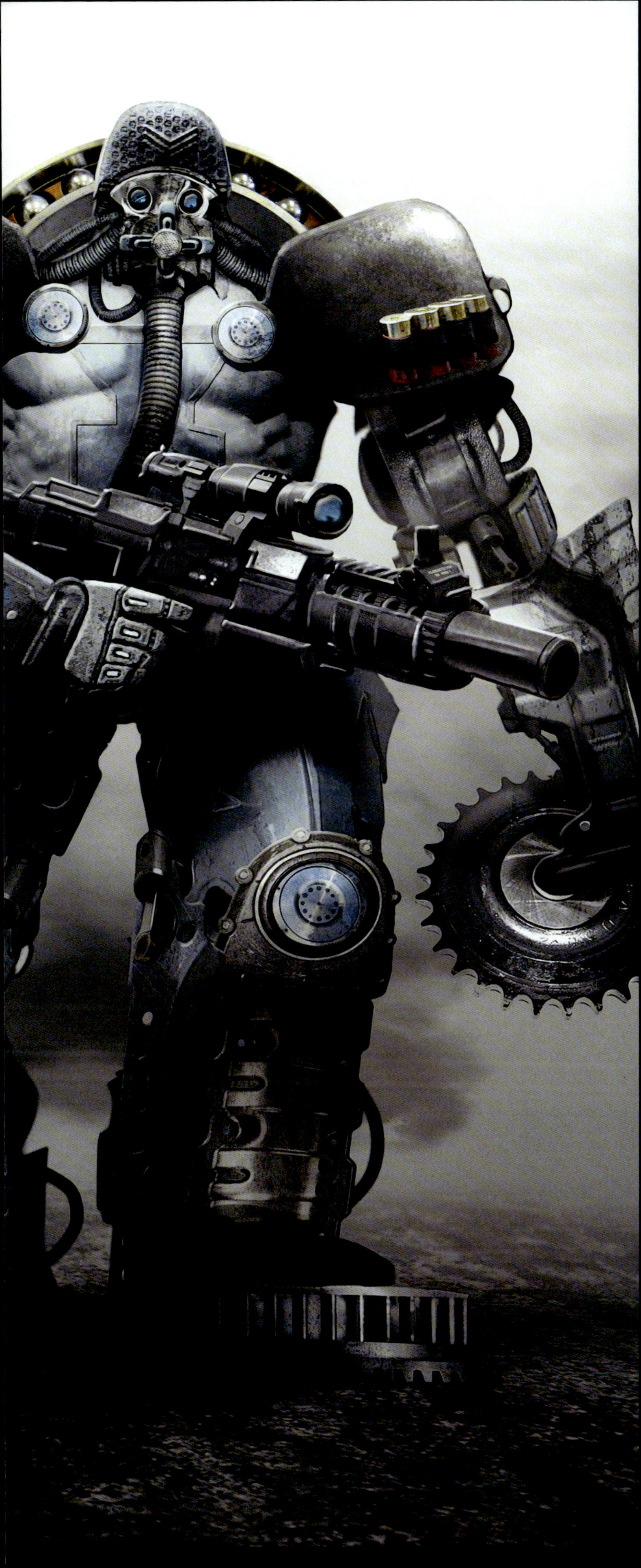

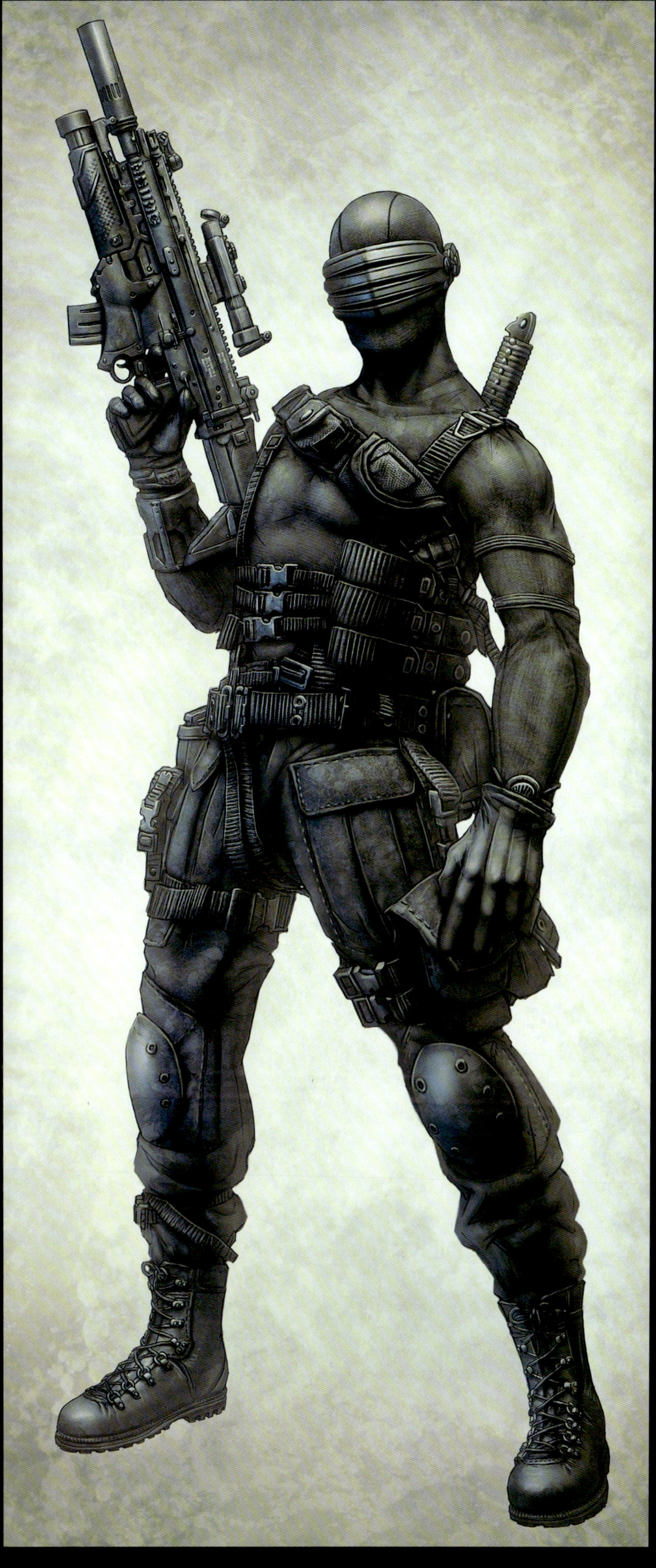

Snake Eyes
Photoshop
Kerem Beyit, TURKEY

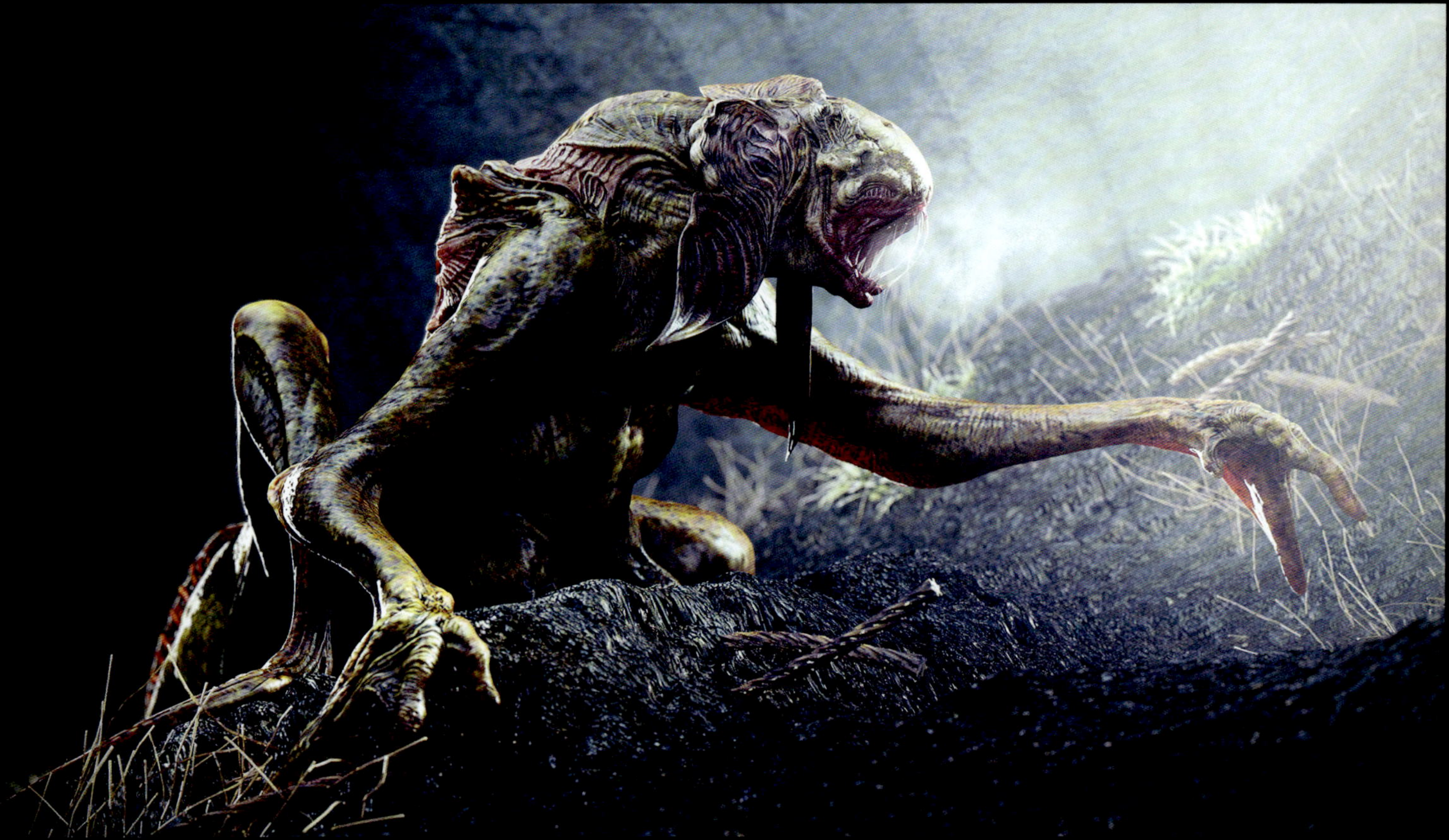

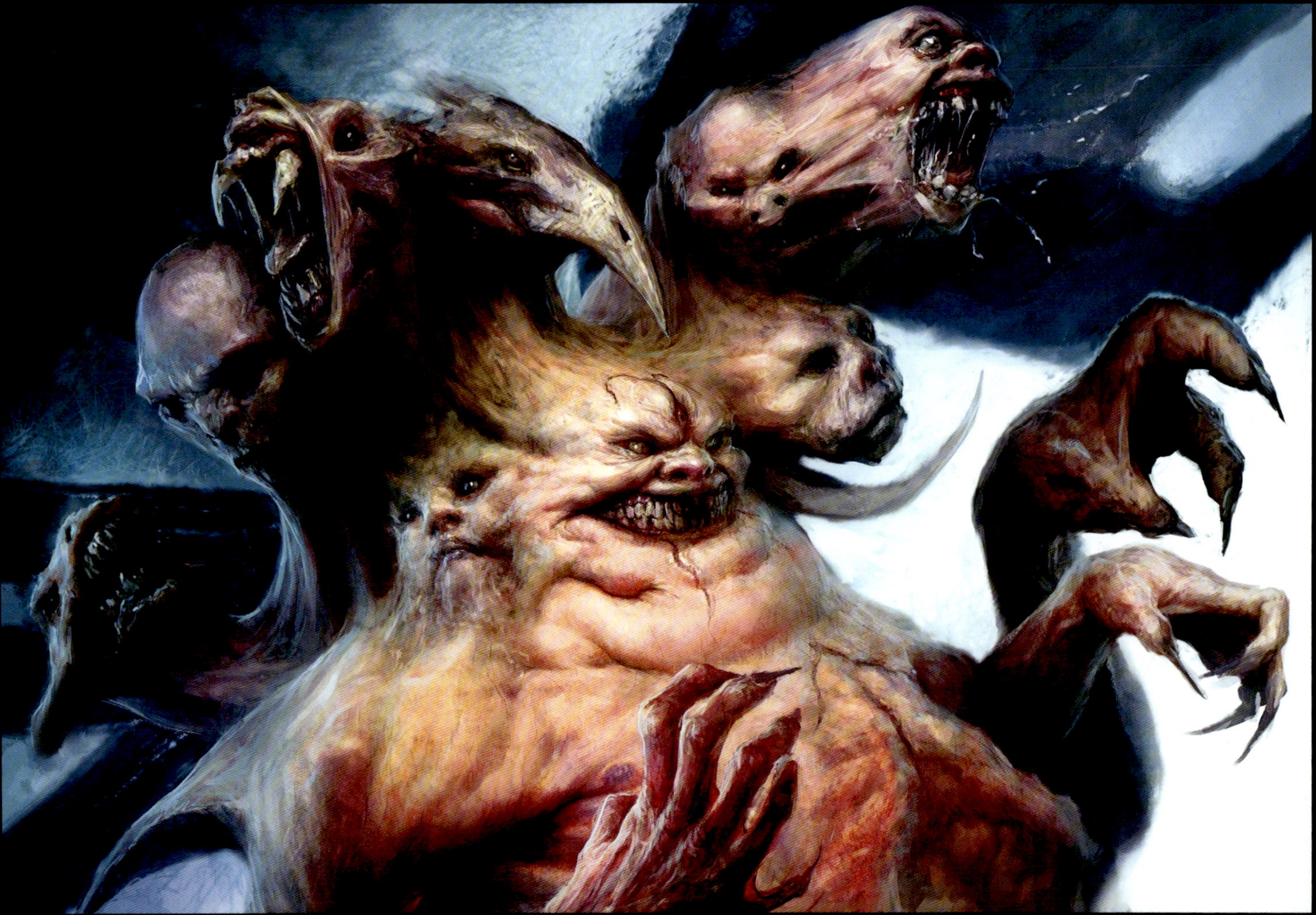

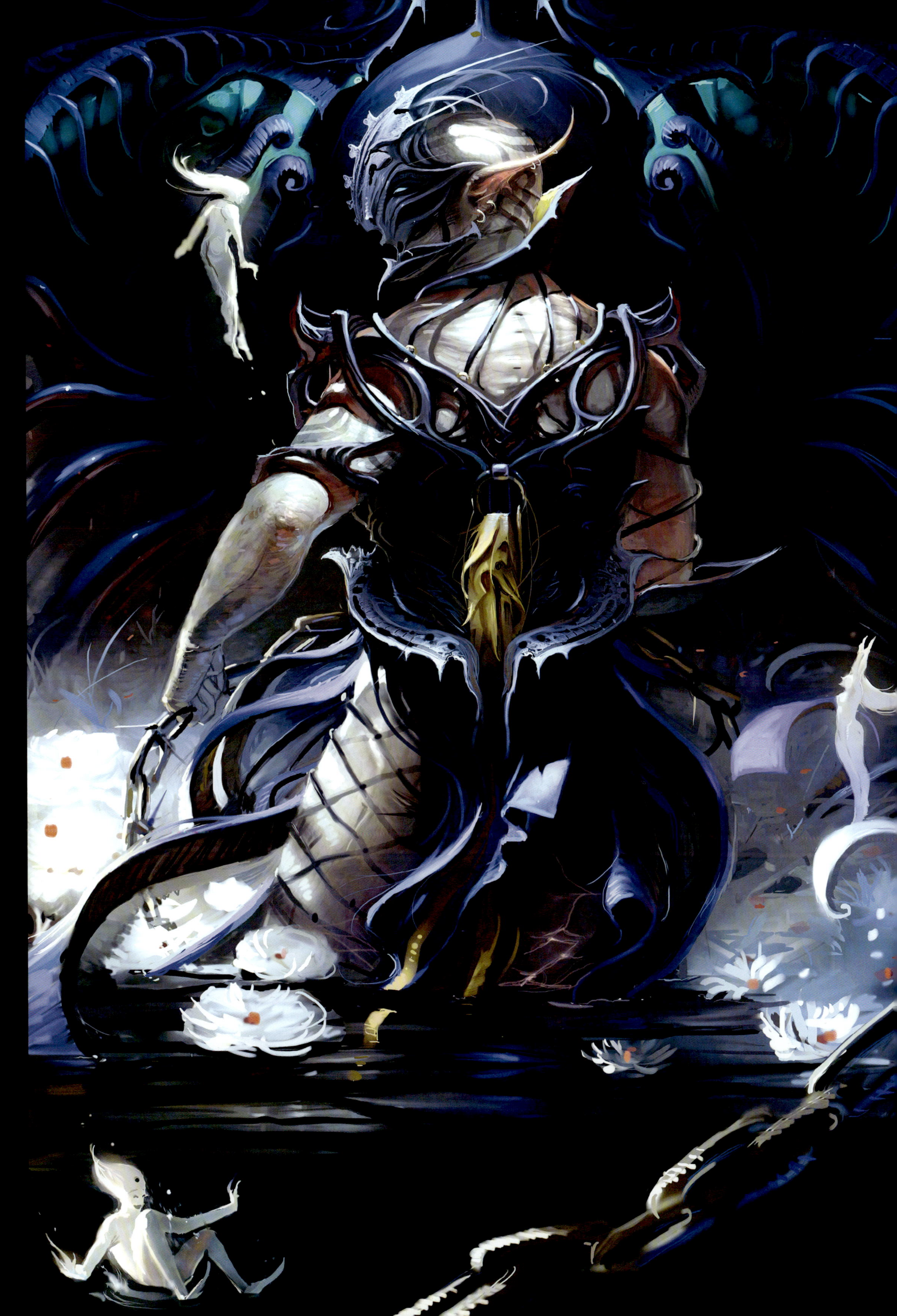

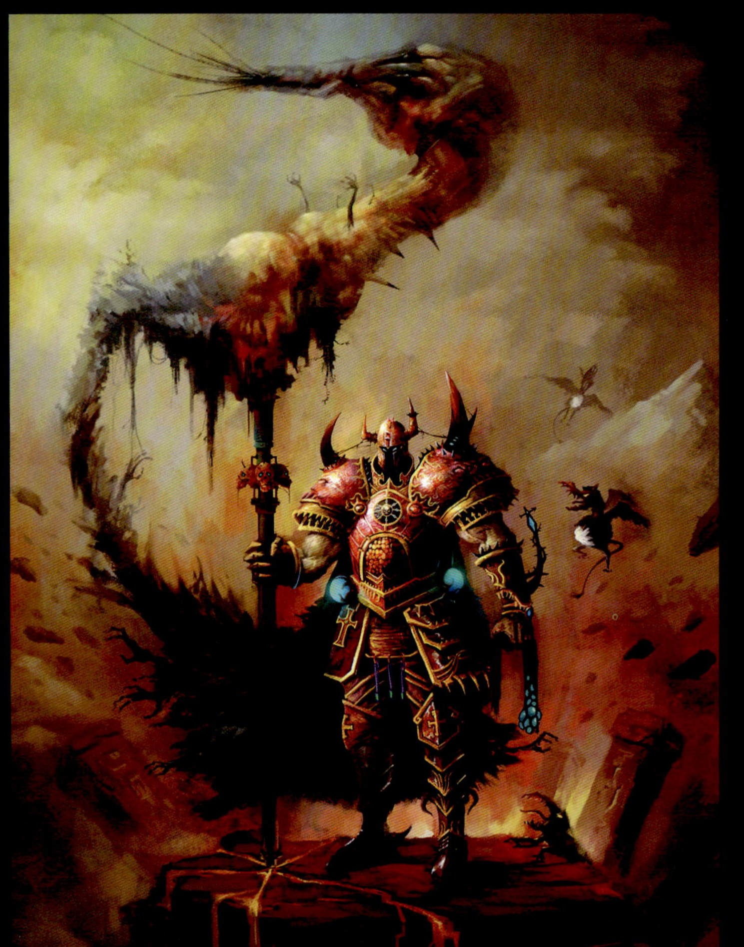

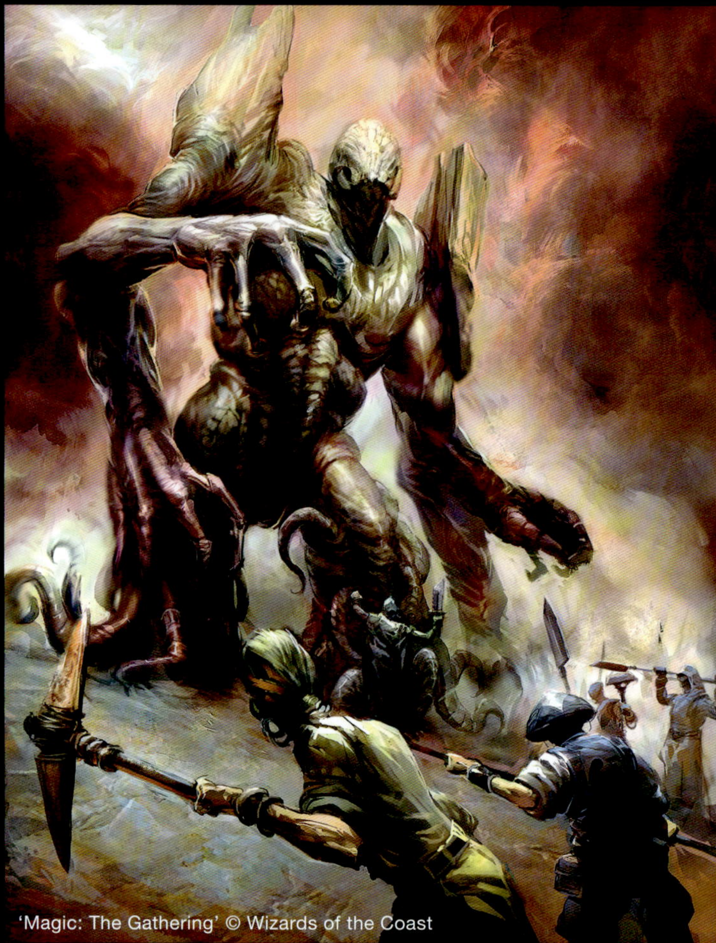

'Magic: The Gathering' © Wizards of the Coast

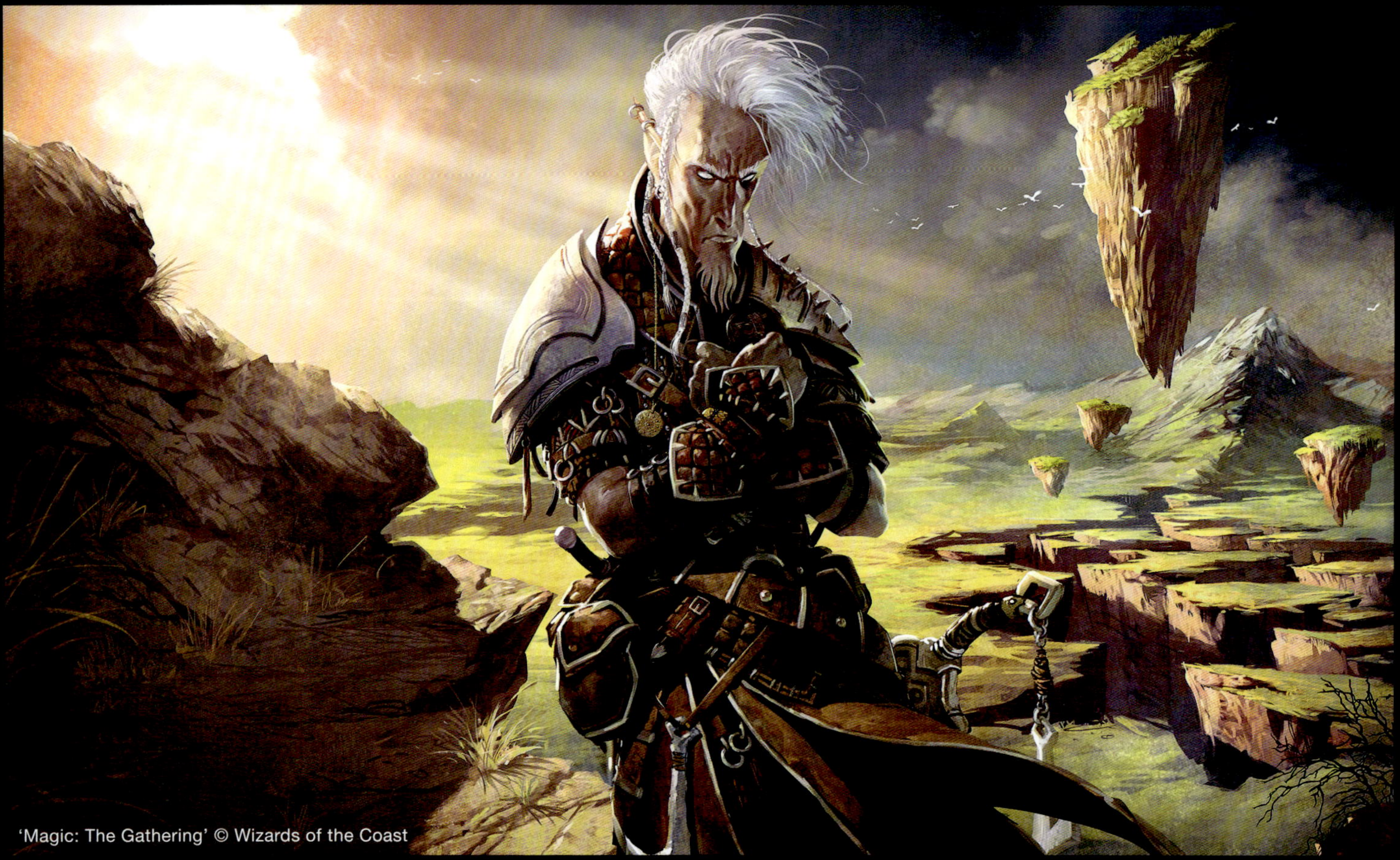

'Magic: The Gathering' © Wizards of the Coast

Guard
Photoshop
Chuan Zhong,
CHINA
[top]

Magic: The Gathering (Lone Missionary)
Photoshop
Client: Wizards of the Coast
Svetlin Velinov, BULGARIA
[above]

Magic: The Gathering (The Maker Of Paths)
Photoshop
Client: Wizards Of The Coast
Goran Josic, SERBIA
[top]

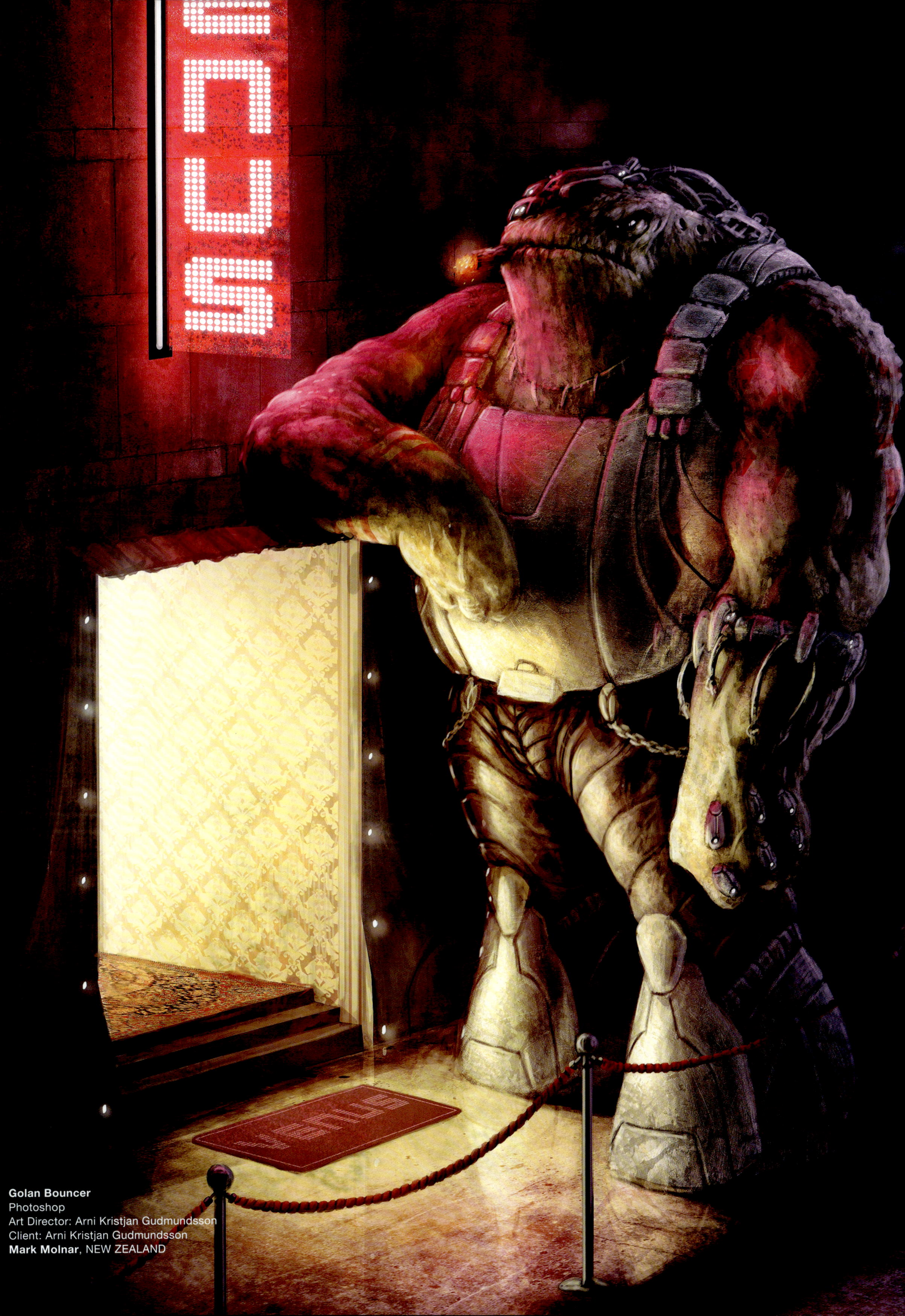

Golan Bouncer
Photoshop
Art Director: Arni Kristjan Gudmundsson
Client: Arni Kristjan Gudmundsson
Mark Molnar, NEW ZEALAND

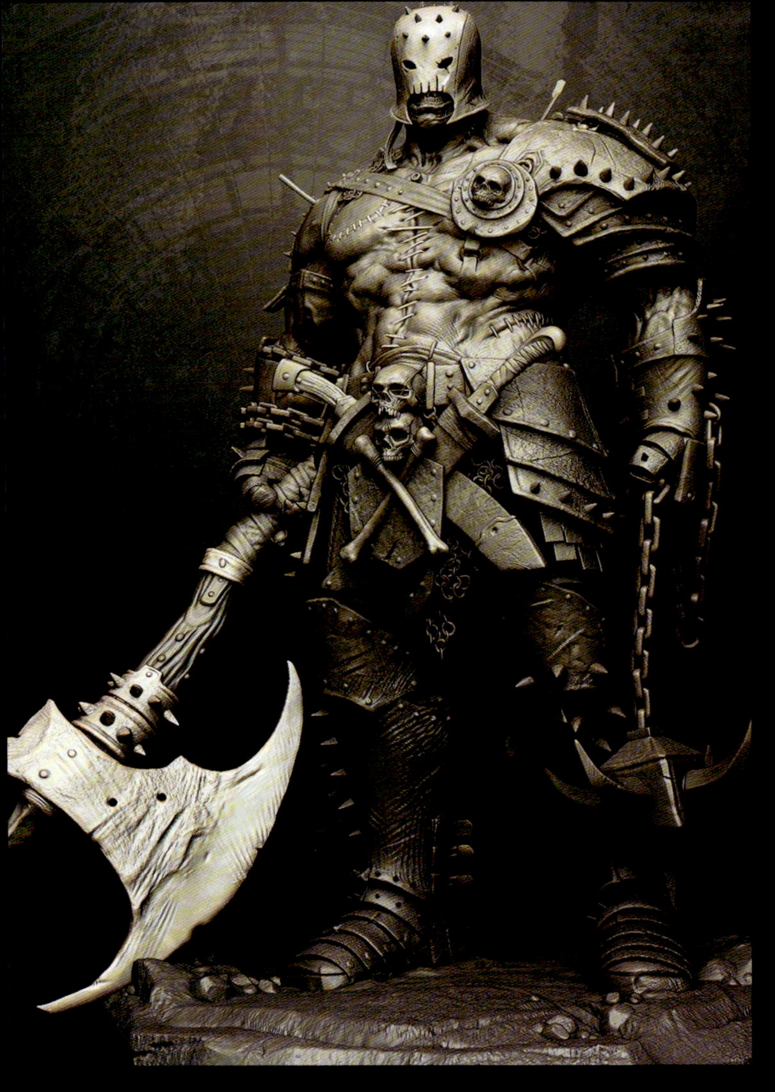

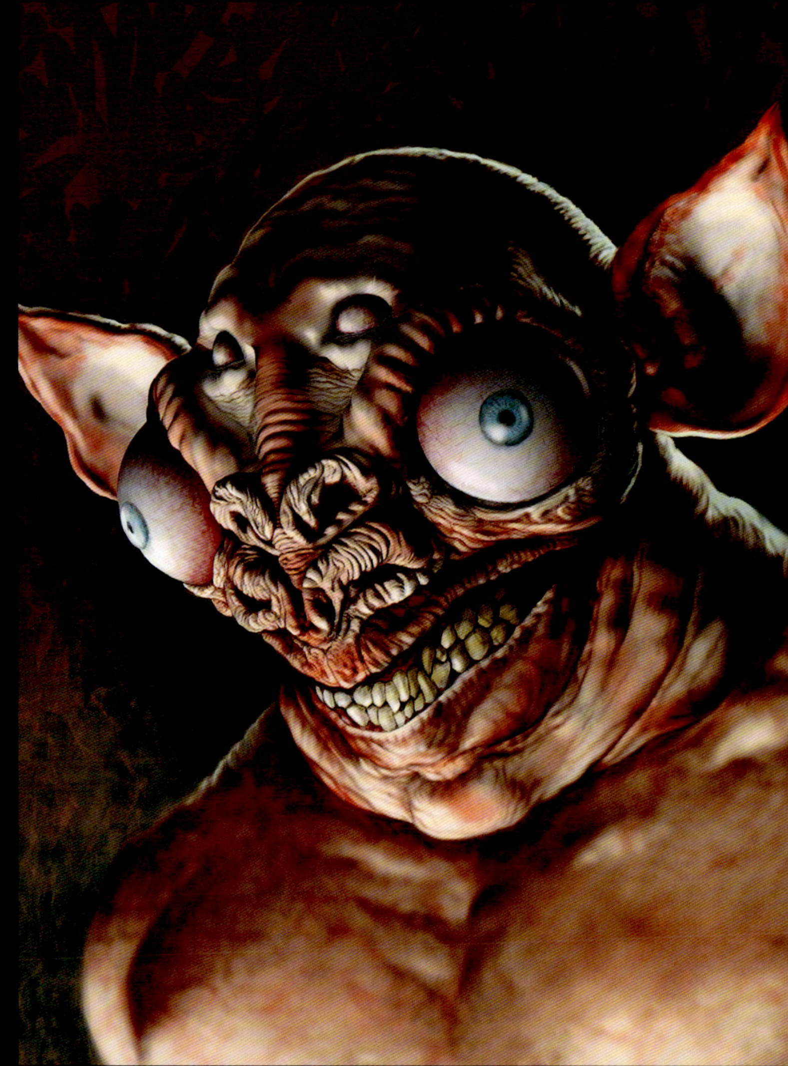

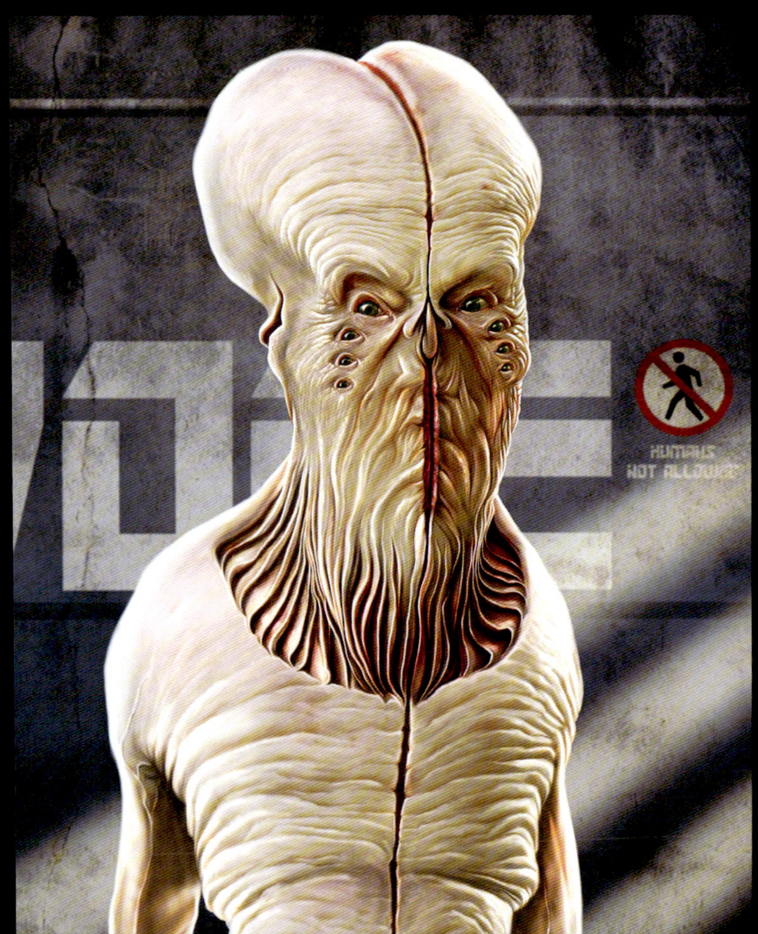
HUMANS
NOT ALLOWED

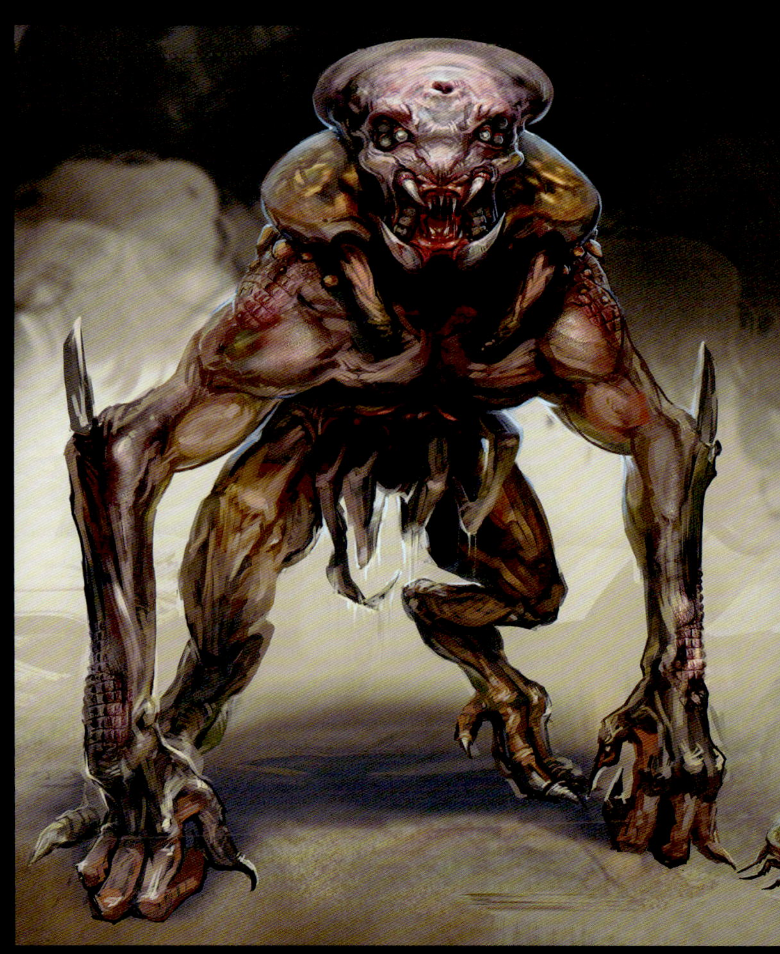

Frankenstein Warrior
Maya, ZBrush, Photoshop
Rishikesh Nandlaskar,
INDIA
[far left]

Devil Mask
Photoshop, ZBrush
Susana Villegas,
BOLIVIA
[left]

Monster
Photoshop
Shichao Huang, CHINA
[right]

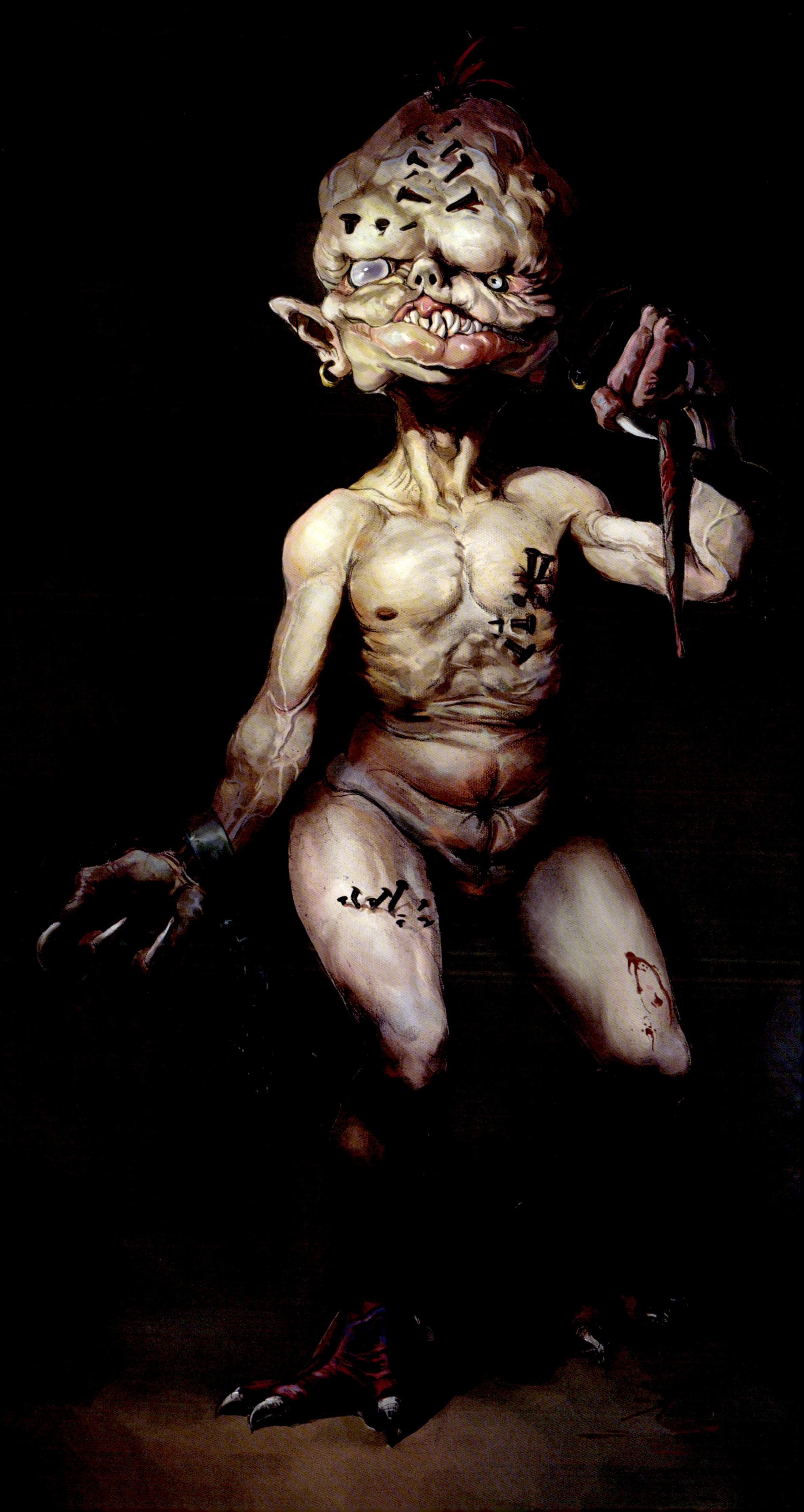

Humans not allowed
Photoshop
Paulo Araujo, PORTUGAL
[far left]

Reanimator Tick concept
Photoshop
Li Jia Tan, USA
[left]

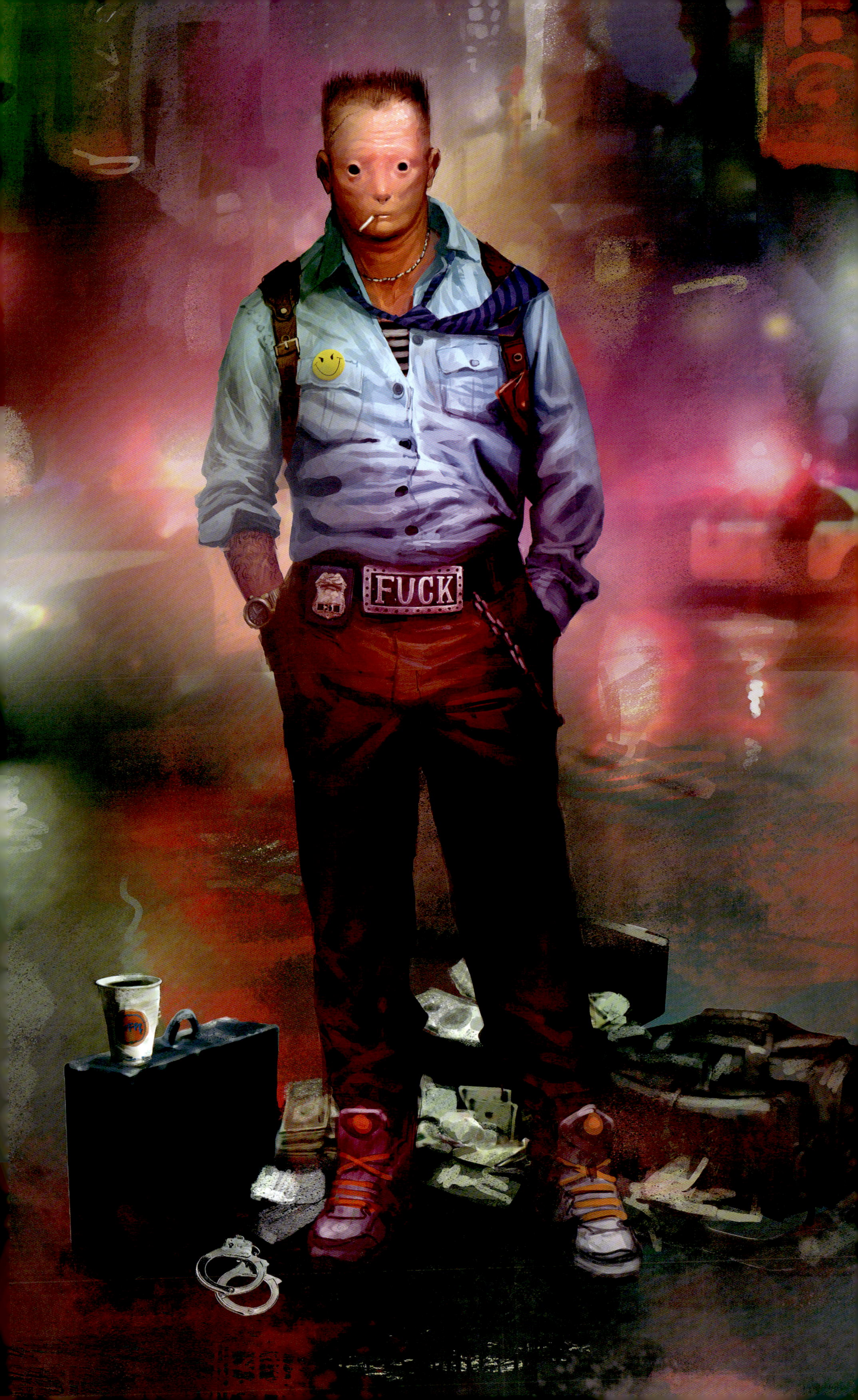
FUCK

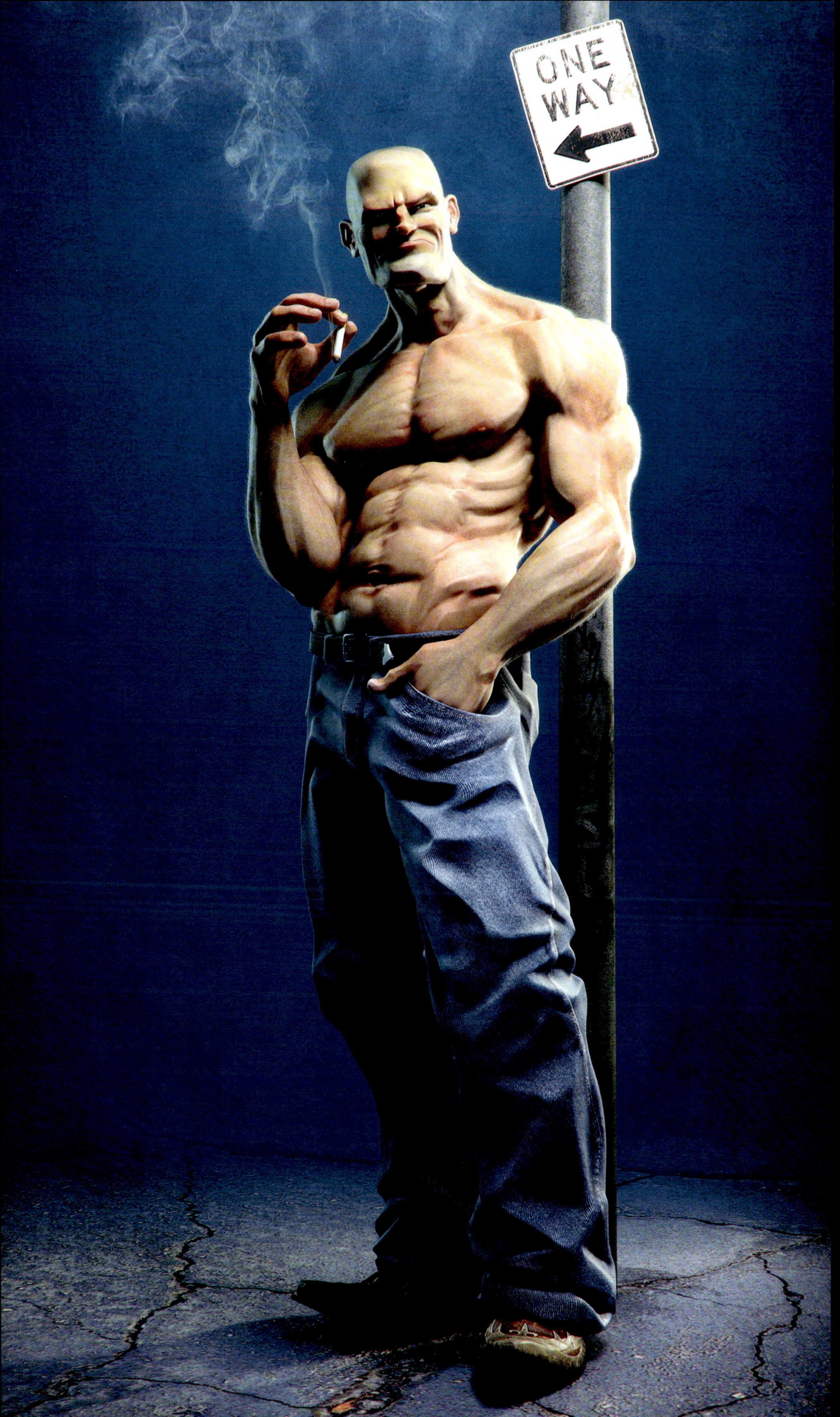
ONE WAY

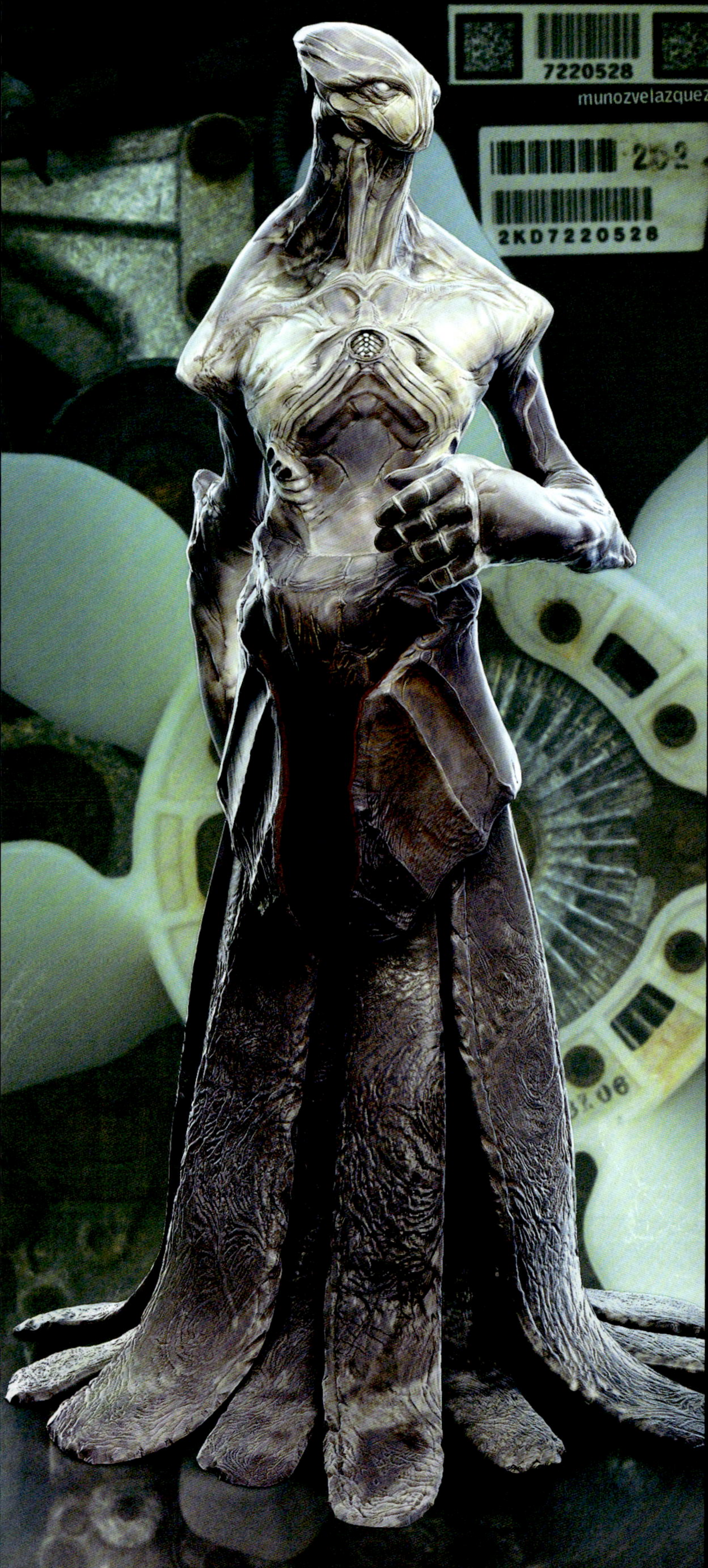

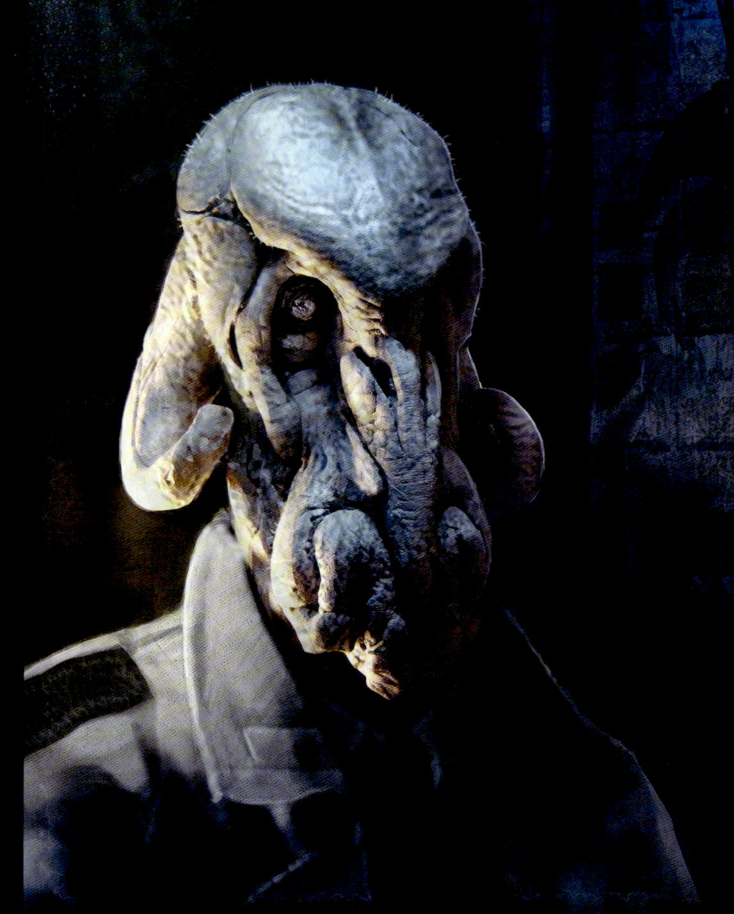

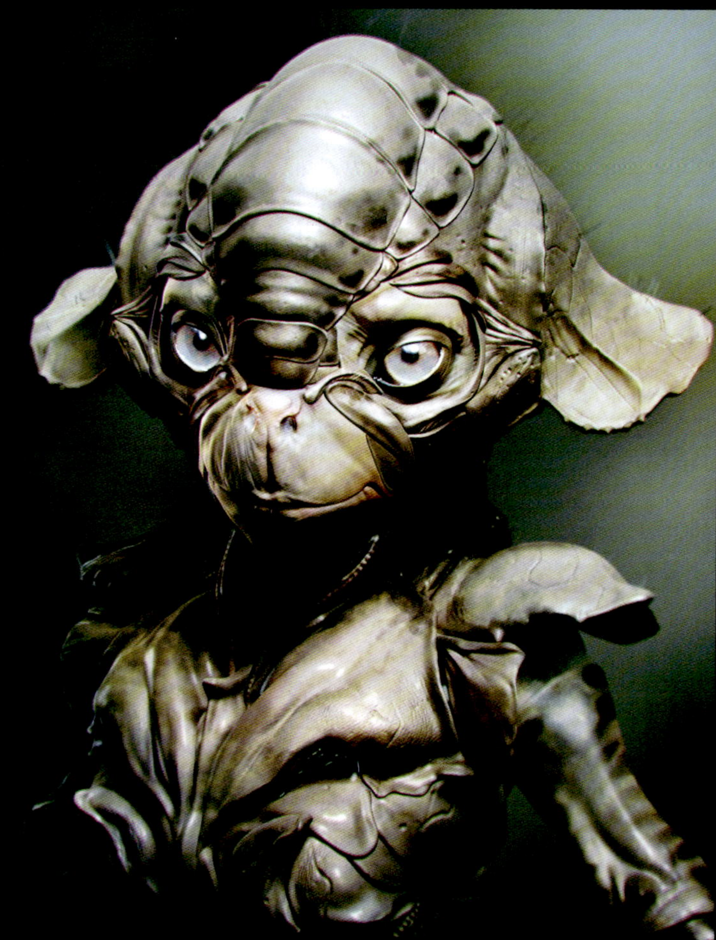

Jambone
ZBrush, Photoshop
David Munoz Velazquez, SPAIN
[above]

Alien detective
Photoshop
Sebastian Meyer, USA
[top right]

Madamme Crab
ZBrush, Photoshop
Jelmer Boskma, THE NETHERLANDS
[above]

Fish Man
3ds Max, mental ray, ZBrush, Photoshop
Fabricio Moraes, BRAZIL
[right]

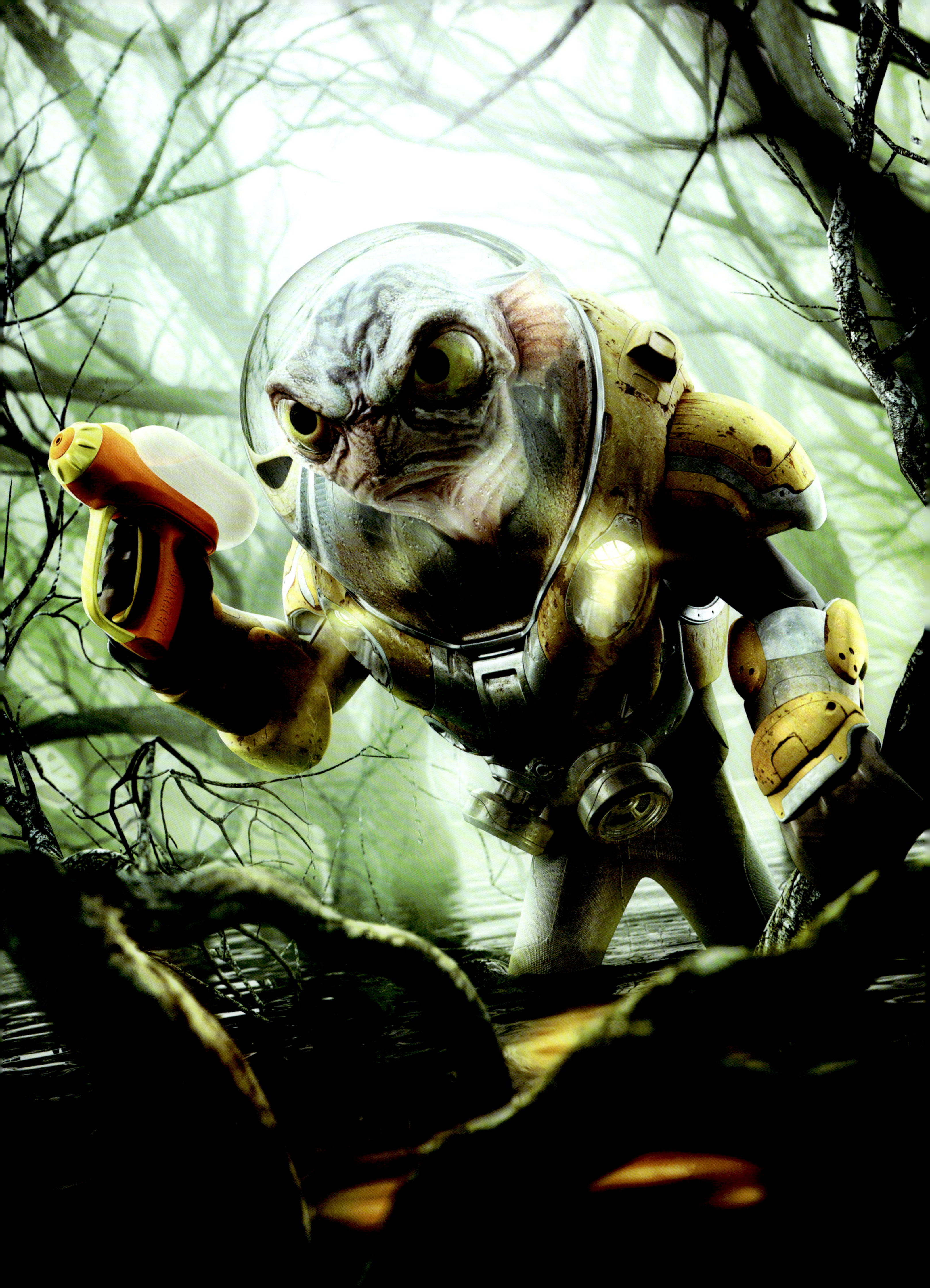

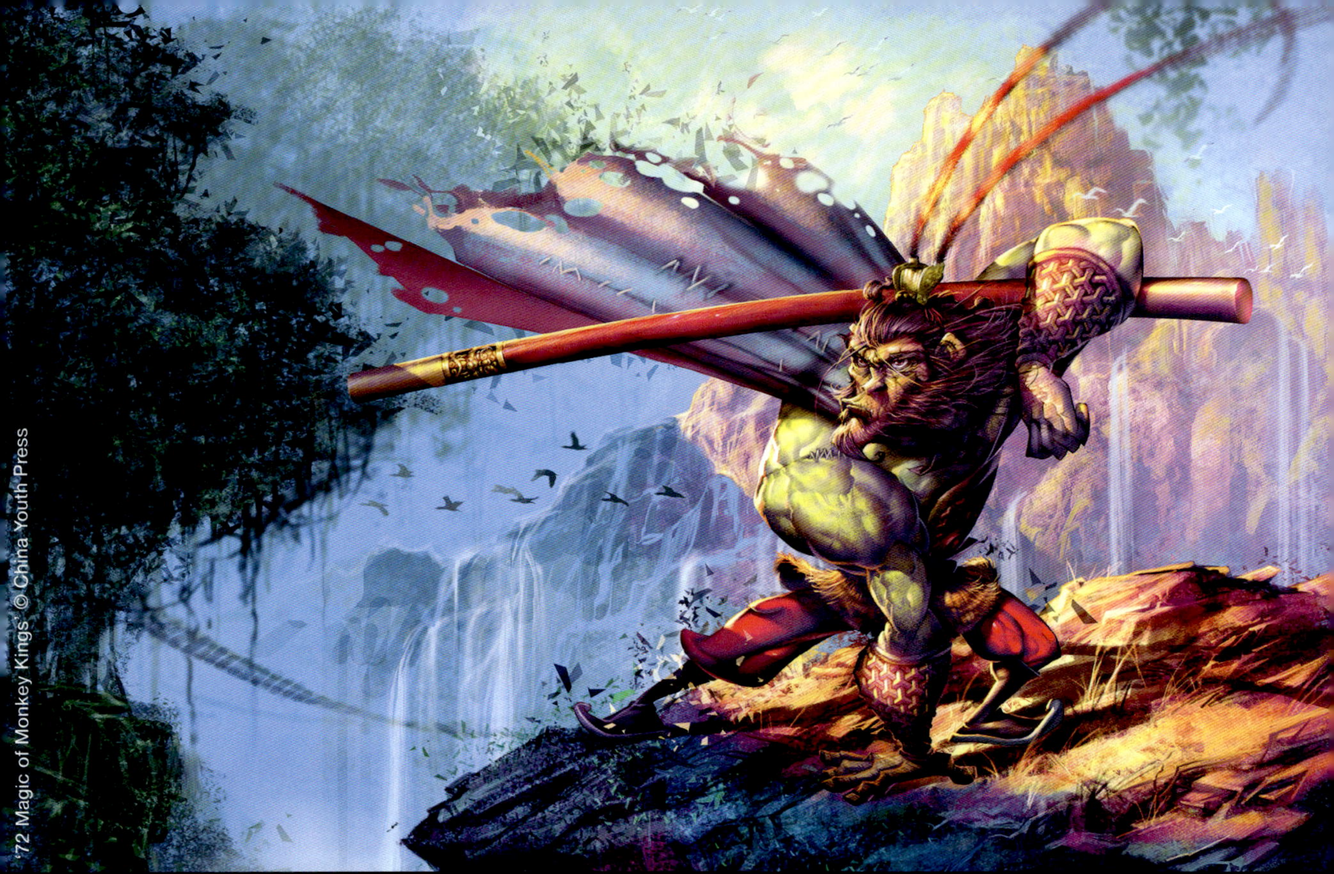

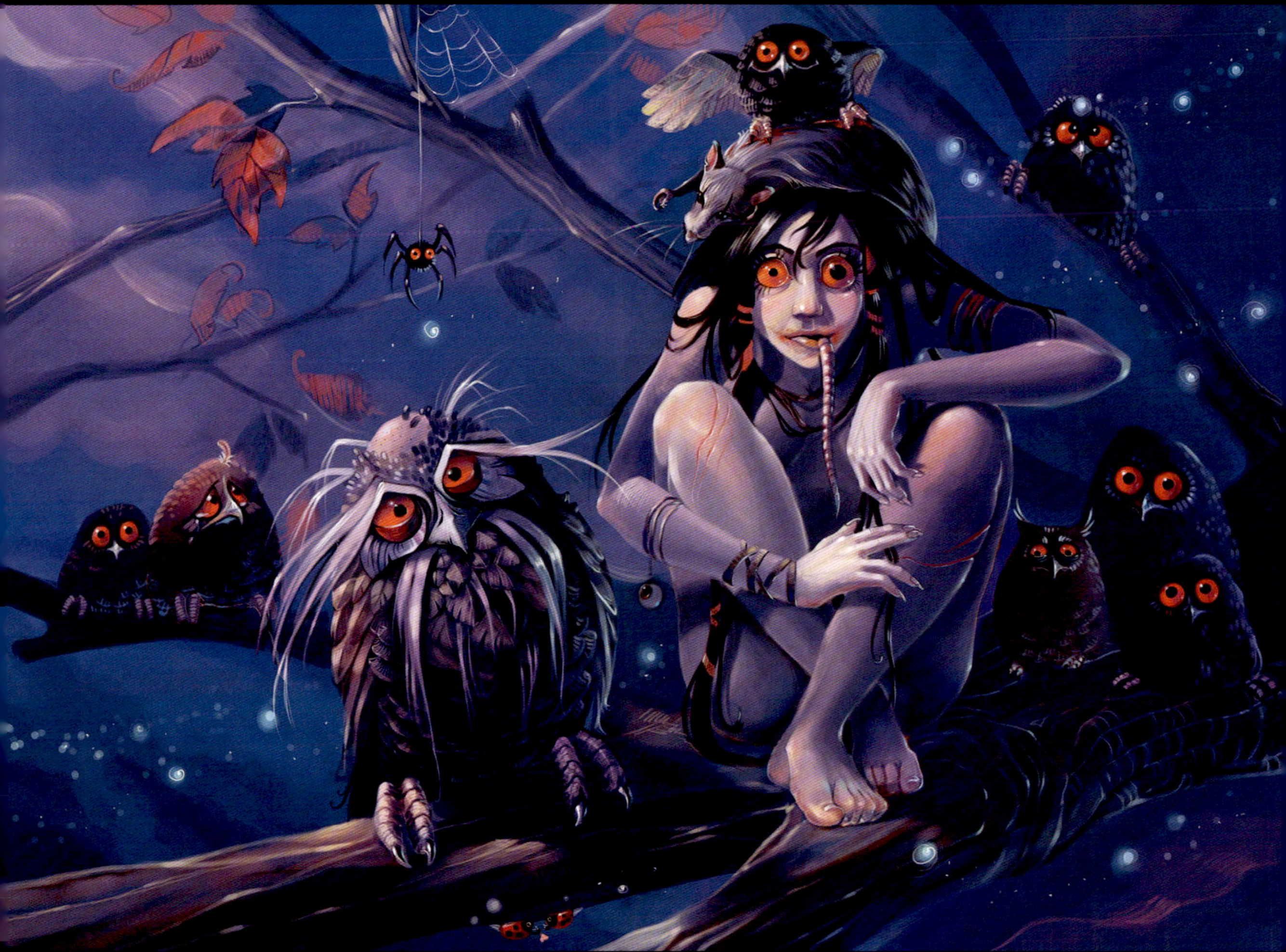

'72 Magic of Monkey Kings
Photoshop
Client: China Youth Press
Haitao Su, Suhaitao Studio, CHINA *[top]*

Owl vampires
Photoshop
Ekaterina Shapovalova, RUSSIA
[above]

Beauty vs Alien
Photoshop
Client: hxsd.com
Haitao Su, Suhaitao Studio, CHINA *[right*

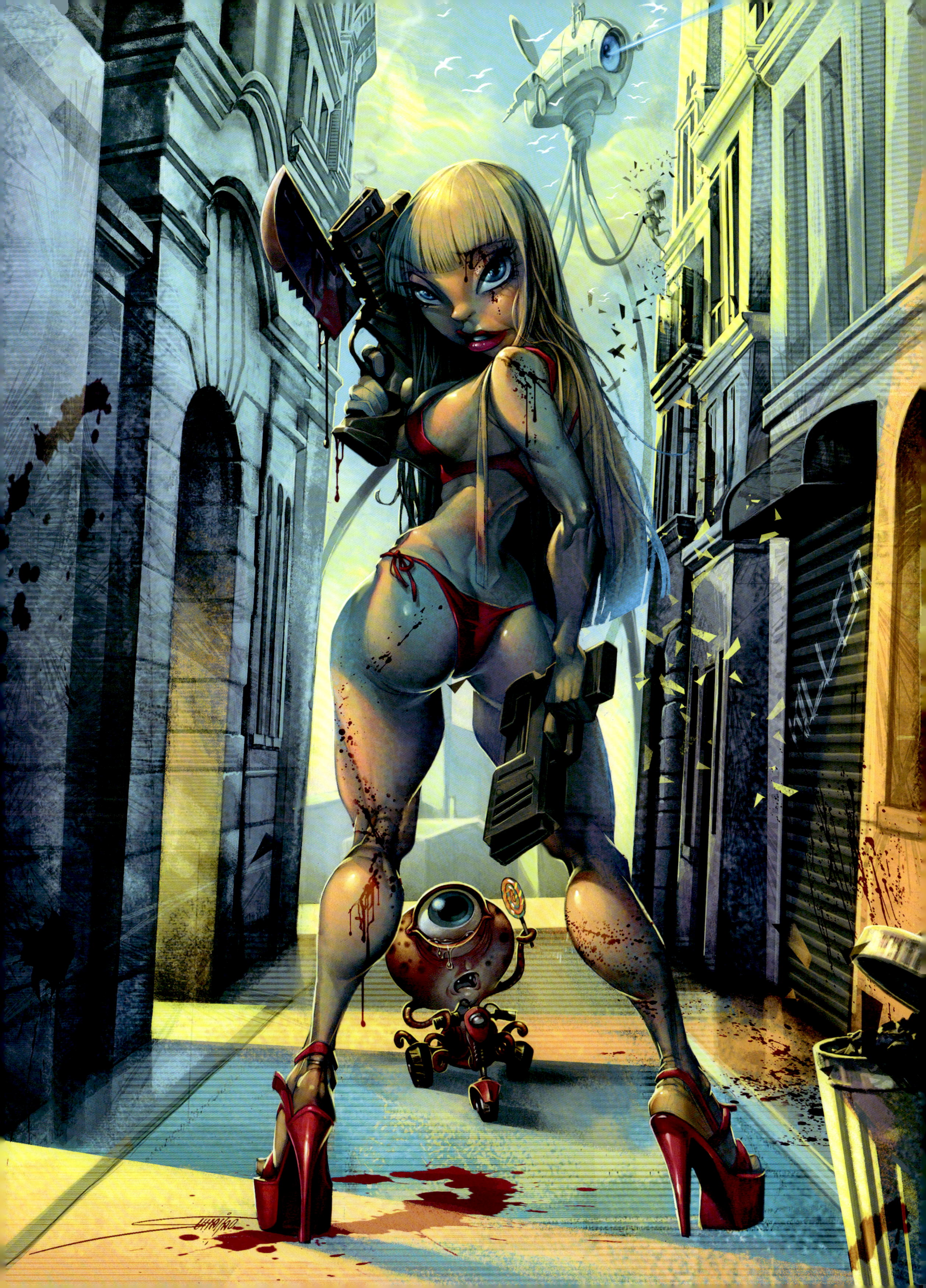

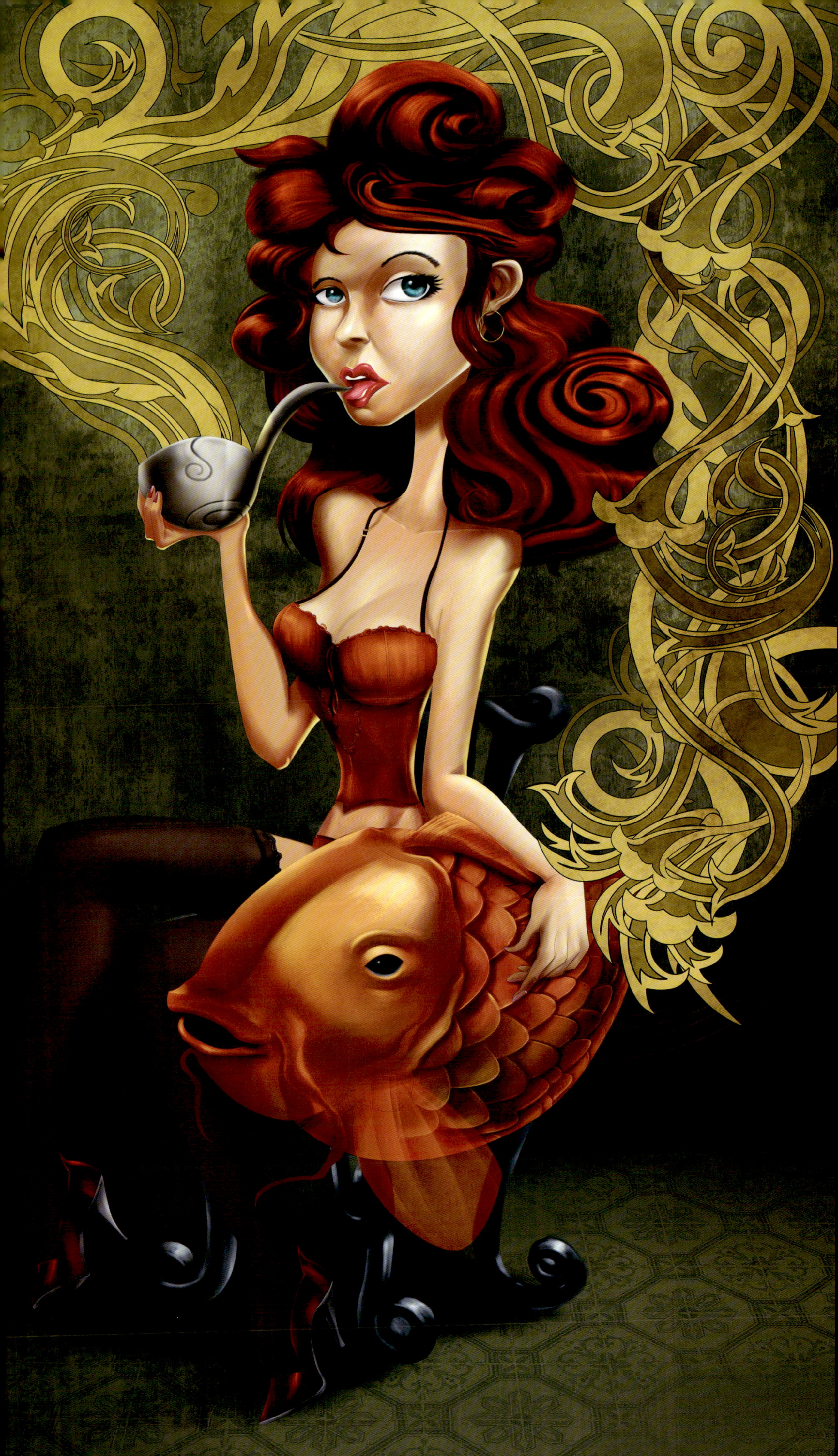

Smoking Koi
Photoshop
Timothy Jeffrey Terrenal, THE PHILIPPINES
[left]

The Seamstress
Photoshop
Leslie Dalton, CANADA
[right]

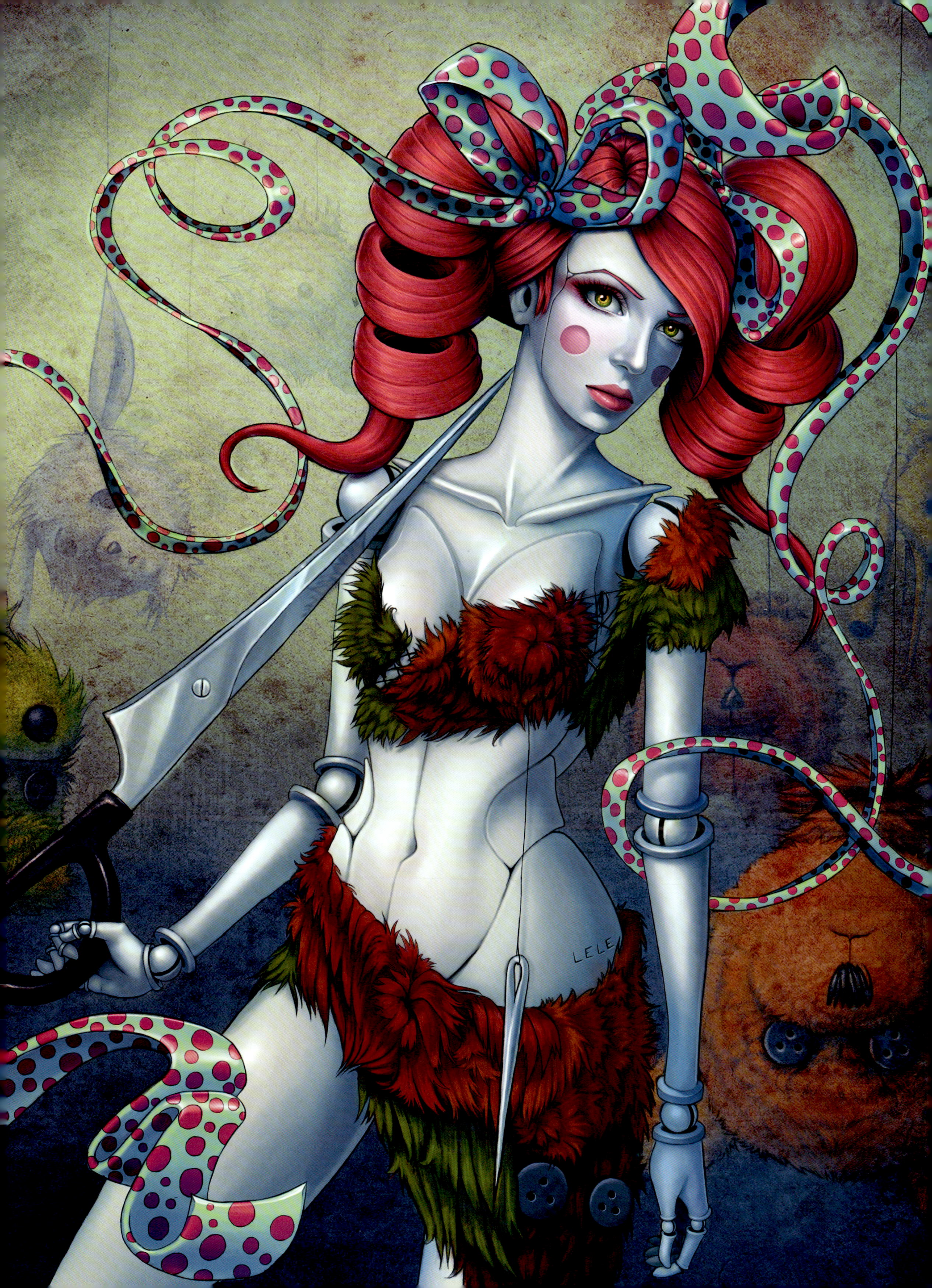
LELE

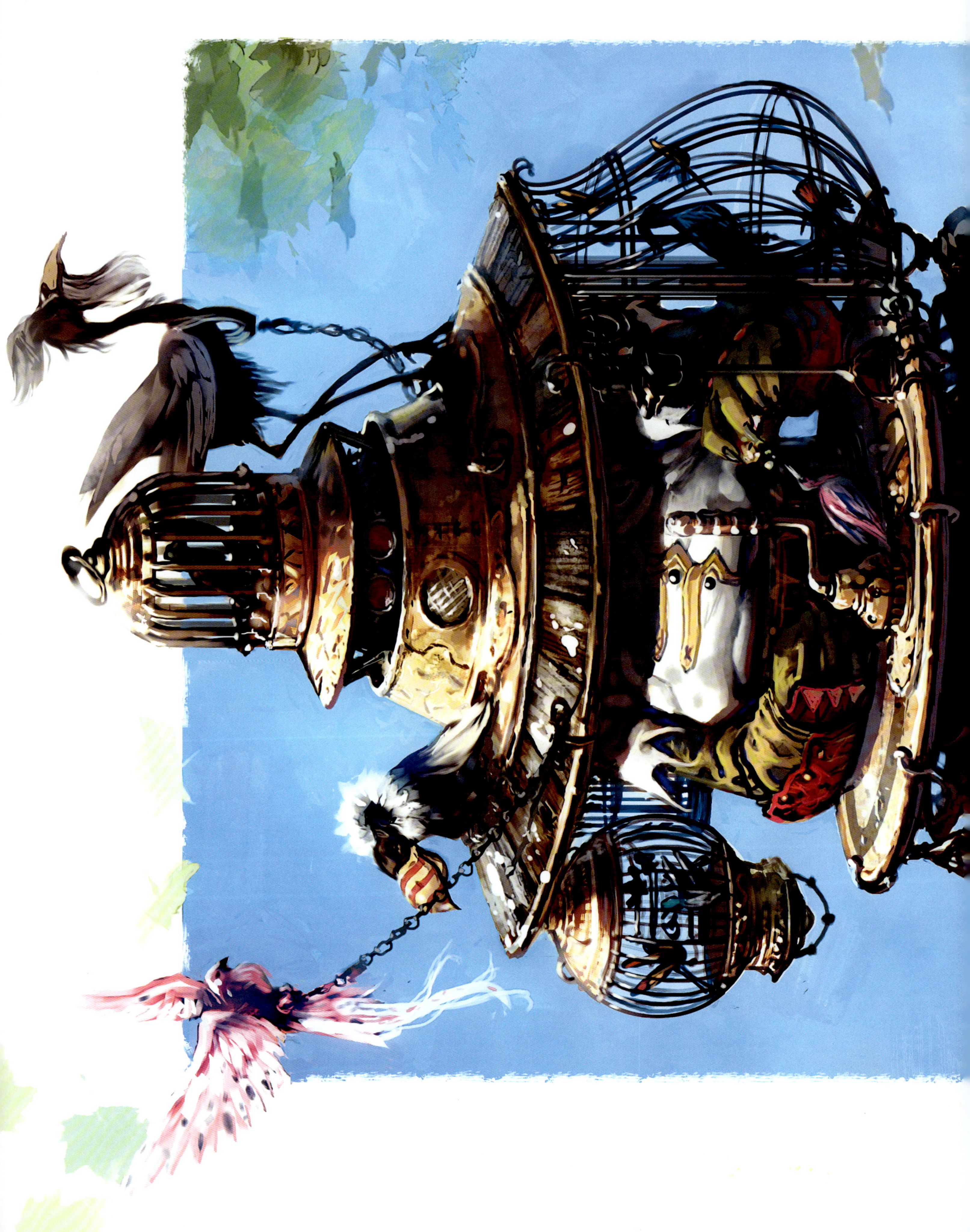

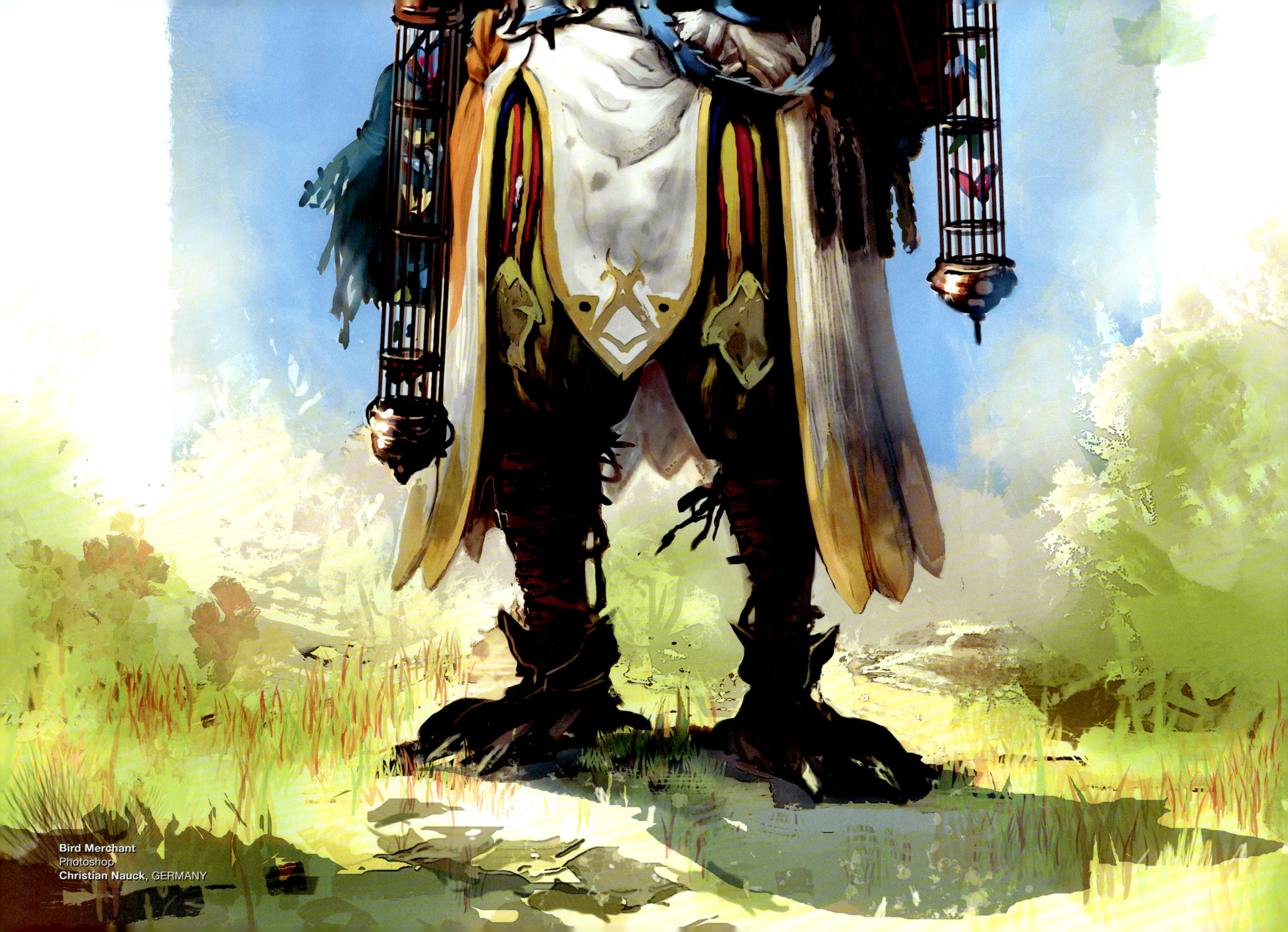

Bird Merchant
Photoshop
Christian Nauck, GERMANY

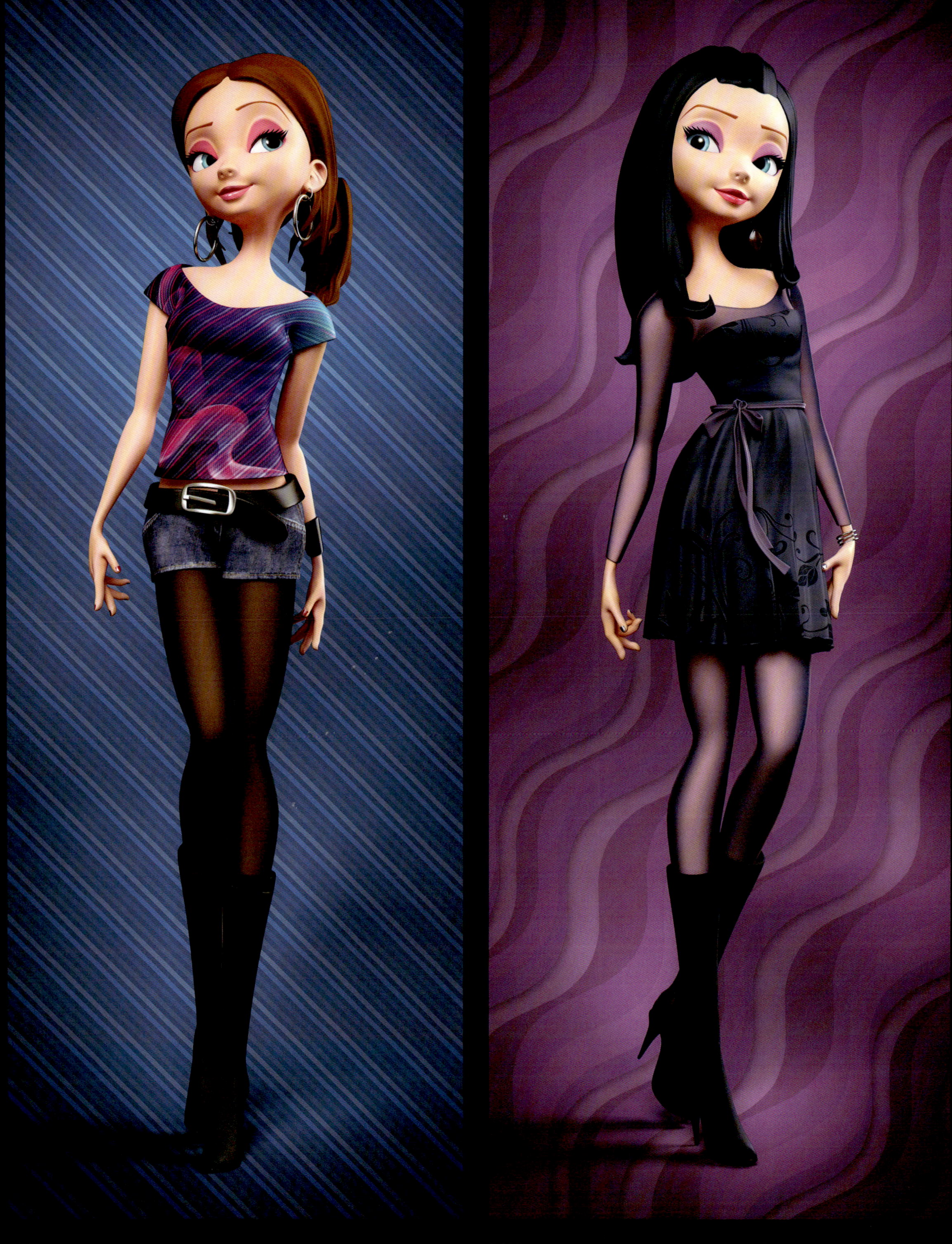

4 Girls
Maya, mental ray, Photoshop
Carlos Ortega Elizalde, MEXICO

4 Girls
Maya, mental ray, Photoshop
Carlos Ortega Elizalde, MEXICO

Ooh la la!
3ds Max, V-Ray
Andrew Hickinbottom, GREAT BRITAIN

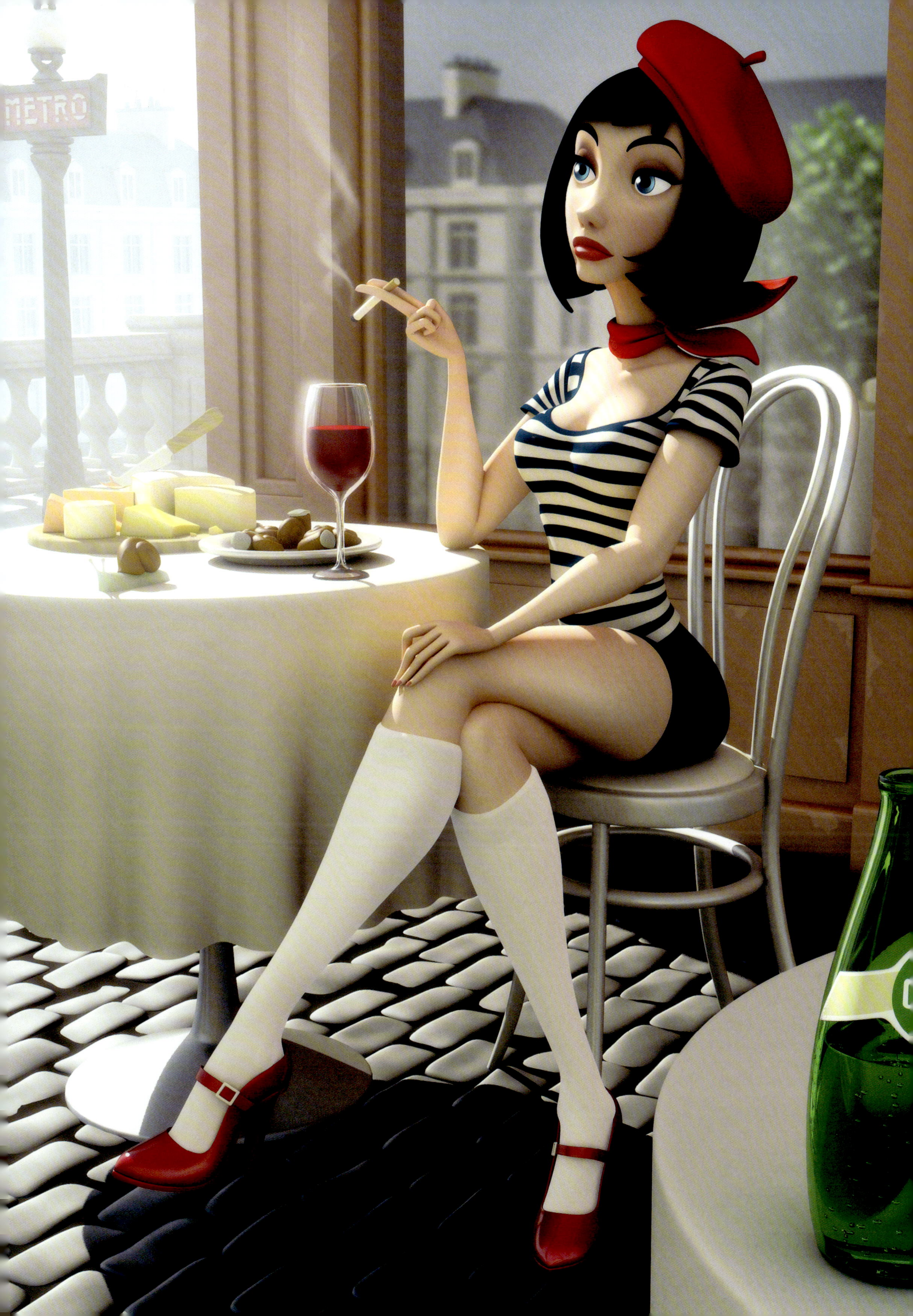
METRO

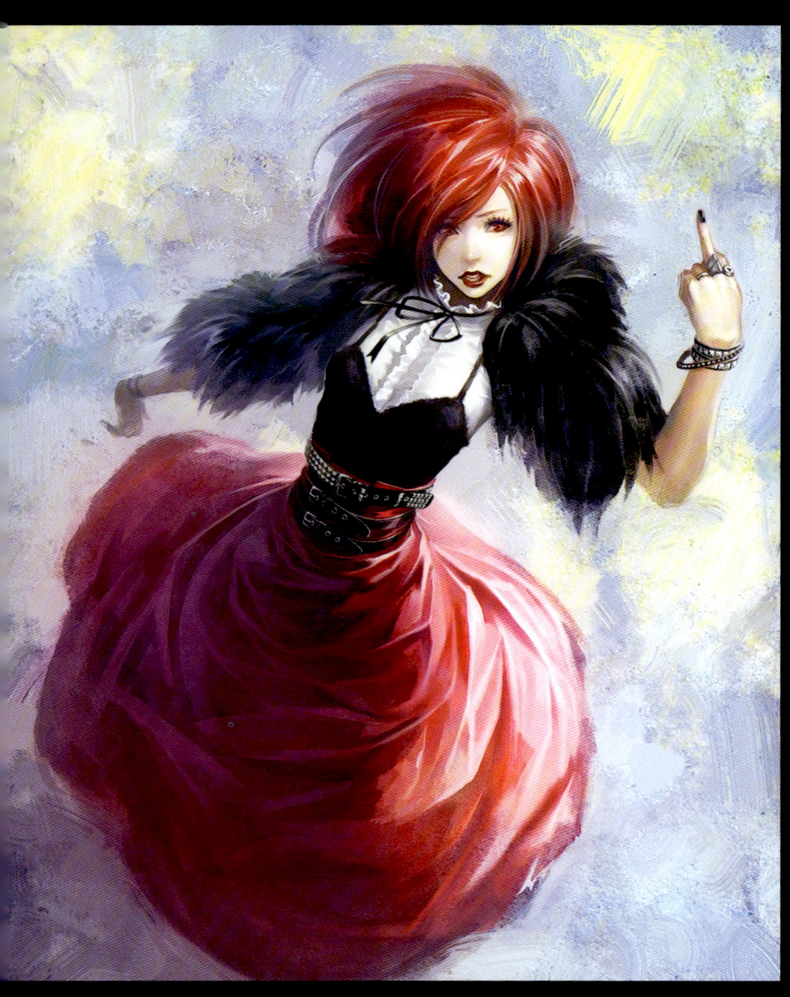

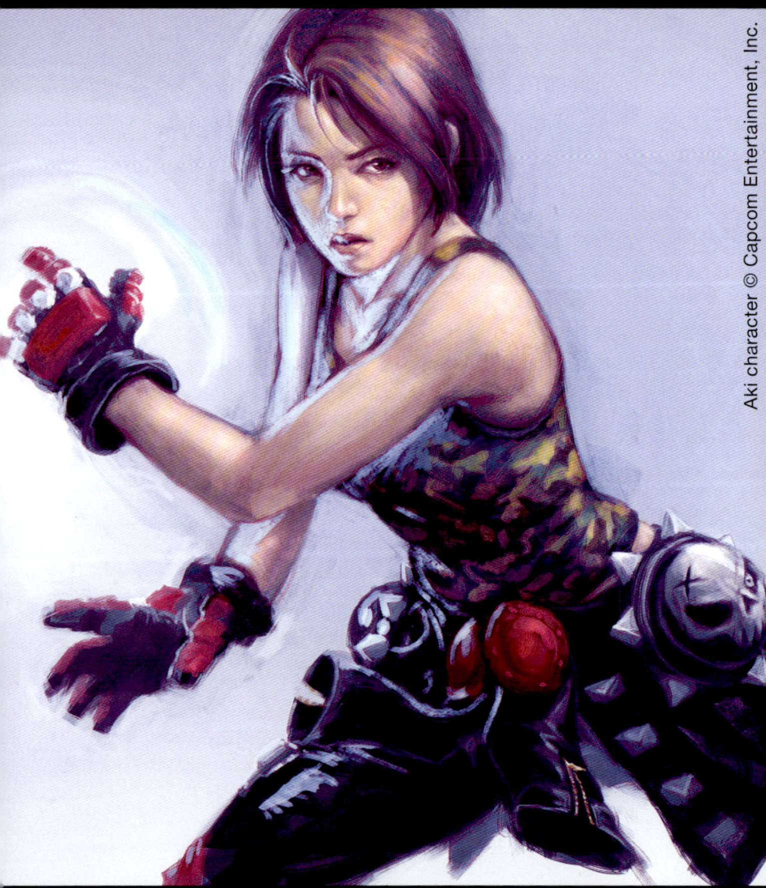

Aki character © Capcom Entertainment, Inc.

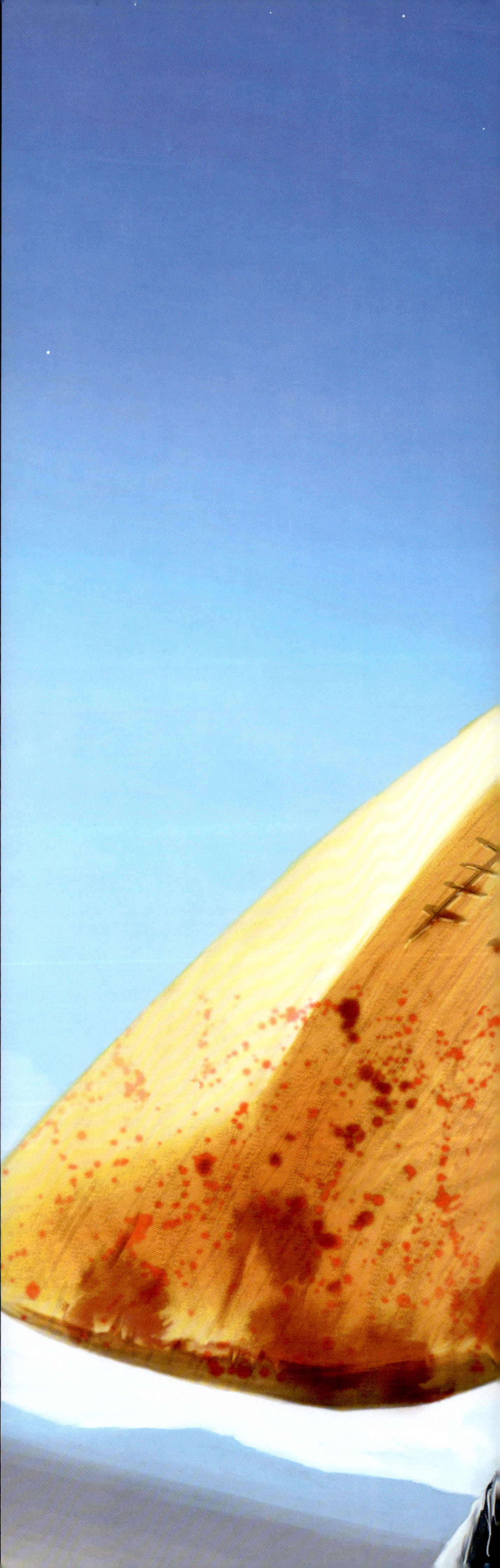

Gothic Punk
Photoshop
Shuichi Wada,
JAPAN
[top]

Rival Schools: Aki
Photoshop
Inspired by: CAPCOM character
Rafi Adrian Zulkarnain, INDONESIA
[above]

Willow
Photoshop
Andy Jones,
GREAT BRITAIN
[right]

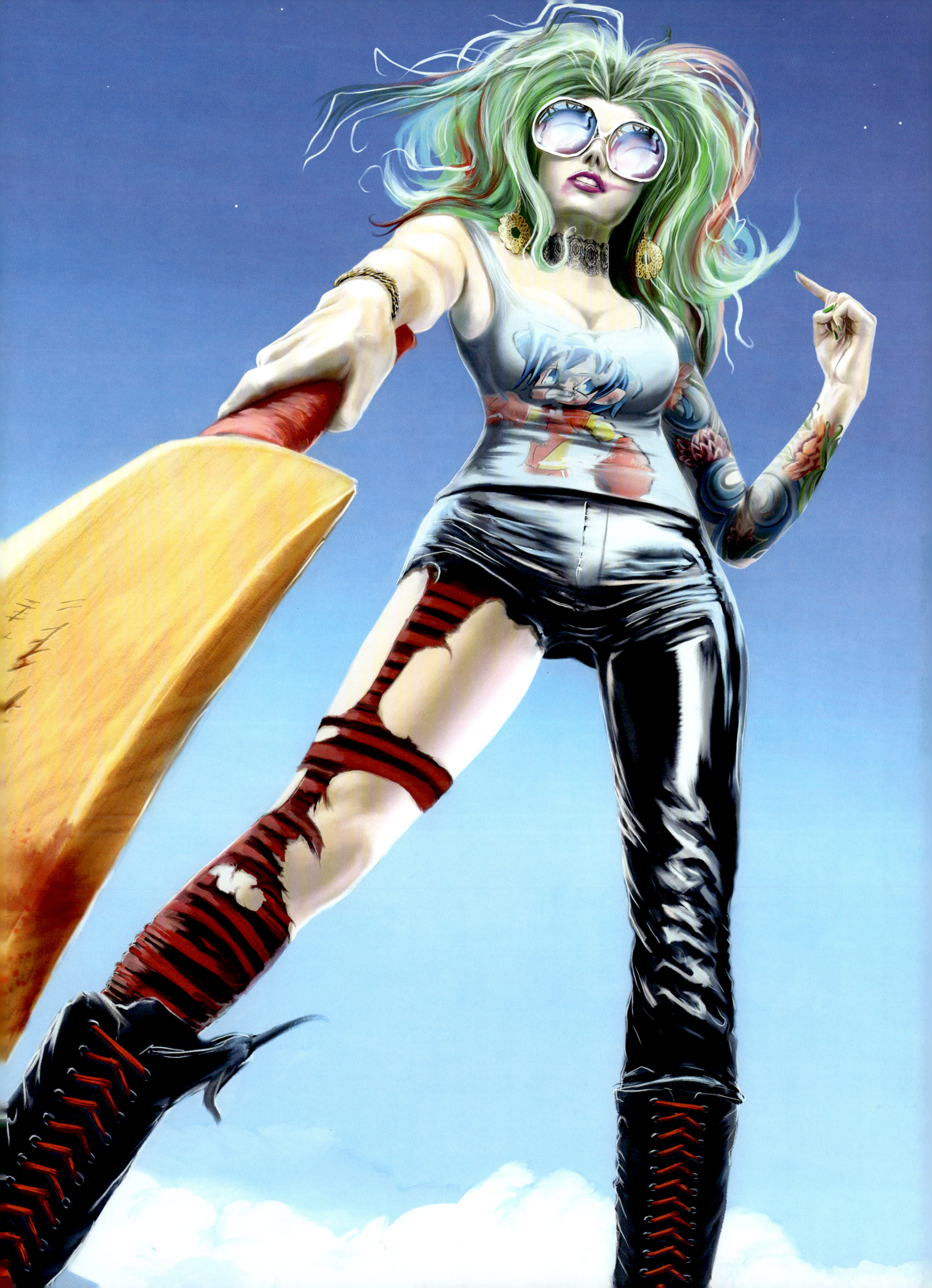

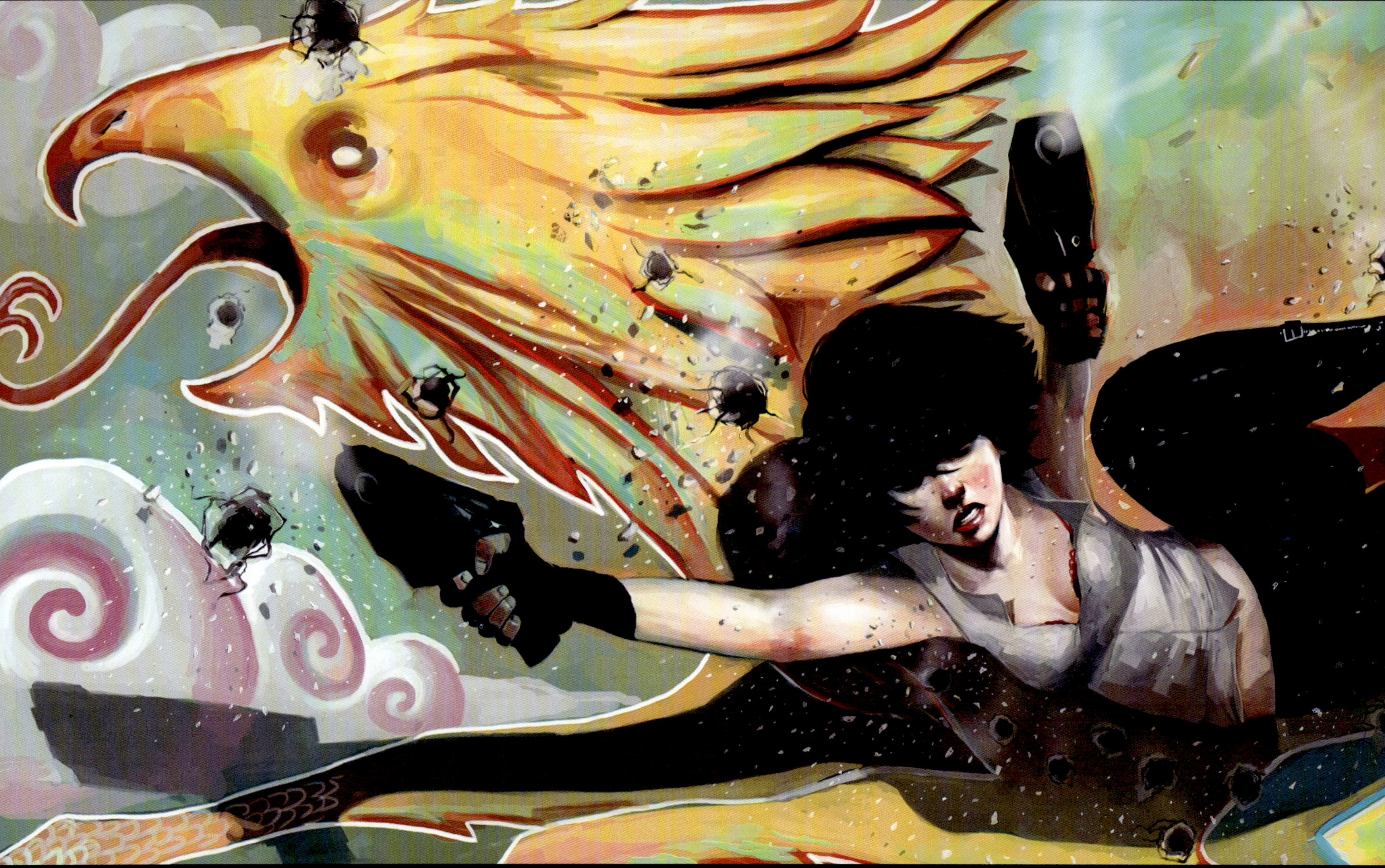

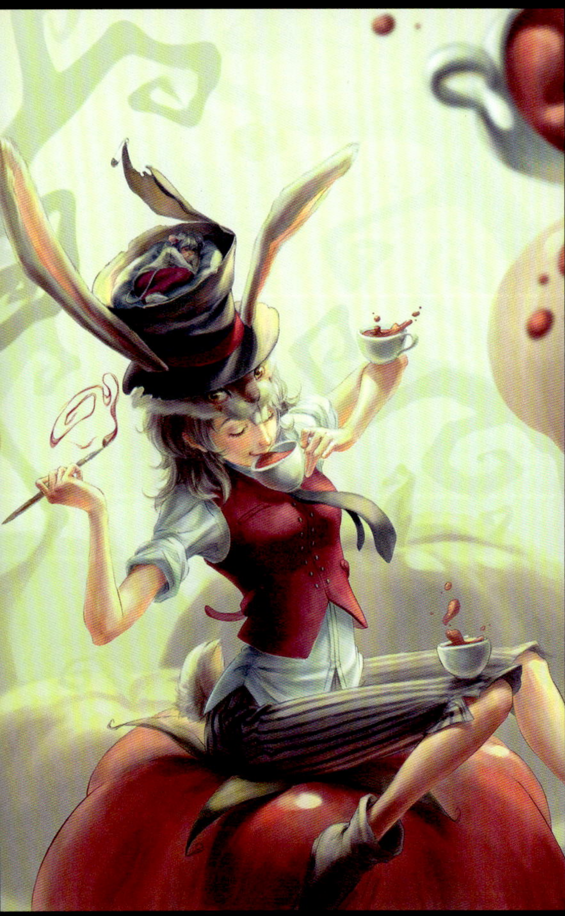

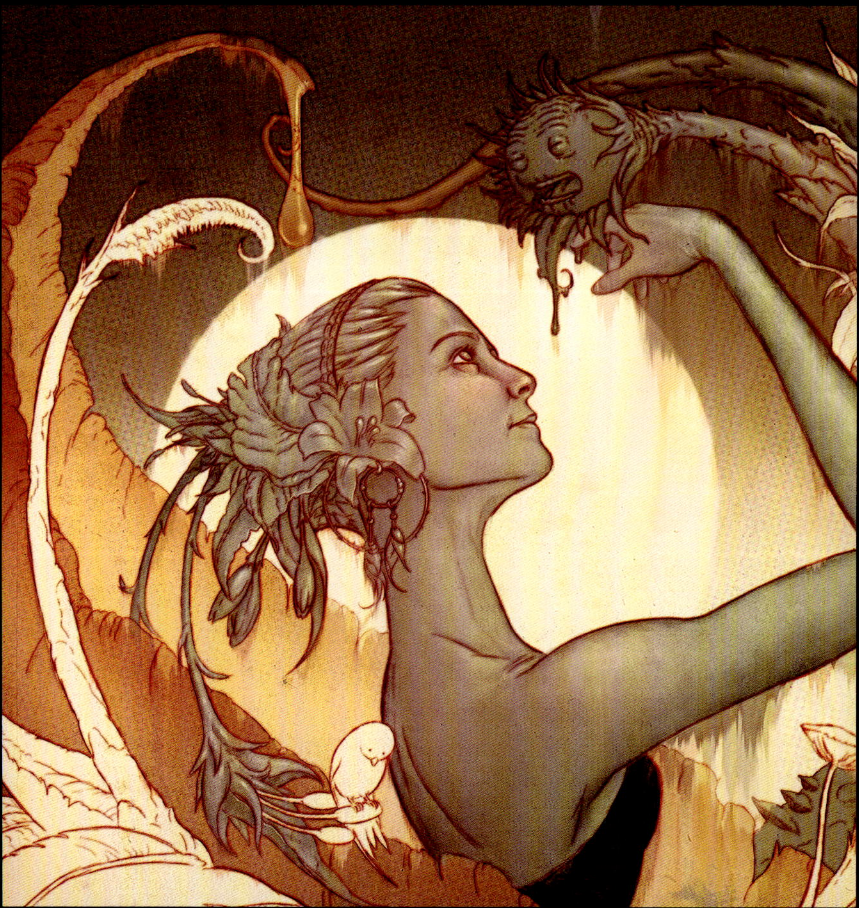

Maggie Will Kill You!
Photoshop, Painter
Rudy-Jan Faber, THE NETHERLANDS
[top]

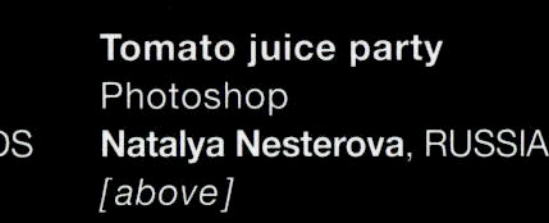

Tomato juice party
Photoshop
Natalya Nesterova, RUSSIA
[above]

Crows' Parliament: Titania
Photoshop
Juan Parra, SPAIN
[above]

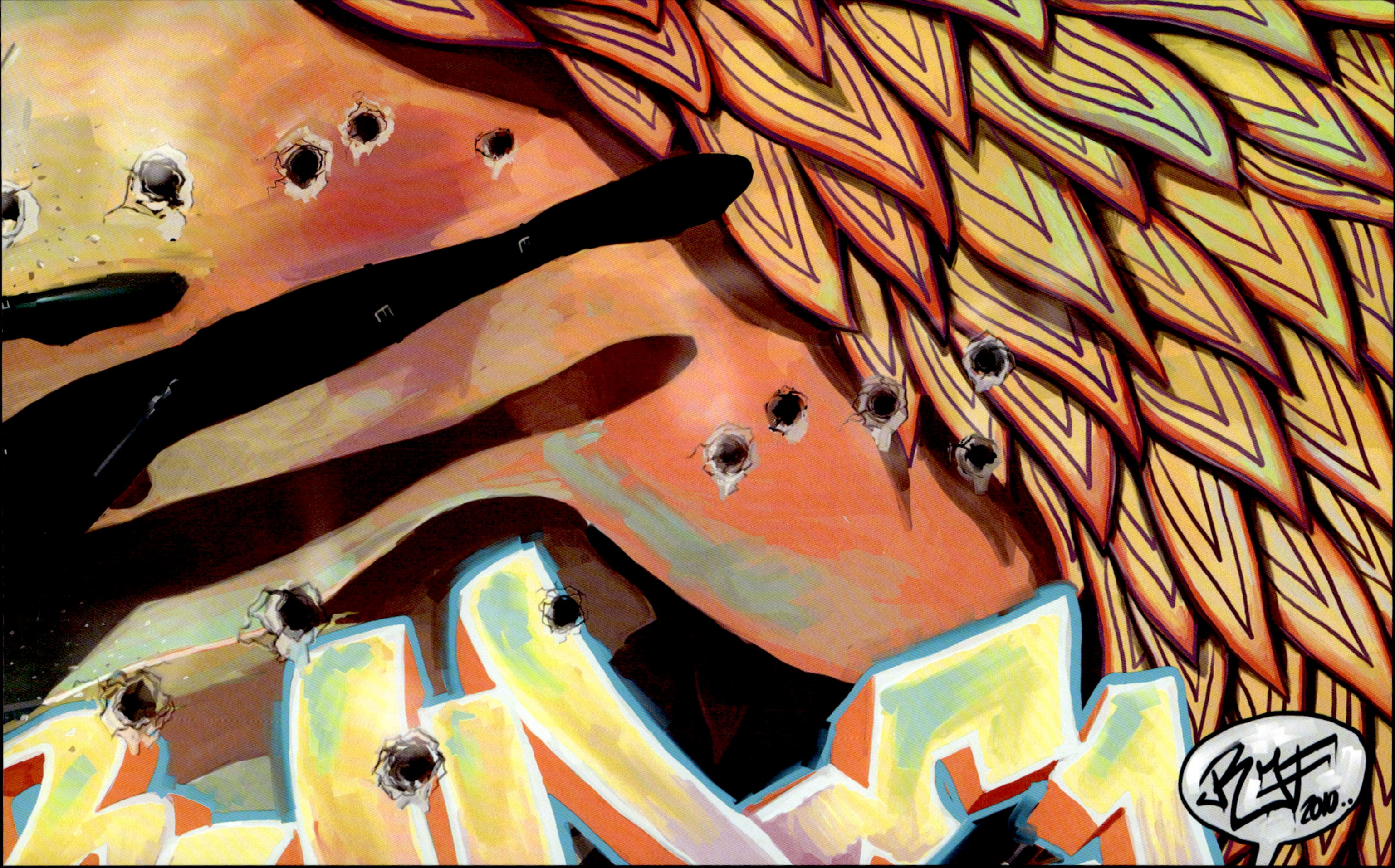

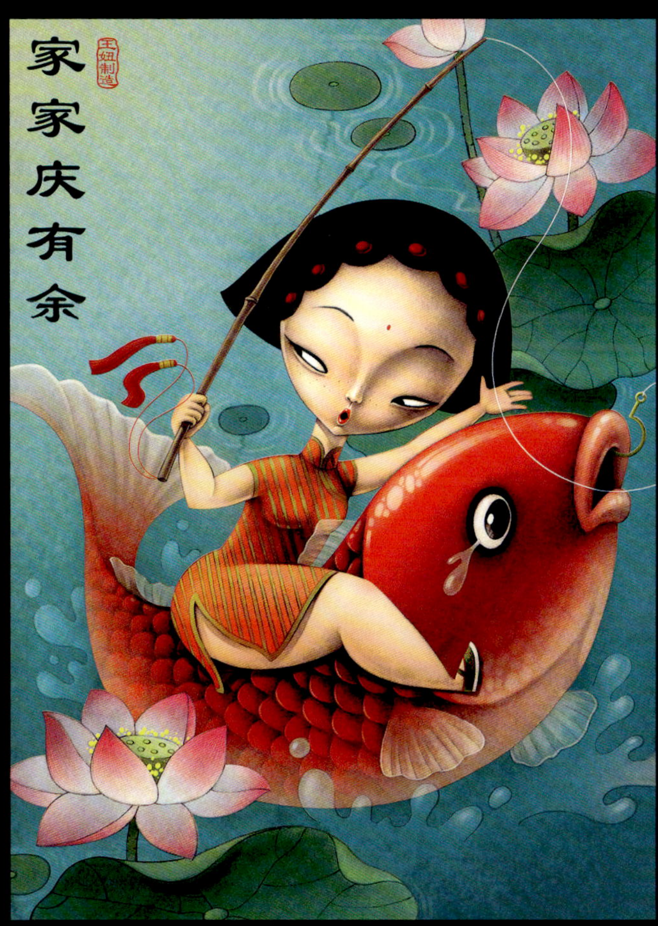

Families Celebrations
Photoshop
Fangwei Wang, CHINA

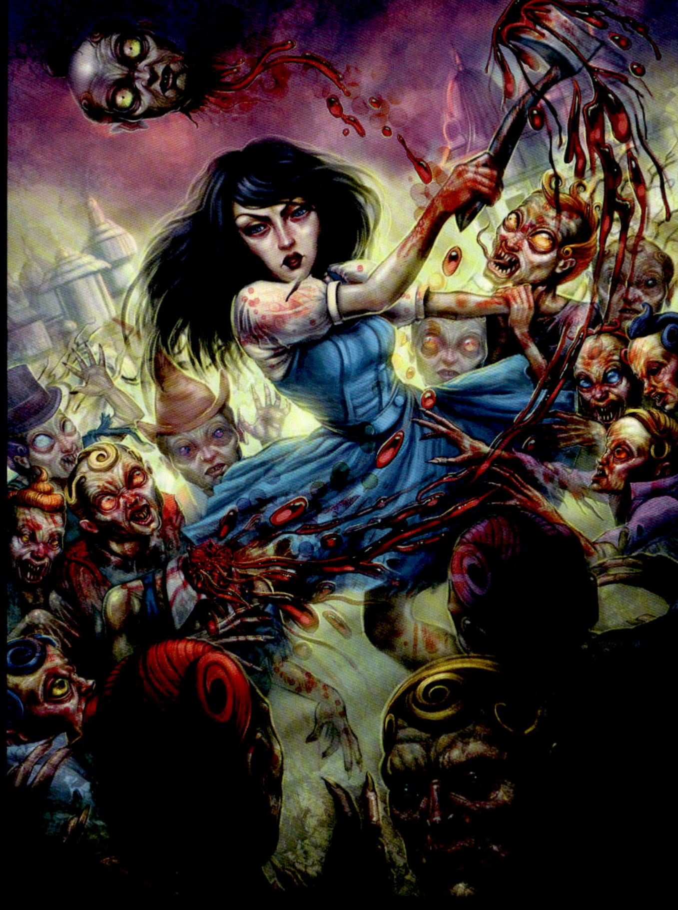

Dorothy vs. the Munchkins
Painter
Client: Ryan Fuller

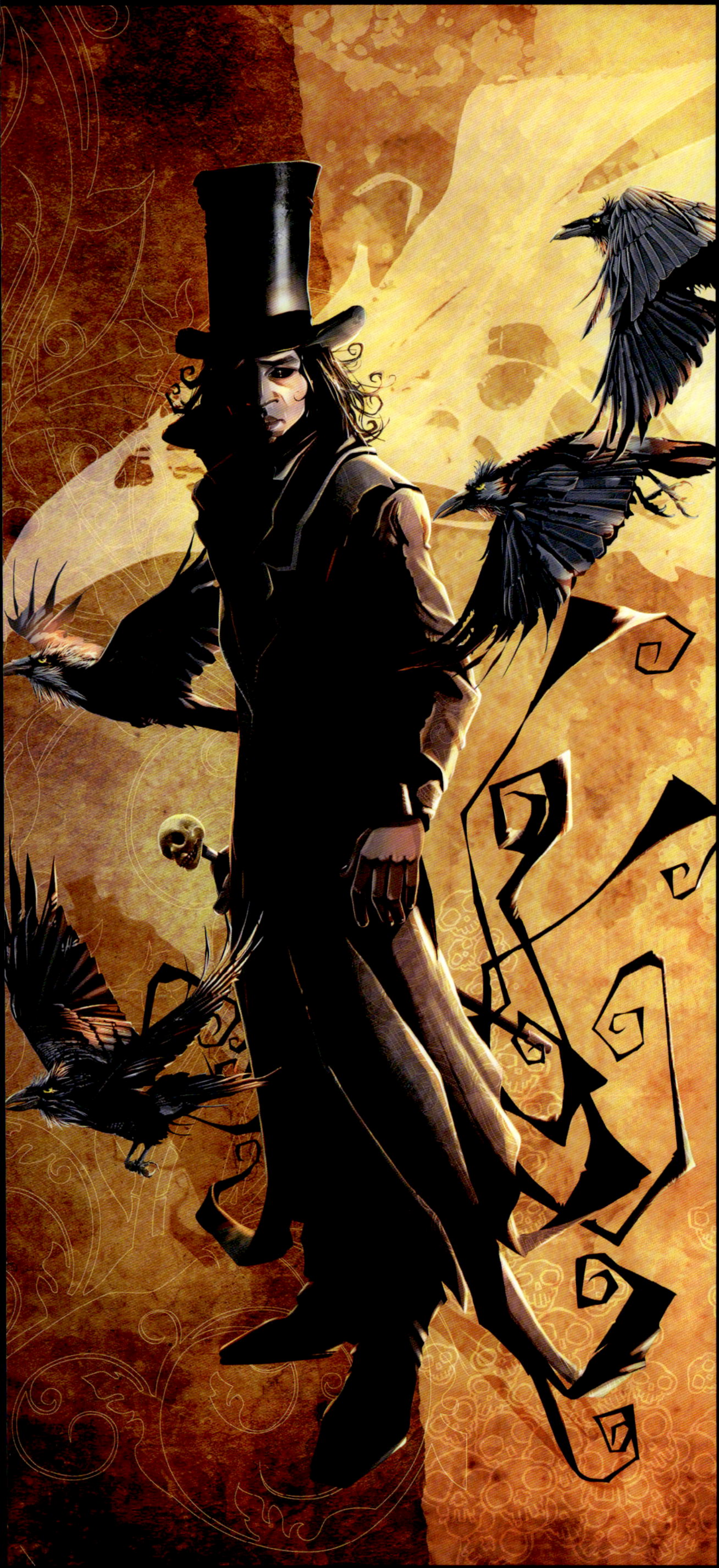

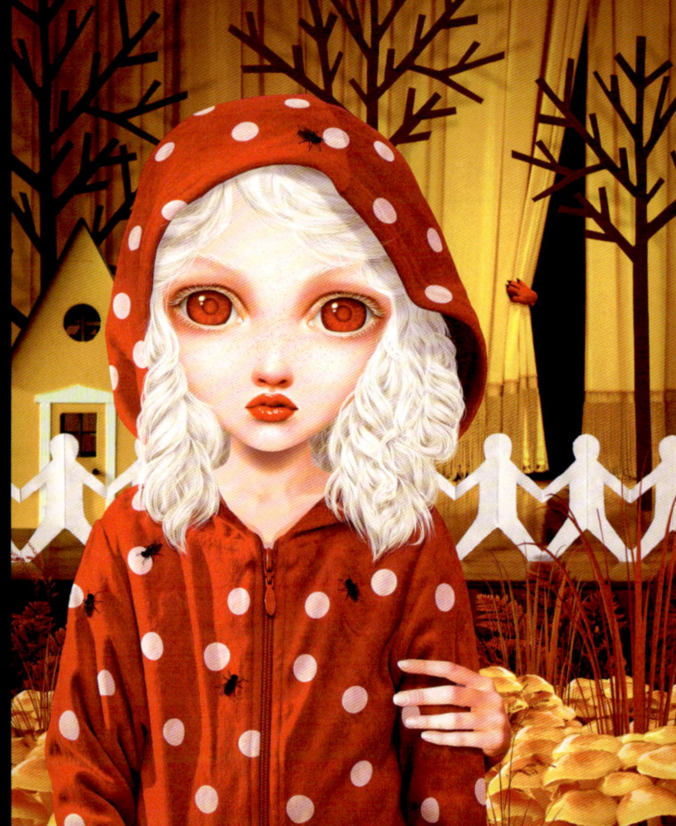

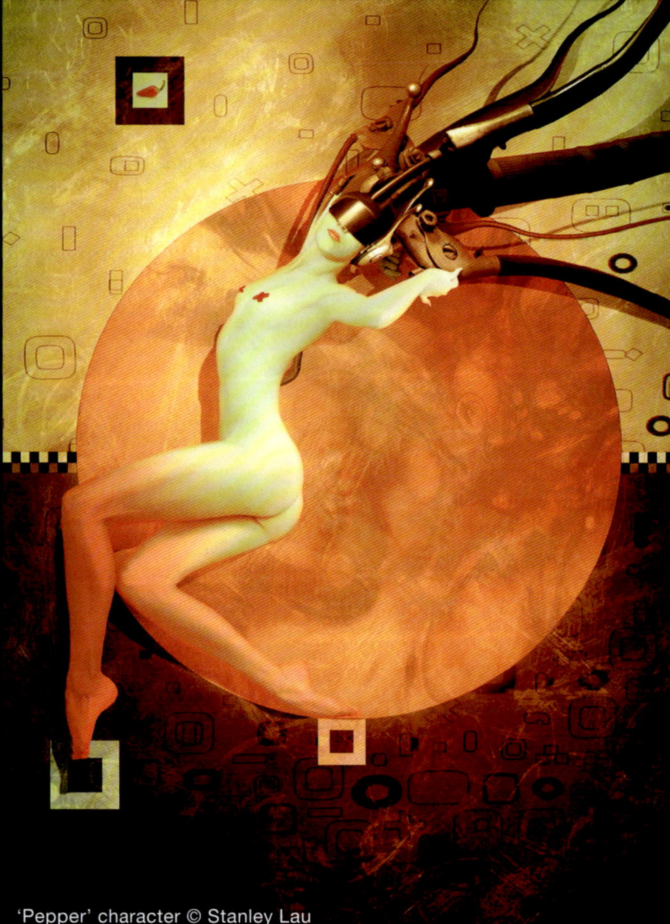

'Pepper' character © Stanley Lau

The Dark Inker
Photoshop, Illustrator
Steve Sampson,
GREAT BRITAIN
[above]

Life is Like a Theater
Photoshop
Margarita Surnaite,
LITHUANIA
[top right]

Cyberpepper
Photoshop
Oliver Wetter, Fantasio fine Arts,
GERMANY
[above]

Tattoos
Painter
Phillip Gerlitz, NA,
CANADA
[right]

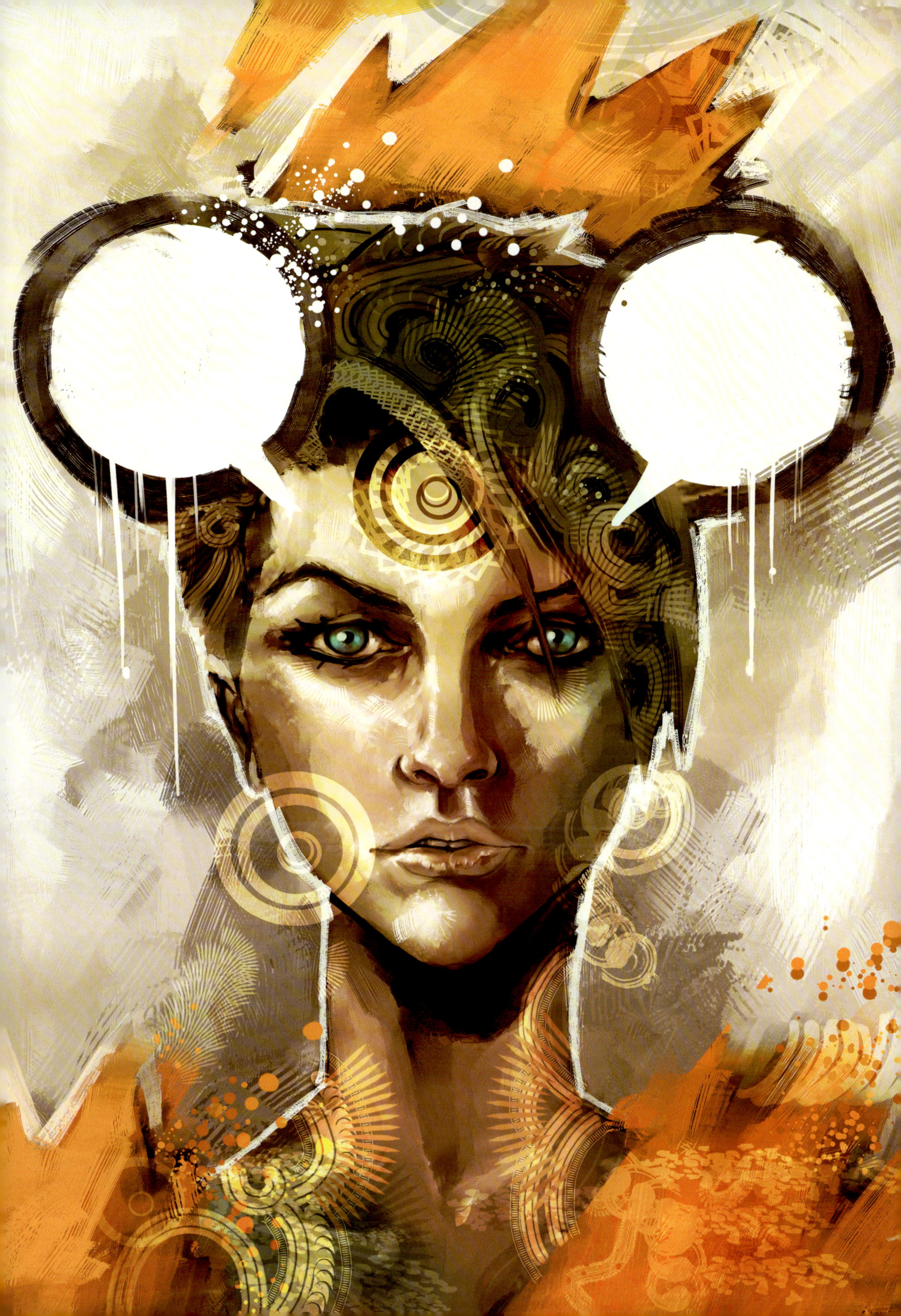

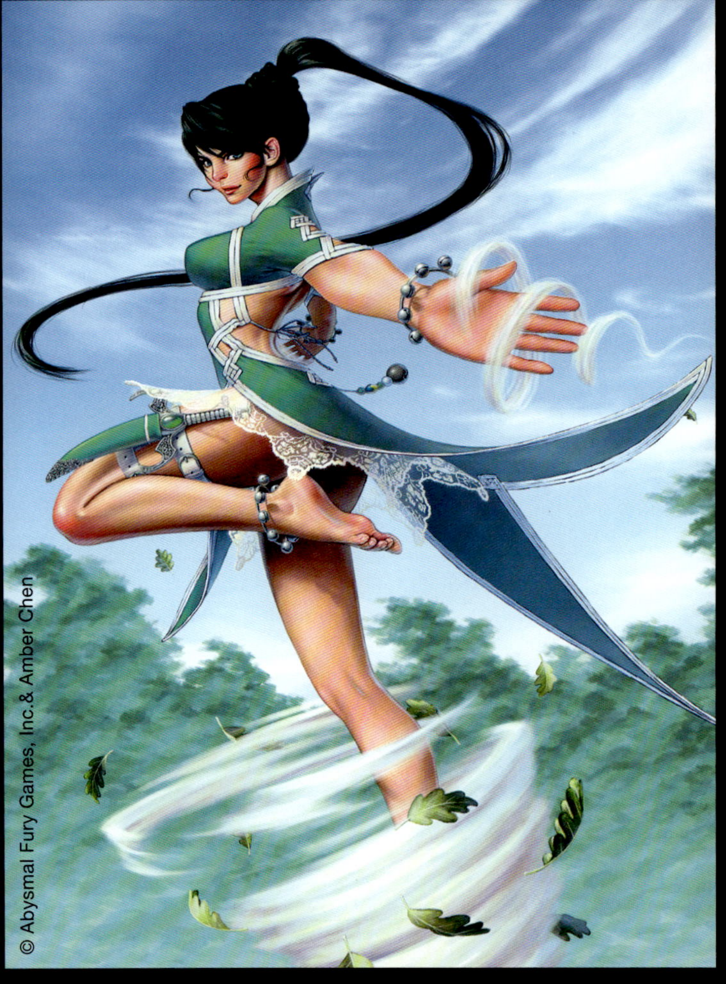

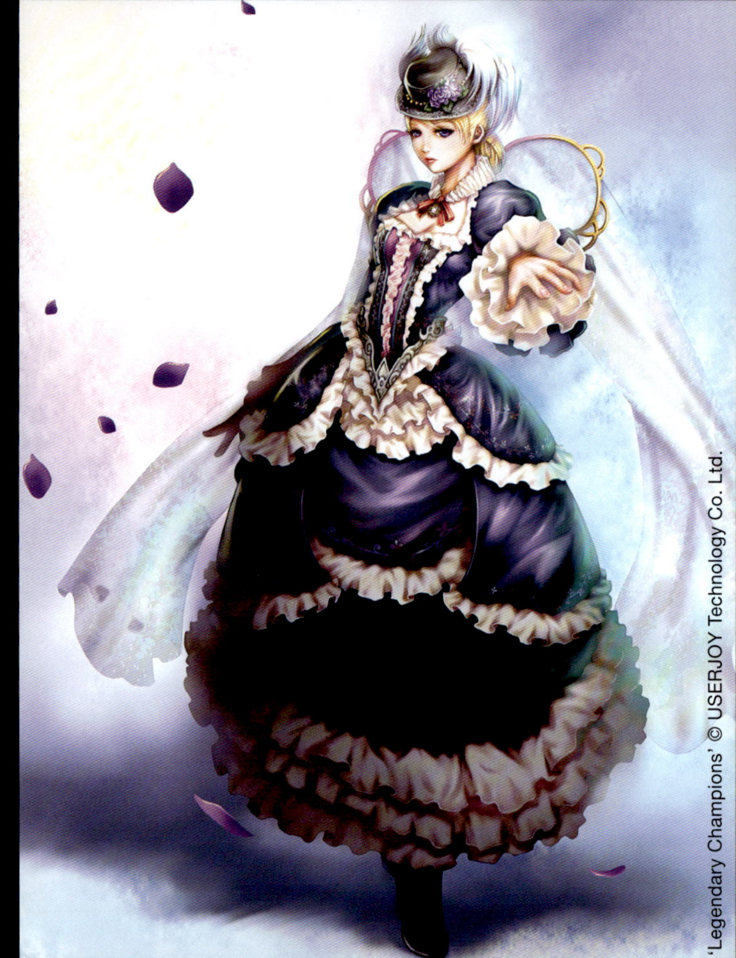

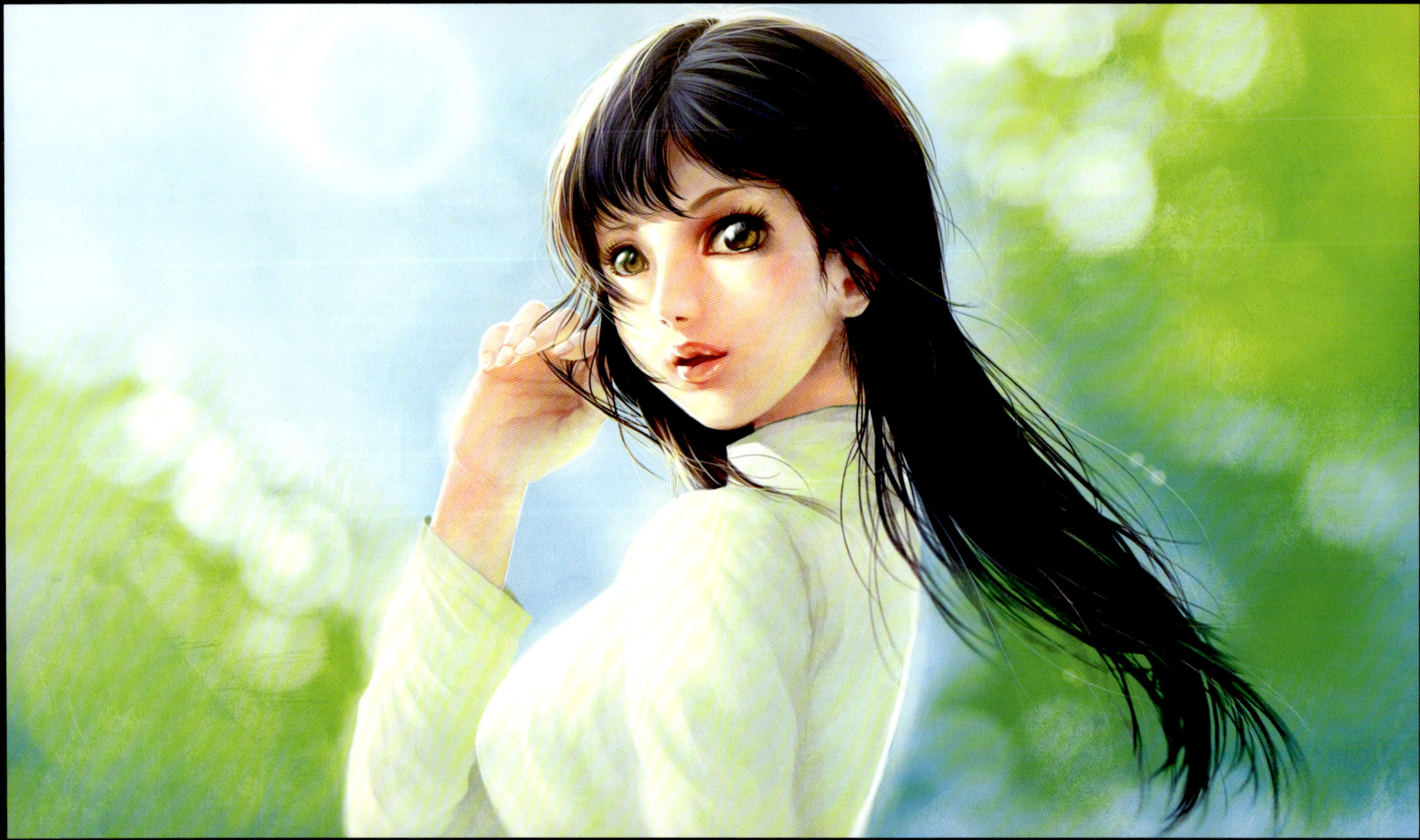

Ride the Wind
Photoshop
Client: Abysmal Fury Games, Inc.
Amber Chen, USA
[top]

Sunshire
Photoshop
Dzung Phungdinh,
VIETNAM
[above]

Legendary Champions: Of ivory song (Josepha)
Painter, Photoshop
Wan Hsienwei, USERJOY Technology Co. Ltd.,
TAIWAN
[top]

Green hair young girl
3ds Max, Photoshop
Wen Chen Yen,
TAIWAN
[right]

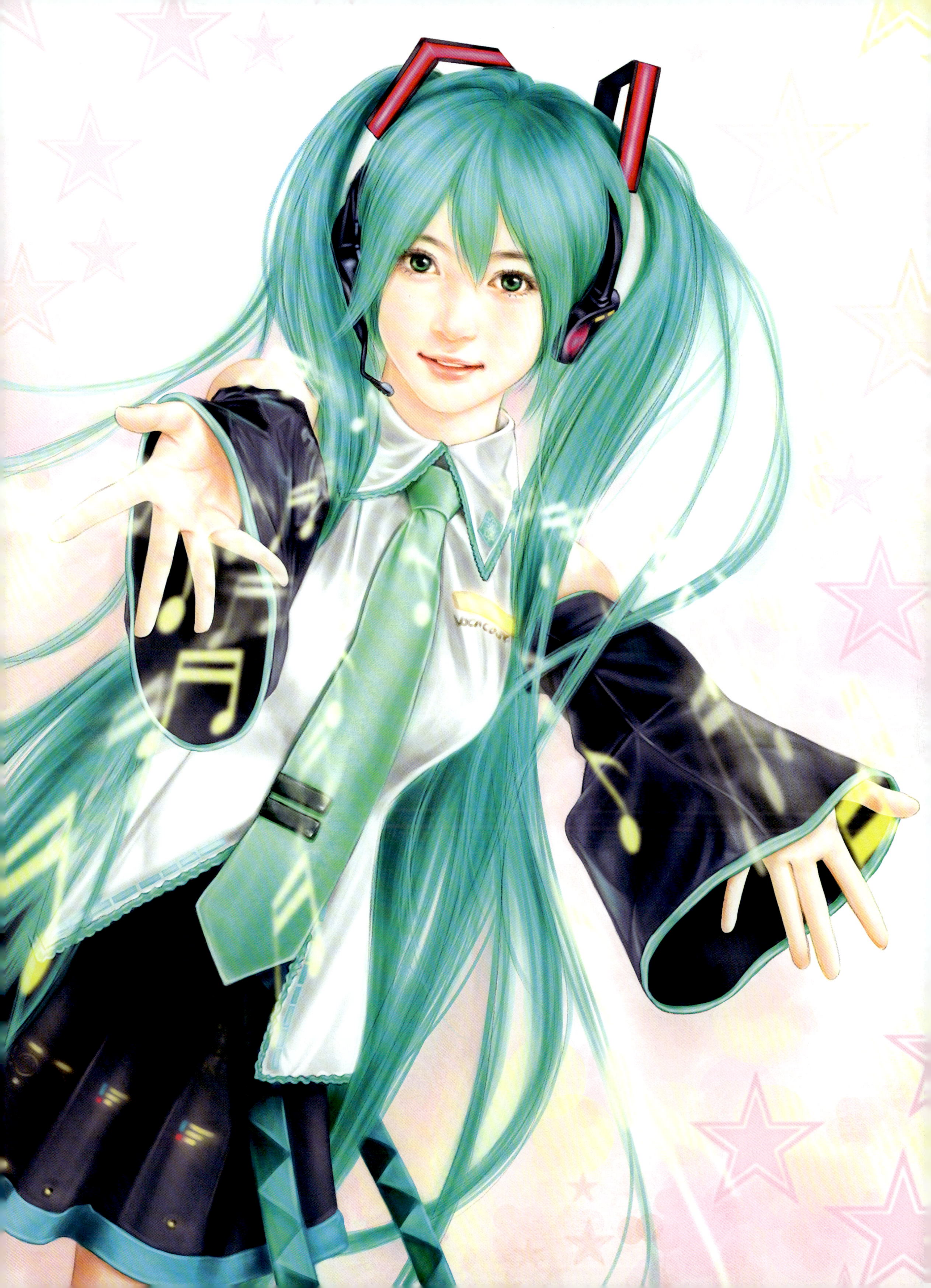

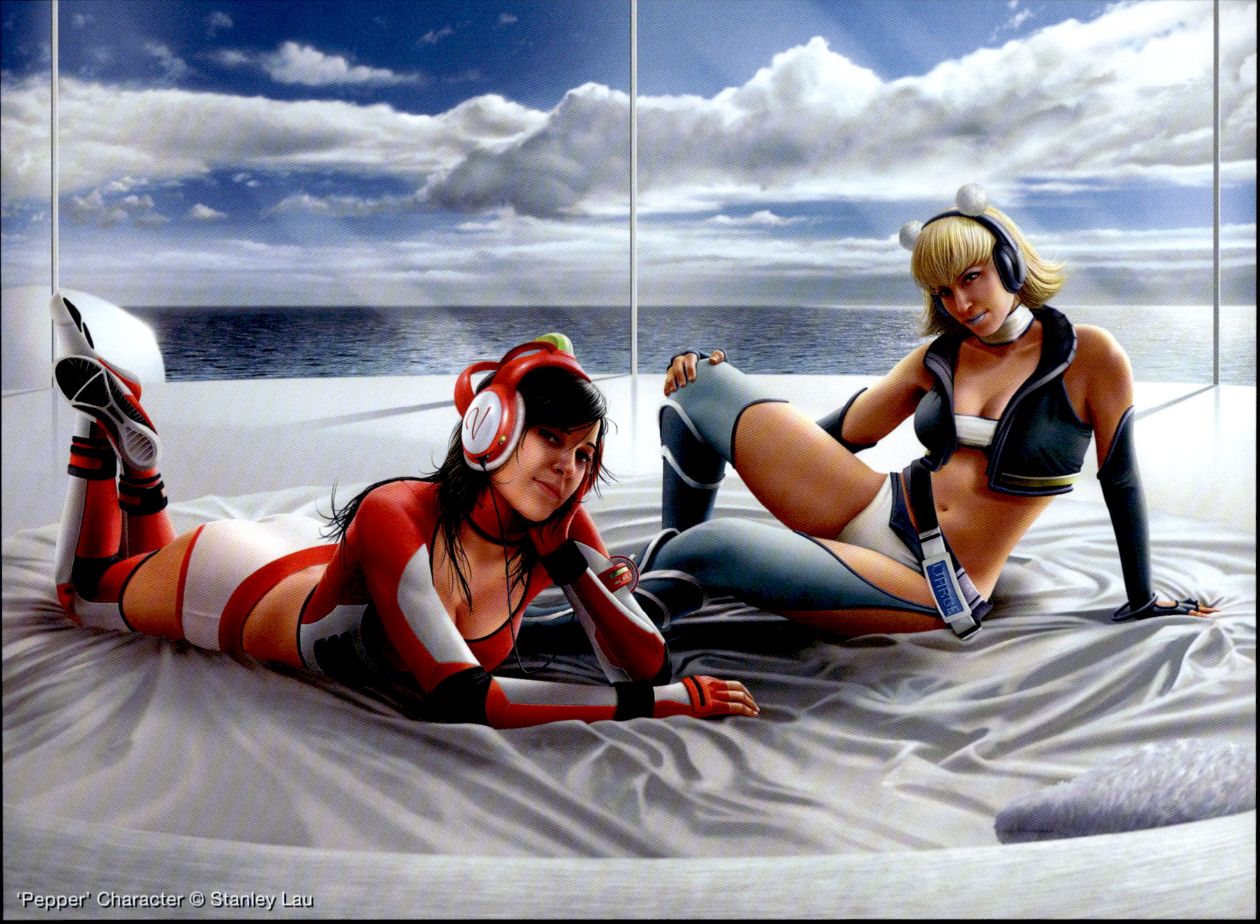

'Pepper' Character © Stanley Lau

Pepper and Wanda
Photoshop, Painter
Toni Rodriguez,
SPAIN
[left]

Corel Girl
Painter, Photoshop
Client: Corel
Wan Hsienwei,
USERJOY
Technology Co. Ltd.
TAIWAN
[right]

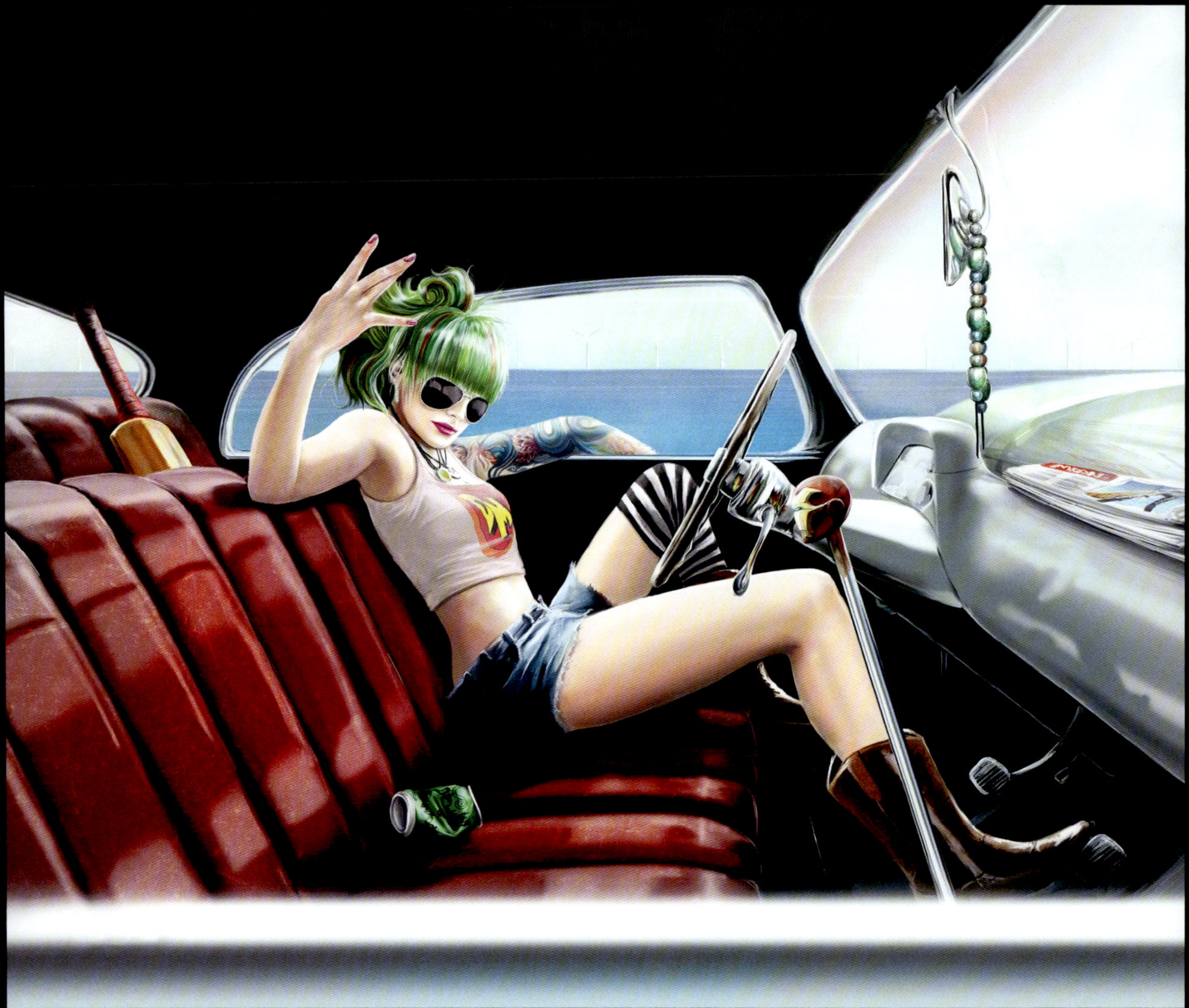

Willow, Wheels and Windmills
Photoshop
Andy Jones,
GREAT BRITAIN
[left]

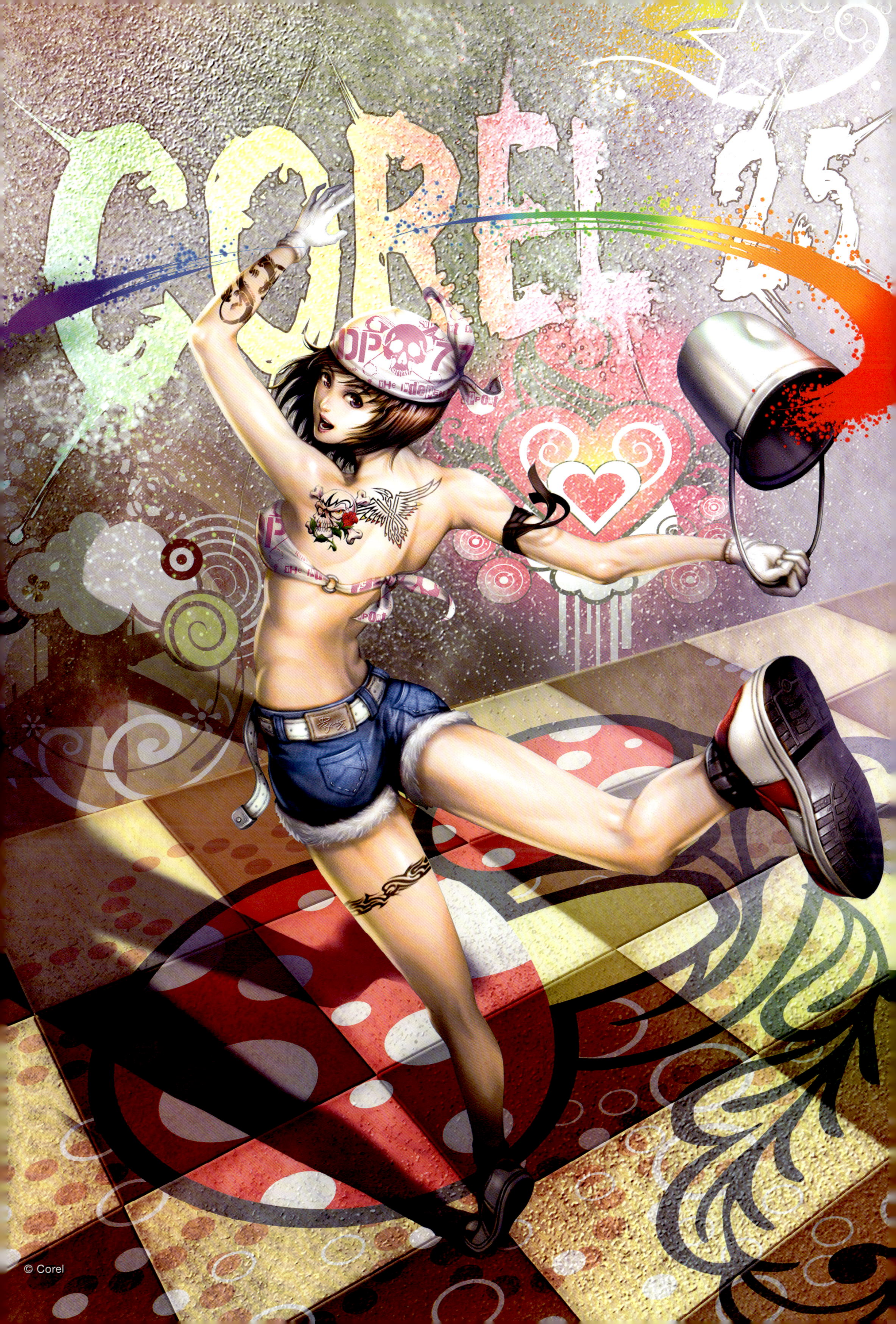
COREL 25

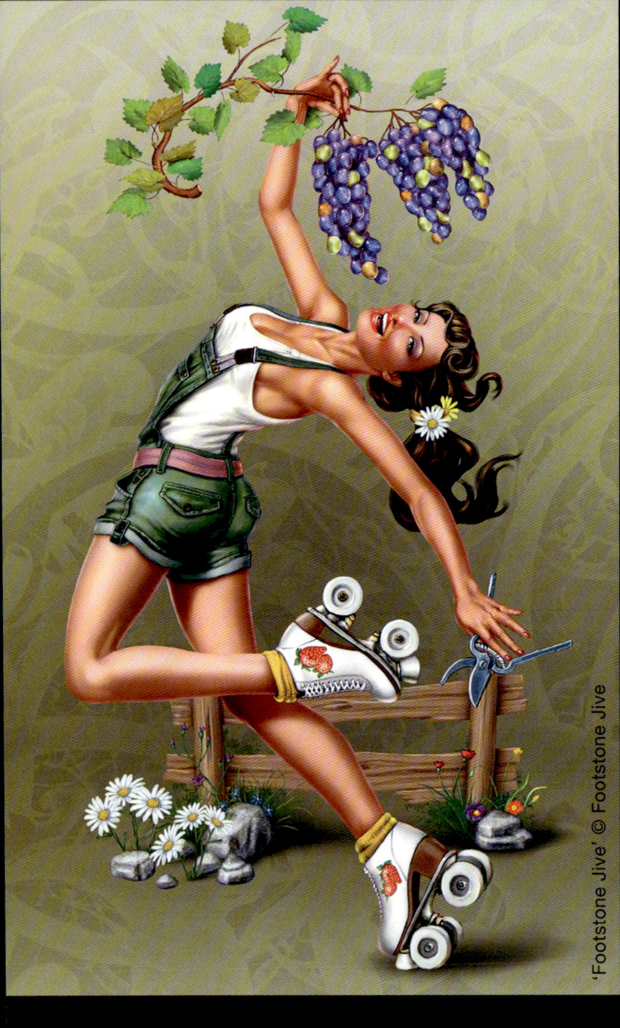

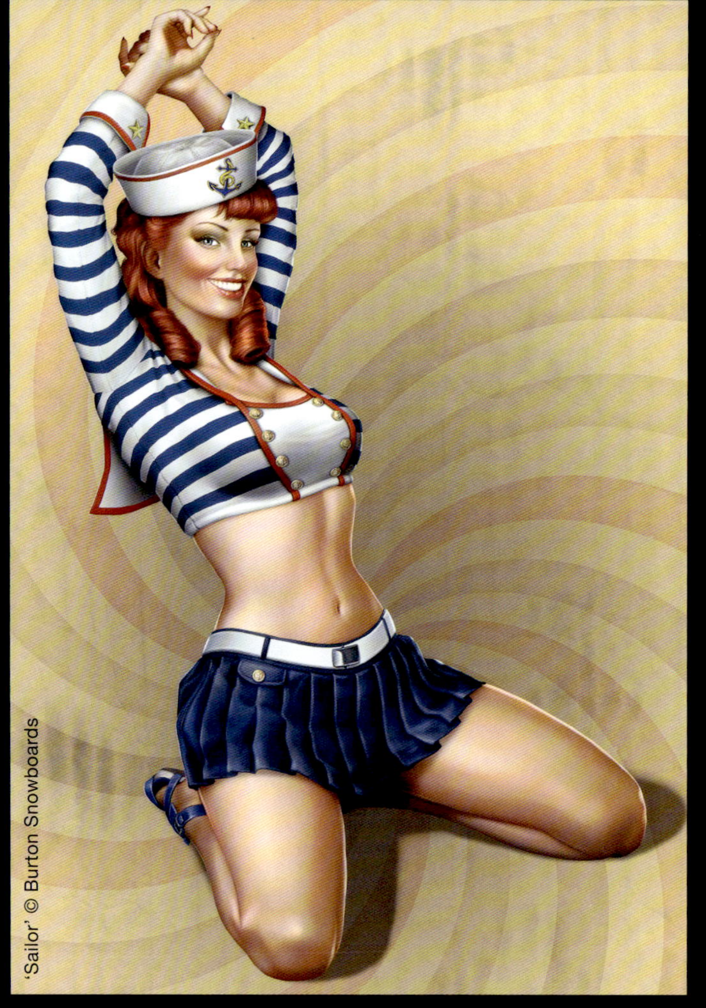

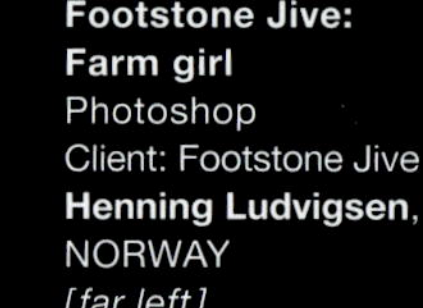

Footstone Jive: Farm girl
Photoshop
Client: Footstone Jive
Henning Ludvigsen, NORWAY
[far left]

Burton Snowboards: Sailor
Photoshop
Client: Burton Snowboards
Henning Ludvigsen, NORWAY
[left]

La fuoriclasse
Photoshop
Marco Fantechi, MeduNecer, ITALY
[right]

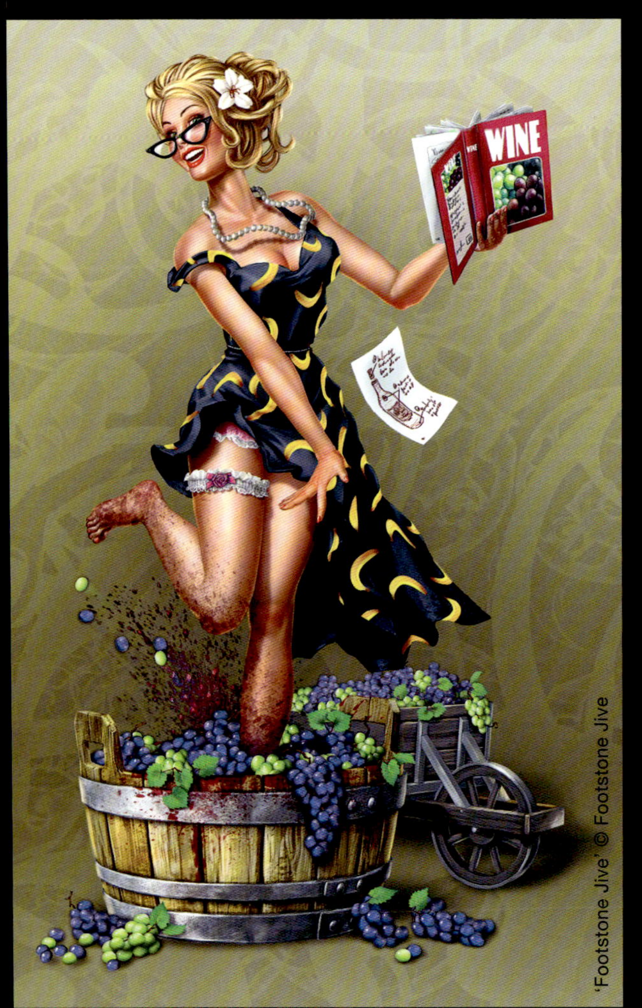

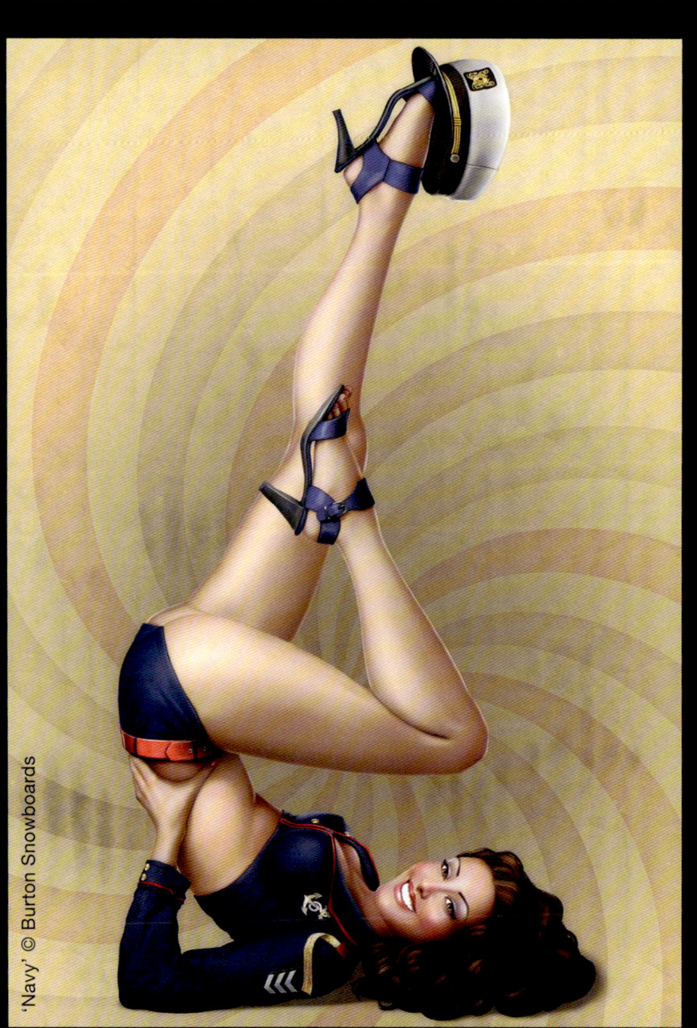

Footstone Jive: Librarian
Photoshop
Client: Footstone Jive
Henning Ludvigsen, NORWAY
[far left]

Burton Snowboards: Navy
Photoshop
Client: Burton Snowboards
Henning Ludvigsen, NORWAY
[left]

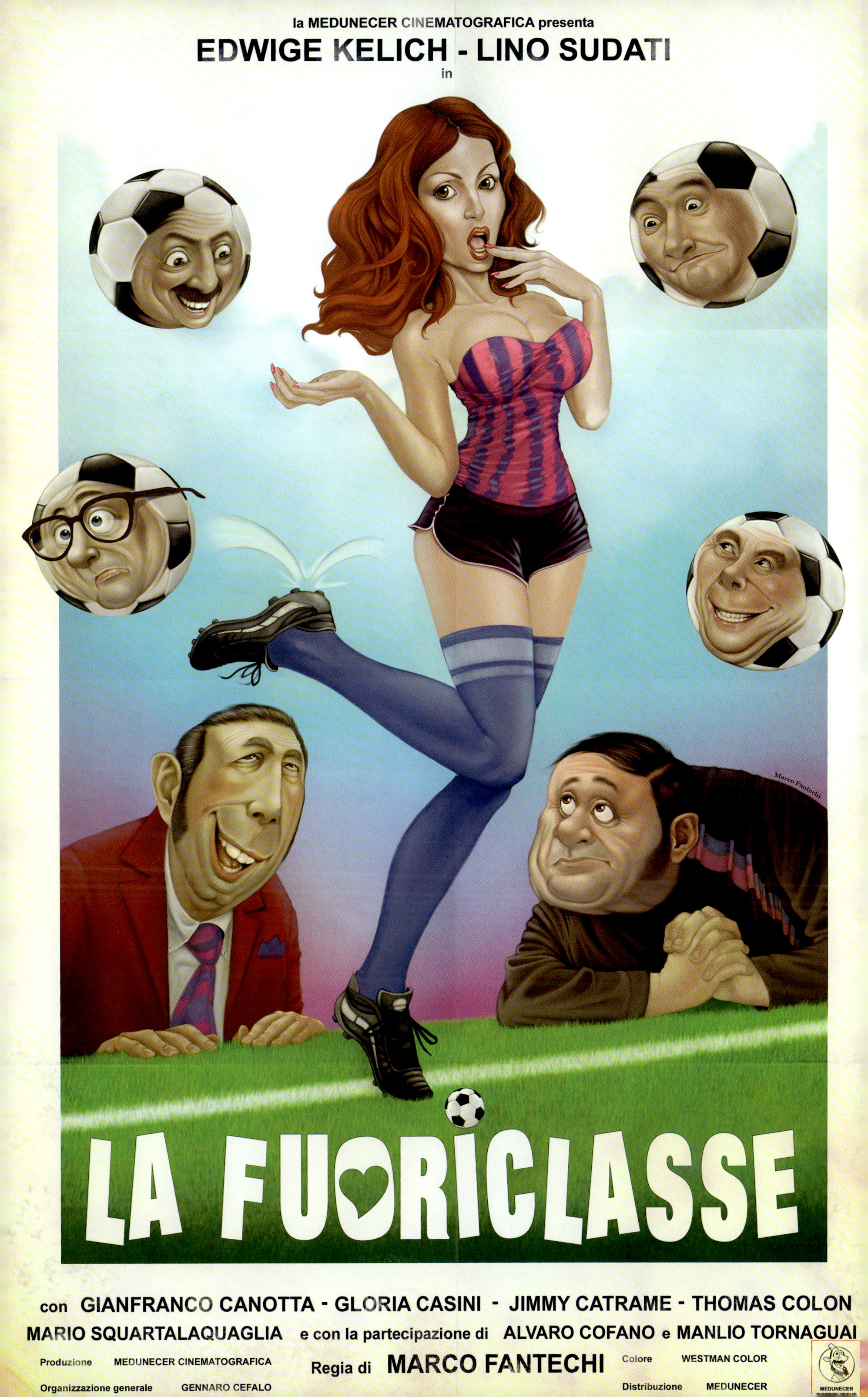

la MEDUNECER CINEMATOGRAFICA presenta

EDWIGE KELICH - LINO SUDATI

in

Marco Fantechi

LA FUORICLASSE

con **GIANFRANCO CANOTTA - GLORIA CASINI - JIMMY CATRAME - THOMAS COLON**
MARIO SQUARTALAQUAGLIA e con la partecipazione di **ALVARO COFANO** e **MANLIO TORNAGUAI**

Produzione MEDUNECER CINEMATOGRAFICA

Organizzazione generale GENNARO CEFALO

Regia di **MARCO FANTECHI**

Colore WESTMAN COLOR

Distribuzione MEDUNECER

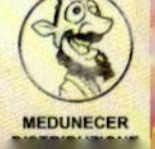

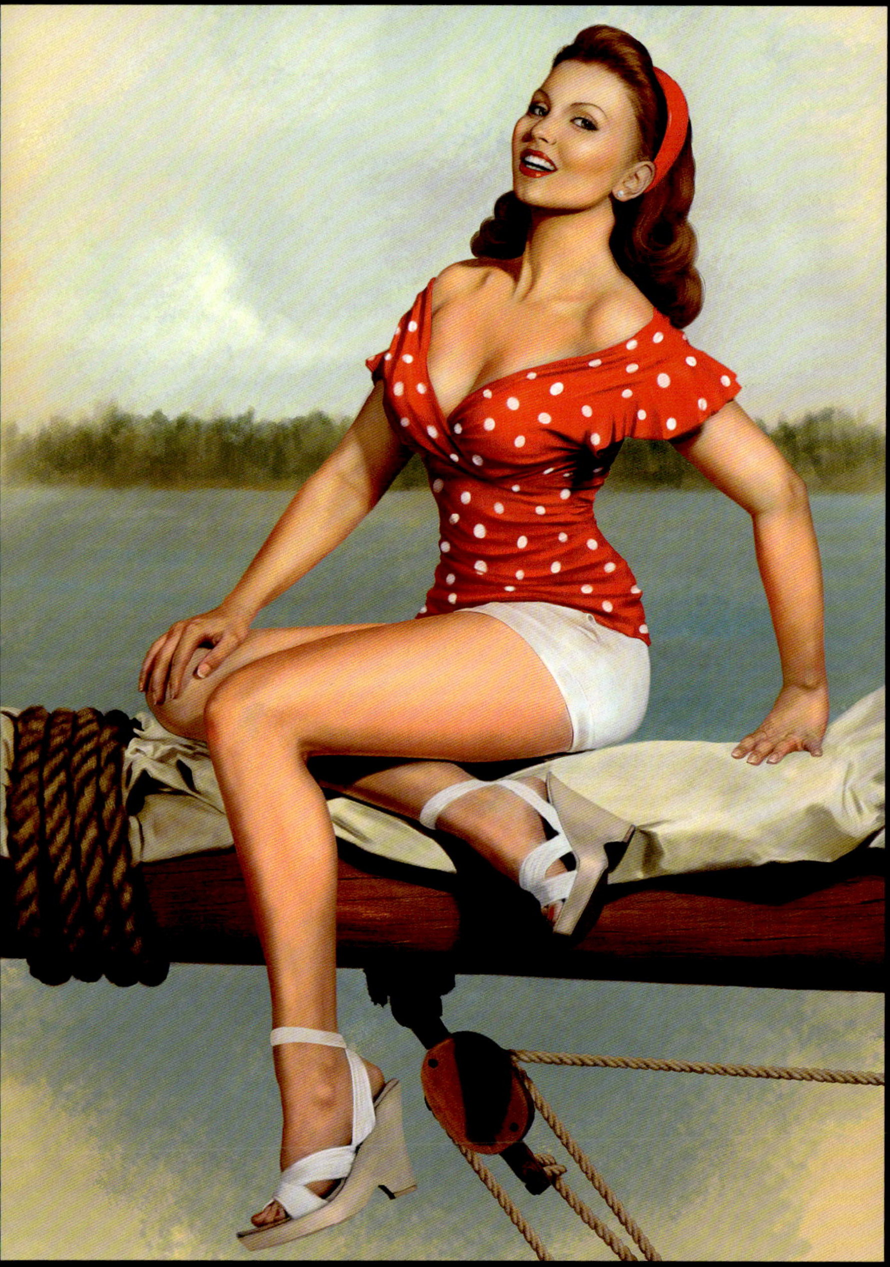

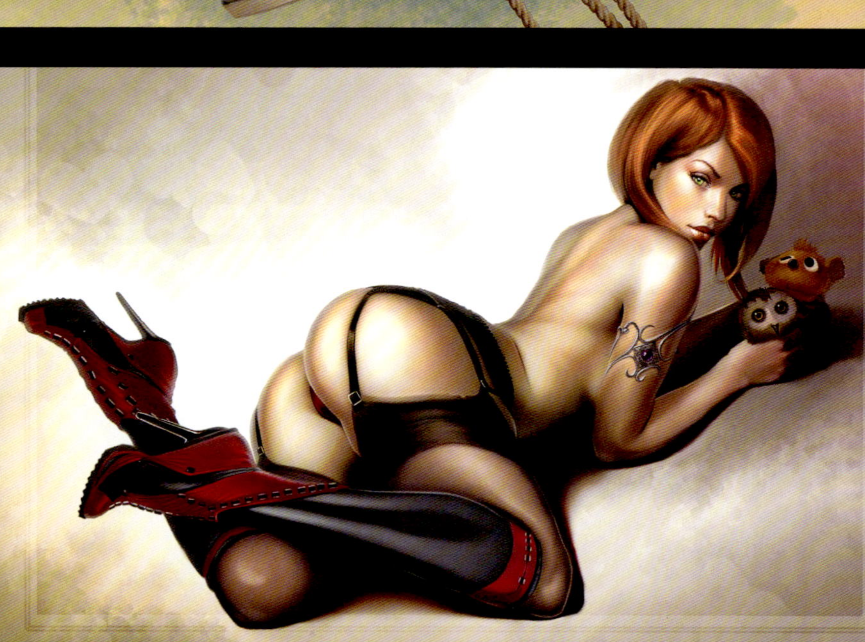

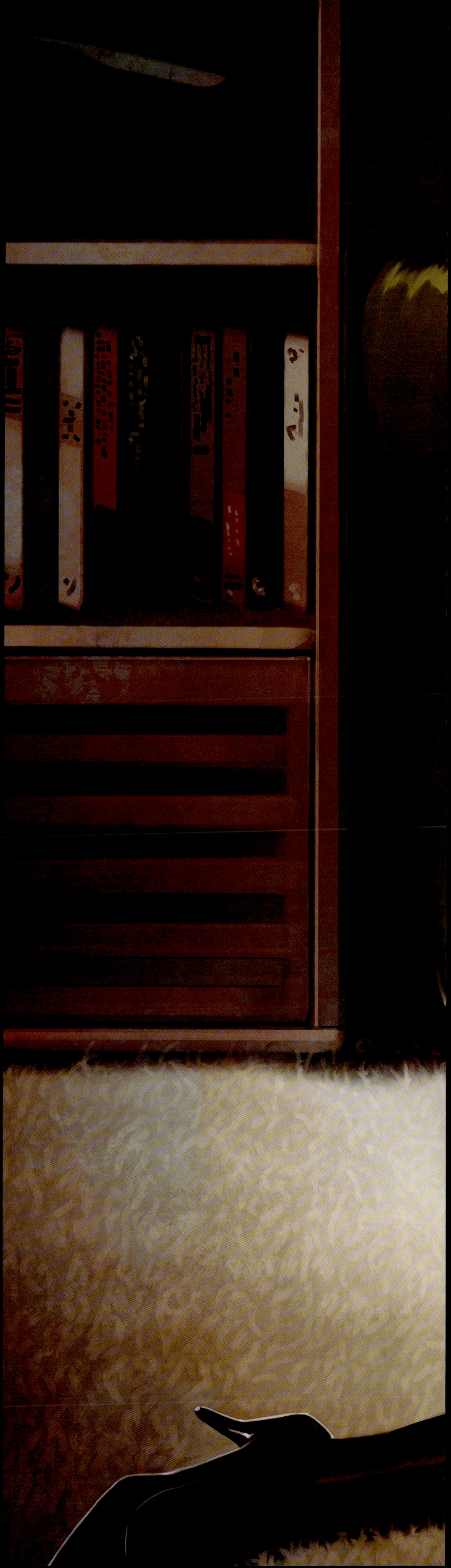

50s Pinup
Photoshop
Client: Photoshop Creative Magazine
Jeffrey M. de Guzman, THE PHILIPPINES
[top]

Virago
Photoshop
Client: R. Spaans
Andrew Hibner, USA
[above]

Gaming girl
Photoshop
Andrew Hibner,
USA
[right]

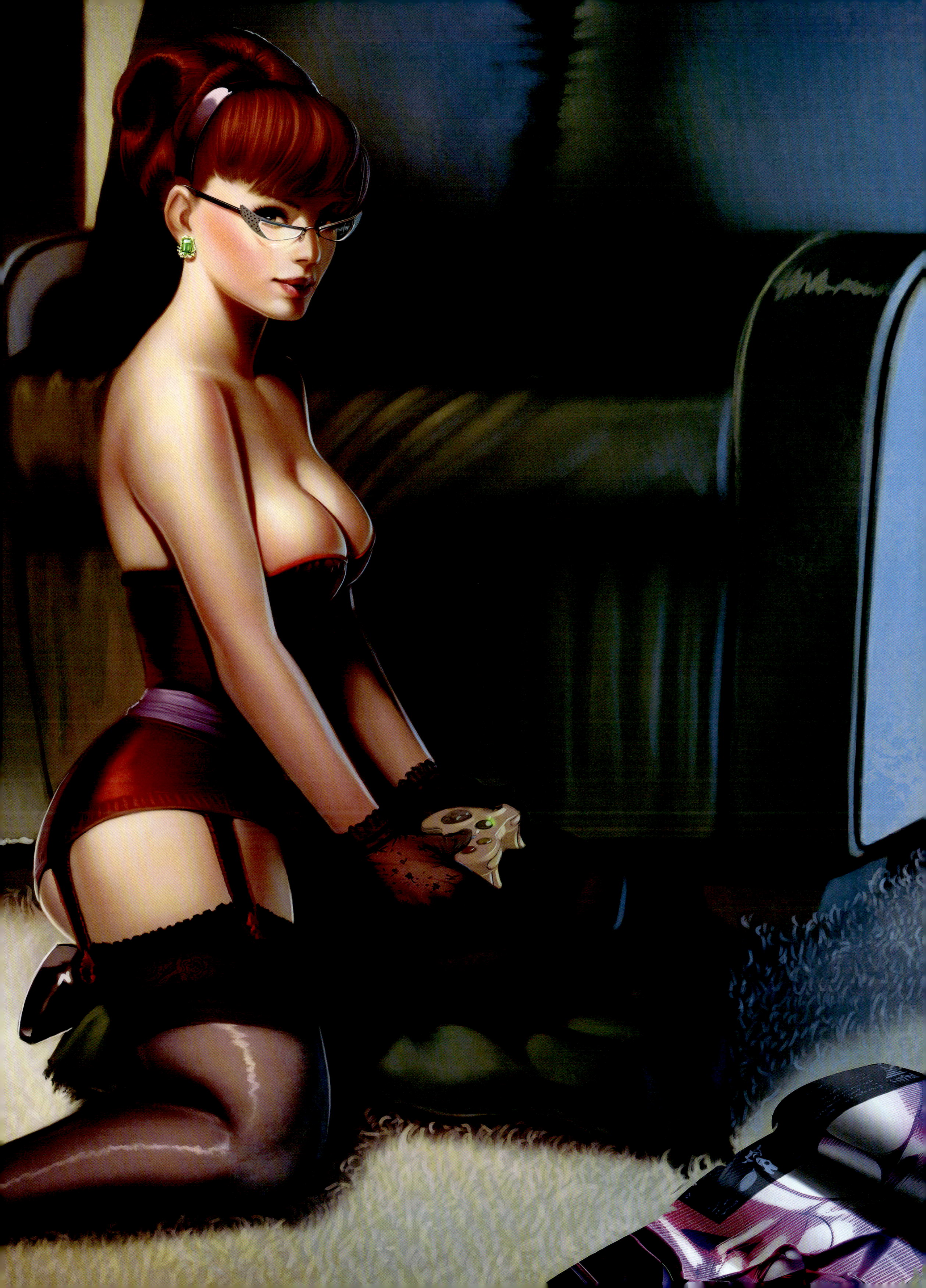

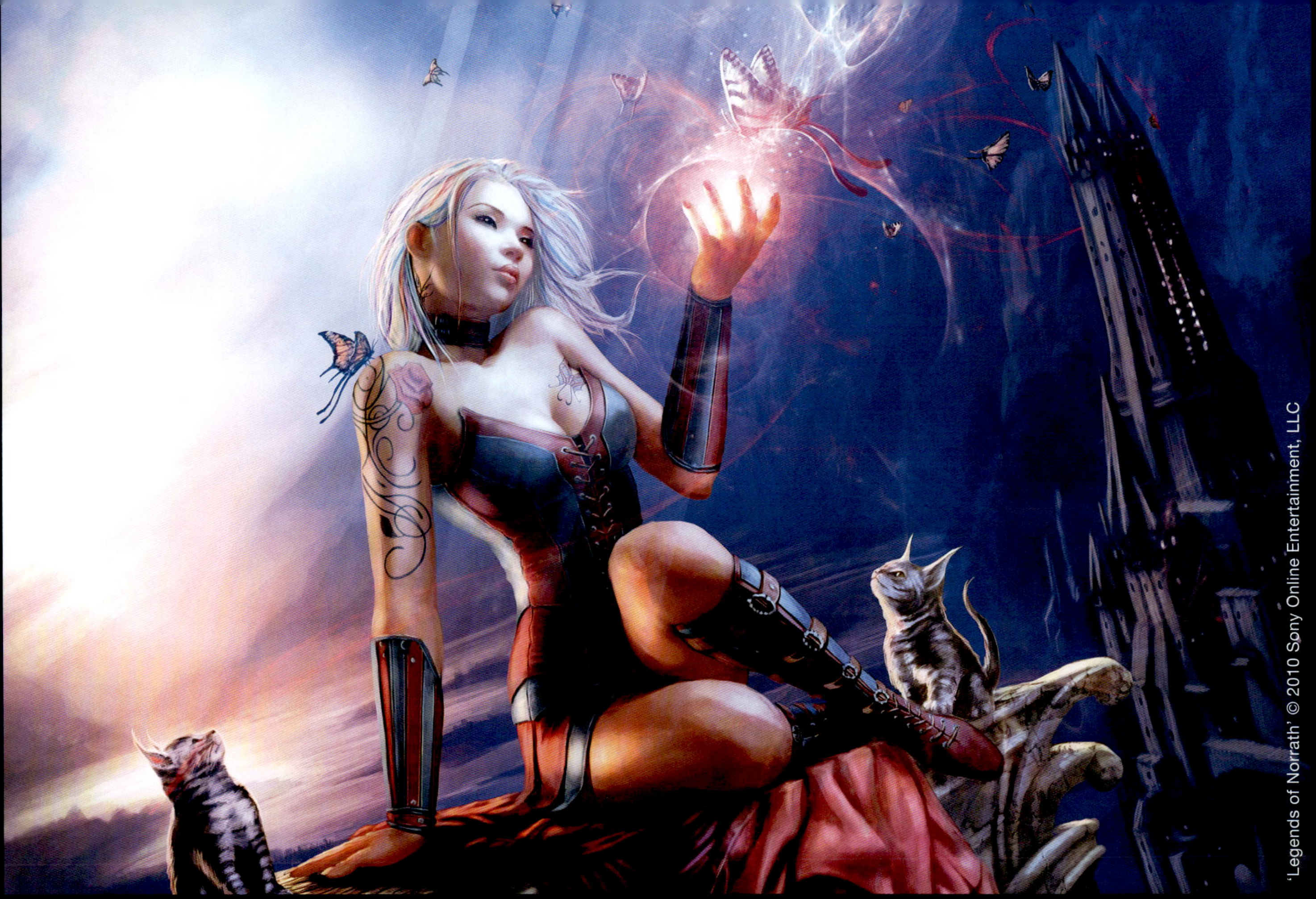

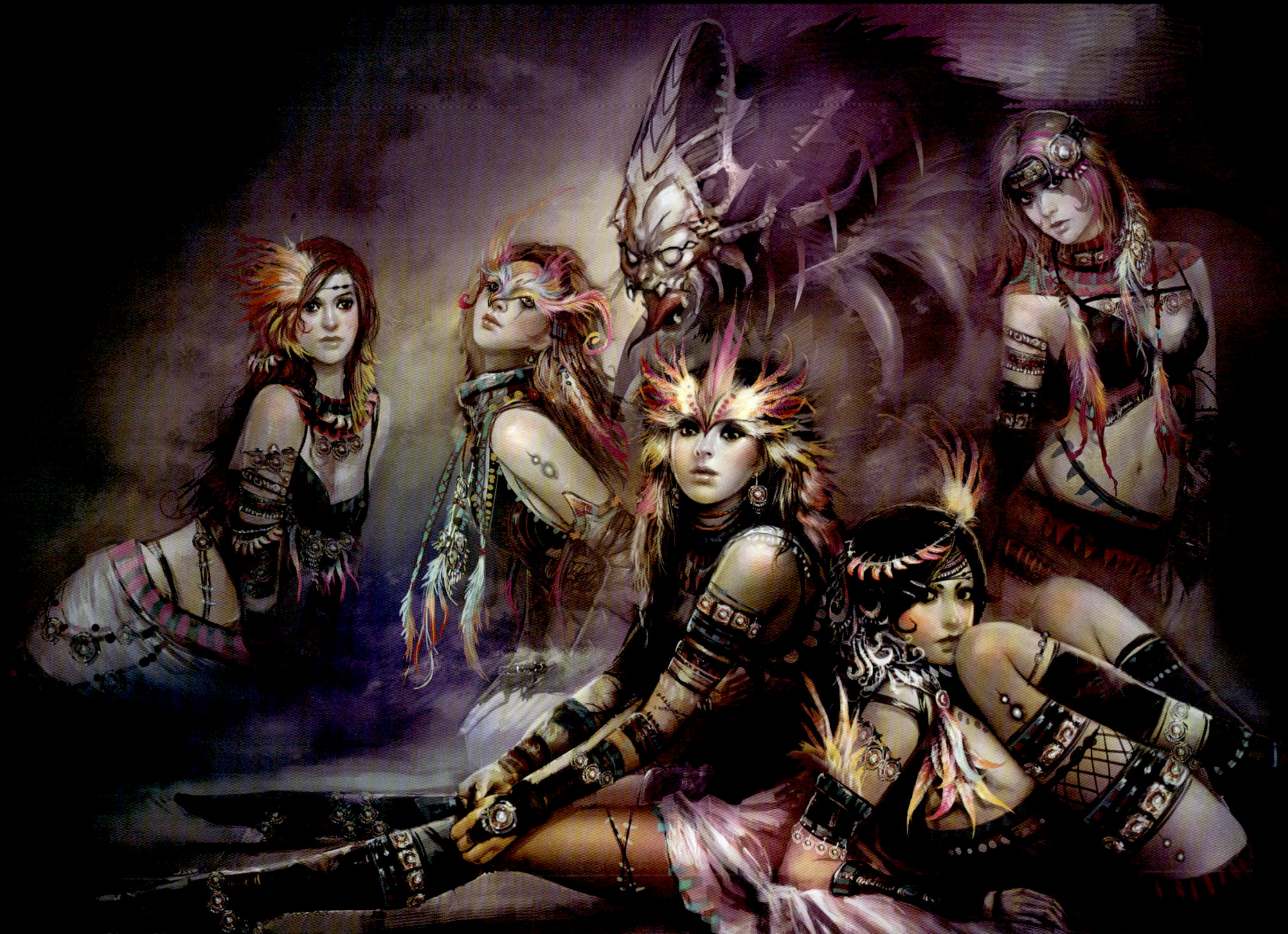

Legends of Norrath: Summoning Trainer
Photoshop
Art Director: Roger Chamberlain
Derek Herring, Sony Online Entertainment, LLC, USA
[left]

The Living Dead: Go, girl!
Photoshop
Client: Taylor Holloway
Gracjana Zielinska, POLAND
[right]

Feather
Photoshop
Huang DaHong, CHINA
[left]

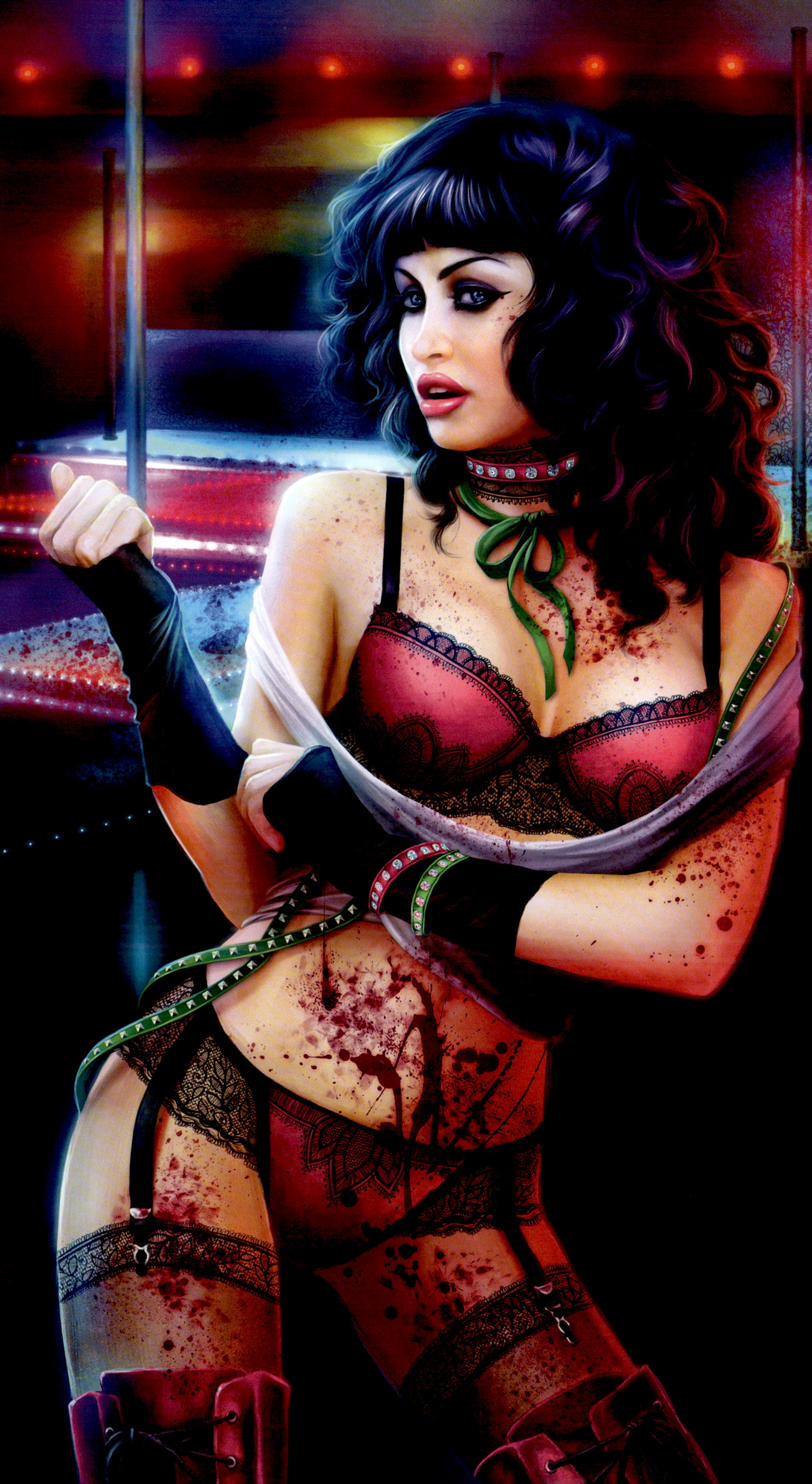

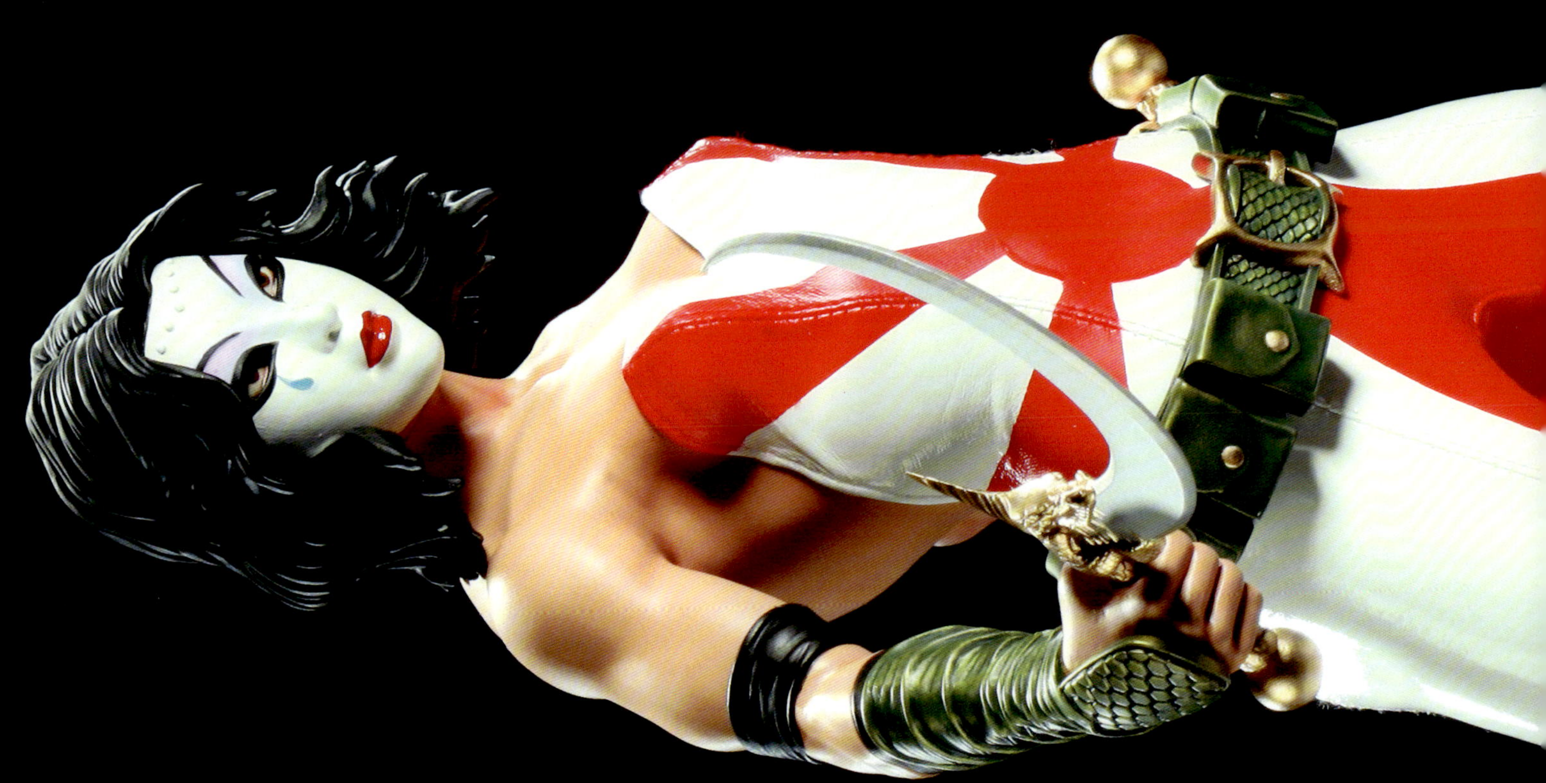

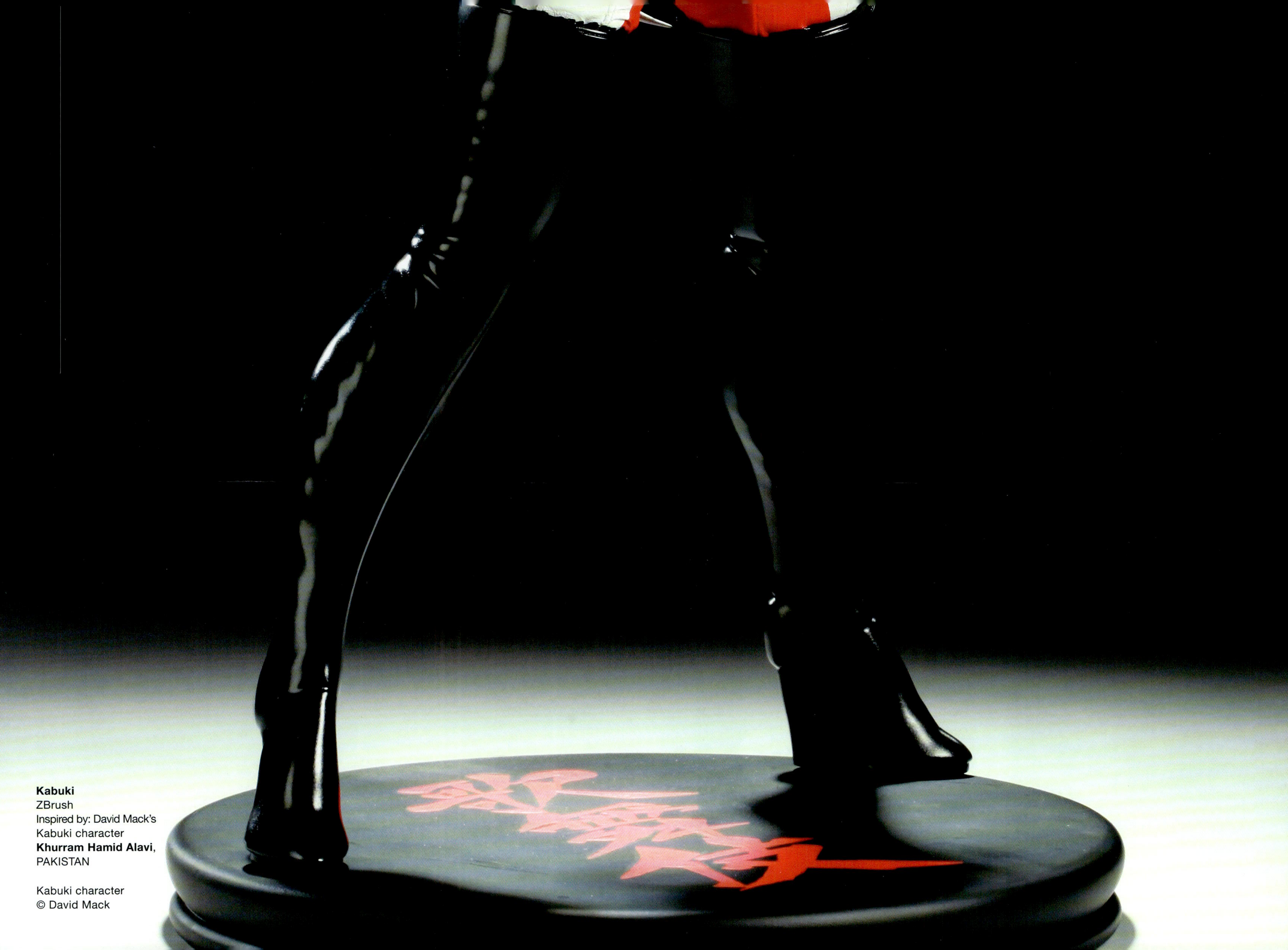

Kabuki
ZBrush
Inspired by: David Mack's
Kabuki character
Khurram Hamid Alavi, PAKISTAN

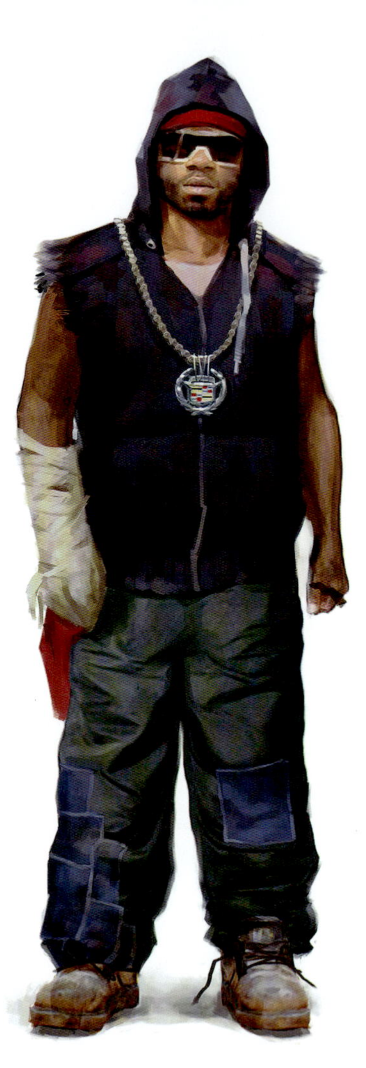
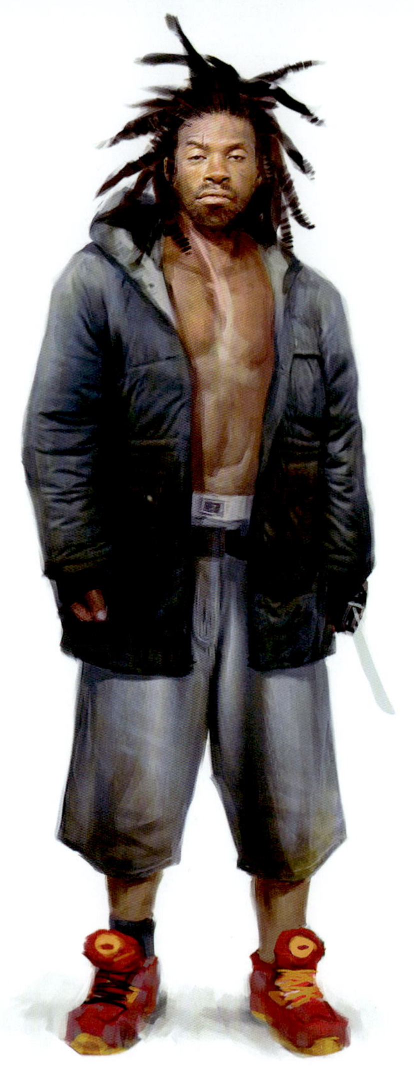
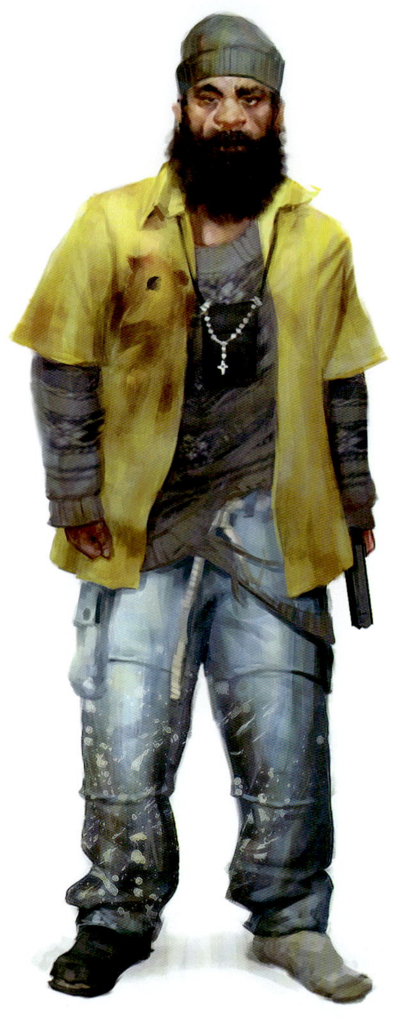
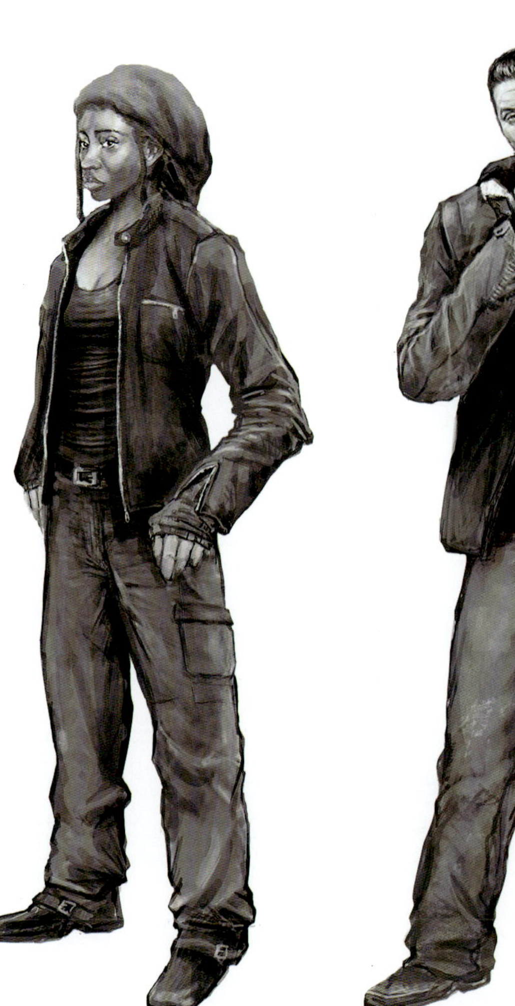
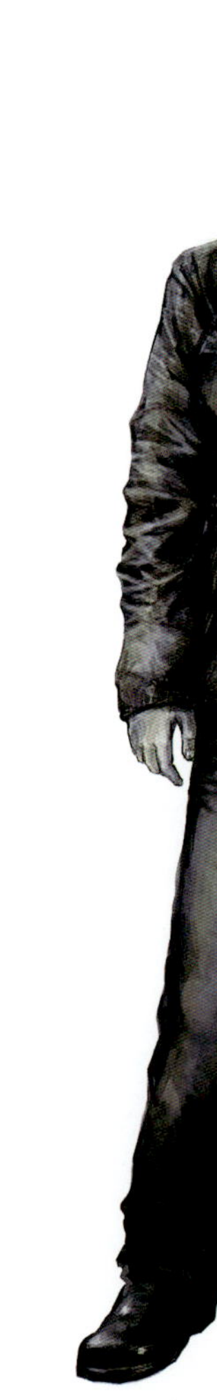

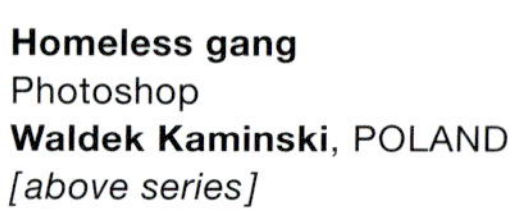

Homeless gang
Photoshop
Waldek Kaminski, POLAND
[above series]

La Loi Humaine: Shanna
Photoshop
Scriptwriter: Arnaud Tourangin
Cyril Terpent, FRANCE
[right]

La Loi Humaine: The drug dealer
Photoshop
Scriptwriter: Arnaud Tourangin
Cyril Terpent, FRANCE
[center right]

La Loi Humaine: Lilian
Photoshop
Scriptwriter: Arnaud Tourangin
Cyril Terpent, FRANCE
[far right]

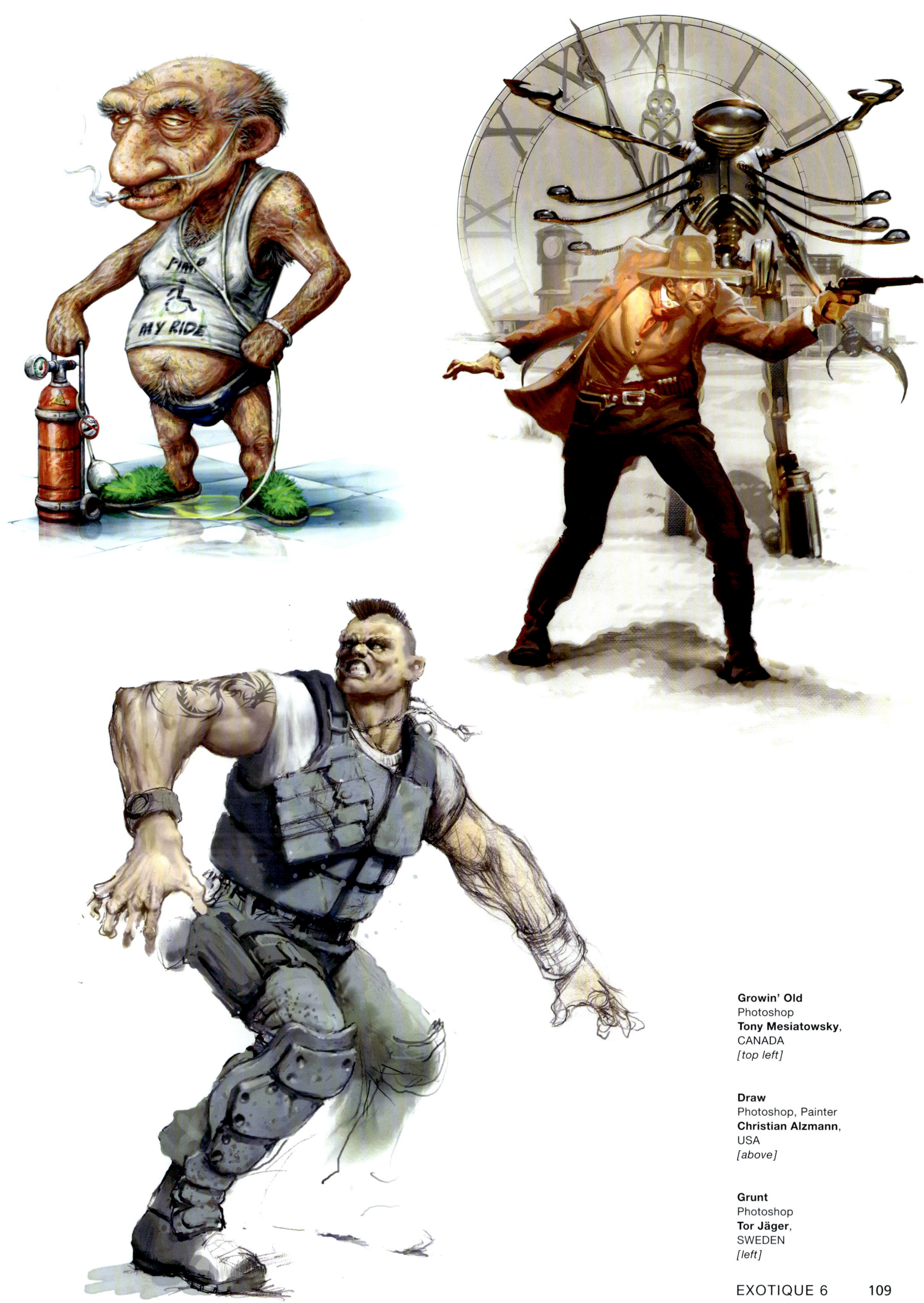

Growin' Old
Photoshop
Tony Mesiatowsky,
CANADA
[top left]

Draw
Photoshop, Painter
Christian Alzmann,
USA
[above]

Grunt
Photoshop
Tor Jäger,
SWEDEN
[left]

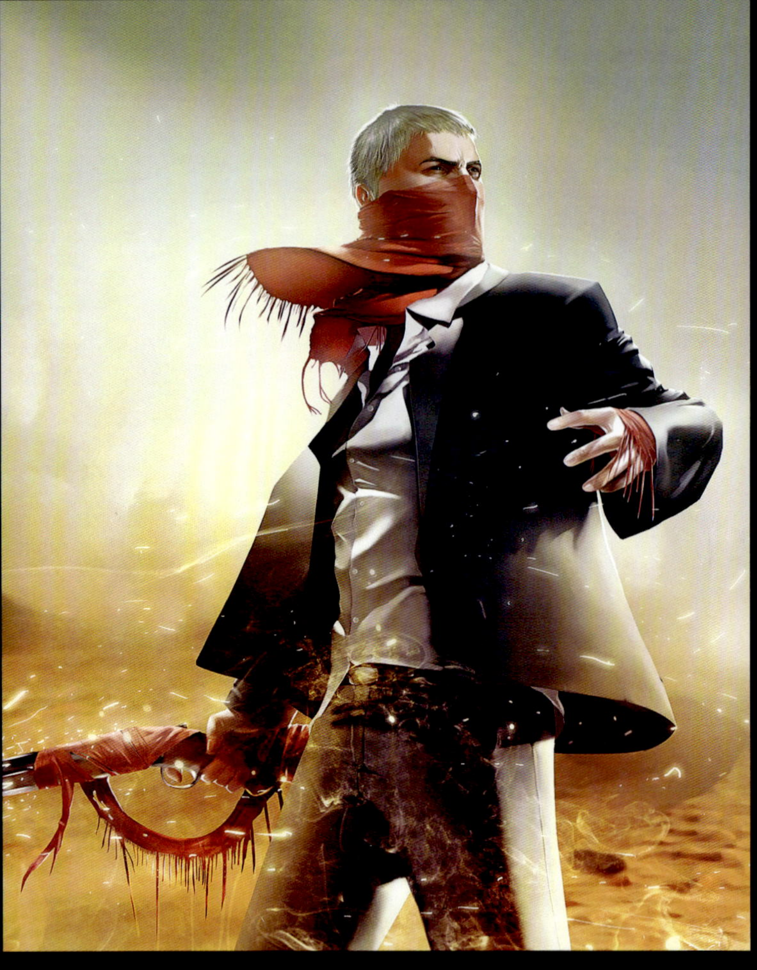

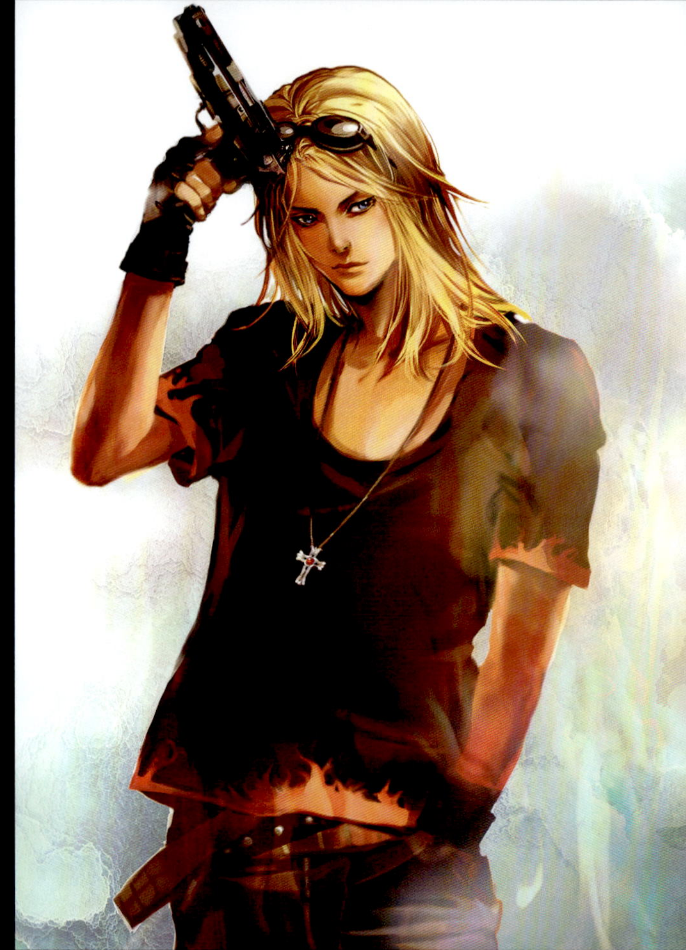

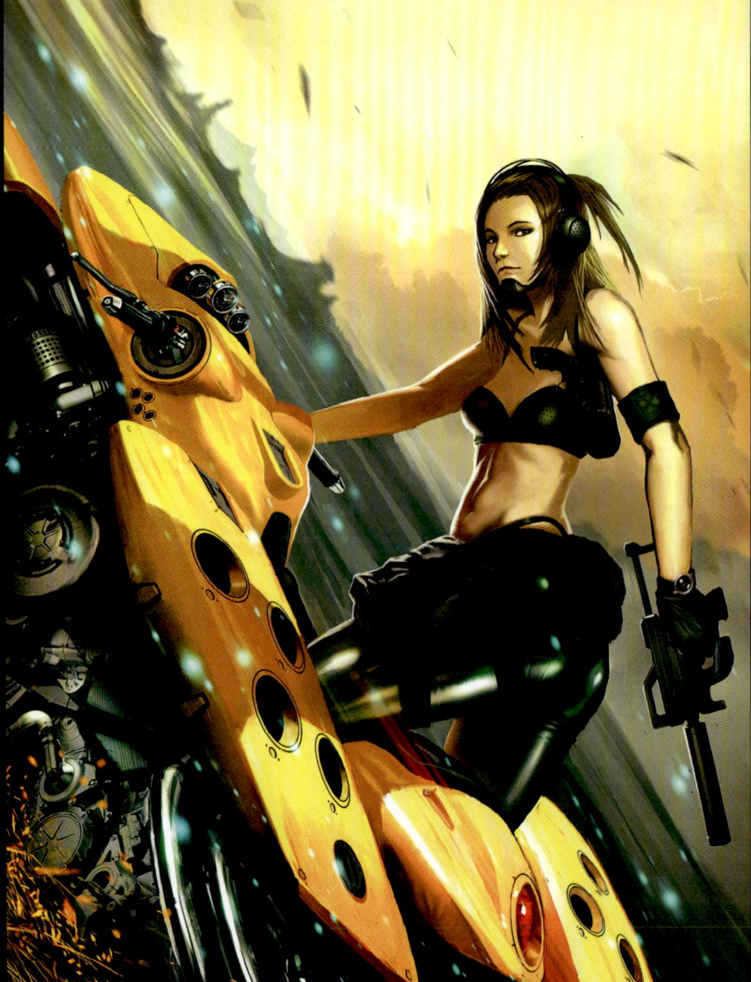

Desert Hunt
Photoshop
Mehran KHAN, Trango Interactive,
PAKISTAN
[top left]

Burn
Photoshop
Athena, GERMANY
[above]

Vertical Rising
Photoshop
Hoi Mun Tham, Passion Fruits
Animation, MALAYSIA
[left]

Guild Wars 2: Sniper
Photoshop
Client: ArenaNet
Horia Dociu, USA
[right]

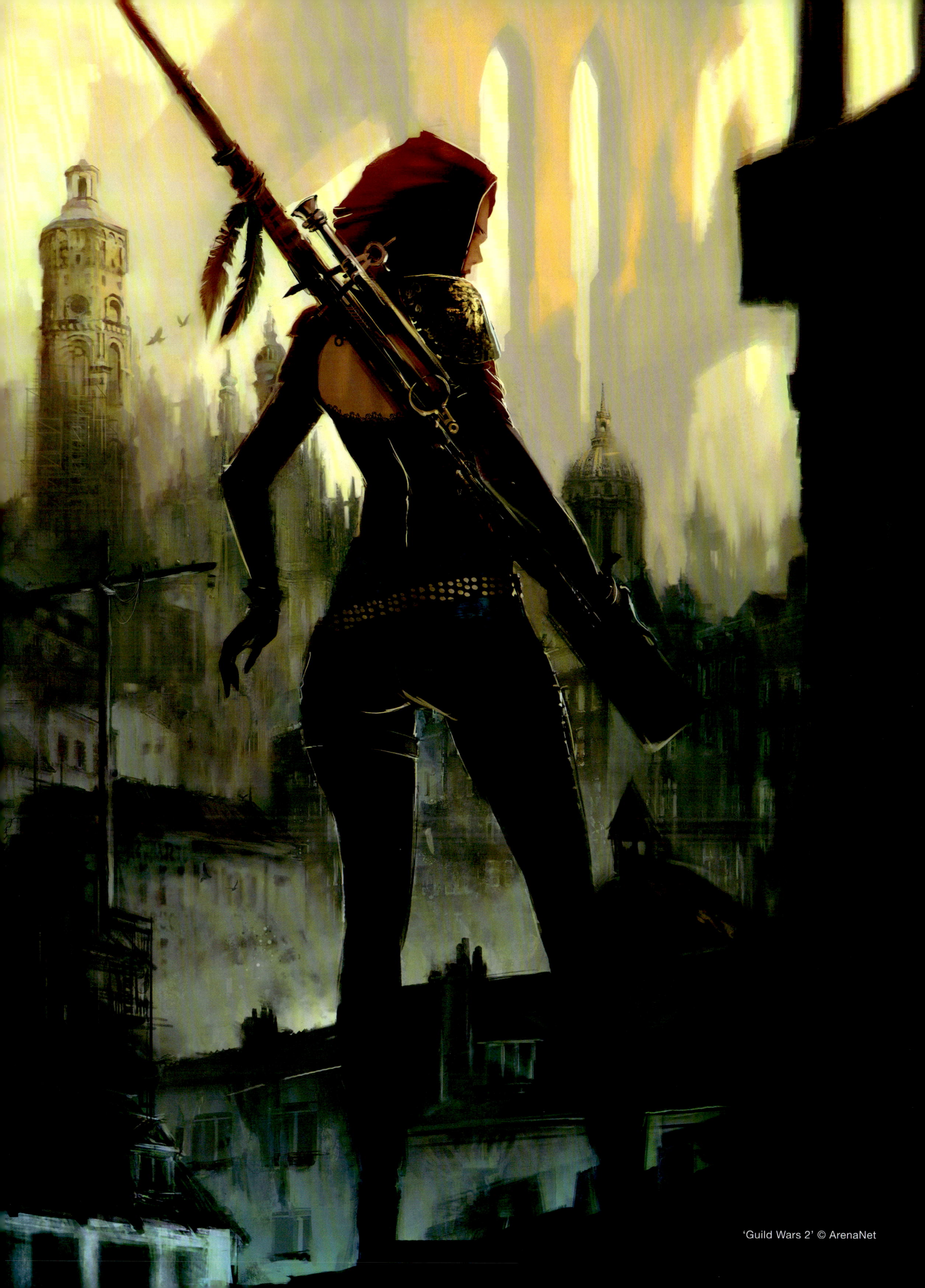

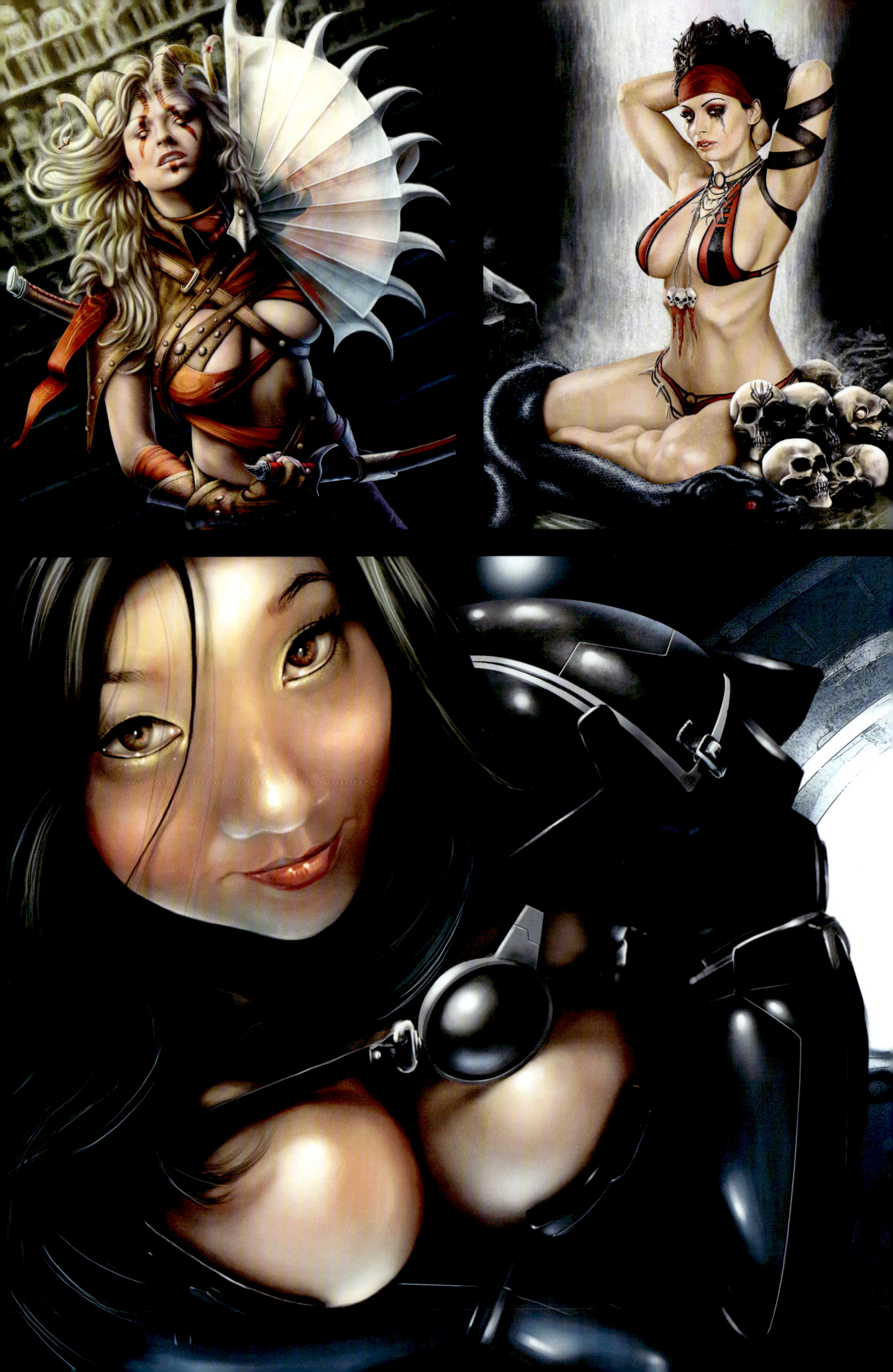

Reflections
Painter, Photoshop
Model: Veronika Kotlajic
Tiziano Baracchi, ITALY
[far left]

Demon Of The Lake 3
Photoshop
Esau Murga, USA
[left]

Uterus
Photoshop
Yigit Koroglu, TURKEY
[right]

Akina in Gas Station
Photoshop
Michel Victor Oliveira, BRAZIL
[left]

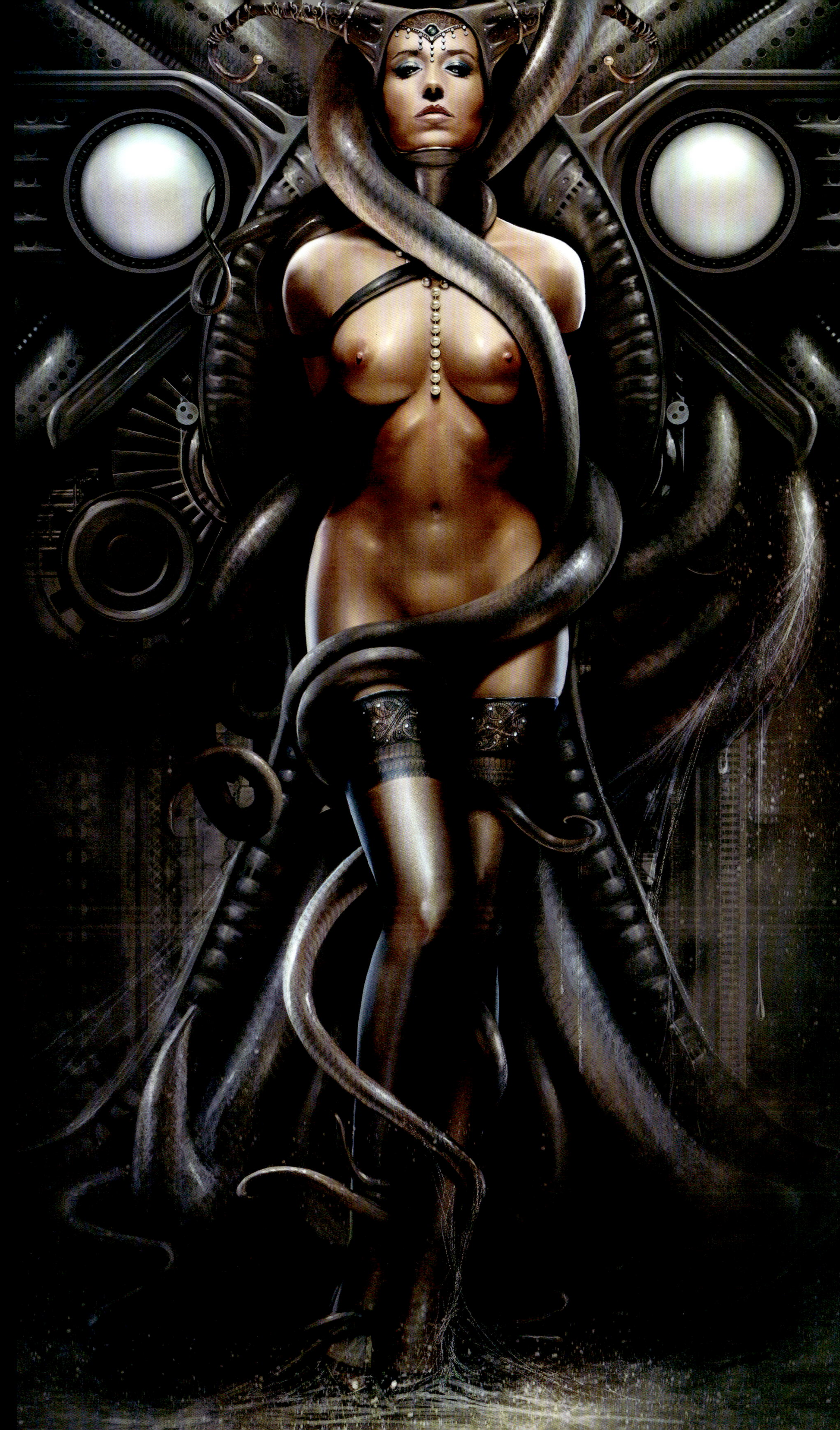

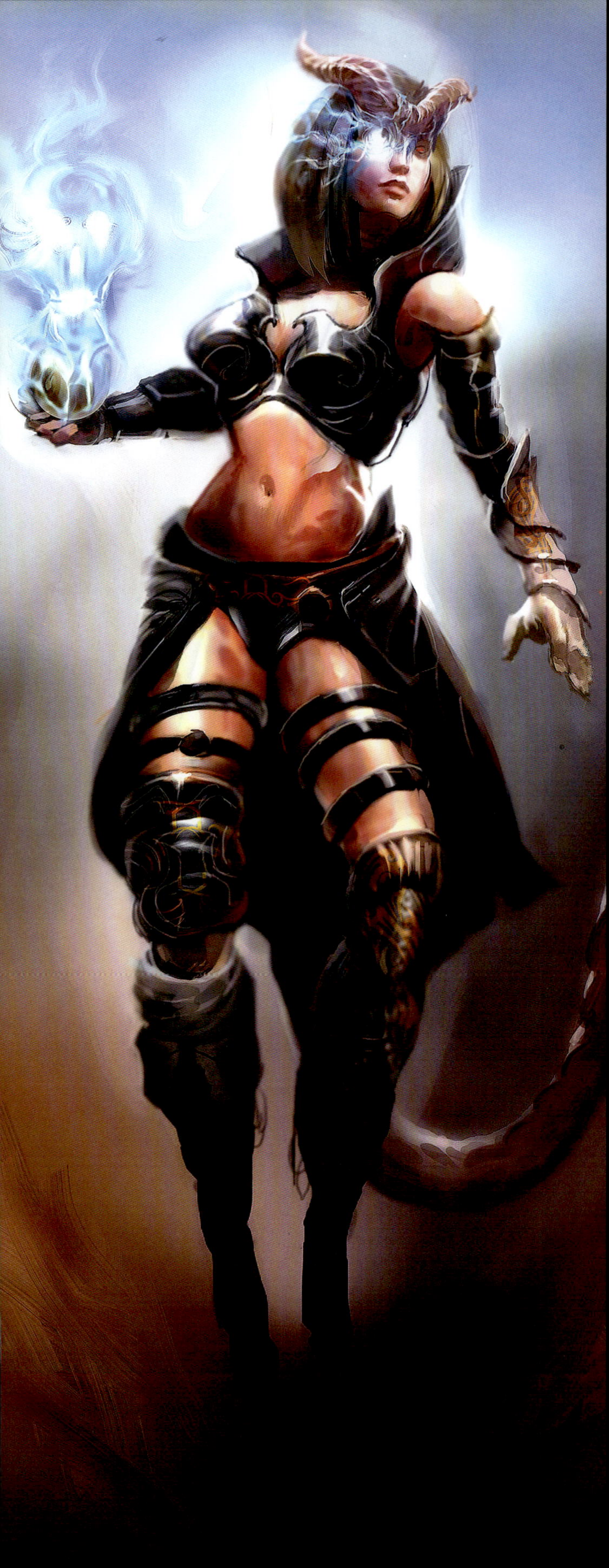

Dungeons & Dragons: Tieflings (Infernal eye)
Photoshop
Client: Wizards Of The Coast

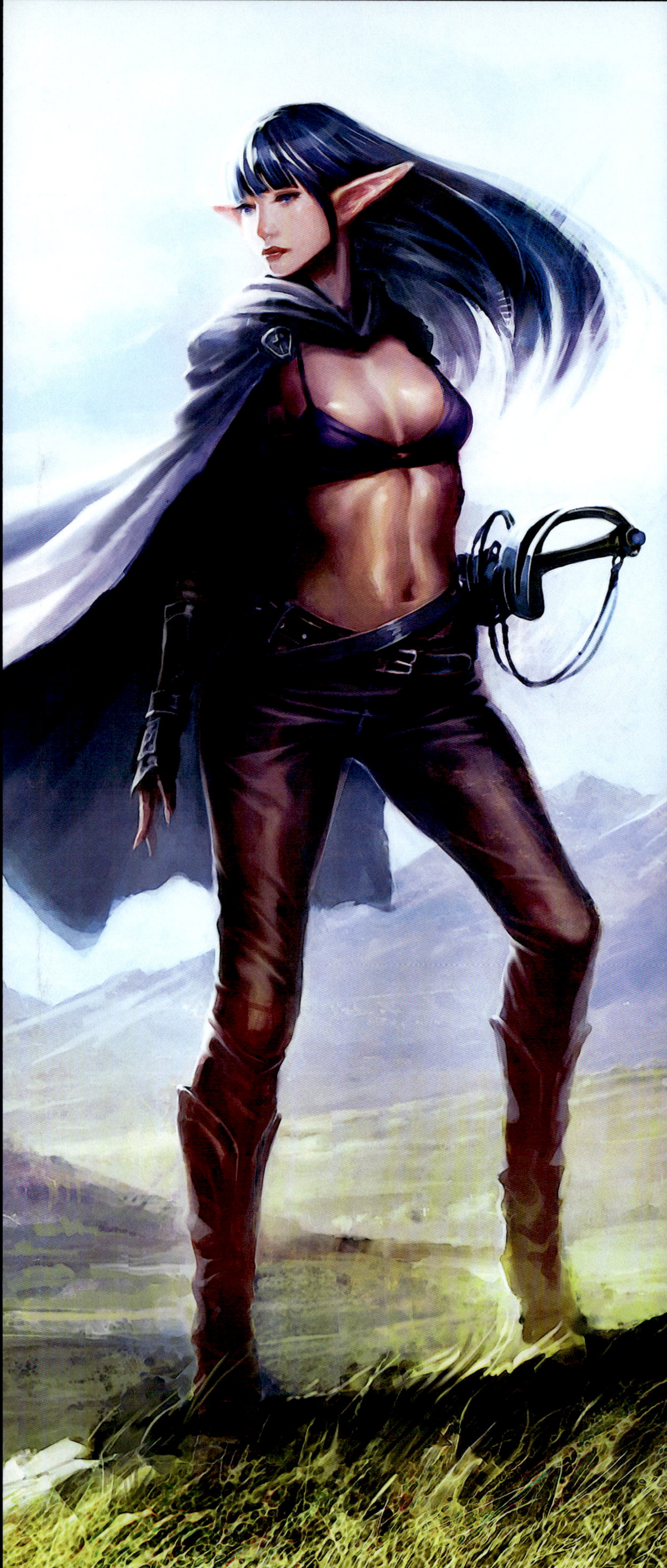

Elven seeker
Photoshop
Shuichi Wada, JAPAN

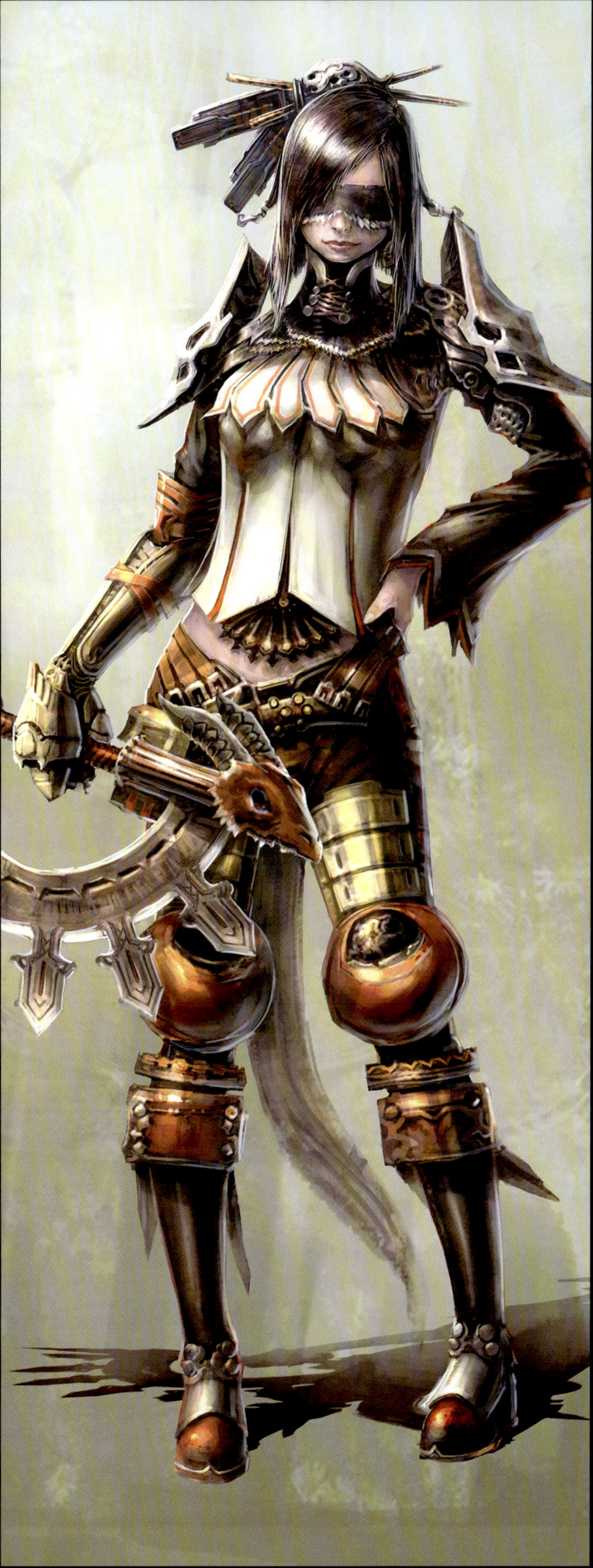

Illidan
Photoshop
zao li, CHINA

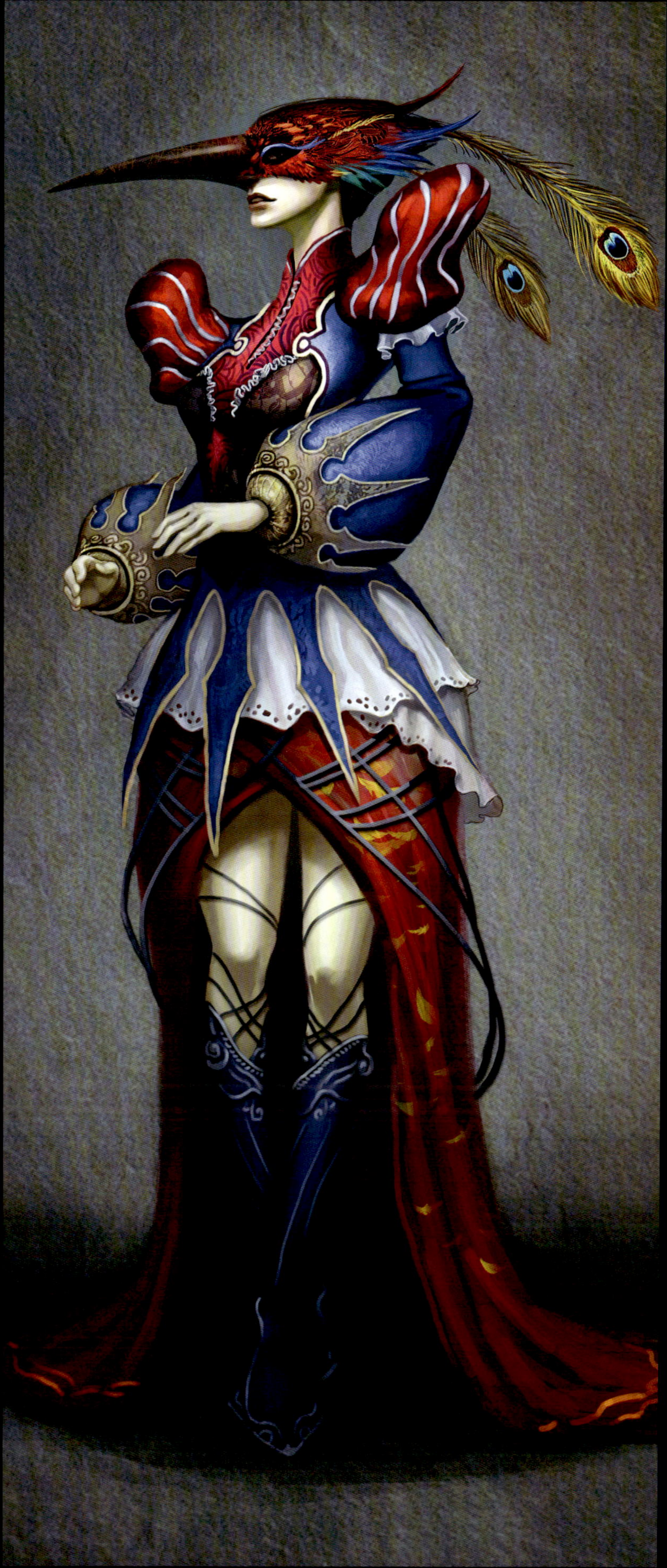

Courtier
Photoshop
Ben Ho, GREAT BRITAIN

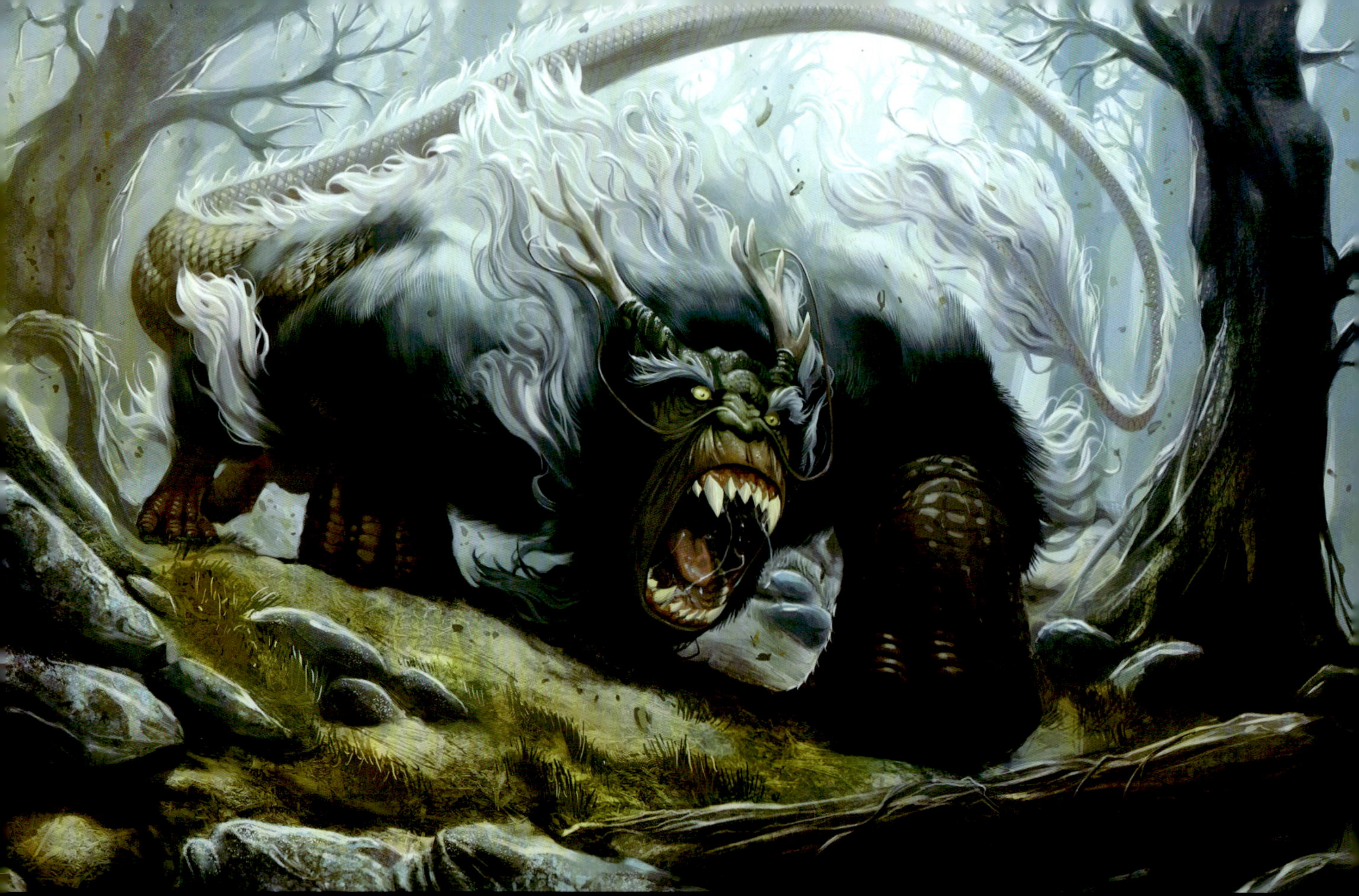

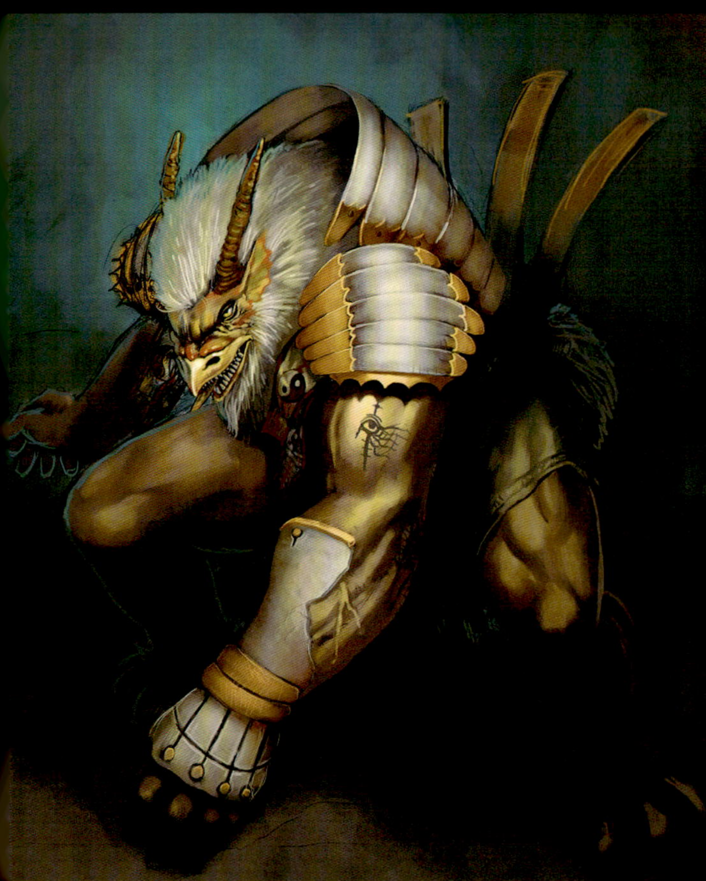

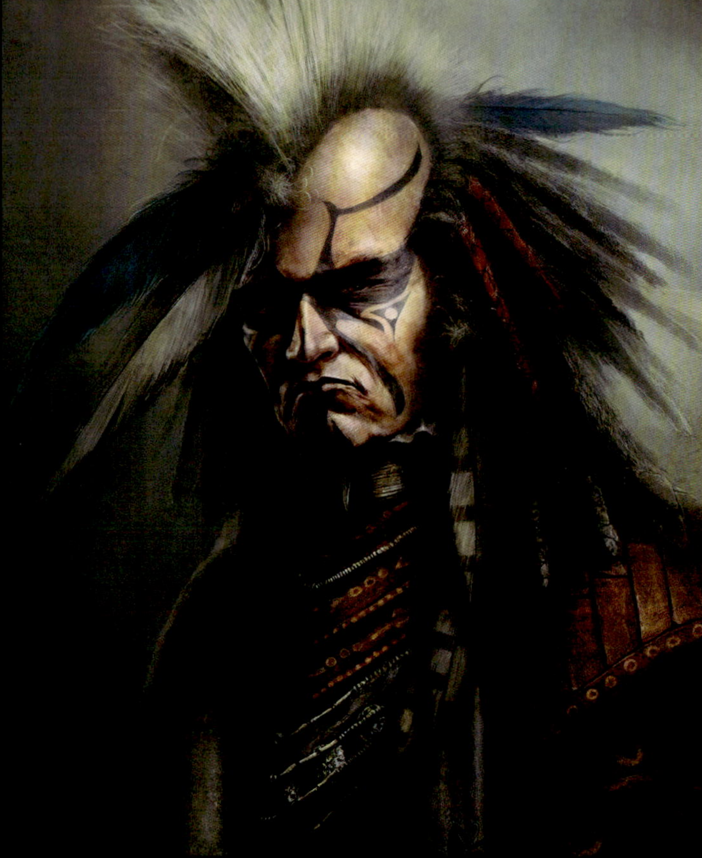

Dragorilla
Photoshop
Jon Bosco,
BRAZIL
[top]

Birdman
Photoshop
Huang DaHong,
CHINA
[above]

General
Photoshop
Artem Borisov,
RUSSIA
[above]

PoxNora: Stitched Concealer
Photoshop
Art Director: Bryan Rypkowski
Client: Sony Online Entertainment, LLC
Jakub Kasper, POLAND *[right]*

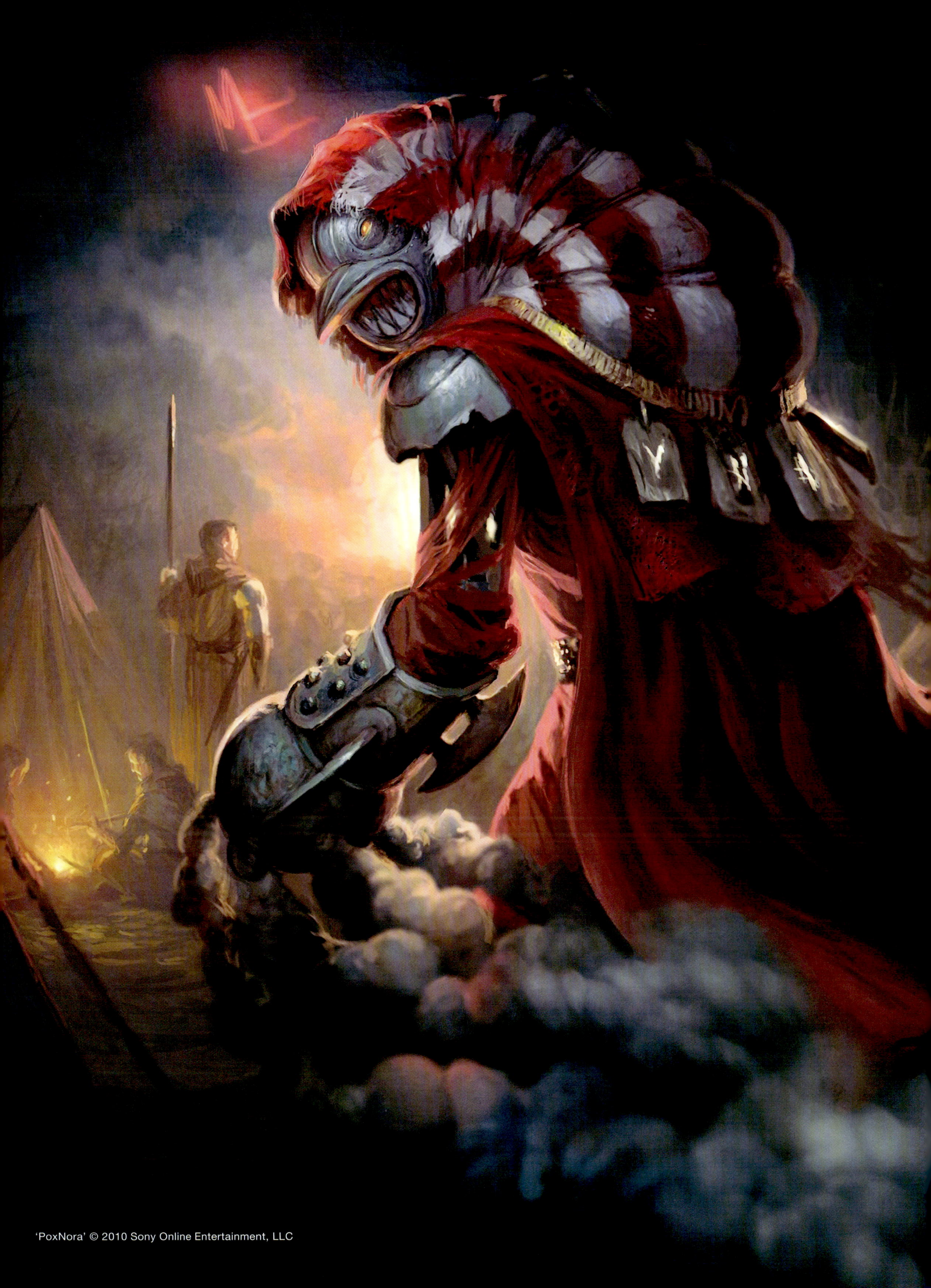

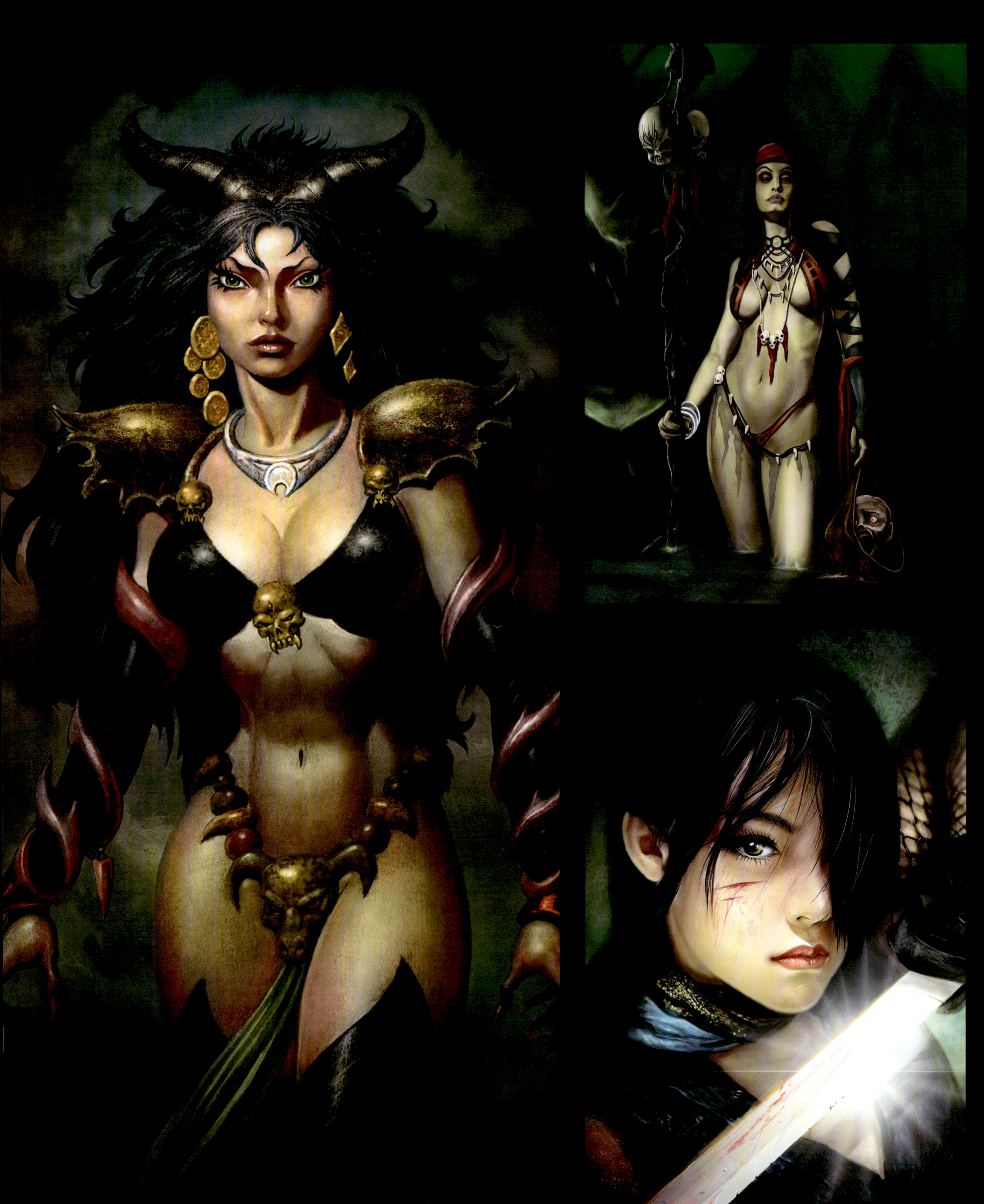

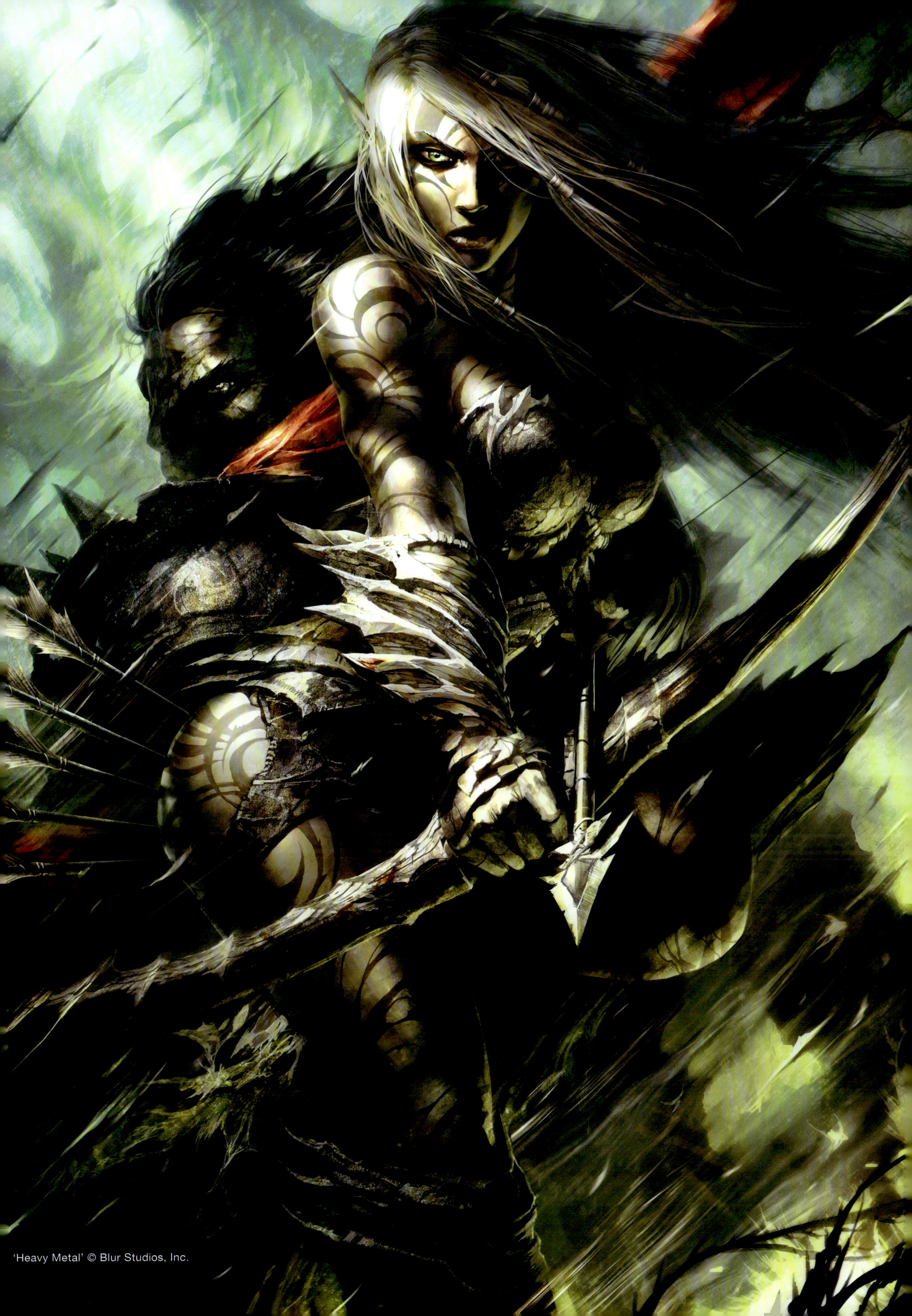

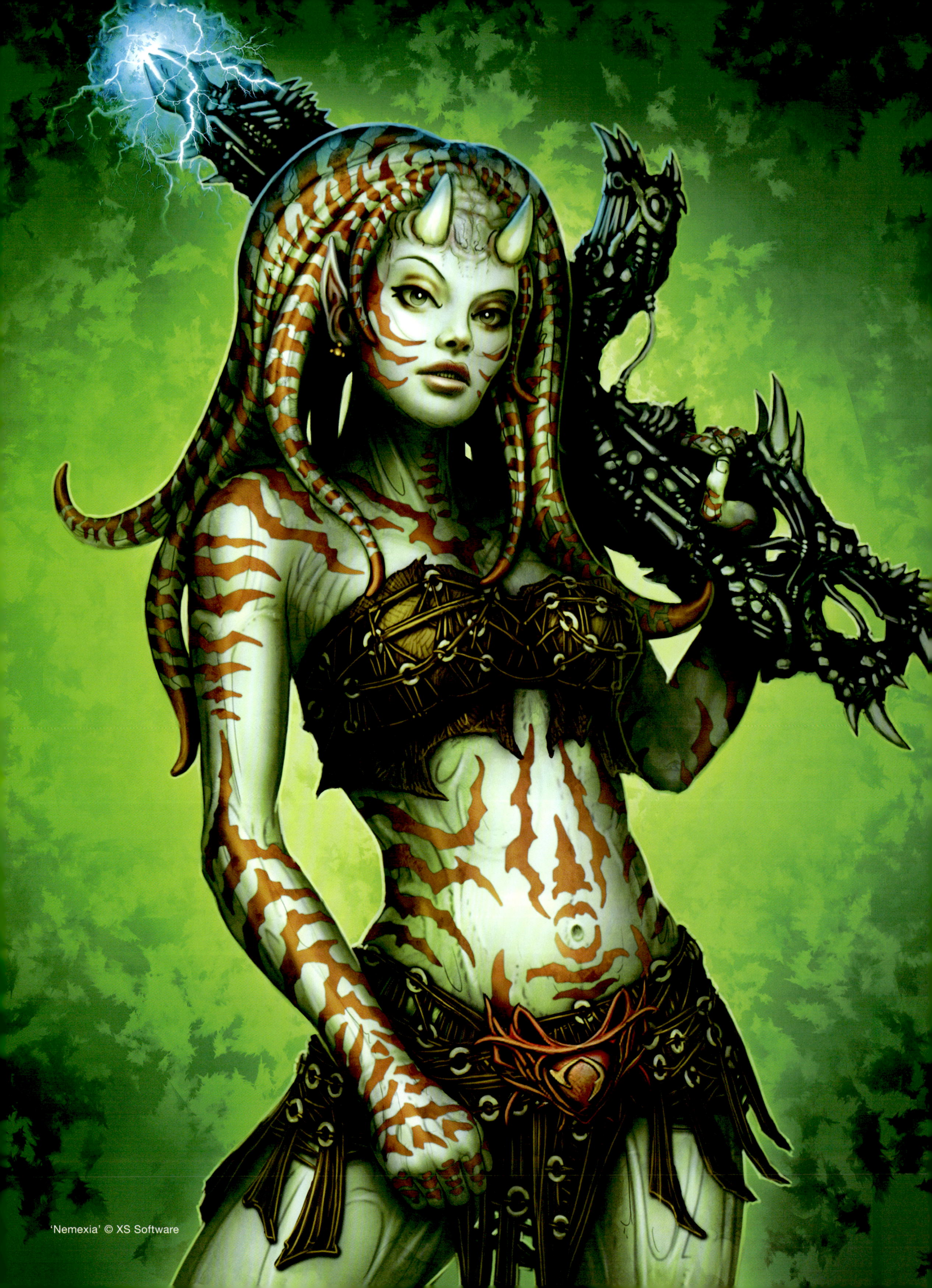

Nemexia: Noxis
Photoshop
Client: XS Software
Kerem Beyit,
TURKEY
[left]

Daemon
Photoshop
Amélie Hutt, USA
[right]

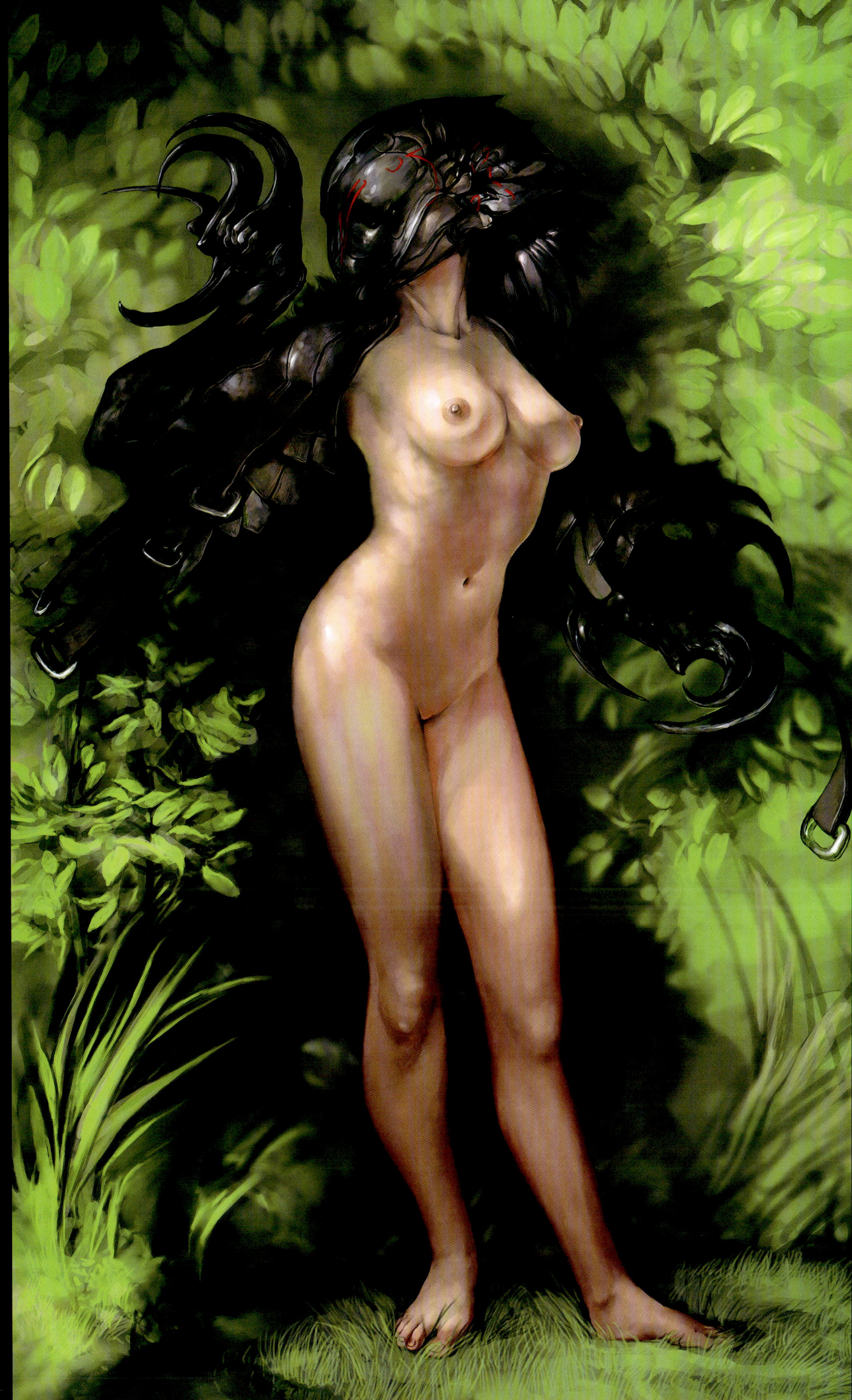

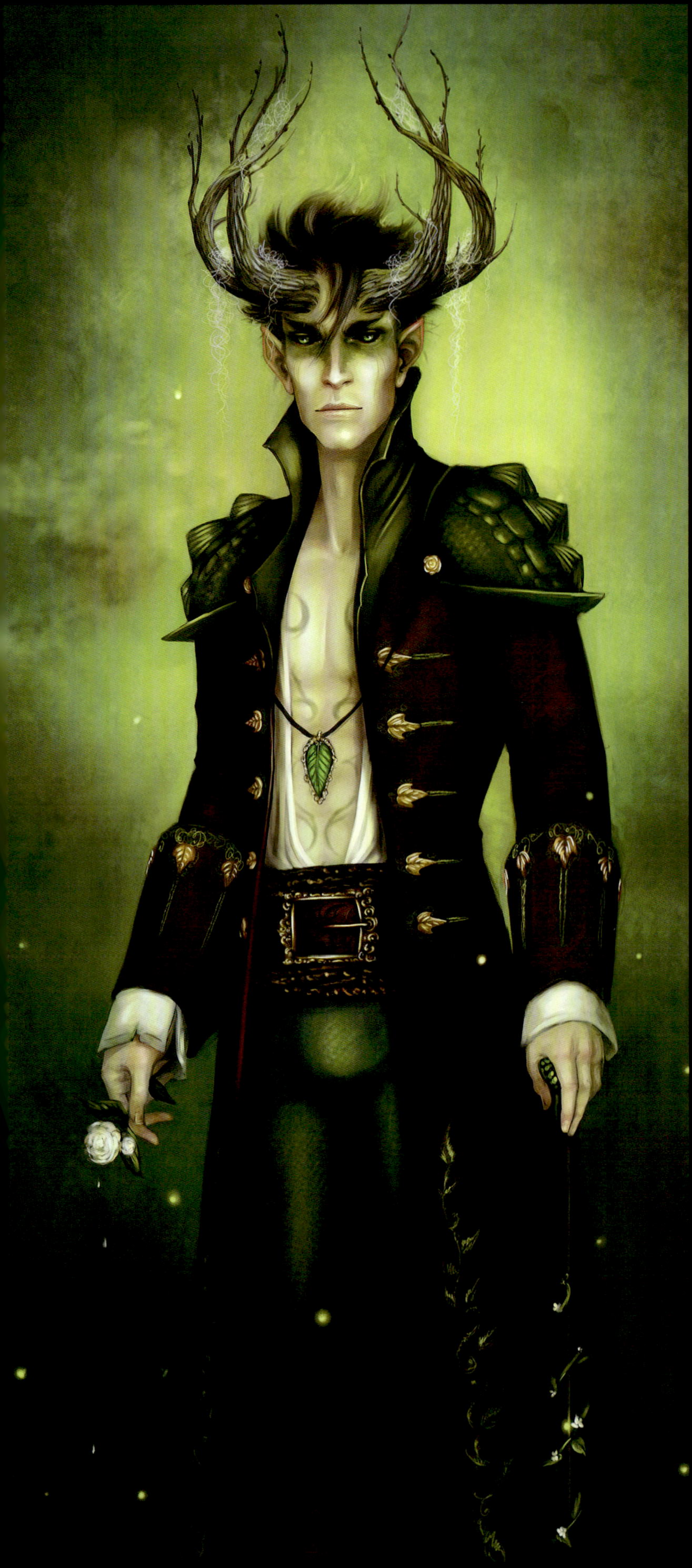

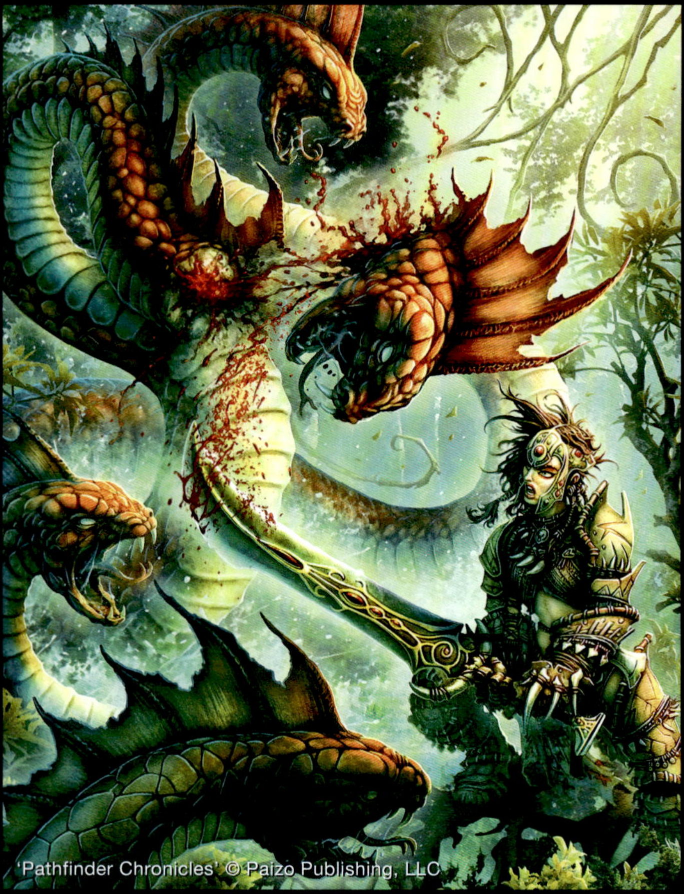

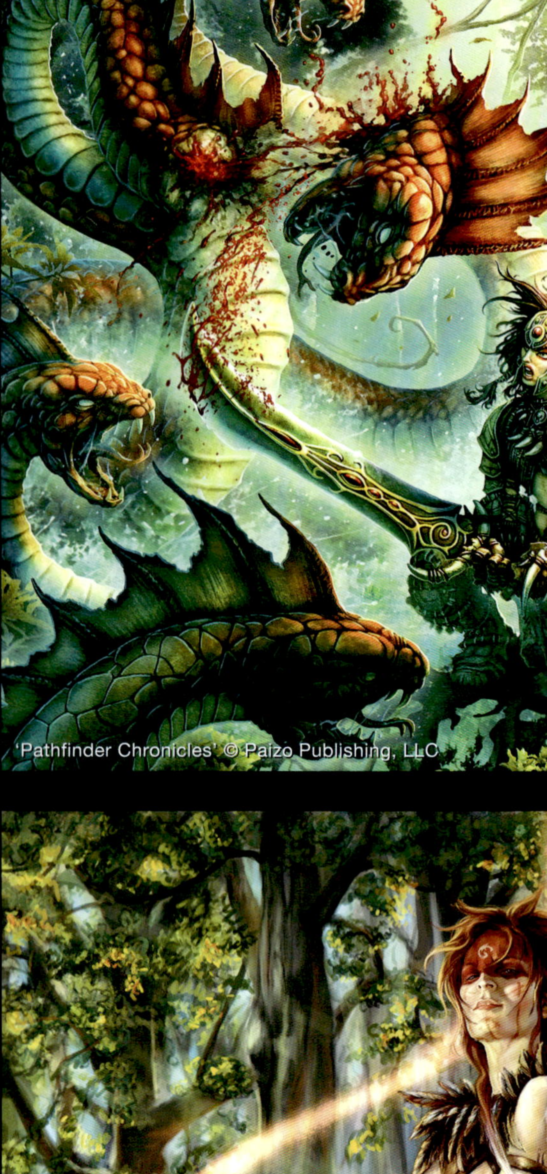
'Pathfinder Chronicles' © Paizo Publishing, LLC

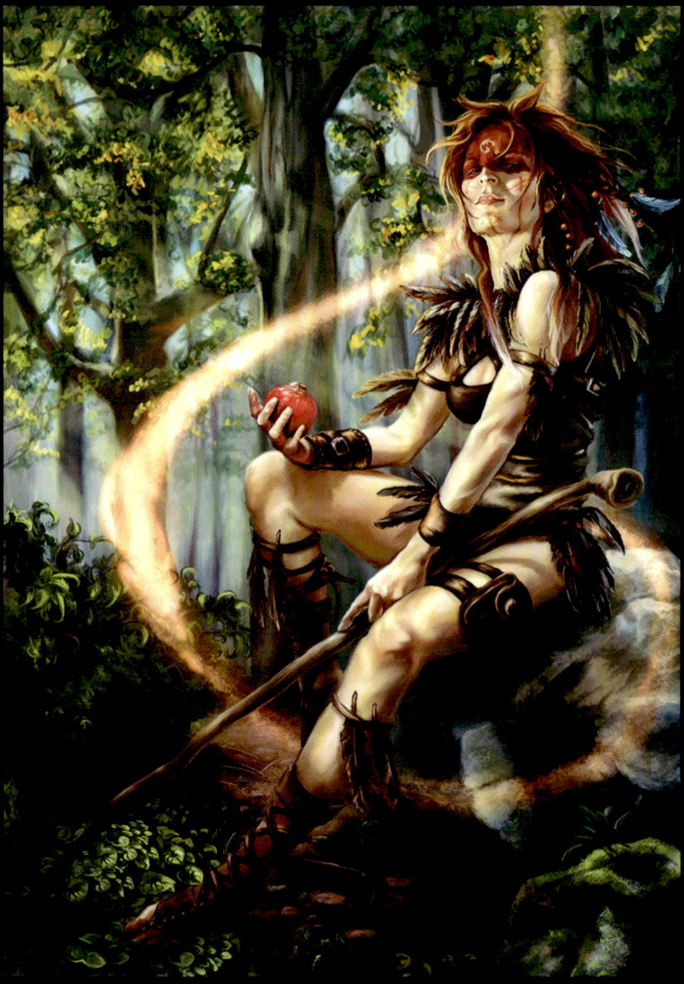

Oberon
Painter
Melissa Findley, USA
[above]

Pathfinder Chronicles: Classic Treasures Cover
Photoshop
Client: Paizo Publishing, LLC
Kerem Beyit, TURKEY *[top right]*

Fox Shaman
Photoshop
Zsuzsa Tasi, HUNGARY
[above]

Queen of the Drowned
Photoshop
Caroline Laplante, CANADA
[right]

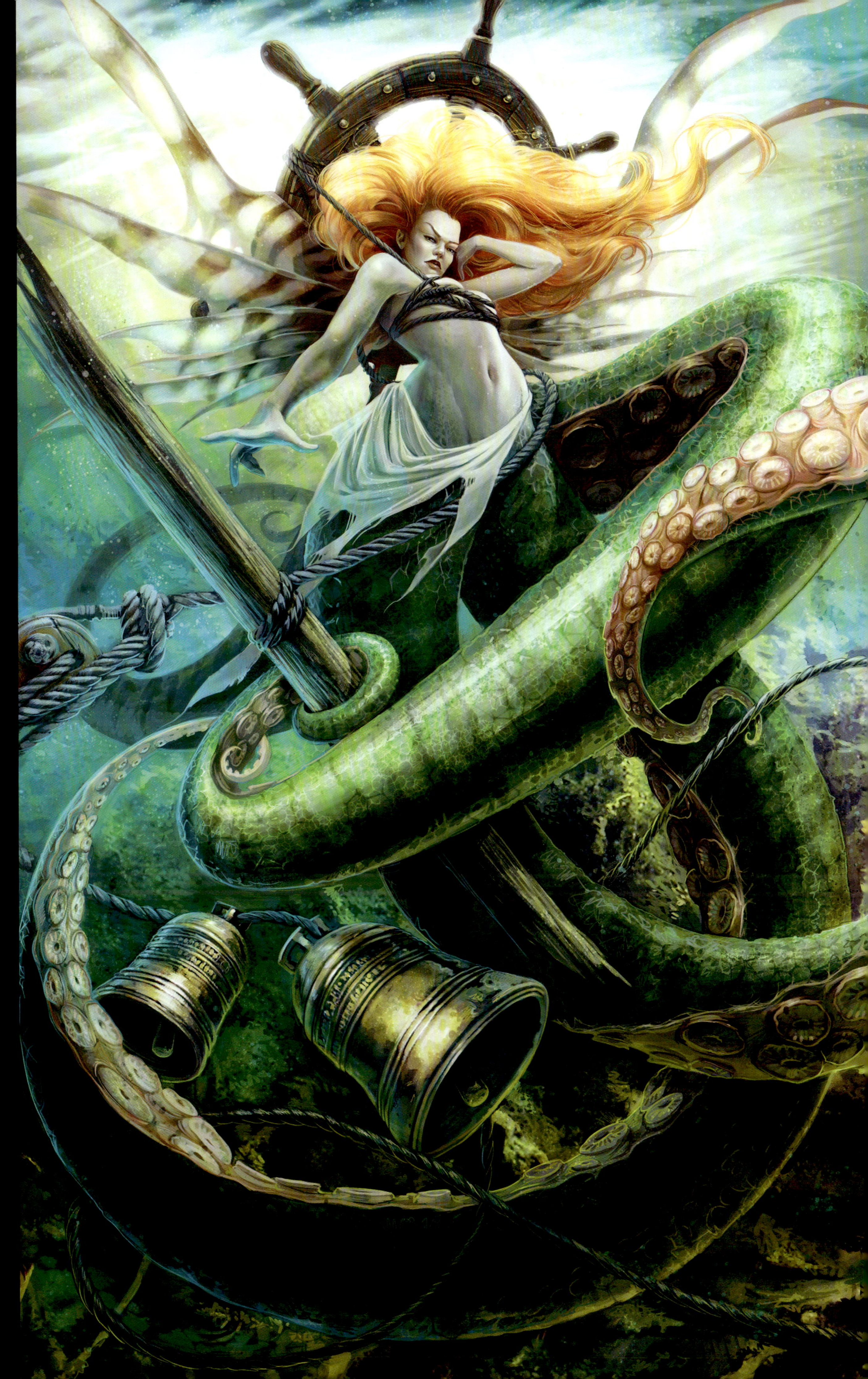

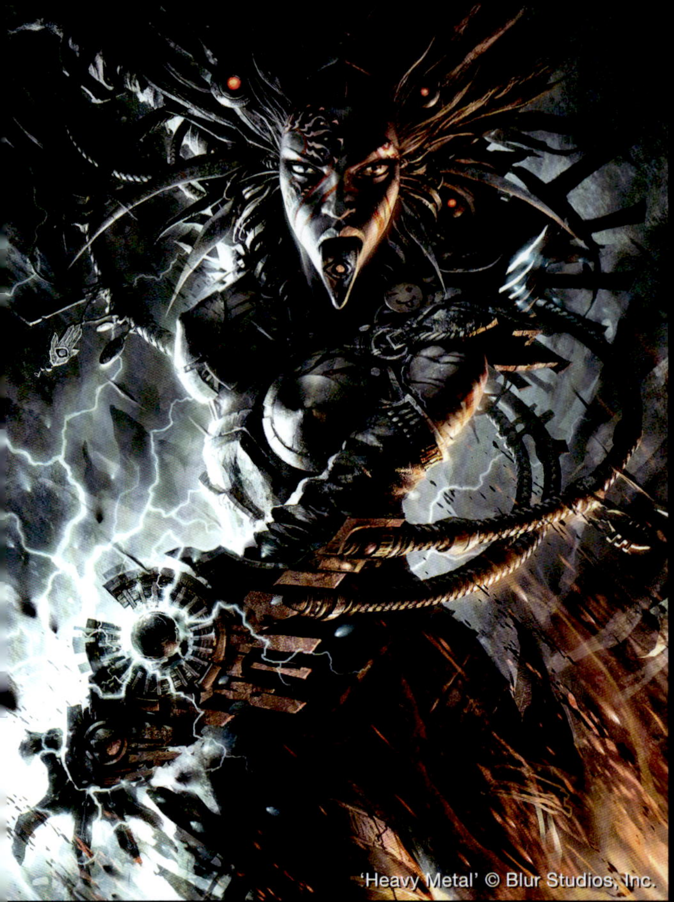

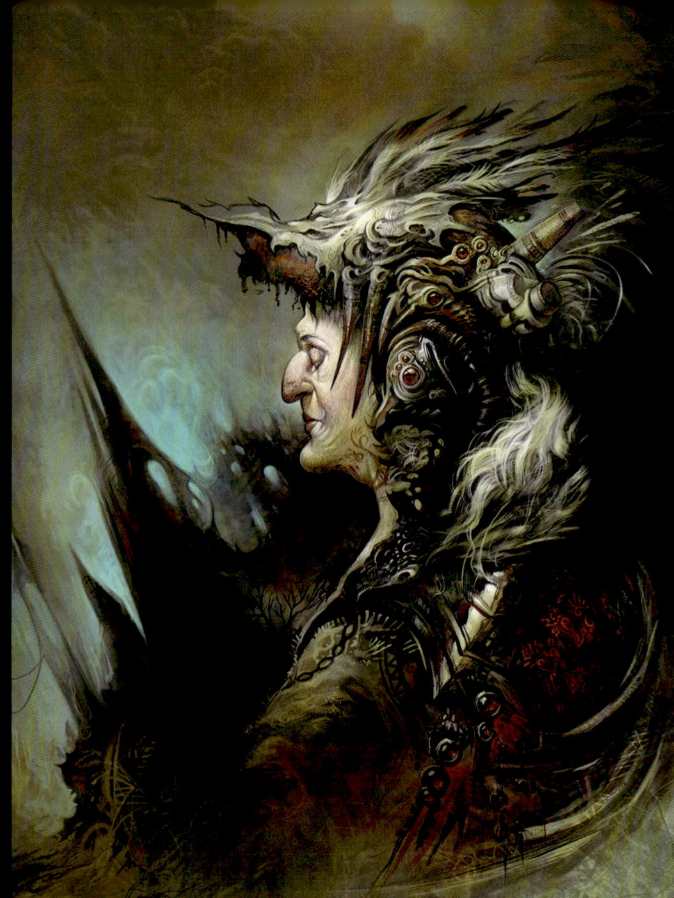

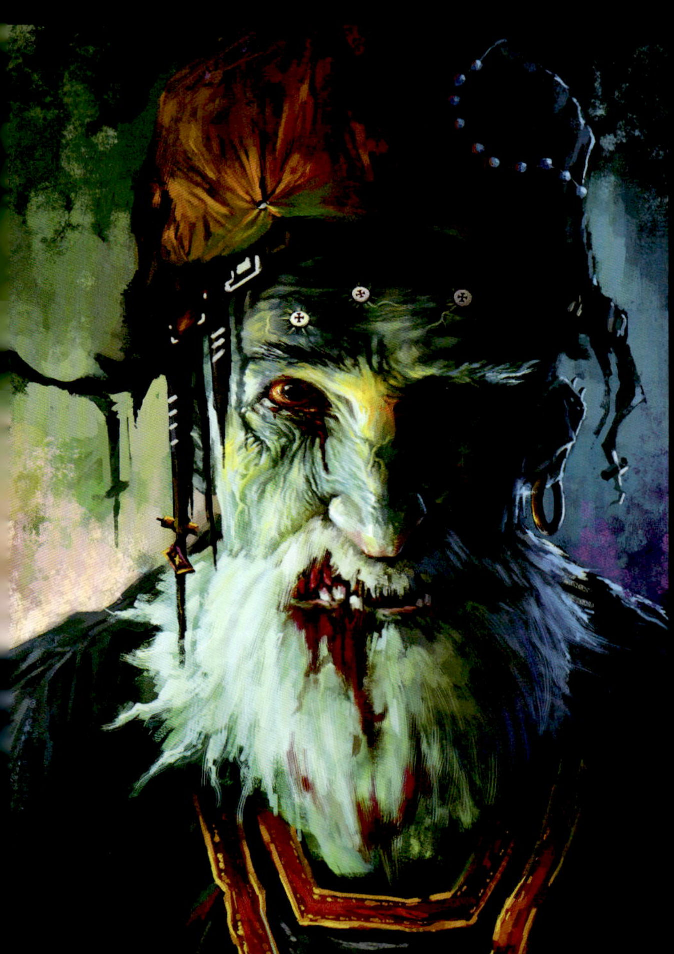

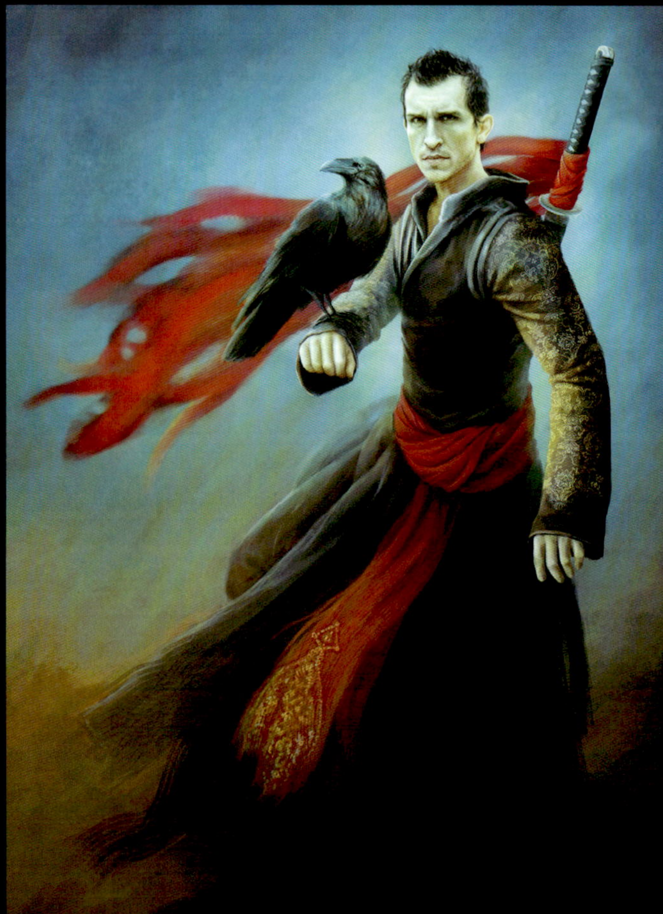

Heavy Metal Teaser Poster 2009
Photoshop
Client: Blur Studios, Inc.
Raymond Swanland, USA
[top]

Bloodthirsty Godfather
Photoshop
Chuan Zhong,
CHINA
[above]

Portrait of a magic warrior
Photoshop
Chaichan Artwichai,
THAILAND
[top]

The Guardian
Photoshop
Model: Francisco Randez
Photographer: PatriciaChica.com
Nykolai Aleksander, GREAT BRITAIN *[above]*

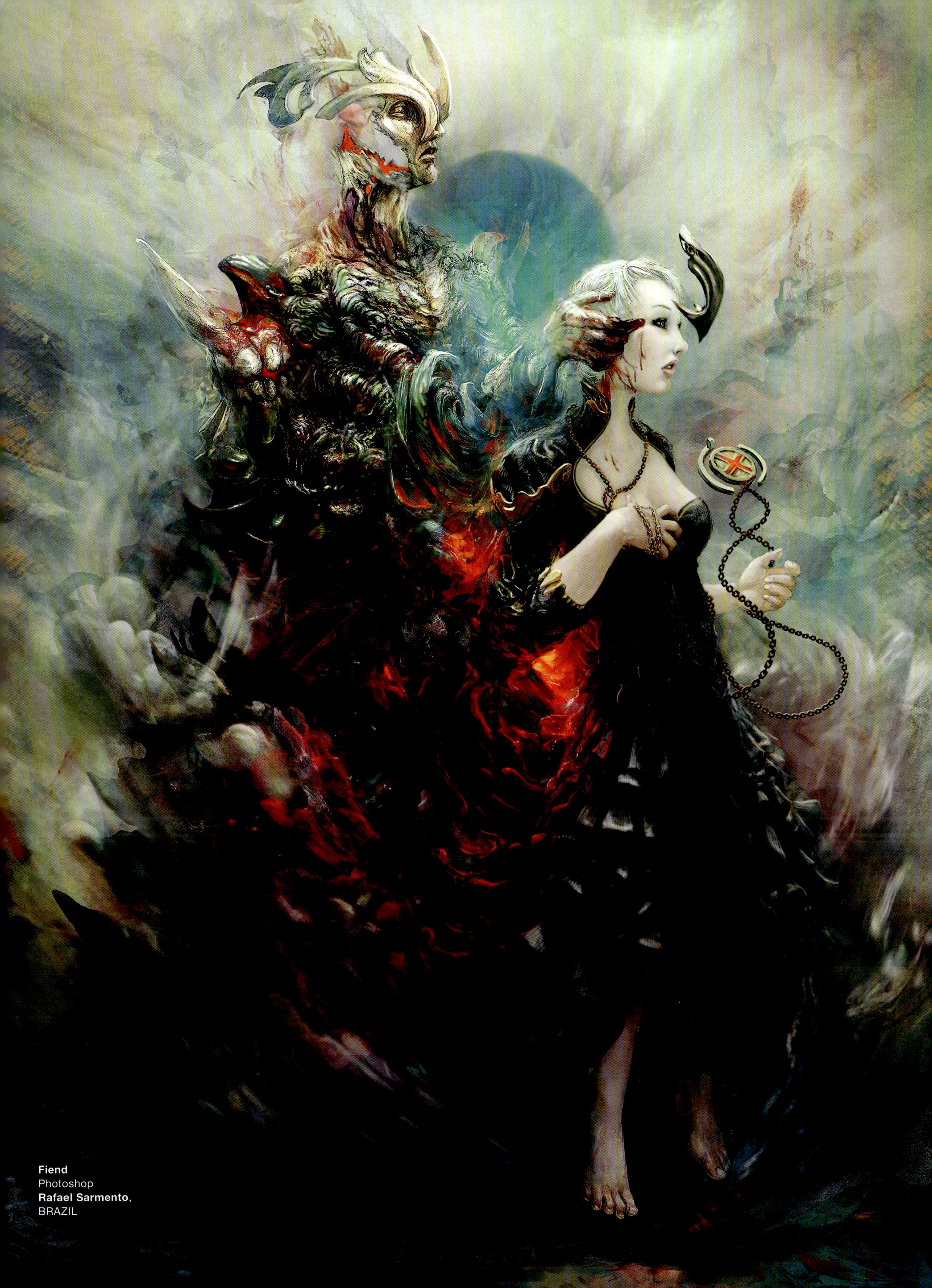

Fiend
Photoshop
Rafael Sarmento, BRAZIL

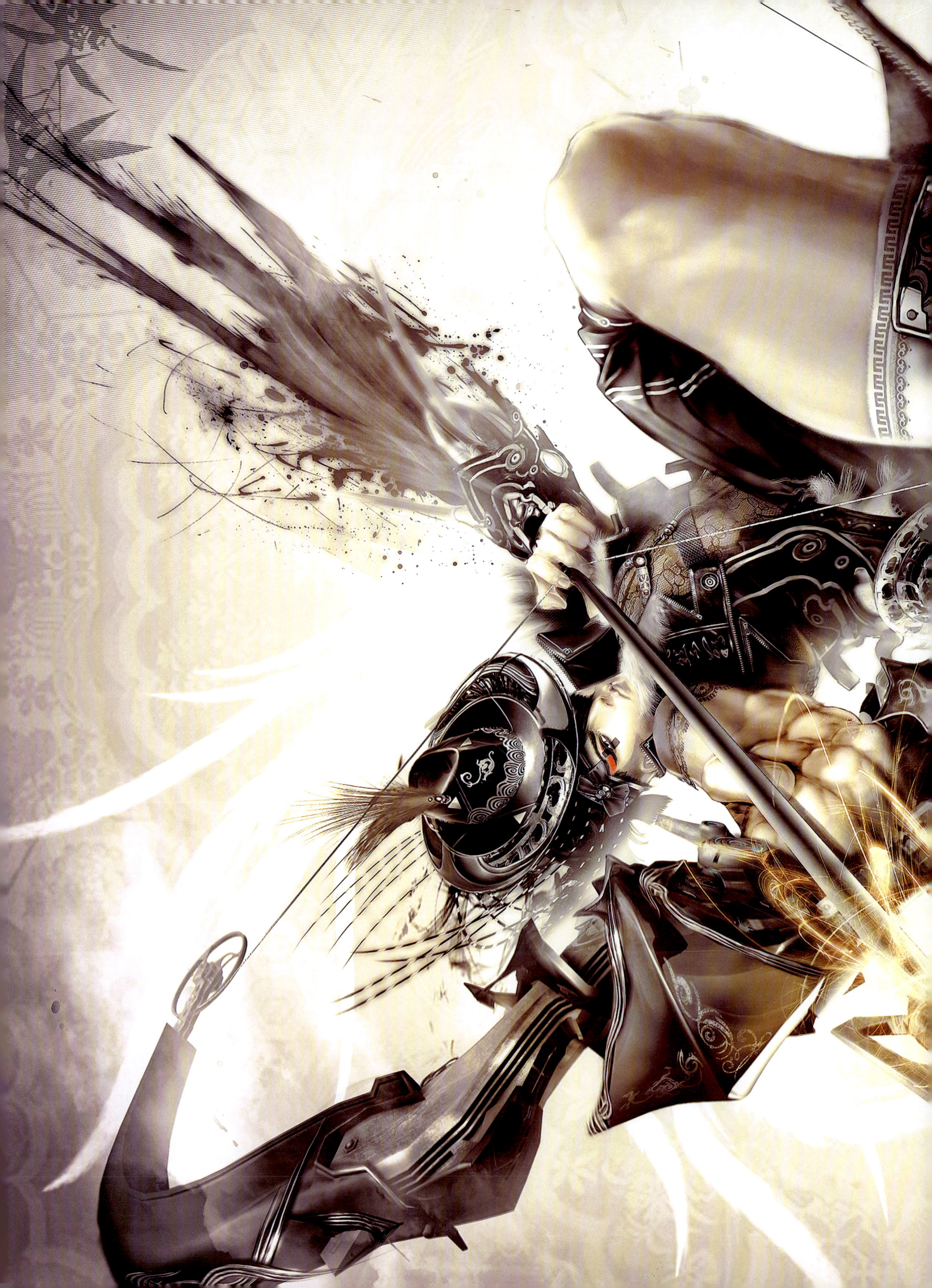

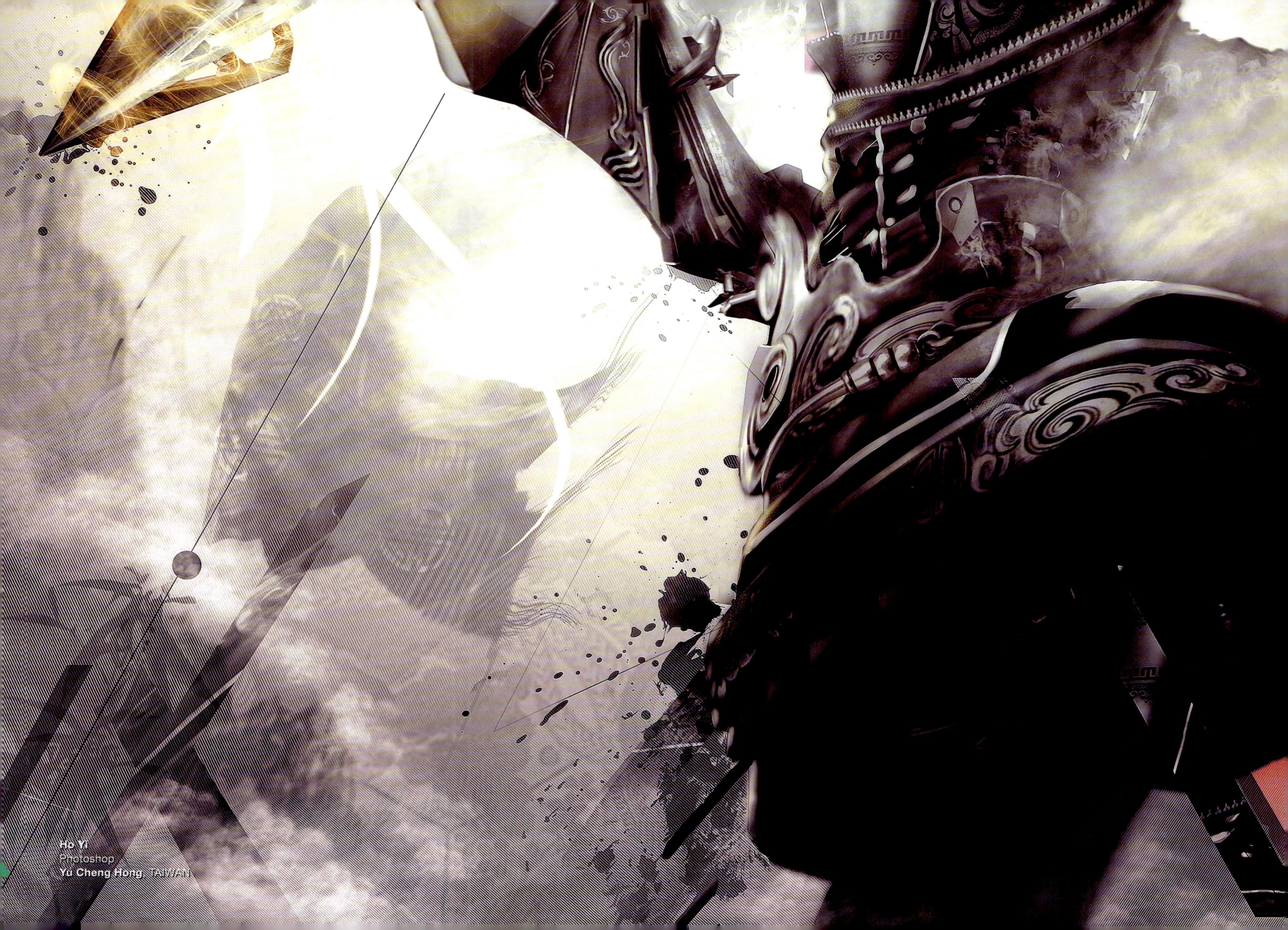

Ho Yi
Photoshop
Yu Cheng Hong, TAIWAN

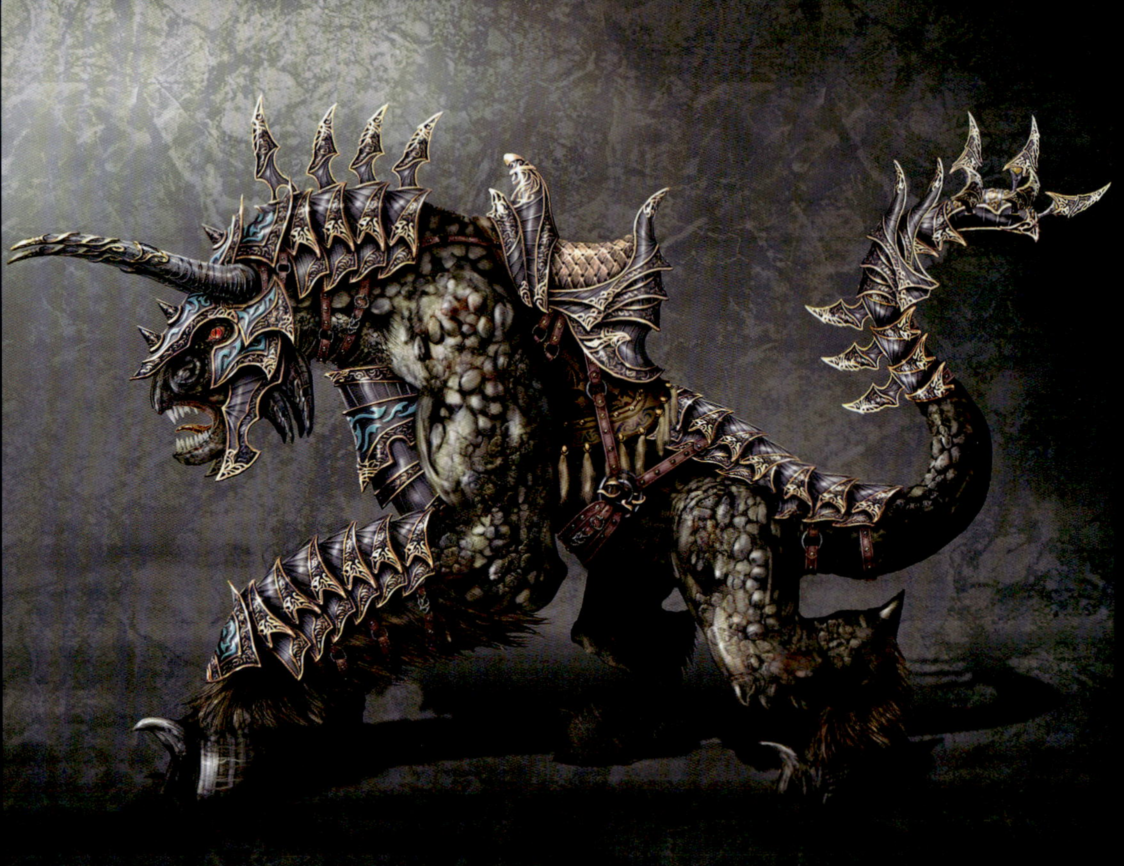

Epic: Fantasy Mount
Photoshop, SketchUp
Ken Nguyen, USA
[left]

DeathBringer
Photoshop
Tu Bui, USA
[right]

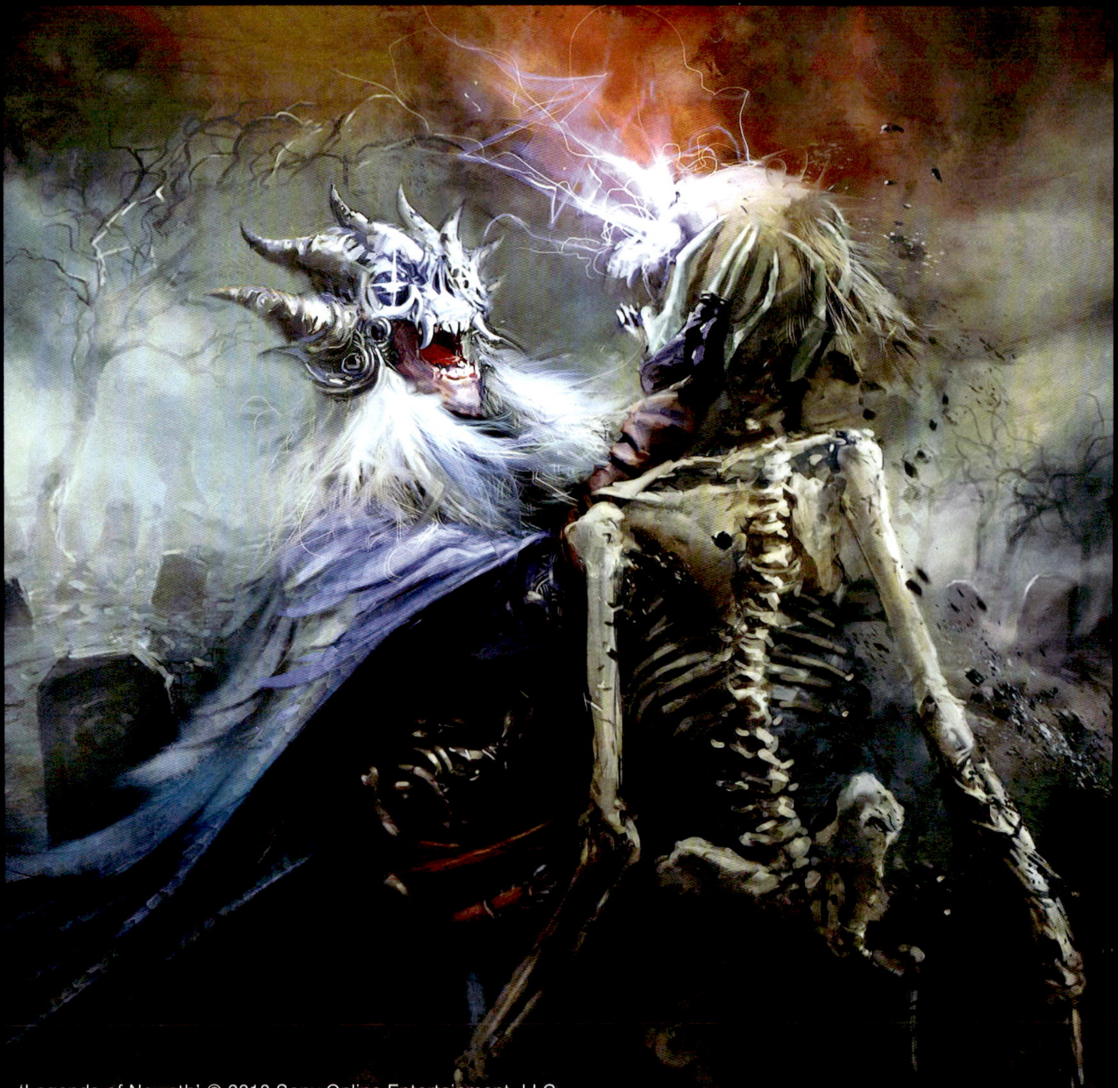

Legends of Norrath: Erudite Necromancer
Photoshop
Art Director: Roger Chamberlain
Client: Sony Online Entertainment, LLC
Fred Rambaud, Volta Creations, Inc., CANADA
[left]

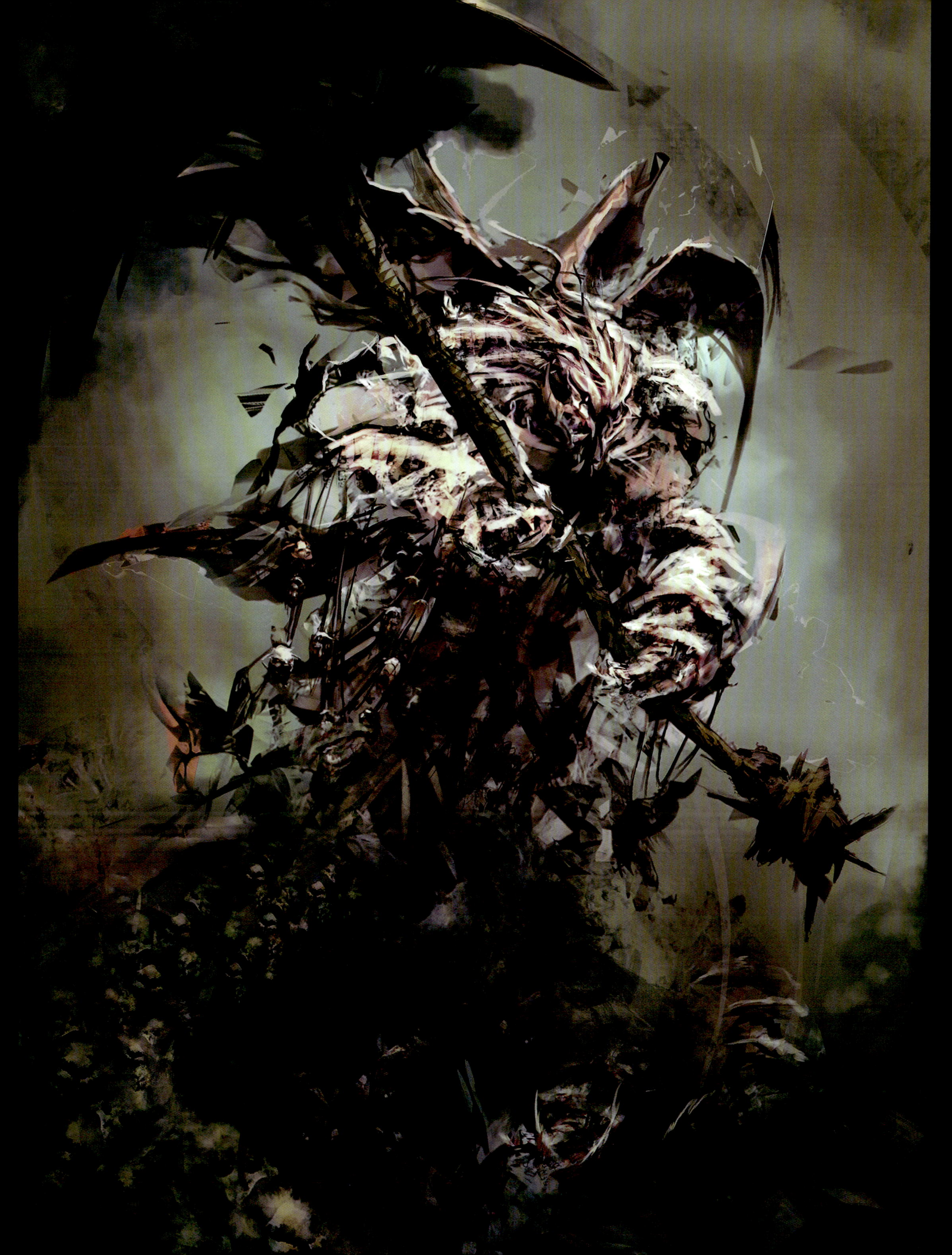

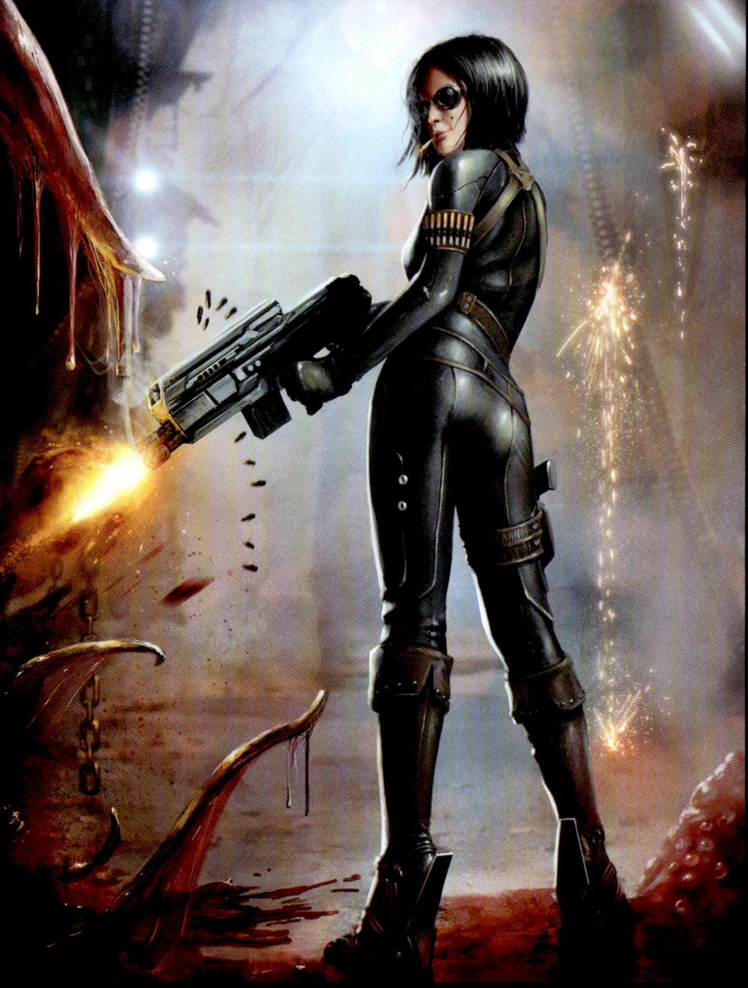

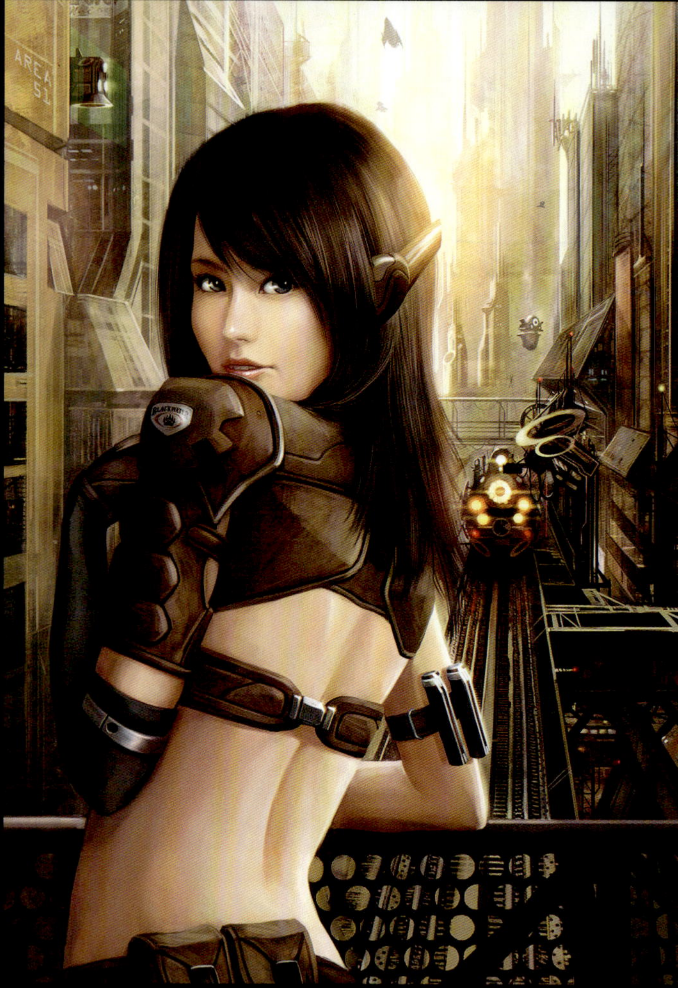

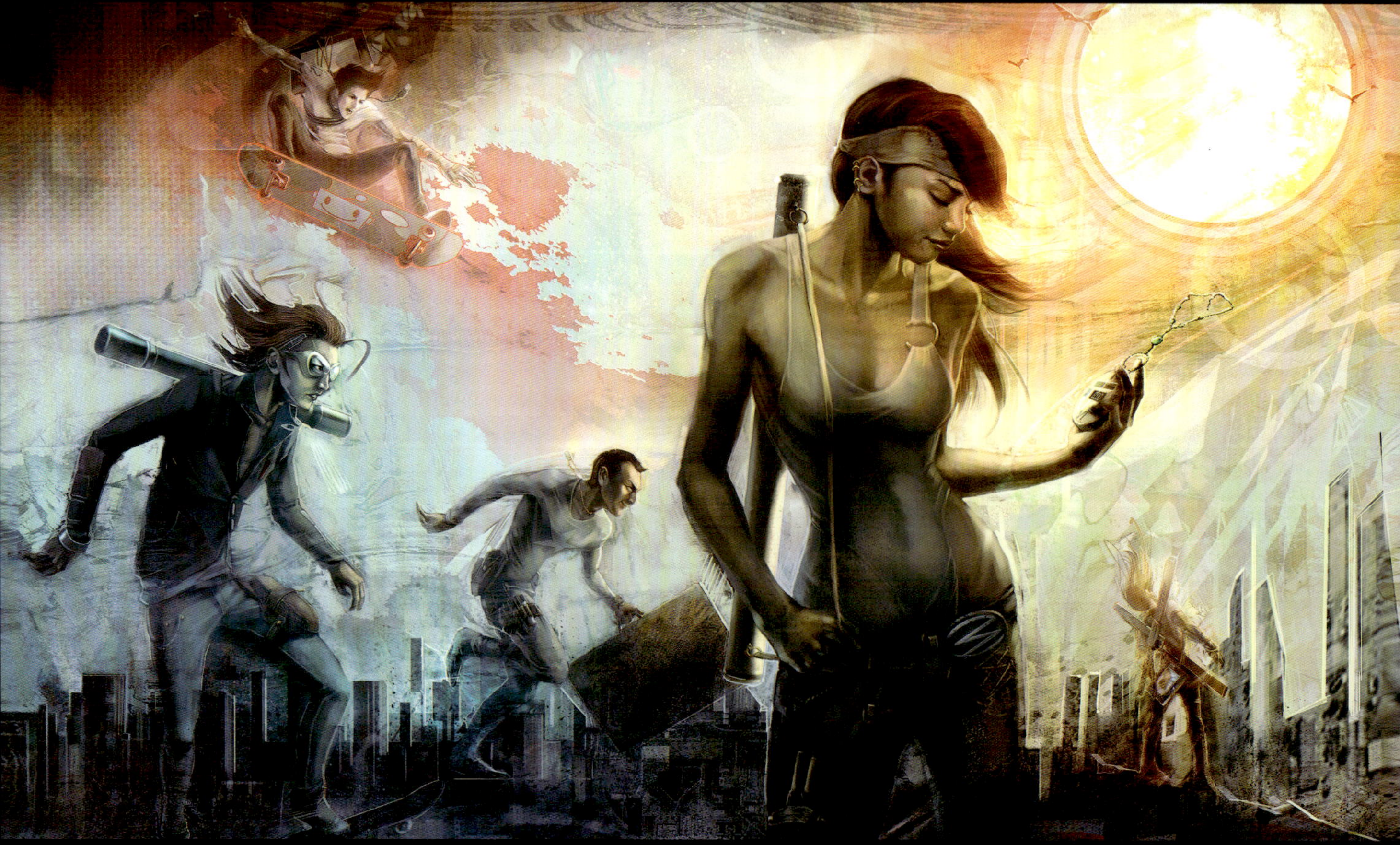

Oh no more tentacles
Photoshop
Yigit Koroglu, TURKEY
[top]

Artiz
Painter
Ivan Tao, The One Academy, MALAYSIA
[above]

Future Girl
Painter, Photoshop
Fei Giap Chong, MALAYSIA
[top]

Gun Slinger Girl
Photoshop
Paul Kwon, USA
[right]

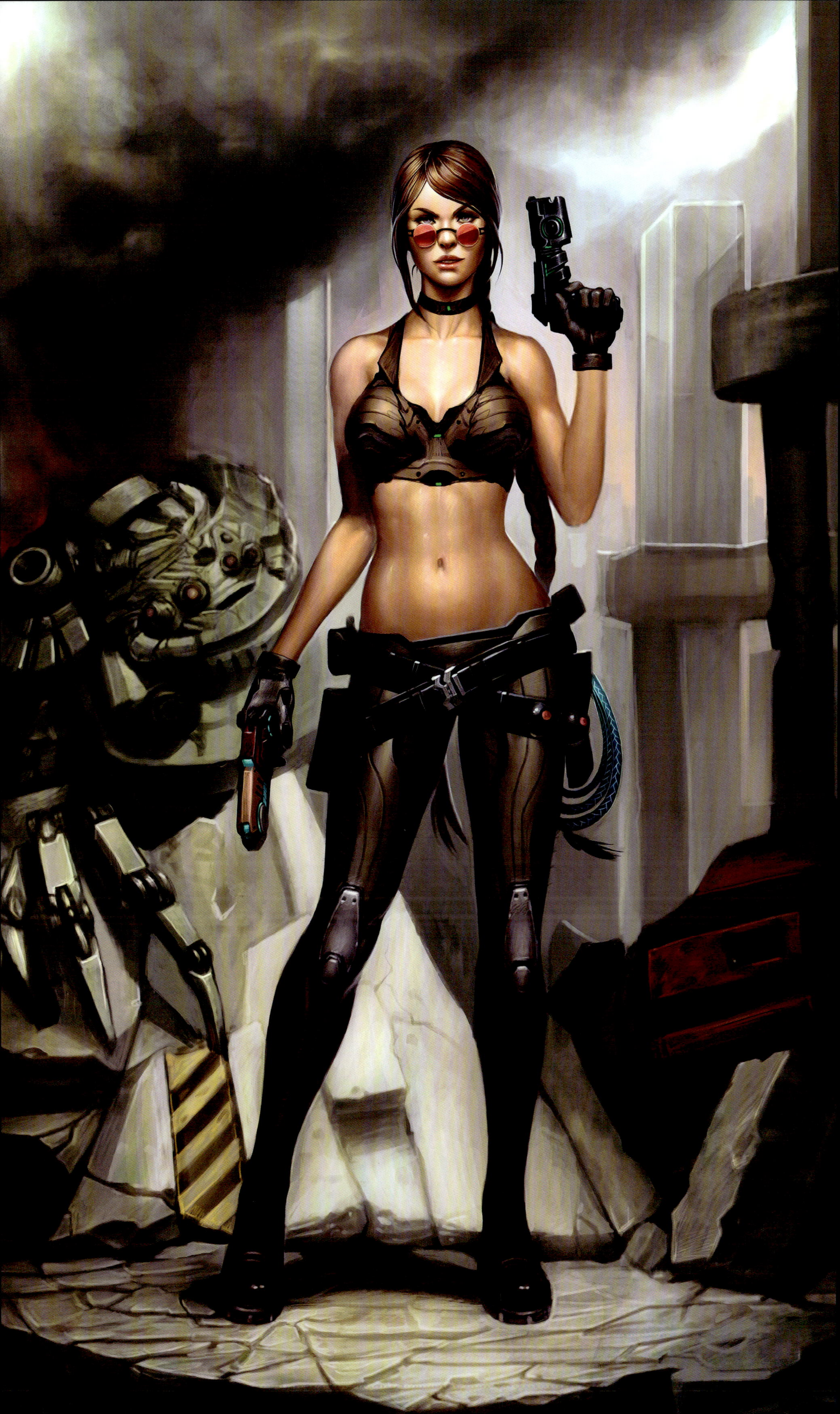

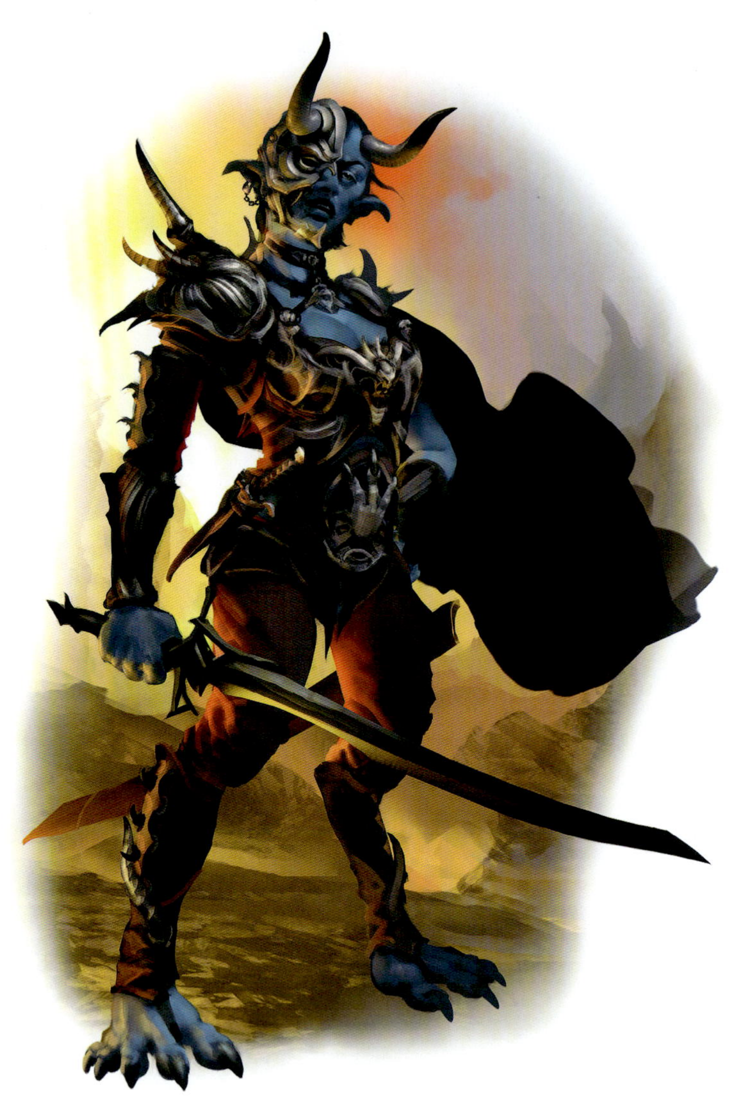

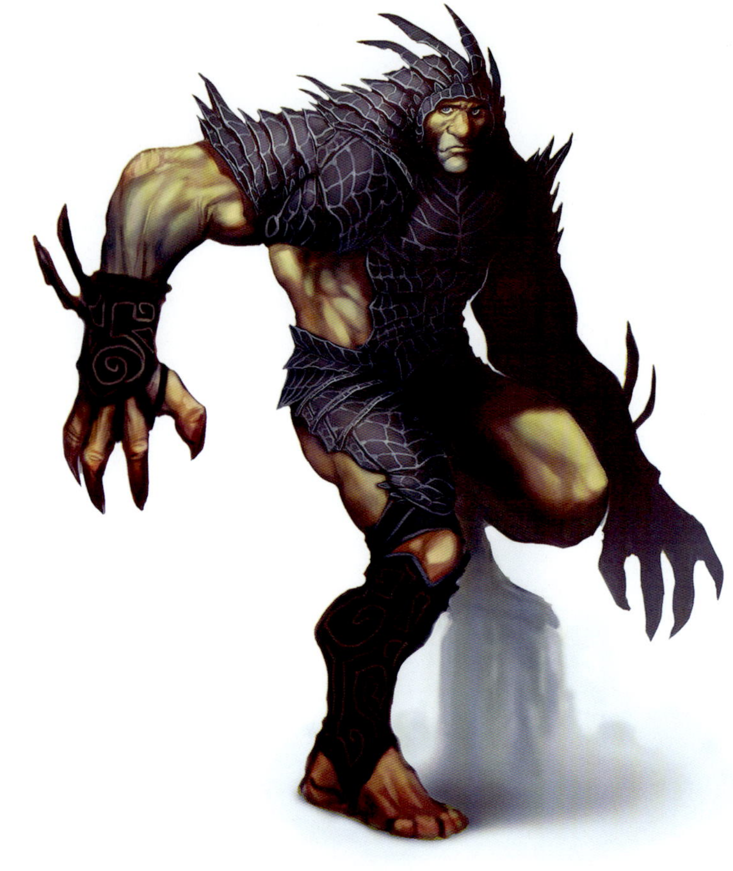

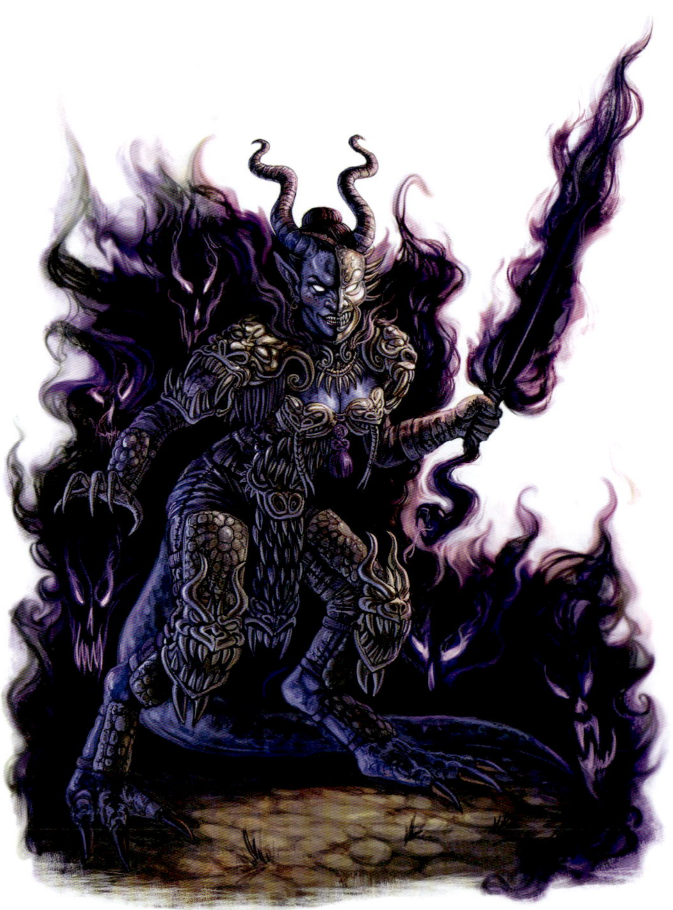

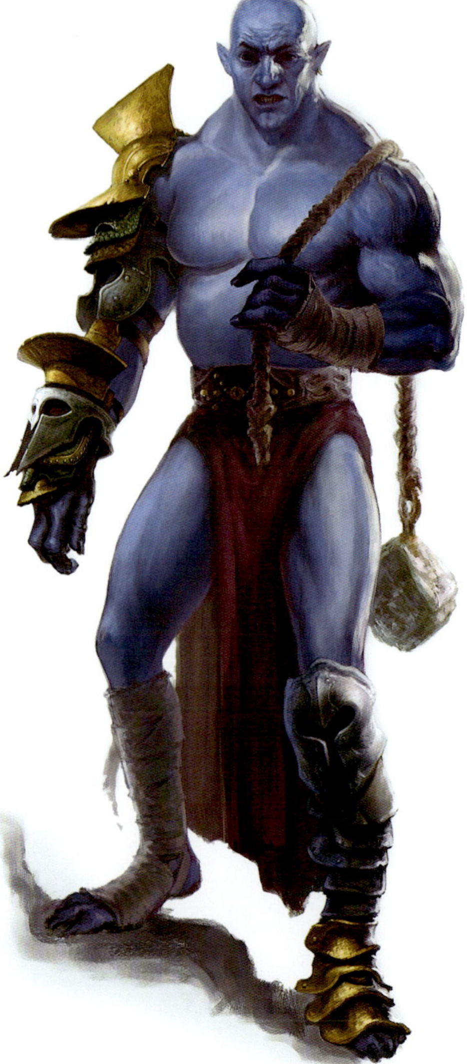

Demoness
Photoshop
Lukasz Jaskolski,
POLAND
[top left]

Armor
Photoshop
Patri Balanovsky,
ISRAEL
[top]

Assassin Devil
Photoshop
Felicia Cano,
USA
[far left]

Monstro
Photoshop
Jim Moore,
USA
[left]

Beast Summoner
Photoshop
Lukasz Jaskolski,
POLAND
[right]

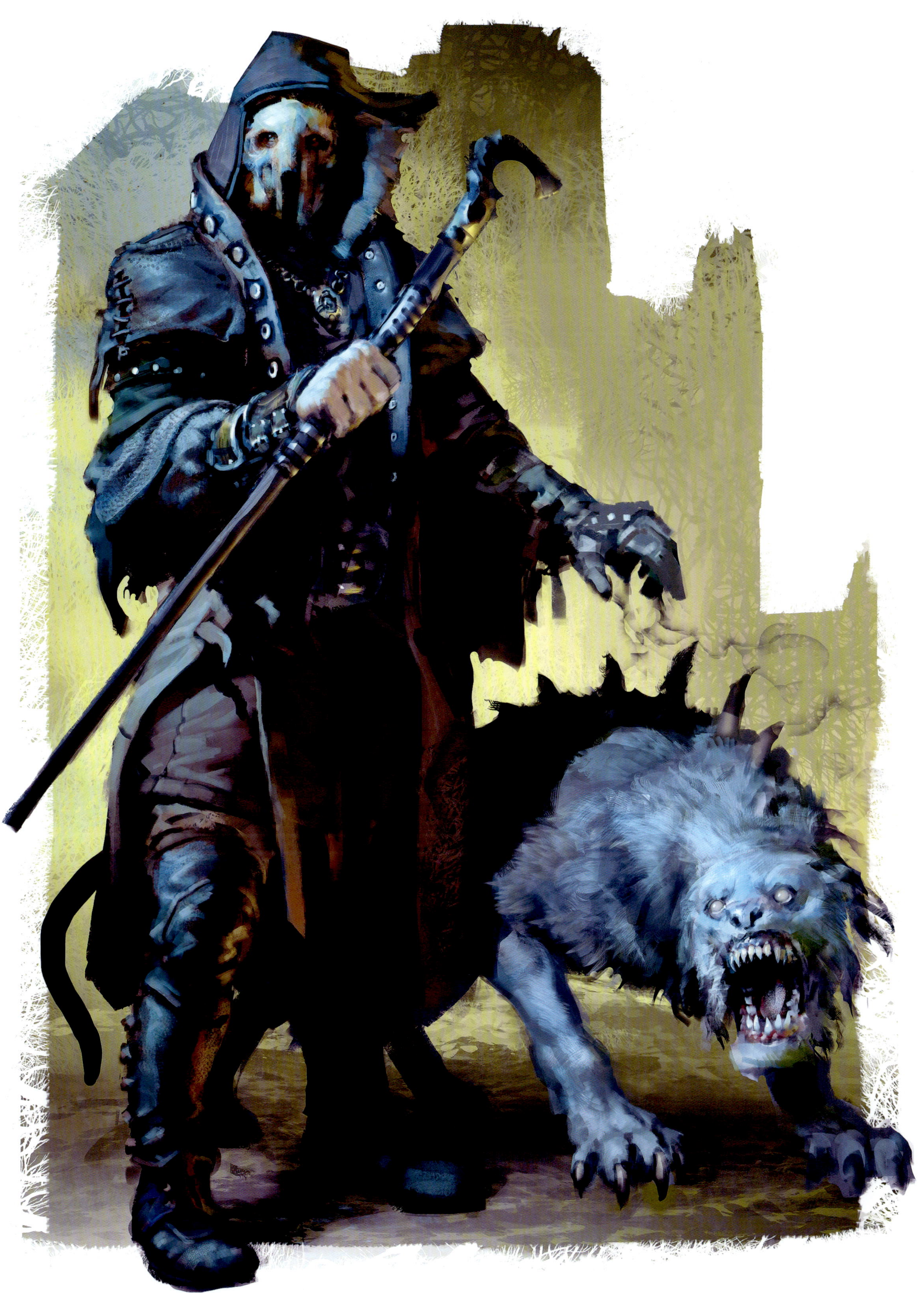

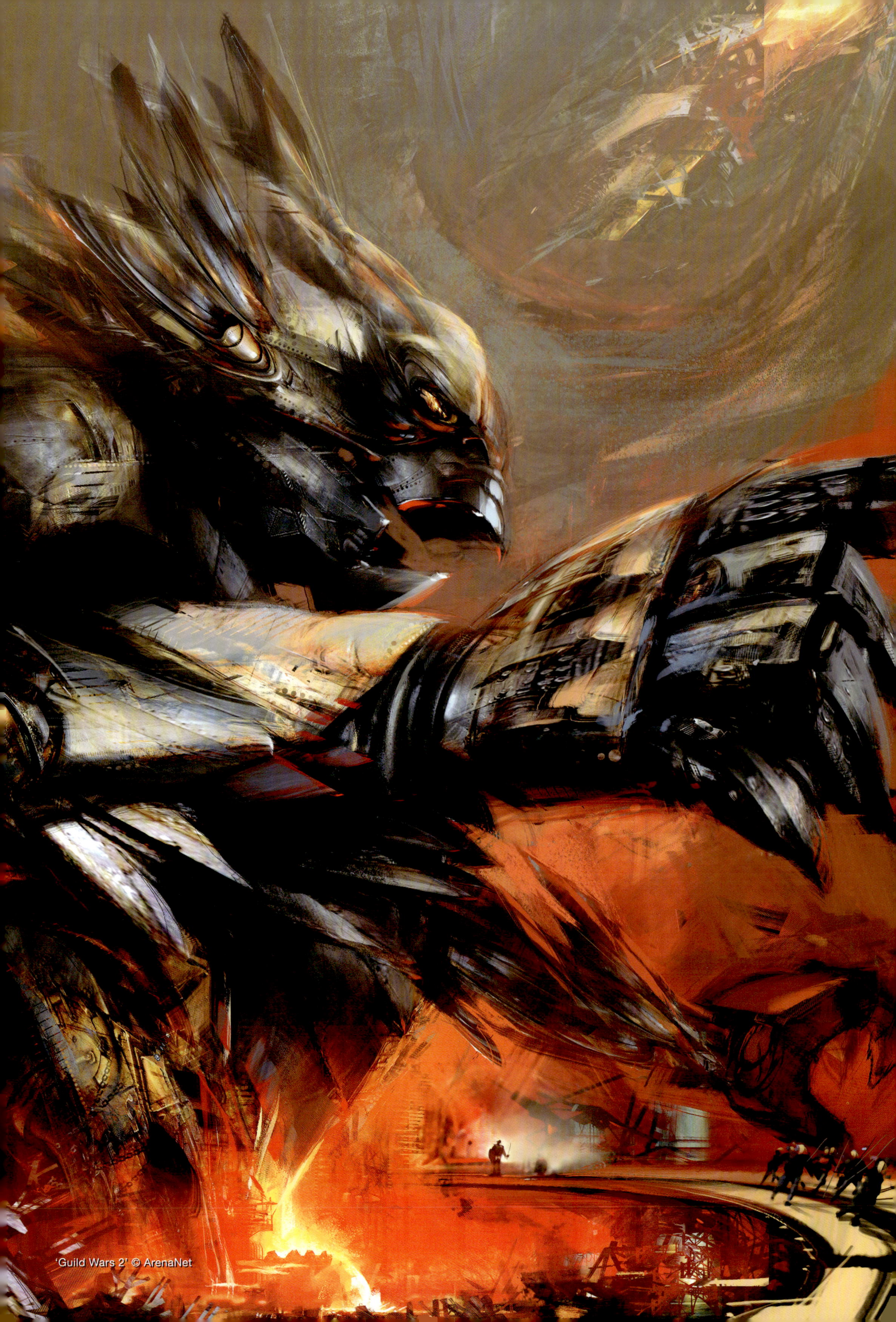

'Guild Wars 2' © ArenaNet

Guild Wars 2: Dredge Robot 2
Photoshop
Daniel Dociu, ArenaNet, USA
[left]

Judgement
Painter, Photoshop
Alejandro Diaz, FRANCE
[right]

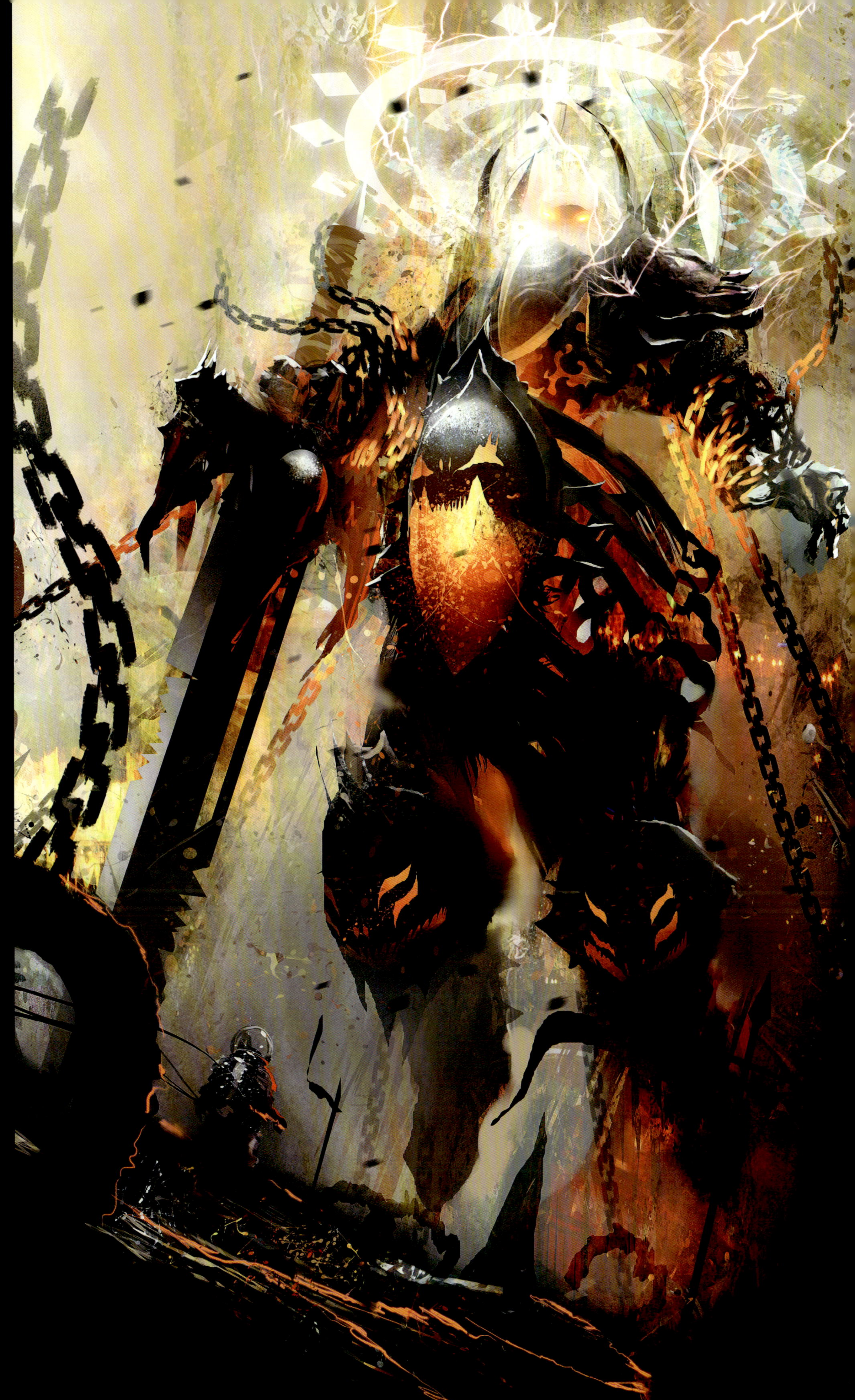

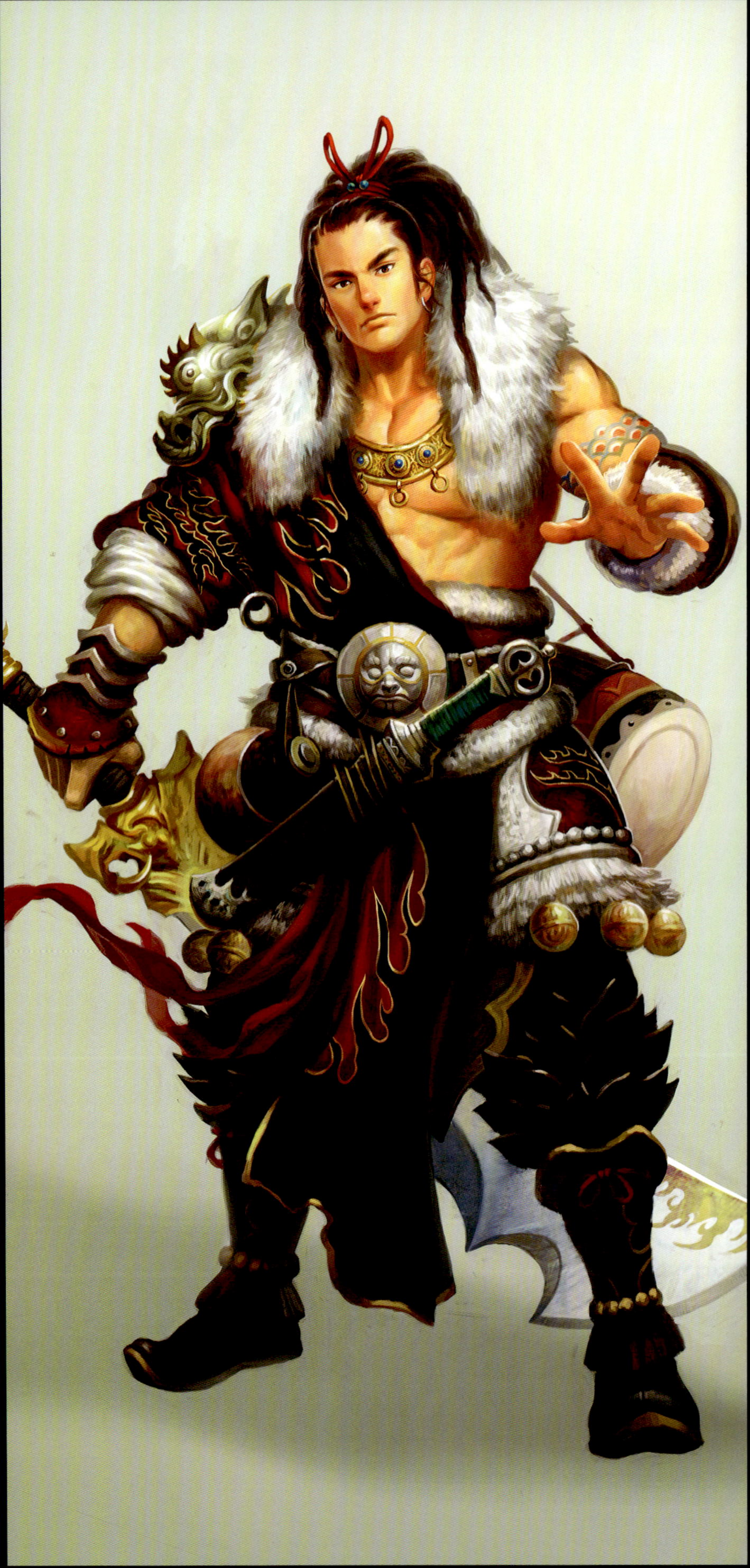

Swordsman
Photoshop
Jiansong Chain, Perfect World Co. Ltd, CHINA

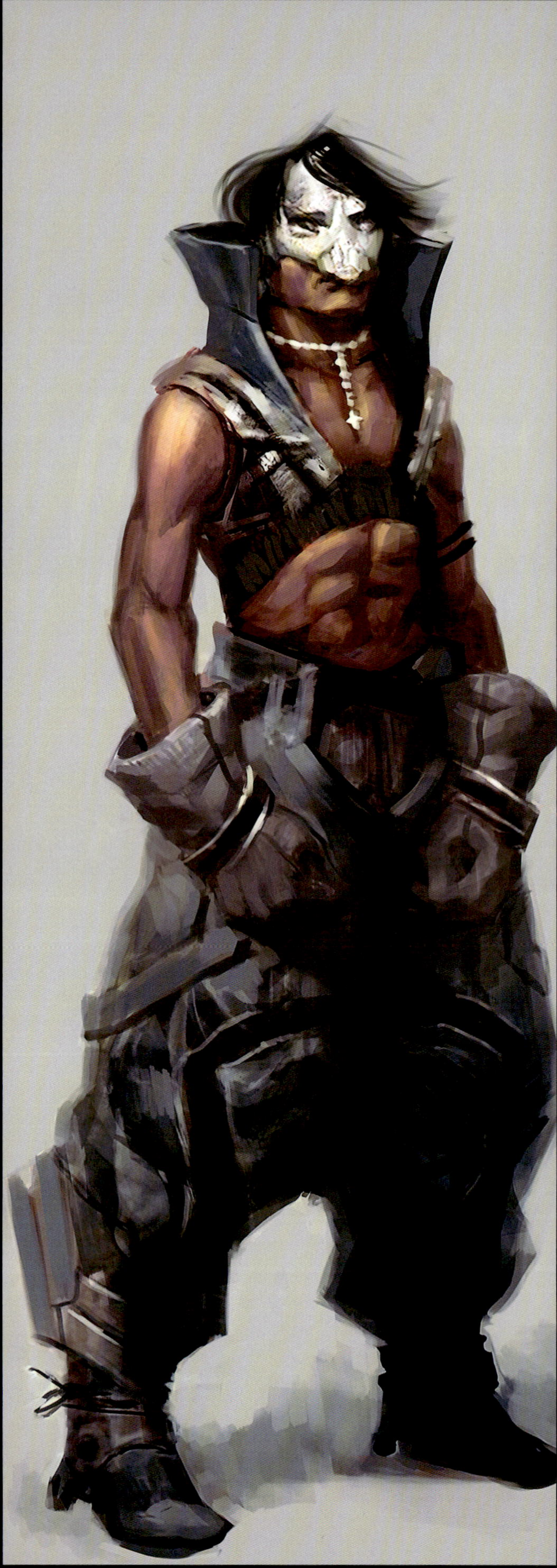

Wizard
Photoshop
Waldek Kaminski, POLAND

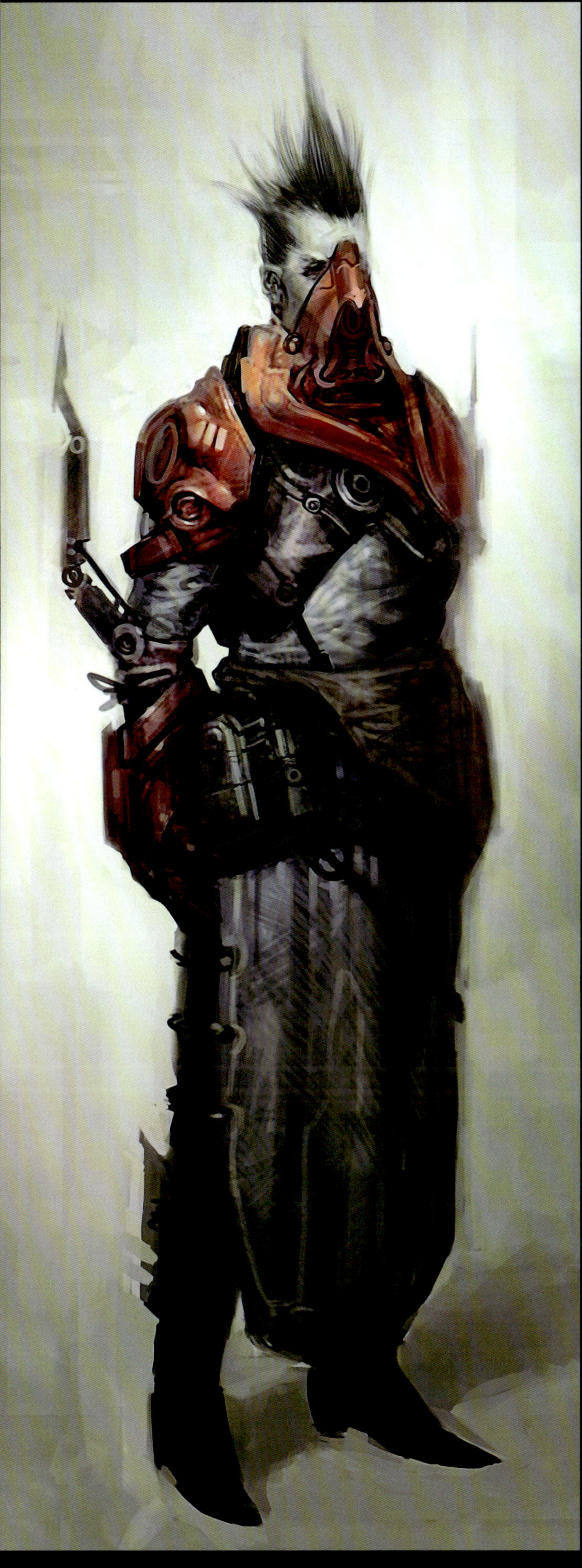

Cyborg
Photoshop
Waldek Kaminski, POLAND

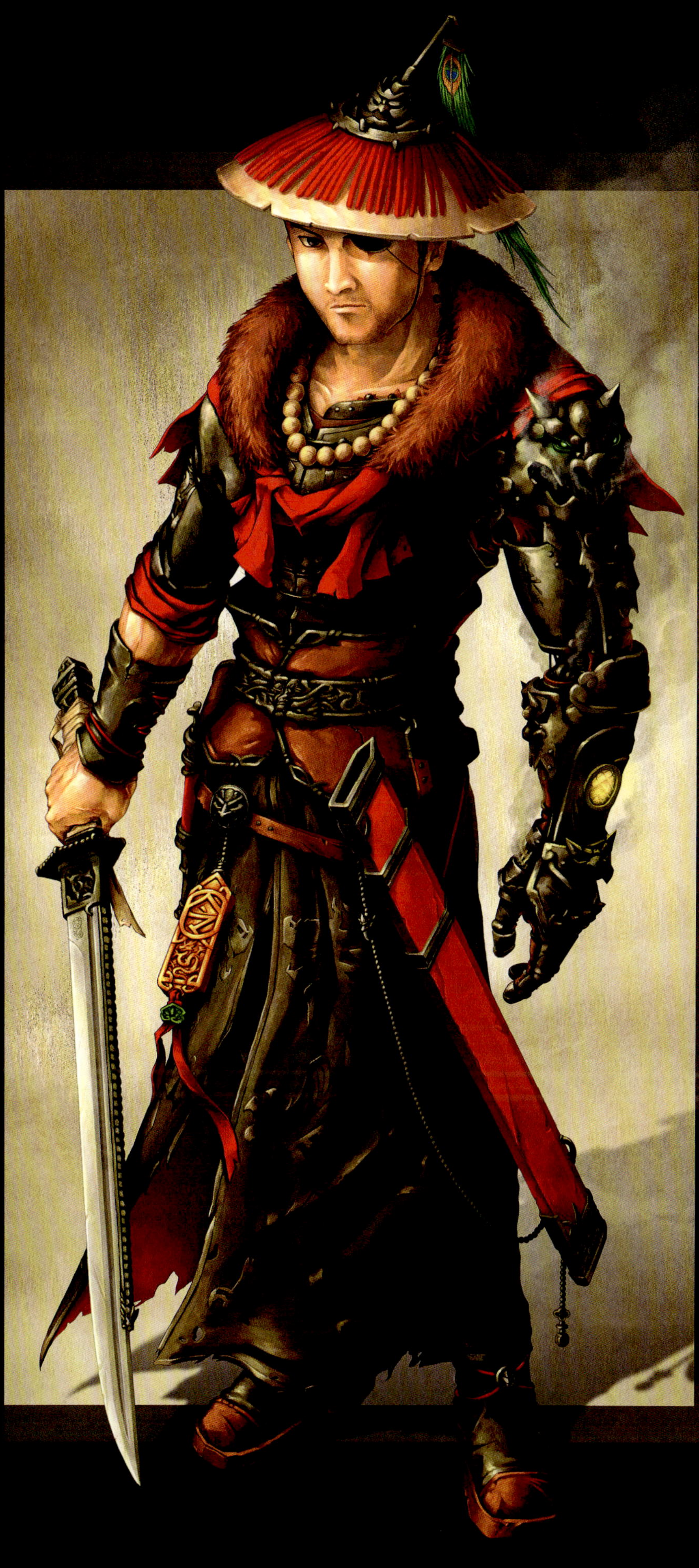

Imperial Sheriff
Painter, Photoshop
James Ng, CHINA

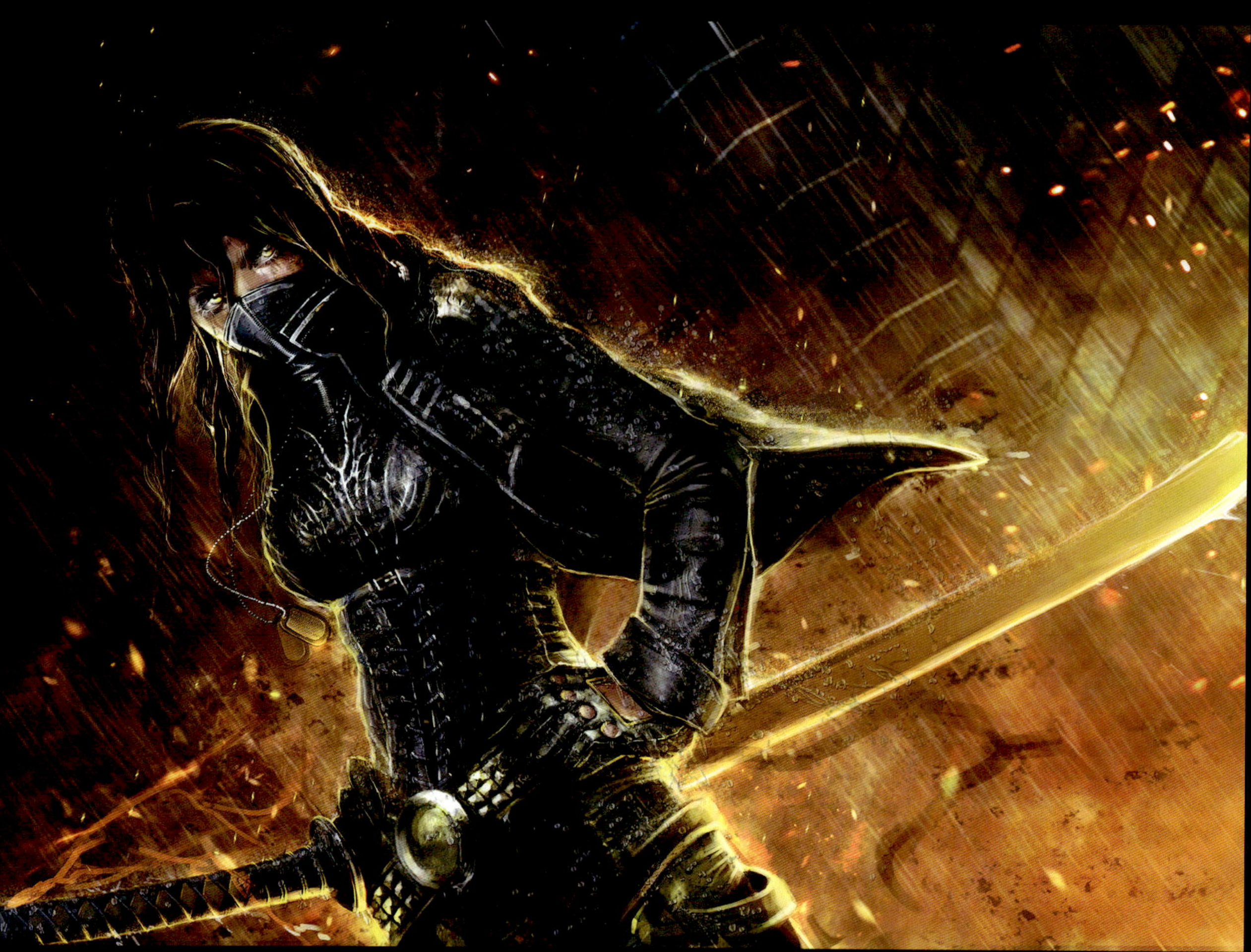

Rain runner
Photoshop
Helen Rusovich, UKRAINE
[left]

Dragon Knight
Photoshop
Eko Handriyanto,
Imaginary Friends Studios,
INDONESIA
[right]

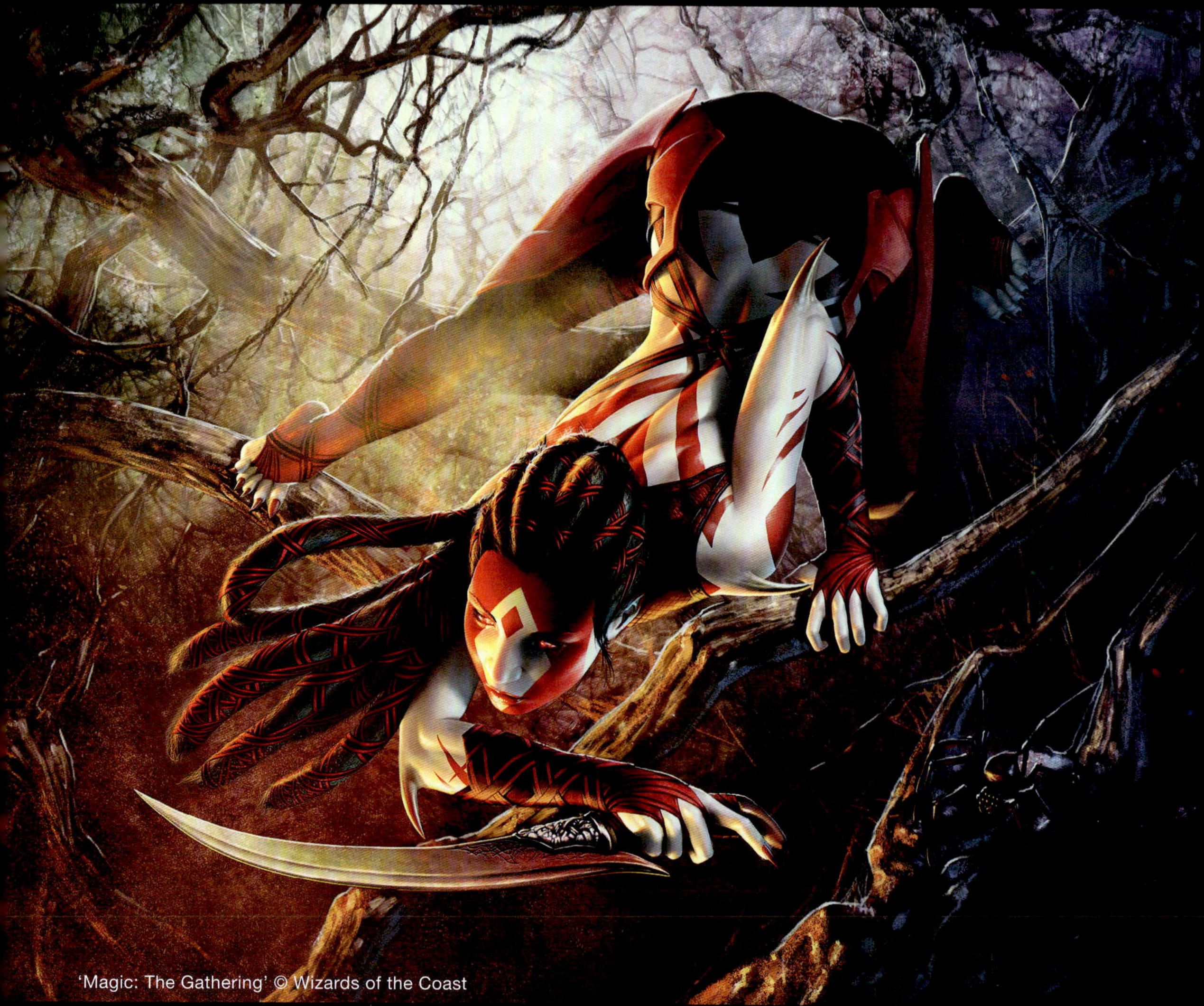

Magic: The Gathering
(Guul Draz Vampire)
Photoshop, Maya
Client: Wizards of the Coast
Art Director: Jeremy Jarvis
Steve Argyle, USA
[left]

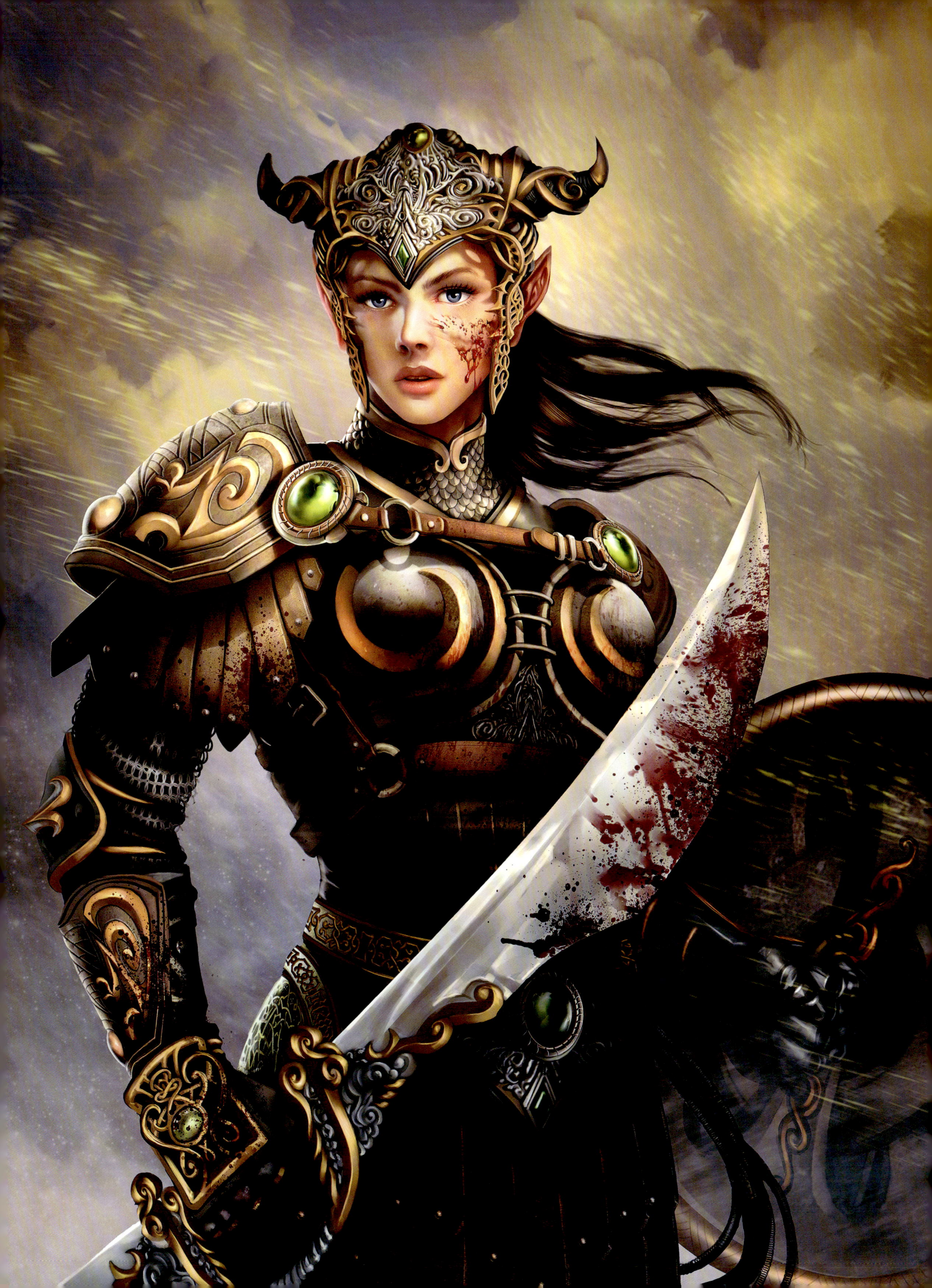

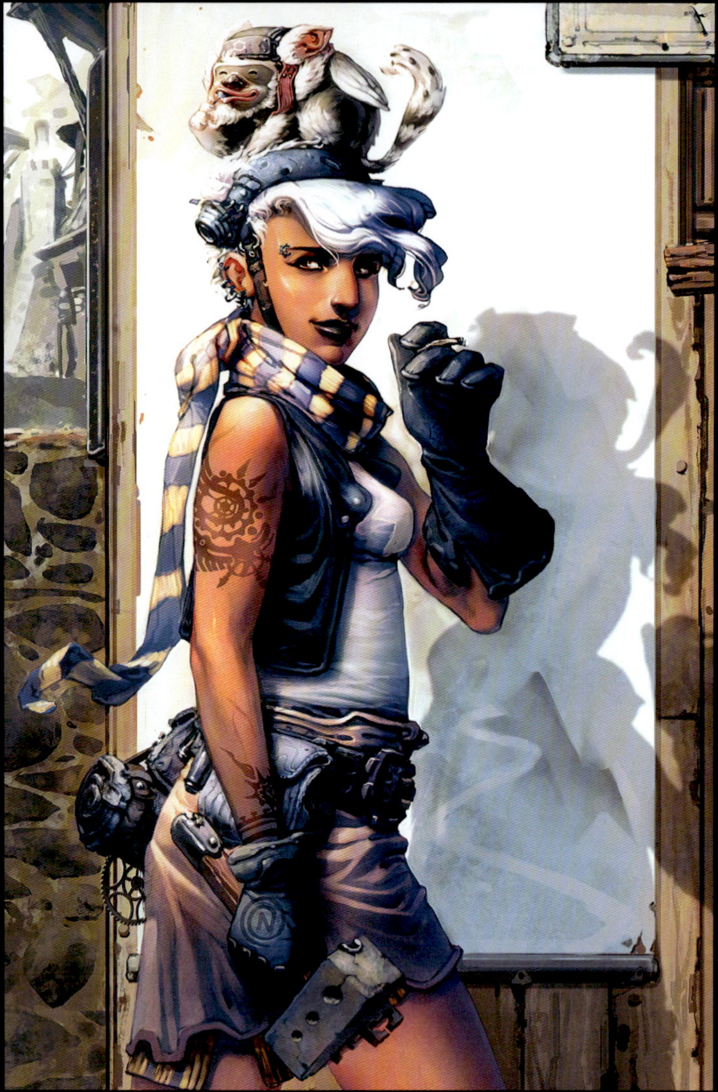

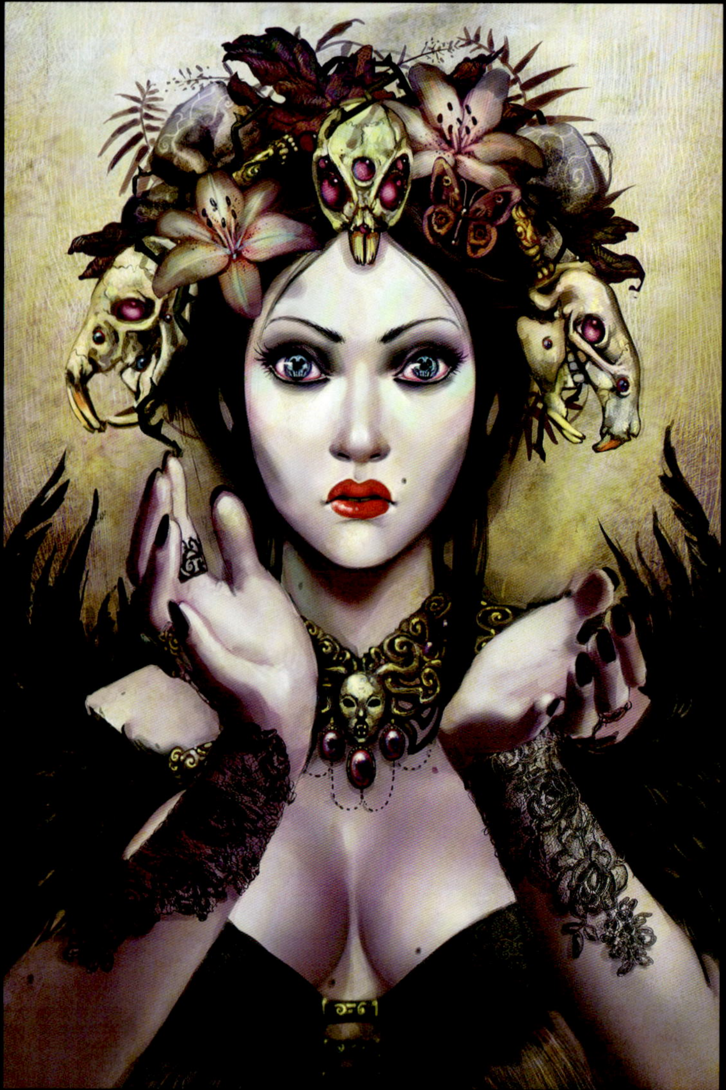

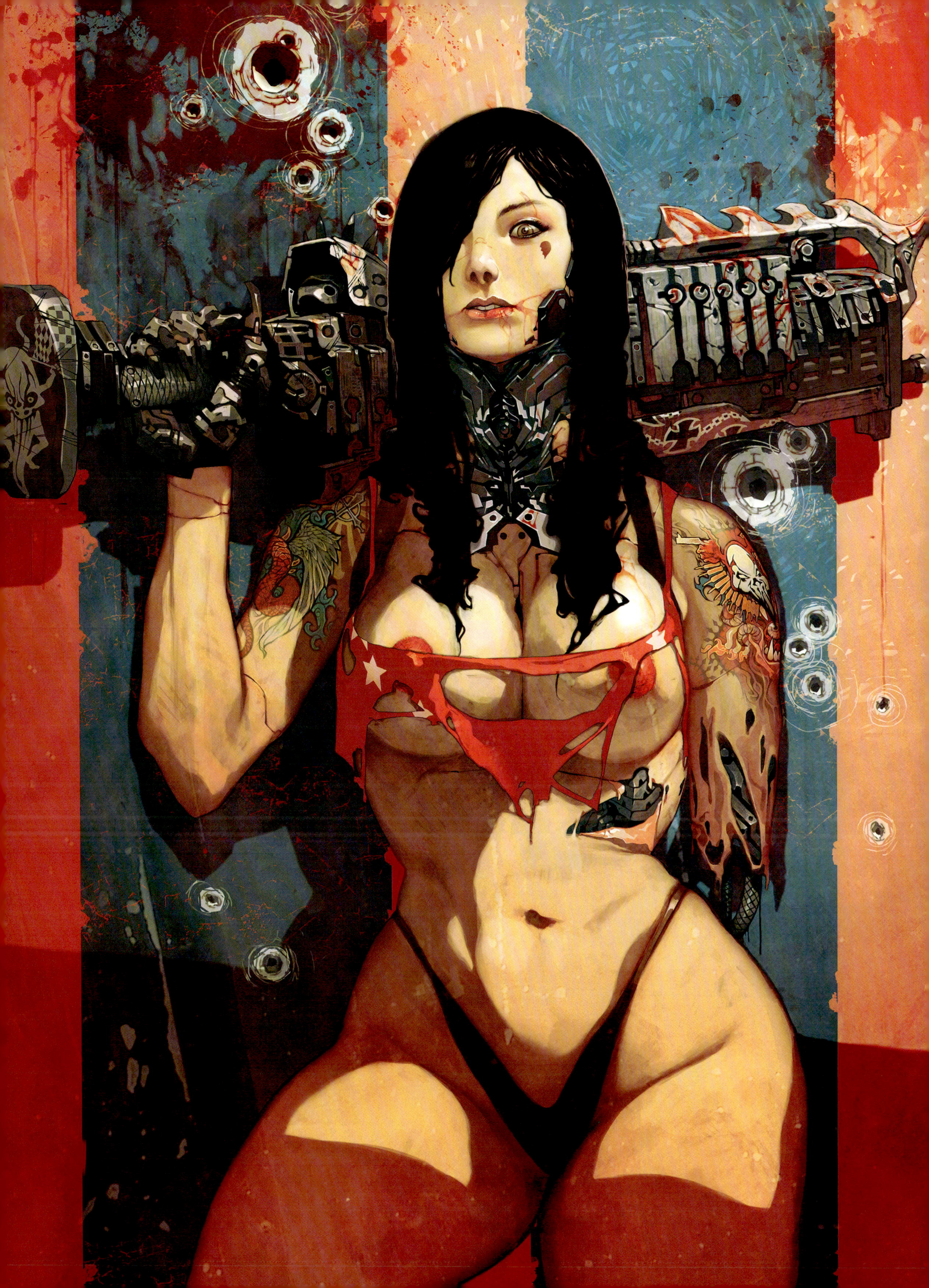

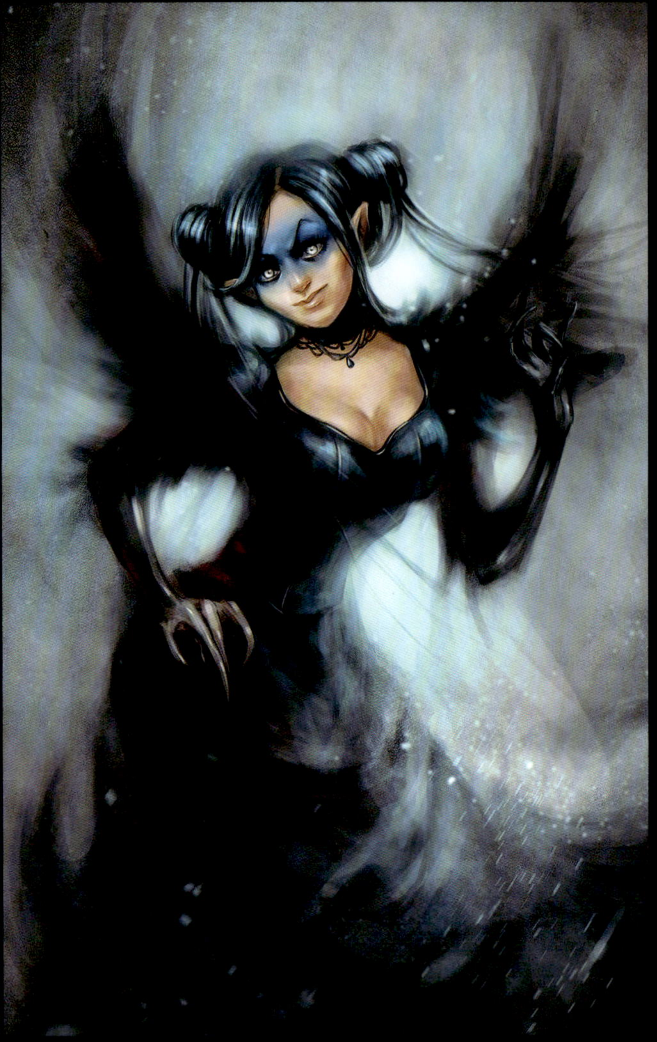

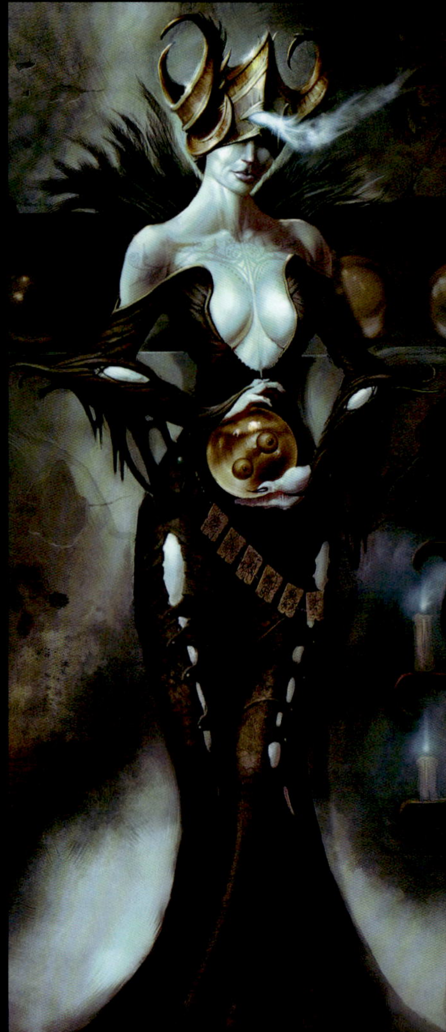

MadBird
Photoshop
Tatiana Vetrova, RUSSIA
[far left]

The Fortune Teller
Photoshop
Tyler James, USA
[left]

Call animal
Photoshop
Huang DaHong, CHINA
[right]

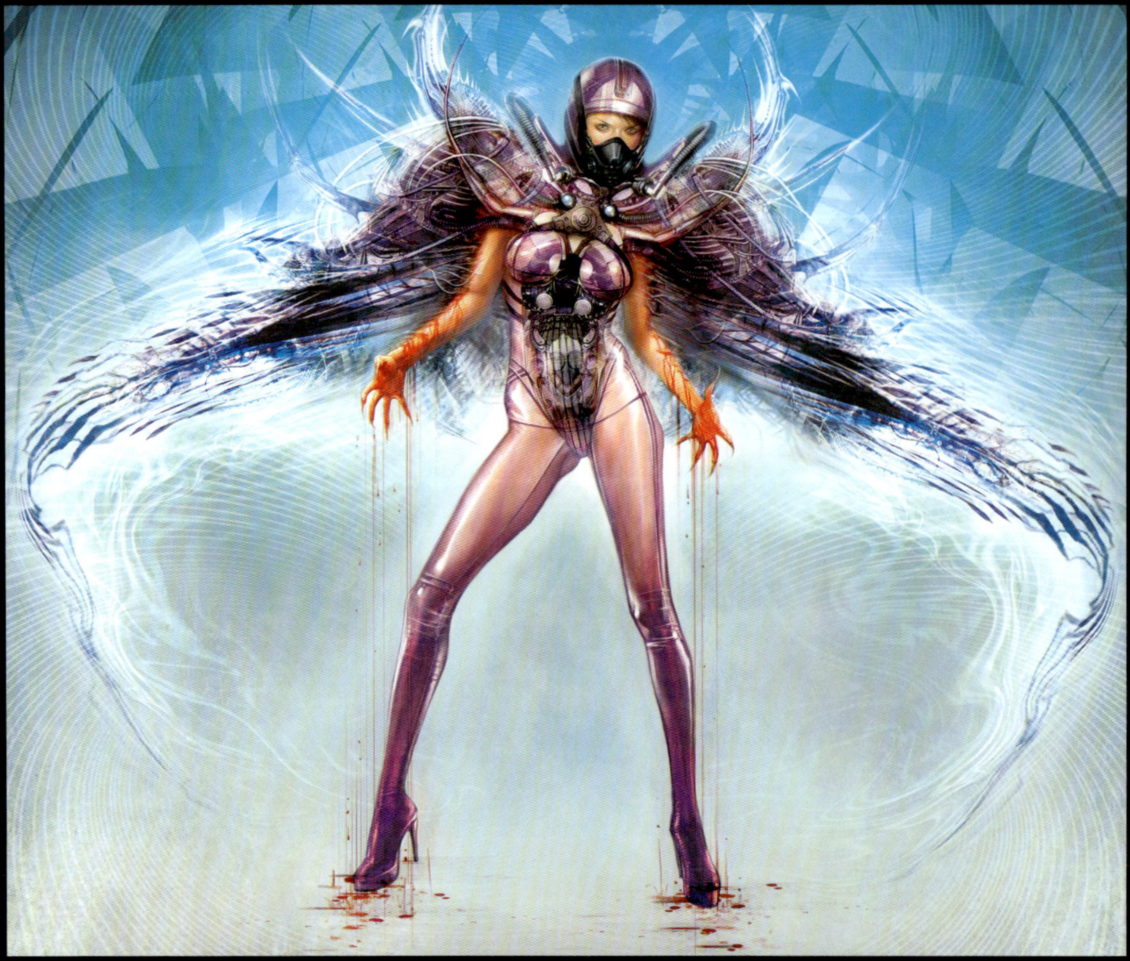

Biomechangel
Photoshop
Michael Leonard, USA
[left]

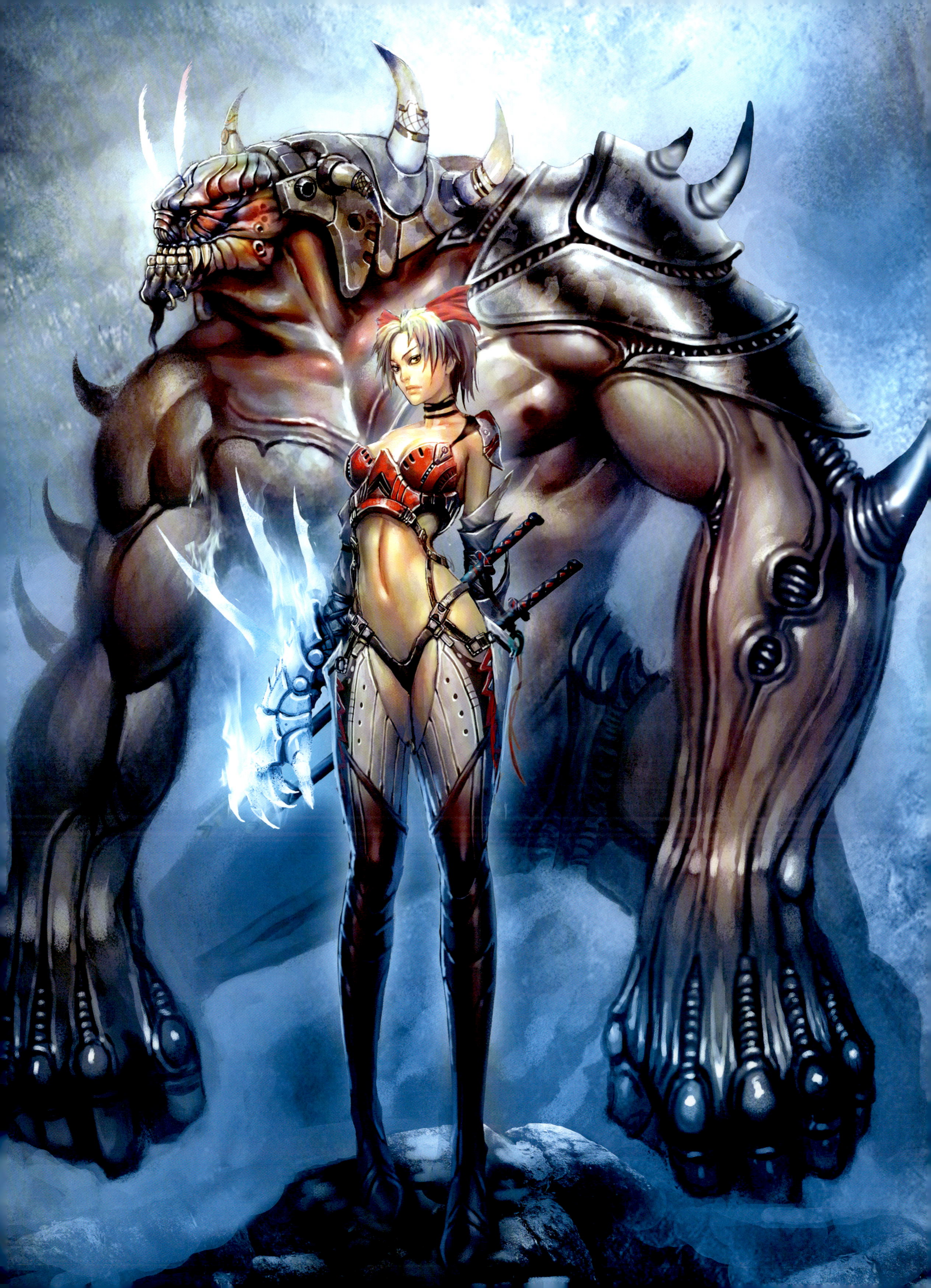

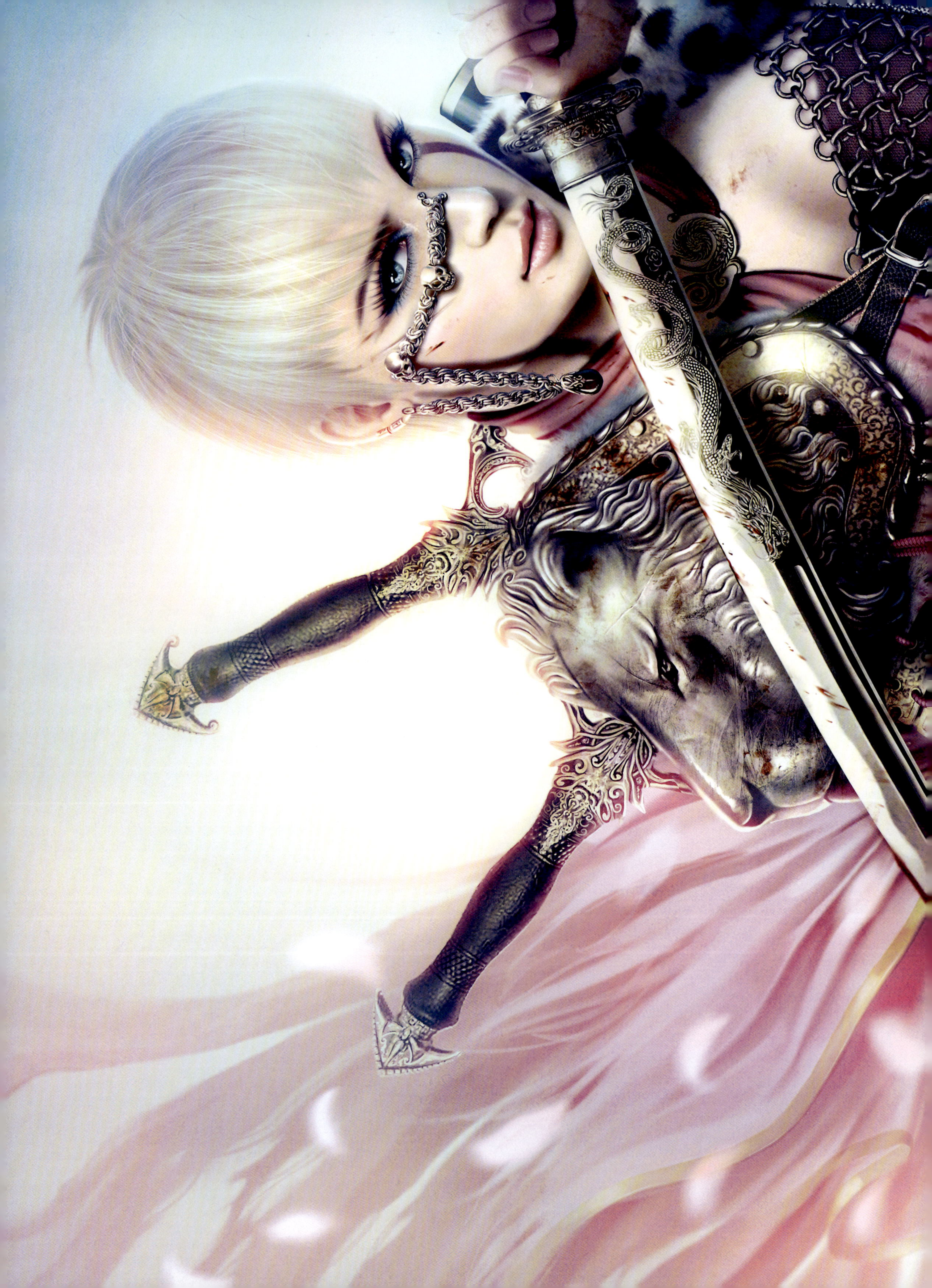

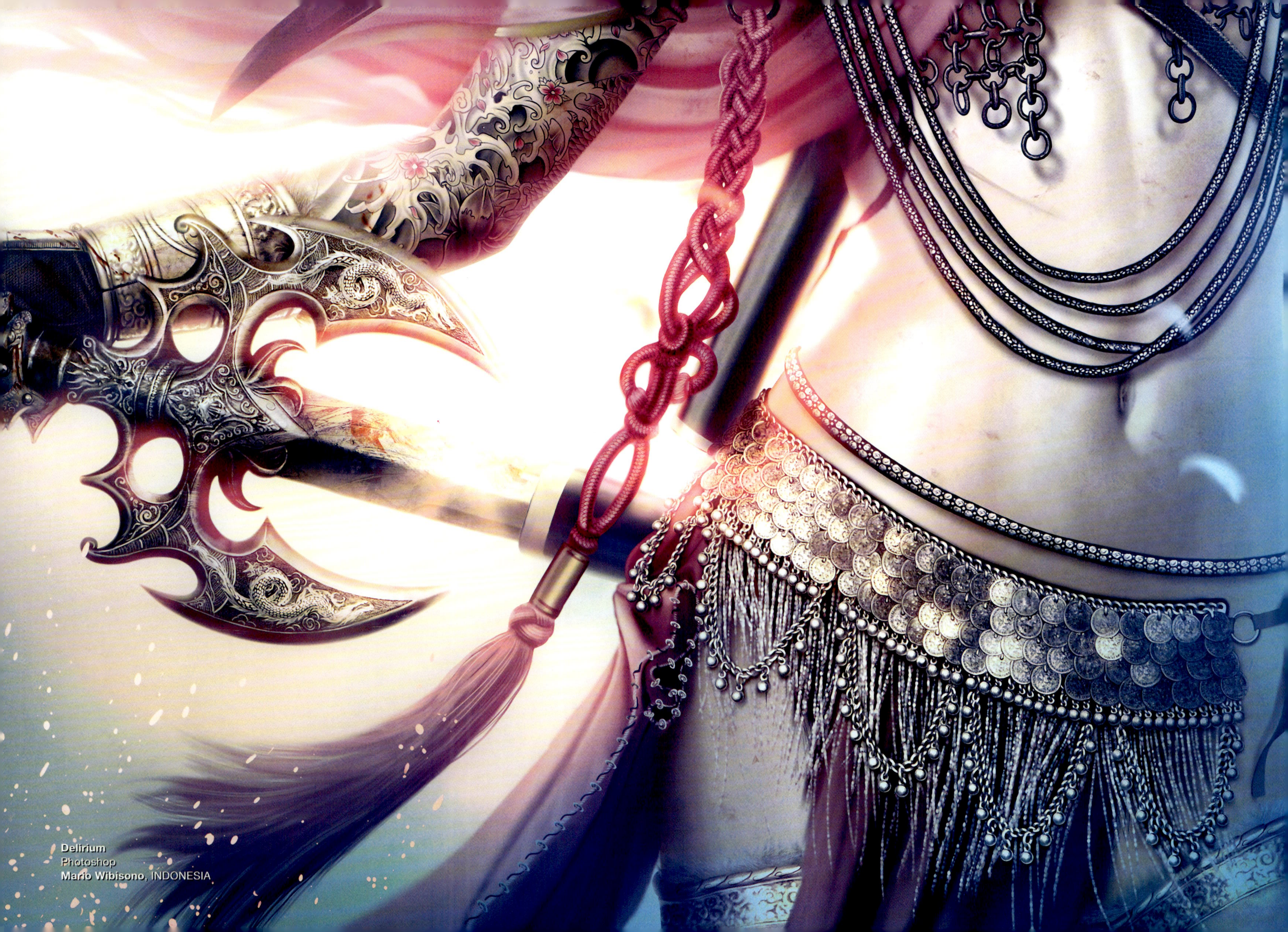

Delirium
Photoshop
Mario Wibisono, INDONESIA

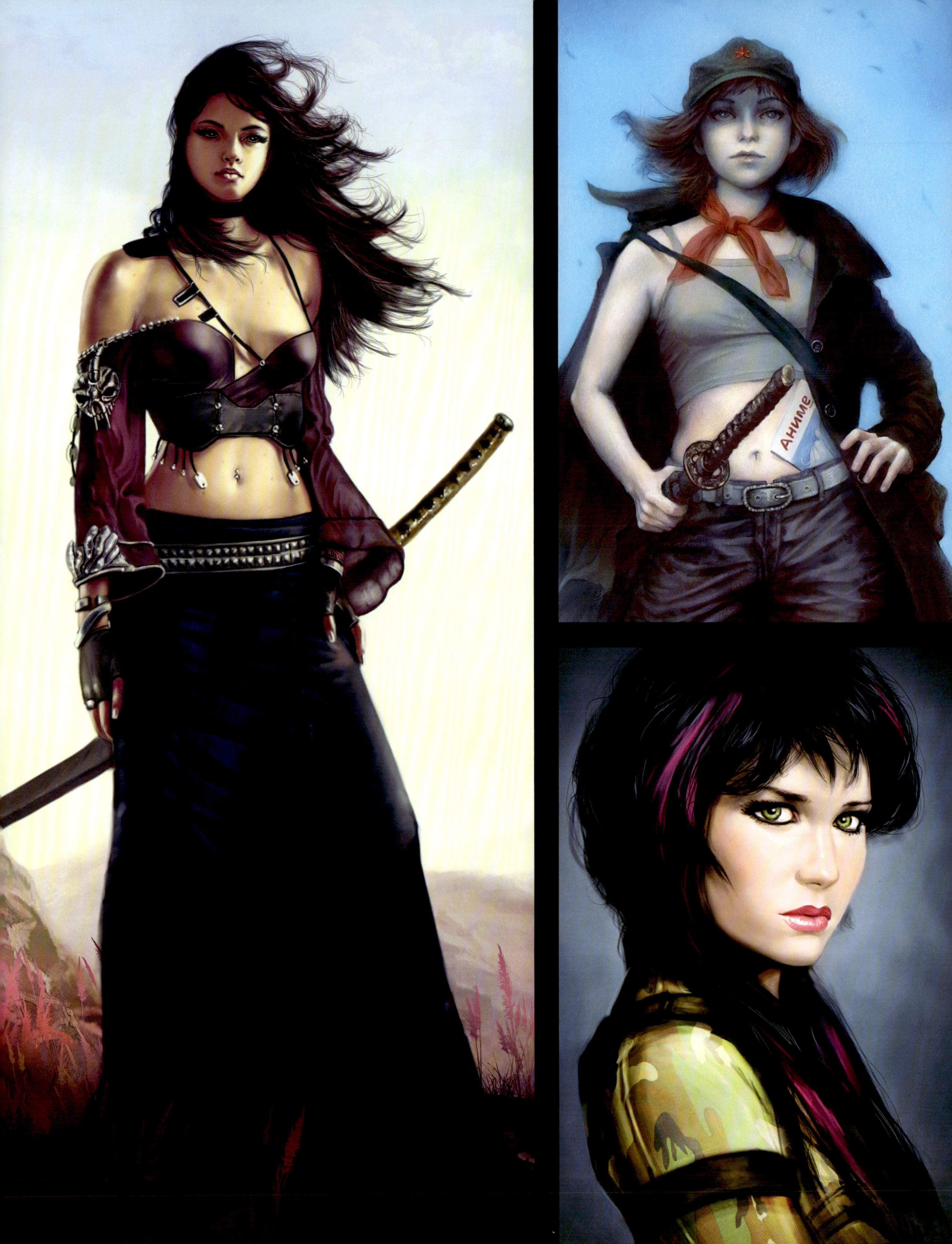
Аниме

Fantasy girl
Photoshop
Aldo Martinez Calzadilla, CANADA
[far left]

Rising
Painter
Client: AnimeGuide magazine
Eva Soulu, RUSSIA
[left]

Northlander
Photoshop
Chao XU, CHINA
[right]

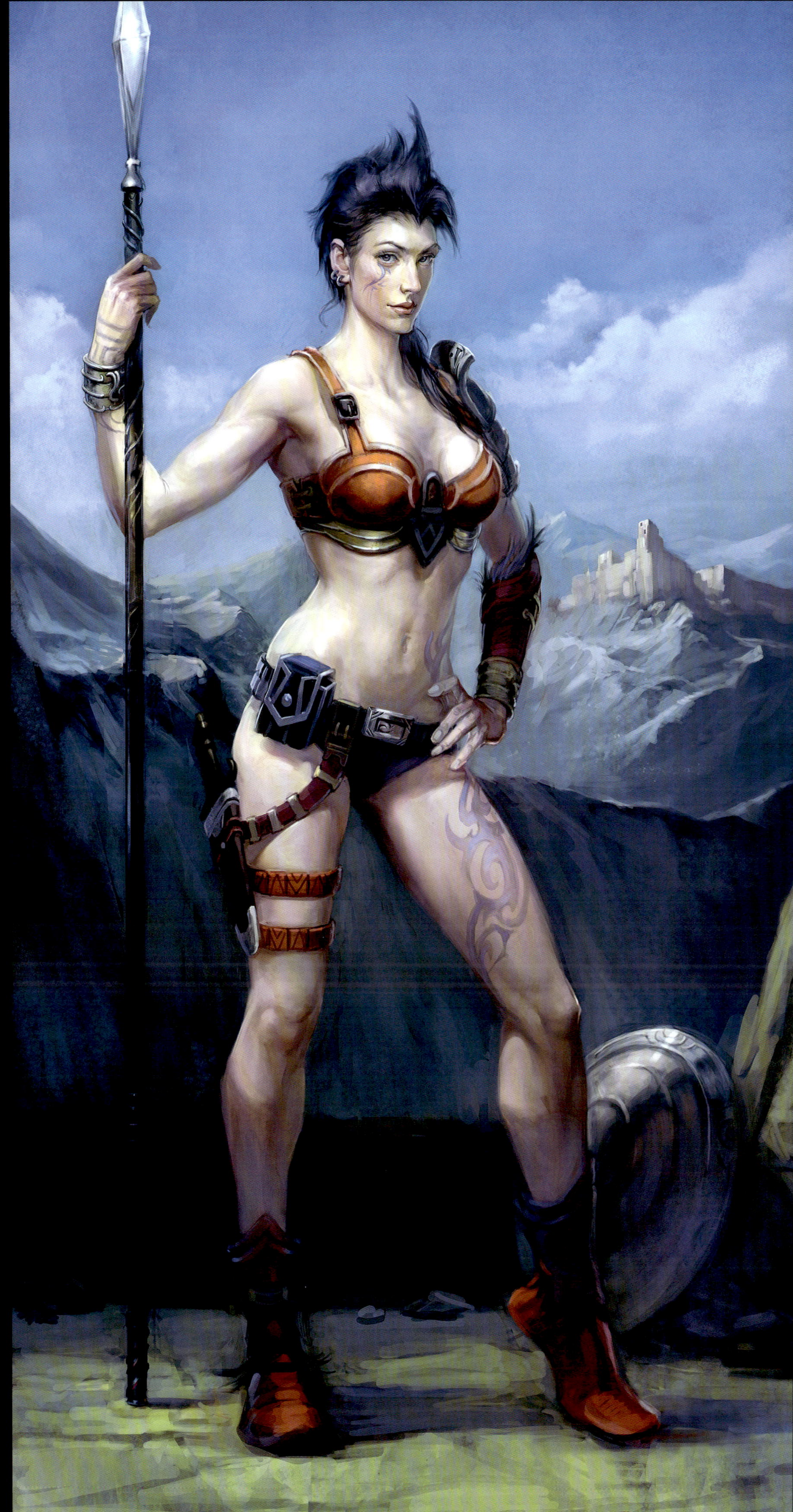

O.k.s.y Military
Photoshop
Ivan Kashubo, RUSSIA
[left]

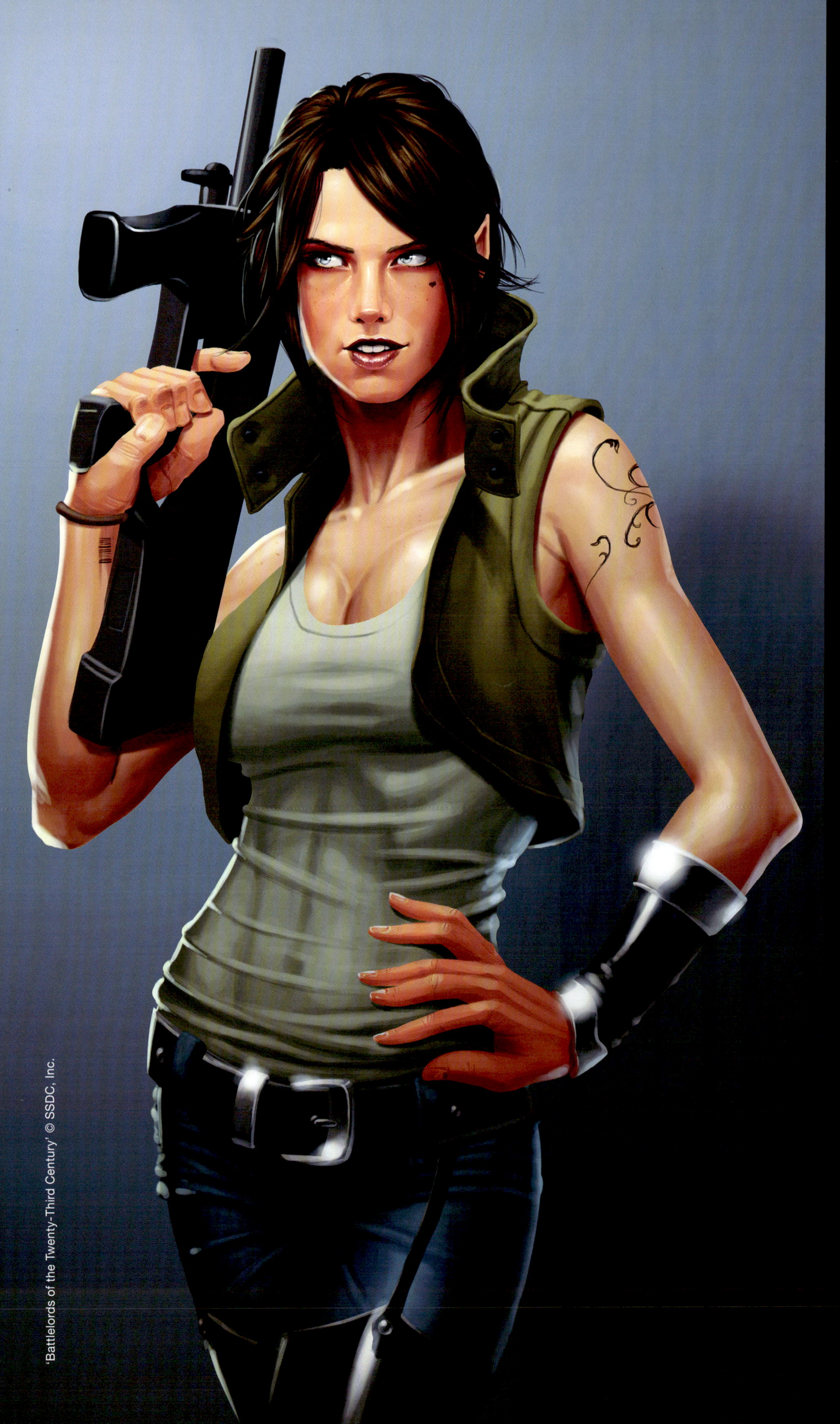

Battlelords of the Twenty-Third Century: Orion Gunner
Photoshop
Client: Athena Virtual Productions, Inc.
Ryan Hawkins, Hawkins Design Concepts, USA
[left]

Mission Completed
Photoshop
Sung Yan 'Frankie' Yip, CHINA
[right]

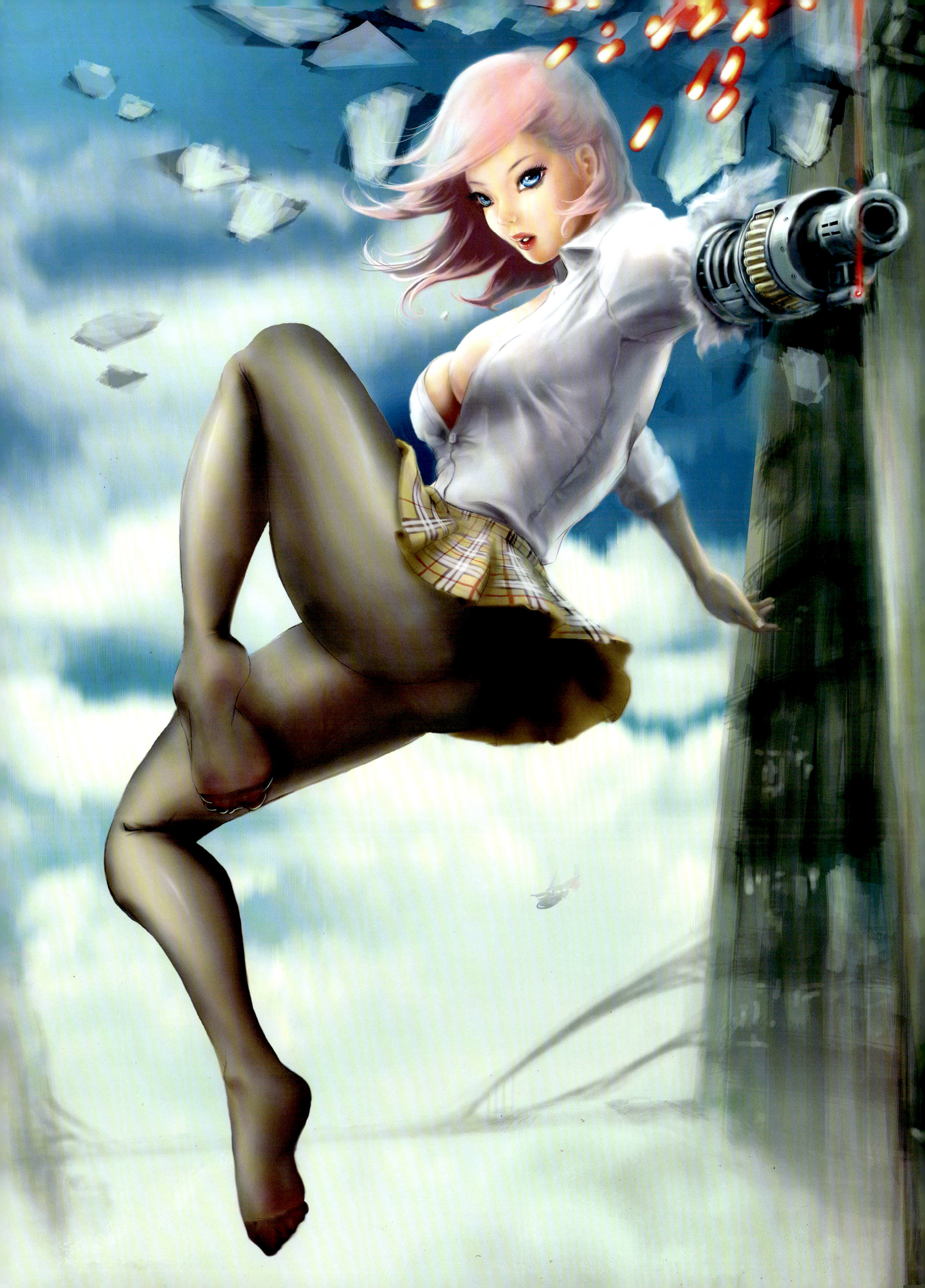

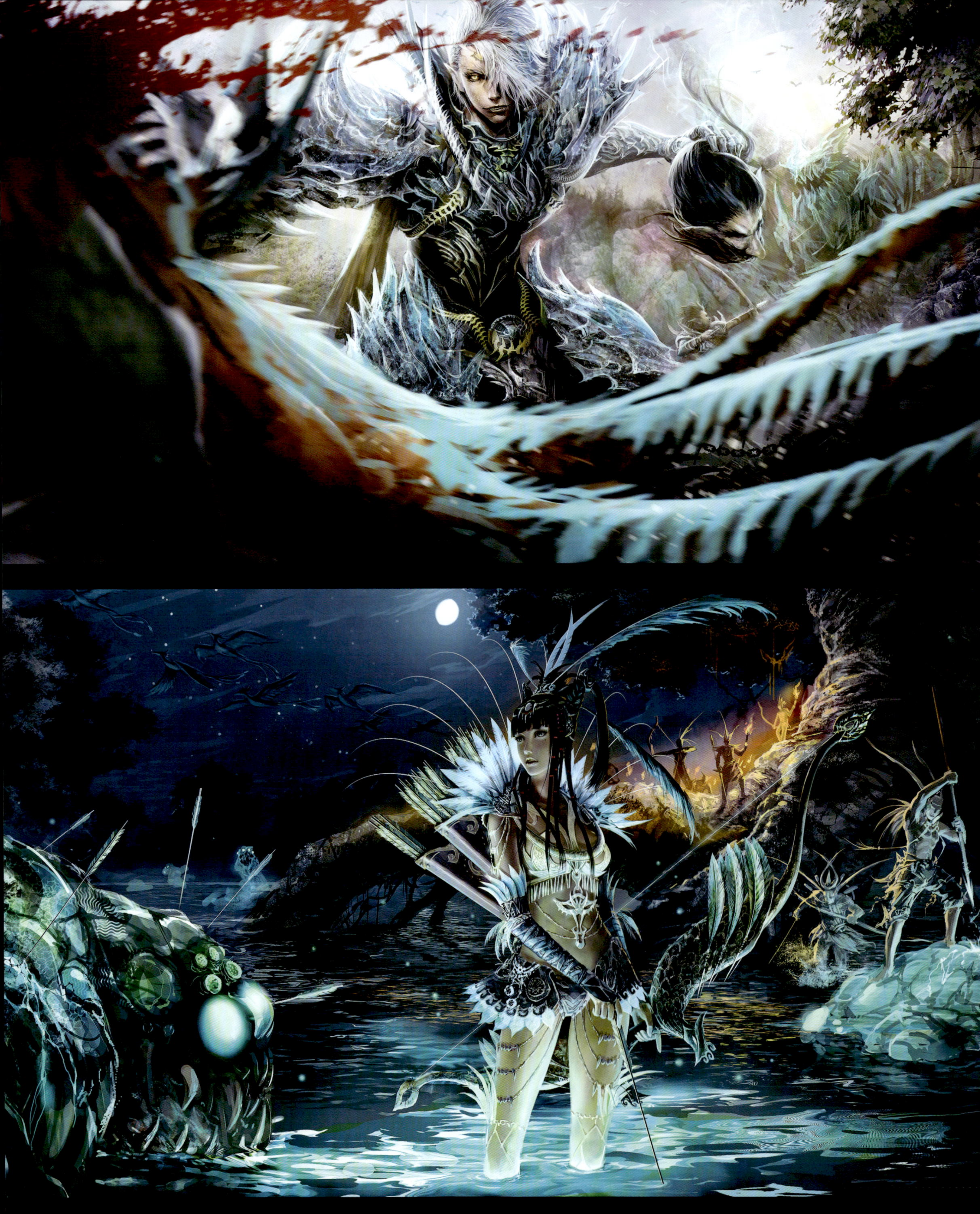

Hunter of Salgador
Photoshop
Buddy Jiang, INDONESIA

Luminous
Photoshop
Jia Tian Yu, CHINA

Wizard Girl
Photoshop
Wenjun Lin, CHINA

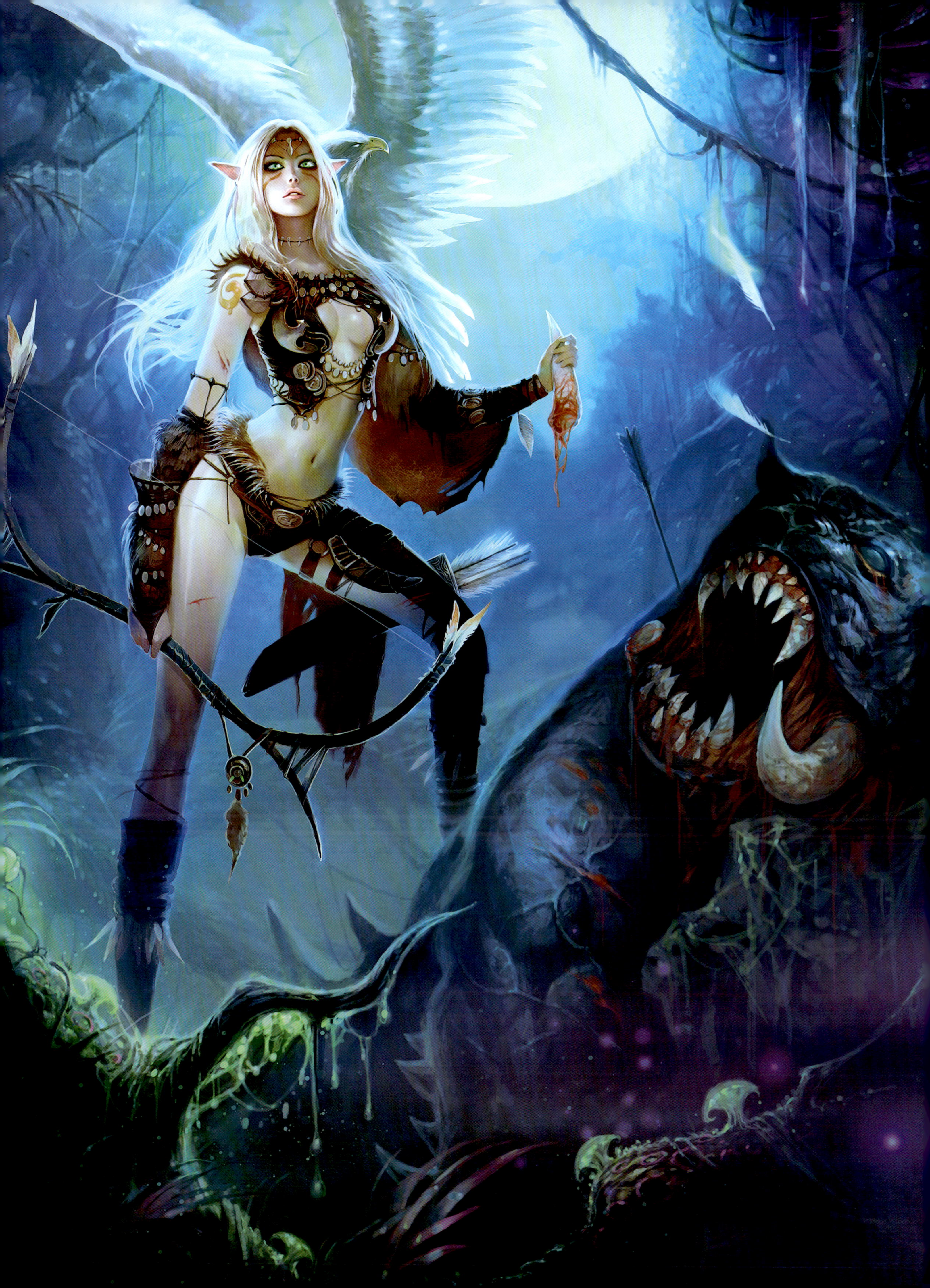

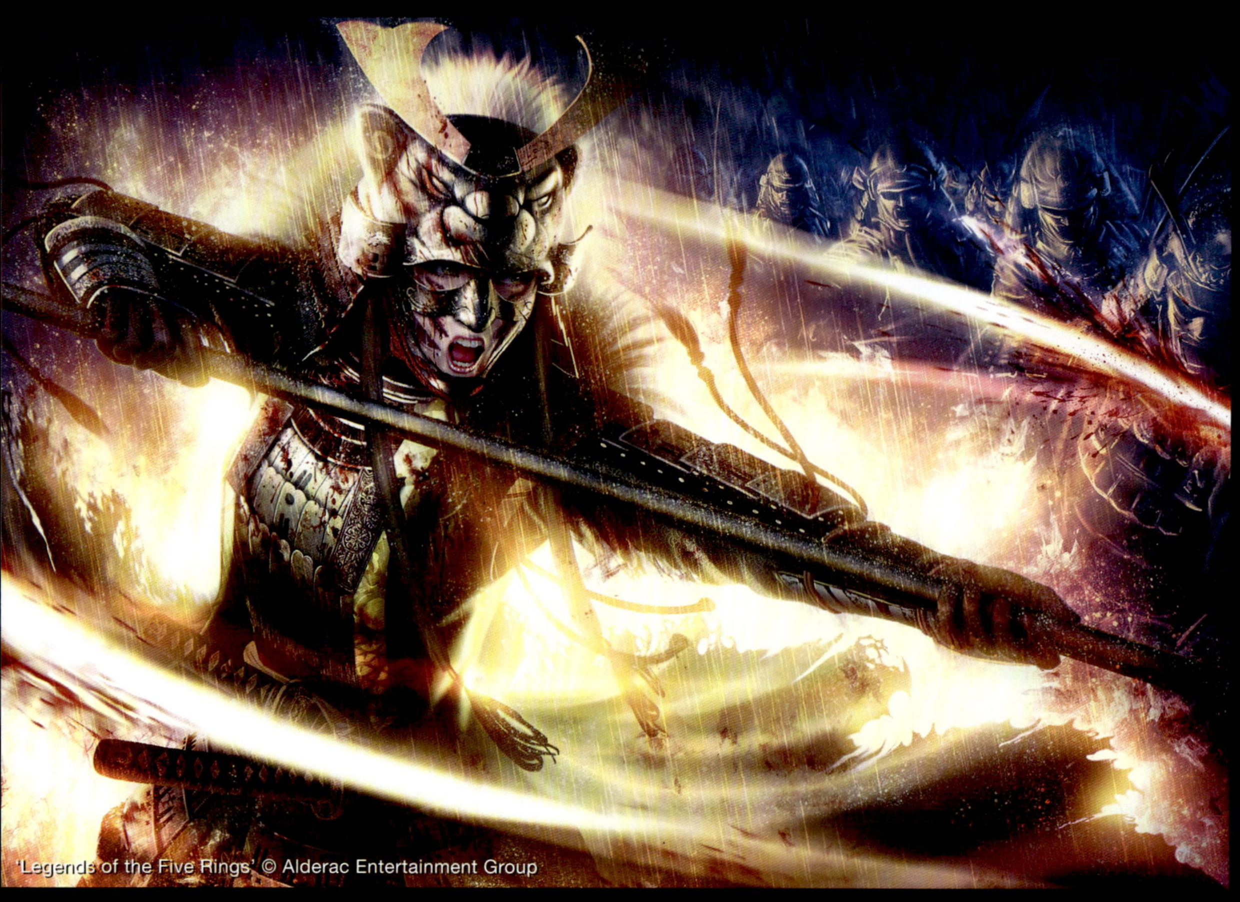

Legend of The Five Rings: Matsu Kita
Photoshop
Client: Alderac Entertainment Group
Mario Wibisono, INDONESIA
[left]

Archer
Photoshop
Michal Ivan, SLOVAKIA
[right]

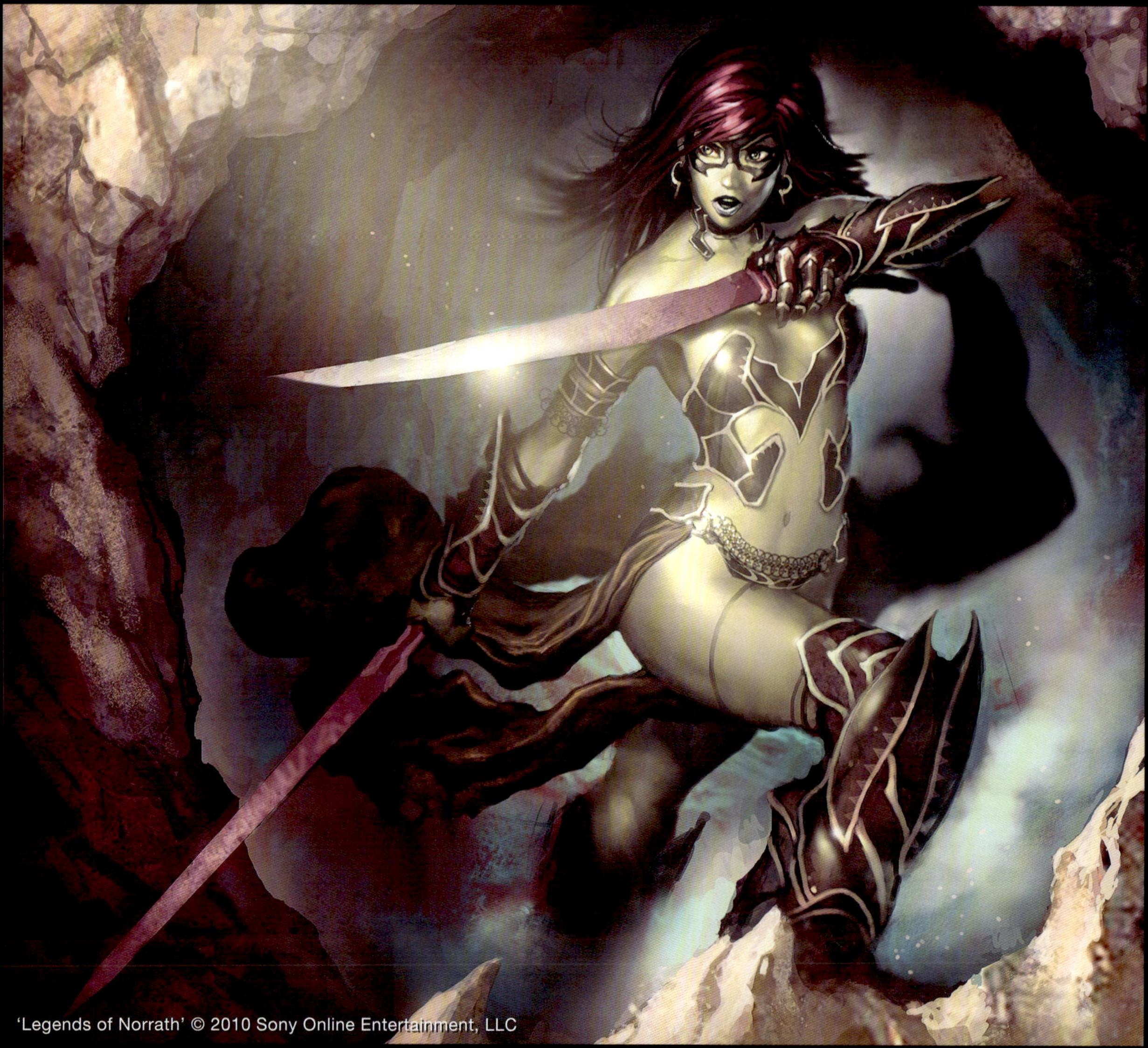

Legends of Norrath: Black Widow Stance
Photoshop
Art Director: Roger Chamberlain
Mike Pedro, Sony Online Entertainment, LLC, USA
[left]

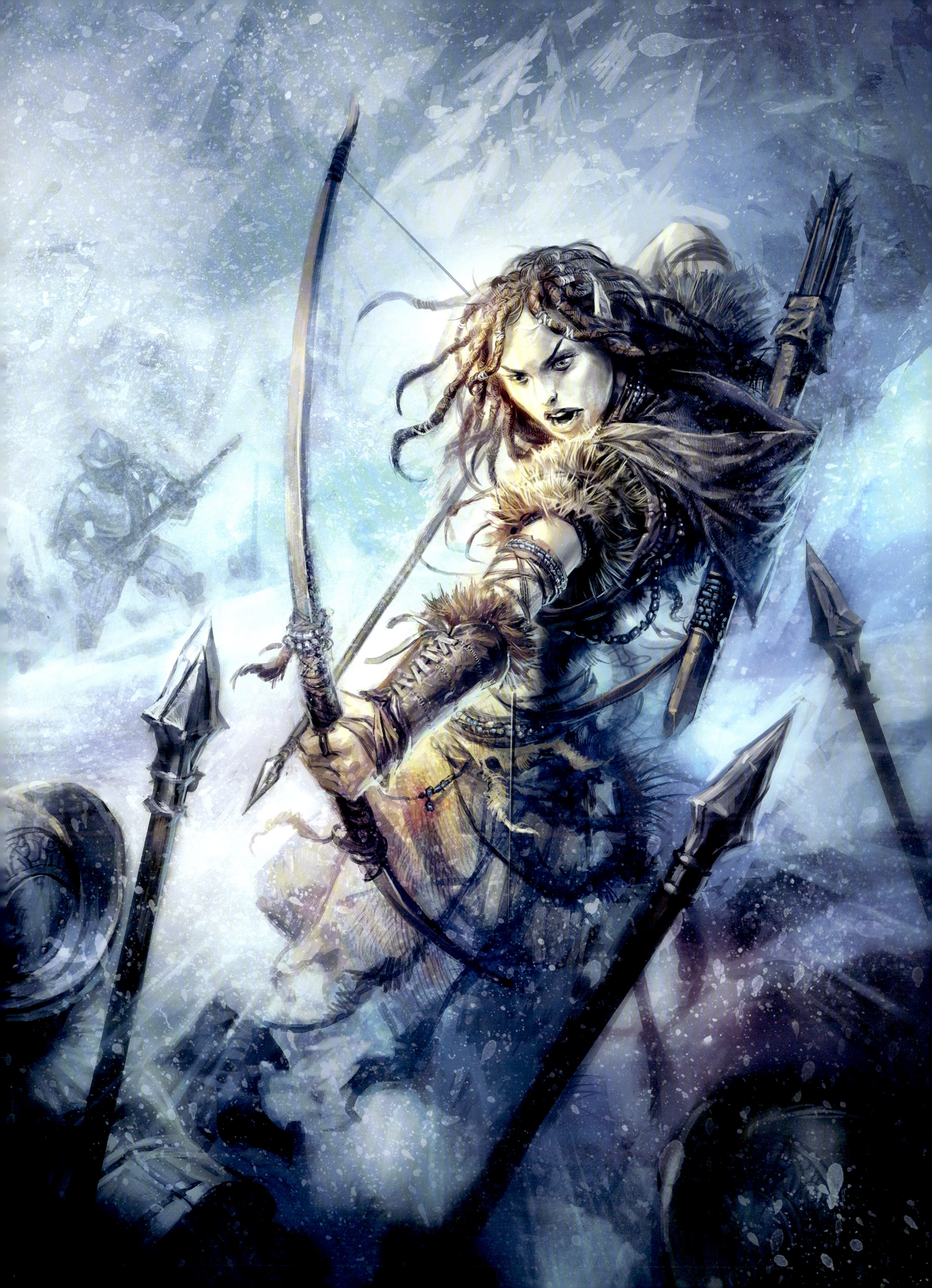

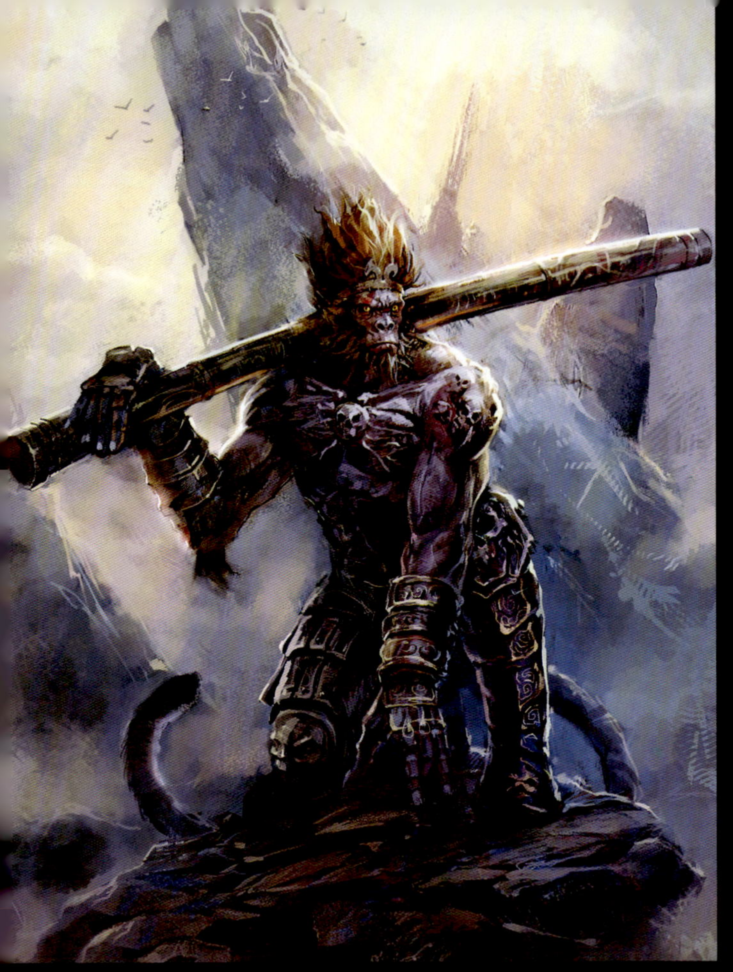

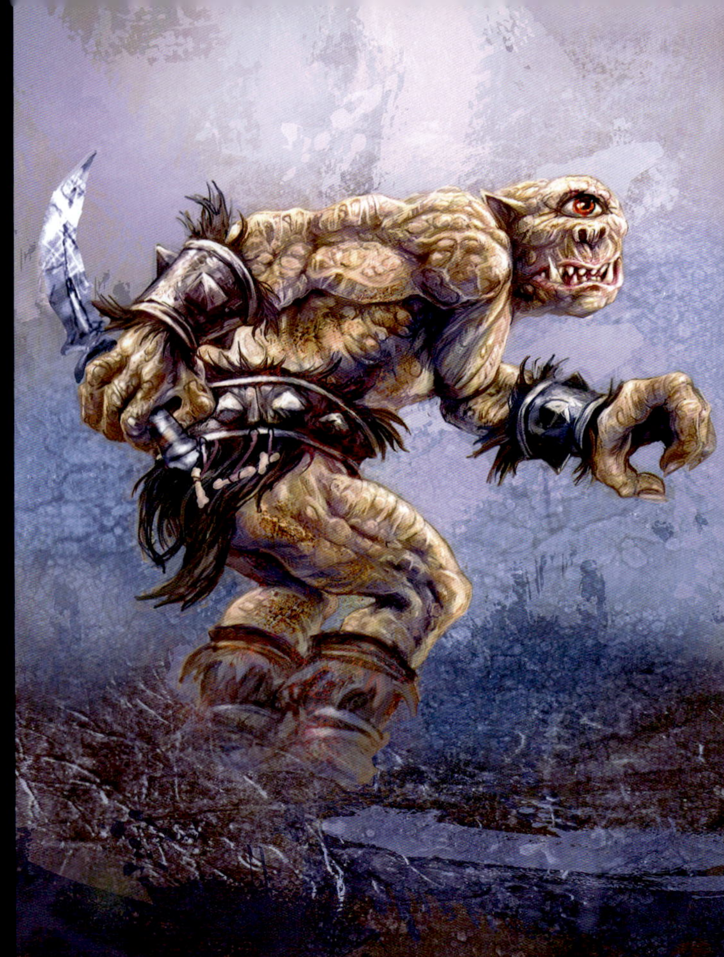

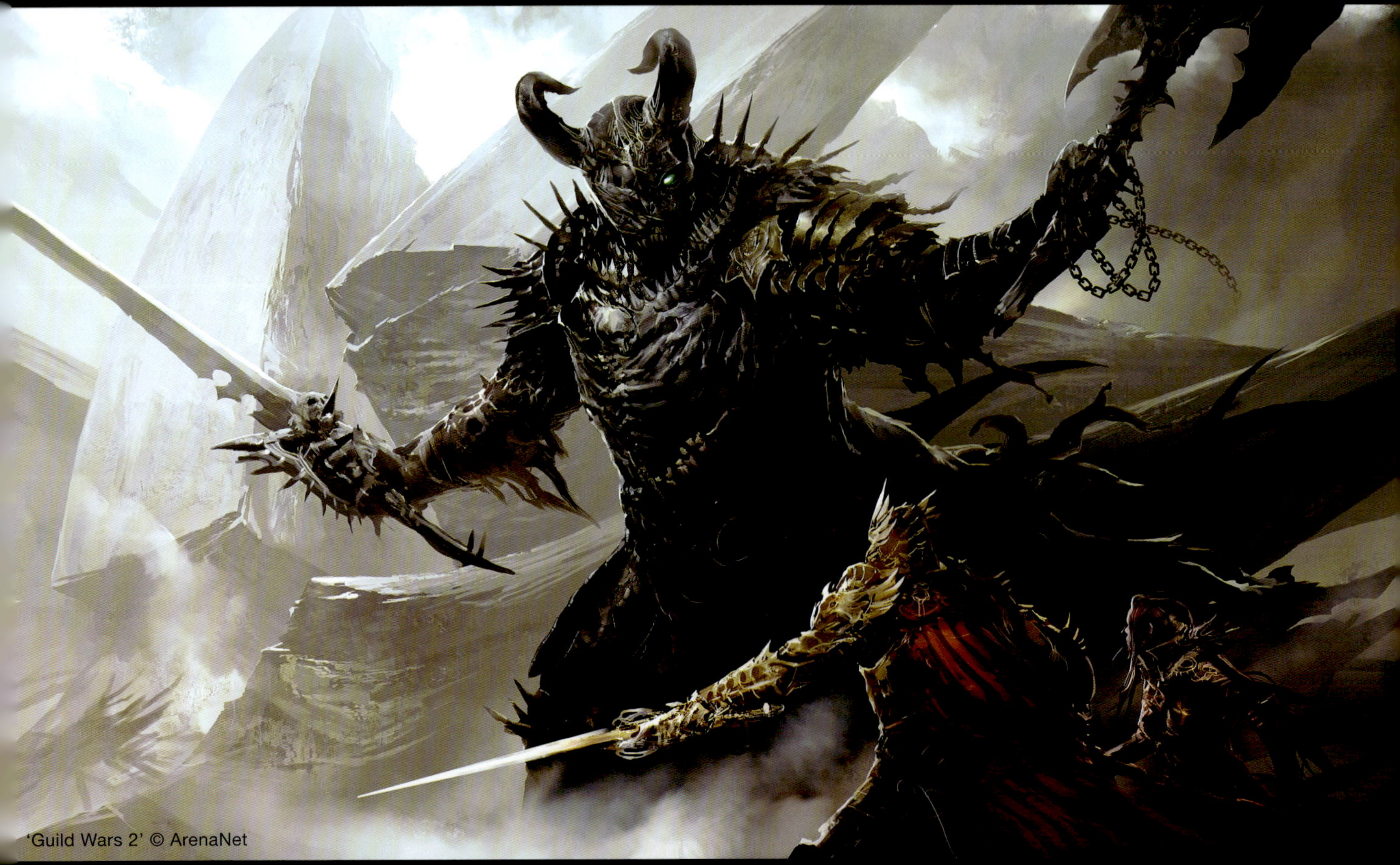

Monkey King
Photoshop
Songnan Li, CHINA
[top]

Undead Warrior
Photoshop
Kekai Kotaki, USA
[above]

Colossal Arena: Cyclops
Photoshop
Client: Altar Games
Jan Patrik Krasny, CZECH REPUBLIC *[top]*

Undead
Photoshop
Client: Irregular Magazine
Ricardo Guimaraes, BRAZIL *[right*

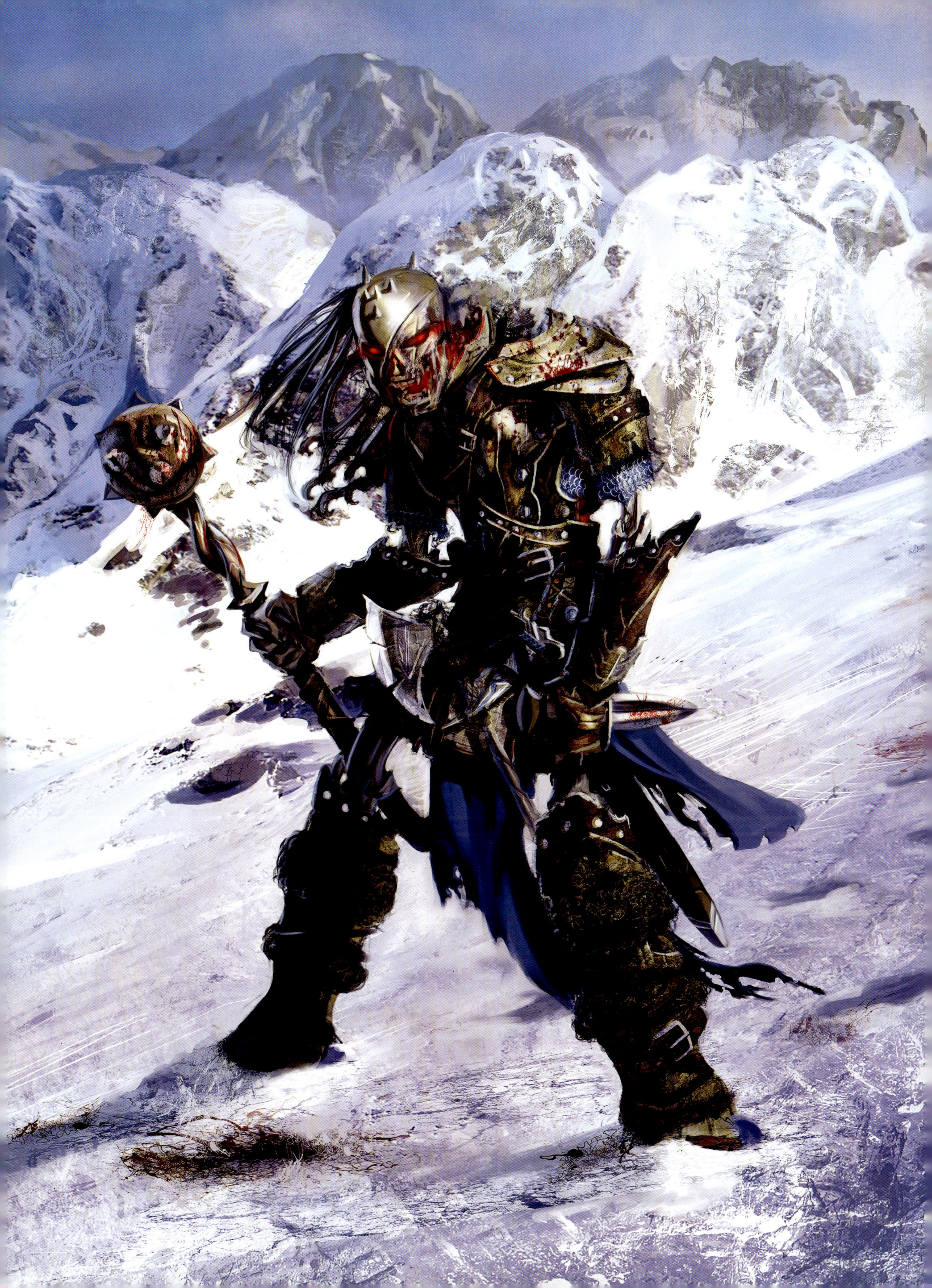

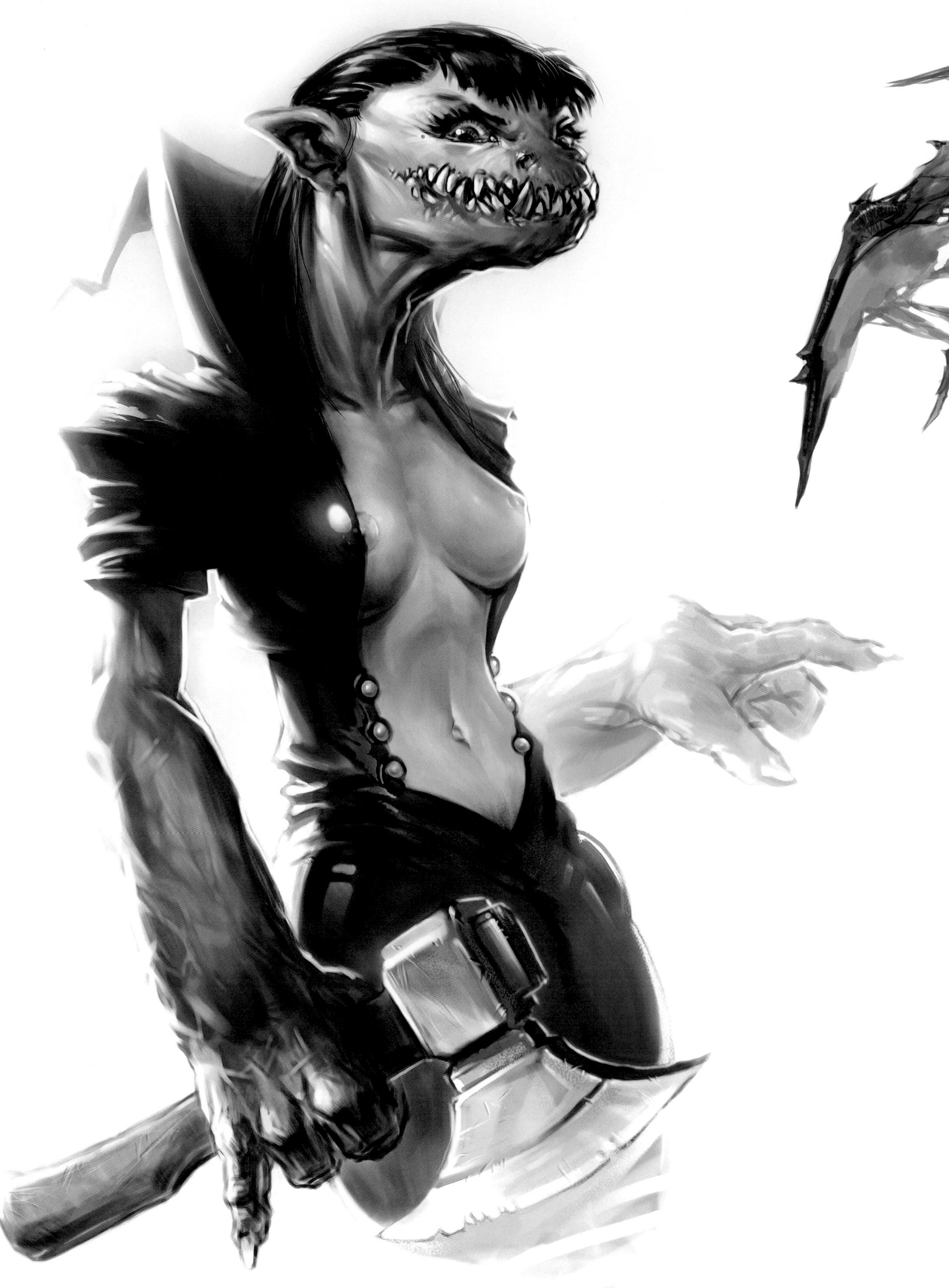

Monstro 'Wom'
Photoshop
Ivan Kashubo, RUSSIA
[above]

IllidanStormrage
Photoshop
Qiu Jian Yuan, CHINA
[opposite top left]

Inuit Mythology Project: Child Stealer
Photoshop
Client: Inhabit Media
Kerem Beyit, TURKEY
[opposite top right]

Giant Traveller
Photoshop
Lukasz Jaskolski, POLAND
[opposite bottom left]

Goblin
Photoshop
Henrique Mamede, BRAZIL
[opposite bottom right]

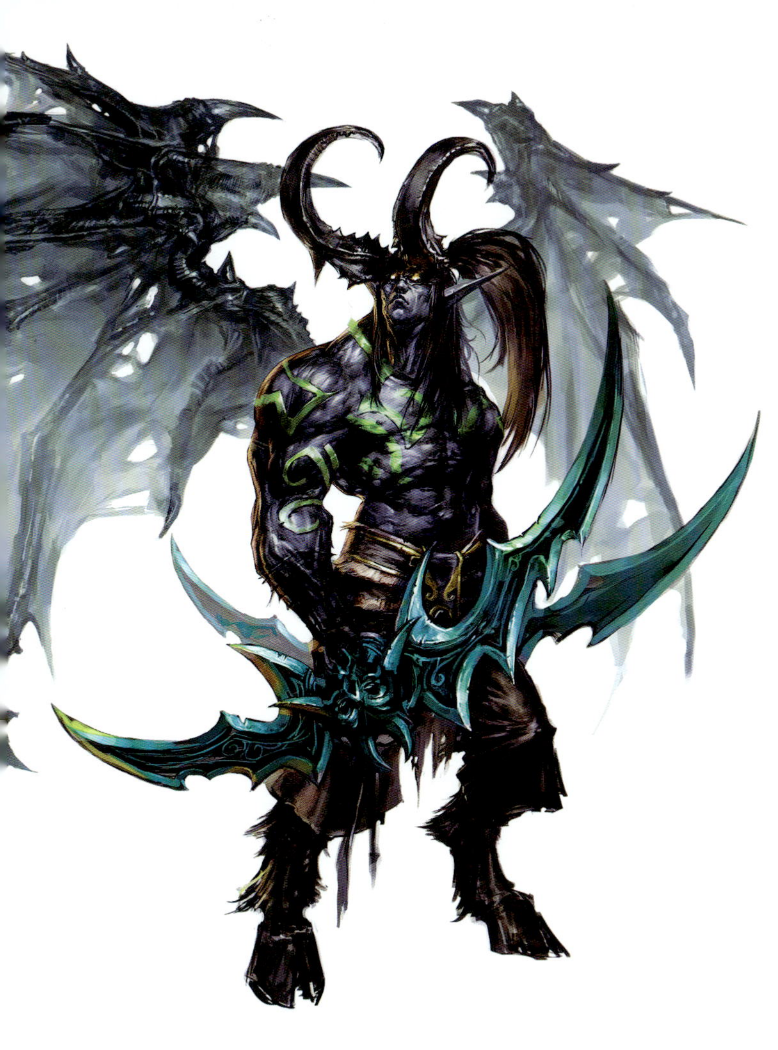

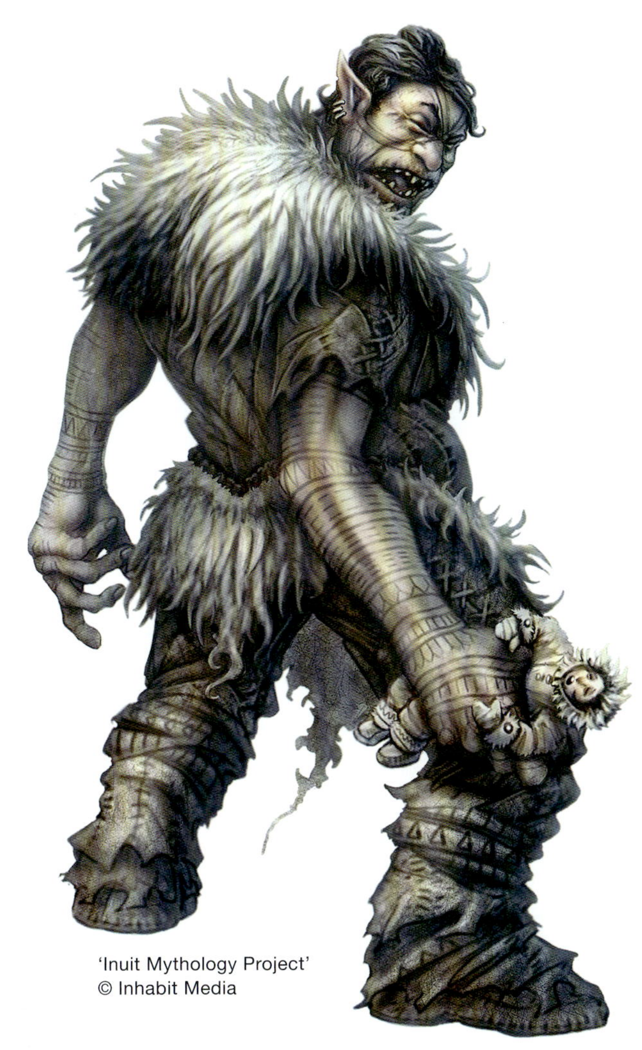

'Inuit Mythology Project'
© Inhabit Media

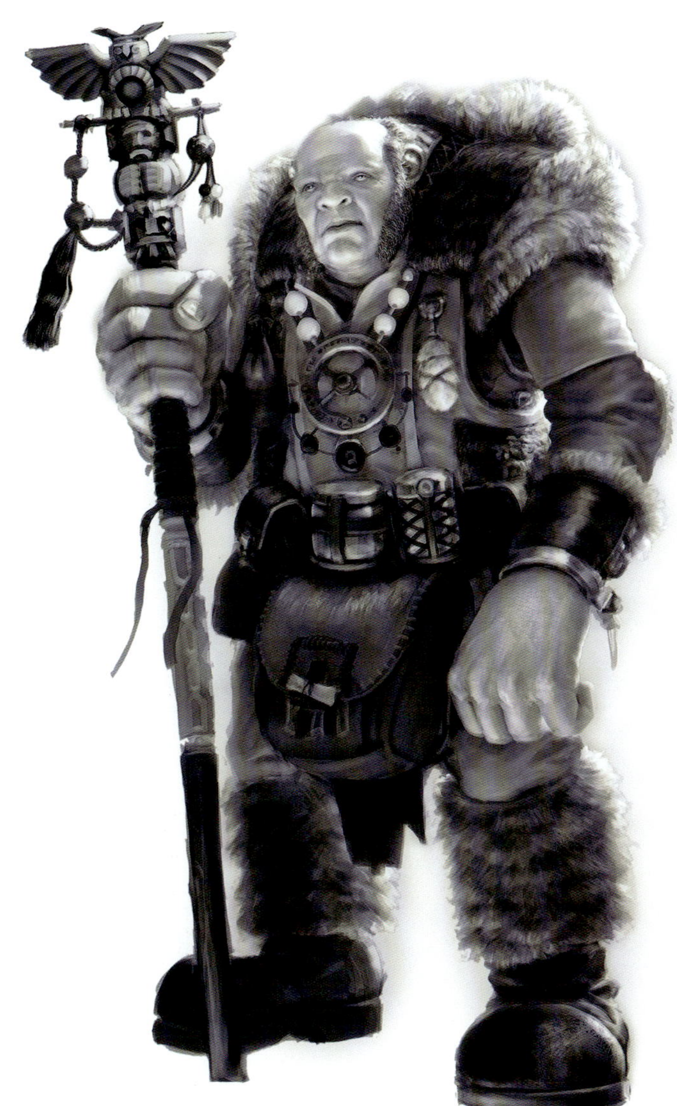

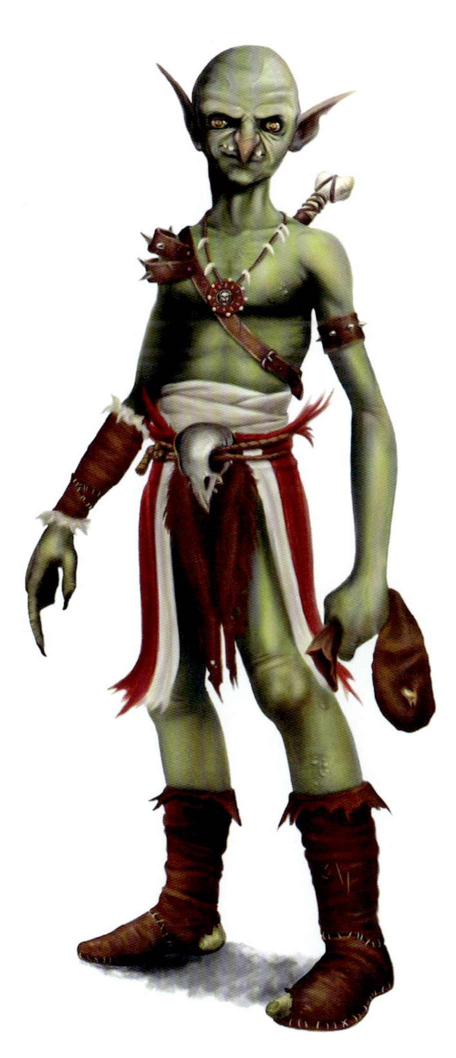

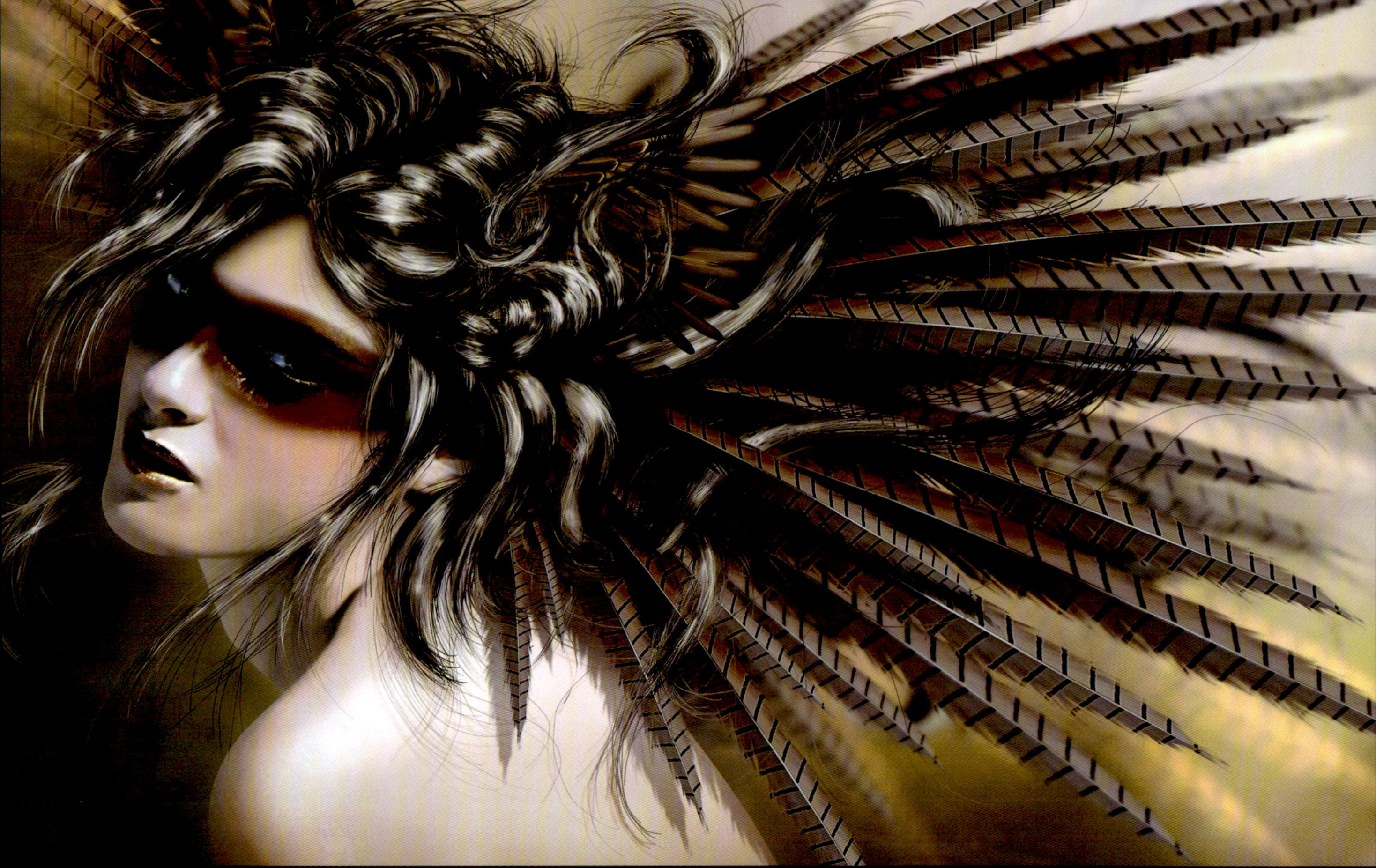

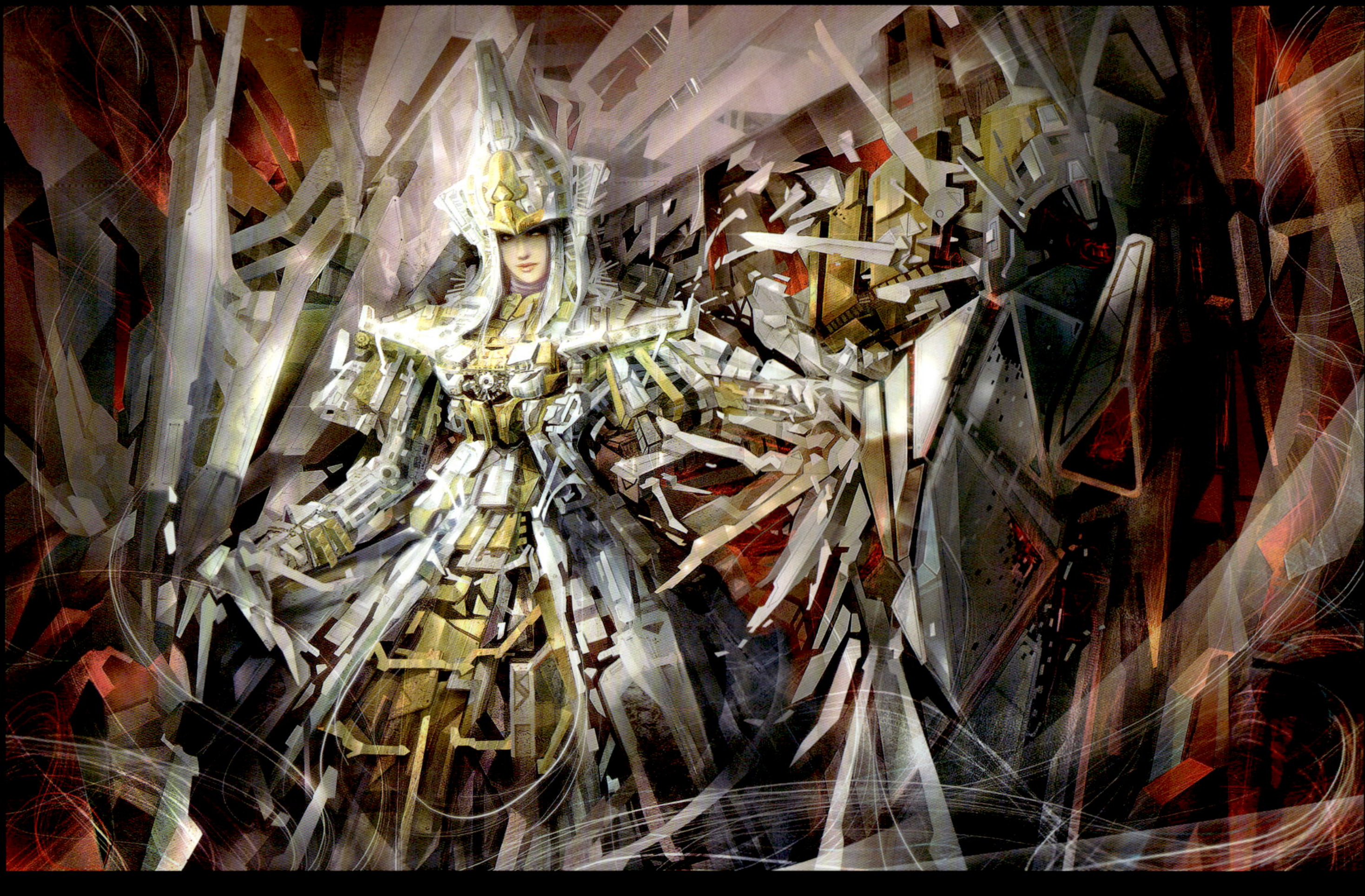

Faisan
Photoshop
Carine Grasset, FRANCE

Shining Castle
Photoshop
Au Yeung Chun Hay, CHINA

Stem
Painter, Photoshop
Hong Kuang, CHINA

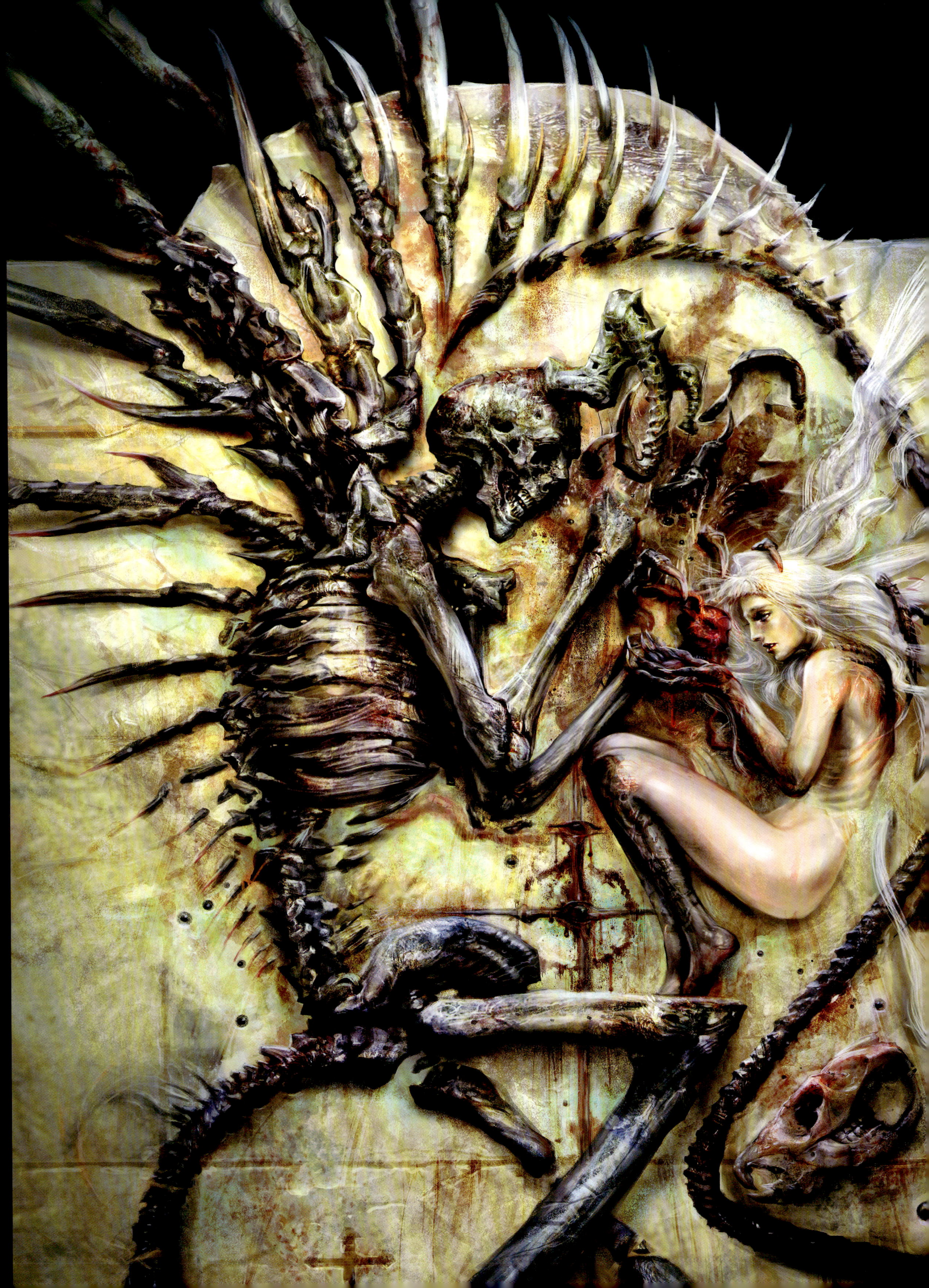

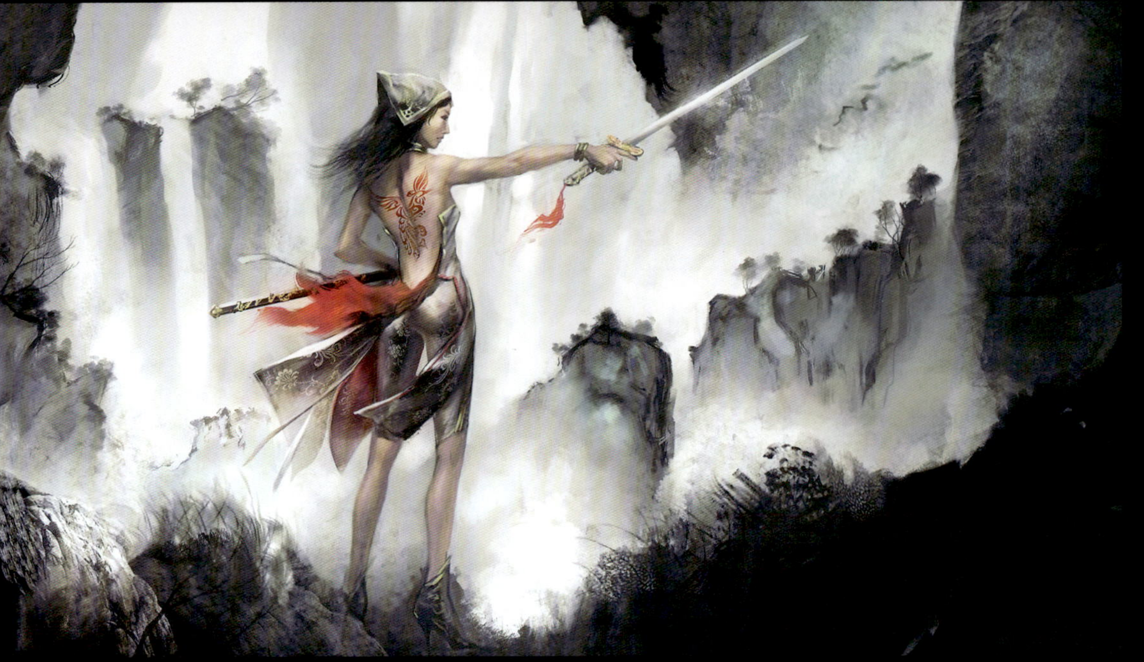

Dynasty
Photoshop
Frank Hong, CANADA
[left]

Mala Estrella
Photoshop
Inspired by:
Henar Torinos's 'Mala Estrella' character
David Laguens, SPAIN
[right]

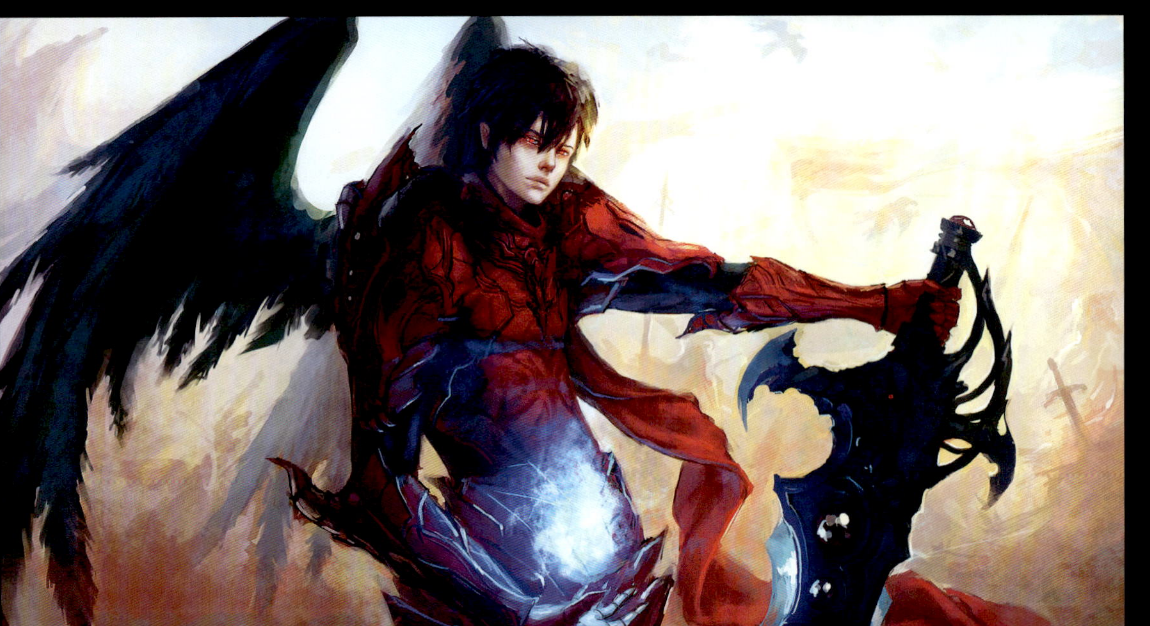

Untitled
Photoshop, Painter
Katrina Lin, CANADA
[left]

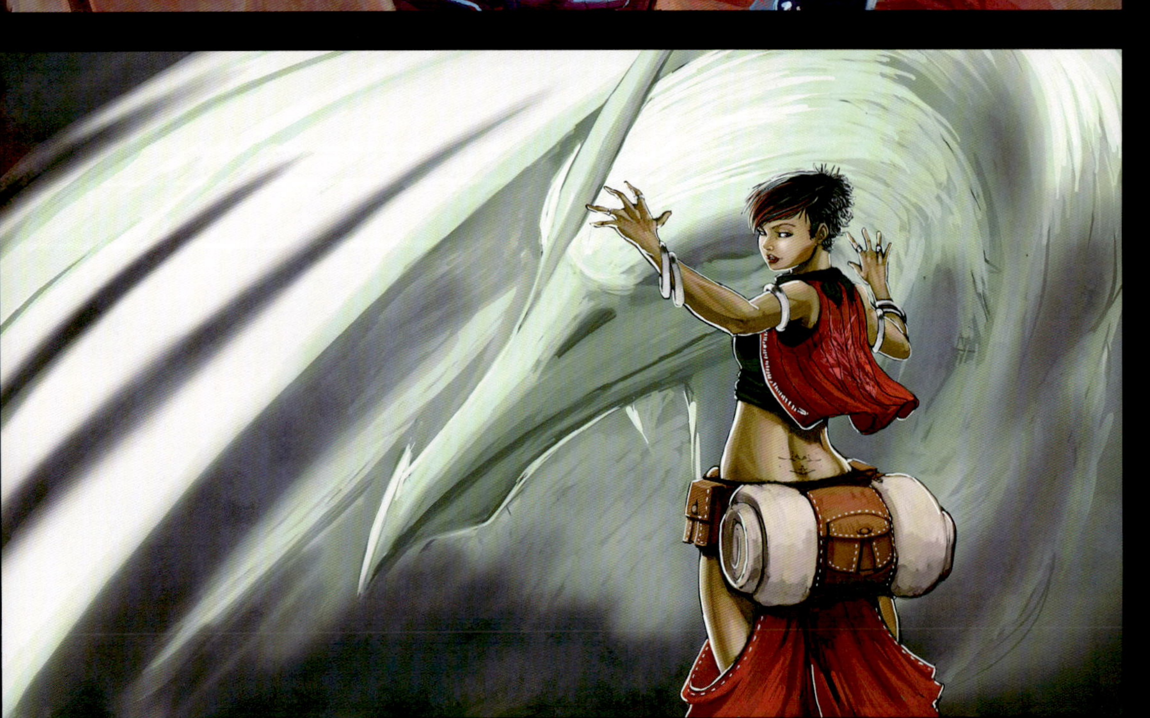

Her beAst friend
Photoshop
William Jones, USA
[left]

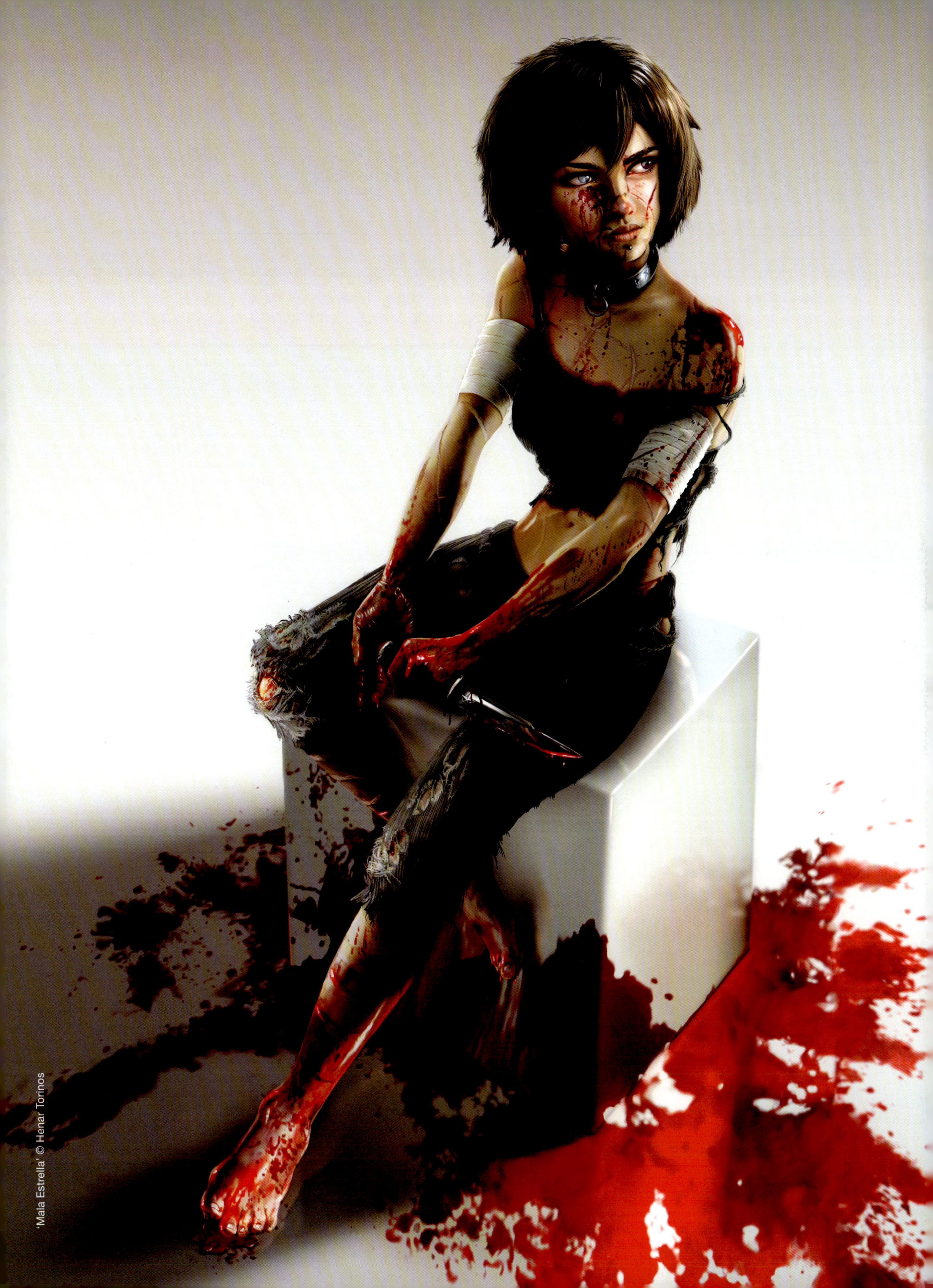

'Mala Estrella' © Henar Torinos

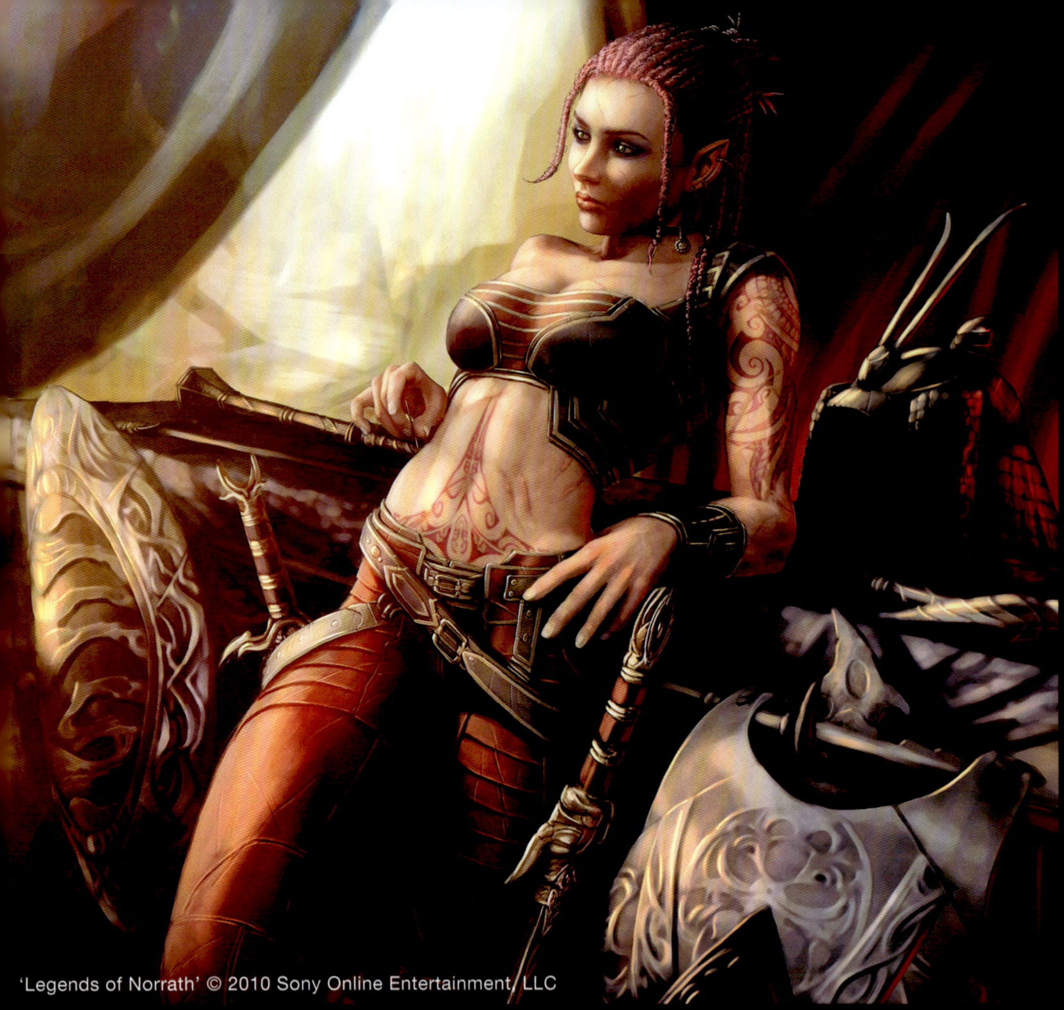

'Legends of Norrath' © 2010 Sony Online Entertainment, LLC

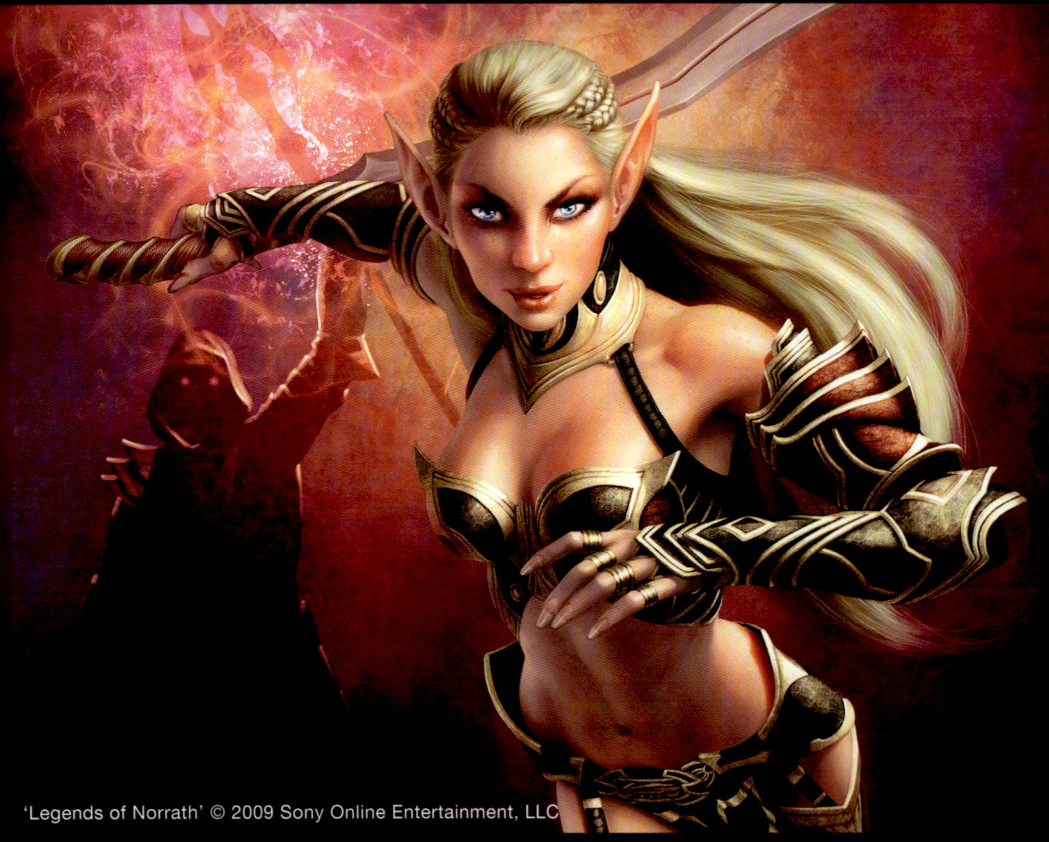

'Legends of Norrath' © 2009 Sony Online Entertainment, LLC

Legends of Norrath: Weapons Master
Photoshop
Art Director: Roger Chamberlain
Derek Herring, Sony Online Entertainment, LLC, USA *[top]*

Legends of Norrath: Aggressive Advance
Photoshop
Art Director: Roger Chamberlain
Client: Sony Online Entertainment, LLC
Steve Argyle, USA *[above]*

Legend of The Five Rings: Shiba Tsukimi
Photoshop
Client: Alderac Entertainment Group
Mario Wibisono, INDONESIA *[right]*

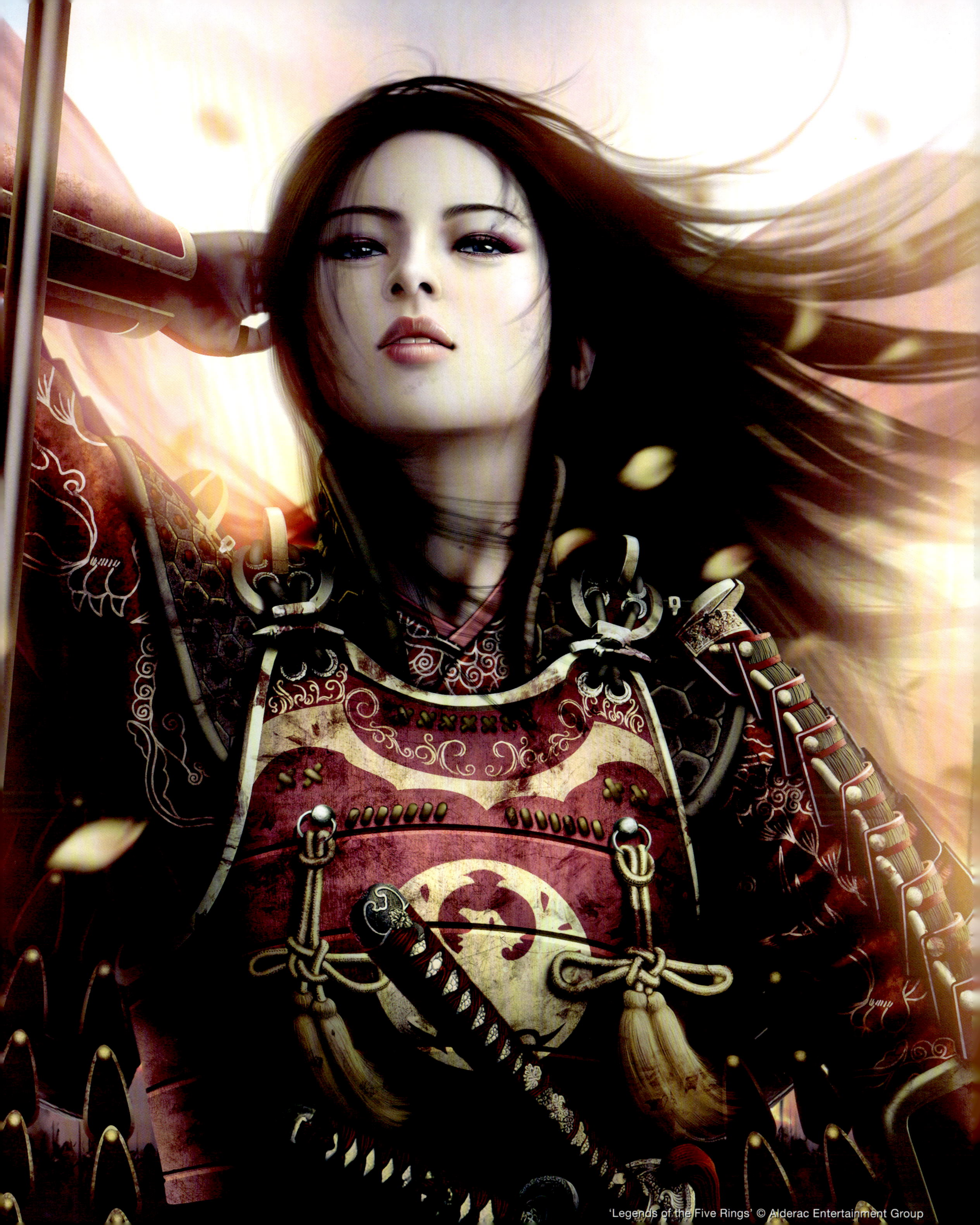

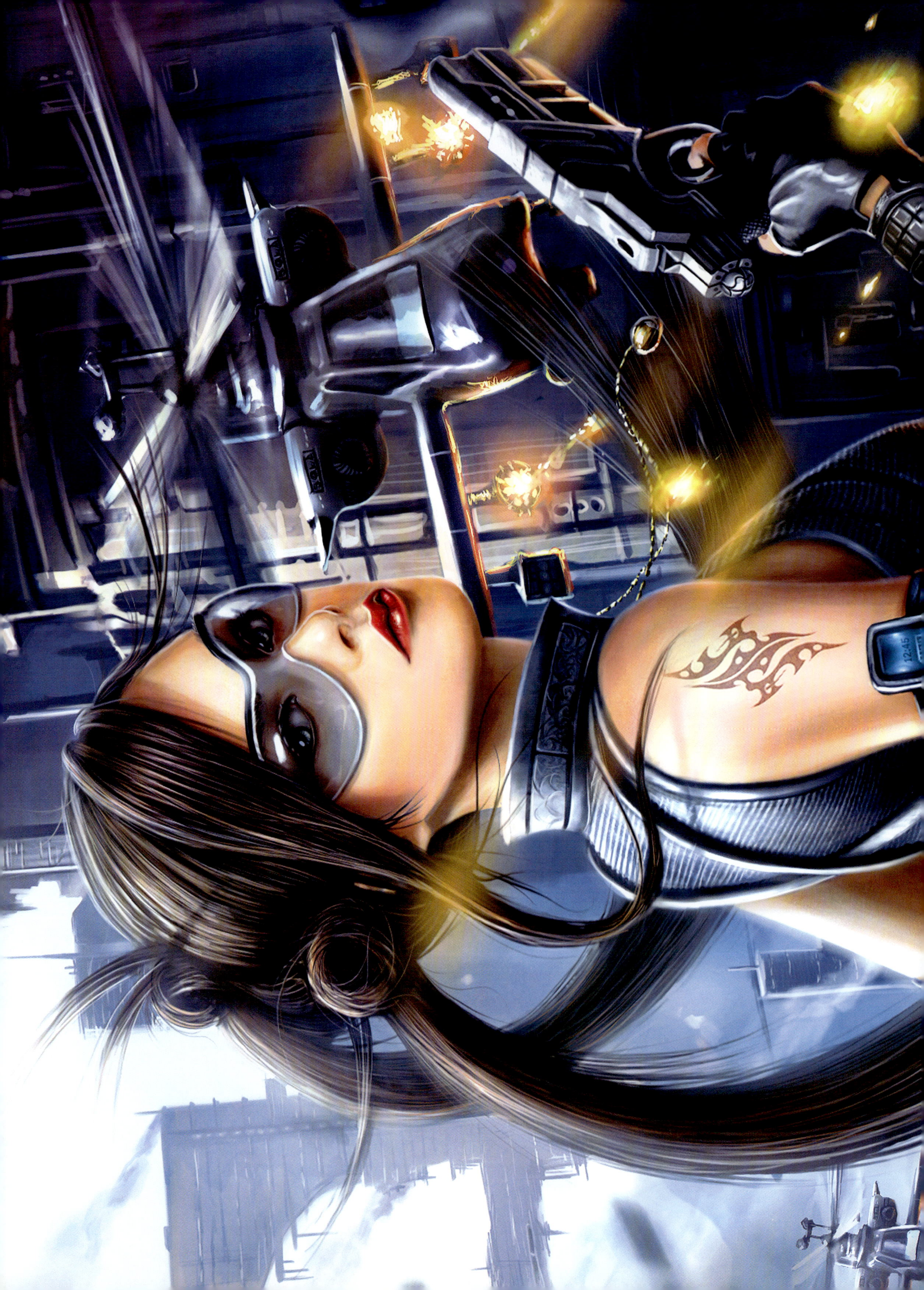

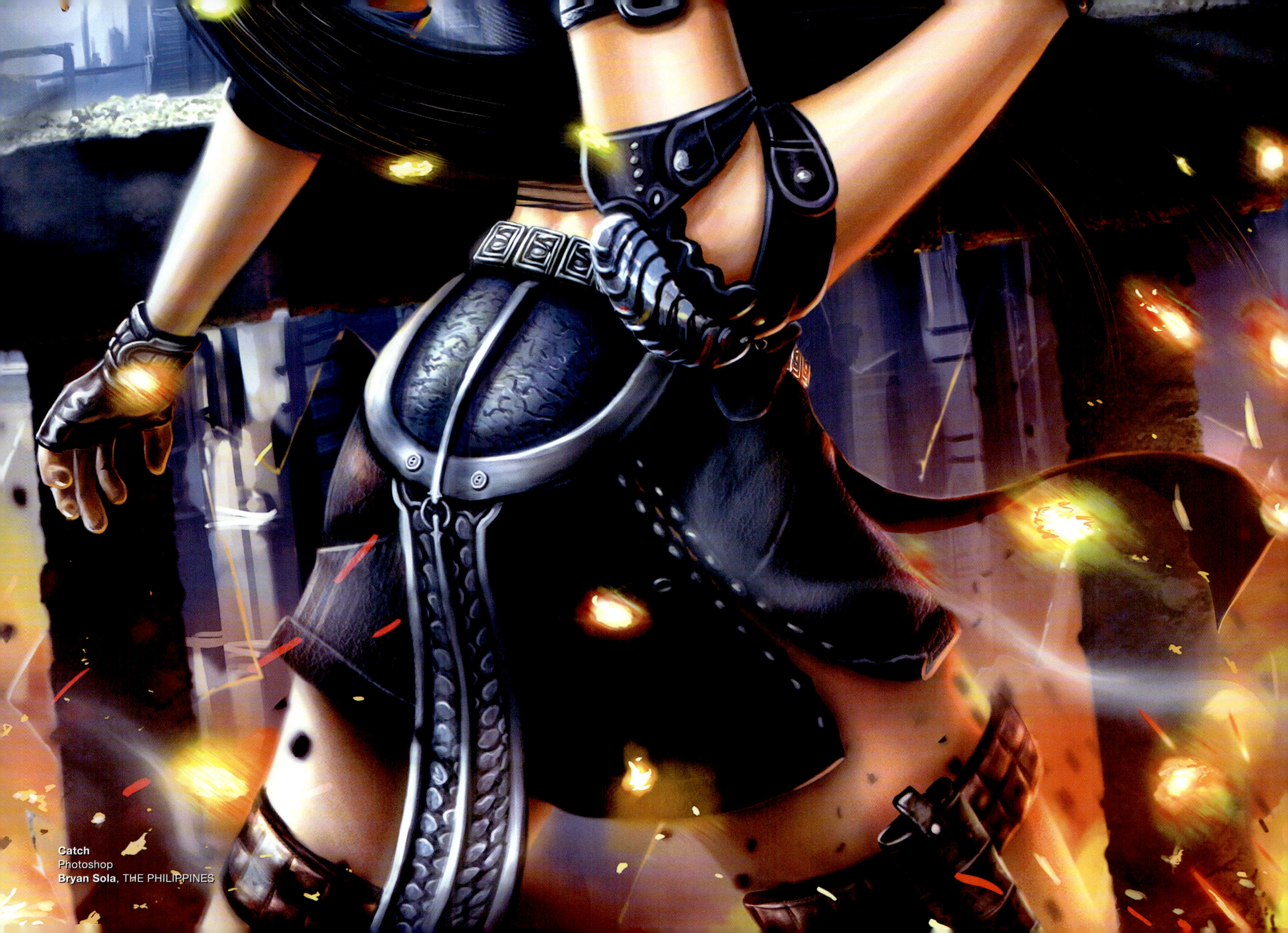

Catch
Photoshop
Bryan Sola, THE PHILIPPINES

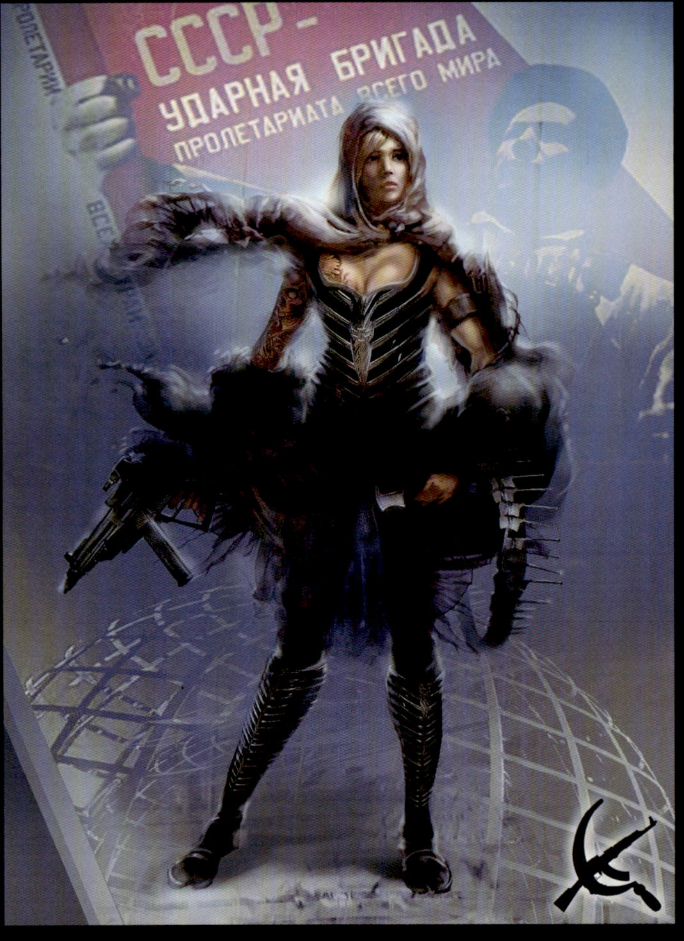

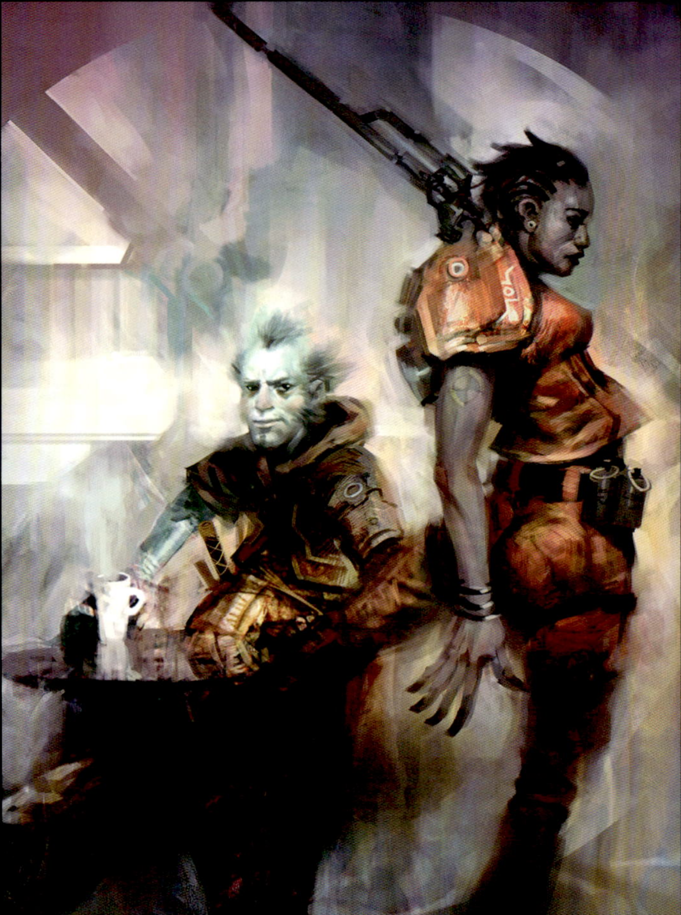

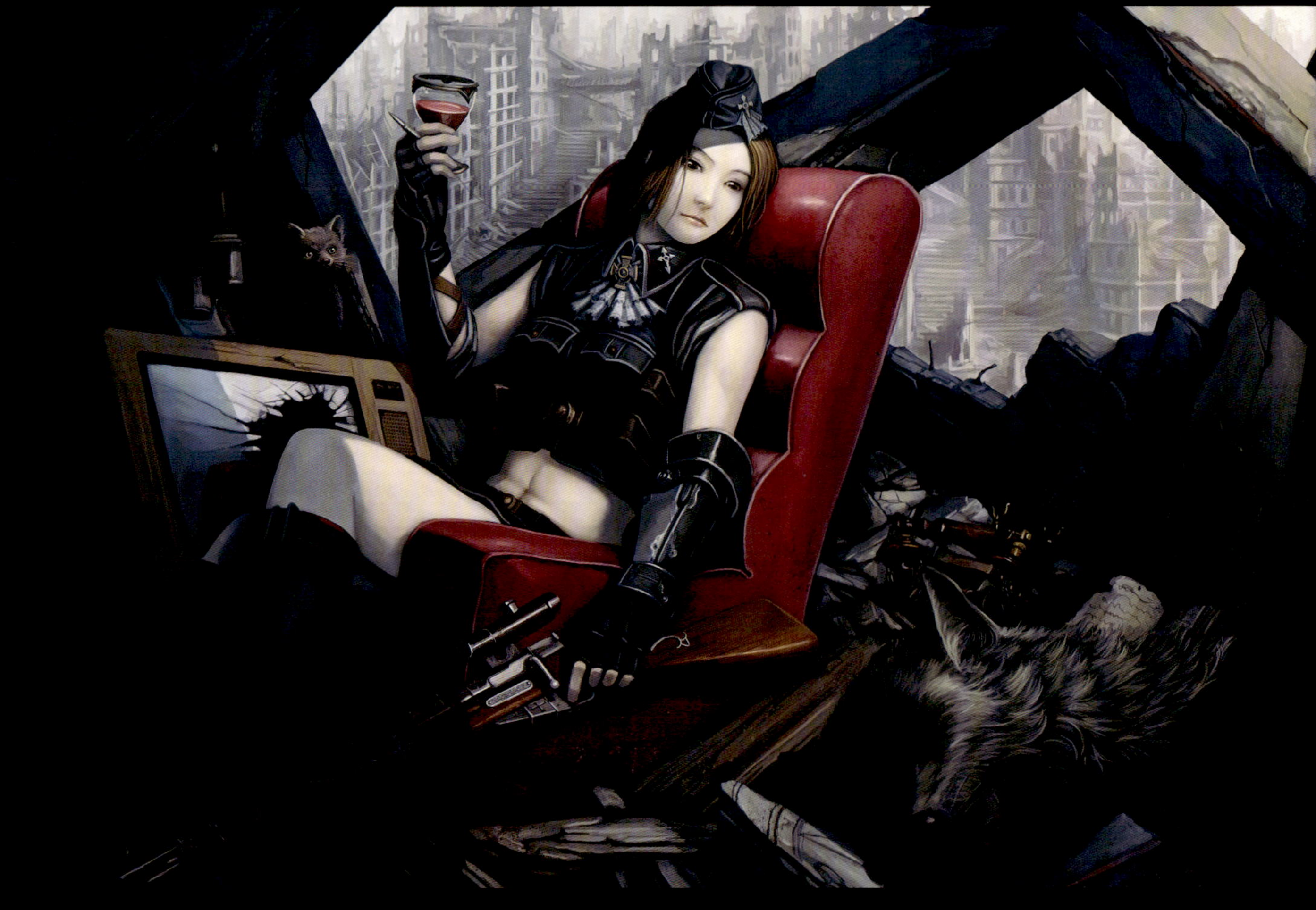

Soviet Covert
Photoshop
Li Jia Tan, USA
[top]

The Last Piece of Silver
Photoshop
Leos Ng, Imaginary Friends Studio, SINGAPORE *[above]*

Morning coffee
Photoshop
Waldek Kaminski, POLAND
[top]

SE-test025
Photoshop
Yee-Ling Chung, MALAYSIA
[right]

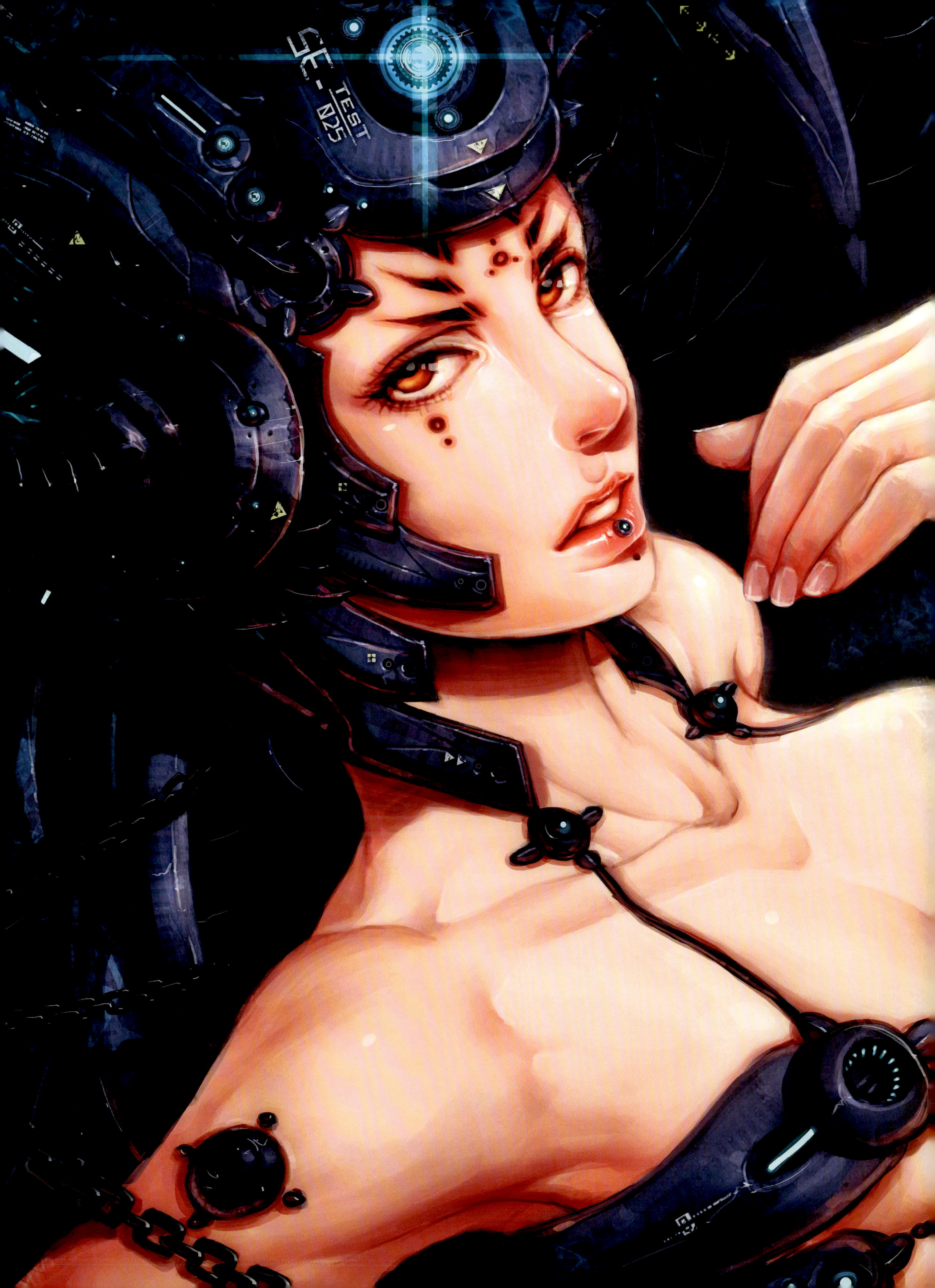
SE-
TEST
Ø25

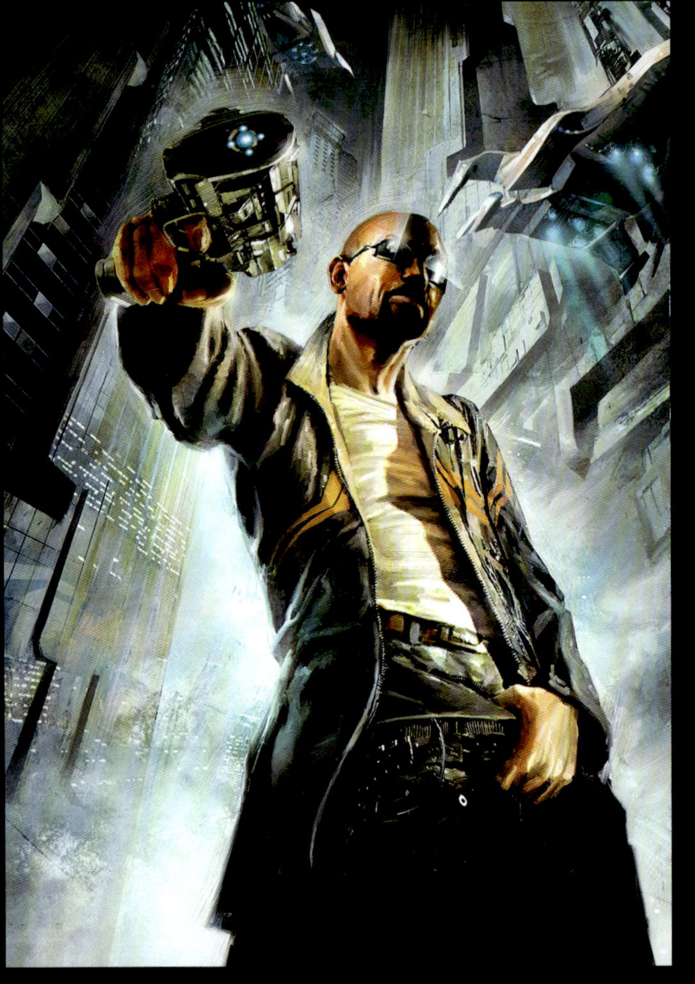

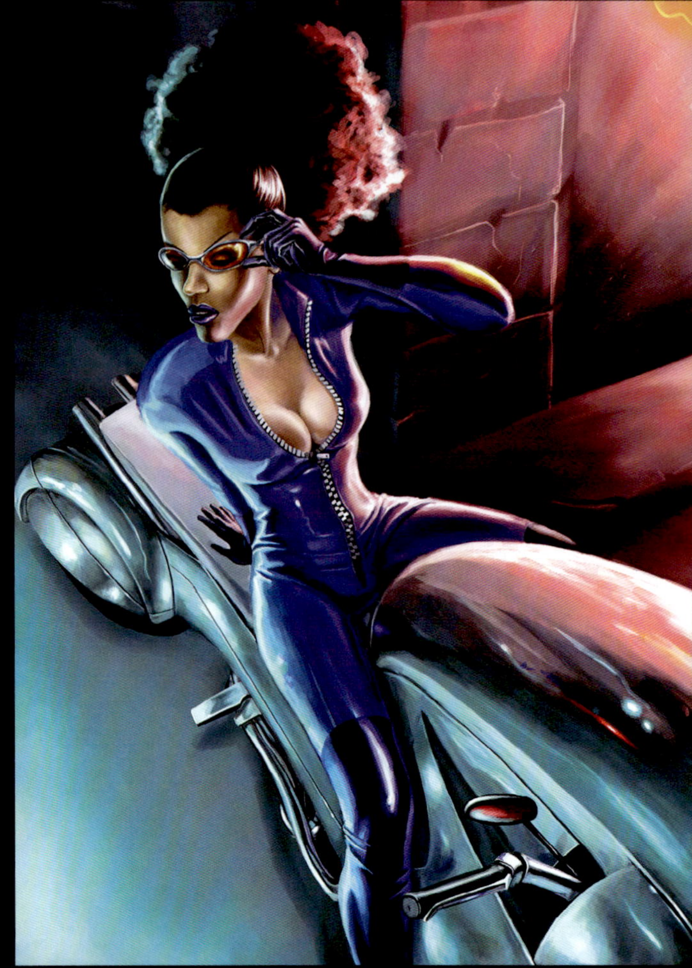

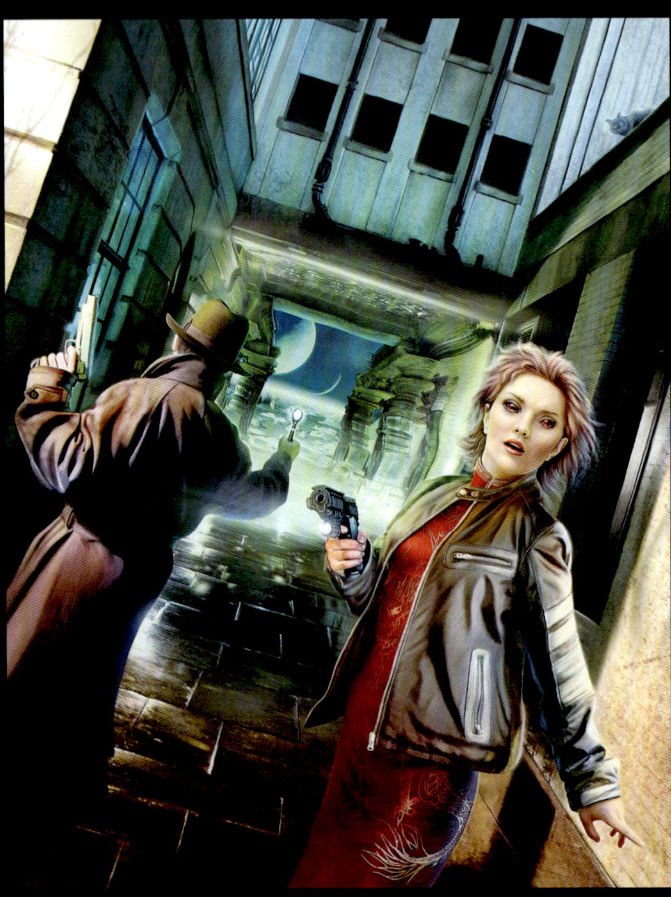

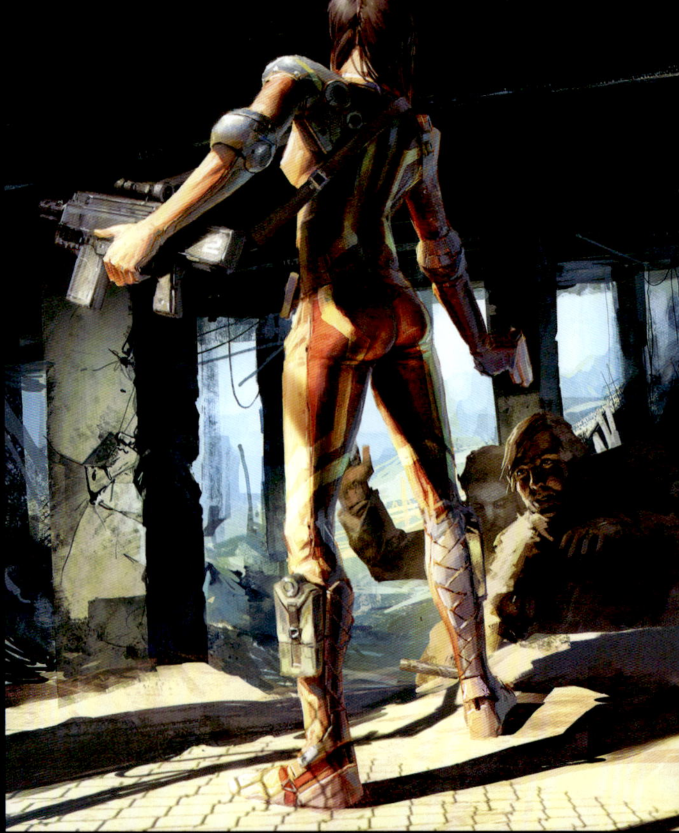

Black Man
Painter, Photoshop
Client: Bragelonne Editions
J.S Rossbach, FRANCE
[top]

Nameless Streets
Photoshop, Painter
Art Director: Dario Corallo
Client: Alephtar Games
Tiziano Baracchi, ITALY *[above]*

Cotton Candy
Photoshop
Andrew Blackman,
BARBADOS
[top]

Breaking Lines
Photoshop
Michal Lisowski,
POLAND
[above]

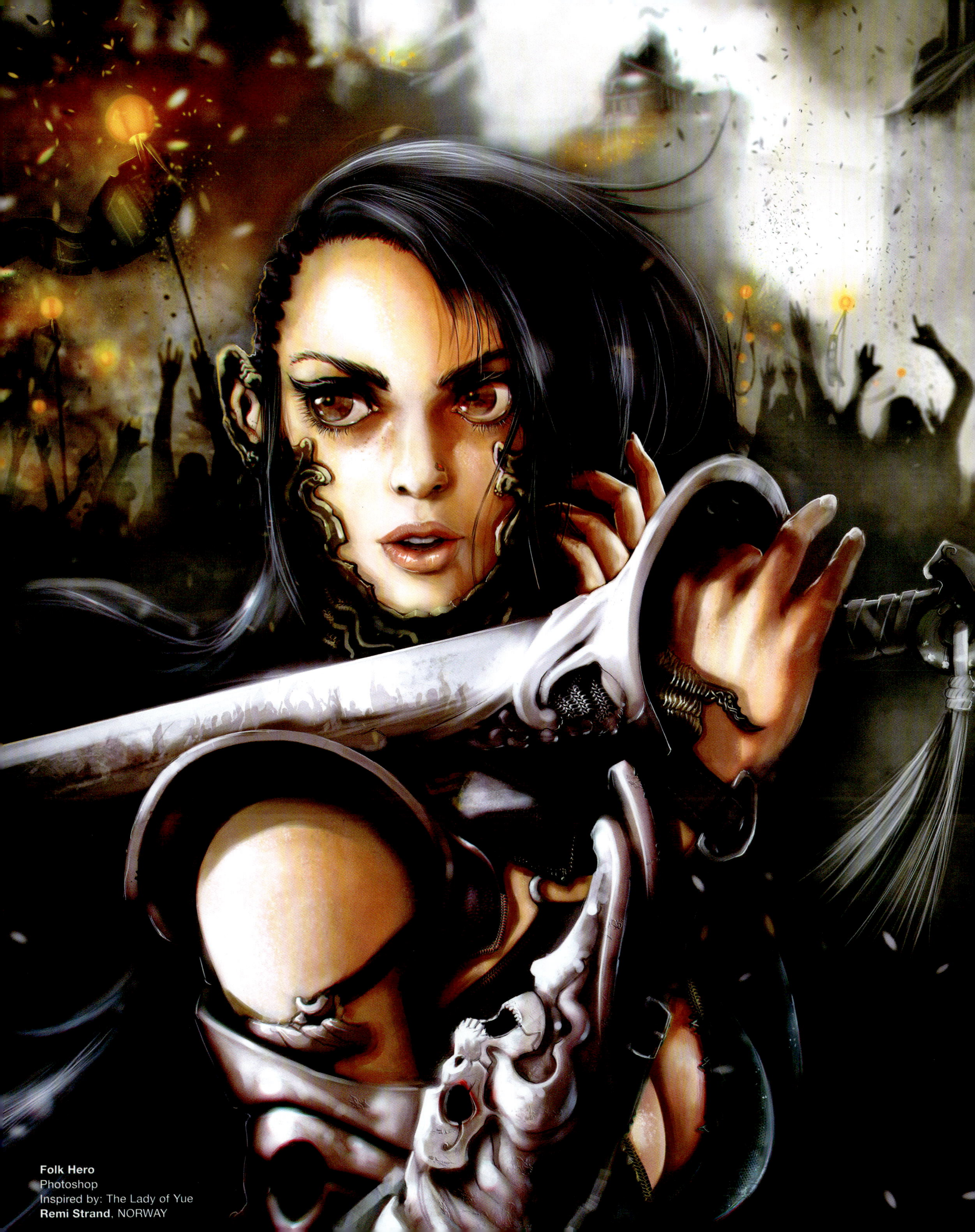

Folk Hero
Photoshop
Inspired by: The Lady of Yue
Remi Strand, NORWAY

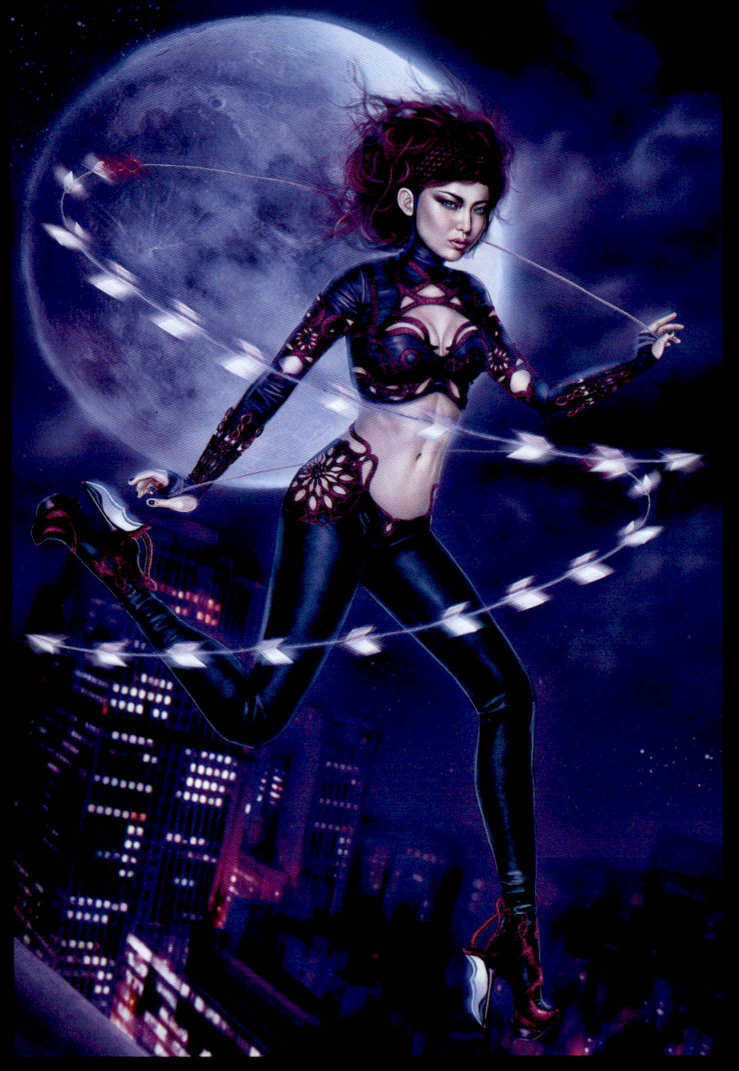

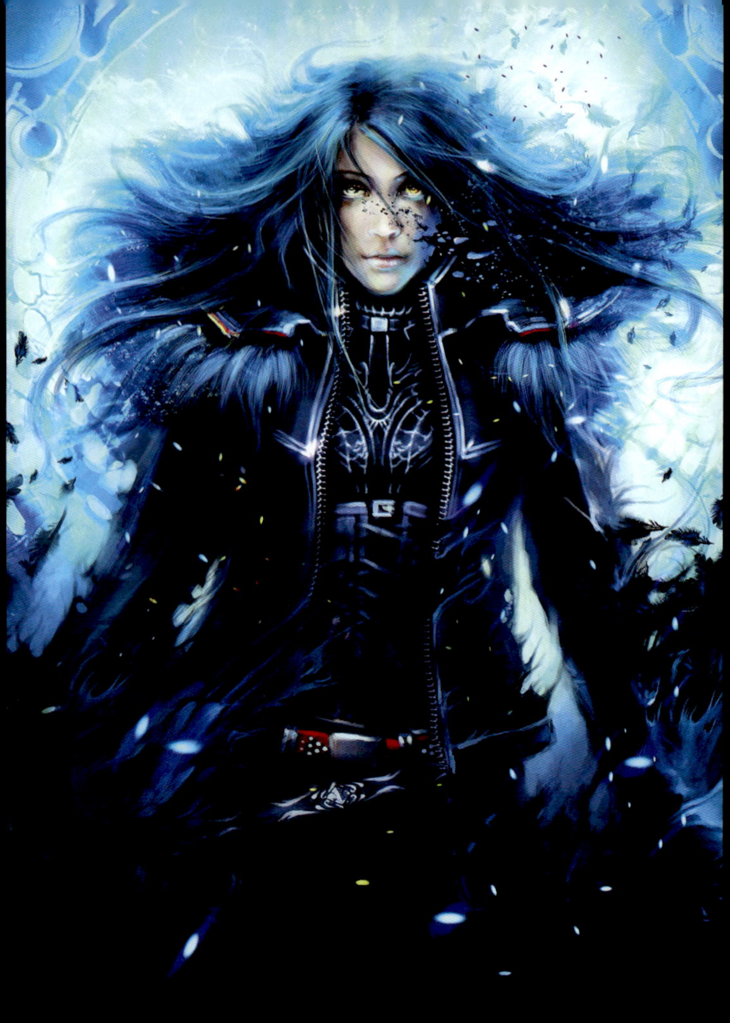

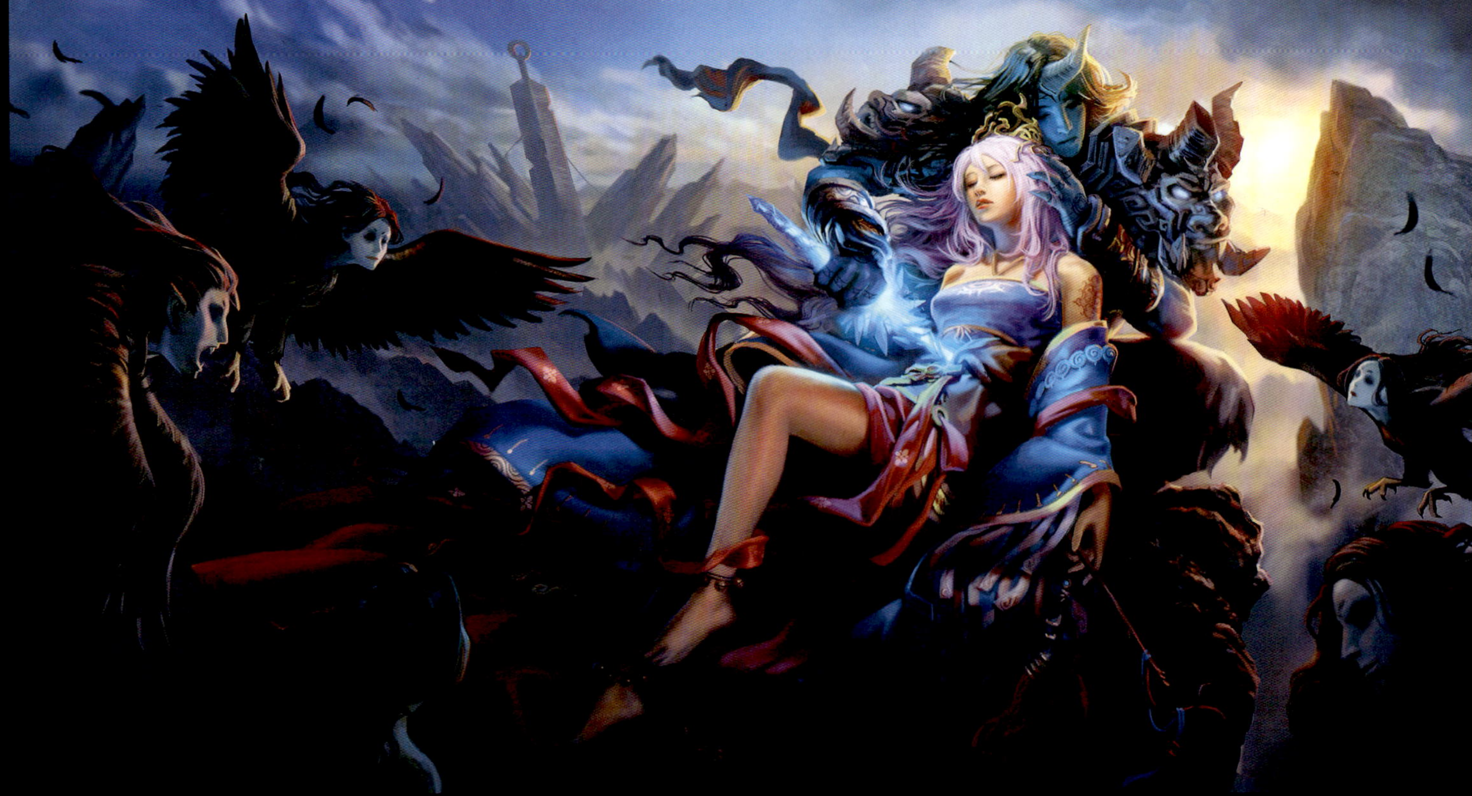

Fashion Assassin
Photoshop
Lisa Jenkins, CANADA
[top]

My Lover
Photoshop
Chen Kai, CHINA
[above]

Blue storm
Photoshop
Helen Rusovich, UKRAINE
[top]

Blue flame
Painter, Photoshop
Bin Wee, CHINA
[right]

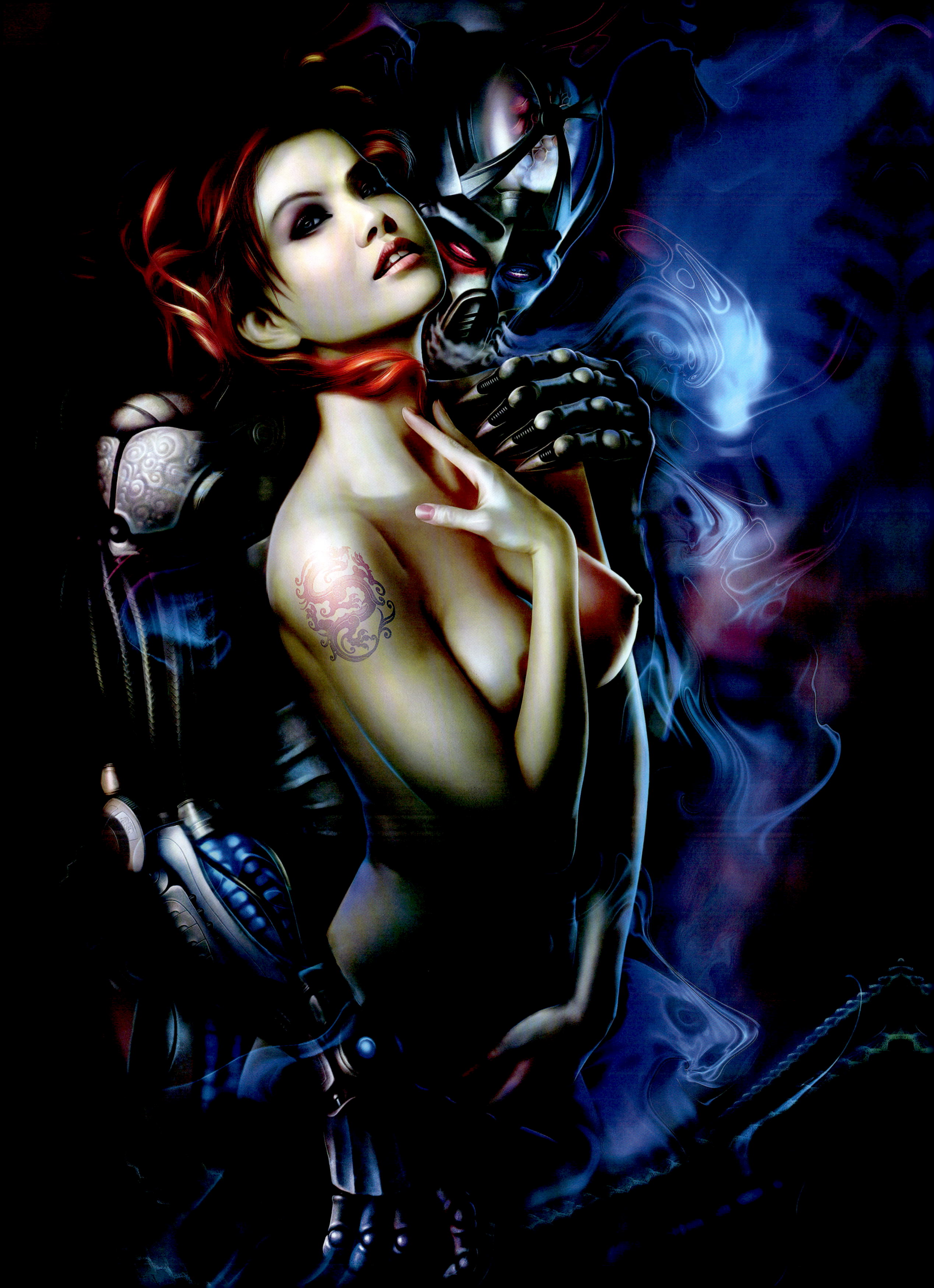

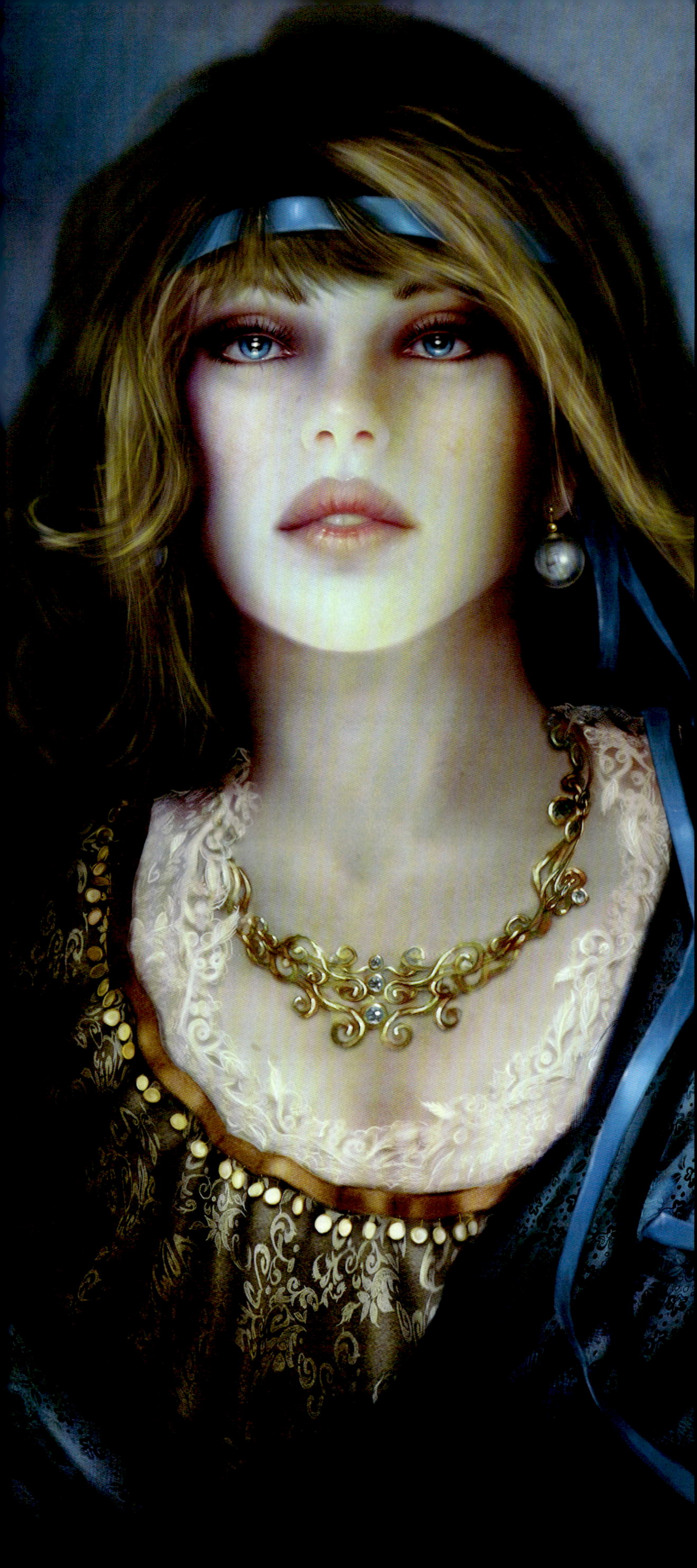

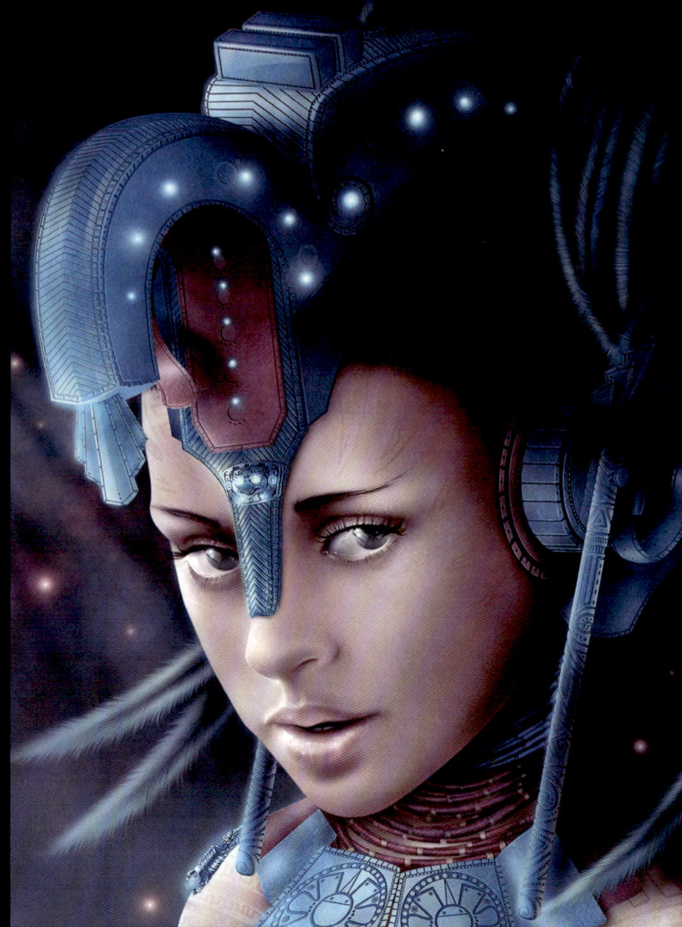

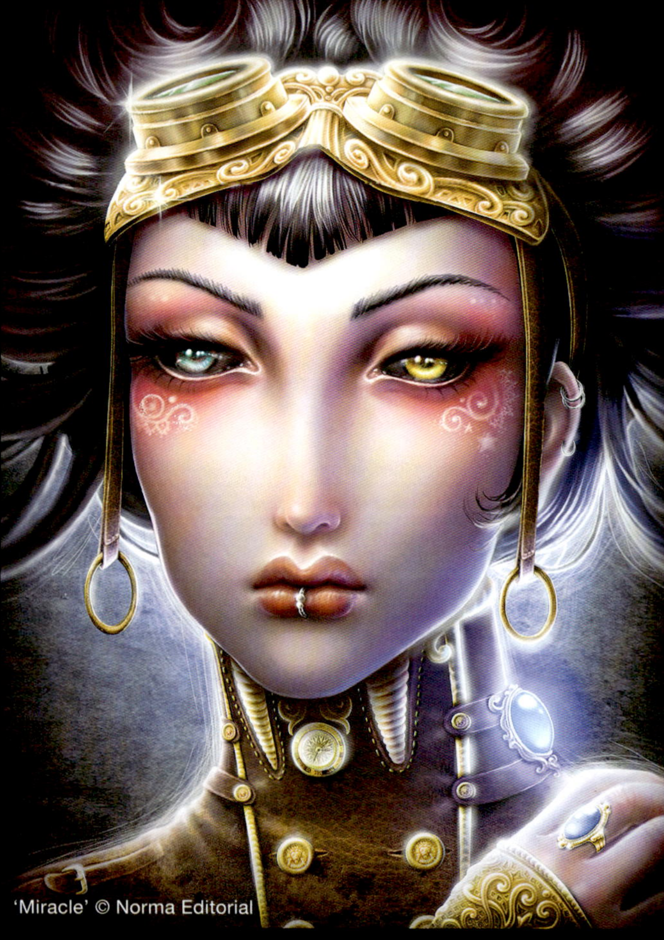

'Miracle' © Norma Editorial

Blue Pearl
Photoshop
Sue Marino, GREAT BRITAIN
[above]

Xiom
Illustrator, Photoshop
Jared Castro, GUATEMALA
[top]

Miracle: Nauta (cover)
Photoshop
Client: Norma Editorial
Asuncion Macian Ruiz, SPAIN *[above*

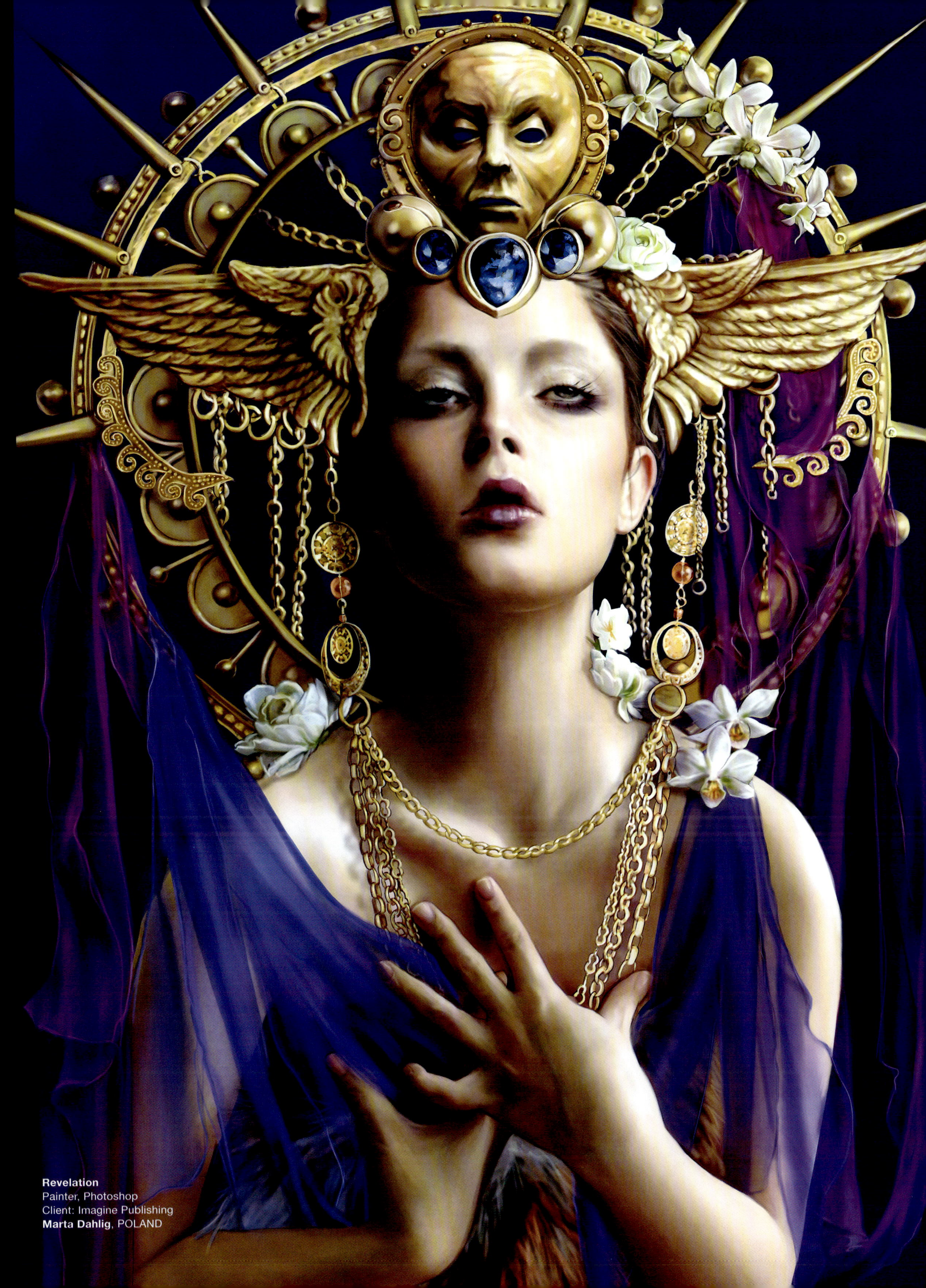

Revelation
Painter, Photoshop
Client: Imagine Publishing
Marta Dahlig, POLAND

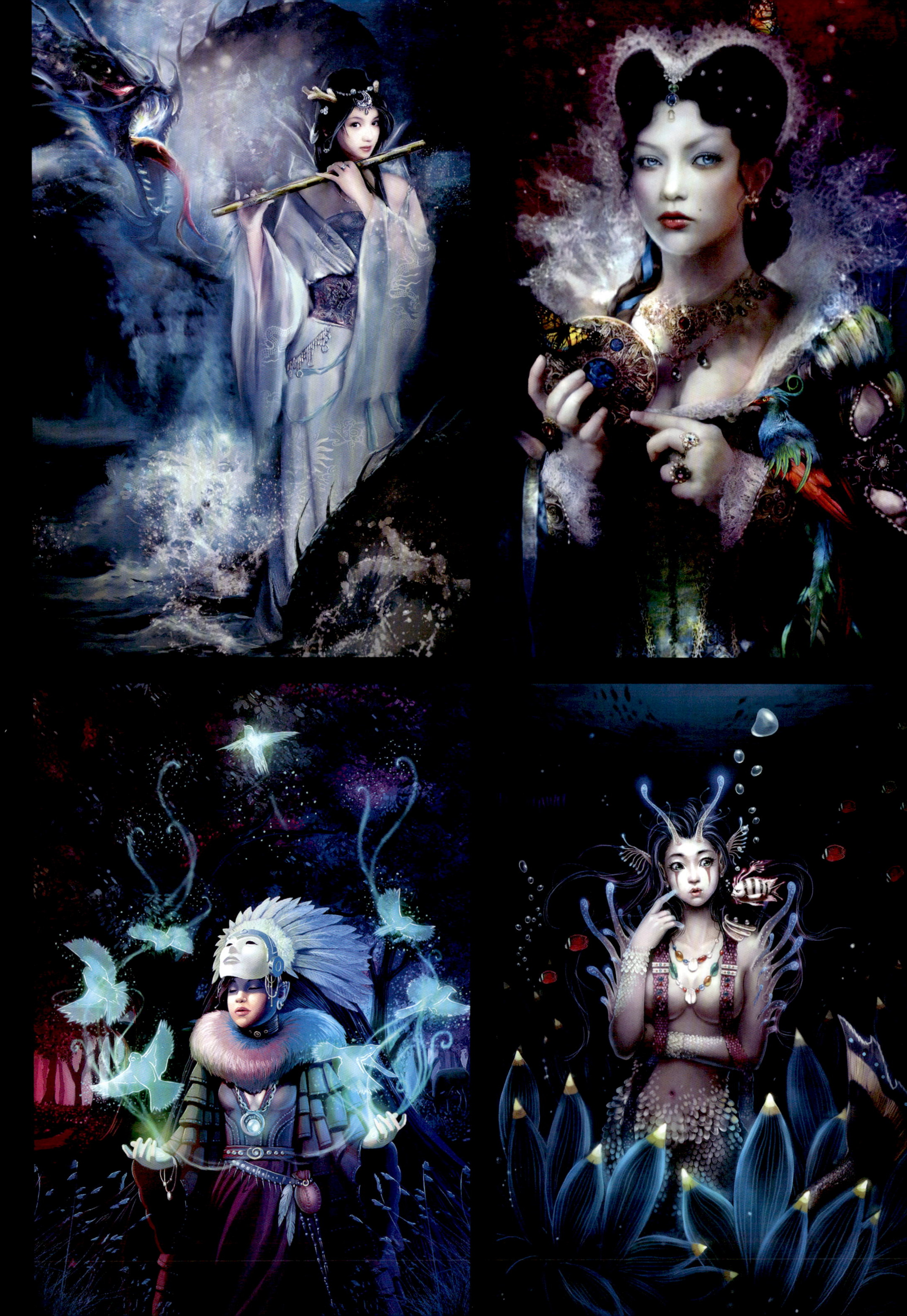

The dragon girl
Photoshop
Ping He, CHINA
[far left]

Lady Mordarante
Photoshop
Rochelle Green,
NEW ZEALAND
[left]

Eva
Painter, Photoshop
Mélanie Delon,
FRANCE
[right]

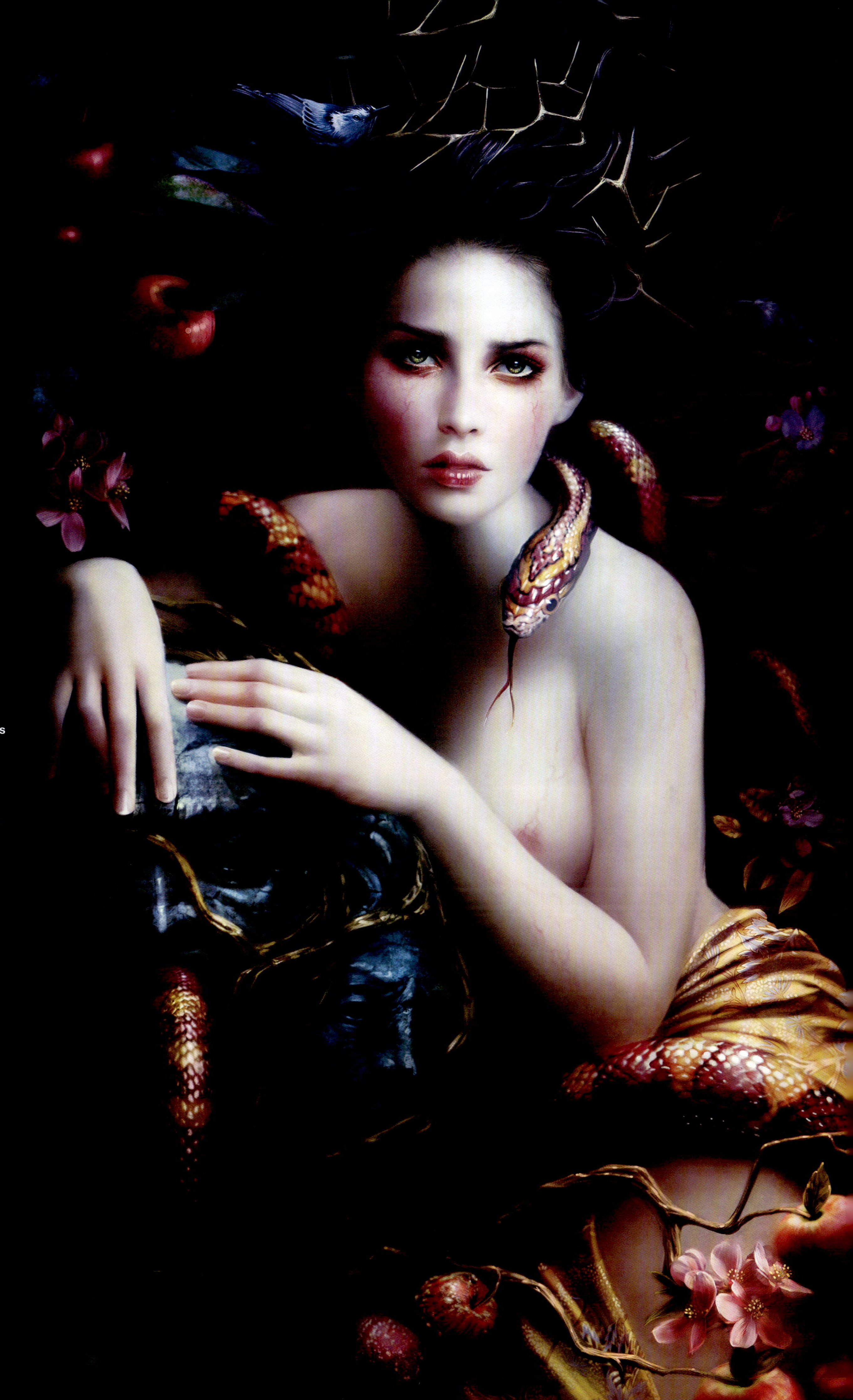

Summon the Sparrows
Photoshop
Traci Cook, USA
[far left]

I am the brightest fish
Photoshop
Hui Tian, CHINA
[left]

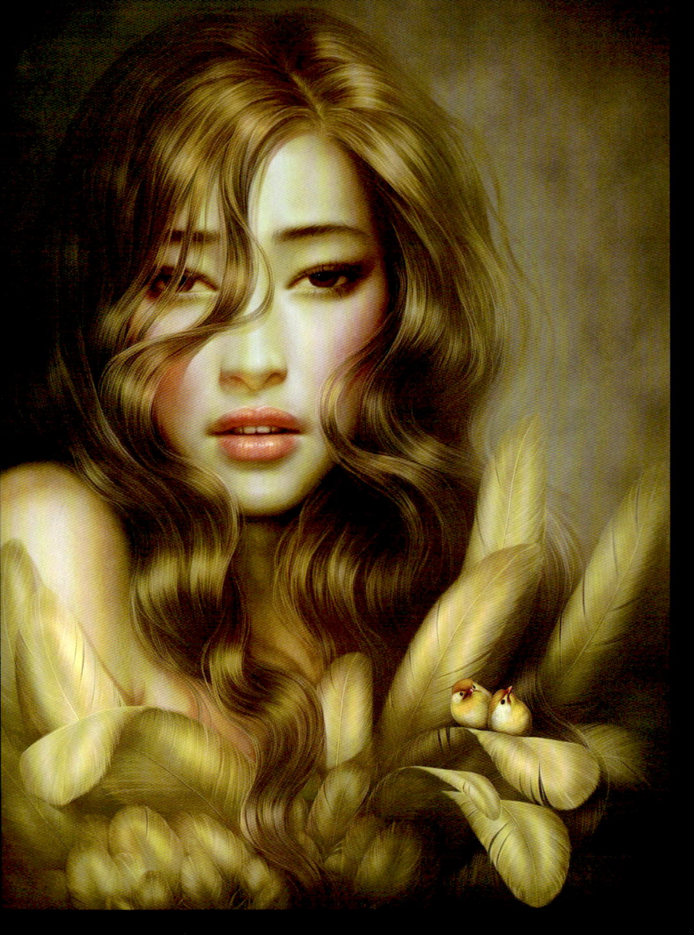

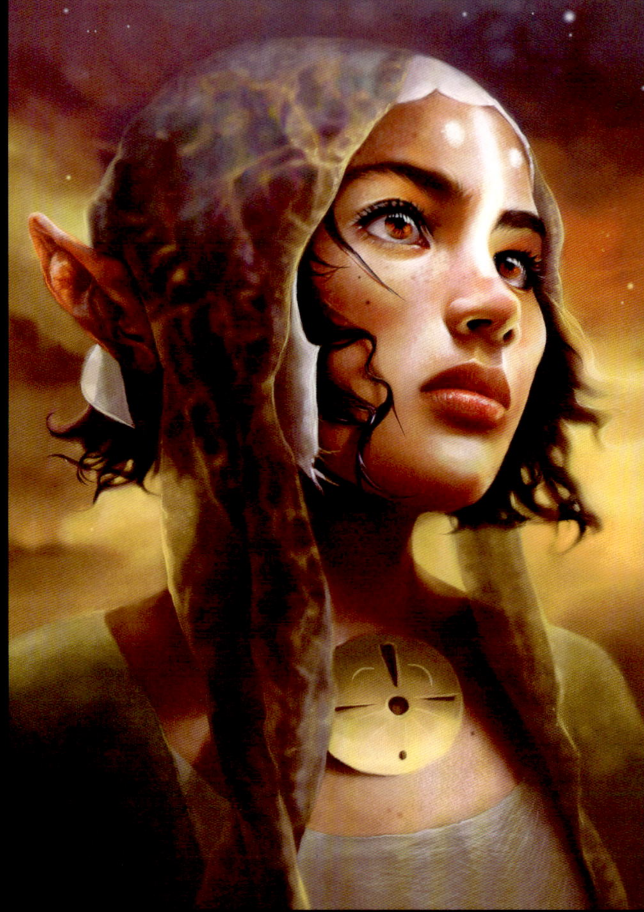

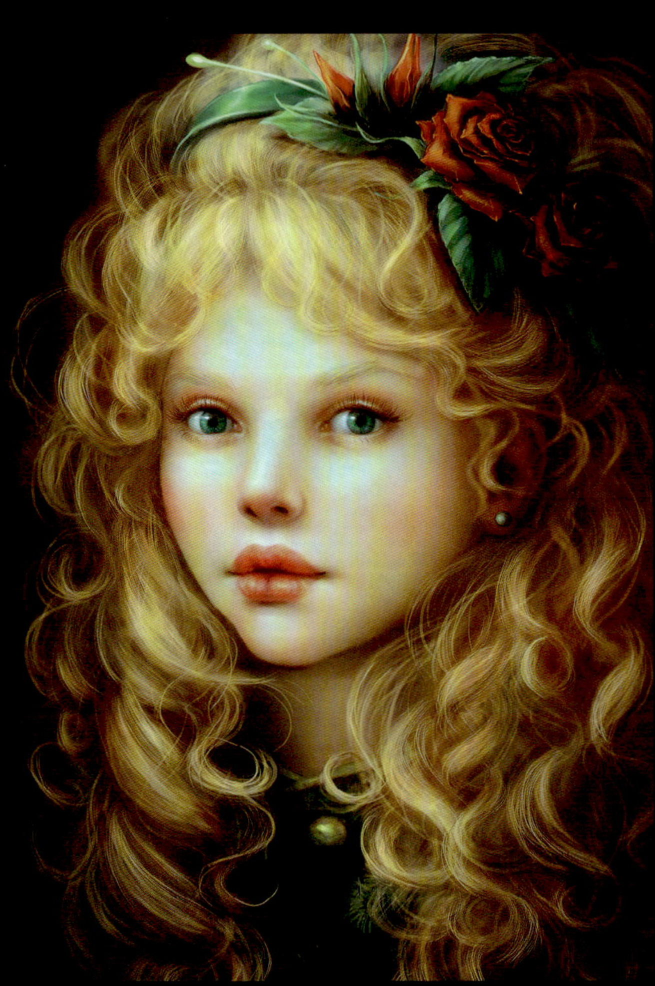

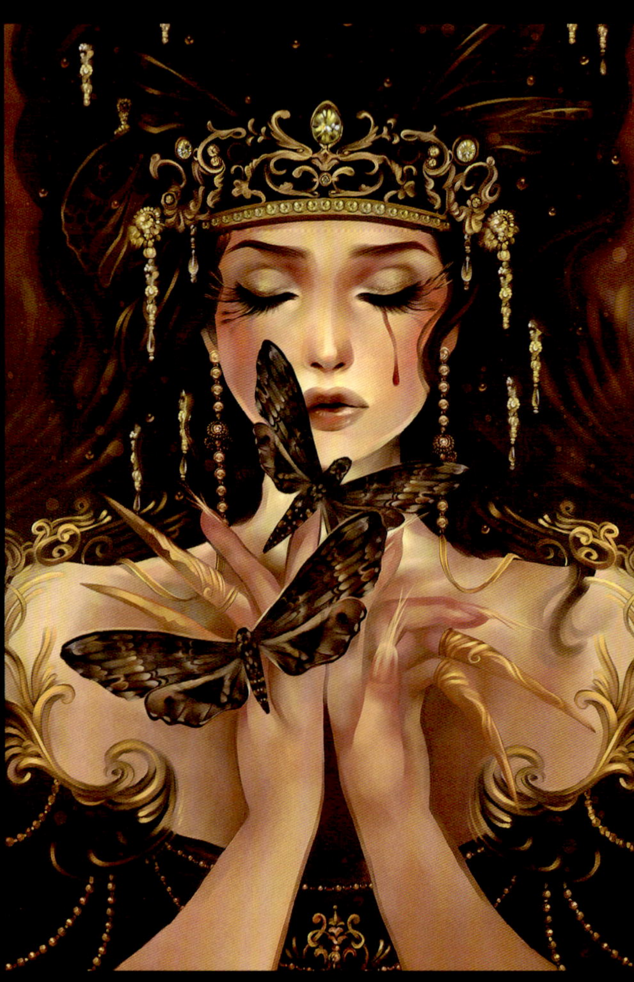

Phantom
Painter, Photoshop
Tang Yuehui, Tang Yuehui computer

Rose
Painter
Tanya Wheeler, USA

Gia
Photoshop
Sini Pakarinen, FINLAND

The Moth Eater
Painter, Photoshop
Schin Loong, USA

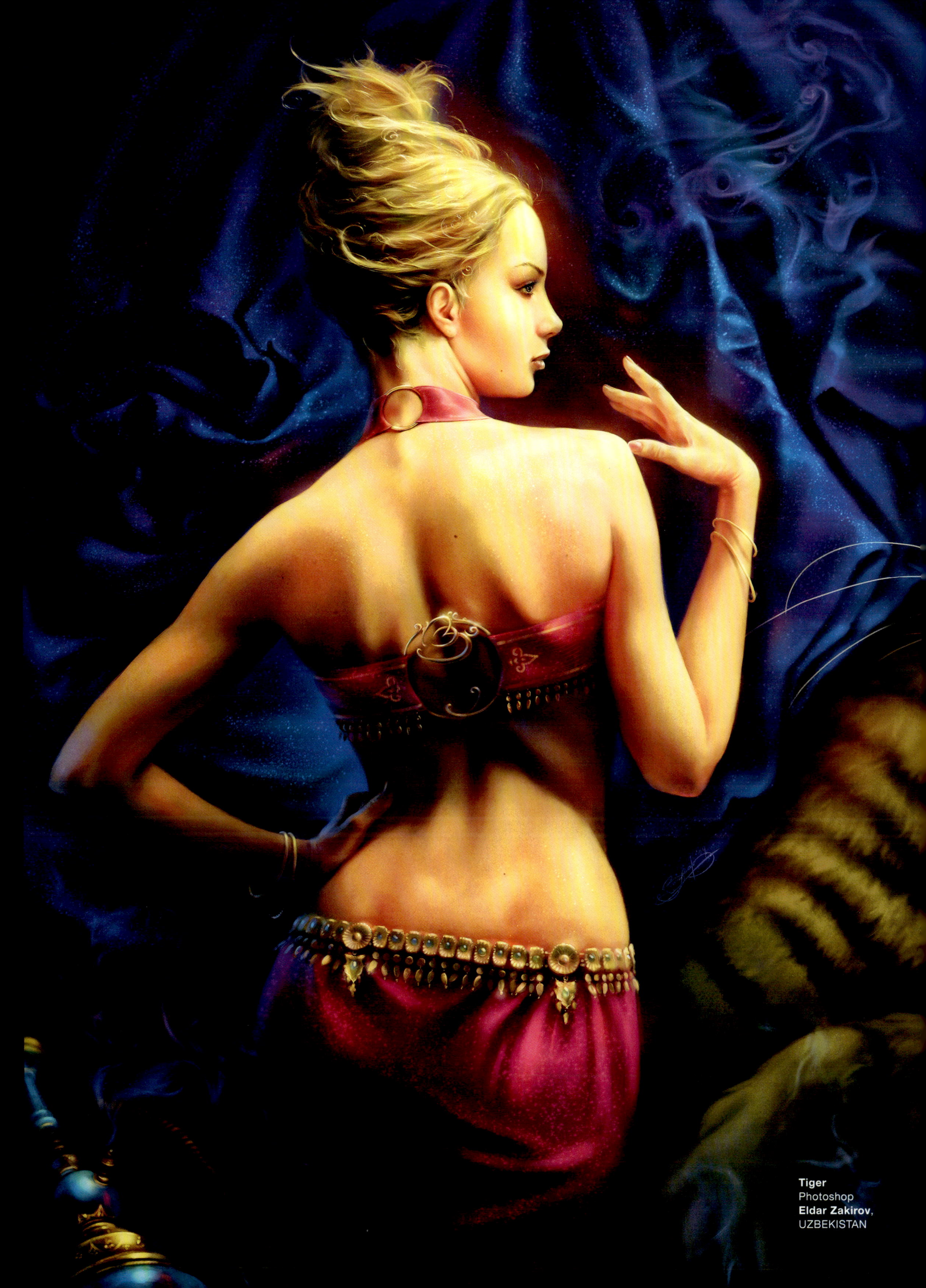

Tiger
Photoshop
Eldar Zakirov,
UZBEKISTAN

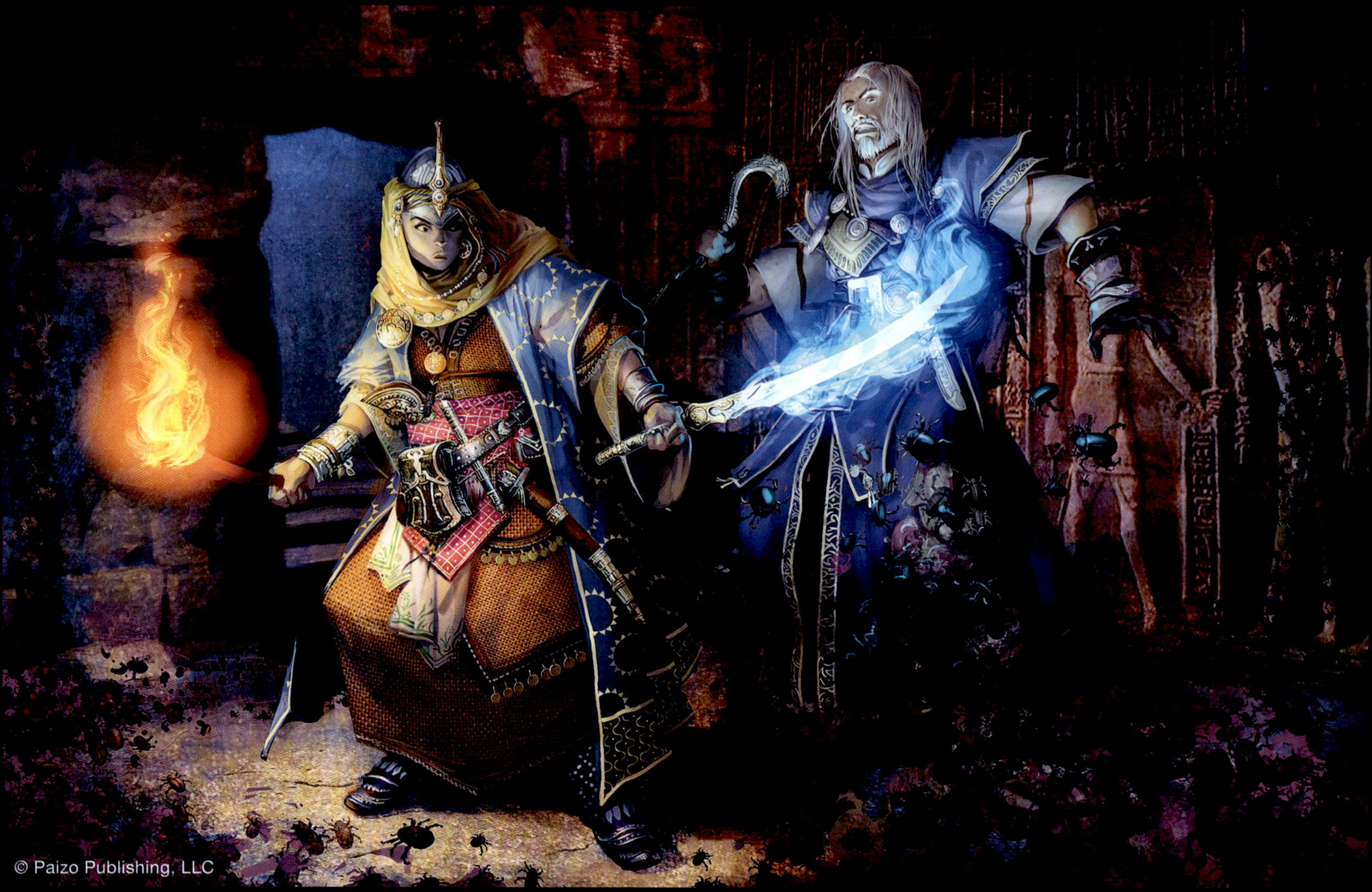

© Paizo Publishing, LLC

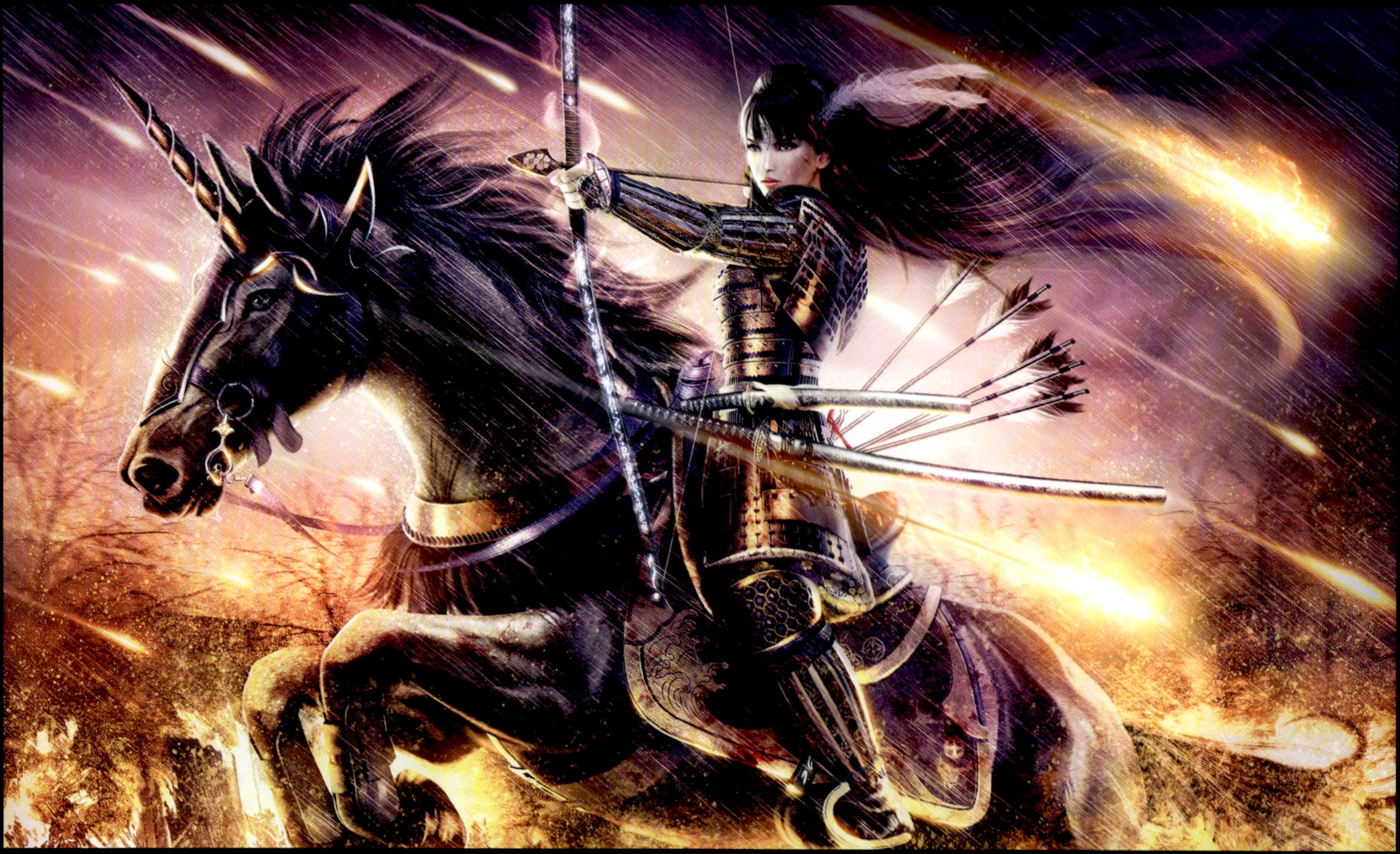

Consumed by beetles
Photoshop
Client: Paizo Publishing, LLC
Svetlin Velinov, BULGARIA
[top]

Legend of The Five Rings: Otako Naoko
Photoshop
Client: David Frantz Adrien
Mario Wibisono, INDONESIA
[above]

The Gypsy
Photoshop
Nakai Wen, Funny Lab, TAIWAN
[right]

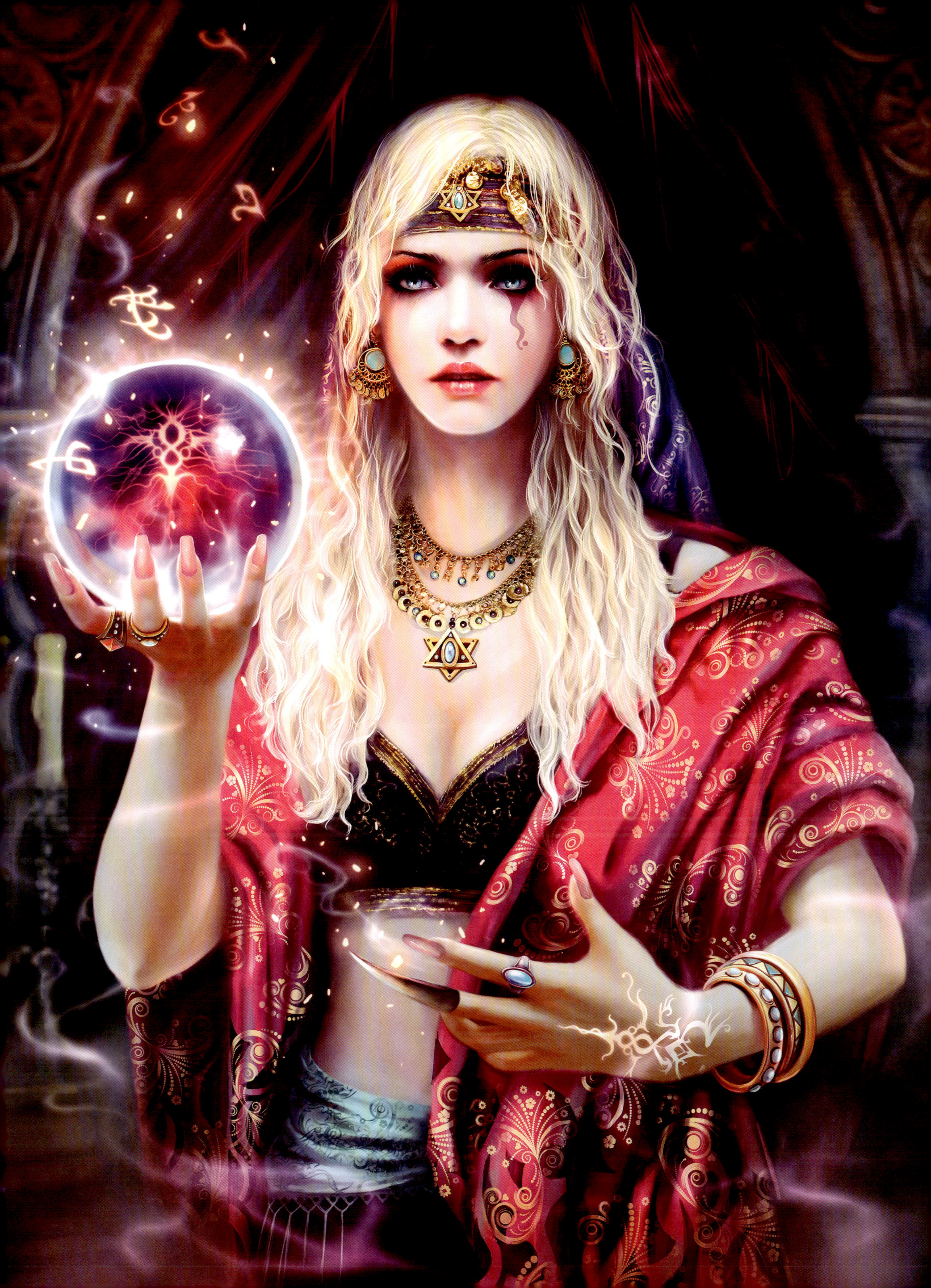

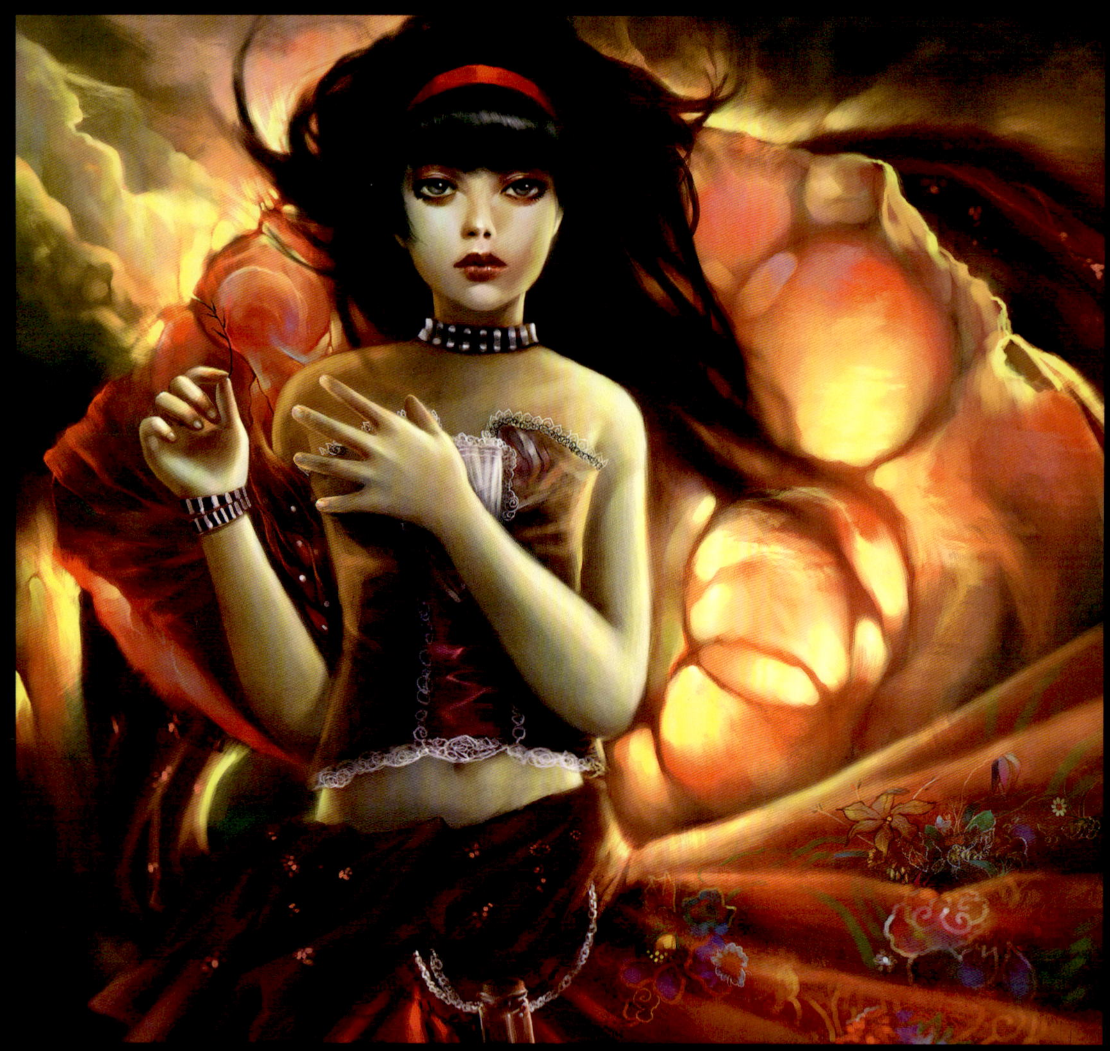

Windmill
Photoshop
Sida Chen, USA
[left]

Morrigan
Photoshop
Inspired by: Darkstalkers' 'Morrigan'
Andrew Hibner, USA
[right]

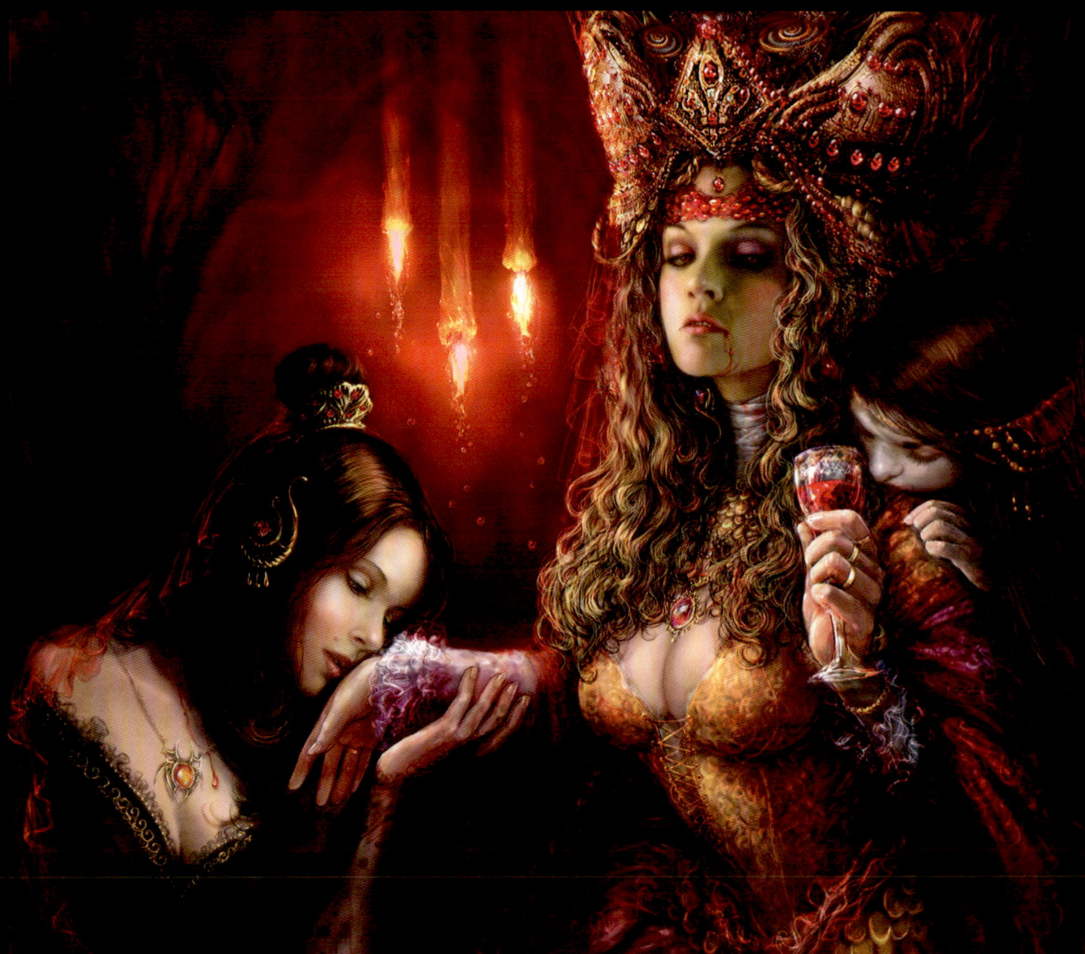

Vampqwin
Photoshop
Elena 'Fish-KAart' Klementyeva, RUSSIA
[left]

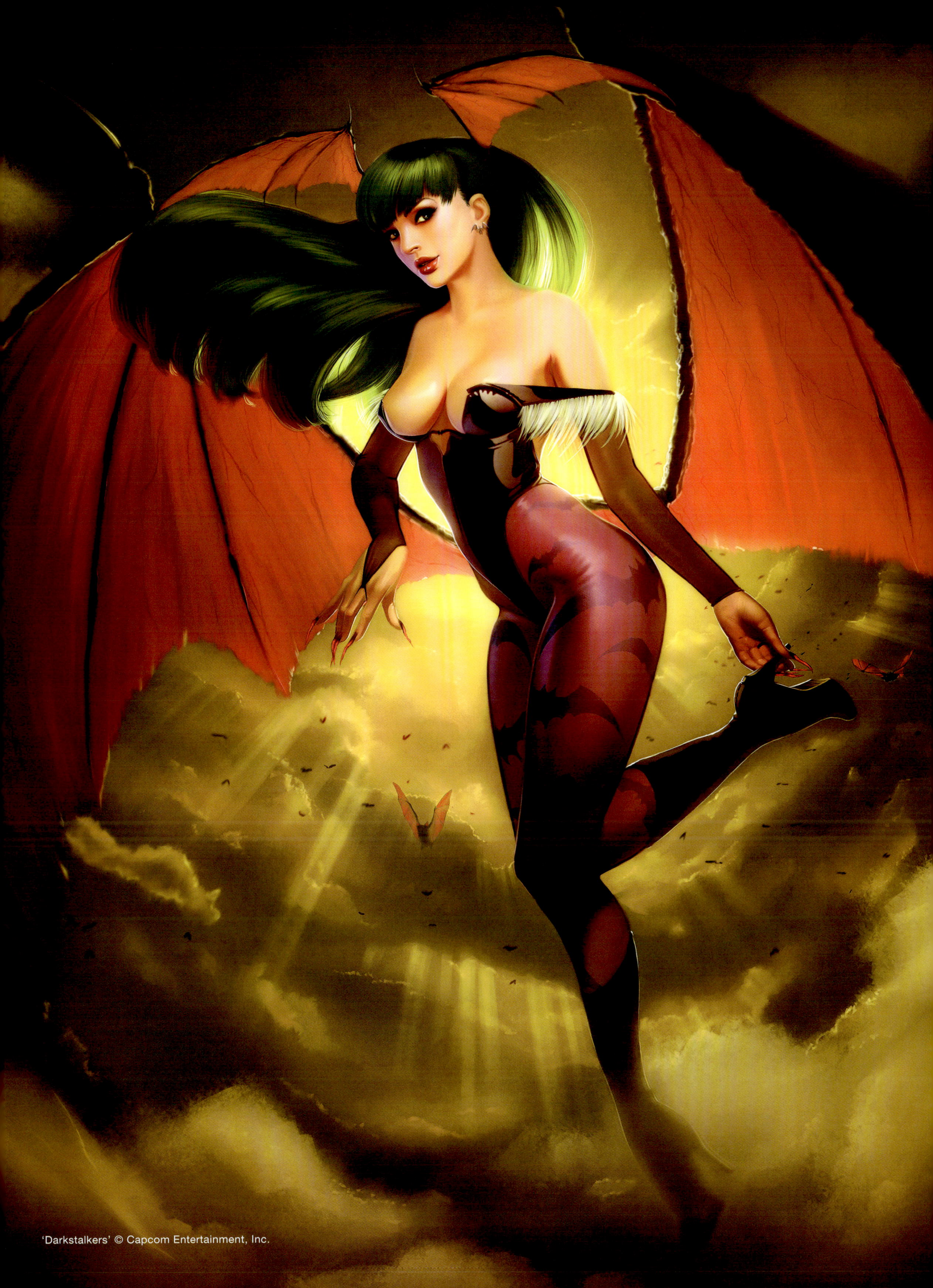

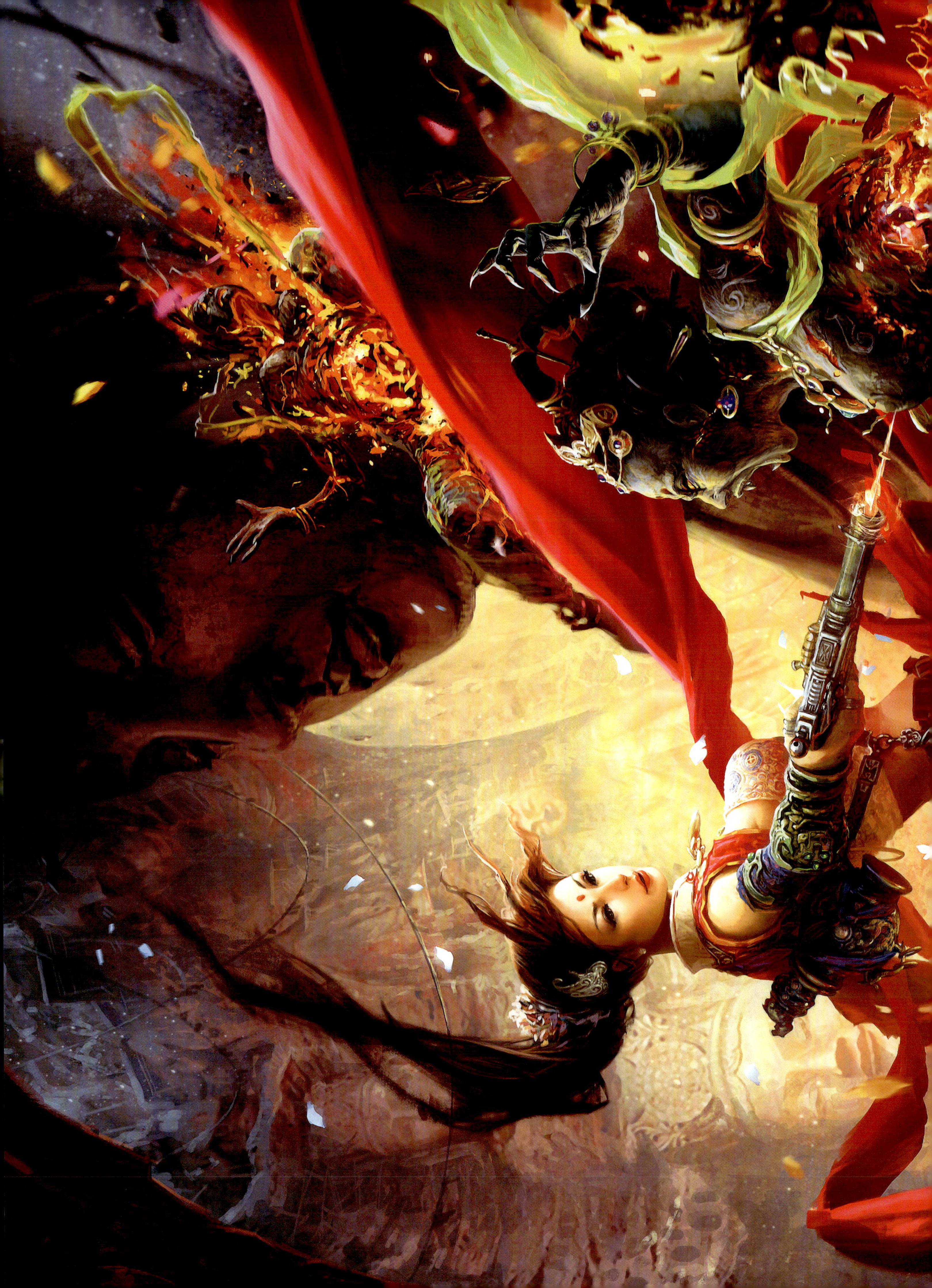

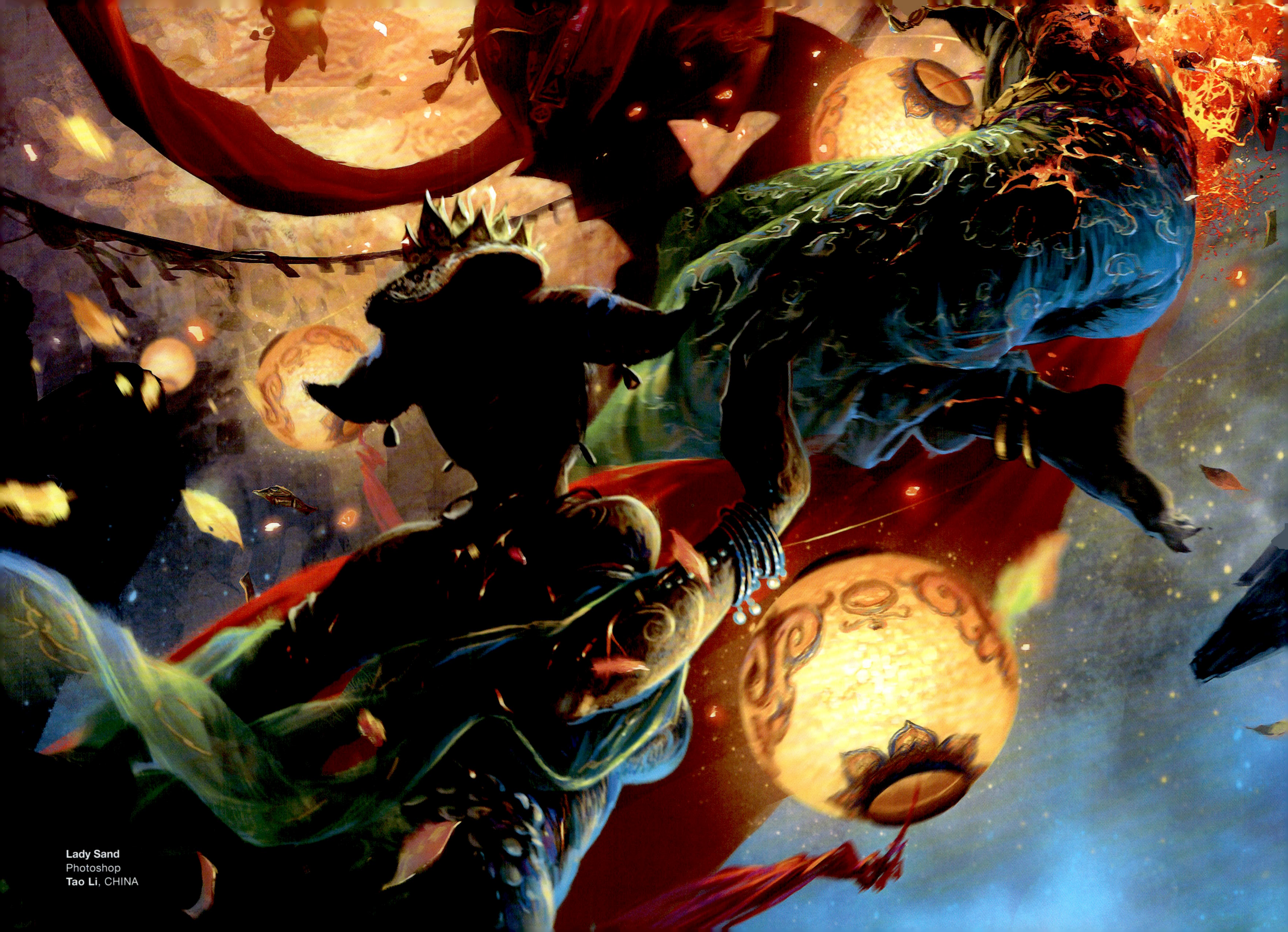

Lady Sand
Photoshop
Tao Li, CHINA

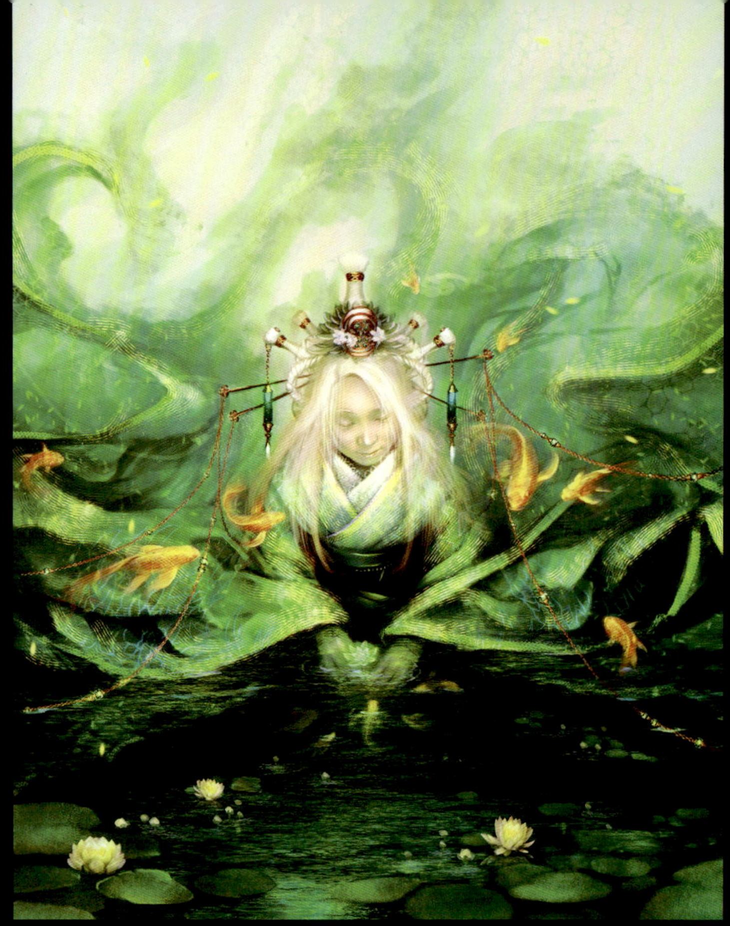

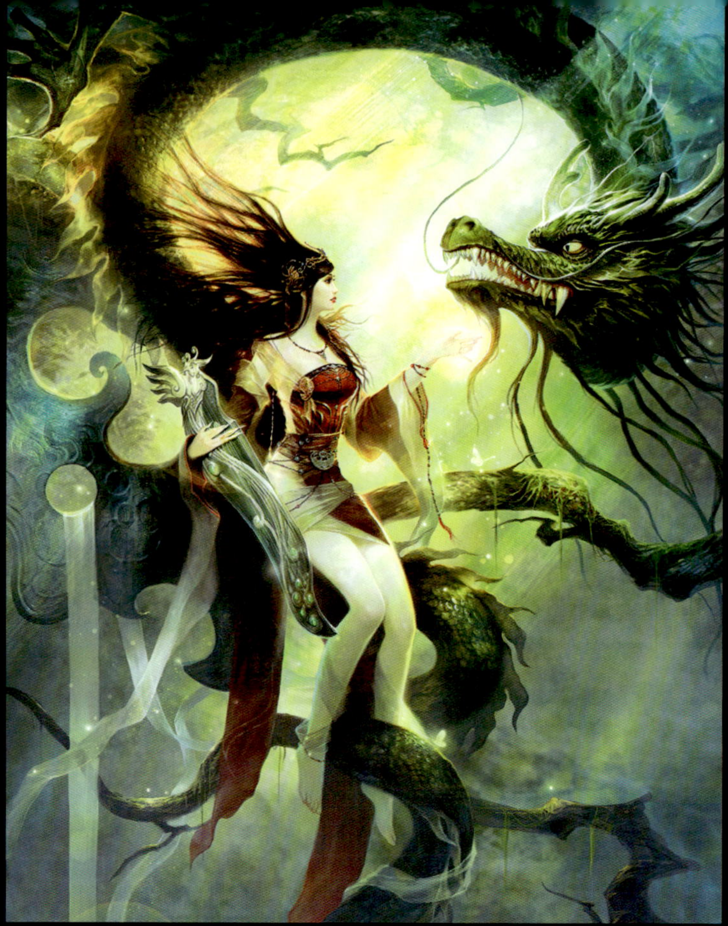

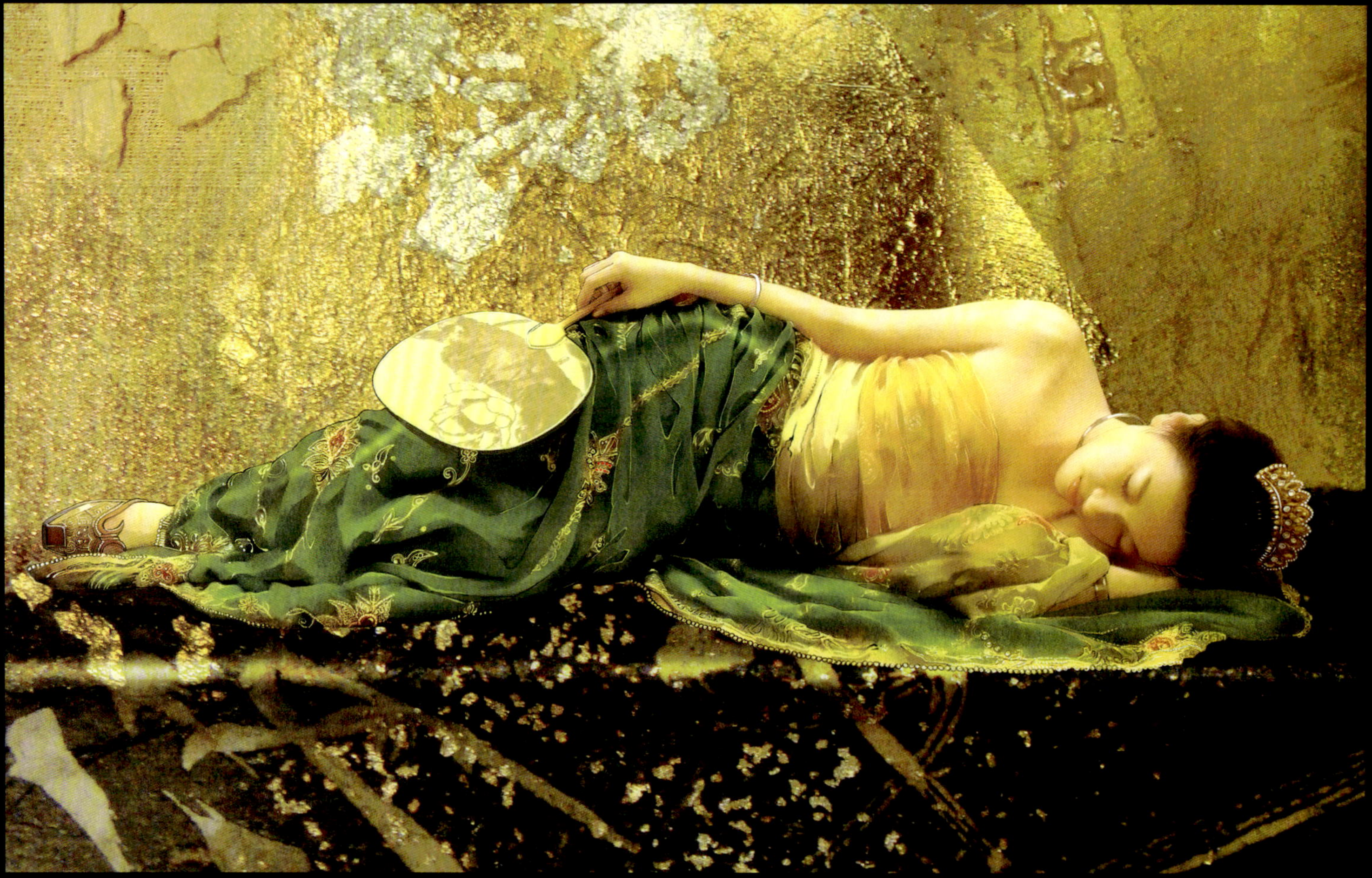

Koi Lady
Photoshop
Helen Rusovich, UKRAINE
[top]

Slumber
Painter, Photoshop
Der Jen, TAIWAN
[above]

Goddess of Light
Photoshop
Wenjun Lin, CHINA
[top]

Yang Yuhuan
Photoshop, Painter
Tang Yuehui, Tang Yuehui computer graphic workshop, CHINA *[right]*

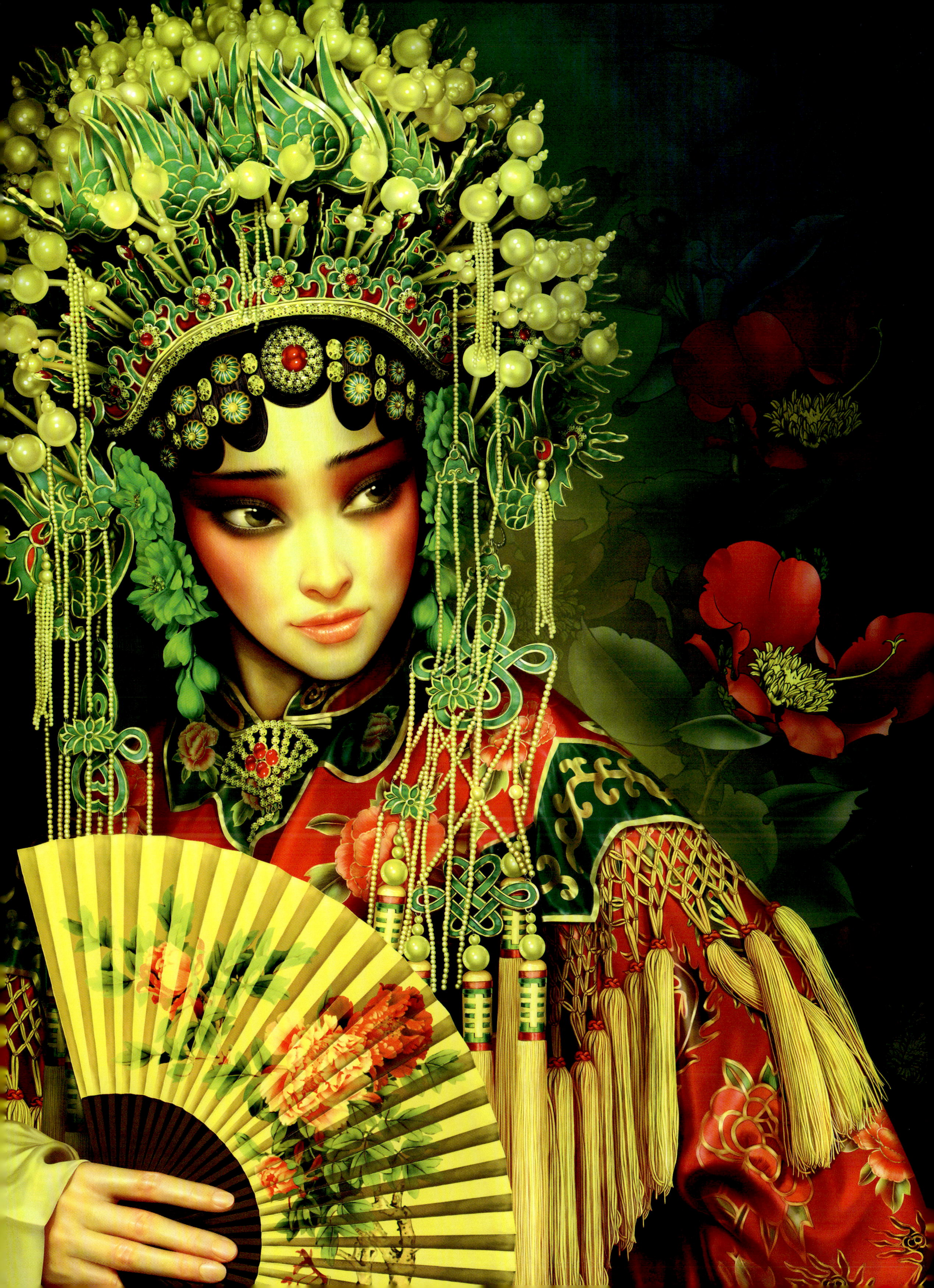

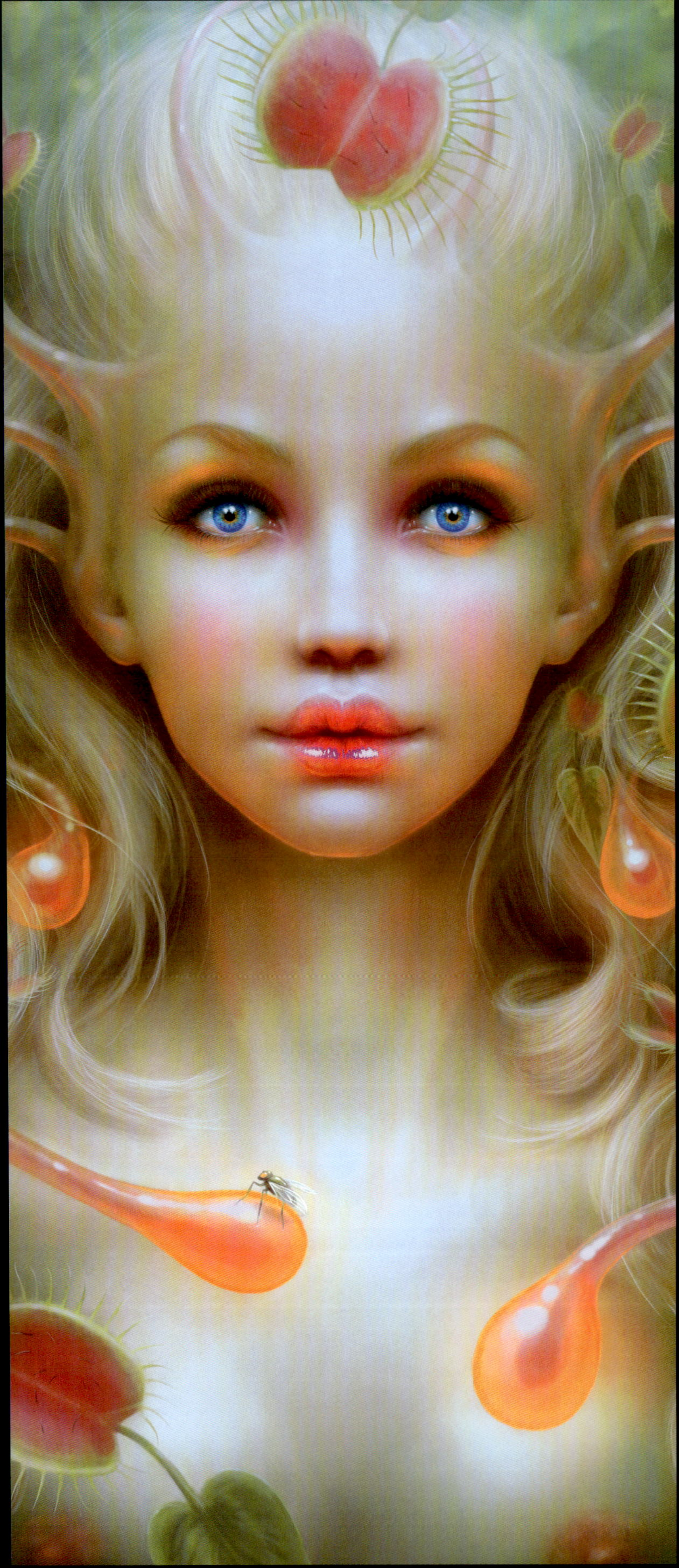

Dionaea
Painter, Photoshop
Tanya Wheeler,
USA
[above]

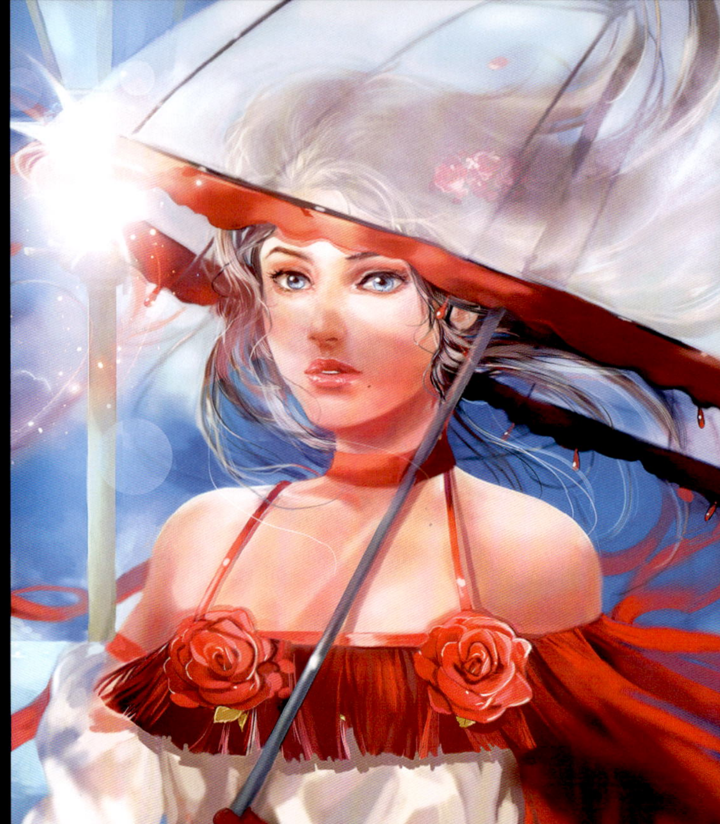

Fairytales
Photoshop
Athena,
GERMANY
[top]

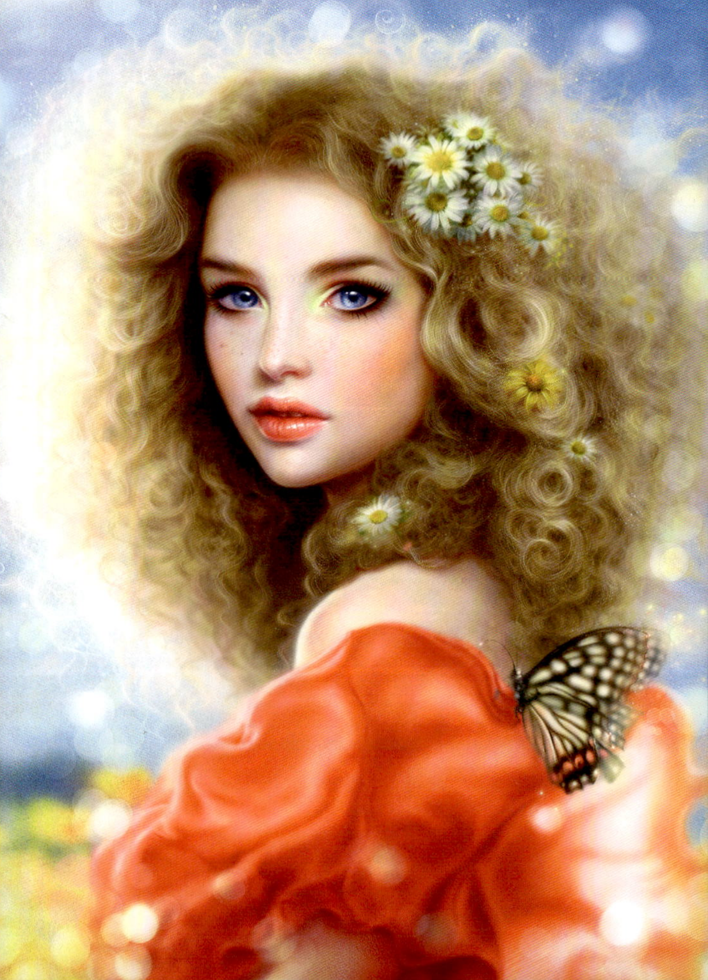

Orange smile
Photoshop
Ruoxing Zhang, Shanghai HuaQi
network technology Co. Ltd, CHINA
[above]

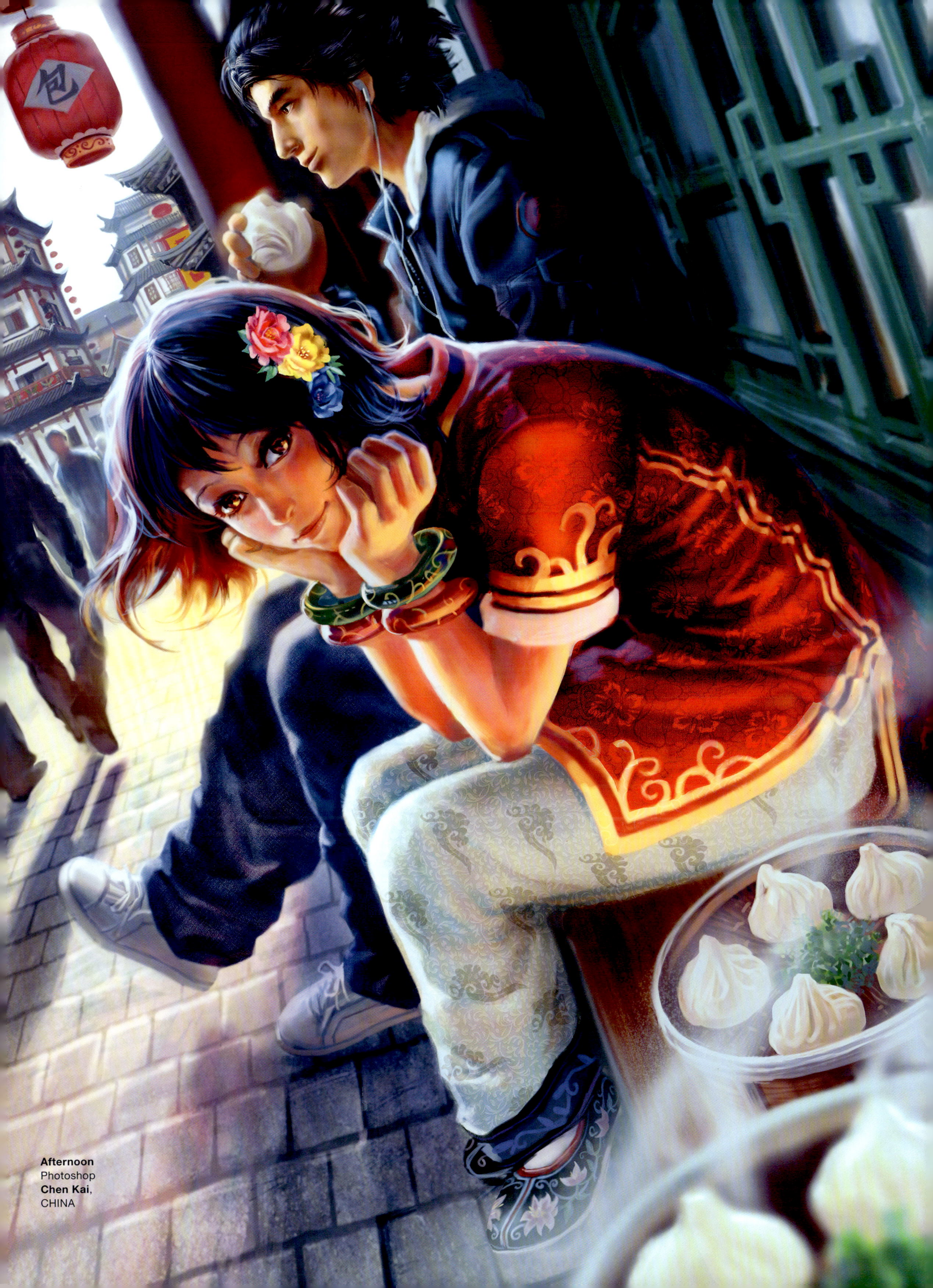

Afternoon
Photoshop
Chen Kai,
CHINA

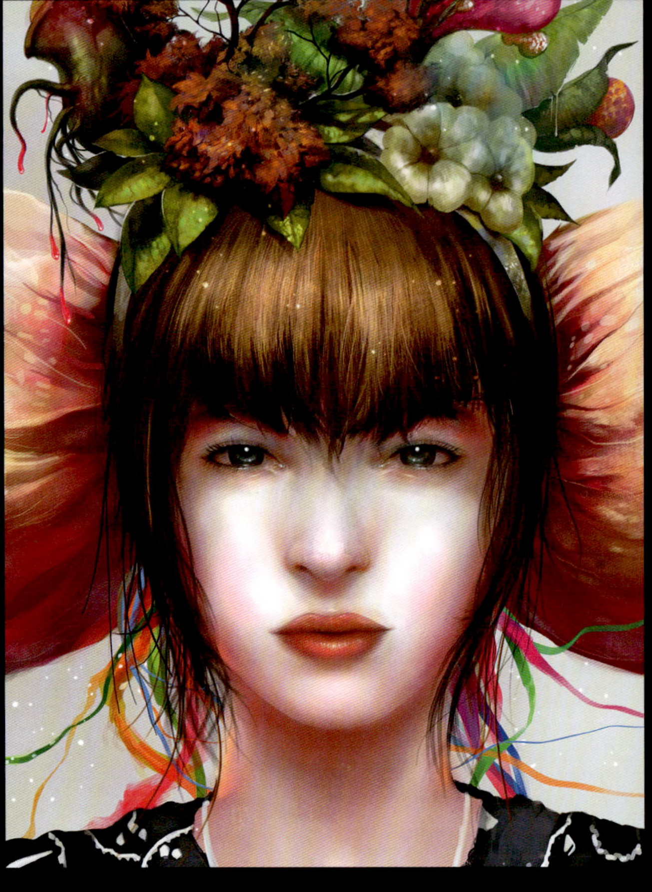

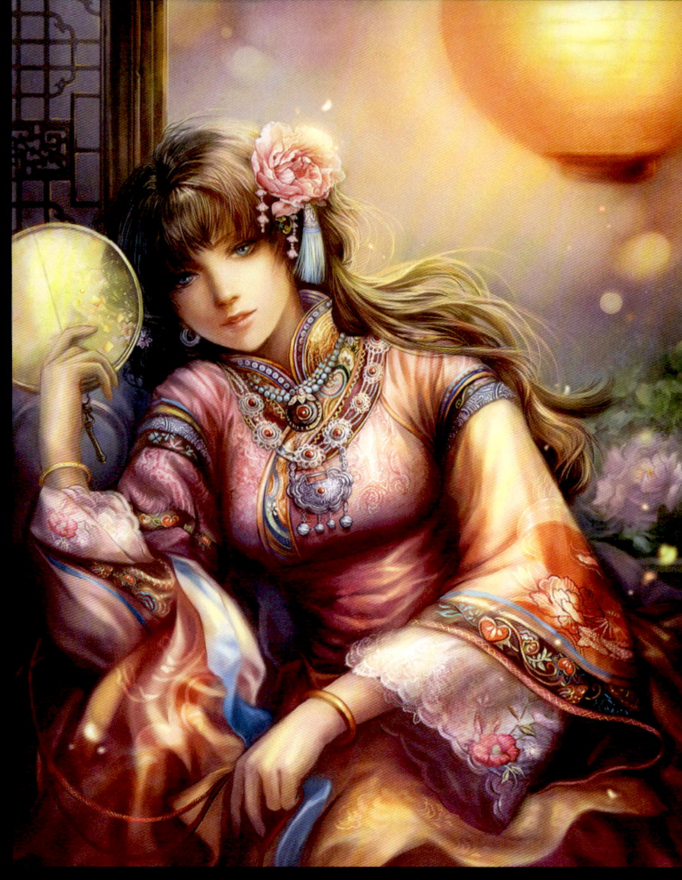

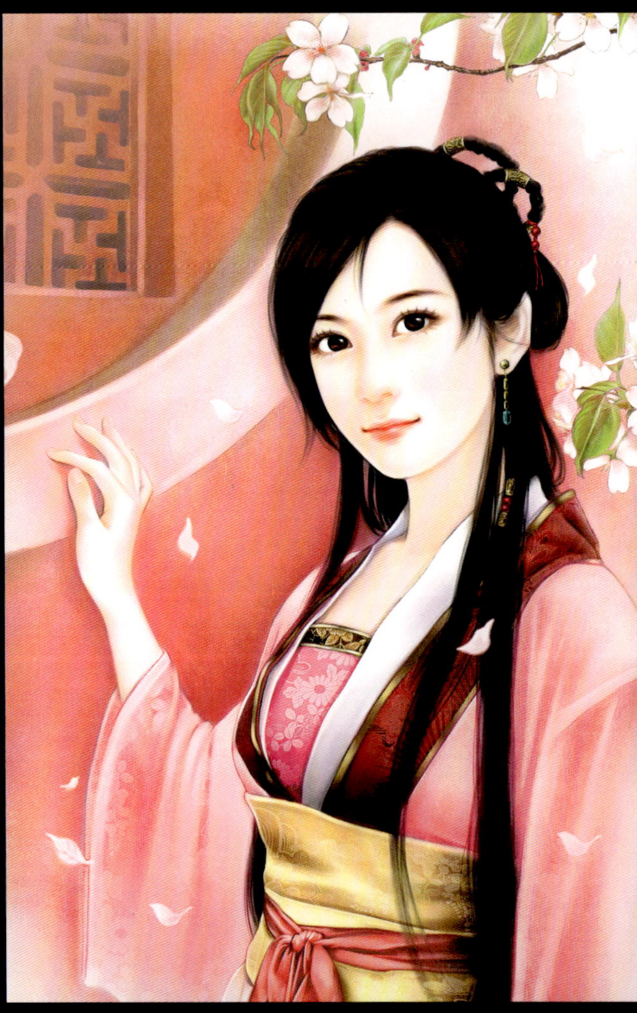

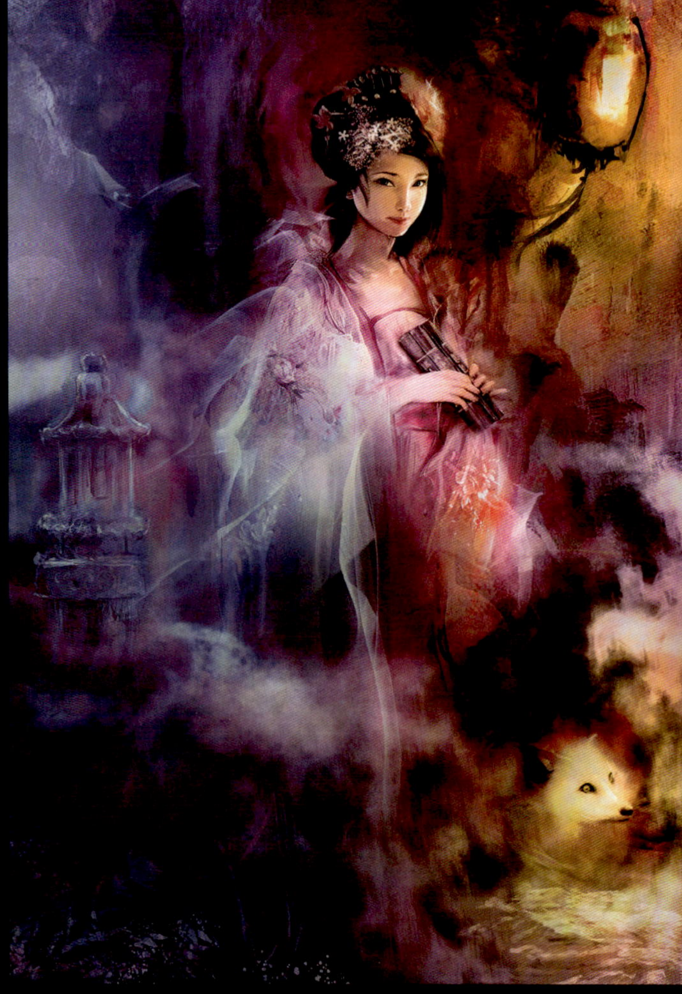

Shanghai bandana
Photoshop
Redi Murti, Nudeface, INDONESIA
[top]

Wait for a gentleman
Painter, Photoshop
Wen Chen Yen, TAIWAN
[above]

Whisper of the Night
Photoshop
Fan Yang, USA
[top]

Fox beauty
Photoshop
Ping He, CHINA
[above]

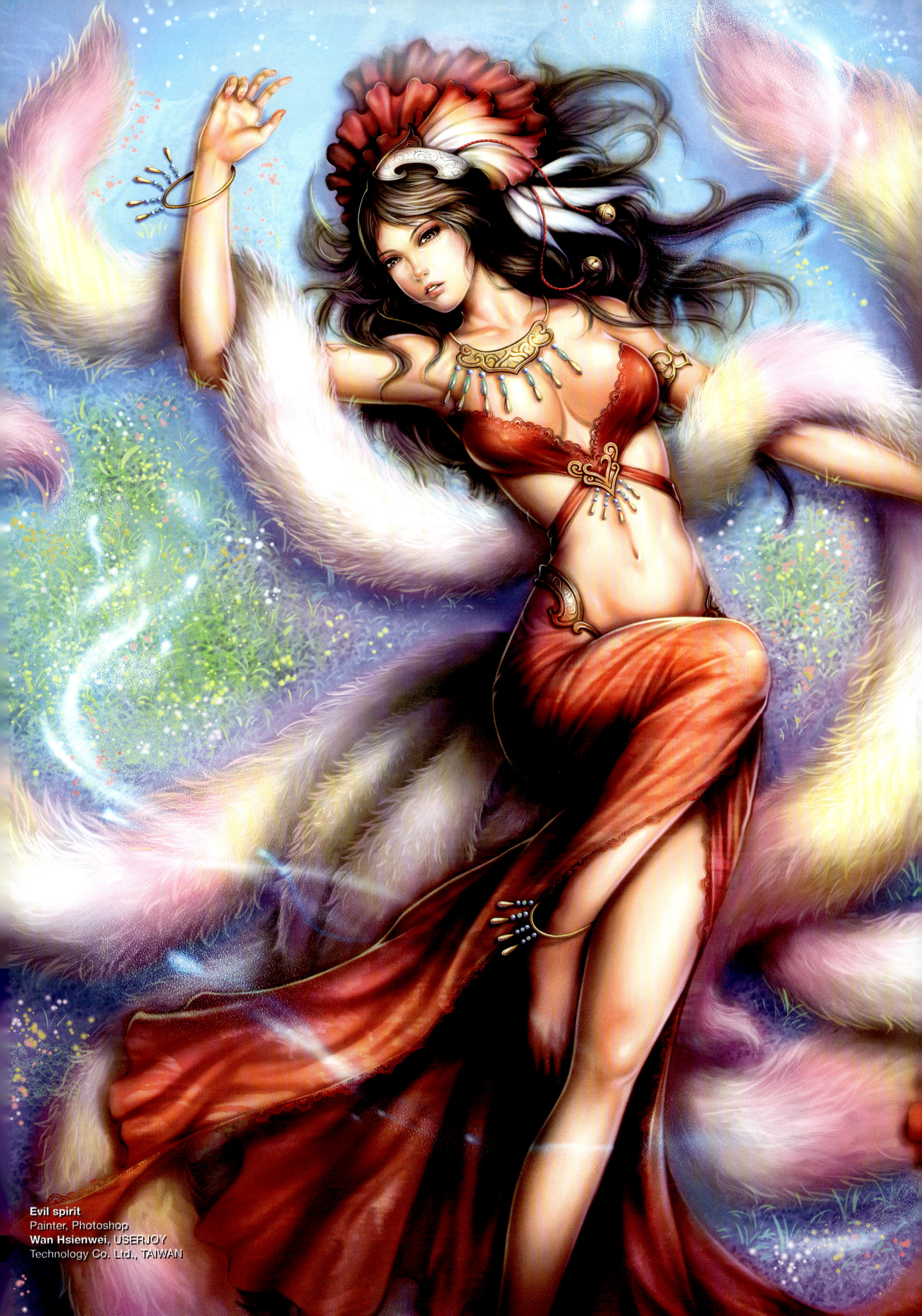

Evil spirit
Painter, Photoshop
Wan Hsienwei, USERJOY Technology Co. Ltd., TAIWAN

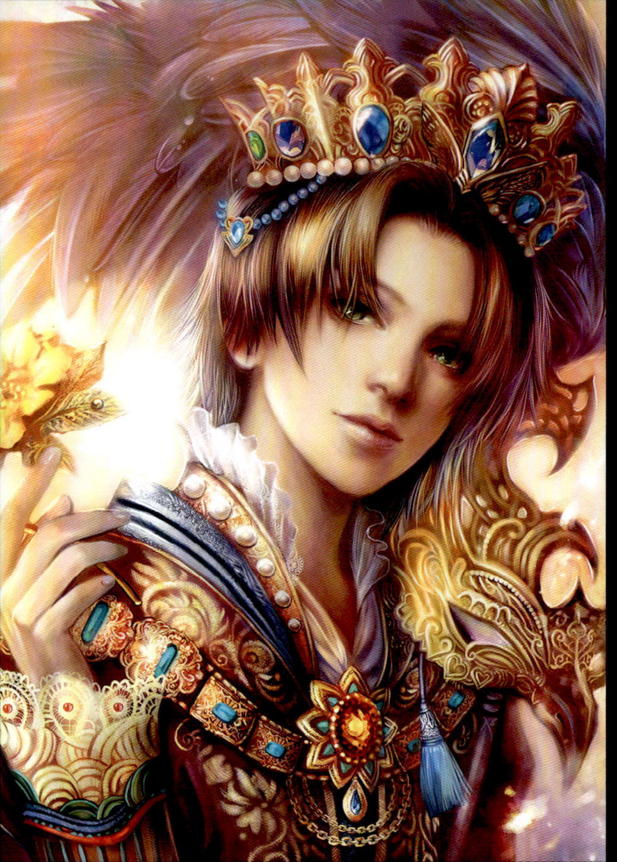

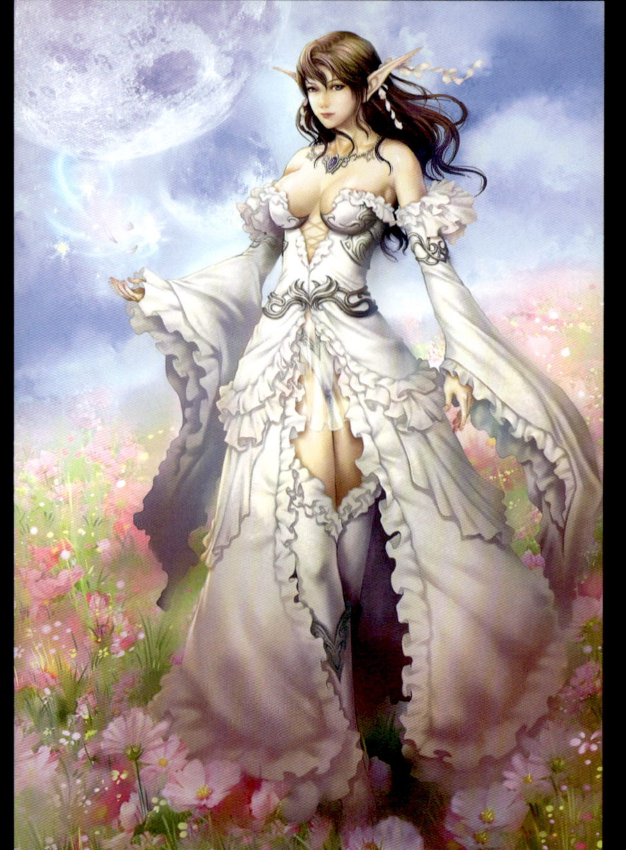

Mask
Photoshop
Inspired by: Axis Powers Hetalia
Fan Yang, USA
[far left]

Luna
Painter, Photoshop
Wan Hsienwei, USERJOY Technology Co. Ltd., TAIWAN
[left]

The queen of the sea
Photoshop
Chen Wei, CHINA
[right]

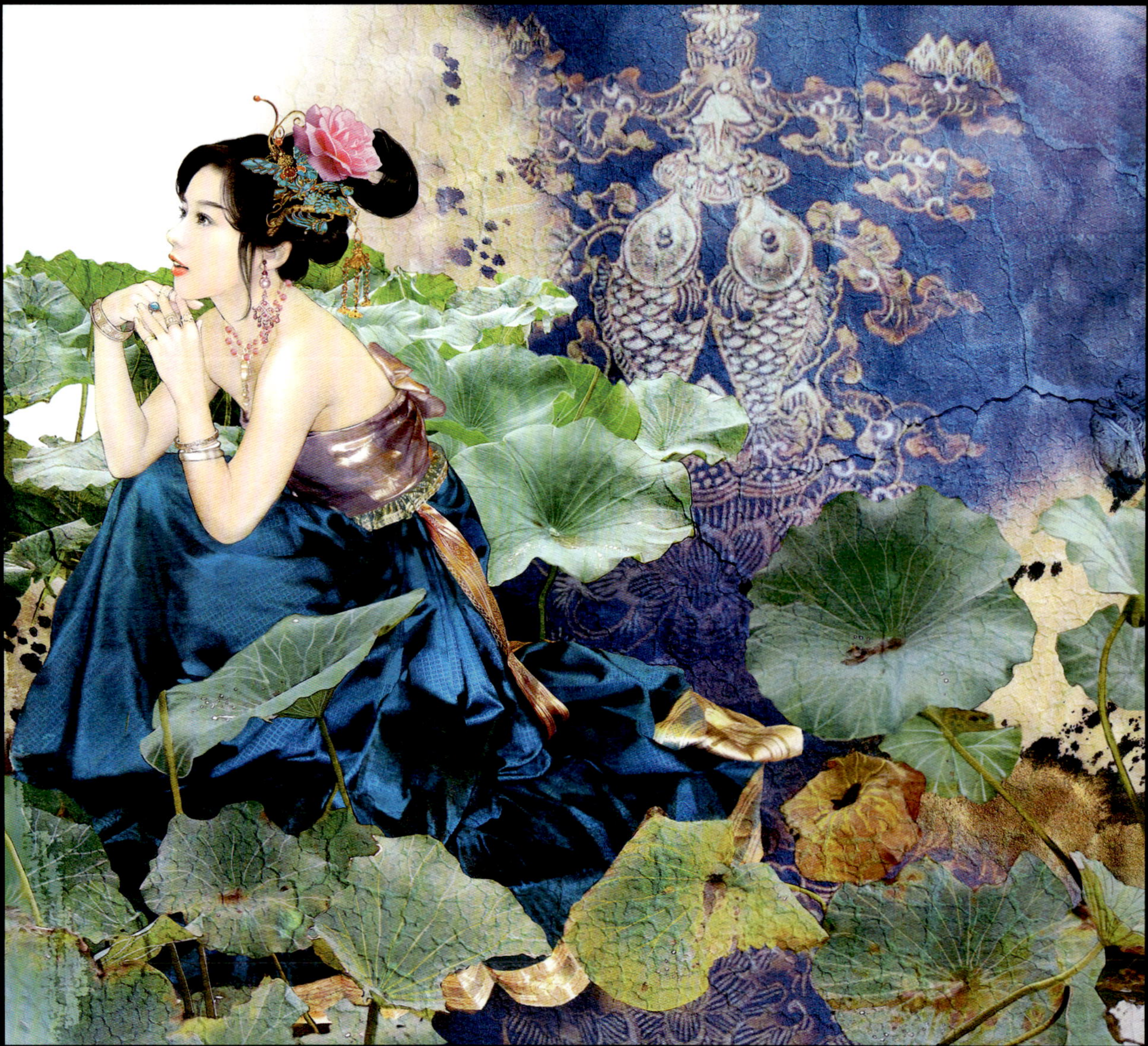

Lotus Peri
Painter, Photoshop
Der Jen, TAIWAN
[left]

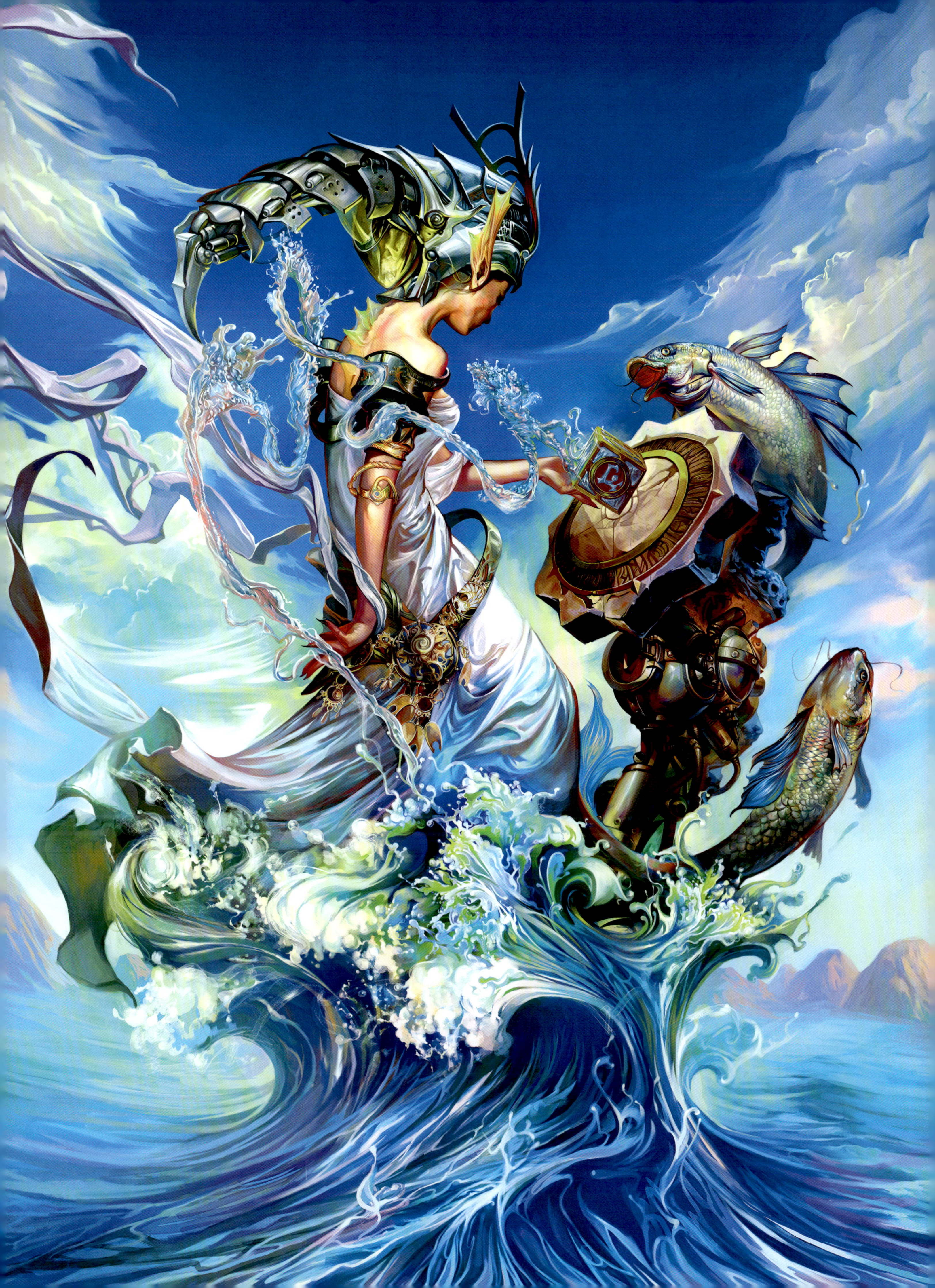

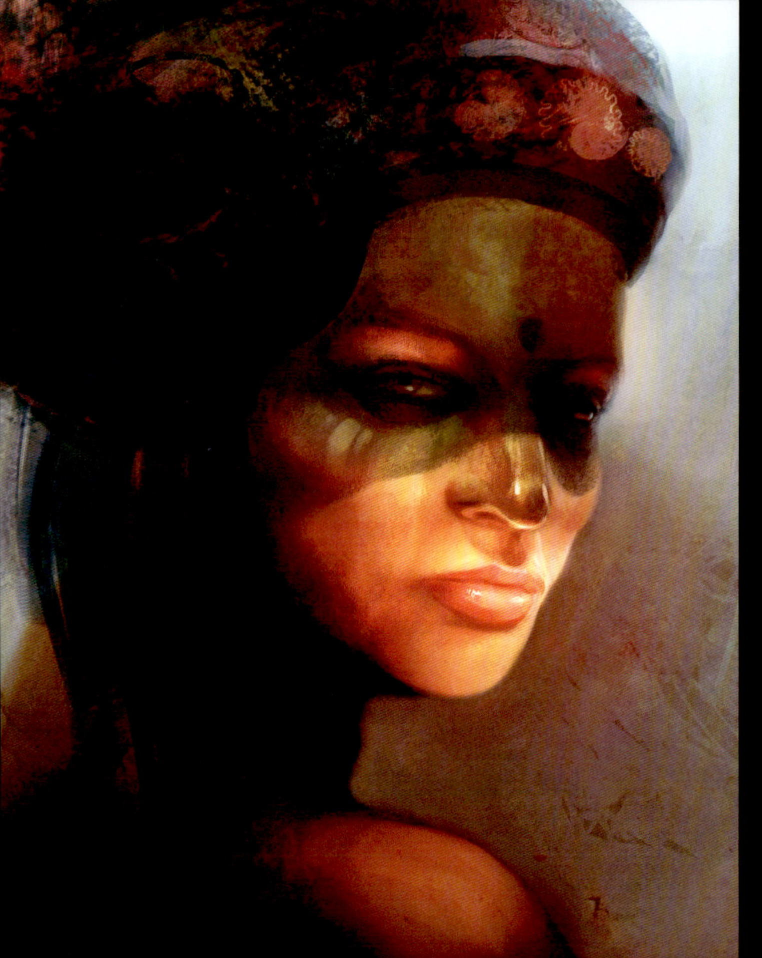

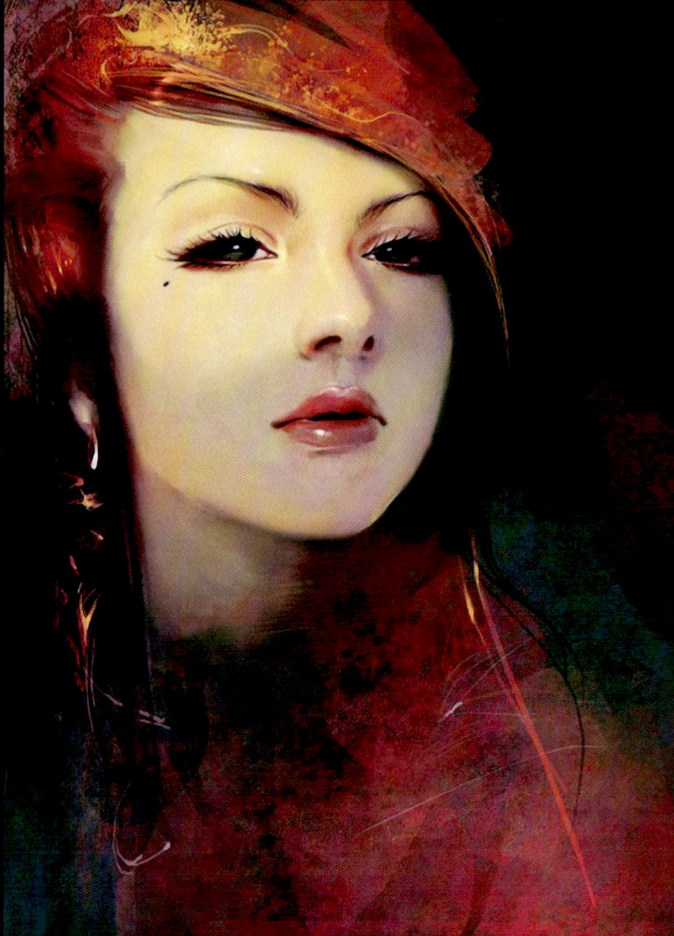

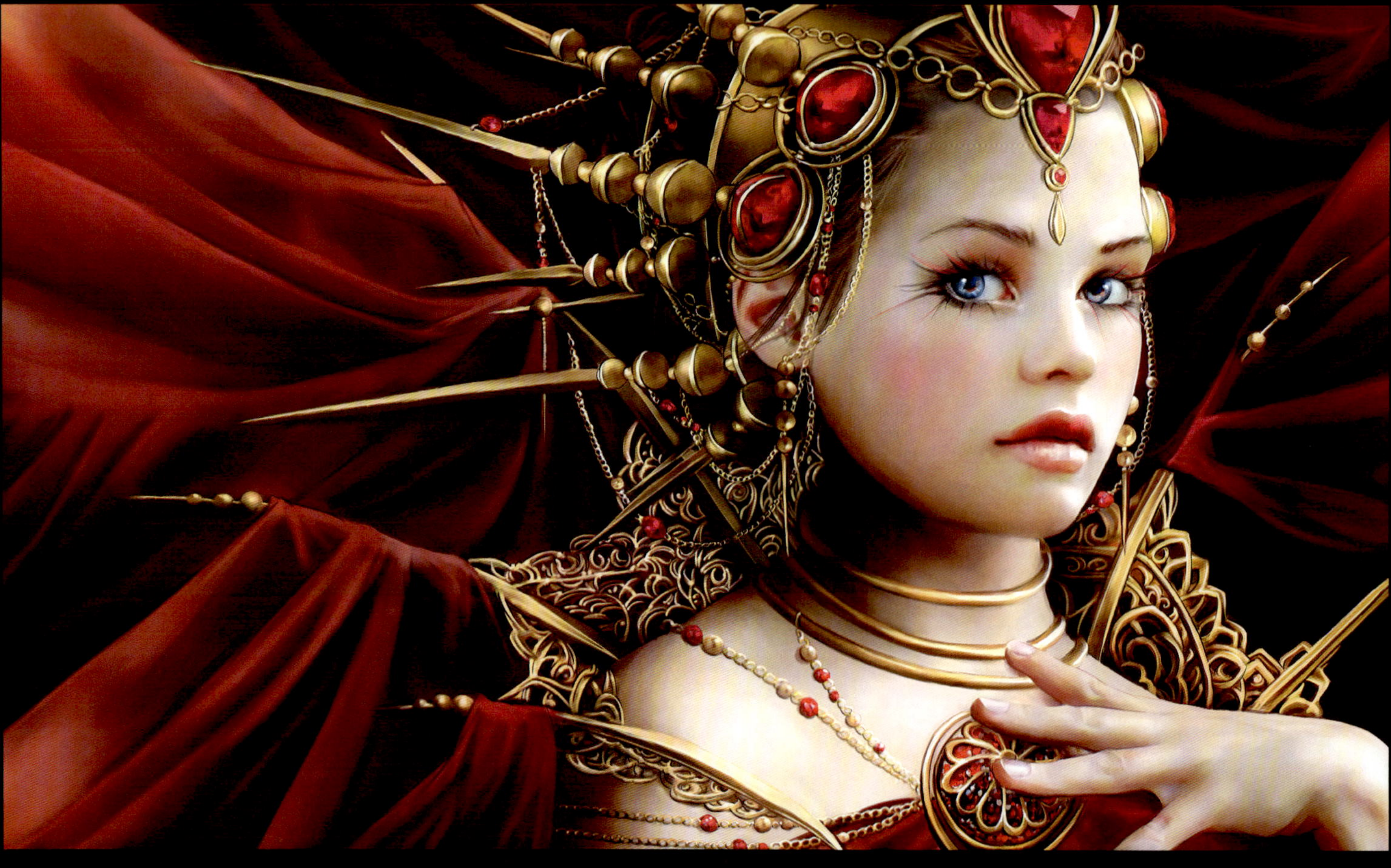

Cold Peach
Photoshop
Przemyslaw Kotynski, POLAND

Golden
Painter, Photoshop
Marta Dahlig, POLAND

Monica
Photoshop
Wenjun Lin, CHINA

The fragile world of a geisha
Photoshop, Painter
Ekaterina Pushkarova,

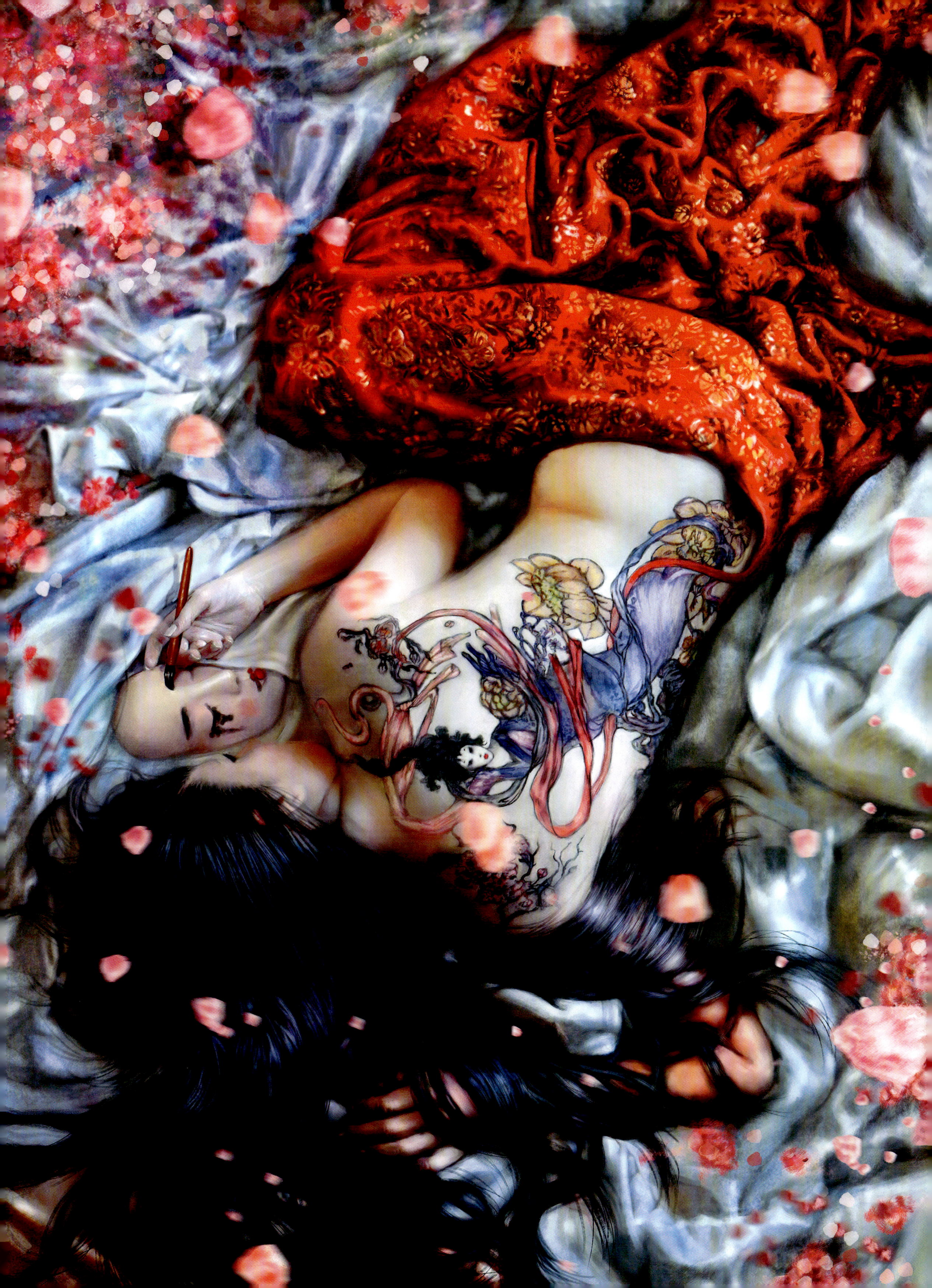

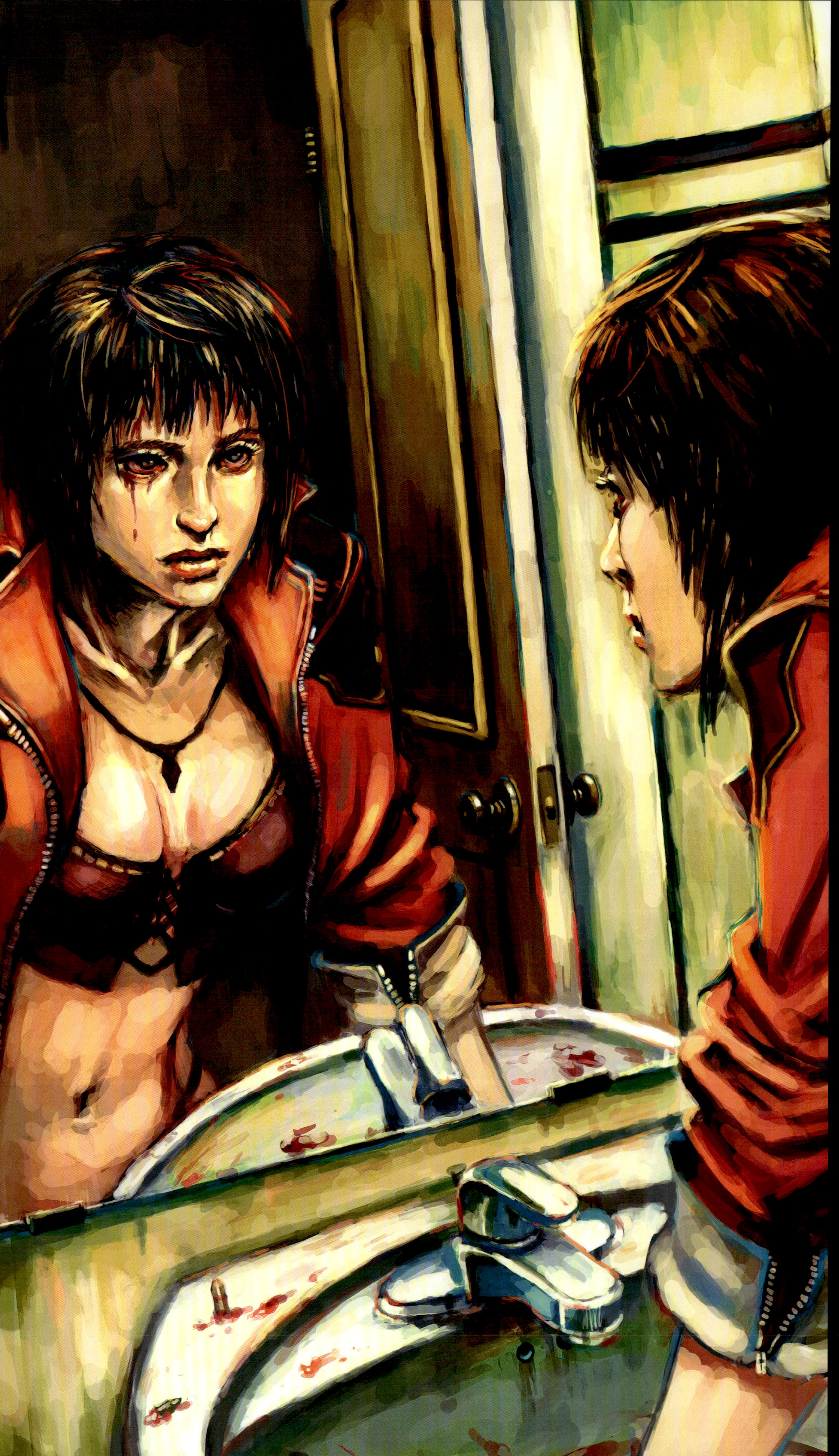

Reflection
Photoshop
Leon JO, CANADA
[left]

Rock the Casbah
Photoshop, Painter
Rudy-Jan Faber,
THE NETHERLAND
[right]

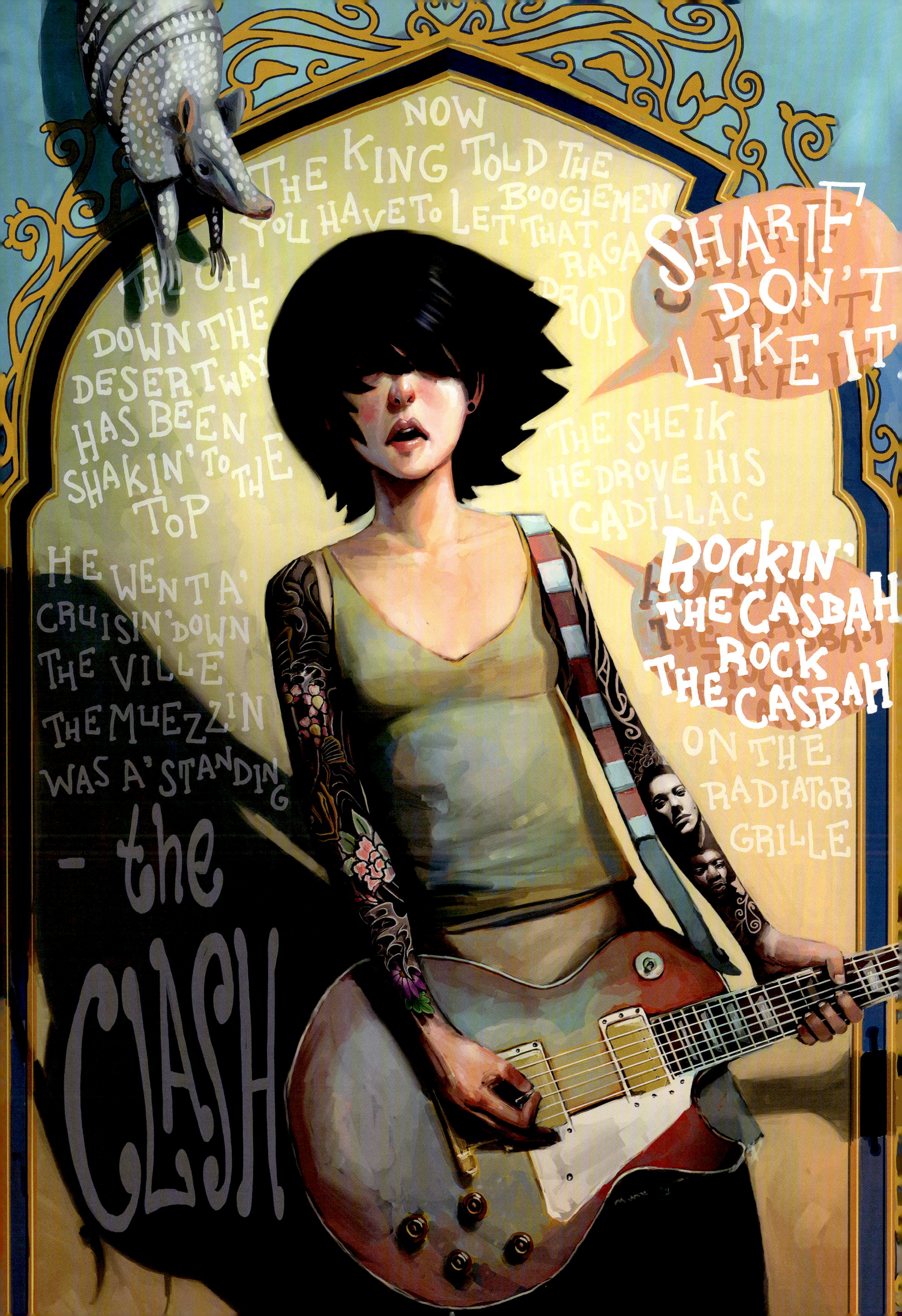
NOW
THE KING TOLD THE BOOGIEMEN
YOU HAVE TO LET THAT RAGA DROP
THE OIL
DOWN THE DESERT WAY
HAS BEEN SHAKIN' TO THE TOP
SHARIF DON'T LIKE IT
THE SHEIK HE DROVE HIS CADILLAC
HE WENT A' CRUISIN' DOWN THE VILLE
THE MUEZZIN WAS A' STANDING
ROCKIN' THE CASBAH
ROCK THE CASBAH
ON THE RADIATOR GRILLE
- the CLASH

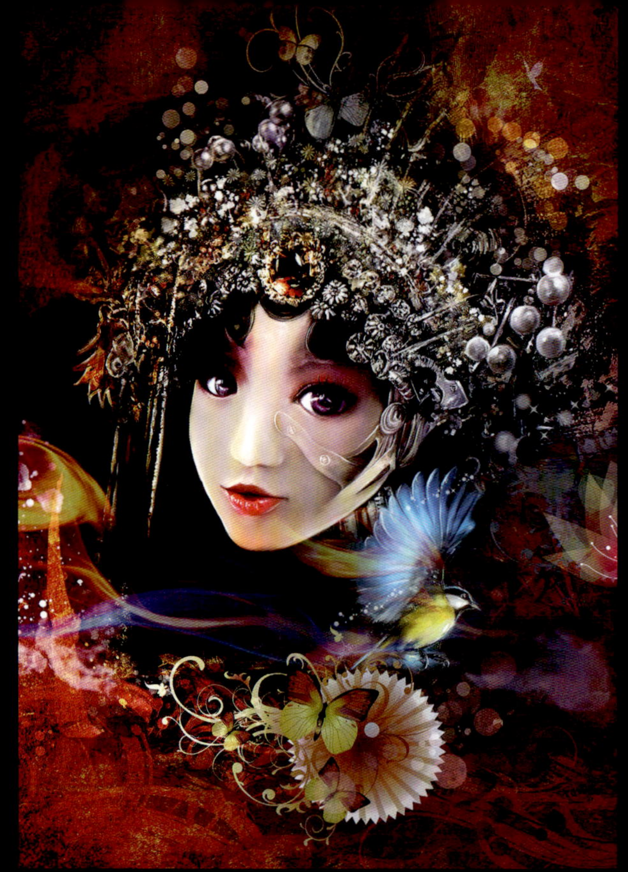

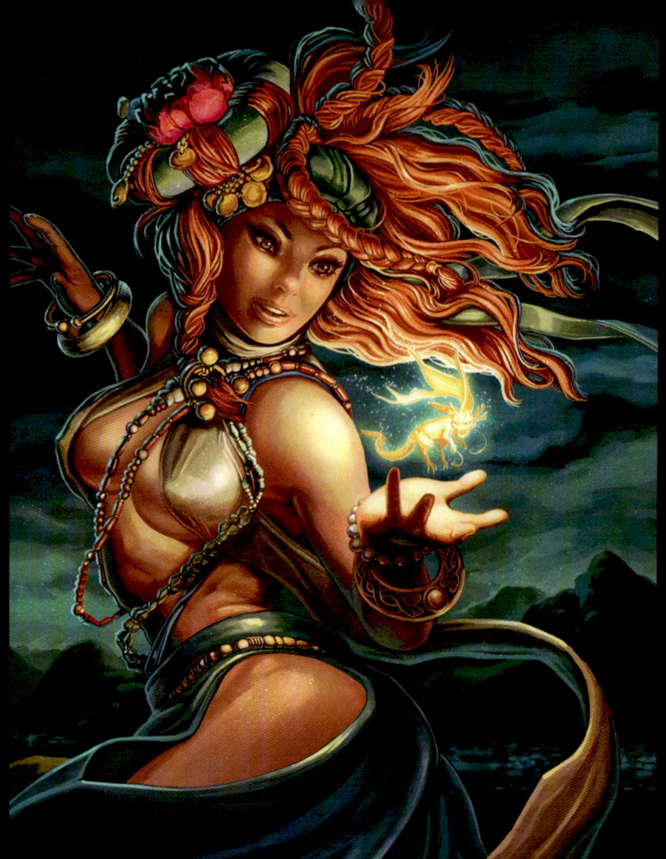

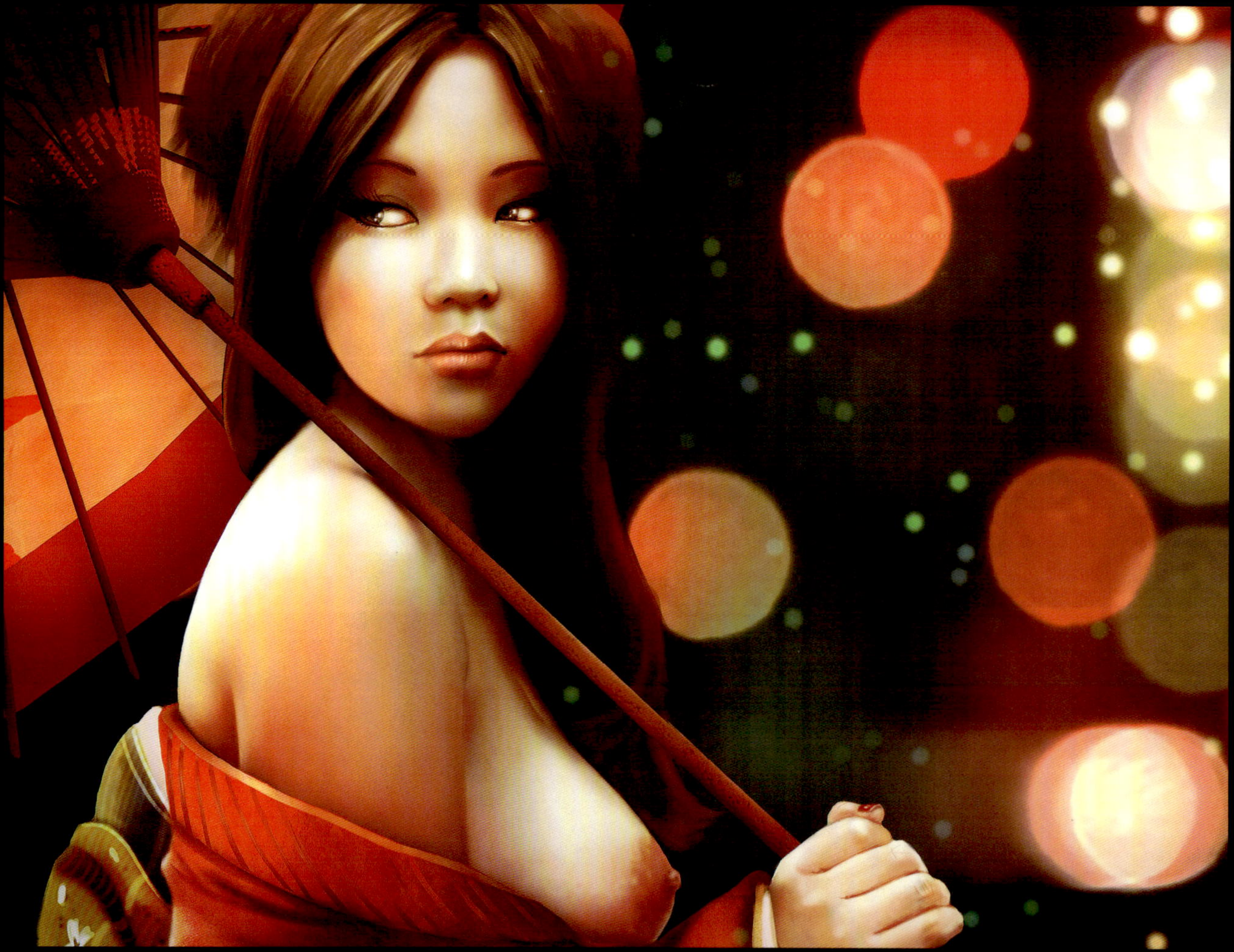

Female lead
Photoshop
Ping He, CHINA
[top]

Sonhos
Photoshop
Michel Victor Oliveira, BRAZIL
[above]

Spirit Dance
Photoshop
Benjamin Ang, SINGAPORE
[top]

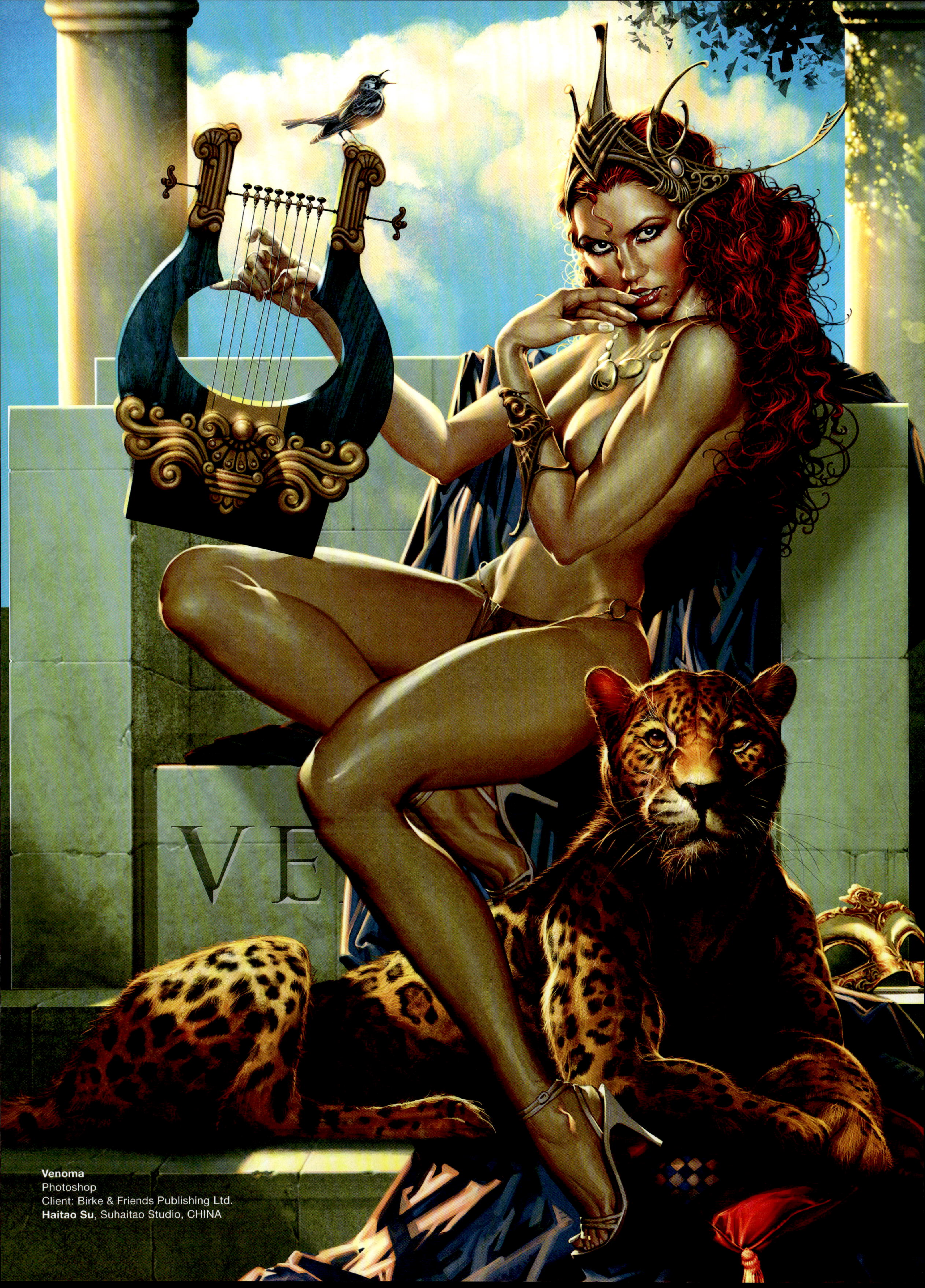

Venoma
Photoshop
Client: Birke & Friends Publishing Ltd.
Haitao Su, Suhaitao Studio, CHINA

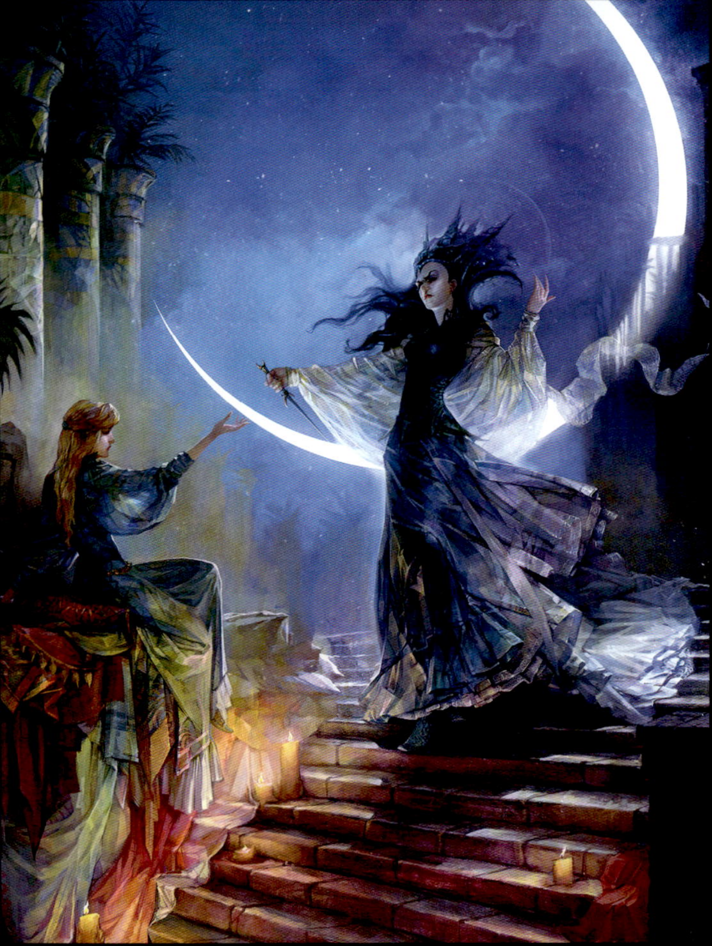

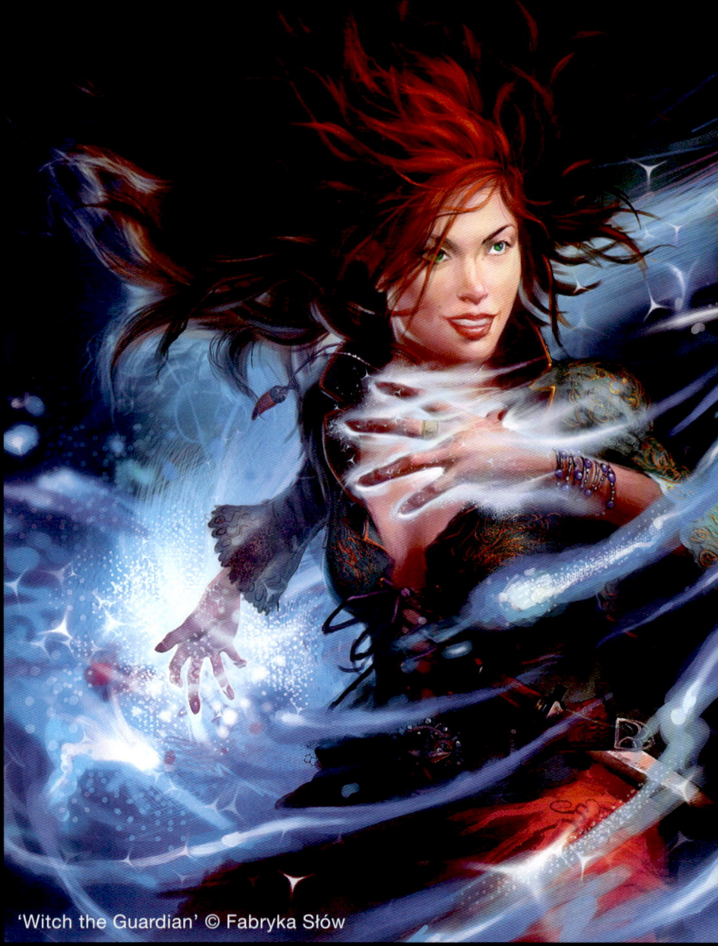

'Witch the Guardian' © Fabryka Słów

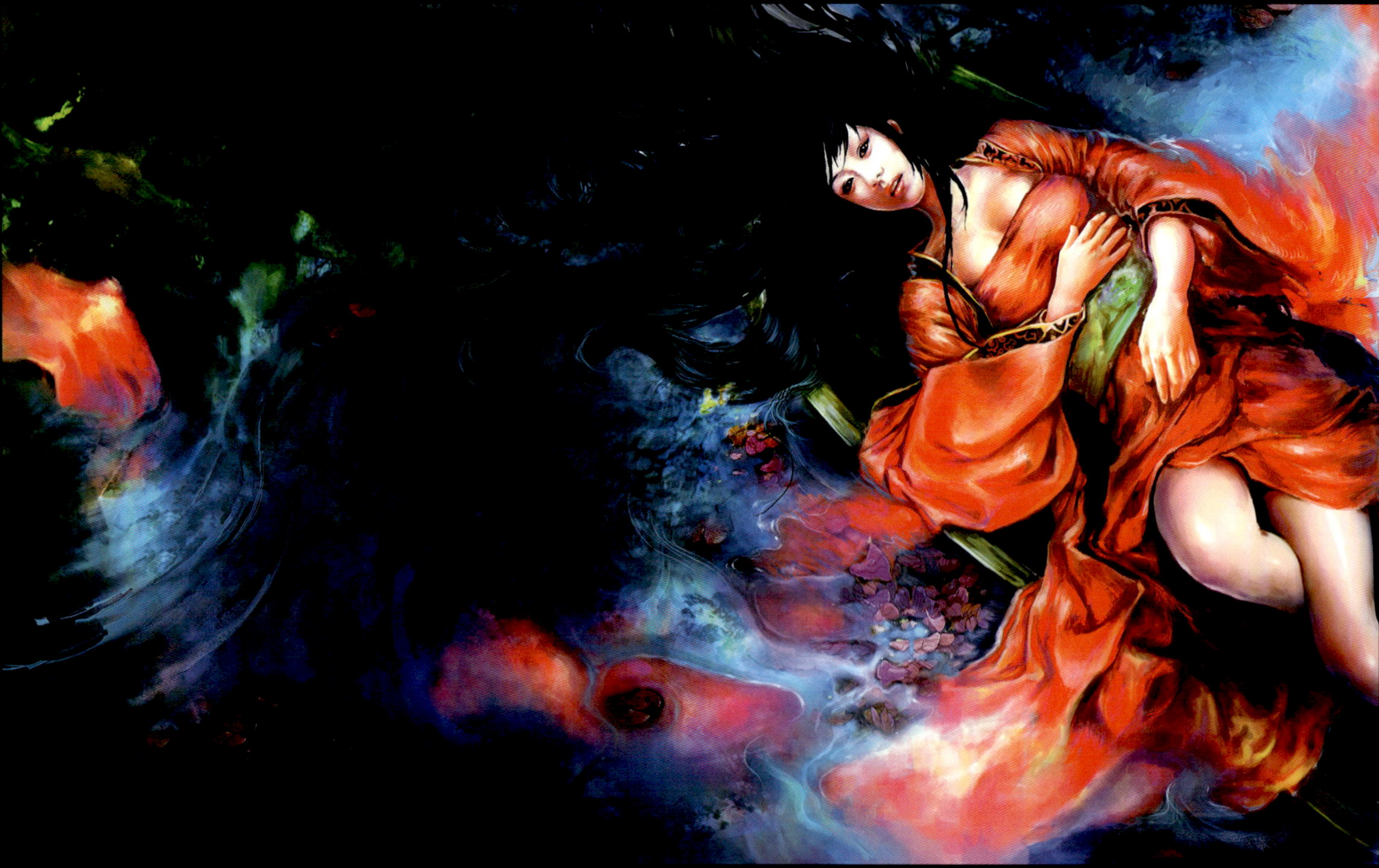

Hell's vengeance boileth in mine heart
Photoshop
Ksenia Mamaeva, RUSSIA
[top]

Silent
Photoshop
Shuangyue Li, CHINA
[above]

Witch the Guardian Vol.2: Cover
Photoshop
Client: Fabryka Słów
Artur Sadlos, POLAND *[top]*

Asian-inspired
Photoshop
Gracjana Zielinska, POLAND
[right]

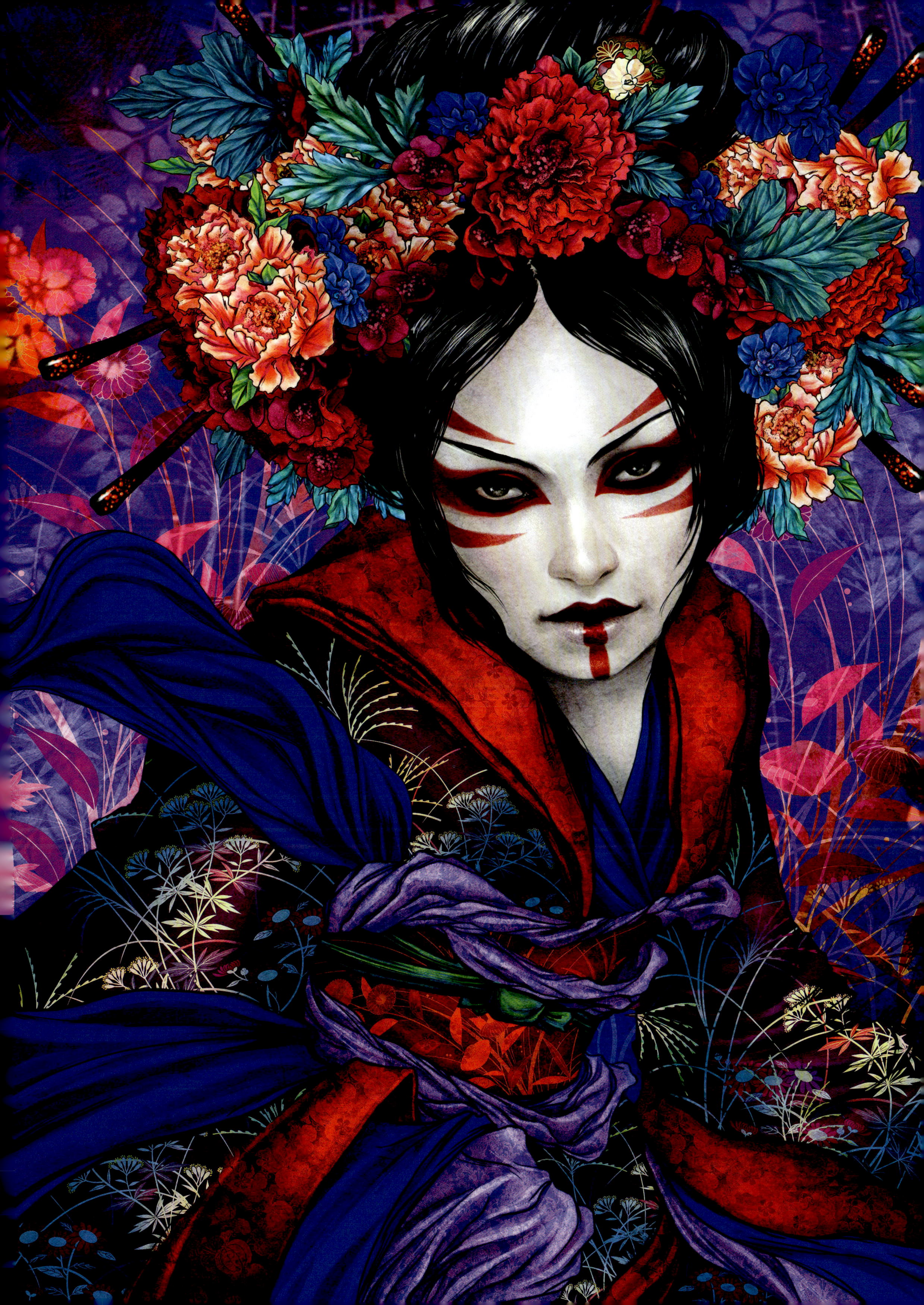

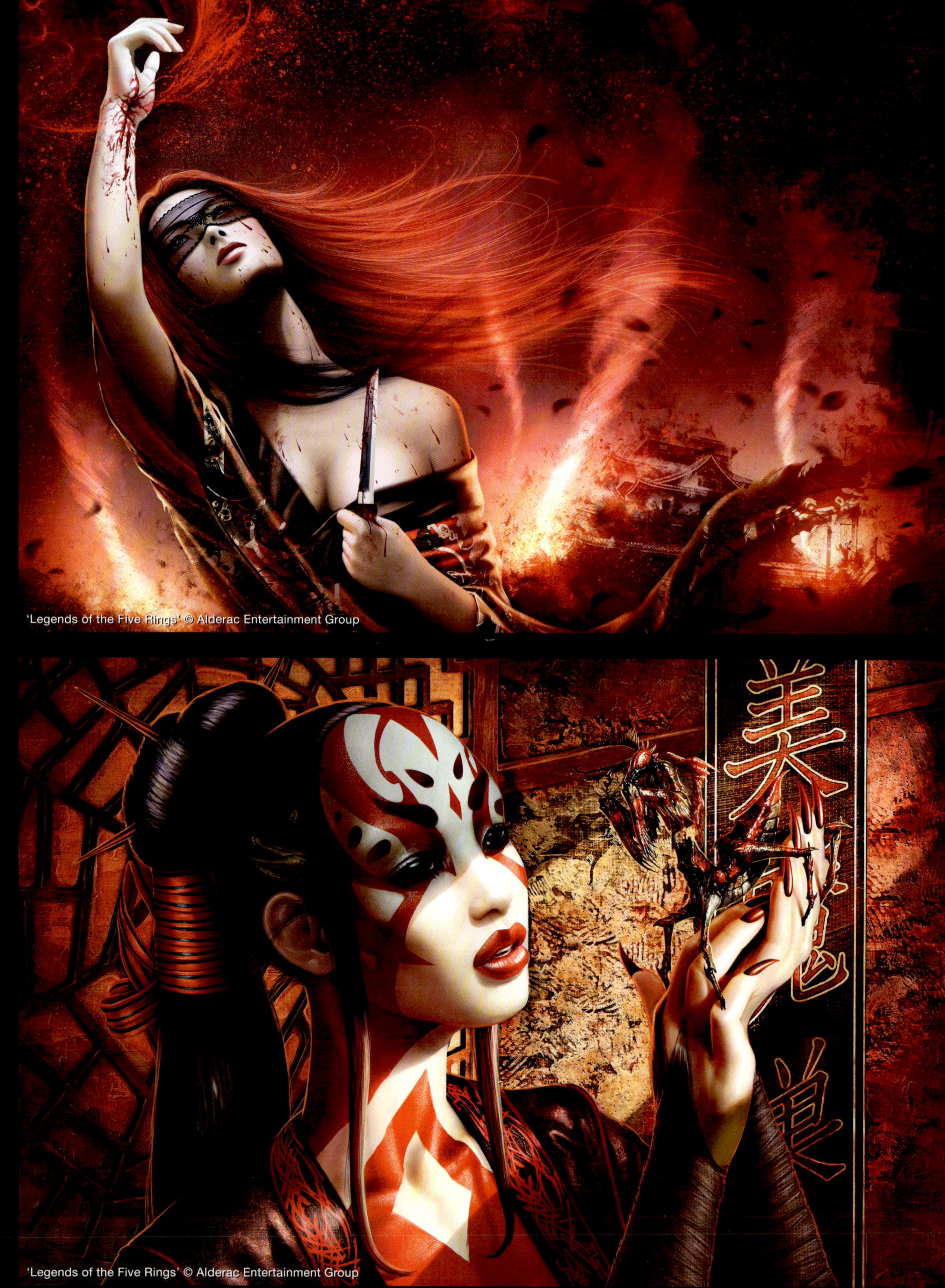

'Legends of the Five Rings' © Alderac Entertainment Group

'Legends of the Five Rings' © Alderac Entertainment Group

Legend of
The Five Rings:
Soshi Miroki
Photoshop
Client: Alderac
Entertainment Group
Mario Wibisono,
INDONESIA
[left]

RedRum
Photoshop, Illustrator
Steve Sampson,
GREAT BRITAIN
[right]

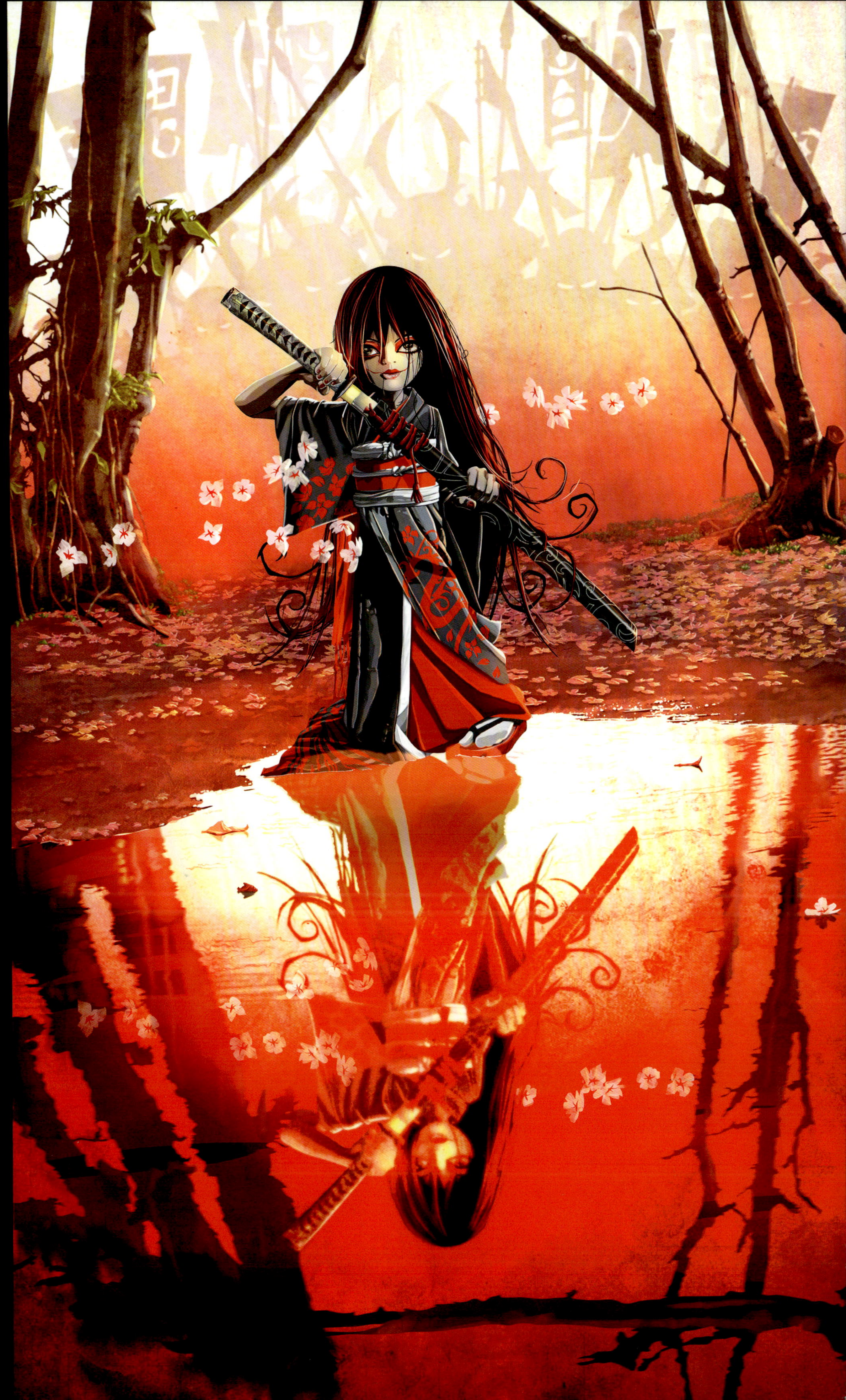

Legend of
The Five Rings:
Eyes of Obsidian
Photoshop
Client: Alderac
Entertainment Group
Steve Argyle, USA
[left]

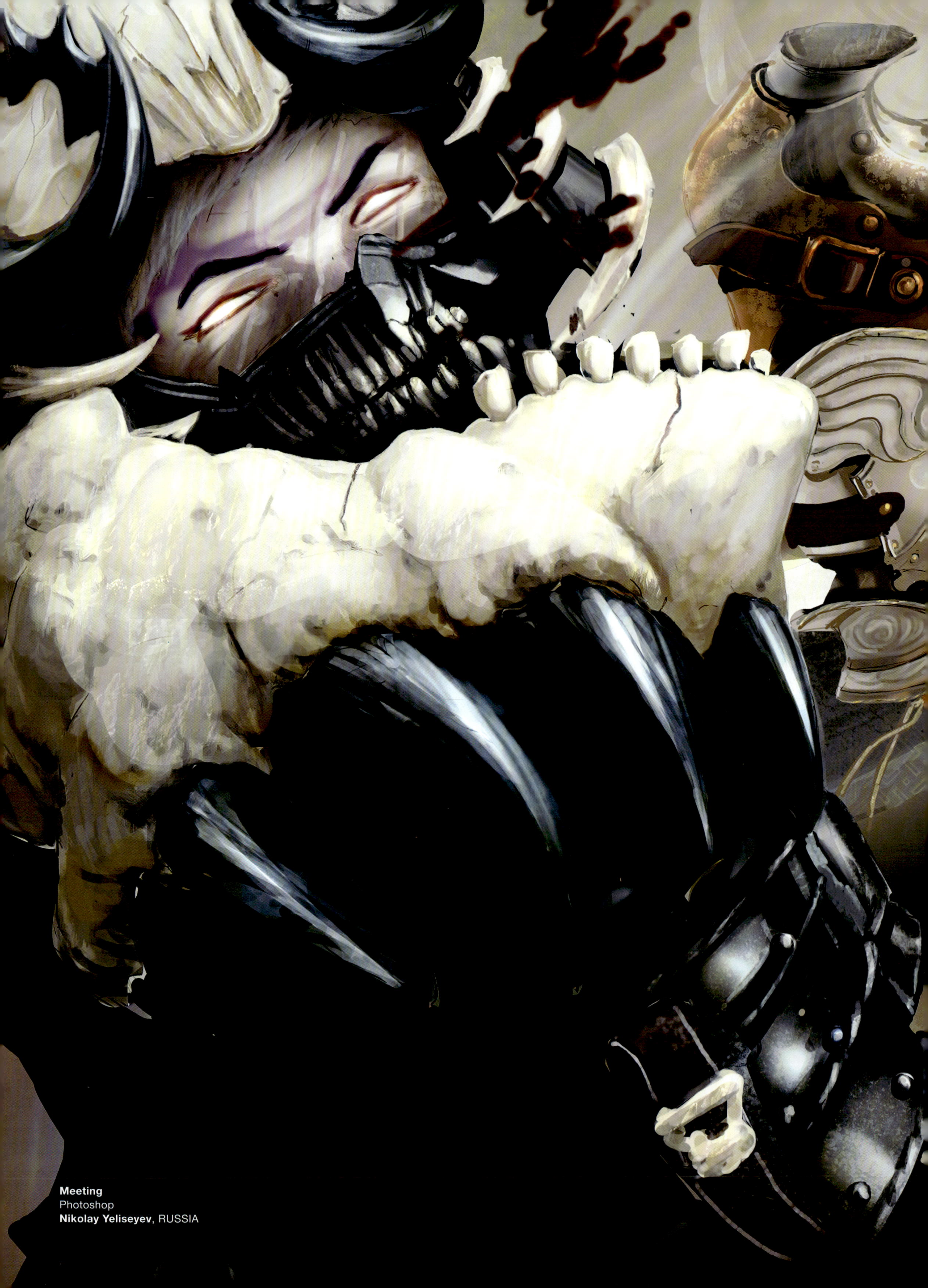

Meeting
Photoshop
Nikolay Yeliseyev, RUSSIA

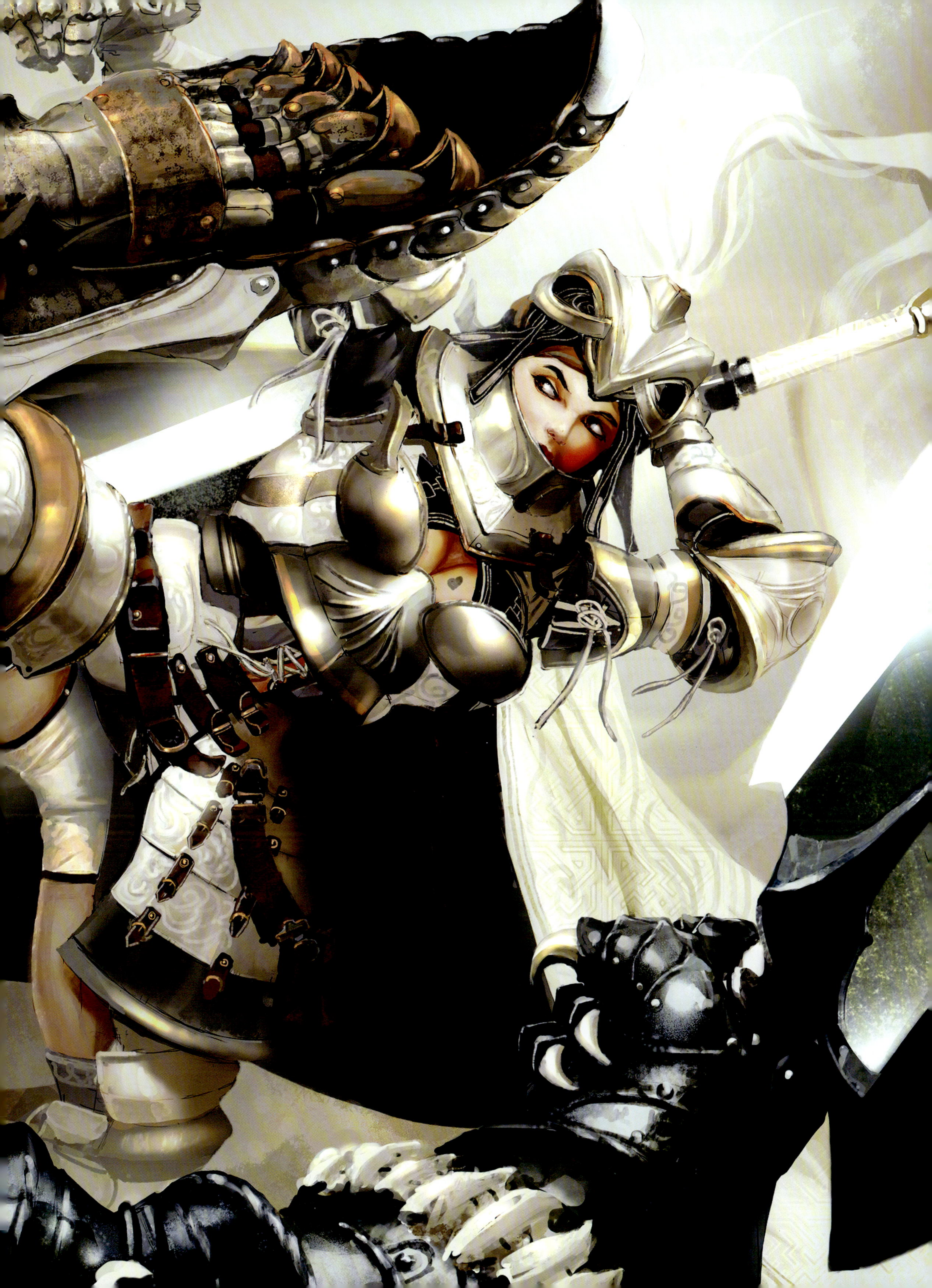

A

Athena
Bonn, GERMANY
110, 186

Paul Abrams
Kingston, NY, USA
obliviongrin@yahoo.com
paulabrams.com
118

Khurram Hamid Alavi
Karachi, PAKISTAN
khalavi@gmail.com
leviathon.cgsociety.org
106

Nykolai Aleksander
Scarborough,
GREAT BRITAIN
x@admemento.com
www.admemento.com
124

Jose Alves da Silva
Lisbon, PORTUGAL
joalvessilva@netcabo.pt
79

Christian Alzmann
San Rafael, CA, USA
www.christianalzmann.com
109

Benjamin Ang
Singapore, SINGAPORE
benjaminang.com
196

Christopher Ang
Cebu, THE PHILIPPINES
cierseruwal@yahoo.com
10

Paulo Araujo
Vila Real, PORTUGAL
pabloarau@gmail.com
76

Steve Argyle
Salt Lake City, UT, USA
steveargyle@gmail.com
steveargyle.com
16, 30, 52, 138, 162, 200

Chaichan Artwichai
Mukdahan, THAILAND
t_artwichai@hotmail.com
124

B

Sanjana Baijnath
Auckland, NEW ZEALAND
www.sanjanasart.com
93

Patri Balanovsky
Arad, ISRAEL
pat2005b@hotmail.com
www.artofpatri.com
132

Tiziano Baracchi
Sona, ITALY
eginardus@hotmail.com
www.tizianobaracchi.com
112, 168

Claire Beard
Toronto, ON, CANADA
claire.b.art@hotmail.com
www.clairebeardart.com
50

Gabriel Belluco
Sao Paulo, SP, BRAZIL
gabriel.belluco@gmail.com
48, 60

Kerem Beyit
Ankara, TURKEY
kerembeyit@hotmail.com
www.theartofkerembeyit.com
71, 120, 122, 157

Branko Bistrovic
Toronto, ON, CANADA
bisvic@gmail.com
72

Andrew Blackman
Bridgetown, BARBADOS
rivenis@hotmail.com
rivenisart.blogspot.com
168

Artem Borisov
Novosibirsk, RUSSIA
jackalyo@yandex.com
www.artemborisov.com
66, 116

Jon Bosco
Fortaleza, CE, BRAZIL
bosco.penciller@gmail.com
boscoart.blogspot.com
116

Jelmer Boskma
Leeuwarden,
THE NETHERLANDS
3d58jelmer@vfs.com
www.jelmerboskma.com
80

Tu Bui
Los Angeles, CA, USA
2buiart@gmail.com
129

C

Felicia Cano
El Monte, CA, USA
feliciacano@gmail.com
www.feliciacano.com
132

Jared Castro
Guatemala City, GUATEMALA
castrochew@hotmail.com
castrochew.deviantart.com
38, 172

Roger Chamberlain
Sony Online Entertainment
Denver, CO, USA
www.soe.com
59, 104, 128, 152, 162

Jiansong Chain
Perfect World Co. Ltd.
Beijing, Haidian District,
CHINA
chain_jane@126.com
www.chainandjane.com
18, 136

Michael Ting Yu Chang
Hong Kong, CHINA
p_spprigan@hotmail.com
www.michaelcty.com
46

Amber Chen
Marietta, GA, USA
kagaminoir@yahoo.com
www.kagaminoir.com
96

Sida Chen
Syosset, NY, USA
onomatopoeiaparadox@
yahoo.com
lappisch.deviantart.com
180

Yi Zhong Chen
Taichung City, TAIWAN
fapweb@yahoo.com.tw
www.fap-web.com
19

Fei Giap Chong
Seremban, Negeri Sembilan,
MALAYSIA
dsngiap@hotmail.com
www.dsngiap.deviantart.com
130

Au Yeung Chun Hay
Hong Kong, CHINA
purehay@hotmail.com
purehay2008.blogspot.com
158

Yee-Ling Chung
Kuala Lumpur, Wilayah
Persekutuan, MALAYSIA
syncmax.deviantart.com
167

Traci Cook
Portland, OR, USA
traci.l.cook@gmail.com
www.tlcookdesigns.com
174

Dario Corallo
ITALY
scravagghiupilusu959.
deviantart.com
168

D

Marta Dahlig
Warsaw, POLAND
blackeri@poczta.onet.pl
www.marta-dahlig.com
173, 192

Huang DaHong
ChangSha, CHINA
hjk-gl@163.com
41, 55, 104, 116, 143

Leslie Dalton
Ottawa, ON, CANADA
lele@lesliedalton.com
www.LeslieDalton.com
85

Jeffrey M. de Guzman
Makati City,
THE PHILIPPINES
jeffreymdg@yahoo.com
www.jeffmdart.com
102

Mélanie Delon
Drancy, FRANCE
contact@melaniedelon.com
www.melaniedelon.com
175

Alejandro Diaz
Arles, Boches du Rhone,
FRANCE
alejandrodiazcardoso@gmail.com
adconcept.blogspot.com
135

Omar Diaz
Madrid, SPAIN
omarenovatio@gmail.com
www.dark-adon.deviantart.com
20

Anna Dittmann
San Francisco, CA, USA
escume.deviantart.com
40

Daniel Dociu
ArenaNet
Redmond, WA, USA
daniel@arena.net
www.tinfoilgames.com
64-65, 134

Horia Dociu
Redmond, WA, USA
hdociu@hotmail.com
www.BADiDEAfactory.com
111

Marga Donaire
Cartagena, Murcia, SPAIN
karmalizzard@gmail.com
karmalizzard.deviantart.com
28

E

Ejiwa Adaeze Ebenebe
Auckland, NEW ZEALAND
ejiwa_ebenebe@yahoo.com
peppermint-pinwheel.
deviantart.com
32

Embiro and Jaysin
DPI Studios.net
Calgary, CANADA
jay@dpistudios.net
www.dpistudios.net
37

F

Rudy-Jan Faber
Leeuwarden, Friesland,
THE NETHERLANDS
contact@rudyfaber.com
www.rudyfaber.com
rudeone.cgsociety.org
49, 92-93, 195

Marco Fantechi
MeduNecer
Rome, ITALY
info@medunecer.com
www.medunecer.com
101

Melissa Findley
Tallahassee, FL, USA
mercuralis@bynkii.com
www.wickedfae.com
122

Jeremie Fleury
Lyon, FRANCE
jeremiefleury@laposte.net
www.trefle-rouge.fr
10, 140

Benjamin Friess
Privas, FRANCE
benf07@free.fr
benf.deviantart.com
28

G

Dani Garcia
Barcelona, Catalunya, SPAIN
woody@woodys3d.com
www.woodys3d.com
31

Cosmin Genete
Constanta, ROMANIA
cosmin.genete@gmail.com
34

Wei Geng
Beijing, CHINA
coldduke@hotmail.com
62

Phillip Gerlitz
Burnaby, BC, CANADA
crimson_phill@hotmail.com
www.phillgerlitz.carbonmade.com
95, 140

Carine Grasset
Vitrolles, FRANCE
carine.art@free.fr
carine.art.free.fr
158

Rochelle Green
Palmerston North,
NEW ZEALAND
caelicorn@gmail.com
caelicorn.cgsociety.org
174

Arni Kristjan Gudmundsson
Reykjavik, ICELAND
75

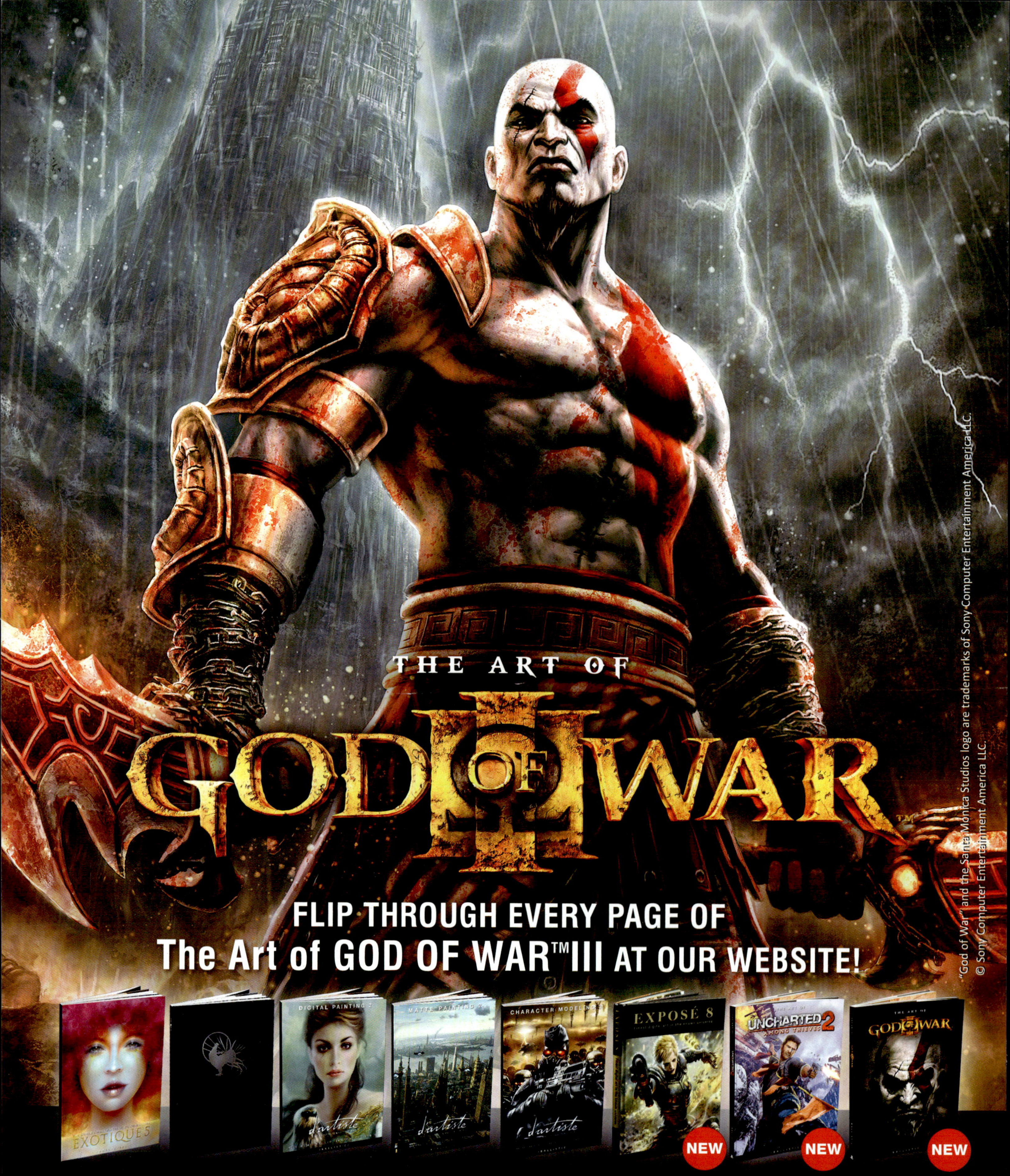